Elyot

With best wishes
from

Roddy Braithwaite

"Strikingly alive..."

The History of the
Mill Hill School Foundation

1807-2007

"Strikingly alive..."

The History of the
Mill Hill School Foundation

1807-2007

Roderick Braithwaite

Phillimore

2006

Published for

The Mill Hill School Foundation

by

PHILLIMORE & Co Ltd

Shopwyke Manor Barn, Chichester, West Sussex, England

www.phillimore.co.uk

ISBN 1 86077 330 3

Designed by Ravenscourt Design LLP

Printed and bound in Great Britain by

CAMBRIDGE PRINTING

Contents

Part Two
Appendices

A. Abbreviations

B. Heads of the Foundation: 1807-2007

C. Building Mill Hill: 1807-2007
1. Presidents
2. Vice-Presidents
3. 'Chairs of the Court'
4. Hon Treasurers and Bursars/ Directors of Finance
5. Trustees
6. Second Masters/ Deputy Heads
7. Architects and Designers

D. Our Mansion has Many Houses

E. "The Book of Millhillisms"
Extracts from Information Supplement No.1

F. Classical Heritage
Mill Hill's Inscriptions & Quotations

G. Money Values 1807-2004

H. Belmont's History
An Overview

I. List of Figures

J. Picture Credits and Details of Personalia in Illustrations

Bibliographical Note

A Mill Hill Bibliography

OPTIONAL [POST-PUBLICATION] INFORMATION SUPPLEMENTS

1. THE BOOK OF MILLHILLISMS

2. A GALLIMAUFRY OF MILL HILL CHARACTERS

3. EDUCATION AT MILL HILL: THE FORMATIVE EXTERNAL EVENTS

4. MILL HILL'S PORTRAITS

5. THE ECOLOGY OF MILL HILL

6. THE COMPETITIVE RECORD: SPORT

7. MILL HILL DRAMA: 1876-2005

MILL HILL'S BICENTENNIAL YEAR
(Separate MHS Publication)

"An Institution strikingly alive..."

Entry in William Gladstone's diary,
following his successful visit to Mill Hill as guest of honour,
New Foundation Day, 11 June 1879 (see Chapter IV).

Acknowledgements:

Sources, Witnesses and Subscribers

Sources My debt to the many authorities in the UK and the US who have facilitated the research, and the quotations, for this History, is gratefully recorded in the end-of-chapter Notes. Particularly helpful have been the Keeper of the Royal Archives, Windsor Castle; Archivists at Westminster Abbey; the Mercers' Company and Royal Exchange; the PRO, Kew (the National Archive); the HMC, Leicester, and ISCis; the O.U.P.; the British Library, its Newspaper Library and its Rare Manuscripts Department; and Barnet Borough Archive; also Archivists/ Librarians/ Information Officers at these institutions: the Bodleian and Cambridge University Libraries; Dr Williams's Library, London; the Archives of St Bartholomew's, *OM* J.Michael Phillips – Archivist at the Maudsley and the Royal Bethlem Hospitals, Beckenham; Oxbridge Colleges Balliol, Mansfield, Pembroke OU, Queens', Wadham, Westminster (the Cheshunt Foundation); RIBA; Wiener Library; the London Metropolitan Archive; the Westminster City Archives; British Film Institute; RAF Museum, Hendon; National Portrait Gallery; the College of Arms; the Koestler Archive, Edinburgh University; Bedales, Marlborough, Tonbridge and Caterham Schools; and the London and Reform Club Libraries.

A personal debt for academic and general guidance is owed to: the late Prof Roy Porter, The Wellcome Institute, London, the late Prof R.E.Kendell, and the late Prof S.Holt, Roehampton University; the late Prof Francis Crick; Prof Clyde Binfield, Sheffield University; Alan Argent of JICHS; the sons of two former Headmasters – John Whale, Dr John Moore; and Dr Pamela Taylor, MHS Archivist. I am also grateful to the Mill Hill Historical Society for permission to quote from a paper presented on 9 January 2002. If inadvertently any other sources have been omitted, the author hereby asks forgiveness.

Witnesses Members of the wider Mill Hill Community must come at the top of my Acknowledgements. At their head are those eight *OMs* whose knowledge has paved the way – E.R.Tanner, "Dickie" Buckland, Norman Brett James, Rev. Ernest Hampden-Cook, George Timpson, David Smith, "Dick" Walker and Gowen Bewsher; their writings are also credited in the Notes. To the latter Mill Hill devotee, together with Esyr Lewis QC, I owe an especial thank-you for acting as 'Nominated Readers' of the draft text, before that task was taken up by Dame Angela Rumbold and Bill Skinner. I have also been fortunate to benefit from the recollections of several *quondam* Head Masters – the late Kingston Derry, Michael Hart, Alastair Graham, and Euan MacAlpine. In parallel, many of the School's former staff and their wives have contributed mightily – Donald Hall, Edward and Peace Stanham, Tony Turnbull, Chris and Christine Sutcliffe, Ted and Mary Winter, Alec Robertson, Tim Stringer, Paul Hodgson, Chris Kelly, Ian Brownlie, David Franklin, Pauline Mills, Alan Prosser-Harries, Tim Dingle, Alfred Champniss and Judith Herbertson. Dr Lena Brown and Peggy Phimester have also graciously helped with regard to the times of Michael Brown and Allan Phimester, as have two predecessors of the current Chaplain, Rev. James Fields – Rev. Paul Hunt, and Rev. & Mrs Henry Starkey. This is not to forget John Hawkins, Lynn Duncan, and two previous Masters of Belmont – James Burnett and Gordon Smith, and also Pauline Bennett-Mills at the Pre-Preparatory School.

To the hundreds of *OMs* and their families who gave their energy, and hospitality over the past ten years, I record the warmest of 'thank-you's', especially the late Michael and Jean Berry, David and Clova Morris, the late Stanley and Kate Farrow, and Stephen and Pat Roberts. Their reminiscences could have formed a separate 'Un-Official' story of Mill Hill, although that anecdotal gap is being filled by the growing custom of mini-histories –

David Clifford's "St Bees Remembered", and Chris Sutcliffe's "Winterstoke", "Burton Bank", and – with David Franklin – "Collinson". I have where possible incorporated the 'gems' of these eye-witness accounts.

Sadly, since these interviews started, some of those articulate 'Old Boys', like Eric Dangerfield and Walter Isaac, have already gone on to *their long home*, to use the Ecclesiastes phrase quoted in the Reports of the Protestant Dissenters Grammar School. The deaths of those informants prevented my showing them the sections which bring in their material. It means too that they will not have lived to see their eras in print. At least many of their surviving families who have invested in this project as Subscribers can see their names recorded within this History.

The living witnesses included members of some of the *OM* families who related stories from the two World Wars, of men who died, like the eldest Batty, in Ypres in 1916, Frederick Charles – his Head Master's letter to his parents is recorded in *McClure of Mill Hill*; or men who fought in both wars like his second brother, Philip, a captain at the end of that war, to be brought back, as he put it, *like an old war horse* in 1939, only to die in the Dunkirk retreat of 1940; or their youngest brother Donald, who could recall the ill-fated Narvik expedition in 1940, the Desert War in the early 1940s, and the Arnhem parachute operation of 1944, in which one of the School's most popular post-war masters, Alan Bush, was decorated; or surely two of Mill Hill's most modest heroes, Francis Cammaerts and John McGavin. The History salutes them all.

Some aspects of a History of Mill Hill might now seem so unfamiliar to the world of 2006/7 that they would appear at first sight discontinuous with the Mill Hill of today. Some Public School histories even vaunt such discontinuity. Yet those earlier *OMs*, whose names and thoughts play their due part in these pages, lived, laughed and ran in the same grounds, in many of the same buildings, and under many of the same trees, that present-day Millhillian boys and girls, and their parents, regard, quite understandably, as 'theirs'; significant parts of the natural setting and the built environment are still the same as those which were experienced even by the very earliest of Millhillians, albeit that Mill Hill's terraces are by now more plentiful, and (somewhat) more level. (Top Field and even the new "Fishing Net" still have their tolerated Western 'slopes'). Without committing the historian's sin of teleology, there is clearly a continuity rather than discontinuity in those memories, making their testimony all the more worthwhile. To the younger *OMs* of both sexes who have contributed, whom I also thank warmly (not least Annie Williams, Mill Hill's first Old Millhillienne Governor, and David Goodwin and Austin Vince, creators of the Millennium Video), this sense of an underlying continuity may give their own memories an added dimension.

The Foundation staff who gave me their scarce time are duly acknowledged but first and foremost the former Director of Administration and Finance, Lt Col Beverley Morgan, and his most helpful wife Pam, who put themselves out to make the workings of the Foundation both accessible and comprehensible to me. Warm thanks are also due to Penny Hill, Dr Roger Axworthy, Bob Taylor, Wilma Davis, Renate Kapur, Anthony Norrington; Andrew Gaylor, Peter McDonough and Sarah Ward, Trevor Chilton, Harry Barnes, Tim and Robin Corbett, Paul Bickerdike, Richard Allain, Dr Anthony Armstrong, Berinda Banks, Mark Dickinson, Bruce Dickson, Lindsey and Joe Shaw, Simon Hughes, Peter Lawson, Jason Lewis, Andy Luke, Jamie Monaghan, Mark Northen, Steve Plummer, David Proudlock, Tony Slade, Philip Thonemann, David Woodrow, Daniel Bingham and the first of Mill Hill's two TV-starring Staff, Andrew Phillips (*vide* the 2002 BBC2 programme on his father, Leslie Phillips: the second was Austin Vince in the C4 2003 series, *That'll Teach 'Em*). This book is very much about the institution which, each in their own way, they have sought to make "strikingly alive".

The wider Community The donation, via Dr David Thompson, by the URCHS Marquis Fund is much appreciated. Picture credits are noted in Appendix J. I record the permission to quote from many publishers listed in the end-of-chapter notes.

I am indebted to many others outside the School, above all: the Village's eminent local chronicler – the late Ralph Calder, David Bailey, J.Ronald Davies and other MHHS colleagues; the MHPS; Dr Michael Worms, churchwarden, St Paul's Church; Mr & Mrs Gordon Wallis; artists Sheila and Peter Hume; at St Bees, Douglas Sim, Old St Beghians Bill Gough, Tony Cotes and John Bell, but especially to Jean Clarkson and all her family for their warm Cumbrian hospitality which will never be forgotten. I am also indebted for discussions with Old Philologians, Raymond Berger, James Bidwell; help from MHSF PAs – Sonia Gribble, Betty Dove, Di Mills, Sue Pope, Heather Baim, Jill Clarke, Sylvia Day; also the Hon Brenda Robbins, former wife of A.E.Rooker Roberts. Other names, including many parents, notably Mrs Elizabeth Tinker, and Mrs Carol Minnis, are identified in the Notes.

Warm thanks for help and advice go also to successive officers of the OMC: John Watkiss – Chairman, Roger Gardner – Treasurer, John King – former Editor, *Martlet*, and to recent Presidents Ronnie Samuels, Jim Roberts, Roy Mills, Tony Bell, Ray Hubbard, Stuart Hibberdine, David Rodda, Ronnie Aye Maung, Terry Allan, and John Elliott but above all to Bill Skinner; to the former Assistant Secretary, Janet Scott, for her assistance in updating me on the whereabouts of the younger 'Old Millhilliennes', whose position within the OMC we both did our best to promote when I was Hon Secretary of the Club, and she was first appointed: equally warm thanks too to her ever-unruffled successor, Viv Wood.

Gratitude must lie with the Headmaster, William Winfield, and to successive Chairmen of the Court, Rt Hon Dame Angela Rumbold DBE and Sir Robert Balchin DL, for the remit they have meticulously adhered to – to read anything and to set down what I felt to be relevant to a true History of a unique modern educational enterprise. Some of that material must inevitably remain archival, for Mill Hill's third Historian to appraise. Many other Governors too have lent me their time in a private capacity – in particular Eric Harvey, Howell James, Bob Stewart, Graham Chase, Veronica Simmons. Apart from some suggestions, which have enhanced the story, this book, albeit sanctioned by the Court, is the author's own responsibility: any acts of commission/omission are mine alone.

Likewise, my thanks go to Phillimore & Co. Ltd, in particular to Noel Osborne and Nicola Willmot; above all to Kathy and Christopher Turrall of Ravenscourt Design, for their highly imaginative professional help in bringing this project to fruition.

Penultimately, a personal dedication: to my own parents whose decision it was to sacrifice much for my enjoyment of Mill Hill's intellectually fertile pastures for over five years, thereby giving up many comforts. I remain grateful to them for their investment in Mill Hill, a school whose story I later came to discover had several unknown connections with my own family. I hope this History will play a small part in further convincing future parents of sons and daughters that an investment in the all-round humane education which is part of Mill Hill School's ancient and yet very modern tradition is indeed one of those decisions that really matter in life.

Subscribers The final acknowledgement must lie, however, with all those who have subscribed in advance to this History – many of them also contributors to its contents – thereby reinforcing the Governors and the Headmaster in their commitment to its publication. I list their names overleaf, and hope that their lead will be joined by many thousands more over the years of Mill Hill's third century.

R.B., Reform Club,   June 2006

Subscriptions and Commemorations (*)

P. Achan
R. Achan
G.J. Adamis
S.J. Adams
M.J. Addison
J. Addison Smith
D. Ahmed
S. Aintaoui
A.J. Alcock
T. Allan
A.S. Al-Rais
M.J. Anderson
K.L.W. Armistead
P.B. Armitage
A.H. Armstrong
C.C.M. Arnold
D.R. Atchley
Adrienne Attree
P. Audemars
Dr R. Axworthy
R.M. Aye Maung
J.E. Ayto
D.A. Bailey
R.M. Bailey
Mrs Glenda Baim
Mrs Heather Baim
N. Baker
Sir Robert Balchin
M.O.T. Baldwin
R.F. Ball
Berinda Banks
A.J. Barlow
J.M. Barlow
R.M. Barlow
A.D. Barnes
Dr C.G. Barnes
H. Barnes
D. Beckett
Hannah Beckett
C. Beckingham
A.J.W. Bell
C.J.S. Belshaw
Mrs P. Bennett-Mills
M.R.W. Berry*
S.F.M. Berry
T.R.J. Berry
H.B. Berwin
J.T. Berwin
L.A. Berwin
M.I. Berwin
J.I. Besent
H.E. Beven
J.G. Bewsher
P.S. Bickerdike
Mrs Jan Bidwell
M.K. Biggs
Prof C. Binfield
S. Bird
A.N. Black
E.J. Black
J.P. Bolton
A.J. Bonner
C. Bowell
C.M.L. Bowen
J.M. Bowen
Clare Braithwaite
Isobel Braithwaite
Phoebe Braithwaite

A. Breeze
N.G. Brett-James*
A.H. Briggs
J.O. Brilliant
A.L. Brooke
D.A.B. Brown
I.C. Brownlie
B. Buckingham
D.M. Burke
P.S. Burns
R.W. Burns
J. Bush
D. Butler
Capt J.G. Butler
J.E. Campion*
H. Cannell
Prof T.E. Carlstedt
Dr D.E. Carnegie
J. Carr
G.F. Chamberlin
Dr R. Chapman
Sir Sydney Chapman
A. Chard
C.A. Charalambous
C.A. Charalambous
G. Chase
G. Chase
M. Chase
Dr A.H. Chatoo
Mrs Bridget Chawner
P.N. Christie
C.D. Clarke
Jean Clarkson
D.J.H. Clifford
J.D. Coakley
R.J. Coffin
D.N. Cohen
J.B. Cohen
M.W.H. Cohn
R. Cohn
Mrs Ann Cook
J.E.P. Copley
T. Corbett
M.W. Corby
R.J. Cotton
J.H. Cranwell
C.E. Creager
Prof F.H.C. Crick*
G.L. Cross
R.P. Cross
M.J. Cuming
C. Davies
J.E. Davies
Marjorie Davies
J.O.M. Davy
E. de Mesquita
G.H.R. de Sausmarez
R.N. Dean
D.I. Deuchar
C. Dicks
B. Dickson
N.J. Dinham
R.L. Dinham
J. Dinsdale
D.W. Dixon
Betty Dove
A.C. Downer
S. Dreyfuss

Susan Drummond
P.M.Z. Duck
S.T.G. Duckworth
Mrs Lynn Duncan
P.M. Durán
A.B. Eason*
B.D. Edmond
D.R.E. Edwards
N. Edwards
J.V. Ellen
Lady Margaret Elliot
A.D.V. Elliott
G.N. Elliott
J.C.K. Elliott
Mrs Clare Erskine-Murray
Dr E.J.M. Evesham
D.A. Fahimian
J.D. Farmer
N.E.G. Farmiloe
L.J. Farrant Shaw
S.C. Farris
N.T. Farrow
J.E. Feasey
V.B. Feteris
E. Fiddy
Rev. J.T. Fields
A.P.B. Figgis
E.S. Fischer
J.R. Fitzgerald
J.N. Fleming
K.R. Fletcher
P.S. Flood
J.F. Flower
G. Fokschaner
B.R.W. Foottit
M.R. Foottit
P.C. Foottit
S.M. Forster
J.F. Fortune
N. Foulger
A.P.S. Fox
R.M. Francis
D. Franklin
B.D. Fraser
Susan Freestone
J.L. Fry
R.A. Furness
J.D.E. Gallagher
R.J. Gardner
H. Gaved
A. Gaylor
M.I. Gee
Dr A.R. Gellert
A.C. George
T.D. Geron
D.R. Gewart
A. Ghadiali
D.J. Gibson
D.L.M. Gilbey
P.M. Gilliver
A.I.F. Goldman
P. Goldman
G.E. Goodchild
J.B. Gould
C.S. Goyder
D.A. Graham
G.M.R. Graham
J.H.M. Graham

N.H. Graham
P.A. Graham
R.W. Graves
F.S. Greenslade
J. Grimberg
I. Gundry*
Penelope Gundry
Suzanna Gundry
A.H.D. Gunning
A. Gupta
A.D. Guthrie-Jones
R.J. Hailey
D.M. Hall
P. Hamilton-Gray
P.W. Hancock
H. Hansen
Dr B.J.S. Harley
H.M.A. Harrington
Nikki Harris
Dr P.A.C. Harris
D.A.R. Harrison
Dr H.P.C. Harrison
E. Harvey
D.O. Hawes
W.G. Hawes
J.R. Hawkins
J. Hellinikakis
J. Hemingway
Rev. J.S. Henderson
M.D. Henderson
Judith Herbertson
S. Hibberdine
W.D. Hicklin
R.E. Higginson
Dr F.D. Higgs
Penny Hill
N.J. Hillman
C.R. Hilton
R.M. Hime
A.P. Hodgson
K.J-D. Hoefkens
M.W. Holden
M.A.L. Holmes
Dr A. Holmes Pickering
O.C. Holt
Rev. M. Hopkins
Mrs P. Howard
N.J. Howe-Smith
R.C. Hubbard
N.P.S. Hughes
W.D.F. Hughes
P. Hume
Rev. P. Hunt
P.J. Huston
Maria Hvorostovsky
Dr D.G. Ismay
P. Ivey
R.A. Jackson
B. Jakober
R. Jakubowski
M. Jambour-Sadeghi
H.M.P. James
M.F. James
I.W.H. Jarvis
S.D. Jenkins
B.D. Jenkinson
B.R. Jessup
L.O. Johnson

M.G. Johnson
R.J. Johnson
M.F.M. Jones
R.S. Jones
M. Jourdan
Nathalie Kadhim
B.K. Kakkad
Renate Kapur
C.R. Kelly
J. Kelsall
Rev. H.D. Kendal
J.D.M. King
S.C. Kinnersley
E.M. Kirk
R.A. Kirk
Mrs S.H. Kirk
Prof D.W. Knight
C.W. Knights
Mrs L.M.S. Kon
M.R. Lackie
A. Lakhani
Jaroslava Lambert
A. Lambie
A.B.H. Lamplugh
J.A. Lane
P. Lawson
C.J.E. Leach
M. Leon
D.R.O. Lewis
E. ap G. Lewis
S.J. Lewis
J. Living
Dr K.N. Lloyd
M.P. Lloyd
S. Lohrasb
P.A. Long
P.K.M. Longley
B.A. Loudon
G.C. Loudon
B.E.S. Mabbett
N.W.O. Mabbett
A.J. Macfarlane
Lt Col A.M. Macfarlane
K. MacInnes
T. Mackenzie
A.S. MacLennan
N.K. Maile
N.D. Marcou
D. Marks
C.T. Marx
J.A.C. Mason
Lynda Mason
P.A.C. Mason
A.M. McCarry
A.G. McClure
D.A.F. McDougall
G.H.K. McNeil
P.M. Merody
K. Metzer
A.M. Micklem
Brig J.H. Milburn
N.R.A. Millard
W.R. Mills
J.A. Milnes
K.F. Miyazaki
G.A. Mizner
M. Montague

J. Moore
A.C.P. Morgan
Lt Col B. Morgan
His Hon D.G. Morgan
D.E. Morris
A.S. Mortimer
J. Mowbray
Maj C.P. Murray
Sir James Murray*
S. Najle-Rahim
R.J. Nettleton
J.M. Newson
L.C. Newton
N. Nihat
J.D. North
G.E. Nosworthy
J.L. Nunn
B.H. Oak
Prof R. Olby
J. Oldroyd
Dr C.G. Owen
J.E. Owen
T.C. Oxenham
Dr A. Padfield
C.D. Parker
J.R. Parkhouse
P.T. Parr
S. Parry
E.P. Payne
G.K. Payne
O.V. Pearce
D. Penson
S.M.J. Peskett
M.P. Peskin
D.M. Petrie
L. Phillips
T.D. Phillips
Peggy Phimester
R.C.M. Piercy
D. Pike
S.T. Plummer
T.B. Poole
Mrs Susan Pope
J.W.H. Prentice
Mrs Karen Prichard
Maj E.B. Prince
Ursula Pulham
Mrs M.E.M. Pye-Smith
Dr I. Reekie
J.D. Rees
G.D. Regan
J.D. Reid
J.M. Relf
Dr J.D. Riddell
D.C. Rigby
O.A.L. Ringguth
Hon Mrs Brenda Robbins
G. Roberts
G.H. Roberts
J. Roberts
Mrs Sarah Roberts
W. Roberts
A.L. Rodbert
D. Rodbert
M. Rodbert
D.W. Rodda
J. Rodger

D.A. Roe
N.R. Roe
J.H. Rogers
C.G. Rose
T. M. Rothery
G. Elyot Rowland
S. Ruhemann
P.J. Rumball
P. Ruthven-Murray
K. Rybicki
C. Salmon
Dr D.H.R. Salter
S.R. Samuels
Mrs Jane Sanchez
P.Y. Sanett
H.M. Saunders
A. Savage
P. Schwitzer
M. Sellers
V.K.N. Shah
A.J. Sharp
R.A. Shaw
D.M.V. Short
S. Silver
M.S.H. Simmonds
N. Simpson
R.D. Simpson
C. Sing
W. Skinner
A.H. Slade
A.B. Smith
Mrs Anne Smith
G.C. Smith
S.L. Smyth
A.J. Soning
E.P. Stanham
A.R. Stanley
G.A. Stannard
Dr B.P. Stark
Rev. H.W. Starkey
L.T. Steele
D.J. Stevens
R.L. Stewart
Mrs M.J. Stibbe
D.A.S. Stonebanks
R.A. Stout
H.S. Stringer
R.J. Stringer
M. Stuart
G.C. Sutcliffe
M.C. Sweetman
S. Takeda
S. Takeda
N.A.J. Tandy
Dr B. Taylor
N. Taylor
P.D. Taylor
W.J.M. Taylor
D. Tennet
M.R.J. Thomas
P.H. Thonemann
F.E. Thorne
R.J. Thorne
Dr S. Thwaites
D.R.W. Tillyard
J.F. Tippett
A.K. Toulson

A.A. Turnbull
A.G. Turnbull
I.J. Turnbull
J.A. Turnbull
D.J. Turner
Fiona Turner
J.J. Turrall
W.B. Tyler
K.E. Ulgen
K.Y. Ulgen
A.B. Vaughan
Z. Vazifdar
G.O. Vero
A. Vince
C.K. Vincent
M.M. Vincent
P. Wakeham
M.P. Walker
T.D. Walker
B.H. Warmington
H.D.B. Warner
S.J. Warner
B.A. Wates
F. Watkinson
J.B. Watkiss
R.B. Watts
A.W. Welch
D.T. Welch
P.M. Welch
G.J.M. Westoby
P.R.M. Westoby
M.J. Weston
I. White*
D.H. Wickenden
I.M. Wicks
G.L.E. Wild
A.P.T. Wilkinson
C.E.R. Wilkinson
A. Williams
C.H.M. Williams
G. Williams
C.J.B. Wilson
F.N. Wilson
N.J. Wilson
E.W. Winfield
Frances Winfield
W.R. Winfield
A.N. Winmai
E. Winter
W. Wolfson
Katharine Woodrow
Philippa Woodrow
B.J. Woolf
A.K. Woollaston
M.J. Worms
G.B. Wren
D.J. Wright
S.R. Wright
T.J. Wright
W.M. Wright
D.J. Wrottesley
R.W. Wyeth
D.F. Yadgar
N. Yates
C. Zitcer

FIG. A(I) OUTLINE OF PETER COLLINSON'S WORLD FAMOUS MILL HILL CEDAR (SEE CH.I) SYMBOLISES THE GROWTH OF
THE MILL HILL SCHOOL FOUNDATION FROM THE ROOTS OF 1807.

A Beginning:
The Mill Hill Perspective

"Everything leaves a residue: every residue is a new beginning":
Playwright Tanika Gupta [pupil 338 at Mill Hill]:
"The Waiting Room"; National Theatre, The Cottesloe: June 2000

The wasps – and Master Goyder – had got there before me ...

This History is not just another narrow, inward-looking account of that most elusively British of institutions, a 'Public School' – in current non-vernacular 'pc' an 'Independent' – appealing only to nostalgia. Educationally, Mill Hill can, in fact, claim a unique 'Middle Way' all its own; and that role began with a vision. One of Mill Hill's most visionary pupils is the contemporary playwright Tanika Gupta; it is perhaps fitting for her words to preface this History, for Mill Hill's story will indeed prove to be a series of brave new beginnings.

Yet why start at all? Why does any institution or 'brand' – State, regiment, corporate entity, or even political party – that seeks primarily to be judged by what it is doing for its current 'market' – also feel a need to recognise any preceding time? Why not just accept, in L.P. Hartley's often-quoted words that *the past is a foreign country: they do things differently there?* One aspect of that difference, developed in the final chapter, is the contrast between today's more transient, facilitative view of the secondary phase of education, and the beguiling, introspective end-in-itself outlook that characterised many comparable schools in the past.

However, a school history is not the oxymoron that might at first appear. The academic outcomes for today's pupils and their parents, and the plans for tomorrow's, are grounded in processes that could only evolve over the medium-term; the principles underlying the development of those processes lie further back still, in the minds of generations of Governors, Heads, teaching staff, and – peculiarly vital for Mill Hill – Millhillians. The present is predicated on a long-running film, not a snap-shot, and a theme emerges: it is one of adaptation, to be educationally appropriate to the community served. In its chronicle of success in that process, the History of the Mill Hill School Foundation reveals – not that 'foreign country' – but a continuity, spiritual and intellectual. As Mill Hill's Chaplain, Rev. James Fields, expressed it on Foundation Day 1997, *there is no future but that we remember our past.*

Although this is a very English story, strangely – for a school whose origins are so bound up with England's, indeed Britain's own religious and social evolution – this History has no need to doff its cap to many preceding Histories, the lot of some even older schools: only at the 1907 centenary did Mill Hill first appoint a Historian. Without falling into the trap of a sentimental determinism – the School could have foundered more times than its one closure – the Bi-centennial History, as its sole forerunner claimed, should enable the Mill Hill community to *feel not isolated units, but parts of a great whole.*

As befits a school born of an enlightened, pioneering, interdenominational tradition, with a Nonconformist – and nonconformist – style all its own, this story of

Mill Hill's first 200 years breaks the mould of what is often a sober genre of literature, opening with lines such as 'The School was founded in ...'. Although due pride has its proper place in the recital of events, the responsibilities that go with privilege are confronted. There will be less statistical analysis than in such works as *Winchester and the Public School Elite* – indeed elitism itself is not a Mill Hill keynote. The timing has been fortuitous: millennial scholarship has yielded insights into Mill Hill's origins in the Enlightenment which were not available in 1907 – special even if in no way elitist.

Although the work of ten years' continuous research, oral and archival, including interface with nine of the dozen 20th-century leaders of Mill Hill, this is not a severe 'historians' History. The narrative speaks to 'the reader for pleasure'. Its task is to interpret Mill Hill to Mill Hill as well as to the outside world. The aim is to evoke as well as to record, to be accessible to all the sections of the wider Mill Hill community, as well as to the educational and social historian; footnotes and bibliographical details are banished from the page, to appear as Source Notes at the end of chapters, as are former pupils' school dates. Above all, the exclusive pronoun 'we' has itself been excluded, and the erstwhile excluding concepts of 'great' and 'major' now properly give way to the holistic yet many-faceted criterion of a 'good' school.

The focus encompasses the Italian concept of *campanilismo* – the loyalty to what can be seen from the local church tower: and also various Millhillian core-groups – what another *OM,* Tony Fitzjohn, termed "the Mill Hill mafias" – who have combined for a range of shared altruistic purposes, from his own, dedicated Kora Wildlife Trust (see Ch.IX) to London's Alford House (see Ch.VI), or the St Bees OMA (see Ch.VII). To borrow an all-but untranslatable concept from a language of increasing importance to the School, the History celebrates what the Hispanists call

Portico of Tite 1825
MHS Schoolhouse
from west at sunset;
oval plaque records visit of
HM Queen Elizabeth II at
the 1957 Sesquicentennial.
(For data on all Illustrations,
see Appendix J, p.369). *Intro.a*

2

conmoción – here that feeling of resonance with Mill Hill which unites generations and ages. However, it also embraces the view of those for whom their own education was merely a phase to be enjoyed, or endured, not investigated. An historic past has had to be newly assessed, and its relevance reasserted, for the world of League Tables, however their value may be measured.

In contrast to the still visible Harrow School across the valley, with whom a kind of love-hate relationship has persisted over the years, Mill Hill is not burdened with having to maintain a reputation as a world-famous school. This school has no monarchical, aristocratic, or monastic origins, no funding by any company, foundation or livery, nor origination in the gift of any Bishop, Field Marshal or Oxbridge College. There could be no glorification of the 19th-century call of the Anglican Ascendancy – 'Church and Empire': true independence, with the *pro's* and the *con's* so implied. Here is a school, bred in pursuit of the spirit of tolerance, which embodies to a unique degree two of the even greater *Leitmotive* of English history, and of the Enlightenment in Europe – the fight for religious and intellectual freedom, and respect for diversity. The institution which evolves is a balance of the intrinsic and the extrinsic, between what Mill Hill has stood for, and what the given market will stand. It is outward-facing, and still 'strikingly alive' for a 21st-century audience: the liberal, truly European philosophy of the author of the quotation which forms the book's title is even more apt for Mill Hill's educational 'Middle Way' today than it was in Gladstone's time.

That independence demands that there will be no sole reliance on a school's equivalent of diplomatic history – Minutes of Governors' Meetings: what the historian A.L.Rowse has called *unilateral history... history in only one dimension, with the*

'Mill Hill On Sea' – wartime exile in St Bees village, Tomlin Head in background; St Bees School (r.). *Intro.b*

Sir James Murray,
Dr Weymouth's Assistant
Master at MHS, 1870-85,
originator of the *O.E.D. Intro.c*

whole heart, soul, and substance left out. There will, however, be messages about what the Governors have achieved for this one 'Public School' – the most celebrated contribution the English have made to educational practice. What is both a social and a corporate history must span the four levels of perception that a school community embodies, from the would-be wider Governors' vista and the broad perspectives of the core academic staff, through to the inevitably short horizons of pupils and parents, and – without being confined by them – the time-limited visions of many Headmasters: there is also need to balance a natural sense that their Mill Hills were *the* sole, permanent Mill Hill.

There will be a focus of interest too for those who cherish this surviving 'London Village' environment – well described by the biographer of one of Mill Hill School's most famous world figures, Sir James Murray: *still surprisingly rural… above all there were views… on each side of the ridge the land drops away and the school occupies a magnificent site…*

Although the Foundation is now analogous to a train with three component carriages, each important in itself, it is the front engine, and the destination, that must be salient. Yet the full 200-year trainload only comprises some 15,000 pupils: it could be visualised as being contained within Lord's – the ground on which Mill Hill's first "Blue" of 1885, Sidney Pauling, played cricket for Middlesex. This small but diverse army is united by a single truth: that its history is greater than the sum of its parts – it has a significance beyond a Mill Hill seen merely as a school. It is a story that will at times look back, to trace the ongoing linkages, but – in the epithet favoured by one of the School's past leaders, Sir John McClure – its thrust will always be *forwards*, highlighting the ideas which have equipped Mill Hill for a competitive, consumerist world. Anticipating later chapters, the evolution of terminology through to 'Independent' is brought in here, **Fig. B**, showing the flows into membership of 'Public Schooldom' – this obstinately surviving nomenclature, with its still evocative but non-'pc' undertones, being retained in the narrative; the Mill Hill of the 21st century is, however, happily freed from the 'effortless superiority' that this term once embodied.

But to return to the wasps, and to Cecil Goyder…

A narrow, rickety little-known stairway in Mill Hill's School House, possibly still the well-worn unpainted woodwork of the William Tite building of 1825, leads up to the attic above the Portico and the main Dining Hall. Up these same stairs in 1923, in the small hours of the morning, awoken by the alarm clock under his pillow, the 17-year-old Cecil Goyder, soon to become the youngest in the long line of Mill Hill's alumni to achieve international celebrity, would tip-toe his way to check the array of aerials on the roof. Initially from there, and later from the newly-built Science Block, he would try once more to make wireless contact with the far side of the Atlantic, and with schools at the opposite end of the globe : 'England's Marconi', as the newspaper billboards were to proclaim him, at a time when that inventive name was synonymous with success (and not yet associated with Mussolini's anti-semitism). *The Times* would hail him in 1988 as the 'schoolboy who broke the rules' when the plaque commemorating him was unveiled.

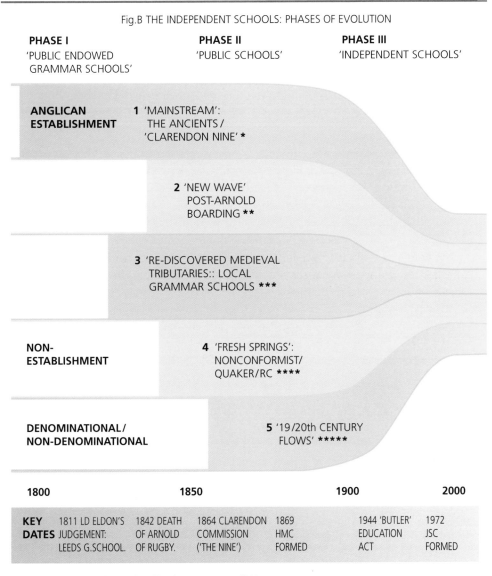

Fig.B THE INDEPENDENT SCHOOLS: PHASES OF EVOLUTION

PHASE I	PHASE II	PHASE III
'PUBLIC ENDOWED GRAMMAR SCHOOLS'	'PUBLIC SCHOOLS'	'INDEPENDENT SCHOOLS'

ANGLICAN ESTABLISHMENT — **1** 'MAINSTREAM': THE ANCIENTS / 'CLARENDON NINE' *

2 'NEW WAVE' POST-ARNOLD BOARDING **

3 'RE-DISCOVERED MEDIEVAL TRIBUTARIES:: LOCAL GRAMMAR SCHOOLS ***

NON-ESTABLISHMENT — **4** 'FRESH SPRINGS': NONCONFORMIST/ QUAKER/RC ****

DENOMINATIONAL/ NON-DENOMINATIONAL — **5** '19/20th CENTURY FLOWS' *****

1800 — 1850 — 1900 — 2000

| KEY DATES | 1811 LD ELDON'S JUDGEMENT: LEEDS G.SCHOOL. | 1842 DEATH OF ARNOLD OF RUGBY. | 1864 CLARENDON COMMISSION ('THE NINE') | 1869 HMC FORMED | 1944 'BUTLER' EDUCATION ACT | 1972 JSC FORMED |

Much of this table will be explained in Chapters I to IV, and VIII

* 1. WINCHESTER, ETON, WESTMINSTER, HARROW, RUGBY, CHARTERHOUSE, SHREWSBURY, ST. PAUL'S, MERCHANT TAYLOR'S.
** 2. e.g. MARLBOROUGH, CHELTENHAM
*** 3. e.g. UPPINGHAM, OUNDLE
**** 4. QUAKER (ACKWORTH 1779); RC (AMPLEFORTH 1802); NONCONFORMIST INTERDENOMINATIONAL (MILL HILL 1807)
***** 5. e.g. CATERHAM, WOODSIDE GROVE, SILCOATES, BOOTHAM, WOODARD SCHOOLS, CRANLEIGH

Perspective

To the north-east of the loft, on the right, are the original 19th-century rafters, charred but sturdy, that withstood the School's first incendiary raid in the Second World War – on 16 November 1940. Between the wars, this was the bedroom of the School Major-Domo; later on, a small select group of boys had slept, laughed, ragged and scragged up here, in a kind of dormitory extension; for a time in the 1970s it was

5

even mooted to house a senior monitor. Facing you, to the north-west, a narrow sash window gives onto the roof, officially out of bounds to all, but where carved initials on the brickwork tell of many an infringement after 'Lights-Out', before the days of Health and Safety regulations. Negotiating one's way over a window-sill full of another set of former inhabitants – that ever-accumulating pile of long-dead wasps, trapped for all time – a visitor would emerge, with effort, into the sunlight.

From a patchwork of slates whose faults over ensuing centuries, until the would-be final re-roofing of 2005, had been a running theme – and indeed more often than not, a theme of running water – there is a simply breathtaking view. This is Mill Hill's horizon: it dawns where the dream of Mill Hill was first dreamed, in the busy City of London, to the east. To quote the biography of one of the first of Mill Hill's distinguished pupils – the 19th-century American merchant prince, Henry Shaw (his public gardens in St Louis, echoing the gardens, and the Portico, at Mill Hill): *the site offered a magnificent view over four counties. From the terrace the students could make out Epsom Downs and Windsor Castle in the distance and the spires of Harrow.* A long-cherished Mill Hill custom grants a half-holiday if, on an exceptionally clear day, Windsor can actually be seen from Top Terrace: a reward more honoured in the breach than in the observance, it was last disallowed by a hard-pressed Head Master of the 1980s. In the far distance, the blue ridges on the skyline are the Surrey Hills. There Leith Hill, touching 1000 feet above sea level, bears its equally English links to a very different generation of 'Wasps' – those of Aristophanes (recalled in the incidental music by

Only extant copy, *Evening Standard* headline on MHS custom of half-term holiday if Windsor Castle is visible from Top Terrace. (l.) Arnhem hero Alan Bush, former Oxford "Blue" – later Ridgeway Housemaster – coaches rugby on Top Field; (r.) RQMS "Dasher" Crouch instructs CCF Band. *Intro.d*

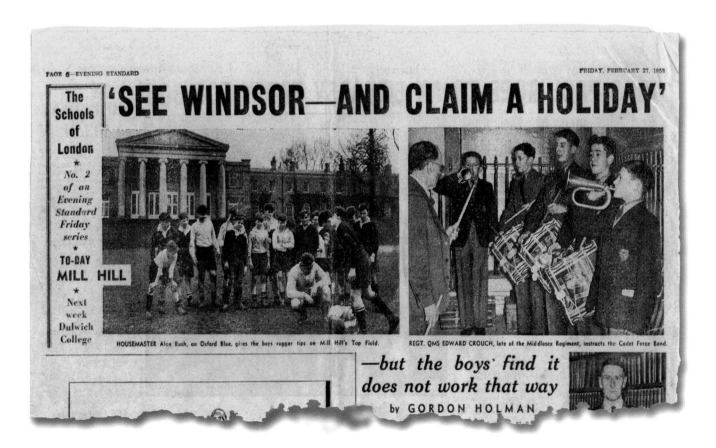

PAGE 6—EVENING STANDARD   FRIDAY, FEBRUARY 27, 1953

The Schools of London
★
No. 2 of an Evening Standard Friday series
★
TO-DAY
MILL HILL
★
Next week Dulwich College

'SEE WINDSOR—AND CLAIM A HOLIDAY'

HOUSEMASTER Alan Bush, an Oxford Blue, gives the boys rugger tips on M.ll Hill's Top Field.   REGT. QMS EDWARD CROUCH, late of the Middlesex Regiment, instructs the Cadet Force Band.

—but the boys' find it does not work that way

by GORDON HOLMAN

Vaughan Williams, a musician of special interest as the teacher of Mill Hill resident and opera-composer, the late *OM* Inglis Gundry).

This perspective was also enjoyed by generations of the Common Room, not least by the longest-serving Head, Sir John McClure, and by that one-time Assistant Master, Sir James Murray, creator of the *Oxford English Dictionary*, both commemorated in eponymous Day-Houses. It also embraces three of the major educational establishments that were constantly in their minds, starting with the site of the first St Paul's School, next to Wren's cathedral, to the left. More or less half-way, in the middle distance, beyond Harrow upon its own adopted hill-top but some 20 feet lower, is Senate House, the tall focal point of Britain's largest tertiary educational body, London University, for a long time one of the few universities to which the sons of Mill Hill's 'Dissenters' could aspire. Many other establishments of learning, both public and 'Public', lie down there on the Thames Valley bed. These include, far to the east, and now obscured both by trees, and by history, the location of a once-active 18th/19th-century academy, Homerton College (today part of Cambridge University), whose role in Mill Hill's origins will shortly be explored.

The great 20th-century temple to Mammon, Canary Wharf, in Docklands, also comes within this horizon, to the distant east: intended to be Europe's highest building, thereby to proclaim the continuing predominance of London as the heart of the world's financial markets. As Shelley's Ozymandias exclaimed, with intended irony, *Look on my works, ye mighty...*

The McClure era: 19C skyline seen from the School, looking across Cinder Path towards the old Gears Cricket Pavilion: chapel of Harrow School on middle horizon. *Intro.e*

Symbolically, in that one glorious, imaginative sweep of the eye, much of Mill Hill's history, and significant elements of a testing future, are discernible. Even the House of Windsor itself, from a 21st-century vantage point, offers parallels – if this is not *lèse-majesté* – with Mill Hill's own lesser story. Both these institutions, albeit in their very different ways, have been able to surmount the difficulties facing them in the last and uncomfortably questioning quarter of the 20th century. Each has succeeded in doing so by drawing deep from the complementary wells of principle and flexibility fashioned in earlier eras; Mill Hill, and the monarchy which would be a gracious visitor on several occasions, have both been able to reinterpret their traditions, thereby to face a new century with renewed confidence in their purposes, and restored faith in themselves; one aspect of that will be the resolution of what can be justifiably seen as a battle for the soul and identity of Mill Hill, waged in the late 20th century.

Setting the scene

Even within the context of the strange Public School culture, Mill Hill has always engendered a special kind of feeling, very akin to the intimate closeness that naval people experience towards their ships. To refer to Mill Hill merely as 'it' does not do justice to such a relationship. In the setting of a History which is affectionate as well as critical, the feminine pronoun seems more appropriate; that was certainly how the most mystical, the last *OM* and the only triply-serving of the Foundation's Heads, Rooker Roberts, and the School's first Historian, Brett James, always referred to their *alma mater*.

Science School commemorates award of 1962 Nobel Prize to Prof Francis Crick *OM*, appointed to the Order of Merit, 1991: (plaque was an outcome of research for the History). *Intro.f*

PROFESSOR FRANCIS H.C. CRICK, F.R.S., B.Sc LONDON, PH.D CANTAB

WINNER OF THE NOBEL PRIZE FOR MEDICINE 1962

FOR HIS PART IN THE DISCOVERY OF THE MOLECULAR STRUCTURE OF DNA

APPOINTED TO THE ORDER OF MERIT 1991

PUPIL AT MILL HILL SCHOOL 1930-1934

Mill Hill commands an incomparable position along an historic Ridgeway, the highest landmark across Europe, as the proverbial but over-credited crow flies – not quite to the Urals but 100 miles west – to the *Timanskiy Kryazh*. Yet Mill Hill has never looked down on her rival schools, in either of the two sectors, in anything other than a purely geographical sense. Figuratively, the School has always looked 'across' to them, respectfully selecting 'the best of the best' – as the first *Mill Hill Magazine* of 1873 put it – when describing the design of the School's original Out-House, Burton Bank. From the very earliest days, Mill Hill's Founding Fathers, men of the 18th-century Enlightenment, sought to emulate whatever good things the bulwarks of the Anglican establishment had developed: schools with whom they would later compete both sportively and academically – Eton, Rugby, Charterhouse, Winchester, Westminster, Harrow and many more (see Information Supplement No.6). They would also innovate in four areas which the older regimes had not yet understood. The School has been hailed as one of the 'science pioneers' – that new field epitomised in "England's Marconi" or in the sole *OM* holder of the OM, Nobel Prizewinner Francis Crick (see Ch.VI); others were music – to become one of Mill Hill's oldest traditions; or the value of smaller classes; or the teaching of modern languages. At that stage of Mill Hill's first century, these were the factors through which the 'Free Church schools' (as they would become known by the 1860s) would be regarded as the finest in Britain.

Of the many analogies that may be offered for a school, the most descriptive is that of a closely-textured tapestry, with its many intimately interwoven strands. Within that tapestry, a school's identity can be hard to define, part fact, part emotion and sentiment; part prose, part poetry. Viewed from one perspective, it is today yet another man-made construct, a business in search of a mission statement; from another point of view it is itself such an indefinable, unstructured, spiritual mission that no simple statement can enshrine it. James Murray offered this basic definition, among the 18 columns of philological erudition which initially his own Mill Hill boys, and then later other Public Schoolboys, scholars and undergraduates, helped him to compile about what he called 'schooldom' – it has a pleasantly forward-sounding ring for the co-educational Mill Hill of today: 'an establishment in which boys, or girls, or both receive instruction'. As the History unfolds, other problems of definition will be explored: buildings and grounds: Heads and teaching staff: officers and servants: pupils – all the 'unknown warriors' and not merely those with their names in the far-too ephemeral lights of school, together with their supportive parents: traditions, language and ideals – these are all part of the picture. Yet economic and practical considerations require that a line be drawn, both chronologically and geographically, to determine how far each of the constitutent strands is unravelled and examined. The trees of Mill Hill are a significant part of her heritage – albeit today also part of a burdensome cost-base: to borrow from that metaphor, it is vital that the many individual 'trees' making up Mill Hill's story are not allowed to obscure the 'wood' itself – the essential spirit and character of an institution which is still unique among the Public Schools.

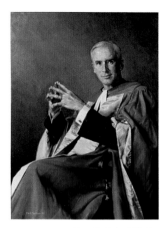

Rev Dr John Whale,
the last ordained and sole
graduate of both Oxford and
Cambridge as Head Master,
1944-51. *Intro.g*

The Public School

Although the 1944 'Butler' Act defined Public Schools as the members of HMC – the Headmasters' and Headmistresses' Conference in England and Wales – a millennial review from the Independent Schools Council's *Annual Census 2000* showed the HMC group of 242 opting, with six other bodies, including the Girls and Preparatory Schools, to be embraced as 'ISC' members. 2,400 'Independents' educate some 600,000 pupils (7% of all children) in the UK; 30 per cent enter from State schools, 70,000 become boy or girl boarders. 90 per cent of Independent A-Level leavers go on to higher education. Of 1,271 'ISC' Independent Schools, (serving 80 per cent of independently-educated pupils), Mill Hill's universe now lies within the mere 1,052 having 'charitable status'; (see Chs. IV, VII, XII).

The study of this small but politically highlighted world, seemingly – in the words of a most recent researcher – a place of *myth, fantasy and legend*, is never-ending in its fascination. It is also somewhat daunting for the unwary, and beset with paradoxes. For a start, unlike its foreign counterparts, a Public School although nowadays open to any pupil of either sex with the right ability and capacity, is not 'Public' in the sense that it is free to every taxpayer. The Mill Hill of the 1840s was worried about the proposal to build a 'public school' (a local school) on the opposite side of The Ridgeway. It is therefore 'Private' in the American sense, yet some of its exponents also have a long tradition of making themselves available through bursaries to particularly deserving sections of 'the public'. What can justifiably be termed Mill Hill School's pathfinding 'Middle Way' in bridging the two sectors in Britain's national educational policy – itself a characteristic expression of her tradition – will be explored, with all its due importance, throughout the text.

The classical concept of an academic *Gymnasium* is one which has meaning for Mill Hill, particularly, as the History will relate, at that most critical time for the School, the period of upheaval and the ferment of ideas during and after the Second World War. It was that concept – (pronounced of course with a hard 'G') – which inspired Richard Buckland and the Court of Governors in its bold initiative with Middlesex County Council in the 1940s. The author had great difficulty in 1950 in explaining the semantics of 'Public' Schools to a country which still retains that ancient term to this day for part of its educational system. This was in the *Gymnasium* in the Rhineland, to which he was sent, as one of the leaders of a Foreign Office Educational Interchange, to start to heal the divisions of war, by the then Head Master, the world-famous theologian, Dr J.S. Whale. (A somewhat lesser aspect of his fame was the fact that he was and still is the sole Mill Hill figure to have graced the front page of *Radio Times* by reason of his then daily peak-hour religious broadcasts.)

The School donated from her hard-pressed coffers the princely sum of £6 6 shillings towards this ambassadorial exercise. It was one of the first steps that Mill Hill took to start thinking European again, and so to enhance the broad internationalism that had long been yet another important, and still growing, part of her story. For a German, 'public' can only mean *öffentlich* – open to all. Here was clearly yet another indication of how peculiar – and still not quite continental – the English, or the British, really were.

Another semantic problem is thereby introduced. The literary and legendary part of the vast schoolboy, and schoolgirl, literature is set unmistakably in England: from the work of one of Mill Hill's earliest visitors and prizegivers, Thomas Hughes MP, the author of *Tom Brown's Schooldays*, or the girls' equivalent, Angela Brazil, to the more contemporary but equally cad-infested Flashman sagas – all of these celebrated fictional works are unequivocally 'English'. Yet the Public School is not just an English – and Welsh – phenomenon, nor is it merely British, although 29 other great rival schools are to be found in Scotland, Northern Ireland, the Isle of Man and the Channel Islands. The British Public School concept has been replicated the world over, including the non-capitalist countries (and sometimes even subverted – see Ch.VI); 12 European Schools, and 67 schools in the Commonwealth are also HMC members.

Although these establishments have become one of the UK's most enduring invisible exports, pupils from overseas still often prefer to come to Britain, and to Mill Hill, to sample the product in the land of its birth, the export thus also acting as an invisible reverse import.

Again, and perhaps this actually is a true aspect of British idiosyncrasy, quite baffling to many social reformers, although in theory this system is exclusive to a relatively small percentage of the population – just over half a million pupils continue to attend the Independent sector – yet countless millions of British schoolboys and schoolgirls will have read such fictional accounts of Boarding school life as Kipling's *Stalky & Co*, and Vachell's *The Hill*, during their formative years. Like many of the parents of the 'Middlesex' boys of the 1945-70s era, they will have come to regard these schools as very much part of their own personal inclusive experience. (One of these fictional works has undertones for Mill Hill, possibly being based on aspects of the School: *The Fifth Form at St Dominic's* by Talbot Baines Reed, a member of the vast Pye-Smith clan of Mill Hill families. Edgar Anstey's story of the Bultitude father and son, *Vice Versa*, of 1882, was also at one stage thought to enshrine a famous Mill Hill Head, Dr Weymouth, in the figure of 'Dr Grimstone'; this pleasant myth was however – unfortunately – later disproved.)

Whilst Mill Hill had not yet become quite popular enough to qualify for the cartoon series of Victorian Headmasters by 'Spy', an early example of this paradox of perception is the inclusion of Public Schools, and Mill Hill, in those indicators of popular Edwardian culture – the *Punch* joke, and the first 'commercial breaks' – the world of the former Cigarette Cards.

There is a parallel in the cult of the modern film and TV star – so often also reflected in such ephemera, a kind of vicarious ownership; in that sense, the Public School system in its own right, argued by historian Vivian Ogilvie to be a formative element in British history, has seemed to belong to everyone.

One of the strongest though not consistent characteristics of the early Public School system, dating from its medieval and monkish origins, was that it was primarily for Boarders, not for that minority which was once termed, with an unjustified sense of tribal superiority, "Day bugs". Indeed, as the History shows, an early decision by Mill Hill's Founding Committee, in 1806, to switch their focus from

Popular cigarette card *c*1907: MHS Coat of Arms No 3 – *Excelsior* – replaced by *et virtutem et musas*, but without monogram in centre of the cross: the motto was much plagiarised. *Intro.h*

Maurice Jacks, the only Head Master to serve twice, 1922-37, and 1943-4 during WWII evacuation in Cumbria. *Intro.i*

Day to Boarding was one of the first indications of an essential Mill Hill characteristic, the ability to adapt to circumstances – and to be inventive at the same time. One national survey has suggested that the Boarding experience, with its ambivalent blend of epic endurance, akin to people's perception of a sustained war, is still the preferred ideal for 50 per cent of parents. Yet today that process has been reversed, and Day pupils are the dominant inheritors of the Public School system. Mill Hill's part in that evolutionary process will unfold in Chapters XI and XII.

More than 150 learned works, many of whose insights inform this History, explore that legendary system. There are still many vital distinctions about the Independent Sector in which parents continue to be prepared to invest significantly. Nevertheless Mill Hill, taking a traditionally individual line, has sought, from well before the First World War, and certainly from the days of educationist Head Master Maurice Jacks, and of the Churchillian vision of the 1944 Education Act, to be compared increasingly with the best in the wider State Sector. This has been done in terms of curriculum, academic achievement, and managerial technique, but also most critically in terms of the 'value added' offered to each highly differentiated pupil: this is a central concept, to which the History returns.

Mill Hill has been a member of that Independent system, through the HMC – and also now AGBIS (see Appendix A: Abbreviations) for nearly 150 years, by personal invitation to the then Head Master Dr Weymouth. Yet the system is no monolith. HMC and its counterpart, the GBA, encourage, through the ISC, what business and industry talk of as bench-marking and 'best practice'. It can provide a framework, often on an area basis, for civilised co-existence between competing

Mill Hill Preparatory School, Belmont, The Ridgeway, from east, one of the major Grade II listed buildings of Mill Hill Village, with its cedar (attributed to Peter Collinson) – sadly cut down for safety reasons in 2005.
Intro.j

members – it cannot enforce any mandatory rules; this system is at the very least a most permissive one. Needless to say, there are similarities between Mill Hill's features and those of other Public Schools. The fortunes of war provided a special window, in two senses, on one school, St Bees (see Ch.VII); over the intervening 65 years, their history reveals many parallel customs and themes. Nevertheless, the freedom with which Mill Hill's Heads and their Governors have been able, over the generations, to decide what should be recommended to one specific though constantly changing market-sector – Mill Hill parents – is another facet which has made the School very much an institution of itself, *sui generis*, and not directly comparable with any peer-group.

Definitions and territory

It may be useful to offer a few commonsense explanations at this point about the way this History chooses to use its words.

'Mill Hill': as one local history has related, many towns with a famous school in their midst tend to be forever linked with that institution. Here, the School's own colloquial title 'Mill Hill' is used throughout to identify not the territory occupied, but today's three-stage educational establishment, the Mill Hill School Foundation, whose 200-year growth was shown in **Fig.A(i)**: first, the secondary Grammar School of 1807, still retaining a 'Boarding ethos', Mill Hill School; second, at one end of The Ridgeway, Belmont, the Junior/ Preparatory School (1912); third, since 1995, the Mill Hill Pre-Prep at the other end, or to be more precise, at the top of Wills Grove (in old Winterstoke House, now coupled with another Millhillian name,

Mill Hill School Foundation's Pre-Prep School, Grimsdell (created from the MHS Winterstoke Boarding House, 1995). *Intro.k*

"Grimsdell"). This History sets out to complement, not duplicate, the local story: that has been well told by a long line of local historians, including two Millhillians (Brett James, and the celebrated international architect Martin Briggs – see Ch.V). The most recent, Bernard Oak, pays this compliment about the linkage: *apart from its renown as a seat of learning, Mill Hill School has had other beneficial influences upon the neighbourhood and has done much to preserve the rural and gentrified air of the Village.*

'The School': this colloquially shortened version will indicate 'Mill Hill School'. (For earlier eras, the peculiar acronym 'GC' would have served that purpose, but its use is now out of fashion: see 'Millhillisms': Appendix E.)

'The Village': Mill Hill Village is still signposted at the foot of Bittacy Hill. What has been called 'the proper Mill Hill on The Ridgeway' is the part of the larger district which has most value for the School; consequently that is the focus as far as this History is concerned. By the 1920s the two entities were almost synonymous: a post-card to Herbert Coates, a revered Head of Maths, was addressed to: 'The School, Mill Hill, London, England'. The School took pains between the Wars to assert this rusticity in her postal address, and also, through Martin Briggs, to set up the two picturesque Village signs that mark its ancient boundaries, from the top of Milespit Hill, to the top of Highwood Hill above The Forge.

'The Mill Hill Community': again, for local historians this use of the term 'Community' may occasion an initial problem, yet it is hoped that they will respect the underlying thinking; (from John McClure onwards, many have used the term 'Greater Mill Hill' for this same purpose). The School, from the very earliest days, was conscious of the need to work with the world outside any formal bounds. The young ladies of Miss Russell's Academy were a respected visiting part of Mill Hill's chapel services in the 19th century, as well as of the science and other lectures; their presence underlines the fact that the two sexes were never so abstracted from each

Road-sign at Mill Hill East: 'Mill Hill Village'. *Intro.1*

other before the 1970s, as legend might lead one to suppose. As another example, the permission of the owner of Moat Mount for boys to walk over its fields was carefully monitored to ensure the relationship held good; in what the Founding Founders described as *a situation peculiarly pleasant and salubrious*, the School has always been concerned about the surrounding environment, and Community Service has been high on the agenda for over 80 years. Moreover there is little evidence – either at Mill Hill or at the wartime Cumbrian exile – of the kind of stand-offish behaviour that some other local neighbourhoods around the country complain about from time to time, in relation to a major school, with a strong Boarding element, in their midst.

However, today the sense of outside Community goes wider. As part of this concept the History visits that Cumbrian setting which Mill Hill and Belmont shared from 1939 to 1945/6, and also the Outdoor Studies Centre both enjoyed at Dentdale, in Cumbria. There will be reference to the Young People's Club in Lambeth – Alford House – which dedicated Millhillians have sponsored from 1929 onwards, and also to the *Institution Join-Lambert* in Rouen, and other European schools, where both Mill Hill and Belmont now have well-established links. Even more importantly, Mill

Hill sees her wider community as lying – albeit mainly within Europe – yet also globally, in terms of ongoing educational and sporting linkage, and catchment: from early on, pupils came to Mill Hill not merely from all over the British Isles, but also from overseas, and that tradition has continued happily. Mill Hill Headmasters today travel the globe to talk to prospective parents. The Mill Hill Community also embraces corners of the world such as India, Nicaragua, and Ethiopia, where Voluntary Service tasks have been accomplished: 'Community' is now an important concept – a little wider than the idea of a 'Greater Mill Hill' – for all parts of the Mill Hill School Foundation, not just a territorial term.

A School of Heads

Although the leadership of Mill Hill will be explored as the story unfolds, listed for easy referral in Appendix B are all those members of what Maurice Jacks called 'a school of Heads' who have led the School academically – 'Head Tutors', Head Masters, Heads, Acting Heads.* There have been 34 different reigns, *de jure* and *de facto*, so far involving 32 different individuals: mould-breakers, manager-supremos, mystics, maestros; academics, all-rounders; reformers, consolidators; many successes, and a few relative failures, their relativity open to debate. Over the past 150 years, five came from headships of comparable institutions, four went on to assume similar roles. Of the 27 substantive appointments, only 12 were of significant length; thus the History focuses on 12 *key periods*, all but one of which lasted seven years or more. The average span of just under eight years reflects the unstable early period, when Heads and Chaplains came and went, as frequently as the proverbial cooks, as well as the disruptive years of the Second World War. Acting Heads, as opposed to the two emergency but full-time appointments of the World War two era,

Present-day photograph of still-charred 1825 oak roof rafters above the Dining Hall, after WWII fire raid. *Intro.m*

will be shown [*thus]; even though only taking the helm for an interim of a few months, they bore the exposed and lonely chief executive responsibility, often in circumstances as challenging as those of the normally appointed Heads. Deserving to be acknowledged in retrospect, the often-used Mill Hill term 'interregnum', to depict those times of office, is not used here (see Ch.II).

Overall, no fewer than 10 MHS Head Masters (excluding the early and ambiguous Chaplain-Principals) were Ministers of Religion, of whom nine took office during the first 100 years, and only one during the second period, surely one of the most signal differences between the two centuries and one common to many Public Schools. Of the significant Heads during the first century, only one is not known to have had a College/ University qualification; two gained degrees at Cambridge (including John McClure, spanning both centuries), four at London (excluding McClure's matriculation), two at Glasgow. Over the second century, five appointed Head Masters took degrees at Cambridge University, five at Oxford, one each at London and Edinburgh: two-thirds had been educated at Boarding schools, one-third at grammar schools. Of the academic disciplines, History predominated (Kingston Derry, Rooker Roberts, John Whale, Michael Hart). Two each came from: Classics (Maurice Jacks, Alan Elliott); Maths (John McClure, Euan MacAlpine); Modern Languages (Alastair Graham, and the Head leading the School into the 21st century, William Winfield); and one each from Theology (John Whale again) and English (Roy Moore). At Belmont, all eight Heads held degrees; five came from Prep Schools (one from within Belmont) of which three were Heads; three had taught at Public Schools. At the Pre-Prep, the sole Principal has been Pauline Bennett-Mills, with the appropriate Certificate of Education.

Mill Hill has been a proving ground for at least 20 other seats of learning over the past 100 years; senior staff have gone on, to head up such distinguished schools as Eltham; Merchiston; Plymouth College; King Edward VI Grammar School, Birmingham; Glasgow Academy; King Edward VII Grammar School, Sheffield; Christ's College, Finchley; Queen's College, and King's College, Taunton; Hampton School; Royal Grammar School, High Wycombe and Culford School. Although no longer to be circumscribed by the Brett James' idealised concept of 'the schoolmaster as a leader of boys', the History is certainly about what these many generations of Mill Hill staff and their Heads have tried to do for the young, sometimes very young, people in their care, in this brief, formative and intensely memorable phase of their lives. Despite the negative image that some writers have projected in the past – Etonion George Orwell wrote that *they never really get over that frightful drilling they go through at public schools* – things have changed radically: it is also part of the History's role to record how those young Millhillians have gone on to do interesting and valuable things in later life, without, however, claiming too direct a part in such evolutions. Nevertheless, this is not primarily a record of each cohort's achievements; nor does it cover the workings of the vibrant Old Millhillians Club, itself one aspect of the Mill Hill tradition (apart from the Order of Merit, the initials 'OM' also connote an Italian car, a Swedish corporation, and a magazine); the careers of former pupils, like those of former staff, only enter these pages in so far as they illustrate Mill Hill's own ongoing corporate story.

Summary and plan

The story of the Mill Hill School Foundation is not simply one of eclecticism, picking and choosing according to circumstance – although, as the History will reveal, flexibility is a key aspect of that constant inventiveness, exemplified in the young Cecil Goyder, which remains a Mill Hill characteristic. Manifesting themselves strongly through the chronicles of these first 200 years – sometimes waxing, sometimes waning – there run two central threads, without which Mill Hill cannot be understood: a vein of moral values, deriving from that early conditioning, the 'Nonconformist conscience'; and, perhaps even more educationally productive, a questioning attitude, deriving from her intellectual origins in the Enlightenment.

Those wasps on the School House window-sill had long since lost their sting: in contrast Mill Hill's pupils have continued to make fresh new impacts on the world. Many follow in the steps of the entrepreneurial Henry Shaw, with sights set on the world's opportunities; some, like the modest but brilliant Cecil Goyder, have held to a single aim. For others, the role model might well have been Herbert Ward – gifted sculptor and artist, intrepid explorer and celebrated author of *Mr Poilu: a rebel against the rigid mould of the day... he left with little to indicate the variety and success of his future career.* He was also one of those – not forgotten in this story – who have ended their lives in the service of their country.

Herbert Ward *OM*, Congo explorer, writer and adventurer: died of wounds, driving ambulances in France, WWI. The contemporary Ward Art Bursary was named in his memory. *Intro.n*

Three overlapping phases emerge: 'religion and learning'; 'sport and imperialism'; 'culture and vocation'. Seven parallel dimensions can be traced: the spiritual base; the sociological catchment from which the intake has been drawn; the School's evolutionary role in the wider national system; the erstwhile Boarding/ Day dichotomy; the European factor within a broad internationalism; the 'distaff' side – co-education; and the element bridging these dimensions – the educational outcome or 'product'. In contrast to the practice of some other Histories, the institution itself is not seen as 'the product'. Infusing these lines of development, the ongoing values are identified that make Mill Hill different, the abstract yet energising qualities that continue to inform the thinking of all parts of the Mill Hill School Foundation of the year 2006/7.

The course of the story divides logically into a sequence of 12 chapters, building on the philosophical origins, to create today's many-sided institution: a direct line from the pre-19th-century roots of the tree, to the flourishing young branches of the new century. Whilst covering all the mainstream events, the History also chronicles for the first time some of the unresolved sub-issues arising from the School's odyssey: the 'Murray/Weymouth' mystery; the strange pre-war interaction with the *NSD Oberschule;* 'The Case of Dr Derry'; the 'Eldorado Island' of the Emergency Hospital; and 'The Guinea Pigs' through whom Mill Hill helped to make educational history.

Whilst valuing each of the three parts of the Foundation in its own terms, for its appointed contribution to the teaching of its pupils, the balance will inevitably reflect the varying lengths of time over which these three parts of the 'Trinity' have been in the ownership of the Court of Governors. Belmont, though closely linked with the School since 1912, has only been within the Court's custody for 44 of the 200 years, after the purchase in 1963; the Pre-Prep was not invented, thus to extend that vision for the Foundation, until 1995. It will be for the last chapter of the story to embody this third stage: a conclusion that will depict in many ways a happy turning of the wheel of history. For here is a Foundation in tune with the society of the new millennium, seen to be confidently seized of a fundamentally liberating idea and one which has the appearance of still being relevant for its time: that idea, custom-built, yet custom-based, is independent education.

This then is a first glimpse of the perspective that Mill Hill has offered to all those 15,000 pupils: distinctive, serious, properly sceptical, non-establishment. That grouping is the chief constituent but also the end-purpose of this colourful, complex tapestry. To them belongs the story which now unfolds.

All Chs: for the detailed sources which inform this History, see Notes at chapter ends, also the Mill Hill Bibliography, and the Bibliographical Note; subsequent refs to quoted titles = (*op cit*).

All succeeding Chs. have four standard sources – The MHS Archive (#); *Mill Hill Magazines* ('*MHM's*) 1873-2006; Committee or Governors' Minute Books (GMs) 1805-2006; MHS School Registers – 'RR1' (1807-1926); 'RR2' (1926-1957); 'RR3' (1957-1983); 'RR4' (1983-2000).

Sources for Introduction include: R.Porter, *Enlightenment – Britain and the Creation of the Modern World* (2000), Chs.I, II, V & passim; U. Henriques, *Religious Toleration in England 1787-1833* (1961); J.A.H.Murray, ed *New English Dictionary* (1888+) (the 'OED'); K.M.E.Murray, *Caught in the Web of Words* (Yale U.P., New Haven, 1977), 104; G.F.Timpson [1906-10], *Sir James A.H.Murray – A Self-Portrait* (1957); Whitakers Almanack, 2005; HMC Records; N.G.Brett James [1894-8], *The History of Mill Hill School 1807-1907* (1909), ... & *1807-1923* (1923); G.Smith, *Belmont 1912-1994* (1994); J.G.Bewsher, [1948-52], *Nobis, The Story of a Club* (1979); V.Ogilvie, *The English Public School* (Batsford, 1957), 1 etc; R.Wilkinson, *The Prefects* (O.U.P. 1964); C.J.Shrosbree, *The Public Schools and Private Education: The Clarendon Commission 1861-64 and the Public School Acts* (Manchester U.P., 1988); T.J.Bishop & R.Wilkinson, *Winchester & the Public School Elite ...* (Faber & Faber, 1967); London Metropolitan Archives: MxCC, Education Committee Minutes, 1942-6; W.B.Faherty, *Henry Shaw, His Life and Legacies* (U of Missouri, 1987); G.A. [1922-51] & Rosemary

Goyder, *Signs of Grace* (Cygnet Pr., 1993); archival records of C.W.Goyder [1920-4], MHS Science School; *Times World Atlas; Times*, 28.iv.1988 (Goyder Plaque). H.F.E.Ward [1877], *Mr Poilu, Notes & Sketches with the Fighting French* (1916) – Intro, S.S.Pawling [1873-7] for MHS dates. For custom of 'Windsor Castle' holiday, see corr with Michael Hart, Alastair Graham, Chris Sutcliffe, Clive Fox [1957-62], 1998, #. Corr with Mrs H.Riddiford, NZ, 1999 ref Rev. Evans, HM. A.L.Rouse, 'Beneath the whitewash, the same old Hitler', *New York Times* 7.i.1962, q. in W.R.Louis ed, *The Origins of the Second World War: A.J.P.Taylor & His Critics* (1972); *ISIS Annual Census 2000*, ISCis; M.S.Briggs *(Middlesex, Old & New)* (1934); N.G.Brett James, *Story of Hendon* (1932); B.H.Oak, *Mill Hill, A History... in its Environment* (Edinburgh, 1994); L.P.Hartley, *The Go-Between* (1953), 9; Letter from E.S.Weymouth [1869-74], *MHM* Jn 1934, for Grimstone story – because "F.Anstey" <= Guthrie> had a cousin at MHS, W.H.Guthrie [1873-5], <father = Th. Anstie Guthrie>, rumour attributed character to Dr Weymouth; in fact = an HM of "Anstey's" own Prep S, at

Highgate). ISCis Report on parents' preferences: *Guardian*, 26.x.2001, Marconi/ anti-semitism, see *Guardian*, 19.iii.2002: 'Marconi blocked Jews from *Il Duce's* academy'; J.Gathorne-Hardy, *The Public School Phenomenon...* (Hodder & Stoughton, 1977), 276; Inglis Gundry [1918-23]: *New Grove Dictnry of Music...* (1980) v.7. 847/8; *New Grove Dictnry of Opera* (1997) v.2, 578. ISC report, 'Independent Schools & Charitable Status', Sept 2002.

Other *OM* references [dates at MHS]: H.L.Berry [1819-22]; M.S.Briggs [1896-9]; R.W.B.Buckland [1878-84]; F.H.C.Crick [1930-4], see also Chs.VI, VIIi; J.T.Fields [1973-8]; T.Gupta [1981-3]; G.Kemp, later Lord Rochdale [1877-81]; A.J.Rooker Roberts {1893-1900}; A.E.R.Roberts [1921-6]; H.Shaw [1811-17], (see also *Financial Times*, 12.viii.2000, R.Lane, 'Victorian implant' blooms in a foreign land'); P.Smith [1829-34?].

(There is also a selected glossary in the Appendices, with an Abbreviations guide: separate companion Supplements deal with certain specific issues).

Service of National Peace Thanksgiving, steps of St Paul's Cathedral, 6.vii.1919: (c/l.) King George V, (c/r.) Queen Mary,
the Archbishop of Canterbury (lwr r.); (extreme l, with scarlet gown),
Sir John McClure, sole Public School Head Master invited; (l.) the Bishop of London. *Intro.o*

19

Busts of the Co-Founders of Mill Hill,
positioned pre-WWII in School Dining Hall;
note individual place-settings. *1.a*

Chapter I

School of the Enlightenment

A fresh look at the background to the founding of Mill Hill

'... those who were excluded from the full membership
of the Anglican Church-state because of their dissent ...
were clearly modern men of the Enlightenment.'

Two marble busts now perch, precariously, high up on the walls of Mill Hill's beautiful Main Dining Hall. On 17 March 1806 the Committee of the Protestant Dissenters Grammar School had declared their intent *to provide for the temporal and Eternal Interests of their Children's children to the remotest Generations*; for all but the very earliest of those generations, these two busts have been the sole visible reminders of Mill Hill's foundation. The silent remoteness of those cold white figures belies the earnest volubility and energetic commitment with which Samuel Favell and Rev. Dr John Pye Smith would start to meet and plan their brave new educational institution, in the London coffee houses of the year of Trafalgar, 1805.

A keen eye might also spot Favell's name on the tablet in the Honorary Treasurers' pew in the Chapel. To a passer-by in the Village, the only vestiges of the establishment of 1807 are the older sections of the brick wall to the garden by The Ridgeway (the oldest of over a dozen 'Grade-II' elements which the grounds preserve from Britain's list of 361,000). Behind it is a desolate stump, all that remains of the glorious 18th-century Cedars which it once guarded. Aided by the Peter Collinson blue plaque, the eye of the imagination might perhaps picture where his mansion, the original "Ridge Way House", abutted onto what was then a rough and muddy highway, at the start of the curved entrance drive to the Tite building of 1825: the last surviving brick is in the Bartram Museum, Philadelphia. But that is all.

The task of this opening chapter is to reveal for the first time the true intellectual origins of that distant act of bravery, the key to the uniqueness of Mill Hill School.

Edwardian viewpoint

Archival copies of Mill Hill's first *History* of 1909 still exist. It has many endearing features; Norman Brett James's erudite local history background, and the stories of the masters during the formative years of the School are two of them, providing a welcome source for much additional early detail. The historical picture it painted had half a dozen main elements: a school of religious origin, founded at the start of the 19th century, but tracing its causes back to the 17th, and thus an institution to be seen in the patriotic tradition of the Glorious Revolution of 1688, and of the more contentious Puritan Revolution of 40 years earlier. Its aim – to teach the sons of 'Protestant Dissenters', whose chance of a good education was otherwise restricted: its guiding spirit, a reassuring talisman for all later eras – tolerance. Under the critical eye of the 21st century each of those elements deserves re-appraisal, including that concept of 'tolerance': Lord Moran (successor, as President of The Royal College of Physicians, to the *OM*, Sir Russell Brain) pointed out to a Foundation Day audience in 1955 that at least as far as their 17th-century Puritan

Treasurers' Pew, MHS Chapel, showing incumbents from Samuel Favell to *OM* "Dick" Walker (see Appendix C). *1.b*

forebears were concerned, 'tolerance' was not necessarily the most outstanding of their virtues.

The first History, serene within its Edwardian world-view, was content to pose just two basic questions: what was the aim behind the actions of those Protestant Dissenters; and how did they tackle it? These are proper questions. The first merits rehearsal here. The second falls more naturally into the next chapter. Yet that approach now seems too limited to provide a real continuity across the intervening two hundred years: what was being protested, and what were they dissenting from? Above all, the vision of 1907 was denied the insights presented by recent European and American scholarship about one of Mill Hill's most critical influences: the British 'Enlightenment'.

Indeed, the words themselves, causes for which ordinary people were once prepared to die, now form a barrier to understanding. The 'Puritans' of the Mayflower were those who sought a *church more pure from the corruptions of popery* – the Old Faith, the catholicism of Rome, which was ever the *red rag to John Bull*. Puritanism was the spiritual frame of mind common to the poet John Milton, the bicentenary of whose birth in 1608 would happily coincide with the actual opening of the new school, and also to John Bunyan, whose words from *Pilgrim's Progress* still resound across that ancient Ridgeway every November, when the School honours the dead of all Mill Hill's wars.

Puritans who were unable to accept the Established Church became known as 'Nonconformists' when, after the restoration of the monarchy, parliament passed the Act of Uniformity of 1662. Over 1,000 ministers resigned – and 960 were ejected – from their livings within the Church of England; the reason – they could not in conscience, and literally, *consent to everything in the Book of Common Prayer*. After the 'Glorious Revolution' of 1688, and the Toleration Act of 1689, those Nonconformists – Presbyterians, Independents (soon known as Congregationalists) and Baptists, then also embracing Quakers – were tolerated as 'Dissenters', with the right to attend their duly licensed meeting houses. While a Dissenter's actions were visible to all, being seen to *turn his back on the steeple, and to go to the conventicle*, that *vigourous 10% of the nation*, 'The Dissenting Interest', never narrowed down as a political party.

New meanings obscure the issue further. For a wider United Kingdom embracing Ulster, the 'Protestant' banner has carried overtones which can conceal its noble roots. 'Dissent' has of course honourable antecedents: for the American authors of *The Dissenting Tradition* it is still *the most exciting feature of English history*. Again calling in aid the *OED*, Murray's words are straightforward: '*The open expression of difference... to that which is authoritatively established*'. Yet as Prof Clyde Binfield puts it, Dissent, as a religious term, can have an off-putting ring to it: *Dissent is querulous, refusal to conform is manly*. Only in a political context does it still carry general value, encompassing the resistance of ideological dissidents, such as Solzhenitsyn or Sakharov in Soviet Russia, Mrs Aung San Suu Kyi in the former Burma (Myanmar) or, as the Headmaster's sermon on 11 November 1999 recalled, the earlier figures of the Scholls or Pastor Bonhoeffer in Nazi Germany. In that wider sense, dissent is a flourishing, living concept, as relevant to the world today, and to Mill Hill, as it was then.

As late as the 1920s, a popular novel could describe its scene in these terms: *the village is prosperous. There are two general stores, one London emporium ... a bank, a dissenting chapel.* In 1951, *OM* Martin Briggs would speak on Nonconformist Architecture to the 'Protestant Dissenting Deputies'. Some individuals still today openly espouse that ancient tradition: Robert Bath, one of the oldest *OM* interviewees for the History, opened with the words, *I'm a Dissenter, too, you know!* These fine 20th-century assertions of the continuation of Dissent – the 'Free Church' – also illustrate a characteristic of those early roots: this can sometimes find modern expression in a certain doggedness, going beyond a wholesome pride in the past, akin even to a siege mentality – the defensiveness of a hilltop stronghold. Yet Dissent has largely gone out of the vocabulary of religious matters today. As Mill Hill's greatest theologian-Head Master, Dr J.S. Whale, expressed it in his address at the unveiling of his portrait on 29 October 1983: *it would have been a mistake ... to have stressed the historic Dissent which was Mill Hill's foundation and raison d'être in 1807: times change.* For the Britain of the 21st century, the intolerant passions which had formerly focused on religion would also be extended to politics, nationality, race and colour, all areas of contention still all-too familiar to the world of 2006/7.

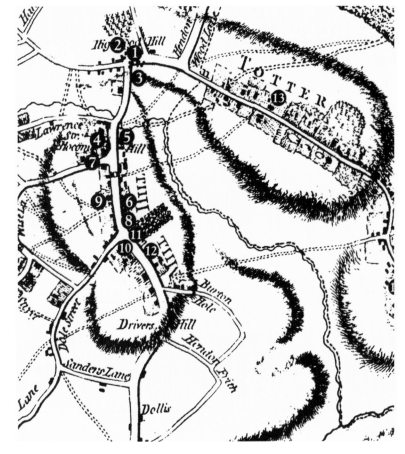

Mill Hill Village c1792 (part): (see Appendix J). *1.c*

Dissent, the Enlightenment, and Samuel Favell

This History is not the place for a detailed account of that many-faceted 'Dissenting' tradition, waged against religious intolerance, through and beyond the century of Hume and Gibbon. Nor is there space to explore the equal relevance of 'Dissent' to the other minority religious communities of that time – the Roman Catholics and the Jews – even though their eventual 'Emancipation' from civil and religious disability has historic importance for the broadly-based Mill Hill of today; for many, the real contemporary 'Apartheid' was not between Church and Dissent, but still that far older divide between Protestantism – the very building block of Great Britain – and Catholicism. The historical phenomenon of significance for Mill Hill is what millennial scholarship now sees as the British Enlightenment, in particular the English rather than the

Sam.ᵉˡ Favell

CO-FOUNDER OF MILL HILL SCHOOL, 1807

Dissenting lawyer Samuel
Favell, progressive Member
of Court of Common Council,
City of London, Co-Founder
of MHS in 1807. *1.d*

Scottish version of that *widely disseminated attitude of mind*, although American historian Arthur Herman has sought to deride the *intellectual goings-on south of the border*. English in origin, principally through Locke (notably in his *Letter Concerning Toleration*), the Enlightenment then became so centred on the *philosophes*, that the French 'school' appeared to be 'The' Enlightenment. The Dissenting tradition had of course preceded the Age of Enlightenment by almost a 100 years; then, during the later 18th century, it became embraced as one of what Roy Porter illuminated as the *competing elites* within that movement of ideas, enabling *the mutual reinforcement of faith and reason. To some, enlightenment was primarily a matter of emancipation from religious bigotry...*; for others, that movement was to politicise across the Atlantic to inform the Revolution in America, as it would influence the Revolution in France.

The Enlightenment is now recognised as 'broad church', with different national forms. The source of the chapter's opening quotation – *Enlightenment and Religion, Rational Dissent in 18th Century Britain*, by Boston historian Knud Haakonssen – establishes its character as the natural format for dissenters, above all for the Rational Dissenters. These included *wealthy merchants on the edge of county society and a scattering of professional men*; they *prided themselves on their enlightened up-to-date attitudes* – a demand for civil liberty, the questioning of the *status quo*, and the rejection of a coercive state religion (be it Anglican or Catholic) – but foremost the belief that things could and must change. This last attribute was crucial for the Dissenters. The reinvigoration of Dissent's aims was a direct outcome; one part of that outcome was the Protestant Dissenters Grammar School at Mill Hill.

For the context of Mill Hill's history, there is no need to delve back further into the convoluted account of Dissent than the year 1789, five years after the death of that ambivalent figure of the Enlightenment century, Dr Johnson; (his was '*the* Dictionary' for Dr Murray, paving the way for his own great work). It was in that year that Samuel Favell first came into prominence. Typical of the coffee-house based, emergent 'middle class', Favell was at this time still only 29 years old; 'Independent' by religious persuasion, the School's first Register omits that he was a member of a profession – the law – which counted some significant representatives in the field of reforming 'rational dissent'. He became politically active as a Freeman, a member of the Clothworkers' Livery, and later, from 1810 to 1829, like many Millhillians after him, served on the London Court of Common Council, representing Aldgate as a Commoner; he was notable for his pursuit of good causes, such as the Repeal of the Corn Laws, as well as being a lay member of the 'General Body' of the London Dissenters. His role in Mill Hill's foundation has hitherto appeared less salient than that of his future co-founder, Rev. Dr Pye Smith, mainly because the clerical factors within Dissent have been taken as the dominant influence, (but perhaps also due to his caricature depiction in the first *Register*). However, John Pye Smith was then (without the hyphen, the family bought it) a mere 15 years old, pursuing his studies as a true polymath at Rotherham Academy, and on course for his career in the hothouse world of the famous Dissenting Seminaries, *the best system of education in England*, whose excellence would prove crucial to Mill Hill.

On 4 December, in the year of the French Revolution, 1789, Samuel Favell was one of 44 laymen and ministers to sign a petition for a first-ever meeting of the representatives of Protestant Dissent, by now fervently reviving countrywide; the 'Dissenting Deputies' were *England's first permanent extra-parliamentary political lobbying group*. As revealed in the Journals of the Common Council at Guildhall, at that date the institution whose Library he would later help to create had not yet turned to this particular reform. His prominence, not as an Alderman, but within the honourable ranks of the 30 Commoners on that 'pressure group' would only evolve some 30 years later.

The Petition sought at last the Repeal of the discriminatory laws which barred Dissenters from full citizenship, civic office, and the ancient universities. Here was the requirement which would provide the 'inner compulsion' for the founding fathers of Mill Hill. These laws stemmed from the Restoration of Charles II in 1660, and from the perceived need to support the alliance of the Church of England and the Stuart State: the chronic fear was of schismatic dissent from any quarter. The Glorious Revolution, which brought over Protestant William of Orange to give power to the Whig cause in 1688 (under what was in effect a Dutch invasion) gave Dissenters a feeling well-described by the eminent Millhillian diplomat and scholar of Dissent, a product of Maurice Jacks' Mill Hill of the 1930s, Sir Anthony Lincoln: *the Protestant succession [was] ... a blessing enjoyed by their sacrifice.* (His study was developed from a thesis he wrote in 1938 whilst up at Magdalene – *Some Political and Social Ideas of English Dissent ...*; it was complemented by another thesis from the same university 20 years later, which offers further insights for the foundation of Mill Hill – *The Revival of Dissent, 1800-1835*).

Dame Janet's Gate (1928), Peter Collinson Garden, The Ridgeway (former entrance to Head Master's House, now "St Bees House"); ivy constantly threatens (r.) one of the four British Heritage Plaques on Village locations linked to MHS: Peter Collinson. *1.e*

To return to the received but in many ways misleading picture offered about the background to Mill Hill's formation, in terms of education Dissenters did in fact have some 100 outstanding schools to hand, those early Dissenting Academies. Likewise in availability for civil office, a device known as 'Occasional Conformity' enabled many Dissenters of a less uncompromising disposition to qualify for public roles. Indemnity Acts were regularly passed to exempt Dissenters from any penalties attaching to their refusal to take the Anglican Sacrament. Many Dissenters 'got by'.

Some were rich enough to send their sons to the older established 'Great Schools', despite the fact that a university place was not open to them at Oxford, nor a completion of any course at Cambridge, without taking an unacceptable Oath of Acceptance: they could of course still go to Glasgow, Edinburgh or St Andrews, all said to be then scholastically superior to the ancient seats of learning, or to some outstanding European establishments, such as Leyden. Among modern revisionist historians, Linda Colley has expressed the view that *in practice English and Welsh Protestant Dissenters were able to penetrate almost all levels of the political system up to and including Parliament itself.*

Nevertheless they remained second-class citizens, deprived of what the new 'Britons' of Great Britain saw as their birthright – the complete Protestant inheritance. The first half of the 18th century had been a quieter time within the longer-term struggle for toleration; however, some 20 years before Favell's call to action, feelings started to erupt once more with the old 17th-century passion. In 1769 Prof Blackstone had published his *Commentaries...* His attack (later retracted) was on those Dissenters who had *once within the compass of the last century effected the ruin of our Church and State...* .

This rebuke by the great but conservative judge to the heirs of the failed Puritan rebellion of Cromwell's Interregnum (the original and proper use of that term) sparked off a furious riposte by a famous pillar both of the English 'Enlightenment', and of 'Rational Dissent'. No relation to Mill Hill's subsequent Thomas Priestley (a 19th-century Head, see Ch.III), Dr Joseph Priestley had been a tutor at Warrington Academy, and then a minister at the Congregational Chapel at the (also unrelated) "Mill Hill" in Leeds. Rational Dissent was not just another doctrinal position within the more than 40 fissiparous branches of the Dissenting movement – ranging from 'Ranters' and 'Jumpers' to two generic groups which were to be of initial concern to Mill Hill's founding committee, 'Paedo-Baptists' and 'Anti-Paedobaptists'; rather it has been described by the historian John Seed as *a voluntary association of individuals who recognised the right of others to full religious liberty.*

In contrast to the emotional 'Evangelical' trend then starting to run in parallel, questioning English thinkers like Priestley, and Gibbon, *the pure crystal of Enlightenment*, and in Scotland, David Hume and Adam Smith, all provided through their writings a new rational temper to radical reform. They thereby deeply influenced the Baptists, wealthy Presbyterians and Favell's Congregationalists; (significantly for Mill Hill, Ursula Henriques, the accepted authority on the process of religious toleration, noted that *the Quakers held themselves aloof from the activities of the Three Denominations*). The emerging 'enthusiastic' Evangelicalism of 'New' Dissent, viewed at first askance by this more rational 'Old' Dissent, would infect it in the next century, blurring the boundary between.

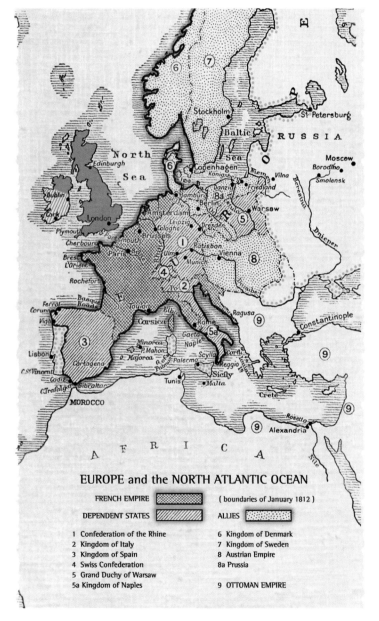

Beleaguered Great Britain facing Europe at the time of the founding of MHS (blue areas: Napoleonic domination). *1.f*

EUROPE and the NORTH ATLANTIC OCEAN

| FRENCH EMPIRE | (boundaries of January 1812) |
| DEPENDENT STATES | ALLIES |

1 Confederation of the Rhine
2 Kingdom of Italy
3 Kingdom of Spain
4 Swiss Confederation
5 Grand Duchy of Warsaw
5a Kingdom of Naples

6 Kingdom of Denmark
7 Kingdom of Sweden
8 Austrian Empire
8a Prussia

9 OTTOMAN EMPIRE

One of Anthony Lincoln's arguments was that the English Repeal movement, with which Favell had now become involved, was akin to the French Revolution in its massive impact on British society. For others, the campaign to repeal the discriminatory religious legislation should better be seen simply as parallel with the Constitutional Movement, which found its culmination in the great political Reform Acts of the 19th century. However Lincoln did succeed in highlighting the divisiveness to which – in Asa Briggs' phrase – these *proud and quarrelsome Dissenters* gave rise. They became vilified as regicides – a *Jacobin fifth column*; Dissent was *spiritual republicanism*.

Their loyalty to the Crown had been amply evidenced by their service to the Hanoverians during the Catholic uprisings of 1715 and 'The "45"'. Yet, however sincerely they protested that loyalty, the political coloured the religious: indeed, as Linda Colley has established, *Protestantism determined how most people viewed their politics*. There was much more of social, political, and indeed intellectual content in this Dissenting movement than Mill Hill was able to identify in 1909.

Why 1807?

Three questions are posed by the year 1807 – which also saw the Slave Trade Act, and an abortive Congregational Union (denounced as *a violent attack on the British Constitution*):

* What was the process whereby that courageous, even rash-seeming, decision came to be taken at that time – indeed, why not earlier – or later? Why specifically then?

* Why did that first Dissenting Foundation, which started so boldly, with an apparently clear view of its educational 'market', fall so far short of its original aims that it had to close in 1869, giving way to the New Foundation?

* Thirdly – most puzzling of all – why would an institution which was ostensibly formed in a firm anti-'Establishment' mode so 'accommodate' its own Nonconformist 'educational establishment' as to align with the Anglican Establishment, scarcely more than half a century after its inception?

The two latter points are best answered in succeeding chapters, although the first clues will shortly emerge; the question 'Why 1807?' has to be explored here.

In terms of the state of the nation, that choice of a 'launch year' seems at first glance to 21st-century eyes conditioned by market-driven decision-making, not merely unpropitious, but highly unlikely. Even if most of Jane Austen's nicely insular contemporary novels could be written as if no state of war existed, the mass of the people – including her brother, at sea with Nelson's fleet – was only too well aware of the threat from a nation three times larger. Children were still going to bed with the fear of 'Boney the Bogeyman' – the Emperor Napoleon – on their lips, just as they were to fear the very name 'Hitler' in the next century. The poet John Clare recorded that people in his village were *chin-deep* in invasion fears, as well they might be, given the barbarity and 'Revolutionary' violence which Napoleon's *Grande Armée* was to display in its invasion of Britain's ally, Portugal, only a few years later.

Celebrated botanist Peter Collinson FRS, age 75, former owner of "Ridge Way House" on The Ridgeway, later to become the first – though not surviving – MHS building. The 'School of the Enlightenment' was the serendipitous beneficiary of this quintessential Enlightenment figure. *1.g*

The Church and Crown in danger!, even the beloved but by now semi-senile Crown of 'Farmer George', and the nation's established Church – this was still the patriotic cry of the hour; half a million Volunteers had rallied to it. As Graham Sutton put it (a writer from Cumbria, that distant part of the country which would be linked with Mill Hill a century and a half later), *war tainted every act of statesmanship and stultified every dream.* Religious differences needed to be sunk; the consequent disabilities, however intrinsically unjust, now seemed to many a minor diversion, even a self-indulgent luxury, at such a time. Romantics and artists were revising their earlier idealistic endorsements of the Revolution: Beethoven had to re-dedicate his *Eroica* Symphony to the *memory* of a great man. As *The Annual Register* for 1807 stated: *Austria, Russia, the Ottoman Porte, Prussia, and Denmark have in the present year been added to the already formidable host of our enemies.* It was *Little England against the World!* In Wordsworth's rallying cry *we shall be left alone*, as would happen again, over a century later in 1940.

Excluding the claims of the Seven Years War of 1756-63 as *the Very First World War*, in this first 'Great War', there were 23 years of ongoing hostilities from 1792 to 1815, twice as long as the wars of 1914-1918 and 1939-1945 combined: why should anyone try to found a school of any kind, in the middle of such a national struggle for survival? What forces combined to make that date special for the ongoing character of Mill Hill? It is clear that any attempt fully to understand today's Mill Hill School Foundation must first establish why the year 2006/7 is indeed an anniversary at all.

Compounded by their championship of the American war, the first impact of the French Revolution on England – and the new wars that ensued – were a real setback for the Dissenters. Although, to quote Lincoln again, *the closing years of the 18th century were impassioned with expectation*, Dissenters were seen as *a foreign group ... whose ways were not as other men's.* They became even more unpopular; Priestley's house and *philosophical apparatus* in Birmingham were burned by a mob in 1791, and he eventually emigrated to Pennsylvania, leaving his intellectual legacy to work on after him. Dissenters' chapels were sacked: they were seen as mixing politics and religion.

Despite an initial humiliation, when William Pitt, while still Prime Minister, refused to propose a Bill to end the infamous 'Acts', liberal feeling still ran high. In Henriques' phrase, *there had been a slow hardening of the differences between Dissent and Church ... sooner or later, sleeping dogs would awake.* Yet Nelson's triumph off Cape Trafalgar was offset by the French dictator's victories against the Third Coalition at Ulm and Austerlitz, and there was, in the words of J.H.Plumb, an *atmosphere of disaster and defeat.* The period from 1807 to 1810 would constitute *years of great hardship and peril.* As *Nobis* expresses it, the Continental System of blockade, the first large-scale attempt at economic warfare, meant that *the civilised world from the Pyrenees to the Urals* was in theory closed to British ships. Under the French dictator's Berlin Decrees, *England was feeling the pinch*; yet even though the threat of invasion, this time from Antwerp, in what Asa Briggs calls the *dark decade*, would be raised again in 1809, and in 1811, the blockade *failed to break her strength or spirits*.

One central factor underlay Dissent's revival at this *caesura* in time. The generation of Dissenters then in its prime was probably the last to manifest the benefit of Academy education: *the upper classes of Dissent were better educated than their social and economic equals in the country as a whole*; they *were in a good position to hold well-informed views*. Favell's friends within both 'Rational', and 'Orthodox' Dissent (the opposing, so-called 'Trinitarian' view which is embodied in several later Mill Hill Head Masters), felt themselves *fitted to be a governing class*; they could take up the cudgels again. But what was the real nature of the cause they now espoused?

An unique identity

One of the ongoing strengths of the Public Schools is their innate diversity; every school's history argues for its own particular, much-prized brand of specialty. Yet even within this context, Mill Hill achieves a unique historical identity.

Mill Hill's uniqueness has several aspects. The 'Protestant Dissenters Grammar School' was the first school whose avowedly non-Anglican Head was ever to be admitted to HMC membership from a foundation outside the Anglican

Original Palladian villa, "Belmont", designed for owner, Peter Hammond c1760 (bought by *OM* Rooker Roberts 1912). *1.h*

'Establishment' (see Ch.IV): an immense achievement, albeit a surprising one. (The Wesleyan Methodism that created Kingswood School, in Somerset, was, of course, at the time of its formation in 1748, within the Church of England. John Wesley, a 'true-blue Anglican', detested 'Dissent', by which he understood 'Old' Dissent.) The School of 1807 thereby represents another unique element: it was certainly the first Protestant foundation in today's HMC membership to be built in the 19th century (Catholic Ampleforth had been founded in Yorkshire three years before the Dissenting Committee's first discussions, in 1802). Yet that simple fact raises a further problem: in educational terms, that time was a kind of void, suspended between the 'Ancient' schools, and the later 'Victorian' schools.

Mill Hill has also been described by the leading authority on Free Church history, Clyde Binfield, as *the oldest as it was the grandest of the Dissenting boarding schools*. (The Quaker School, Ackworth, founded in the buildings of the former Yorkshire 'Foundling Hospital' in 1779, but only admitted to the HMC in 1987, does not seek to enter this comparison: as its Archivist has written, it was *outside the influence of both established and non-conformist protestant establishments*.) Mill Hill's Free Church lead was followed by 10 other Nonconformist schools, three of them purely Congregational foundations (*), five of them also later HMC members: Caterham* (1811), Silcoates* (1809, 1820, 1831), Walthamstow Hall (1838), Eltham (1842), Taunton (1847), Tettenhall (1863), Bishops Stortford (1868), and The Leys (1875); there were also two girls' schools – Milton Mount* (1873) and Wentworth (1879). (Unlike some, Mill Hill spurned the name 'College': that would have smacked too much of the medievalism of Eton and Winchester.) Mill Hill's story has interrelated with many of these sister-schools, through a Chair of Governors, two Head Masters, and a Master of Belmont, as well as through other staff, benefaction or competition. However, that particular, and by definition unique, pathfinding role within what evolved as a broad Nonconformity has never been one that Mill Hill has sought to assert: the School was happy then, as today, to plough a broad, individual and – most significantly for the School's underlying identity – interdenominational furrow.

Yet all these wholly legitimate statements conceal the essential nature of the real difference that first typified, and still distinguishes, Mill Hill from all other English – or indeed Scottish – Public Schools, with their characteristic Boarding school ethos. For the period of some 50 years from the end of the 18th century onwards, the new ideas and questioning ways of thinking that have created a recognisably modern western world – Roy Porter's *Enlightenment within the Enlightenment* – were starting to revolutionise Europe. It needed a Royal Historical Society Symposium in the year 2000 to re-value the English stream within this cross-cultural movement of ideas, now seen as 'The British Enlightenment'.

No other educational foundation such as Mill Hill has evolved from this formative period. There were many Anglican Day Grammar Schools, falling into disrepair as the 18th century proceeded. Lord Kenyon wrote in 1795: *whoever will examine the state of the grammar schools in different parts of the kingdom will see to what a lamentable condition most of them are reduced*. Although numbers varied (Winchester's

Roll was eight in 1751), the 'Ancient Schools' still dominated, serving the aristocratic and landed classes, limited in the subjects taught, and prey to riots and abuses of all kinds. Countless smaller private Dissenting Academies sprang up, catering for local Day pupils, many with strongly commercial curricula: all were later to founder. 'Dame' schools, and 'private' education at home filled the gaps. However, no future inter-denominational 'Public School' had emerged to break the mould: by 1791, *English education had sunk to almost its lowest point.*

Strengthened by a wider view of the time than was available in the 1900s, it can now be seen that Mill Hill's true claim to an historical identity, that still has meaning for today, lies not just in the plain fact of her Founders' actions, nor simply in their stated reasons for them, wholly valid in themselves: it was in the fact of their intellectual provenance. The eyes of the island race were focused externally on the survival of the state, invasion still fresh in the memory of all; the tents of the enemy which, right up until August 1805, could be seen sprinkled like confetti over the cliffs of Boulogne, had concentrated the English and – still to many a novel concept – the 'British' mind. The choice of timing seems quixotic for the launch of a new, intentionally challenging institution, set not in the far-off countryside but in the purview of a capital city, whence ideas, and reputations, spread fast.

The historic Peter Collinson Cedar, Head Master's Garden, MHS, *c*1907 (cut down for public safety, 1997).*1.j*

The only answer that finally fits the facts is that those exceptionally-educated Dissenting minds nevertheless worked on 'other-worldly' lines, a theme whose full meaning will only transpire as the story unfolds. The founding of the Grammar School at Mill Hill was not a nicely calculated act, thought through carefully for maximum impact by a mature, shrewd-thinking Court of Governors. Lent new energy by the spirit of the age, it was the final outcome of generations of cumulative frustration and anger, enhanced by Dissent-dominated 'media', and interrupted only temporarily by the panic reaction to the French Revolution. Of its very nature it had to be the decision of a group of individuals, necessarily inward-looking, glorying *in the dissidence of dissent*, firmly – even obstinately – determined not to compromise, holding, as *OM* Ernest Hampden-Cook wrote in 1926, *unflinchingly to their own Puritan faith*.

Under this perspective, the timing had its own logic, reaching fruition in those years leading up to 1807. This was the year when for Mill Hill's founders, all the civil deprivation, social stigma, and religious injustice of more than a century, accelerated by the increasing prosperity now starting to flow from the Industrial Revolution, came to a head. Above all, it was the act of men, brought together from all walks of

Renowned Dissenting
educationist, cleric and writer
Rev. Dr John Pye Smith,
Co-Founder of MHS with
Samuel Favell. *1.k*

life, *widely tolerant of opinions from which they differed*, yet finally intolerant of intolerance, liberated into action by the profound, pervasive intellectual forces of the Enlightenment.

What kind of school?

Is there then a legitimate historical framework which describes the improbable actions of those embattled Dissenters at this momentous time in British history? Even if many have argued that 'Victorian' habits of thrift and hard work were already in evidence by the end of the 18th century, yet in a strictly chronological sense, the Mill Hill of 1807 cannot – at that stage of her evolution – be thought of in the framework of the 'Victorian Public Schools'; Queen Victoria's accession lay exactly 30 years in the future, indeed the term 'Victorian', applied at first only to architecture, was itself not coined until some time into Victoria's reign. This is the reason why, in contrast to the ample (yet even there still misunderstood) coverage in today's classic Public School history, some would-be overviews, focusing either on the medieval schools or their mid-Victorian successors, contrived to by-pass the Dissenters' foundation: they have not understood how to place Mill Hill.

Quite apart from the fact that the future George IV was not formally appointed Regent until three years later, the year 1807 could scarcely be seen as anticipating the full 'Regency'; Mill Hill's severe and pious founders could by no stretch of the imagination be associated with the stereotype of rollicking, reprobate 'Regency men'; here was no Regency school. Again, despite the fact that 1807 coincided with the continued resilience of the House of Hanover, the term 'Georgian' with its connotations of easy, comfortable landed wealth, riding on the back of a grim social undertow – *affluence and effluents*, as Roy Porter graphically put it – just does not fit Mill Hill.

Were the founders of 1807 simply '18th-century men'? They were men of that century, for sure, and with the conditioning of the years of Dissent lying further back in their consciousness. Although the increasingly progressive, metropolitan nature of the latter decades did indeed act as their backdrop, the 18th century had, as its foreground, a character of rural living – endemic violence and crudeness, inegalitarian and hierarchical; the rich magnates ruled, a royal Court, albeit constitutional, still disposed. From the writings of the pious Founders, they do not sit easily in such a setting: nor can Mill Hill be type-cast merely as 'a school born of the 18th century'.

The key to a fresh understanding of the intellectual origins of today's Mill Hill lies in the view that historians now take about those marked changes that started to gather speed in the country's mood and manner some 25 years before the idea of Mill Hill was conceived. From about 1782 onwards, continental upheavals notwithstanding, the British economy began to move up a gear. Although the Industrial Revolution was no sudden thing, this was the moment when, in anachronistic nuclear terms, its 'critical mass' was achieved, through what the historian J.B.Owen has called *a concatenation of favourable circumstances*: technological advance; sharply increasing productivity in agriculture and in the new factories; sudden population growth; and above all the existence in Britain, in contrast to other continental countries, of flexible political structures beneath an apparently restrictive surface, whereby change gradually became possible. This was the peculiar nature, until recently misunderstood, of the English Enlightenment at work: it aimed at intensely practical outcomes – in Roy Porter's words, *faith in progress throve within piety*.

Social mobility

One other factor, identifiable as a contributing cause of this 'industrial' revolution, is of especial importance for a revised view of Mill Hill and her Founders: the presence of growing numbers of careful, sober, hard-working Protestant Dissenters of various persuasions and denominations within the successful commercial and industrial 'middling people', the new 'middle classes' – Mill Hill's future constituency. *Bankruptcy in a Dissenter was almost unknown.* As Roy Porter has neatly expressed it, there was a *deepening of consumption down through the social spectrum.* Consumption included education.

Religion, and social and economic standing, linked up with what was both a theme of 19th-century capitalist society and also a fundamental aspect of the story of Mill Hill: social mobility. The French historian, Elie Halévy, wrote with the insight of a friendly outsider: *If a successful man of business wished to enter the governing class ... he must not be a Dissenter ... Puritan nonconformity thus tended to become a transitional creed, a stage in the history of an English family.* That later Head Master, Thomas Priestley, would suffer much anonymous calumny *because some of our Pupils have joined the Established Church.* Asa Briggs goes further: *It was frequently a sign of social advancement for a nonconformist businessman to abandon the chapel and turn to the church.* At the risk of some over-simplification, the relationship of 'class' to the various strands within Dissent, which together produce this evolution in the history of Mill Hill, can be represented graphically: **Fig.C.**

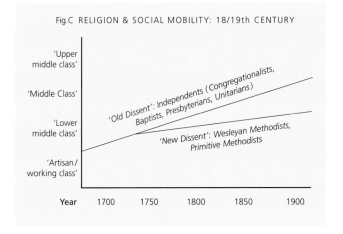

Fig.C RELIGION & SOCIAL MOBILITY: 18/19th CENTURY

Social mobility combined with another factor. The collective effort of will, called upon across all classes, to withstand the threat of invasion, meant that energies which had been turned inward had to be re-turned outwards. Those who until the end of the 18th century had been more conscious of what divided them, were now increasingly having to concentrate their minds on what united them: as Linda Colley has put it, *the Volunteer Corps ... also attracted ... Protestant Nonconformists and Roman Catholics, men who had every reason to want the British state to be reformed, but no reason at all to want to see it invaded by the French.* This trend to patriotic 'middle-class' convergence would have major consequences; inevitably, a 'social history' flavour characterises Mill Hill's story.

Protestant School of the Enlightenment

Ideas that had already taken root in the British mind now reached their flowering time. The event which coincided with Mill Hill's foundation – the Act abolishing the Slave Trade – is a signal international example of this era of breakthroughs in what had seemed to be intractable areas for reform.

Change was at last in the very air, and the Founders of Mill Hill, whilst intent on their specific goals, were in no way immune to it. Regardless of the internal pressures of Church and State – defying the opposition of Blackstone, Pitt, and even the redoubtable Edmund Burke – Napoleonic Alliance or no – a school like Mill Hill now demanded to be born. Once the idea of creating their new school had entered the collective agenda, it was no longer a question of whether, or even when, but merely 'where, how, and how soon'.

Samuel Favell had now got together with Dr John Pye Smith, who in 1801 had been appointed as classics tutor at Homerton – which liked to be regarded (dubiously) as *the most ancient of the Dissenting Colleges*. They and their group of busy, earnest Dissenters formed one more expression of the broad process which was turning the Age of Enlightenment into what Asa Briggs has aptly titled '*The Age of Improvement*'. Inevitably Mill Hill's founding Nonconformity was not synonymous with all the characteristics of Enlightenment thought, yet many themes were common: *a better world and a happier life was what the dissenter envisioned ...; dissent may be characterised best by noting its dedication to liberty of conscience, intellectual freedom and the right of free expression.* The effects of these themes, part of the ongoing fabric of contemporary Britain, are still the stuff of many an address in the Chapel at Mill Hill, not least by the current Chaplain, Rev. James Fields, who described himself in his inaugural sermon in 1997 as *a Presbyterian with a good head for the rational*.

In this sharper focus, the historical void of those early 19th-century years is filled. Mill Hill emerges not merely as the 'Protestant Dissenters Grammar School', by which deliberate title the School was first identified: an emergence which ranks her – for what such statistics are worth – as the 119th in the long list of today's HMC foundations, the 25th oldest among all those founded originally as boys' Boarding schools, and the 10th oldest within the Greater London/ Home Counties area. The School can today be seen as something more significant: a fresh concept which lay beyond the awareness of her pious founders, but which they would surely have recognised and found illuminating. At the traditional level, the Dissenters' small, ambitious establishment, with an unwavering confidence in that unseeable future epitomised in Bunyan's Celestial City, has of course long been recognised as part of those sources depicted earlier [**Fig.B**], which would, in one historian's phrase, *contribute a fresh and healthy element to English education.*

It is pertinent here to recall that Boarding was not new to Protestant schools in Europe – it was well-established under the *Collegium* concept of the Reformation – but they were church-funded. Others were public-funded, wholly or in part; (for example Mill Hill's former 'link' school, Goslar's *Christian von Dohm Gymnasium* of 1804, with founders who also *felt indebted to the European Enlightenment*, was a partly State-funded girls' Day school). This has meaning for the broader view of Mill Hill's origins which has now crystallised.

Britain's first major independent Nonconformist school, with an interdenominational aim: that Enlightenment-inspired religious identity is itself sufficient cause for a modest pride. (It was once honoured briefly in a late 20th-century competition for Inter-House hymn-singing, named after the Nonconformist hymnist, Isaac Watts.) Befitting the European dimension of the School's current vision, however, it is now possible to balance that spiritual concept with a parallel philosophical, intellectual perspective.

Defined in this broader sense, the first independent Protestant Boarding school of Europe's Age of Enlightenment: that is the highly relevant uniqueness of Mill Hill's origins – her historical laurels.

This History will show those hard-won laurels to be of continuing significance for the Foundation of the Bicentenary. It will also emphasise that no one in the Mill Hill of the 21st century seeks to rest on them.

I am indebted for insights re this Chapter to Prof Clyde Binfield, Dept of History, U of Sheffield; Prof Roy Porter, Prof in the History of Medicine, University Coll, LU; and Prof Stephen Holt [1948-54]: also to the Rev. Paul Hunt, & Rev. James Fields [1973-8], respectively Mill Hill's first Anglican and first Presbyterian Chaplains. Re. sources for the historical importance, ref Mill Hill's origins, of the British/ English Enlightenment & Rational Dissent, see Bibliographical Note, p.372.

Sources for Ch.I include: R.Porter, *op cit*; A.Herman, *The Scottish Enlightenment* (Fourth Estate, 2002); 9 pp letter, T.Priestley to Rev. Wells, 27.iii.1846 #; also *MHM* 1997-8; J.G.Bewsher, *op cit*; N.G.B.James [1894-8], *Some Extents and Surveys of Hendon* (1932): *Statutory List of Buildings of Special Architectural or Historical Interest* (Barnet LB, 1998); R.Calder, *Mill Hill, A Thousand Years of History* (Angus Hudson, in assctn with MHHS, 1993); B.Oak, *op cit*; G.Sutton,

Smoke Across the Fell, (1947) 83; 'Invasion', BBC2, 4.xi.2001; Briggs Archv, *op cit*; corr, Bartram Mus., PA/USA, Dr J.S.Whale, & Prof S.C.Holt; Gathorne Hardy, *op cit*, 102, 109, 112, 134, 189, 276, 350; T.Pocock, *Battle for Empire, The Very First World War 1756-63* (1998); G.Orwell, *Coming Up For Air* (Penguin, 1973 edn.) p.67.

Educational & dissenting history: U.Henriques, *op cit*, 16-17, 63-65, 85, 104; City of London Library, Guildhall – Minutes of the Meetings of the Committee Appointed to Conduct the Application to Parliament for the Repeal of the Corporation and Test Acts, 1787-90; Guildhall Records Repository – Journals of the Common Council of the City of London; M.B.Whittaker, 'The Revival of Dissent, 1800-1835, MLitt. thesis, CU (1958); A.Lincoln [1925-9], *Some Political and Social Ideas of English Dissent* (C.U.P., 1938); L.Colley, *Britons...* (Pimlico, 1994);

H.McLachlan, *English Education under the Test Acts: The History of Non-Conformist Academies 1662-1820* (Manchester, 1931); K.Haakonssen, *Enlightenment & Religion...* (C.U.P., 1996); *Jnl of the Untd Refrmd Church Hist Soc*, v.612, May 1998: Alan Argent, 'Nursed by the Church: The Founding of the Congregational Schools'; corr with F.A.Davies, Archivist, Ackworth School; Dec 1999, S.Schmelting, Christian von Dohm *Gymnasium*, 1999-2000; & J.R.Davies, MHHS; R.Warner, *English Public Schools* (1945); J.Potter, *Headmaster – The Life of John Percival...* (1998); V.Ogilvie, *op cit*, 118; Whitakers' Almanack 2005. Ref. James Paine, see J.Fleming. H.Honour, N.Pevsner, *Dictionary of Architecture* (Penguin, 1966), 321, and Paine J., *Plans Elevations ... Gentlemen's House* (1767, 1783).

Other *OM* references: R.W.Bath [1921-6]; W.R.Brain [1908-13]; M.S.Briggs [1896-91].

Original "Ridge Way House" (r.) with (l.rear) additional buildings of
the first Grammar School, probably from S.
The Ridgeway lying beyond the Cedar (c.). *2.a*

The Protestant Dissenters Grammar School

Creating the tradition: the first quarter-century

"It has always been one of the objects of that institution
to lay a sure foundation for moral and religious character:"
Samuel Favell to his constituents, St Mary-Axe, London, 6 November 1829.

There are dangers in trying to paint too broad a backcloth to the history of a school. Apart from the major events in the life of a nation – war, political upheavals, natural disasters, the impact of new legislation, or the eventual perception of some underlying economic trend – the life of a school normally proceeds along a measured course, governed by its own inbuilt agenda: so too with Mill Hill. The 20th century would bring many such extrinsic changes to bear upon Mill Hill, but for most of the 19th century the wider effect of the School's origins – the first formative phase of the History – would give way to a much more intimate story. Yet although the dramas, the heroism, the failures, would be localised, not nation-wide in their nature, the History's role is to remind new generations that Mill Hill's is, in the words of a 21st-century visitor, Prof Duncan Forrester, *much more than a straightforward school story*, a concept bigger than any one era of pupils: it needs to bring out the relevance of earlier experience to a contemporary world whose points of difference *vis-à-vis* the past may seem to be differences of kind, not just of degree.

John Pye Smith

The focus has now shifted from the Treasurer, Samuel Favell, 'a very ponderous gentleman', to the 'very spare figure' of the second of Mill Hill's Founding Fathers, Rev. Dr John Pye Smith, a contrast in every way. The man who has hitherto occupied the dominant position in the accepted legend of Mill Hill's origins had been born in 1774 in Sheffield, the start of a long and honourable connection between the metropolitan school and the north of England. As the 1926 *Register* notes, *he was always serious-minded, and before he was six years old had plunged a knife into his toy drum, in token of his determination to put away childish things.* The story has some significance for later events. Although self-schooled in his father's bookshop, so great was his intellect that, had he not been a Dissenter, and thus barred from advancement within the established Anglican church, he would certainly have become a prelate, and one of the renowned figures in the Church of England. In the *golden age of Nonconformist preachers*, he became one of the best known in London. Even as it was, such was his standing in his day that he would be mentioned by a contemporary writer, Edward Baines (see Ch.III), in the same breath as Luther, Calvin, Wesley and Wilberforce. His training was at Rotherham Academy, which would also be the provenance of the god-fearing Rev. Maurice Phillips, the second Head of Mill Hill, following the three short years of her first, the now re-commemorated Rev. John Atkinson. Rev. Phillips was described in the Diary of a later Chaplain, Rev. Henry March, as a man *whose learning and knowledge are richly mellowed by years of affliction.*

Rev. Maurice Phillips, second
Head Master of the Protestant
Dissenters Grammar School,
Mill Hill, 1811-8. *2.b*

Pye Smith embodied a quality that the Enlightenment historian Roy Porter has highlighted from the writings of John Locke – *'the reasonableness of Christianity'.* Moving to London, from 1803 he was Pastor of a famous Congregational Chapel, The Old Gravel Pit, in Hackney, one of the many leafy villages fringing the capital, with neither the heights of North London, nor the marshes of the south bank, to inhibit easy access by coach or horseback: one reason for its choice as an area for Dissenters to congregate. As Roger, the fifth generation of the surviving Pye-Smiths, made clear, his distinguished ancestor John Pye was a prodigiously hardworking man, albeit suffering from what he called *disabilities and hindrances [arising] from private duties...*: decoded, this alluded to his unhappy marriage to a wife who had private means and did not care to take responsibility for the students in her husband's charge. As with many men pursuing a single-minded religious cause, he may not have been the easiest man to live with – or, by extension, work with; there is a family legend that he would sit and sulk at the foot of the stairs when thwarted. At first sight a rather forbidding man, he was certainly not without his faults.

However, intellectually, the School had a power-house at the helm, bringing to bear all the educational qualities of the 18th-century Academies. A seeming oasis compared with the classics-obsessed desert then presented by the Ancient Schools, an indication of the rich soil from which the new School would be fed emerges from the list of subjects taught in the Academies: Geography, Medicine, Architecture, Jurisprudence, Music, Political Economy: in the sciences, Astronomy, Chemistry, Electricity, Geology, Hydrography, Magnetism, Meteorology, Mineralogy, Natural Philosophy, Optics, Pneumatics, Surveying: within the mathematical field, Algebra, Conic Sections, 'Geodesia', Mechanics, Mensuration and Statics.

Rotherham Academy (not as elsewhere recorded, a College until 1824) inculcated many of these subjects in the mind of the Tutor who was to be 'called' to Mill Hill's service: it was indeed a calling from God. John Pye Smith, summoned from the Student's Desk to become Tutor in 'science and languages' at Homerton in 1801, has been described as *the most encyclopaedic scholar that the Academies ever produced: his scholastic attainments rank him as one of the foremost tutors of the period. He occupied front place amongst the English-German students of his day.* To round off this essentially Enlightenment portrait, *at meetings of the British Association, he was treated as a well-informed and unprejudiced geologist, and in accordance with his scientific convictions he interpreted parts of the Book of Genesis.* Strangely, as noted by the writer about the *OED*, Simon Winchester, both rocks – geology – and language – philology – were thought by the early Victorians to be equally derived from divine origins.

The Committee

Pye Smith did not share the same 'Congregational network', nor the same practical approach to business matters, as Samuel Favell; his advice to the School Secretary in a letter as late as 9 January 1847 was still that *our wisdom and our strength lie, above all, in prayer.* Favell lived at Camberwell, whence his carriage would bring him daily into the City to his two businesses: first, the warehouse embracing his wife's interest, Favell, Beddome & David, at 170 Fenchurch Street; second, Favell & Bousfield, 'slop-sellers' – cheap ready-made clothing – with premises at 120 St Mary Axe, 247 Tooley Street, and 108 Lower Thames Street (now the site of the *Walrus & Carpenter* pub). Clearly, when they did meet up, they *talked of many things* in the area of Reform; Favell brought acumen to the table, Pye Smith in theory brought the understanding of educational matters. They put together a Committee of 27 (with no Chairman), later increased to 28, including six ministers. One early decision was to opt for the first of two routes for school funding in the 19th century – public subscription; many later schools would adopt the proprietary, joint-stock model.

To this Committee, convening successively at Batson's Coffee Rooms in Cornhill, Mr Fox's office in Lombard Street, the *New London Tavern* in Cheapside, and Rev. Gaffee's Meeting House and the *London Tavern* in Broad Street, this must have seemed like a great opportunity. By July 1806 they had spawned a Sub-Committee, and also invested in a relatively new practice – advertising – in order to communicate their intentions to their desired audience: initially defined, understandably but all-too narrowly, as readers of the *Evangelical Magazine*, the *Eclectic Review*, and the *Theological Magazine*. Although subsequent advertisements would run in *The Star* and *The Morning Post*, a framework was being set: the definition – or rather the lack of insight – into the target market for the new Grammar School was crucial. It would affect the School's progress for the next 75 years. Was it an idea before its time, a school too soon, or would it prove to be that great opportunity which they so earnestly sought, the opportunity of the century?

Later that month, on 19 July, an enduring theme was first expressed for what now became referred to as a 'society' (one which would be a major feature over the ensuing centuries): *the power to admit gratuitously a number of pupils who may be in confined circumstances.* This would be repeated at the first Annual Meeting of the loosely formed organisation into which they had evolved, similar to a Nonconformist congregation – the "Society of Subscribers and Friends", in April 1808: a concern for *... meritorious individuals, who may possess the most promising Talents, which would otherwise be lost to the public.* They added – prophetically for the mid-20th century – *This is an object which the Committee will never lose sight of.* Two years later, the Committee recorded their deeply-felt belief that *Talents and Genius are not hereditary Endowments, neither do they exclusively accompany Rank and Wealth... .* Mill Hill was already finding a distinctive voice.

Initially, the Society thought that its "great Object" could be achieved through a Day School run close by in the City. Yet *Dissenters being a scattered body compared with the Establishment, many children must come from a distance ... [and be] exposed to accident.* This scene, preceding Bazalgette's drains, was described by Charles Dickens' biographer: *London resounded to the noises of carts, waggons ... cabs, and the old four-horse staging coaches. There was still the danger from footpads, or street robbers and at night linkboys still bore lights to take the wary pedestrian homewards ... there were no railways and urban sanitation did not exist ... It was a slower paced city ... a city with its heart still in the eighteenth century.* The founders also feared that their pupils *would encounter ... passing twice a day in the streets ... much that no person could wish to be seen or heard by Youth of either Sex.* They might also have passed, to their benefit, the 50-year-old William Blake, or Charles

Lamb in the year of publication of his *Tales from Shakespeare*, or perhaps – a real danger – the poet Byron in his wild 19th year, with his first volume, *Hours of Idleness*, just out. By August 1807 the Committee resolved to be flexible and start to look in *the Vicinage*. Foregoing houses at East Barnet and Winchmore Hill, it would *treat for premises at Mill Hill*: this was Ridge Way House, erstwhile "Goodhews", Peter Collinson's *sweet and calm old Mansion* with its famous garden, now owned by Richard Salisbury of Featherstone Hall, Yorkshire, and George Dobree of Chelsea. By October they were renting the buildings and land for £100 p.a., envisaging an opening in January 1808; the Deeds were finalised on 25 May, at a price of £2,000: an Enlightenment School was the inheritor of a quintessential Enlightenment luminary.

The target market

The choice of the title 'Grammar School', so far from that implication of subsidiarity which confused the first History, constituted on the contrary a clear statement of confrontation: in the words of writer Vivian Ogilvie, *a deliberate attempt to create a modern type of public school*. He related that advice would be taken from Dr Keate of Eton; later also from Arnold of Rugby, whilst never on the scale of the 'Arnold mania' which would sweep the Establishment. The term 'Public School' was in use by the early 19th century, but new scholarship has shown it to be shorthand for the more proper technical description, the 'public endowed *grammar schools*'.

Whilst the Protestant Dissenters were free from the constraints of local endowment that so narrowed the curriculum and obfuscated the finances of these existing Public Schools, the new school also aspired, from the start, to a focus on the classics: they were the major route to the predominantly classical scholarships at the Universities – that full education from which Dissenters had been largely excluded. That the classics were also synonymous with the education of 'gentlemen' was at that stage a lesser consideration for dissenting Mill Hill. The confrontation was also socially oriented: this was to be a Boarding school, partly because the catchment was envisaged as national, but also because 'Day schools' were then widely seen, in class-ridden England, as the form of education best suited for the 'lower classes'; this was despite the inclusion of St Paul's and Merchant Taylor's in the expanded group of the 'Clarendon Nine' by the time of Mill Hill's second Foundation in 1869.

The differences that worked potentially in Mill Hill's favour were three-fold. Firstly, Mill Hill believed, as later Shrewsbury under Dr Kennedy (famous for his Latin textbook) would prove: that the very grammar of the classics could be better taught than at the seven 'Ancients' (Eton, Winchester, Rugby, Shrewsbury, and the 'Free Grammar School' of Harrow, also City-based Westminster and Charterhouse). Learning by rote and recitation were still the main fare there. Secondly, at the time of Mill Hill's formation, the new establishment – without those restrictions of local endowment ordained by Lord Chief Justice Eldon in a classic judgment in the case of *Attorney General v. Whiteley* – could legally extend its curriculum beyond the confines of his definition: *a school founded for teaching grammatically the learned language... i.e. Latin and Greek*. Colin Shrosbree, the authority on 19th-century Public School history, has commented: *science, modern languages and even mathematics... had already gained a place in 'public school' education, but... modern languages and science were rarely established in a formal sense.* Thirdly, by virtue of her very constituency, Mill Hill was relatively free of the pupil attitudes which pervaded the more aristocratic of the older Boarding schools. The same author has written: *for some, the attempt to teach anything well, even the classics, lowered the tone of the school, for it meant that the aristocracy were judged by what they could do, rather than by who they were.*

The imprecise terminology was as confusing then as it is today. From the earliest days, the brave little foundation at Mill Hill was committed to ploughing its own individual furrow within the established 'field': what the Secretary for the Home Office, Sir George Lewis, in the House of Commons in 1861, would term generically the *public endowed schools* (i.e. the 782 schools reviewed by the Taunton Commission of 1868). At their core would initially be that arbitrary 'principal class' of seven; this group, later increased to nine, would be known by the time of the Clarendon Report as the narrowest definition of the 'Public Schools'; the phrase would later come to embrace all the schools that became members of the HMC (its formation itself a by-product of the Clarendon Report) from 1869 onwards.

'Grass walks and fishponds'

Within 'Myll Hylles' – *vide* the Records of 1544 – were 'fields' of a different kind, the first eight acres acquired by the Committee, plots 156, 153, 158 in the Cooke map of 1796 (even Winchester only started with five). Most of the School's future grounds were contained within an almost triangular area, six large medieval fields of Mill Hill's famed pastureland, bounded by The Ridgeway to the north east, 'Ratcliff' Lane (Hammers Lane) to the west, and a footpath not shown on the later Whishaw map of 1828 – (Mill Hill's future private road, Wills Grove) to the south/ south-east]. Three rectangular fields swept down from the top of The Ridgeway on the south-east side of Ratcliff Lane – Broom Field, Bunn's Grove, and Little Gears (a *gaerstun* was a paddock in Anglo-Saxon). The bottom south-east corner (still to the north of Wills Grove) was The Ridgeway Pightle (field) – today's Memorial Field, Collinson Field, and Top Field. A 'Gravel Walk with a row of High Trees' ran in front of old Ridgeway House. Most of the School's buildings lie on these "original lands". The purchase of the Pightle and part of Broomfield along The Ridgeway in 1822 (now Cedars House area) and other fields would come later: great oaks from little acorns ...

By 1814, a fashionable Mill Hill ridge earns the County History epithet, *a considerable village*, with shops at both ends. The first map of the school grounds of 1820, **Fig.D(i)**, is owed to three pupils: James Challis (a stonemason's son, who became Plumian Professor of Astronomy at Cambridge, and the first observer of the planet Neptune); Edward Smith; and Robert Maitland (son of a Bank of England director, who went up to Trinity, Cambridge). The L-shaped villa's longer arm gave

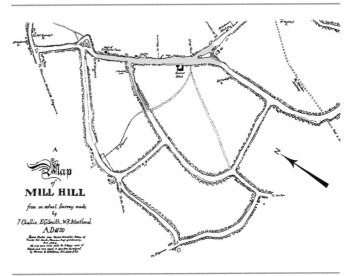

Fig.D(i) MILL HILL TOPOGRAPHY 1820s

onto the road, with a separate stables where the present driveway begins: it was converted to form the first Chapel. A later map by Brett James, **Fig.D(iv)**, (Ch.VI), marked this with a star, purporting it to be the site of 'The Old School, 1525-1825', but he later retracted this: Richard Swift's School (1660-1701), on Drivers Hill, was on the site of "Jeannettes", between "Rosebank" and Burtonhole Lane. Of "Peacock's", at the north-west corner of the later Wills Grove, parallel with the stables, Brett James wrote that the *long low wooden house with its end to the road* was the home of Mr Peacock, a School functionary. It faced *The King's Head*, and also its subsequent fate. Tumble-down even then, it did indeed tumble down later in the century: no trace remains.

As **Fig.D(iii)** will show in Ch. IV, a three-part U-shaped building to the east of that junction with an unfenced path was "Hill Top" (misreported elsewhere as the Head Master's house). From 1816 to 1825, this would be the site of the first Junior School to gain the Committee's patronage, on the basis of a cut-off age of 10 years. Breaching this agreement, 'Wood's Academy' (after the Maths master) had to decamp to Totteridge as it was threatening Mill Hill's own intake; it achieved 53 boys under 13 by 1822, the age-barriers then being in no way clear-cut. It was just as well that Mill Hill did not try to replace it as a separate institution – at least 250 such establishments founded in the 19th century failed (including another 'Belmont' at Brighton), with only 131 surviving into the late 20th; 90 per cent of today's 'Preparatory' Schools (in the British, not the American 'Pre-University' sense) were founded between 1850 and 1950. There would be four other Junior Schools bearing the popular 18th-century name "Belmont" – at Dorking, Glasgow, Hassocks and Hereford. This precursor to both the future Pre-Prep and Mill Hill's later Belmont (then designated as the 'Seat of Sir Charles Flower') would become a bakery towards the end of the century, and then a Cafe in the Jacks' era. It was at first in-bounds, before "Blenheim Steps" was bought (see Ch.VI); next as 14-15 High Street, for staff-rental up to 1962; it was purchased, then demolished in 1967, making way for staff houses.

Village, c1900: castellated "Hill Top", former bakery and in-bounds shop (r.), (now site of MHS staff houses), prior to purchase of "Blenheim Steps" (c.) in 1928 (sold in 1972 as a private house). 2.c

"Sunnyside", later "Murray House", atop Hammers Lane to the west, was shown as "Mr Humphreys House" [*sic*]; this was the dwelling, replete with a basement to cope with the slope, which was occupied first by Rev. Phillips, then by Rev. Dr Humphrys, and finally and significantly by a Chaplain, not by a Head, Rev. Henry March; he moved in on 12 January 1826. By 1893, the time of the publication of the *Dictionary* that would emerge from that humble location, distances in this scene of 'grass walks and fishponds' (probably spring-fed) were still being measured, as the *Dictionary* explained, in 'Chains' of 66 feet: (each made up of 4 'Poles or Perches' of 5 yards: 10 chains x 1 in breadth = 100,000 square links/ rods = 1 acre).

The Octagon of Accountability

By December 1808, at the end of the School's – and Rev. Atkinson's – first year, a small but important event occurred. *Nobis* tells the story: *He, like his staff and boys was doubtless looking forward to the well-earned Christmas break of four weeks. It had been a long hard grind since the month's holiday at midsummer which with Christmas constituted the only times the school was in recess ... As he surveyed his 60 boarders (fees £45 per annum or £30 for the sons of accepted ministers) it is probable that [he] had thoughts for one boy in particular. He had not been an especially distinguished pupil ...* and leaving that December, after just one year at Mill Hill, at the age of 15, he would not go on to *lead an especially distinguished life ... but Richard Baker Aldersey ... became the first of 10,305 "Old Millhillians"*; (see Ch.XII).

Whether a Head's reign is longer, or shorter – like that first and in fact seven subsequent regimes – doing it full justice is an elusive goal. The task is made all the harder by an awareness of the intellectual and 'political' effort involved in accomplishing this most exacting of management tasks. It requires, in the topical words of one of the few Heads ever to have written about *The Art of the Headmaster, the constitution of a carthorse, the nerves of a gladiator and the resilience of a sorbo ball* (as it happens, the kind used in Mill Hill's "Singlehanded"; see Appendix E). There has to be a regret that so much planning and struggle over resources, such sheer dogged leadership, is finally over: at the same time a hope, even a satisfaction, that the good or innovatory achievements will not be forgotten. To witness the ending of the greatest of such reigns is akin to being in the audience for a major symphony, under the baton of a top conductor. Each performance is unique, yet each follows a comparable pattern: the orchestra changes, although the instruments are the same. The scores are familiar: the art is in the interpretation, for a particular audience, at a particular moment in time.

The year 1818, whilst full of unrest in the 'Ancient Schools', passed quietly at Mill Hill. By 1825, the end of the reign of the third Head, Rev. Dr John Humphrys, School Secretary under his predecessor, a new School building would arise: the boldness of this development merits separate coverage. However, one feature of this building would provide a particular piece of symbolism: the Octagon. Its occupants, the cavalcade of Mill Hill's 27 Heads, have had to satisfy a many-faceted constituency. Corporate governance has also imposed some problems peculiar to Mill Hill alone; as the History will relate, some of the magisterial riders in that cavalcade would baulk at the complexity of balancing all those factors. With hindsight, that 'accountability' can be seen

First Octagon, MHS, Tite Schoolhouse of 1825: severe decor characteristic of period up to 1950s: main School House corridor beyond Barrier at second octagonal light-well. *2.d*

anachronistically to have eight main aspects. From 1825, as they stepped every day into that airy eight-sided space, the men leading Mill Hill School had the unintended distinction of being confronted with a symbol in stone of the eight main areas of their task; for continuity, it can be seen as an 'Octagon of Accountability'.

From the earliest days, each of those 'interest groups', with all their subsidiary audiences, demanded a different strand in an ideal Head's capability, even if today's management jargon would accord new labels to familiar characteristics. The link to the parental constituency has always been one of 'recruiter'. For the Feeder schools, the role of 'marketer' (personified today in a separate Deputy Head) has evolved from, but never abrogated, a Head's charismatic ability to engender good word-of-mouth recommendation. Towards the pupils, the role has evolved from the self-contradictory combination of 'instiller of the fear of God' and 'spiritual guardian', to the more genial, and congenial, ones of 'cultural educator' and 'pastoral carer', again supported by other members of the overall 'management' – and indeed gubernatorial – 'team': (today pastoral care merits a Governor's overview, see Ch.XI).

Vis-à-vis the governing body, the role of 'sound administrator' has remained a necessary constant, but the responsibility as 'budget-holder' was extended in 1987 to a member of the non-academic staff, [**Fig.E**]. To be a 'good picker' and potentially an 'effective performance-controller' with regard to the teaching staff, have been added the modern roles of 'enabler' and 'communicator'. As to Mill Hill's relationship with her former pupils, this was important from early on, becoming increasingly delicate in the later stages of the 20th century, as pressures for change mounted. It could never be ignored, and has at times taken on a salience disproportionate to other interest groups. It is a highly sensitive version of that especial Public School sense of ownership, a sense – right or wrong – of the Old Boys ('Old Girls' do not seem to have, or want to have, this quality) being endowed not merely with a unique insight into, but a responsibility for safeguarding the essence of the School's tradition and 'spirit': even, some might feel, her soul.

The greatest evolution within these continuities lies in the role required for presenting a face to the outside world, the 'figurehead' – evolving from a very simple concept, to a major, highly complex and subtle role in today's competitive market. It is asking too much of any one person to possess all these 'competences' in equal measure: the best regimes will be those where each of these functions is professionally covered by at least one or other of the total team. That luxury was not available to those early, often beleaguered and solitary Heads.

Fig.E 'THE OCTAGON OF ACCOUNTABILITY'

Feeder Schools

Parents

Pupils

Governors and the Chair of the Court [The 19C Committee]

Headmaster

Teaching staff: the Common Room

Old Millhillians [Former pupils]

Finance function: [Secretary/Treasurer]

The outside world

The first 'Millhillian' families

Simone de Beauvoir might well have been able to get away with entitling her seminal sociological work, *The Second Sex*, and indeed that is how most of a Public School's male staff and pupils would have thought and spoken for much of the period up to the 1960s. Yet as the story of Mill Hill will reveal, the two equal sexes have never been so abstracted from each other at Mill Hill as tradition would seem to imply. The balancing feminine presence was always there, if often well concealed under the shell of a centuries-old male chauvinism. Even if the female title of 'Millhillienne' could not be properly conferred until 1974, the co-education of Mill Hill's 21st-century life can be seen as part of a long continuum. It dates back, by the modern definition of co-education, to the joint lessons with Miss Russell's girls from the school conducted in association with the Chaplain in his house in 1825, and the demure ribbon-swapping 'Crumpites' of Miss Crump's later establishment of the 1840s. It is a perspective that needs to be borne in mind from the outset: the 20th-century decision to 'go co-educational' was not the precipice in time that some die-hards, for the most understandable reasons, feared it might be.

George Eliot described Dissent as *a foolish habit that clung greatly to families in the grocery and chandlering lines*. The nicely acid humour of her remark apart, the novelist was being less sharply pertinent than usual. The parental background to the Grammar School's first 150 or so pupils reflects far more accurately the complexion of early 19th-century Nonconformity into which Dissent was now developing; members of all five of the top 'classes' sent their sons – even one farmer, and possibly one 'Gentleman'. The pattern is clear: nearly half came from business backgrounds, a third from professional homes, and some 17 per cent from the owner/ retailer class. That second category included six attorneys or solicitors and four surgeons, the start of a long, continuing presence in those two senior callings, and a scattering of bankers, Army officers, and schoolmasters, as well as a stockbroker, and an organist. The pattern embraced *22* ordained ministers, or families of a strong denominational bent: metropolitan Congregationalism is by far the largest of those declared family faiths – at seventeen. There were also four Baptist families, and the first Presbyterian. There were as yet no Methodists, reflecting the difference in wealth and length of existence in the community of 'New' as compared with 'Old' Dissent. As to Quakers, there were none in the first 25 years; indeed the absence of Millhillians in *Quakers in Commerce* seems conclusive; they did after all have Ackworth School to go to, from 1779 onwards. Yet beliefs overlapped: Lord Leverhulme, a later Trustee and Congregationalist, was described as *almost a Quaker*.

Parental businesses indicated the commerce of late Georgian England, and also highlighted the many lost trades: merchants in ostrich feathers, and in ivory; a silk manufacturer, tanner and tallow-chandler; tea dealers, millers and brewers; factors for leather, flour, and hops; warehousemen, like Samuel Favell, and a builder: Thomas Piper (Snr – father of a Thomas – commemorated in the Piper Library of 1999/2000) later to become the School's devoted Treasurer (see Ch.III); and a cutler from Sheffield, the father of Henry Shaw, later of St Louis. The spread of retail trades gives an insight into the potential wealth that could now be acquired as booksellers, apothecaries, drapers, clothiers, glovers, hosiers, jewellers, silversmiths, tailors, bakers, grocers or ironmongers.

Before the advent of the Great Northern railway to 'Mill Hill' [East] in 1867, many families would use their own *équipage* to take their boys up to Mill Hill. Others

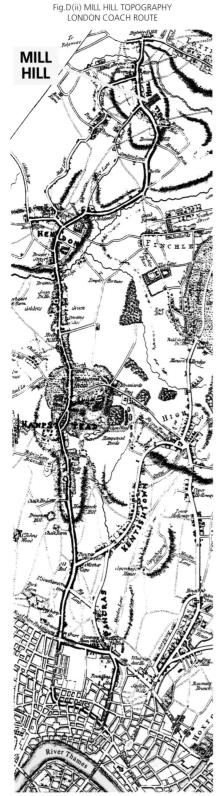

Fig.D(ii) MILL HILL TOPOGRAPHY
LONDON COACH ROUTE

MILL
HILL

would use one of Mr Bowden's 'glass coaches' which left the *Bull Inn* in Holborn just to the east of the City Bar, opposite Fetter Lane, at 10.30 and 3.00 each day. Other start points were *The Blue Posts* or the *Elder Wine House*, Holborn. Later, in 1831, as Frederick Helmore records, there was a coach driven daily by Mr Woolley of Mill Hill, who had three boys at the School himself; possibly this was the 'two-horse Mill Hill coach' of a memoir by Rev. Whitemore of 1825 (Thomas Priestley would later distrust *our only conveyance from the Hill*, due to a fatal accident).

By 1851, writer Bernard Oak reports two-hour fares from Broad Street, St Giles, or Bishopsgate, costing 1s.6d. (7p). The route ran through the open, garden country north of the 'New [Euston] Road', by-passing the domain of rival Highgate, bowling down from Hampstead into Golders Green, and straining up once more to Hendon, **Fig.D(ii)**. Although the nine-mile stone above Engel Park on 'Drivers' [Bittacy] Hill, abetted by the School's first Historian, suggests otherwise, the Village's careful researcher, Ralph Calder, (reinforced by the Cooke map) asserted that an old coach route followed the now impassable line of Ashley Lane to Sanders Lane, Dole Street and Milespit Hill. There is an inference that the gradient up to The Ridgeway escarpment, like that up Haverstock Hill, was too much for the horses; special 'shoes' would be taken out, and put under the wheels to prevent them slipping back; the passengers, by now well jolted, had to dismount while the coach, with their 'boxes' still aboard, made it over the steepest parts of both hills. (Leslie Millard, an *OM* of the 1920s, would recall that even the technology of his time, the municipal bus from today's Mill Hill East, was not equal to this task, with the same need for the passengers to get out and walk, whatever the weather; there is a similar story about the gradient up Hammers Lane.)

What Brett James called 'the Glass Stage-Coaches' carried an interesting cross-section of boys. Most notable to the eye of the 21st century was the spread of their ages – from eight to even in some special cases as high as sixteen. During those founding years they came not merely from London itself, and addresses that today are not primarily residential – Covent Garden, Thornhaugh Street, Oxford Street and Thomas Piper's Little Eastcheap; they also resided in the select villas that the emerging middle classes were already favouring – in Hackney, Southwark, Kentish Town, and Walworth. More significantly, parents as far afield as Scotland, Wales and the Isle of Wight were reading those advertisements in media now widening to include *The Times* and the *Morning Herald*, and deciding to try Mill Hill for their dutiful sons. (For totals over different year-groups, see **Fig.F**.)

They came from towns that already boasted a Public School, Day or Boarding, in their midst – Shrewsbury, Canterbury, Newcastle, Manchester, St Albans; from the busy heart of Britain's Industrial Revolution, the source of her imperial dominance for the next 100 years – Birmingham, Halifax, Leeds; and they came too from the tiny hamlets that still reflected the old rural, peasant England that was slowly but surely passing: Bourton-on-the-

Water, Melbourn, Cerne, Chipping Norton, Stratford-on-Avon. Bath, Margate, Herne Bay, and Brighton also sent their sons. Research for a recent book by a distinguished Lakeland *OM*, the late Michael Berry, *A Sunlit, Intimate Gift ...*, has revealed that the livelihood theme that automatically links them today, to become known as 'tourism', was still virtually unknown, apart from the 'taking of the chalybeate waters' at Bath, Harrogate and elsewhere; as to Brighton, 'Prinny', the young Prince of Wales, was only to bring it into prominence during the second decade of Mill Hill's story. The two provincial cities which had grown rich on Britain's most infamous and only recently outlawed industry, the Slave Trade, also featured: Bristol and Liverpool. As the History has noted, Mill Hill's Founders, not least Isaac and Dr John of the famous Buxton family, were associated with the great movement to abolish both 'the Trade' and Slavery itself.

The opening *Mill Hill Magazine* of 1873 would claim that every county of England was represented. Amongst those counties, the names clustered, suggesting much word-of-mouth recommendation in localities: Essex, Wiltshire, South Wales, Northamptonshire and the Cotswolds area, were frequently mentioned. The towns read like a gazetteer: Aberavon, Berwick, Cambridge, Devizes, Edington, Frome, Hull, Ivinghoe, Kettering, Ludlow, Market Harborough, Nairn, Oxford, Portsmouth, Rotherham, St Ives, Tewkesbury, Wisbech, Yeovil. Even more significant, many of the boys' families came from abroad, the sons of missionaries, traders or diplomats: Batavia, Gothenberg, Calais, Colombo, the East Indies, Madras, Calcutta, Cape of Good Hope (Cape Colony), Vizagapatam, the Sandwich Isles, China. Only by the mid-century would the first of Mill Hill's foreign 'princely' sons arrive.

What could then be legitimately termed 'Christian', or given names, included the usual royal William, Charles and George, and biblical Mark, John, David, James, and Joseph, but also an Algernon, an Archibald, an Augustus, an Aeneas, and a Jeremiah. Some of the surnames were interesting in themselves: a Bacchus; two Fauntleroys; and a Courtauld from Braintree (an early forebear of the family into which the 'RAB' of the 'Butler' Education Act of 1944, married, see Ch.VIII). Many of them were related to the leading members of the Foundation itself: charity began very

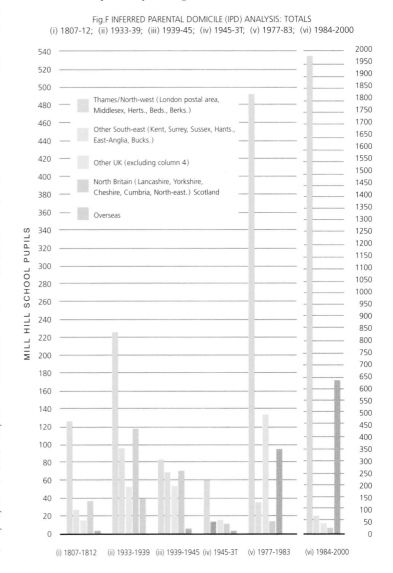

Fig.F INFERRED PARENTAL DOMICILE (IPD) ANALYSIS: TOTALS
(i) 1807-12; (ii) 1933-39; (iii) 1939-45; (iv) 1945-3T; (v) 1977-83; (vi) 1984-2000

Thames/North-west (London postal area, Middlesex, Herts., Beds., Berks.)

Other South-east (Kent, Surrey, Sussex, Hants., East-Anglia, Bucks.)

Other UK (excluding column 4)

North Britain (Lancashire, Yorkshire, Cheshire, Cumbria, North-east.) Scotland

Overseas

MILL HILL SCHOOL PUPILS

(i) 1807-1812   (ii) 1933-1939   (iii) 1939-1945   (iv) 1945-3T   (v) 1977-1983   (vi) 1984-2000

proudly at home, with the Favells and the Pye Smiths, the Pipers, the Sabines, the Dawsons, Hankeys the School's bankers, and many others. Every boy had to be introduced by a main Committee Member, and voted in by him: neither the Head Master nor the Chaplain had the right to do so – they could not control their own intake, yet would be judged by their results with this raw material.

On the surface this might seem to be a very mixed bunch of early Millhillians – an anachronism of course; the term did not evolve until the 1870s. They became known in due course as 'O.P.s', Old Pupils, although in retrospect several 'OP's referred to 'Old Boys' in the context of cricket matches and meetings of this period; in contrast to the assertion made in *Networks*, this would constitute the earliest use of this term, pre-dating the 1868 origination attributed to Haileybury. Yet the fact is that a strong self-selection process had already taken place: the sons of Ministers in the three main Dissenting faiths were always favoured, as well as the sons of other manses, e.g. the Church of Scotland. The backgrounds to many of those early intakes were serious, even pious, and thus they brought with them a propensity for learning and a religious approach to all things; *the youth of so many of our most influential families*, as the Chaplain, Rev. England (himself married to a Miss Butler of Witham) would later describe them. Of various boys credited with different Mill Hill 'firsts', William Cornwell of Oxford Street was 'No.1' on the Roll. Thomas Noon Talfourd is credited as the first to be admitted, though only arriving in June 1808; he became Charles Lamb's friend, dedicatee of Dickens' *Pickwick Papers* and also his lawyer, bearing the second longest 'CV' in any MHS Register, and sole *OM* writer to appear in the *Oxford Companion to English Literature* – see A Mill Hill Bibliography (p.373); (the hero of his book, *Ion*, would find an unlikely resurrection as the multi-media centrepiece of the 2000 Millennium Dome). Samuel Favell's eldest, also Samuel ('No.2'), was the first boy proposed, on 6 October 1807. Of William Lepard Smith ('No.6'), a nice story in the 1938 History, for which there is now no evidence, relates his racing another Millhillian to be first through the entrance in the brick wall on The Ridgeway.

The new Institution

All these 'new bugs' found a vastly different establishment awaiting them from those of later eras, let alone from that which characterises the year 2006/7. An 1810 document promised *a Classical and Religious Education*, comprehending English, French, Latin, Greek, Arithmetic, Geography, Mathematics and History. However, many other subjects were fitted in on the side, later interspersed with what must be regarded as pathfinding lectures – in 'Natural and Experimental Philosophy', 'General Electrical Science', Chemistry, and Astronomy. Of teachers, the least stable was French, although many other Assistant Masters lasted a bare year or two. The most stable was Drawing, held by George Shepherd from 1807 to 1819 and thereafter by a teacher from London, Mr Renton, (appointed by the outgoing Rev. Phillips) with until 1860, still – by a year – the longest-ever tenure over the 200 years, outseeing Thomas Priestley. Several masters progressed to other egregious careers from Mill Hill, most notably Rev. Temple Hillyard; he went on after 1839 to become Canon of Chester. Many long-servers also became much loved figures, including the Writing master, Joseph Newland, *an humble and upright man*, who interestingly, according to Rev. Henry March's Diary, *seems an Israelite*. He was one of two staff commemorated by a marble tablet in the Chapel; it was put up on his death in 1832. No fewer than 41 staff came, and mostly went, during these first 27 years of the School's existence: two evolved to become Head Masters – Corrie and Priestley; one, Mr McLaughlin, from Edinburgh, was said to have come in to act as Head for six months during Rev. Lea Berry's absence through illness, before Priestley took over in October 1834.

The timetable within which this small fast-changing band of pioneers taught was incredibly tough, [**Fig.G(i)**]. First bell was at 5.30 a.m. in the summer 'half', moved forward as a great concession to 6.00 in the winter half; this was later relaxed to 6.00 and 7.00: then about one hour's prep downstairs before Family Prayers and breakfast at 8.00. After a 45-minute break, the day thereafter followed a not unrecognisable pattern: School lasted from 9.30 until 12.30 (with 'dinner' at 1.00 p.m.) and again from 2.30 until 5.30 pm, except on Wednesdays and Saturdays; bedtime was at 9.00 p.m. in summer, 8.00 p.m. in winter. Parents were not expected to visit on the Lord's Day. A comment does eventually surface reflecting some concern for the boys' frailty, not to mention that of the Assistant Masters, in the face of these hours: *Pupils are rather in danger of being overwhelmed by an Excess of Exertion.* Not only were the hours long, but as *Nobis* has commented, the holidays were sparing. No sooner had the summer half broken up in June than they were all back again in July for the second half, to work through until December. No hint of those carefree family holidays that by the time of the first *Magazine* were a recurrent theme. After a mere month, they were all convening once more for the long haul up to "the Hill", as the School was often referred to in the Governors' Minutes.

On arrival boys would alight on The Ridgeway, first of all at the Gate in the old brick wall where Lepard Smith had had his legendary race (today, after the Stancomb-Wills connection, 'Dame Janet's Gate'); with the new Tite Building of 1825, they entered the main entrance to the Octagon. A Housekeeper/ Matron bustled them off to their bedrooms to unpack; by 1831 there were also a Cook, Maids (Kitchen, Parlour, Linen, Assistant and House) and a Porter. Brett James related that the boys' dress was standard: *blue or black jackets and black trousers, except in summer, when they wore white ducks. The collars were attached to the shirt, open and free about the neck, round which they tied coloured ribbons or silk handkerchiefs.*

Patterns evolved. A first Speech Day was held on 18 June 1811. *Over the knee* – the use of the cane by Masters – was much in evidence; rudimentary football and cricket matches occurred, as well as archery, rounders, gymnastics, and 'prisoner's base' in the then playground; there were regimented countryside walks, though few and far between; the privilege of personal 'good conduct plots' for deserving boys in the kitchen garden (on the site of the future schoolhouse) was greatly prized; by 1821 a new Prospectus had been produced. By 1831 and, by inference, in consequence of Arnold's 15-year spell at Rugby from 1827, the earliest forms of 'monitorial' discipline reigned over bedrooms and dining rooms. Disdaining to adopt the

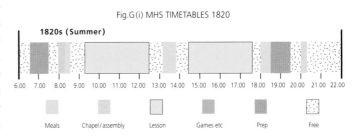

Fig.G(i) MHS TIMETABLES 1820

aristocratic 18th-century concept which Arnold had had to endure as a Wykehamist
– the Wykehamical 'propositours' ranking above 'inferiours' – Mill Hill preferred the
newer Rugbeian 'moralized form', whilst calling them 'monitors', (see **Fig.H**).

Any subsequent failures by the Committee and its School did not come about
for want of trying. As early as 1807 it compared itself with Harrow, St Paul's,
Merchant Taylor's and Eton, and at the 1810 Annual Meeting was claiming that the
new Grammar School was *on a par...with similar Institutions belonging to the
Establishment*. Whatever the faults of the School's embryonic management structure,
one testimony as to academic merit is at least positive; it is that of the Rev. Richard
Hamilton, DD, LLD, as contained in a Memoir by W.H.Stowell. Of undoubted
ability and probity, among that initial experimental intake of 1807 he became, with
the School's first knight (already encountered here – Justice of the Pleas Sir Thomas
Talfourd) one of the School's 38 'OM' entries in the 'old' *DNB*. He left in 1810, aged
16, to study at Hoxton College; comparing it with Mill Hill, he found the lectures
there *too easy*: mathematics was *taught in a very limited and desultory way*.

Notwithstanding the disabilities facing Dissenters, Mill Hill had many successes
from that first four-year cadre, including her first Cambridge graduates: Joseph
Harris, who went up to Clare College, and Rev. Edward Wilton, the pioneer in a long
line of *OMs* to go to Queens'. Mill Hill's first clinician, and her second knight, to
become Sir James Bardsley, MD, FRCP, JP, DL and a graduate of Edinburgh, is
another outstanding professional alumnus of the first decade. So was, five years later,
William Jacobson. He would deserve mention on merit alone – leaving in 1819 for
Homerton and Oxford, he was Lord Palmerston's appointment as Bishop of Chester
from 1865 to 1884. A Foundationer who repaid the costs of his fees, he also deserves
to be freed from an 80-year-old slur on his character. Among the books given by Mill
Hill's first Historian to the Archive was one discovered in the Script roof in 1999,
Burgon's *Lives of Twelve Good Men*. The First Register of 1926 attributes to Jacobson,
as one of those 12, the dubious epithet *the simple-minded bishop*. The text's correct
description – *the single-minded bishop* – reads somewhat better for posterity.

Much of the activity that preoccupied those early 19th-century Governors is now
of more antiquarian than historical interest: indentures of Trusts, Loans and
Mortgages; enfranchisement of that ancient property title, copyhold; or redemption
of tithe rentcharges through the intricate customs of the Lordship of the Manor of
Hendon (in the 18th century, held by David Garrick the actor – also listed in the
Deeds of the first Burton Bank property). References to Doctors' Commons, and the
Courts of Chancery, and Common Pleas, in beautiful copperplate, and in the fustian
language of the 'Jarndyce and Jarndyce' of Dickens' *Bleak House*, bear witness to the
care with which successive Honorary Treasurers and Secretaries progressed the
interests of their institution. The educational often became submerged under the
legal, with up to 25 Governors needing to approve issues.

The documentation is, however, still of enduring value today in four respects:
first, the themes underlying those early dealings – the continuing emphasis on the
need for a moral character in all things, the education of *Youth of extraordinary talents*,
and the evolution of the Dissenting interest; second, the sociological composition of
the Committee, as well as of those prepared to lend them their money –

entrepreneurs, solicitors, rentiers, even farmers; thirdly, a precept is emphasised that, nearly two centuries later, would still be acting as a banner and a reference point for the Court Chairman, Headmaster and Chaplain of the 1990s – the concept of tolerance (see Ch.XI). Lastly, there is the increasing evidence of the School's development as a significant landowner – what an 1892 Surveyor's Report would describe, without intended irony, as *the property in all its peculiar features*; within 18 years of the foundation, that property would acquire its most illustrious enhancement.

Tite's transformations

The Napoleonic Wars had a further advantage for Mill Hill: they enabled Sir Charles Flower to make a fortune – from Government contracts – thus ensuring the survival of the Belmont mansion. However, architecturally, the exuberance of the Regency period had other consequences. London swung to a more restrained style, the Greek Revival; it is evident in the National Gallery in Trafalgar Square of 1824, and in Smirke's facade for the new British Museum, planned in 1826. At Mill Hill, the first School was now bulging at the seams; bedrooms, housing up to 25 boys, had been built over the original structure. The first Chapel was recalled as an *old, ugly red-brick building* by Benjamin Scott (later Chamberlain to the Corporation of London, a prolific writer and a School Governor, President of the OMC – and, incidentally, saviour of Epping Forest). It was enlarged in 1820, for £250, with junior boys occupying a new Gallery, while the seniors sat below (this too had to be superseded – by Tite's Chapel, the future 'Large', opened on 27 June 1832).

Sir William Tite MP, twice PRIBA, leading 19C architect: MHS Governor and building advisor up to 1850s. *2.e*

Increasingly limited by the original Collinson mansion, despite considerable improvements under Rev. Maurice Phillips, in 1824 the Committee took a jump into the unknown future; its bold decision was not just to extend but to transform the site, and build afresh. The new building was in tune with the times, in more ways than one. *Pevsner* gives authority: *The 1820s was the high point for Grecian neoclassicism, adopted as an appropriately serious dress for a variety of institutions...favoured particularly by Nonconformists. Mill Hill School, established in 1807 as the first Nonconformist public school, was provided in 1825-7 with imposing but plain buildings by William Tite, a long frontage with Grecian colonnade dominating a high ridge of North Middlesex.* Tite's second competition-winner in one year, this style would be even more visible in his facade for London's Royal Exchange of 1844, also still surviving today as are his many railway stations.

The Committee ensured that Tite's building marked an advance in educational terms too: *At the beginning of the nineteenth century schools generally consisted of little more than a large schoolroom, with teachers' accommodation and perhaps an additional classroom. Among large boarding schools, Mill Hill was exceptional in providing as many as four* [in fact five] *classrooms in addition to its main hall.* Tite was the son of a City merchant, twice President of the RIBA, knighted in 1869, and MP for Bath from 1855 to his death in 1873, at 75. He is reported to have said to the Prince of Wales, *I inherited a fortune, I married a fortune, and I have made a fortune.* According to the authors of *The Victorian Buildings of London*, he *introduced himself wherever possible*, most outrageously into the final stage of the competition for the Royal Exchange building, whisked from under the nose of C.R.Cockerell, famous for his Harrow chapel. The authors dubbed him

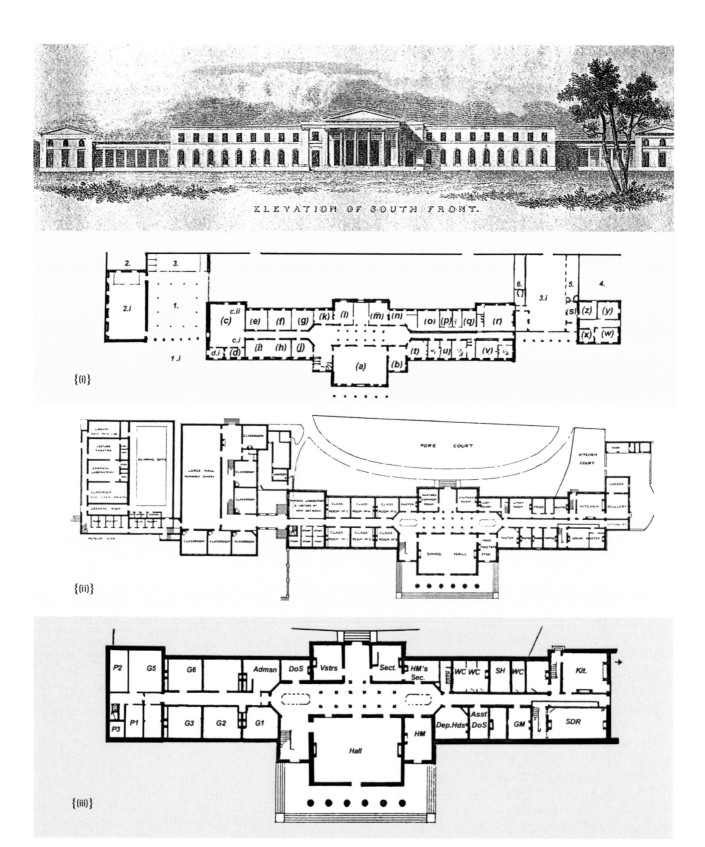

FIG. H MILL HILL SCHOOL HOUSE UTILISATION (I 1825; II 1907; III 2006/7)

the odious and well-connected Tite – opportunistically he dominated the railway boom, with stations such as Windsor and Blackwall to his name – nonetheless his presence as architect, advisor, and Governor for Mill Hill was wholly beneficial, and sustained. He was to be the first of two PRIBAs, and three RIBA Gold Medallists, to design for Mill Hill (see Ch.V; Appendix C).

It was already clear that Mill Hill's location had become an even more sacred *Mons Sacra* than that occupied by the rival Harrow on the south-west skyline; the dominance of the 1825 building would ensure that the site would remain centripetal, never breaking down into the 'Balkanization' identified by Harrow's recent historian. At a grand ceremony on 16 June 1825, the Foundation Stone was laid by Samuel Favell, with a silver trowel, on the site of the Dining Hall; glasses of gold, silver George IV coins, a prospectus, and a brass inscription in Latin (see Appendix F) were entombed for posterity; they still lie there today, undisturbed by Hitler's bombs. The new building was in fact ready for occupation by July 1826, for a cost of £15,000, a remarkable feat. The following year, 1827, Samuel Favell presented the marble bust of himself, the first adornment of the otherwise severe Hall; (11 years later, John Pye Smith's bust would be presented by his son, Ebenezer). An act of the imagination is required in order to visualise the thinking behind the layout of the original Tite building of 1825/7, see **Fig.H**. The rooms planned by Tite are keyed 'a-z', enabling an easier comparison of space utilisation across the centuries:-

a: the Dining Hall, initially with a fifth entrance into...

b: set aside for the Committee's meetings, and a Library, this central location was not seen as the place for the Principal; *c1/c2:* then a single large 'playroom', with disruptive traffic eventually having to pass through from the Schoolhouse corridor to the Covered Quadrangle (today's Loggia) and after 1832 to Tite's new (Second) Chapel, (today the Marnham/ Large area).

d: the sole School washroom; *d.i* monitors' room;
e, f, g, h/i and j: the five innovatory separate classrooms and Writing Room which the Pevsner classic authority praises.
k was a Master's Room, connecting to *l*, an adjacent Office.
m was the first Visitors Room (not, as now, the former *l*).
n: Housekeeper's Room (subsequently the downstairs room of the Chaplain, Rev. William Clayton, 1831 to 1838; currently the Headmaster's Secretary's).
o/p/q: Linen Store /other Stores, abutting the Servants' Hall; *r:* the Kitchen was beyond the stairs, with a Scullery, *s.ii* (part of new buildings *s1/2/3* by 1905).
t was envisaged as a Sitting Room, with three doorways – into the Library; the Octagon, on an angled wall; and into a Master's quarters/ studies, *u.i/u.ii/u.iii.*
v.i/v.ii: beyond the stairs was the Head Master's set of rooms. On the site of the former Collinson mansion (and of the future School House extension of 1928) were planned (but never built) a colonnade; a further Library *w;* a Study *x;* the Head's Dining Room, *y,* with its own Kitchen, *z.* The open spaces were: *1.* the Covered Quad (see Ch.IV), giving onto the Playground *1.i; 2.* Chapel Court [The Ridgeway entrance to the Second Chapel, *2.i,* next to the Bath; *3.i* the Kitchen Court [transposed to the NW by 1905], *4.* the Drying Ground, where washing was hung out from the Wash-House next-door. *5.* The other

Silver chalice and paten, designed for second MHS Chapel of 1832, (still in use for Eucharist and all-faith Communion services today). *2.f*

interesting adjunct was the Brewhouse, 6. The essence of that early layout was that all School activities were closely intermingled. (By the 1980s, the wheel would come round 360 degrees, the School House corridor rooms reverting to their earlier educational role, in the Faculty Block reforms.)

A fight for Principals

Whilst the School was acquiring a generous, newly unified outer shell, the space within it was exhibiting less generous, internecine characteristics. The seeds lay back in the beginnings, when five sub-committees were spawned – 'Printing', 'School', 'Appointments', and two which became the Head Masters' sole channel to the General Committee – 'Visiting', and 'House'; these structures created problems of delegation, access, and communication, whose echoes would still resound, cloaked by modern terms, in the late 20th century.

The Committee were split between 'Godliness', a goal which they could all-too readily recognise (while not yet the Public School 'muscular Christianity' of the later 19th century), and effectiveness, which they could not. Up to 1825, the Head Master was also the undisputed 'Principal', short for 'Principal Tutor'; thus the first Register oversimplifies with its all-embracing statement that 'the position of Principal was above that of Headmaster'. In 1825, the Committee in its wisdom abolished the title of 'Principal', and asked Dr Humphrys to carry on as Chaplain, and minister, while they 'networked' for a new, more powerful Chaplain. After a turn-down by Rev. William Rooker, an ancestor of Rooker Roberts (see Ch.VII), Rev. Henry March accepted. Dr Corrie succeeded as 'First Classical Tutor', to find himself referred to by the new Chaplain as 'Head Master', without any acknowledgment that this title might precede his own role. Both having equal access to the Visiting Sub-Committee, confusion grew to Brobdingnagian proportions: the Head Master had to deal with 'reverence in worship' (i.e. boys' behaviour); the Chaplain led 'religious contributions'. From 29 January to 24 June 1828, the successor Head, (the later Hon Rev. Dr Evans – 'Honourable' as a member of the Victoria State Cabinet), was in charge of the *classical and school department* [*sic*], while the Chaplain was charged with a *domestic and moral oversight* which would seem to overlap directly with that task.

Not surprisingly this tension affected School life; the monitors (reintroduced by Evans) asked to be allowed to resign, and there was a famous incident, to be detailed later. This period's dates are confused by both the 1926 Register and the first History, which also floated – without substantiating – the term 'Interregnum'. There was no Head from July to December 1828, but day-to-day control lay with Mr Wood, the Maths master and *resident master in charge and domestic superintendent*, before he departed for Totteridge. The Committee tried to cut through the impasse by dismissing half the staff, keeping on Messrs Cullen, Priestley, Newland – with the addition of Mr Renton. It was not the first time that the strange bundle of powers that constitutes a Court of Governors had wronged some of its faithful servants, nor sadly, as this History will relate, would it be the last. The celebrated Rev. Thomas Blundell now took over as Chaplain, to be succeeded in 1831 by the first of only three 'OM' Chaplains, Rev. Henry Lea Berry, who was very soon thereafter asked in effect to move sideways to pick up the hot potato of the 'Head Mastership'.

Only with the appointment of Rev. William Clayton later in 1831 as Chaplain and 'Coadjutor' to the governing Committee, and, as will unfold, the seemingly unequivocal appointment of Thomas Priestley as Head Master in October 1834 (not 1835), did peace beckon; they would manage the duality as co-operatively as they could, and at least as well as any Roman consuls. The decisive moment would prove to be Priestley's letter of 1846 (see Ch.III). His successor, Rev. Philip Smith, the second *OM* leader of the School, would make unitary responsibility a pre-condition of his appointment, which the Committee reluctantly approved. After that, power gradually evolved in a form recognisable today, onto the shoulders of a Head Master.

There is thus a strange contradiction at the heart of Mill Hill's early years. For most of those first two centuries, generations of loyal Millhillians have found reassurance in one of the characteristics of the School's founding fathers: their strong moral principles. John Pye Smith, Samuel Favell, and their colleagues and successors could not be faulted in terms of a long list of abstract qualities: they were courageous, ambitious, meticulous. Their *extraordinary act of faith* still deserves the admiration of all who follow them. The noble aspirations that inspired them endure, transmuted into 21st-century terms, to inform and underlie the Mill Hill of today.

To overburden that list of abstractions, they were by the same token characterised by a magnificent zealotry, one overwhelming 'mind-set', which seemed to be handed on unconsciously, like some Holy Grail, from one cohort of Committee Members to the next – a Dissenting concern for the soul before all else. This example of Governors' 'cognitive dissonance' would echo in the later 20th century. Here it created an intractable triangle of relationships between themselves, the 'First Masters' who would work for them, and the Chaplains – and their wives – who were appointed at their side; it was to prove an all-but fatal flaw. As the events of the

Tite's Schoolhouse Portico facade from below Top Field, with second Chapel (l.): note typical boys' dress of long white or grey 'ducks' (trousers), short black or blue jackets. *2.g*

Top Terrace – unchanging under snow at all eras: an anachronism, but no MHS photographs occur before 1873. *2.h*

ensuing 40 years will sadly demonstrate, they were oblivious of the one thing they had set their hearts to do, a problem not confined to that distant time: how to develop a school. There was repeated evidence that might have caused them to hark back to the famous plea for toleration to the Kirk of Scotland in 1650 by that extraordinary Protestant forerunner of their Dissenting tradition, Oliver Cromwell: *I beseech you ... think it possible you may be mistaken.* Deeply believing in their God-given mission, they were ignorant – almost sublimely – of the basic elements involved in running that complex corporate entity, a school: this was a limitation all-too critical to a Boarding Grammar School, aimed originally at a specialised minority market, which even from its inception had the then existing 'Public' schools in its sights as yardsticks. As one of their own number, Rev. Dr John Humphrys, asserted as early as 1825, in one of the myriad critical pamphlets published during those tortuous early years by various forcibly departing Head Masters and Chaplains: *the author knows this Committee too well to expect that they will, at present, acknowledge any error in their proceedings ...*

It was not until the School had nearly reached her first half-century that the real problems and priorities in running an outward-facing, publicly competitive School, as opposed to what at times could almost take on the appearance of an inward-looking self-selecting religious seminary, are allowed onto the cryptic pages of the Committee's monthly reports. It is astonishing that Mill Hill survived the interventions of those successive Committees of good, well-meaning men. As a reading of their Minutes and the hitherto undiscovered tracts and pamphlets of that time clearly shows, the eventual dashing of those early hopes and objects seems to cry out with all the inevitability of one of the Greek tragedies that were still a central part of the scholastic fare of the 'young gentlemen' in their charge. As Mill Hill's first History put it, tentatively and deferentially, in 1909: *The Committee's ... new arrangement of a divided leadership could not work satisfactorily ... yet they continued to try ... their constant interference in all the details of school routine gave no opportunity for initiative in the masters ...*

A question poses itself: if Mill Hill's early committee-men were indeed to be judged as actually unsuited for the task, how did the heritage of their beloved 'Institution', as they preferred to call it, survive? In a legal sense, as the History will unfold, the Foundation of 1807 did not of course last in its original form. Yet in the sense of its basic identity, and above all in the continuity of its glorious territorial setting, the Mill Hill of 1807 did survive what will later be seen as the technical collapse of 1869, to go on to become the major educational foundation of this present century; the ensuing chapters will explore the process whereby that subtle balancing act was achieved, against all the odds.

The heritage

One of Mill Hill's lesser late 19th-century Head Masters, overshadowed both by his predecessor and his successor, offered this insight in a sermon delivered in the

School Chapel around 1880s/ 1890. Charles Vince later published the best 19 of these sermons under the title *Christian Conduct: Every school has a collective character, which is created by the character of its members, yet is in a sense independent of them.*

For the first half of 1828, with a mere 12 boys, the youngest, shortest-ever serving Head Master, 26-year-old George Evans MA, *a gentleman, a scholar, and an able…tutor*, made three colourful contributions to that 'character': he fell in love with and later happily married the lady-housekeeper who had been there for two years, Mrs Harriet Riddiford; he unwittingly provoked thereby an undeserved rebuke from the ill-informed Committee Secretary of the day; and thus became the cause of one of Mill Hill's rare riots. The story of this *fracas* was told by Frederick Helmore in his Memoir on his elder brother, Rev. Thomas, who went on to become a Priest in Ordinary to the Queen, Master of the Children of Her Majesty's Chapels Royal (where he abolished fagging, a century before Mill Hill dared to do so), and teacher of (Sir) Arthur Sullivan (and also the subject of the Music Bursaries from 1999).

THE TRAVELLED MINISTER.
(Probable appearance of the Postmaster-General on his return from New Zealand)

Rev. and Hon Dr George Samuel Evans, Head Master MHS, 1827-8, depicted as a Maori in his later 19C role as Postmaster-General, State of Victoria, Australia. *2.i*

Frederick conjured up the scene vividly: Evans *confided to Helmore (his School Captain, already at 16, at his full height and with 'a very respectable pair of whiskers') that he intended to vindicate his character on "Public Day" … the boys formed in the corridor [Octagon] outside the small door of the hall. At the moment Dr [sic] Evans rose to speak, the boys, forty in number [of whom 24 were new boys], marched to the front of the platform, and gave three hearty cheers for the headmaster. An attempt was made by some of the committee and one or two of the masters to turn them out, upon which they mounted to the platform amidst the screams of the ladies, who fled precipitately, pitched into the committee, some of whom they pommelled severely, and finally cleared the hall. Coachmen, footmen, and school servants were summoned…this they did without coming to a fight; most of them admiring the pluck of the lads, to whom they touched their hats as they retired from the battlefield.* 'Mr' Evans only gained his doctorate in law in 1830, later ordained as a Congregational minister; he resigned in December, after a popular six months, first to start a school at Hampstead, whither several boys followed him (and where Helmore was his assistant). He was then admitted to the Bar, working for the Reform Movement, and emigrated to New Zealand in 1839, subsequently to join the Government of Victoria, then work as Editor of the *Melbourne Herald*, becoming the subject of cartoons in the *Melbourne Punch*. Committee-heavy Mill Hill could have used that ability.

On 20 June 1830, Samuel Favell, the first of the School's Founders and the original contributor to that collective character, had died, at the age of seventy. Seven months before his death, on 6 November 1829, he had delivered an address to his constituents in the Ward of St Mary-Axe, London, fully reported in the prestigious *Gentleman's Magazine* for 1830. Apart from its conceptual linkage to the ideas underlying the School's origins, and its instance of an early evolution from the 'Protestant Dissenters' label, it also has 21st-century interest for the modernity of his thinking, and for a surprising reference to the source of the historic visual feature of the new century's second quadrangle, the Stoa.

Mrs Harriet Riddiford, Cook-Housekeeper, 1820s; marriage to Mr Evans raised eyebrows: emigrated to Australia. *2.j*

The enlightened state of the public mind has arisen in great measure from the power of the press, and the influence of general education. I have assisted to the best of my ability many societies formed to promote this great object … I have laboured with other friends to establish the

Mill-hill Grammar School, which, though not immediately connected with the city, has furnished during the last 20 years the sons of many of its merchants with an education equal in most respects to that supplied by our ancient endowed schools, several Mill-hill scholars having obtained high honours in the University of Cambridge, and one became a Senior Wrangler. It has always been one of the objects of that institution to lay a sure foundation for moral and religious character... He added: *I shall ever consider it an honour to have given the casting vote in the committee for the erection of a new London-bridge.* (The Stoa's granite block, saved by *OM* Ivan Luckin from that same London Bridge (see Chs.IX and XII), provides an additional, unintended but very solid reminder of Mill Hill's first foundation).

Within four years two more substantive Head Masters, and two more assertive Chaplains, would succeed each other; one of them, Rev. Thomas Blundell, then a Baptist, was particularly strident about his right to primacy. As an interesting pointer to the future, he later became the Anglican vicar of Mere, Wilts. These various figures made their input to the emerging Mill Hill tradition. The year 1834 (a year after the Indian Civil Service started to require competitive entry by exam, a key point in 19th-century Public School evolution) marks the conclusion to the second of the 12 discernible phases of influence in the School's story. Yet the School Roll was still a fragile thing, with no firm base for growth. How would those about to inherit that nascent tradition develop it? The next Head Master would be the first of only two 'insider' appointments to the full role in the School's entire history, a man with *a known attachment to the Institution*, the Classics Tutor first brought onto the staff in April 1818: what would be the effects of the reign of Thomas Priestley?

Sources for Ch.II include: J.Bennett, *Sermon... at New Broad St*, Jan 10, 1810. *Gentleman's Magazine*, 1830, 11, 185-6; *Congregational Magazine*, 1807+; letter, 29.iii.1927, to M.L.Jacks from Mrs M.Robson, gt-gt-niece of Rev. M.Phillips, with copy of 1817 sermon #; Pye-Smith Family Archives; Brett James, *op cit*: *English Public Schools – Mill Hill* (1938); Rev. H.March, *Diary of an Ordinary Man* (unpubl., not extant); *DNB* Search, Dr Susan Studd, OUP, 15.xi.2000; corr, T.J.Wright. Corr with author and Prof Duncan Forrester, speaker in Chapel, Fndtn Day, ref significance of Mill Hill's History: Oct/Nov 2003 #.

Background: Shrosbree, *op cit*; C.Hollis, *Eton* (1960); C.Tyerman, *Harrow* (O.U.P., 2000); T.W.Bamford. *Rise of the Public Schools...* (1967); T.Aveling, *Memorials of the Clayton Family* (1867); E.Baines, *Life of Edward Baines* (1851) [PSA]; T.Binney, *Education, two Sermons at Mill Hill... 1842, 1847*, (1847); Rev. T.Blundell. *Narrative of the Appointment of [TB] to the chaplaincy of the [PDGS/MH], and the causes of his removal* (1831); Rev. D.Bogue, *Nature and Importance of a Good Education, Sermon before the promoters of the [PDGS/MH]* (1808); J.W.Burgon, *Lives of Twelve Good Men* (1891)#; W.Clayton, *Charge and Sermons...* (1809): *Rural Discourses* (1814); S.Favell, *Plan and Statement* (1820); *Speech on Reform in Parliament* (1820); B.Flower, *Statement of Facts relative to the conduct of J.Clayton...* (1808); Rev. Humphrys to the *Committee of the [PDGS/ MHS] brought before the Bar of the Dissenting part of the* *Religious Public...* (1825); W.A.Newman Hall [1883-5], *Autobiography* (1901); H.McLachlan, *op cit*; W.Orme, *Address... to the Young Gentlemen of [PDGS/MH] on the appointment of Rev. H.March...* (1826); W.H.Stowell, *Memoir of... Richard Winter Hamilton* [1807-10] (1850); Timpson, *op cit*; C.A.Vince, *Christian Conduct...* (1892); T.N.Talfourd [1807-10], *Ion* (1835), *Vacation Rambles* (1845)#; Rev. J.Medway, *Memoirs of the Life & Writings of John Pye Smith* (1858); F.Helmore [1834-6], *Memoir... Rev. Thomas Helmore* [1825-8] (1891)#; Bewsher, *op cit* #; Ogilvie, *op cit*; corr. with Dr J.Philip 1999, C.H.B.Priestley [1929-34]; corr. with Mrs H.Riddiford, NZ, 1999, & 1868 obits of Rev. Dr G.S.Evans, HM; M.Drabble ed, *Oxford Companion to English Literature* (Oxford, 1985); W.C.Abbott ed, *Writings & Speeches of Oliver Cromwell* (Cambridge, Mass.,1937-47) v.II, 502-3; J.D'E.Firth, *Winchester College* (1949); J.B.Hope Simpson, *Rugby Since Arnold...* (1967); P.H.Emden, *Quakers in Commerce* (1939); W.E.Braithwaite, *Beginnings of Quakerism* (1912); C.S.Horne, *Popular History of the Free Churches* (1903); P.Ackroyd, *Dickens* (publ by Sinclair-Stevenson: reprinted by permission, The Random House Group, 1999); M.R.W.Berry [1943-7], *A Sunlit, Intimate Gift – Low Wood on Windermere* (Windermere, 2002); 'The Great Stink', (Bazalgette & London's Drains), Channel Five TV, 10.x.02; M.F.Tighe, *A Recovered Church: The Mere Papers* (2003, Mere). Dr Williams's Library: Rev. J.Bennett, Sermon, Friends of [PDGS], Mill Hill, 10.i.1810 [3022 B.11].

Prep schools: D.Leinster-Mackay, *Rise of the English Prep School* (Lewes, 1984); I.S.M. Hamilton, *When I Was a Boy* (1939); Lonsdale Ragg, *Memoir of Edwd. Chas. Wickham* (1911); G.Smith, *op cit*.

Topography/ Buildings: R.B.Pugh ed., *Victoria History of the Counties of England*, v.I, 307-8, (Oxford, 1976); Cooke map of Hendon, 1796, & Index; RIBA Library; G.Stamp & C.Avery, *Victorian Buildings of London, 1837-1855* (1980); M.S.Briggs [1896-9], 'Sir William Tite MP... 1, (*Builder*, 13 & 20 Jan 1950); Hendon Local Archives: MH maps – Cooke (1796), Whishaw (1828); Oak, *op cit*; B.Cherry/ N.Pevsner, *Buildings of England..., London: North* (1998): see also Ch.XII (vi), and Appendix C.

Other *OM* references: R.B.Aldersey [1808]; J.O.Bacchus [1816-22]; J.L.Bardsley [1810-?]; R.B.Beddome [1811-2]; H.L.Berry [1819-22]; J.Challis [1818-20]; W.Cornwell [1808-10]; G.Courtauld [1815-8]; N.Dawson [1808-14]; Fauntleroy – R. [1811-4], C. [1811-5]; Favell – J. [1815-20], S. [1807-10]; J.A.Hankey [1814-5]; J.Harris [1808-14]; W.Jacobson [1815-9]; I.F.Luckin [1922-5]; R.Maitland [1817-20]; N.L.Millard [1920-4]; T.Piper Jnr [1811-7]; A.J.Rooker Roberts [1893-1900]; J.Sabine [1807-12]; B.Scott [1822-3]; H.Shaw [1811-7]; E.G.Smith [1818-20]; (Pye) Smith – John William [1820-4], Ebenezer [1814-22], R.E.S.Pye-Smith [1935-9]; W.Lepard Smith [1807]; P.Smith [1829-34?]; J.O.Whitehouse [1825-30]; E.Wilton [1809-12]; T.J.Wright [1934-9].

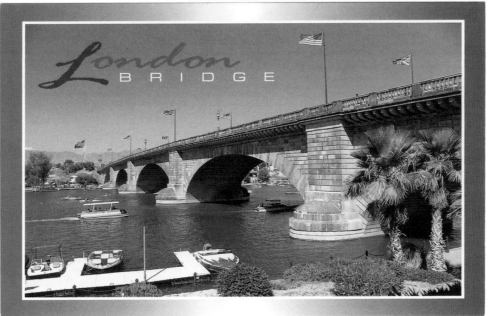

(i) Granite slab from Rennie's Old London Bridge, in new 21C quad,
The Stoa – new ATD Block and Piper Library in background;
(ii) inset: plaque impliedly commemorates role of
OM Ivan Luckin in sale of Bridge as feature for –
(iii) Lake Havasu City, Arizona. *2.k*

MHS Chapel: Priestley window, unnoticed over Visitors' Gallery,
NE (Ridgeway) end; funded with rest of building by
grateful erstwhile pupil Henry Wills. *3.a*

Chapter III: 1834-1869

Rise and Fall of the First Foundation

Thomas Priestley and the emergence of the modern Head Master

"The School was instituted by the enlightened, liberal exertions of that generation
of Protestant Dissenters now fast disappearing ..."
Address by Rev. Algernon Wells (School Secretary), Public Day 1845.

Given the trials and tribulations he had already witnessed during the previous 16 years at Mill Hill, the motivations of the new Head Master, Thomas Priestley, must have been something out of the ordinary; to an outsider, the Chapel chalice (still part of Mill Hill's sacred vessels), now passed on to him as Head, might appear to be somewhat poisoned. Yet he accepted it.

His strong Nonconformist faith was one such, even overriding, motivation. To truly sense from a 21st-century viewpoint the prime impulse behind those early Treasurers, Heads and rival Chaplains, it is necessary to understand the strength that transcendental belief then held over the minds of men – and their 'womenfolk'; people took to it *like ducks to water*. One measure was only to emerge by the mid-century; Sunday 30 March 1851 would see the first-ever national census of religious attendance, not just observance; Mill Hill's Chapel congregation of 200 would be one small part of that picture. As compared with a regular Sunday attendance of just 7 per cent in 1999, the astonishing statistic was that as many as 40 per cent of the population attended a place of worship that mid-Victorian Sunday: (nearly half of those were Nonconformists of one kind or another, the majority being Methodists). That fact hides the real ubiquity, if not the productivity, of religion for those Victorians; (as Thomas Piper would write to Rev. Wells on 28 November 1847, *we appoint, God disappoints*). Historian M.R.Watts has written: *For millions religion determined their marriage partner, the upbringing of their children, and moulded their family life. It pervaded education, shaped morals, motivated philanthropy, controlled leisure, permeated literature, inspired poetry, stimulated music, reduced crime, inhibited class conflict, moderated industrial strife, decided political loyalties and on occasion influenced foreign and imperial policy.* One further aspect of Nonconformist influence was the development of its own gaunt architectural style – "Dissenting Gothic", one from which Mill Hill's buildings are mercifully free.

Hub of the Congregational network

The Founders had begun a process which would reach out to the end of the century; it was to prove powerful for at least a further 50 years. In Mill Hill's wake, 11 schools have been noted as catering for Dissenters' families in general, some for those of ministers or missionaries, working in bodies familiar to Mill Hill – the 'LMS' and the 'BMS'; (an early example was John Robert, son of the Scottish Presbyterian and Chinese missionary, Robert Morrison). Whilst never seeking a leadership role in 'the Nonconformist appetite for education', Mill Hill and her luminaries inevitably formed the hub of what has been called an *intertwined network* of Nonconformist, principally Congregationalist, influence of immense complexity; there were also informal cross-links between many of its adherents. From early on, what can with justice be termed a 'movement' served the various regions of England. Prophetically, it embraced education for girls as well as boys: in this sense, the co-education of the later 20th century had deep roots.

'Networking' surfaced as a management concept in the 1980s; yet England's Nonconformist community had perfected this art at least 150 years before. In 21st-century terms, networks operate at many different layers between today's HMC schools. The 19th-century Nonconformist communications web had all the character of the defensive-aggressive Dissenting battle for equality with the educational establishment. The main aspects are these:

The 19th century Congregational network
([] = original titles; S = School; C = College).

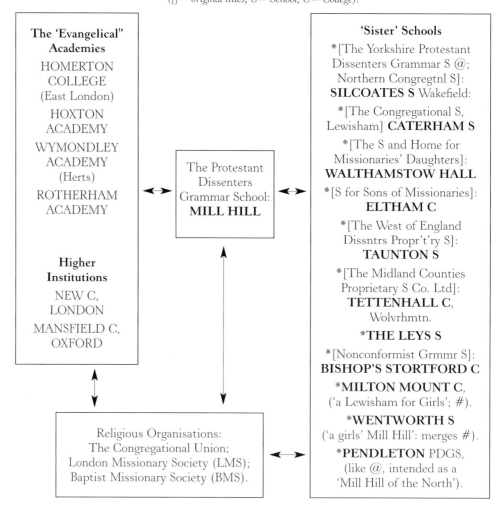

This network operated at seven levels – those of ideas and concepts; benefactors, Governors, and Treasurers; educational origin; Heads and academic staff; 'Old Pupils'; the religious organisations; and finally in terms of the family ties which arose. Firstly, at the conceptual level: Silcoates, and later the 27-year-old PDGS at

Pendleton, Manchester, were both intended to be 'a Mill Hill of the North', and Wentworth 'a girls' Mill Hill'; none of these schools sustained those aims (although Wentworth would still be inviting a Mill Hill Head as Guest of Honour in the late 1930s). For Taunton, Henry Wills requested the use of Mill Hill's Order of Service; his nephew, later Sir Frank Wills FRIBA, and advisor to Mill Hill, was Taunton Chapel's architect. Mill Hill's Life Governors scheme was copied by Caterham, and the subsidy for ministers' sons was widely followed. At a second level, Mill Hill shared the help of John Pye Smith, Samuel Favell, John Townsend, and Henry Thornton with Caterham, and of W.A. Hankey, principal of Hankey & Co, the School's bankers, with Silcoates: he was Caterham's Treasurer until 1859, having served on Mill Hill's Committee from 1806. John Pye Smith, also a Caterham Governor, supported Wentworth; one of Mill Hill's financial saviours in 1869, Samuel Morley, also supported Milton Mount, as well as Tettenhall and Bishop's Stortford. Mill Hill's Thomas Scrutton would become Treasurer of Milton Mount five years after taking on that office for Mill Hill in 1866, continuing for four years after relinquishing this role at Mill Hill in 1895.

In terms of grounding in the Nonconformist Academies, Mill Hill's first Head, Rev. John Atkinson, was a Hoxton Tutor, and when he resigned from the School in 1811, became Classics Tutor at Wymondley; his successor, Rev. Maurice Phillips, had been Classics Tutor at Rotherham: both men had taught Pye Smith there. Edward Stallybrass studied under Pye Smith at Homerton, becoming Head of Eltham. Later, the son of the Principal of New College, Hampstead, Robert Halley, became Head of Tettenhall. Academic staff moved across the network: John Haydon came to Mill Hill as Classics Master from HM Inspectorate, having been Head of Tettenhall up to 1891, when it merged with Silcoates; John Storrar moved from Mill Hill to Taunton in 1857; Francis Young, Science Master, left to lead Bishop's Stortford in 1899; *OM* Rev. John Best was Pendleton's Head for two years.

Family links included the second marriage, to one of Thomas Piper's daughters, of Rev. Thomas Binney (father of two boys at the School) who preached at Mill Hill, and at the foundations of Bishop's Stortford (1868), and of Milton Mount (1873); Miss E. Piper's marriage to Rev. Josiah Viney, progenitor of five Millhillian Vineys; John Pye Smith's second marriage, to the widow of John Clayton, the Mill Hill Chaplain, in 1843; and the marriage of his son Ebenezer, to the daughter of John Foulger, founder of Walthamstow Hall, and Eltham. Benefactors included Millhillian parent Sir Titus Salt, who supported Milton Mount; and *OM* William Henry Wills of Bristol's notable Dissenting community. He supported Taunton too, and endowed it, like Mill Hill, with a Chapel, a Library, and two Houses ('Winterstoke' was Mill Hill's only commemorative House); Wills also helped to found Mansfield College, Oxford. However the religious bodies did not reflect this network: no Secretary of the Congregational Union

Thomas Priestley ("The Pecker"), Head Master MHS, 1835-52, holding Book of Court of Governors' Minutes: c1844. *3.b*

was educated at a Congregational School, although five Millhillians were among Albert Peel's leading 'Congregational Two Hundred': Albert and Evan of the 27 Spicer family *OMs*, H.Arnold Thomas, Edward White, and T.McKinnon Wood.

In the next century, John Whale, of Caterham and Mansfield, would come to Mill Hill as Head in 1944; while Mr Justice Sellers would be simultaneously Chair of the Governors of both Mill Hill and Silcoates, his predecessor, Sir Arthur Pickard-Cambridge, an Anglican, would emphasise the changing of the times by also chairing the Governors at three Anglican schools.

Yet, as the historian Alan Argent well expresses it, *religion was not the sole motive behind the Congregational Schools... an essential ambivalence underlay Mill Hill...* and indeed the other schools in the network. Situated closest of all to the growing metropolis, Mill Hill chose from the start to be financially independent, and not rely solely on subscriptions. Here was a further difference which distinguishes Priestley's Mill Hill from the narrowly Congregational foundations.

Milestone: "The Pecker"

At the heart of that second phase of the First Foundation, 11 years before the quotation heading this chapter, one figure had emerged to change the course of Mill Hill's story. Although now no longer the Head Master with the longest overall tenure, Thomas Priestley's 34 years' service is rightly commemorated in the largest – though rarely identified – window in the 1898 Chapel. After eight years riven by *cabals and intrigues of all kinds, of which the Committee knew nothing*, his value was recognised, first by the commissioning, through a group of Old Boys, of a full-length portrait by Thomas Phillips RA, who had painted John Pye Smith. By coincidence he was also painting three other Public School Heads at his studio during the same period; Priestley used to meet Thomas Arnold of Rugby there, exchanging views on the *Diabolism of Boy-Nature*.

The picture was unveiled in the Dining Hall on 26 August 1843, a date (in the second 'half') that in Lord Winterstoke's recollection was thereafter *kept as a whole holiday in order to cultivate the spirit of loyalty to Priestley (and to the Prince Consort!)*. A year later, possibly spurred on by this voluntary gesture, a public 'Memorial' also marking Priestley's 25th anniversary was offered to him in another ceremony in the Hall, this time by the Committee. Both events, long remembered by the boys, are today a reminder of the quality of his commitment to a beloved 'Institution'. His 18 years as Head, from October 1834 to September 1852, are the second longest on record, to be exceeded only in the following century by the 31 years of Sir John McClure: long by Mill Hill standards, although quite normal among the established Public Schools of that time.

Bachelor Thomas Priestley, a native of Halifax, typified by his clear, regular handwriting, had joined Mill Hill's staff from Pontefract in April/May 1818. Brett James' purported link to Dr Joseph Priestley was disproved in the Hampden-Cook letters to Mary Davies at Leeds of July 1920, and through recent US scholarship on the great Dissenter. A stickler for punctuality, deeply religious, and watchdog for *evil* in any form, from the *persecution* of New-comers to *peculation* in the Kitchens, yet warmly caring for justice, he served up to the relatively brighter days of 1852.

Courage is a quality to which in varying degree many of Mill Hill's Heads can lay claim, yet in the besetting problem of the Chaplain-Head Master dichotomy the courage of Priestley stands out: in 1846 he caused the well-intentioned but narrowly-focused Committee to change its mind. Given the preceding history, that was an achievement. His period is profusely documented, offering an opportunity to discover much about Mill Hill's mid-19th-century inner life.

Priestley was *tall, thin, and with [a] stoop*, as one of his boys, Henry Hinds, then a Maths 'Dux' and later an FSI, recalled him, and as his portrait confirms: a conscientious worrier, he had a sharply pointed nose which when coupled with *his way of looking at delinquents* gave rise to his popular nickname, "The Pecker". To this man more than to any other is owed the evolution of Mill Hill's first recognisable 'Head Mastership'. What had gone before was a nominal Head Master among a group of subservient 'Assistant Masters', not even a *primus inter pares* but yielding precedence to *the representative of the Committee at Mill Hill*, the Chaplain. His eventual memorandum of 13 November 1846 set out his views to the all-too frequently visiting House Committee, urging such a clear division of departments ... *as might obviate ... any co-ordinate authority or blended responsibility.*

His letter to Secretary Algernon Wells of 18 November 1846, on the respective roles of Head and Chaplain, adds up to one of the School's defining documents, to be ranked with similar 'position statements' of the 20th century. *All men of practical experience will advocate that unity of action is essential to the successful government of a large School ... this cannot be secured without visiting the supreme authority in one person.* Thus was signalled the beginning of the end of the amateur era, and the faltering start to a new, more professional age. His vision was simple, and to many other schools at that time – certainly to his fellow-portraitist from Rugby – self-evident: to Mill Hill's fussy, intrusive Committee men, bogged down in the minutiae of household management, invariably failing to see the managerial and corporate wood for the all-too obvious administrative trees, it came as a long-overdue revelation. An entity as fast-reactive as a School had to be run day-to-day, on the spot, albeit within a properly delegated authority and subject to checks and balances: not just a Head among Masters, but henceforth a sole Head Master. The Committee responded at last with its *entire concurrence.*

If the revelation had come earlier in the century, Mill Hill might have been able by this time to pursue the same realistic, opportunistic path that other Boarding schools, old and new, were exploiting, as the opening up of the railways from 1830 provided hitherto undreamed-of expansion in parental catchment.

National access to the Public Schools: 19C transformation through growth of railway network, as satirised in Punch. *3.c*

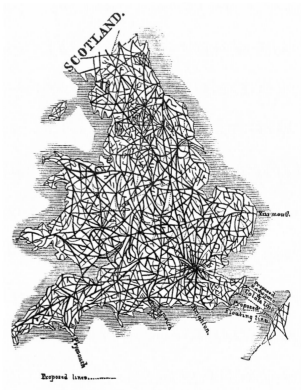

RAILWAY MAP OF ENGLAND (A PROPHECY)

NIKKANOCHEE, PRINCE OF ECONCHATTI,
A young Seminole Indian.
SON OF ECONCHATTI-MICO, KING OF THE RED HILLS.

MHS's first princely pupil, Nikkanochee, a young Seminole Indian from Florida, USA, Prince of Econchatti tribe; last heard-of prospecting in the Australian outback. 3.d

Some 5,000 miles of track had been laid in Britain by 1848; Mill Hill's Midland station, like its Great Northern, came in 1867. At one of Mill Hill's new competitors, Marlborough, the Roll had risen from an enviable 200 in 1843 to an even more enviable 500 by 1848; in the years from 1851 the new Head, Cotton, made organised games part of Public School life. At neighbouring but yet distant Harrow, numbers were to rocket five-fold from 80 in 1844 to 438 by 1859. It was indeed an opportunity wasted by Mill Hill's governing body, but the revelation that gave so much to that first foundation was of a spiritual not a secular nature. All that Priestley could do was to work within the frame in which he found himself, and try to improve it gradually from within. The tortuous path along which the Protestant Dissenters Grammar School arrived at this glimpse of the obvious was nearly 40 years old by the time of this great awakening; many Heads and Chaplain-Principals had twisted and turned down its course, increasingly forced by a dogmatic regime to fall over each other, jostling and elbowing their way towards some semblance of power and authority. When the Committee staged its Memorial ceremony – a 19th-century custom – they were in effect thanking Priestley for staying the course for them. His Testimonial had been hard-earned.

When Thomas Priestley was appointed as Second 'Classical Master' in 1818, Rev. Maurice Phillips was still the Head. Priestley brought many attributes to the part; the solid Yorkshire commonsense, and accent, of his native upbringing were two of them; the first at least was to stand him in good stead. The 1844 Address praised his *strict but not irksome rules of discipline*; he was generous in his commendation of colleagues, particularly the young Classics Masters under his careful tutelage: one new Master, Mr Tucker, was openly commended by him in 1852 *for that prudence and circumspection which his post requires*. He also praised the Chaplains with whom he was forced to work in tandem, above all, and at last, a compliant, co-operative Rev. Samuel England from 1847 onwards.

Priestley's Mill Hill

His time was the launch-pad for some celebrated Millhillians: some 686 can be attributed to his magisterial regime (not 623 as recorded in the First *Register*). They included the Prince Consort's Choirmaster, Prof Frederick Helmore; Sir Walter Medhurst (one of the world's first experts on China and the Far East); Mill Hill's first Prince, Oceola Nikkanochee (a Seminole Indian Chief, 'The Last of the Mohicans': despite Henry Wills' comment – *he would not eat meat because of the cruelties he had seen inflicted on cattle* – others denied his 'vegetarian' tag); Lt Gen Albert Bamfield (to be famed for his exploits on the North-West Frontier, and in the Indian Mutiny); Henry Eve ('School Classical Captain' in 1852, later Head of University College School); and Sir William Hood, Superintendent of the Bethlehem, later to become the Imperial War Museum (see Ch.VII), linking up unusually with Mill Hill's later story.

Foremost was the great benefactor, Henry Wills, the first of *22* members of the tobacco dynasty to go to Mill Hill (according to *The Guardian*, by 1899 second only to Cecil Rhodes in wealth). These alumni are the more remarkable in that from 1820 to 1870 only twice, 1840-41, did the new boy intake exceed fifty. The year 1851 saw the first boy of a family, the Spongs, to achieve fame for a sport, rugby football, not then even played by Mill Hill; the only 'football' Priestley's Second Master, George Sykes, knew was on the 'gravelly playground', with 'downhill cricket' on the sloping play-field. The 1840 entry included John H. Micklem, related back in Spanish Armada days to a family spawning seven Millhillians over the next 100 years. It also ushered in the first of seven Scruttons, Thomas Urquhart, Treasurer from 1863 to 1896; (his son was Thomas Edward, later a Lord Justice, *the greatest English-speaking Judge of the century*, to feature in 1999 as one of two Millhillians – with Rev. Paul Clifford – in the photographic gallery of Liberalism's historic home-from-home, The Reform Club). Thus five of the names of Mill Hill's future Houses had by now emerged in the annals – Collinson, Priestley, Scrutton, Winterstoke and Atkinson.

Samuel Devenish MB, in 1841, was an early son of an 'Old Boy', an honour first achieved in 1826, within Priestley's time, by C. Sabine, son of the Charles Sabine, who had left the School in 1809. Such signs of faith were but one of the ways in which "The Pecker's" parents and pupils would return many times over the compliments which he paid to his own colleagues. W.D.Wills wrote to the Secretary on 4 June 1847: *it will give me sincere pleasure to do what I can to promote the interests and diffuse the advantages of an institution where my dear son has enjoyed such opportunities for improvement.* That son, Henry Wills himself, a great admirer, as the Chapel window bears witness, was one of the most fulsome commentators on his former Head:

THOMAS SCRUTTON. (M.H. 1840-42)
TREASURER OF THIS SCHOOL from 1866 to 1896

OM shipbroker/ shipowner, Chairman of Lloyds, Thomas Urquhart Scrutton, Treasurer of MHS 1863-96, and of other 19C Nonconformist institutions, father of *OM* Lord Justice of Appeal, Rt Hon Lord Thomas Edward Scrutton LlB PC. *3.e*

A fair classic, efficient in general superintendence of the School. Used to like to make the boys think that he knew more about them than he really did ... Laid aside for many months by the accident on the night of [the] first Sunday in [the] 'half', January 1845 ... when he fell over a form in the Hall at the top of the 5th table. As well as being a true teacher of Boarding school boys – he could not have imagined any 'daily Boarders' such as the few admitted by two of his successors, Smith and Weymouth, he was a disciplinarian – (but not in the mode of his Classics predecessor of a mercifully brief two years standing, Mr Reeve, in 1817, notorious for a *floggation of 27 cuts with a cane across the knuckles).* He made sanctions fit crimes: *two boys ran away, and to provide funds one of them sold ... some very beautiful pictures on Chinese rice paper ... Priestley got hold of them ... and tore them up in the presence of the whole school.* As another example, *the glazed partitions dividing the main corridor* [substituted during the early 1840s] *in place of the 'gate' which cut off the classrooms from the Hall and staircase ... could be locked backwards so as to contain a boy for punishment.*

In one of his frequent letters to the School Secretary at the Congregational Library, in Bromfield Street, London, Priestley wrote on 1 November 1847 about the case of Thomas Baines (son of the famous Sir Edward Baines of the *Leeds Mercury*) and a ring-leader, James Gething, who had got *out of bounds, climbed over the cowshed*

roof, torn down a railing... throwing another into the pond: Gething's *spirit of resistance to authority would be fatal to the character and usefulness of the School.* He *had calmly set before him his fault and its penalty;* they departed that December. He never carried the exercise of the rod to the extent to which some of the other, better-known schools indulged; Henry Hinds in 1848-9 could *remember no case of corporal punishment.* With the sole exception referred to above, Mill Hill has no record of those sadistic beatings of boys until blood poured from the weals across their backsides or hands, with which the stories of the 'great Victorian Public Schools' abound. This is one of the areas where, to the critical eye of the 21st century, the religious roots come through, way in advance of their time: *... our peculiar ethos,* as a later *OM* Governor, Sir Ryland Adkins, was to describe it in 1918. Priestley's highly original method of publicly shaming liars has been widely chronicled: *a proven case of deliberate lying was punished by the boy being obliged to wear his jacket turned inside out. This only happened once – one day for one lie, two days for two, but a full week for a third:* it was a sartorial pillory which worked.

Priestley was also full of ideas for new lectures on Geology or 'Chymistry' or 'Natural Philosophy' in general, maintaining Mill Hill's pioneering and very non-establishment role in the field of science teaching, in which he could usually persuade the Committee to back him; at the time of the 1864 Clarendon Commission, only one of the nine apparently leading schools taught Science. His efforts were strengthened by the year 1851 and its Great Exhibition; school servants were allowed time off to see it, though curiously not the boys. In June, Mr Henry Blyth, the maths teacher – no doubt under the Headmaster's encouragement – wrote this letter, raising a totally new concept of liberal education. He was seeking the expenditure of a modest £5 on 'philosophical apparatus': *I have as you know, Sir, endeavoured to interest the Boys at Mill Hill in these subjects... The age is pre-eminent for the application of Science to supply the wants of man... shall the young man have had a liberal education who on leaving school finds himself ignorant of the elements... of Chemistry... and knowing nothing of the laws regulating the movement of the electric fluid [sic]?...* The request was approved, (although it is to be hoped that no too lasting a principle of electric 'fluid' was left to confuse those impressionable minds).

The Head Master had a clear concept of 'the good teacher', as opposed to intellectual merit on its own, and would constantly bring his perception of his younger colleagues' balance of those two dimensions before the attention of the visiting House Committee. He was also conscious of what today would be termed the 'image' of the School to the outside world, showing a rather canny awareness of what constituted a 'policy line' on the ever thorny problem of school health, which is at

"SKIPPERS"
From a drawing by Martin Shaw Briggs, F.R.I.B.A (M.H. 1897-99)

some variance with his straightforwardness in other matters: in fact it was his wish to be straight with the Committee that actuated him to draw this question to their attention in what they readily realised was 'an important matter': how to describe the health of the establishment truthfully, without giving rise to unnecessary apprehensions on the part of the parents. At this period, requisite notice could be given – or not, as the case might be – and boys withdrawn, with vitally needed revenue suddenly stopped, for the most minor of reasons. The scarlatina outbreak of 1849, affecting all but 16 boys, and actually killing three, one of them the School Classical Captain, Perry, shook them all: this was not one such minor reason.

The School was fortunate at this time in having as Treasurer Thomas Piper Snr, a man who also fulfilled that role for the Coward Trust, one of Congregationalism's central charities; a builder, then living at 38 Bedford Square, his portrait now graces the new millennial Piper Library. The Committee faced a continuous 'cash-flow' crisis, needing repeated overdrafts from its bankers, later a bulwark of Liberalism, Hankey & Sons. Priestley was realistic – in his words it was no *'eleemosynary'* institution: he could see that news of what was mostly a passing or minor illness for one or two boys could have quite disproportionate consequences among present or future parents, along the Dissenting 'grape-vine'. "Rose Bank" was a 'safe house' in the village (Mr Skipper's, the farm bailiff), where a boy could be kept apart until his disease had passed, with the local 'surgeon', Mr Holgate, in reasonably constant, if costly, attendance. This procedure would be adopted if the limited resource of the

18C *Three Hammers* pub, top of Hammers Lane, c1900, freehold still owned by MHSF (note gas lighting); (extreme r.), "Sunnyside", former MHS property and home of MHS Chaplains and later of James Murray; site of first Scriptorium of 1875. *3.h*

Sick-room in 'the House' itself, draughty and cold as it was and facing the sunless north-east, was full.

Despite constant vicissitudes, the numbers during the Priestley era had finally, in April 1841, edged back up over the first magical milestone – 100 – a direct product of the relative stability that was at last appearing to characterise Mill Hill's corporate affairs. Outside events had, of course, a major influence on numbers, as always: the long story of Mill Hill is littered with the ascription of falling School Rolls to the departure of Heads, when in fact national economic conditions could well have been the prime cause. (The contrived departure of the benign Charles Vince, after a bad downturn in the economy, later in the century, would be a prime example of this tendency on the part of Mill Hill's 19th-century governing bodies.) The mid- to late-1840s were a troubled time for the country as well as for 'the House', with continental Europe experiencing in 1848 the emergence, and the suppression, of Socialism in its first 'Year of Revolution'.

England's Chartists alarmed the monarchy – and the conservative Priestley – but did not threaten the country. The nation breathed again, although parents, especially Ministers, were stretched financially: as one wrote in 1849, *Trade and Agriculture are now very bad*; right up to 1870 Mill Hill's intakes would regularly fall below fifty.

Attitudes towards offspring or wards varied – and some were as young as eight, many going to school at all for the first time. One father told Priestley he was *glad* that his expelled son was *well-flogged* for not *fagging* (working) hard enough, and arranged for him to be sent to Sydney *next Monday – don't tell him*. Another, with *Xtian principles*, feared *contaminations* for *my, as yet, innocent boy*; another enquired whether they had *separate beds*. Priestley, ever aware of *the best interests of the School*, thought one boy, who *could not amalgamate with his fellows*, a *Spooney* (a softhead). He bewailed to Thomas Piper *our poverty-stricken appearance – many Mamas cry out for blankets*; by 1849, the *pianoforte was a mere tin kettle, deficient in the requisite number of keys*.

Centre of the local economy

All those parochial preoccupations which seemed, at the expense of the main issues of school governance, to dominate the House Committee on their fortnightly visits, provide by the same token the very stuff of local colour and sociological interest. Even by the 1850s, this new employer, itself at the mercy of the economy, was a force in the life of the village; although building repairs were done by the Millhillian Piper firm of 17 Bishopsgate, at least 40 different suppliers were called in. Among the 'Country Bills' to be paid were those of teachers of Drawing, Music and Singing, 'Drilling' (P.T.), and the School Doctor. As well as the normal bricklayer, grocer, cutler, ironmonger, machinist, barber, plumber and slater (two constantly needed inputs), such arcane local trades as cooper, tinman, and brasier were also involved. The House Committee loved to check minute deviations in price or quality, for meat, bread, oil or candles, or any other commodity that caught its business fancy: this also included beer, then a standard part of the Victorian Public Schoolboy's – though not every boy's – diet. New tenders would be sought, and new contracts for the next half-year 'Session' issued, sometimes with capricious disregard for the local interest. The Victorian yardstick was value for money. Little evidence is given for such decisions, which could clearly affect the livelihoods of those losing out.

School Housekeepers or Matrons, some with suitably Dickensian names, came and went: Mrs Couch, 'Mother Kight' and 'Mother Harris' (*every boy loved her* – later to marry Mr Earle), Mrs Tapp, and (despite her *evident predisposition... to give the whole thing up in dispair*) Miss Freeman. Each in her turn was regularly besought to look further afield, to Barnet, Highgate or Hendon, for alternative suppliers. Where members of the Committee had a favoured source in London, for example Carter & Bromley, those services were brought into play: 'drugs' (medicines), printing, wine, books, and the increasingly important and modern professional tasks of accountancy, and advertising, were so handled. The School's annual 80 tons of coal came, of course, from Newcastle.

Henry Shaw of Sheffield, entrepreneur, hardware and sugar merchant prince, by now a multimillionaire, only *OM* to earn an annual commemoration, May 19, date of his arrival at age 19, in the city of his future fame and munificence. *3.i*

In two areas of internal economy for the 23-acre estate, the School at that time was happily self-sufficient – those of the farm and the orchard, north-west of the old Chapel (see Ch.IV). 'Milking cows' were then traded from a dairy farm in Edmonton at seven guineas a head and milk was sold to the village during the all-too short bi-annual vacations. *We have not got Milk enough as the Red Cow gives but v. little,* wrote John Tilburn, the widower gardener-cum-carrier, on 2 August 1849. Pigs were slaughtered, for sale or consumption, in the piggeries in the School's suitably water-logged grounds; at one stage they had been too close to an earlier Chaplain's quarters at the east end of 'the Schoolhouse' for his and Mrs Crump's comfort. Sheep were grazed amongst the cows, where the amount of pasture allowed it. The need for hay was paramount: boys could not play on those parts of the fields until the crops had been taken up, and the 'Rowing', the second and last grass, had been gathered in. Boys were barred from the fields on Sundays: a sacrilege in more ways than one. The stock of fruit and vegetables was routinely described by the inspecting Committee as adequate, although Housekeepers often disagreed.

Itinerant sellers of additional food, notably oranges, would be a recurring feature of the day's routine all the way through to the 20th century, giving rise to constant complaints of orange peel littering the grounds. Three years before Priestley's Headship, in 1831, pedlars of such needed extra vitamins were banned from the premises. However by the end of the 1840s one vendor, 'Old Warby' and his daughter, from Barnet, were once more a welcome aspect of daily school life at the school fence at break times – 11.15 a.m. – bringing "cakes, pies, etc" for purchase out of the 1d. to 6d. a week pocket money, the normal prescribed limit. The indulgent concept of the Tuck-shop had not yet been allowed to soften the resolve of *the most respectable and well-ordered institution which Dissenters possess*; boys stole apples from the orchard, and would have to send to London for a supply of 'Polonies' (Polish sausages).

Tilburn's tasks included the question whether he should *fill the pond in Home Field* (site of future Winterstoke/ Pre-Prep). On 21 October 1847 he asked the Secretary about the *Diseases among the Pigs: Mr Priestley... wished me to wright [sic] to you, waiting your commands."* He accounted initially to the Chaplain, but eventually by the 1850s all servants reported to the Housekeeper: there was a typically 'Committee' blurring of lines between the two for a time, causing the usual confusion and inefficiency. With "Skipper's", "Tilburn's" also doubled up as an isolation house before the days of a sanatorium.

Highway rates and 'poor' rates, as well as church tithes, were all duly paid, albeit not without contesting the rates levied, and sometimes winning respite. The School was consulted as a vitally interested party about the new steam-railway line to run *close to us in the valley*, linking a new Mill Hill to London; its course is still traceable, nowadays a grassy path leading west from Mill Hill East. Mill Hill's interrelationship with her village was very close, even if in individual cases uneasy. Its most visible expression was in the bare and unlovely 'barrack', the 1832 Chapel, on Sundays, where the floor was occupied by the local congregation not wishing to attend St Paul's, the Anglican church of the late William Wilberforce across the road; they were joined by the School's servants and officers, whose presence was not optional but explicitly required by the Committee. Until the 1850s, the boys were relegated to the upper gallery, opposite the pulpit.

Grounds and bounds

The grounds at this period were still little different from the layout already described, save only for the extension in 1847/8 to embrace *The Three Hammers* and Broomfield. When this estate came on the market, it was sought partly, in Dick Walker's words, because *that generation seemed to value the purchase of land as general prudence*, but partly as a defensive action: if the pub continued outside the control of mid-Victorian rectitude, the boys might be tempted to increase their alcohol intake beyond what they already enjoyed as school fare. Much local opposition was aroused, but with the support of the Governors, the sale went ahead: one resident deplored *the sale of intoxicants ... in a village with a class of people neither teetotallers nor bigots.* Also by the 1840s, "West Grove", according to local historian Ralph Calder, *had been let to the junior master of the School*; from 1874 it would again be let, as a Boarding House, and from 1889 to 1924 was the home of the School MO, Dr Martin. There were as yet no properties in the High Street. The bounds ran from the path, later Wills Grove, to the out-of-bounds fir trees at the southeast corner of 'the topfield', alongside what in Dr Weymouth's time would be called "Doctor's Pond" (see Appendix E: 'Millhillisms').

The Ordnance Survey (OS) map of 1863 will appear in the following chapter, but the picture it paints is still similar to the Mill Hill of Thomas Priestley. A farm road is clearly discernible, leading down (past the future site of the San/ Cedars), with farm buildings (the site of the Language classrooms of the 1980s). Top Terrace

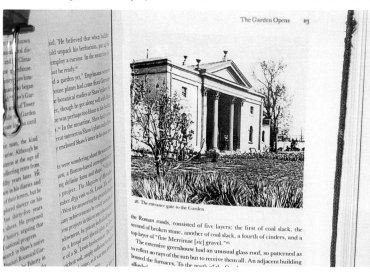

19C protestant work-ethic in practice: Missouri Botanical Garden, St Louis, USA; grounds and pediment modelled on MHS and his schoolboy garden there by OM founder, Henry Shaw; cutting from MHS Linnean cedar planted close by. 3.j

consisted of a path framing a semi-circular lawn, continuing round the grounds of the former Peter Collinson Garden. The School ended at the north-west entrance: *there was a gravel court between this end of the building and the Chapel*; here was the site of the only school game of that time – a locally-adapted form of Eton Fives. Beyond lay the *playground with wood fence all round, and outside these was a large field with hedge and ditch on two sides, abt 4 acres.*

Inside Schoolhouse, down the main ground-floor corridor were classrooms, but as yet no studies. At the north-west end, by the steps down into the notorious basement, was the room, where in the words of Henry Hinds, *every Saturday night after tea the boys went out in relays of about 20 to a grand foot-tubbing. Large wood [later zinc] troughs ran around the sides of the Box-room and a stream of warm water was put through them, the boys sitting round on forms and washing therein* – ['whether', to appropriate Queen Anne's famous words, 'they needed it or not'] and inspected by the Matron. At the barrier, starting with first Roll at 6.00 a.m. in Summer, 6.30 in Winter, boys lined up in correct form order to answer *Adsum*, before entering Hall to be served, as young gentlemen should, by the maids with Breakfast, 'Dinner', and Tea. Dormitories were upstairs: he remembered that *No. 1 had 14 beds, No. 2 – 19 (or 20), No. 9 – 12. No. 5 was the smallest – 8 beds ... The first class boys ...* [possibly scholars] *had No.9 to themselves. It opened on the 'second Octagon', over the Headmaster's study.* Henry Hinds wrote that *each boy had a small bed and at the side was a box seat for clothes, brushes etc ... We were allowed to talk till 9 p.m.* Servants were in the East Wing, with kitchen and domestic quarters beyond the far south-east door of the Octagon.

The Library had by then been removed from where the Head Master's study was now located; it was supervised by the two boys, the 'Captains' – each a 'Dux' respectively of the Classical and Mathematic sides. They had power to impose fines for untidiness, loss of the vital candles, and other damage; the proceeds helped to fund the '*Optimi*' letters (leading to Good Conduct prizes) awarded at the end of each 'Session'.

Although sanitary arrangements were clearly primitive, not to say dangerous, health varied. Chilblains – endemic in the cold unheated dormitories, with doors kept open – *were treated with brandy and salt in the Hall*; other boys, with faulty memories, given the various epidemics, could not recall any illness. As another eminent *OM*, Sir Michael Bishop, would demonstrate a century and a half later, with his hilarious anecdote to a Foundation Day audience, about the legs of an exploring boy suddenly appearing through the roof of The Large during a School House play, the enjoyment of pranks was no respecter of persons (see Ch.XI). The future and eminently responsible head of the Wills tobacco empire could remember, in Rev. Crump's once-a-week evening class in religious instruction, *tying all the candles in the classroom together and so being able to pull them all over with one twitch.* A *Mill Hill Chronicle*, one of the many early attempts, was started up in 1849, under the editorship of Wells Butler, (later to win a Classics First at London University, heading the exams to enter the Bengal Civil Service in 1856). Of bounds, *free run of the field next [to the] playground was allowed out of school hours. A few of the 'Tipper' form [class] boys could by special permission of the Head Master take a walk outside the school limits.* Hour-long walks could be taken, under supervision.

Staff – domestic and academic

Serving this compact community, variously consisting of 'the children', 'the young Gentlemen', 'the Youths', or euphemistically 'the scholars', was a staff of nine servants, hierarchically designated in the best traditions of 'Upstairs, Downstairs'. In 1850 they were the Cook, Mrs Killick, and the Linen Maid, Ann Love, the famous "Betsy", a long-serving institution whose celebrated if uncomfortable cry to dignified returning Old Boys was "I washed you, Sir!" They were complemented by Elizabeth, personal servant to Mr Priestley; Mary, who attended the resident masters' domestic wants; Eliza, the Kitchen Maid; another Eliza, First House Maid; and Sarah, Second House Maid. There were also two 'Indoor Men Servants', who initially slept in a windowless cubicle off the Octagon, before health considerations forced their relocation to a proper bedroom in the far corridor.

The *little band of professors* serving the pupils was also small. In 1841 it too totalled nine members: Priestley himself and Rev. Henry Crump, the Chaplain, each at this stage earning £125 for the 'half'. (Miss Crump, his sister, ran a well-known Nonconformist girls' Academy – where Miss Russell had tutored earlier – 'the Crumpites'). *Arithmetic and Mathematics were very carefully taught* by Mr Earle, an autodidact, and much favoured by the Head, earning £60; there were four junior masters, earning between £35 and £25; and a forever underpaid Modern Language master, then a M. De Lizy. A Mr Bullock *lodged under the roofs* for a year. By Henry Wills' time there were Thomas Carlisle, Classics master from 1843 to 1846 – *quite unfit for his place – haunted the* Adam and Eve *and often was drunk*; Thomas Storrar, Classics, *fat and good-tempered*; and a master omitted from the Register, a certain Holt, who *stayed one half-year, and bolted out of the door up the stairs on receiving his money at Xmas 1842, as his creditors came in through the front door*; Henry Fuge, *writing and 'general attendance', master-minded his work but was not a gentleman*; and the Drawing master already introduced, Mr Renton, painter of the oil painting of the old Ridgeway House – *a kind, painstaking old man, whose fingers, he said, were all thumbs*.

Crime came under the Head's wing. Although technically in the Chaplain's half of the building, not his, Priestley summoned the police over a break-in on 14 November 1847 to his own rooms on the "South front" (by now he had moved in from "Peacock's" house in the Collinson Garden), losing his *little dog and a Time-piece*; (*I miss the poor dog most, and hope that the Party that has him will treat him kindly*). The ninth member of this team was the Housekeeper, on £20, trying to keep all fronts under review: 'druggets' to go over the carpets; replacements for the ever-vanishing cutlery; sofas for the Masters' rooms; a book for the Visitors Room; new bedding. The Committee put off expenditure as long as it could: shelves for the Library were, without any conscious irony, shelved; a couch for Mrs Couch was only ordered with reluctance. The Visiting Committee's attention was directed not to these domestic niceties and necessities, but to the ceaseless list of faults in the buildings. The former Chapel from The Ridgeway House era was, until its demolition in 1843, the main offender, with a damp basement, and a leaking roof, due to poor guttering. There were those chronic faults too in the roof of the Dining Hall, which surface throughout the History. On the dormitory walls patches of 'wet' appeared with monotonous regularity. Draughts swept up from nowhere. At one Committee visit, dust was noticed thoughout the dormitories, then called Bedrooms. One concession to warmth was the installation of a double window in the upstairs sick room. In the winter months, boys were cold – round the clock, an occurrence not unknown in some Houses, in the recollection of one of the last Millhillian Micklems, a century later: Darwinian survival was the unintended order of the day, well before Darwin committed those ideas to paper which would eventually challenge the religion of Mill Hill's formation.

The 'Young Gentlemen'

Something of the 'Young Gentlemen's' weekly timetable has already been examined. **Fig.G(i)** (Ch.II) implies a tiring, virtually unrelieved and, even by 19th-century standards, fairly long day. Classics, Mathematics and Arithmetic – partly in the 1½ hours of early morning 'prep', before a meagre breakfast; some obligatory French and optional German, a smattering of Geography, lecture series on 'Natural Philosophy' – thanks to Priestley, and a weekly drill session: but virtually no English or History. It was an even drearier Sunday, with 1½ hours of Chapel in the morning, exercises in the catechism in the afternoon and a short supervised walk, with work on the scriptures or other strictly permitted 'Sunday reading' up to and beyond Tea, even as late as eight at night. 'Lights out' was at 8 p.m. – 8.30 p.m. in summer. Even though a considerable improvement on the regimes of the 'Ancient Schools', the twice-yearly 20-week 'Sessions' still dragged out, no doubt as interminably for all concerned; in midsummer, one blessed week longer when, much too rarely, there was re-painting under way for the woodwork, the fences, or 'oil' for the iron railings. For Henry Wills *the third month of the half-year was always the most trying both to masters and boys. The 4th was lightened by the hope of the coming vacation.*

Until the 1850s, apart from some desultory games of cricket with nearby 'lower Grade' schools (such as Thorowgoods in 1845), there were no organised sports, nothing remotely resembling sports kit, and certainly no regular competitions against other schools: as to nearby Harrow, they could look, but not yet touch. Boys recalled informal games of leapfrog, marbles and 'football' (not yet of the Rugby variety), as well as some pastimes rarely found in Games Compendiums, such as Prisoner's Base, High Cockalorum, Black Bull, Islands, and Spanish Fly.

Henry Hinds recalled that in 1848 *owing to a fatal accident a few 'halves' before I went to Mill Hill, the game of Hockey [sic] was absolutely forbidden.* This was the earliest recorded manifestation of Mill Hill's unique, informal, and highly dangerous 'Singlehanded', played then within the confines of the small enclosed playground, with its partially protective pillars, behind which one might with luck hide, and the close walls from which balls in a game could ricochet unpredictably. As *The Romance of Hockey's History* demonstrates, what Mill Hill would have to term 'Double-Handed' hockey only really came into being nationally, through the Blackheath Club, from 1861 onwards; prior to that, 'each school seemed to have developed its own version, depending on the type of stick and ball, and the size of the pitch… for example a single-handed stick at Mill Hill, and at Rossall' – (future significance there for the Mill Hill of the St Bees time) – 'a sandy beach'. The effect of this regime was recalled by Henry Wills: *there used to be a great deal of walking round and round the play ground.* An image of prison life comes to mind.

However there were a few special occasions to break the monotony. There was firstly the monthly gathering in Hall for review and determination as to '*Optimes*' letters. (This practice would survive into the next century, with Dr Derry its last recorded exponent, in 1938-9.) Every half-year there were *examinations in June and December, conducted by Dr Smith, Mr Redpath, Mr Yockney, and others* (members of the General Committee, all still very inward-looking). There was an annual Public Day, *on the Wednesday nearest the 21st of June*, when speeches etc were *spouted, prizes distributed*, usually held in the Chapel. To the normal ensemble of the 'black coat and vest', crowned by the traditional and, for the Mill Hill of that time, surprisingly conformist 'Public School' uniform, the Eton Collar, there would be a touch of colour and unwonted luxury: Henry Hinds wrote that *it was de rigueur that on this occasion the boys should wear yellow kid gloves*. George Sykes recalled that *we oiled our hair, perfumed our pocket handkerchiefs, and fed well on boiled beef and rhubarb pie.*

Overall, at the Mill Hill of Thomas Priestley, whatever else he may have stood for, and he stood for much that was enduring, daily life for the boys, in common with the lives of their contemporaries in England's other Boarding schools, was but a dreary thing. It was not exactly calculated to inspire the makers and shakers of Empire. That pattern would only emerge by the end of the century, across the whole face of the legendary late-Victorian Public School: the privileged, status-enhancing coterie which by that time the pro-Establishment Mill Hill of McClure, no longer needing to dissent, would be all-too anxious to join. Priestley had at least laid the foundations, but by the time of his death, in South Kensington in 1864, the new Elysium was not even visible over the horizon. Much water had yet to flow under Mill Hill's awkwardly idiosyncratic bridge.

Character and design: 1845

An early attempt had been made in 1838 to express the inner life of the School through two hand-written magazines – *The Liberty*, by the intellectuals in No 1 classroom (notable for a first reference to 'football') and the riposte (from monitors who subsequently seem to have temporarily disappeared from the scene), *The Herald*. However, the core of what Priestley's Mill Hill stood for – *the character and design of that interesting establishment... in the great intellectual struggle of our own and coming times* – was set out in the address delivered in the Chapel, on 18 June 1845, by Rev. Algernon Wells; he was eighth in the long line of 'School Secretaries', and also the first paid General Secretary of the Congregational Union, at Moorfields. The occasion was Public Day, and the presentation of medals by the 'committee of former pupils'. Here was an indication of the confidence felt by the 'many gentlemen once disciplined in this seminary' (a revealing use of that term):

> *Mill Hill is a public as well as a Grammar School... in the sense that a considerable number of pupils are assembled..., and also being... managed for public interests... It is public property, is under public care, is established for public objects.* However the School had to be *select as well as public. Families... in that class of society from which the pupils of Mill Hill are gathered... are not able to engage competent tutors to reside in their houses.* That was in fact an advantage: *a well conducted public establishment is deemed best for boys...* Those boys were described by the speaker, somewhat hopefully, as *free and*

gladsome, but the authentic voice of 19th-century educational principles comes through clearly. There were *rules, laws and hours that must be kept. Needful discipline is maintained. Salutary fear is established. Boys feel that they are governed. Whoever thinks that boys can be trained without this is mistaken... A misplaced word is a punishable offence.* They studied the classical literature (presumably expurgated) with all the fervour of the Ancient Schools – Greek and Latin were *on the right side of truth,* of whose Grammar it could be claimed: *no other study, mathematics alone excepted, can compete with it as a discipline of mind. Yet the knowledge of things... the facts of history, the discoveries of science... should be neglected at no period of education... the usual requisites to a mercantile education receive due attention. Modern languages take their place... lectures in Science are given...*

The rounded Boarding ethos was already a dominant theme, overlaid with a proper degree of Victorian self-righteousness, and the robust ethics of Public School literature: *the play field is indeed mimic and miniature life... conceit is humbled, mean tricks are scorned, unfair advantage-taking is repelled, arrogant assumptions are brought down, and a lad is made to feel that he must be frank and honourable among his fellows.* To the tender mother of the object of *this rude discipline* there was the reassurance that a '*hardy plant must be the nurseling of free breezes and changing skies...*

Most critically, Wells also touched on, without perhaps fully understanding, what was emerging as the underlying fundamental problem of the School by this time. Although *the importance that the Evangelical [sic] Dissenters should possess a permanent institution...* was still recognised, times were changing. *The... School was instituted to promote an effective rudimental education in the higher walks of literature...* Her existence was owed *to the enlightened, liberal, and strenuous exertions of some of the very first men in that generation of Protestant Dissenters now fast disappearing, of which only a few venerable elders survive.* In his desire to stress the enduring religious base of the School, his use of the word 'Evangelical', to describe the original foundation, was an interesting anachronism. Yet there is a complacency here, which contrasts with the 'market' position of the School, with new competitors, firmly inside the national Establishment, already starting to lap at the heels of all the older schools.

The kindly Rev. Smith

Priestley's kindly successor, *OM* and Governor Rev. Philip Smith, who arrived in 1853 and had some inkling of that situation, added status through Mill Hill's first Coat of Arms: *Azure three martlets or; on a chief argent a cross of St George gules* – a central monogram, and a motto *Excelsior* (see Ch.VI). He came from an erudite Nonconformist family; as the eventual Head Boy during what was probably a five-year time at the School, from 1829, he was said to have drawn a picture of the Head Master's study: he placed his own initials over the door declaring, prophetically, that one day he too would be the Head. He floated the idea of a 'Public School' three-term year, but failed to convince the parents: that advance had to wait 16 years, for one of the contenders for his post, a certain Mr Weymouth, at that time rejected, since he was not ordained.

Of the family relationships which typified the School of this time, some evidence comes from a later *MHM* story of the letters of the 14-year-old William Spooner

Brough, to his "Dearest Papa", a silk manufacturer from Leek. Even if the School was by now on a downward path, the boys within seemed content. He wrote home on 10 August 1854: *It was rather unpleasant on Tuesday night meeting so many new faces, and receiving the comments of the old boys (that is the boys that had been before), but now I am as happy as I possibly can be ... That wooden box that I took my books in is kept in the play room, and is called my play box... I remain, Yours, W.S.Brough.* Two weeks later, on 26 August, at the outbreak of the Crimean War, he reports on a double change of culture: *Mr Smith is going to challenge the Mill Hill club, that eleven of our best cricketers will play against eleven of theirs. A man has been to measure them all for cricket suits... Twenty new boys have come, but one disappeared rather mysteriously. I fancy he must be mammy sick...* Preparing for Public Day, 1 August: *You will have to put your cab up at one of the inns. The Kings Head is the most respectable... Tomorrow is packing up, and pay day... you will wish to know what pay day means... When a boy has been cheeky or saucy,* [the term "guffy" not yet in use – see Appendix E] *in the middle of the term you do not touch him then, but just quietly book it down in our [sic] book, and then leather him on pay day, because it does not matter if he does tell the masters then, they cannot touch us.* By 28 September 1855: *we have* not so many boys *this time... cricket is abandoned now for rounders.* The last letter was on 7 April 1856: *"Dearest sis, Only 3 days more and half of this long term... I am in want of a parcel... I will show you what a very small [one] will be so you can enlarge upon it 1. Biscuits. 2. Gingerbread. 3. Canister of toffee made by sis. 5. Bag of nuts. 6. Figs or dates. 7. Raisins and almonds. Your affect. brother, Will.*

More colour came from the School ads (under 'Public Schools'): *Every pupil has a separate bed. The diet is on a most liberal scale* (1858, '50 gns a term'). That year there was also Sydney Ebbs' letter to his sister, using the peculiar 'across and down' process; with Alfred Carter, son of Governor James Carter, he wrote a *Treasury of Biographical and Geographical Information.* They listed Mr J.S.Barker who *barked but seldom bit,* and two members of staff unknown before Ebbs' great-grandson, Graham Harper-King, unearthed it in 1999: Mr Cook, whose *principles of religions were something approaching infidelity;* and Resident Sergeant, John Brown, who *'put to Coventry'* for swearing. They also wrote of organised walks to Hadley, Harrow and Stanmore, on the whole or half-holidays.

End of the regime of 1807

Four clerical Heads strove to lead the School over the next 18 years. Former pupil Rev. Philip Smith (early 1853 to midsummer 1860) was for Robert Spicer *a scholar and a gentleman with courtly manners and high conversational powers... he was not a success... both as regards teaching and discipline.* The final straw was the great Rebellion of 1860, when *pace* George Whiteley, *all the boys except 5 defied the Head Master, giving in at last as the Captain of the School was the Head Master's son [Charles] and he distinctly stated that he only obeyed him as a Parent.* Smith printed a protest against his sacking, *this new blow to a noble institution.* Next came the ambitious Rev. William Hurndall, a Congregational Minister of Coward College, East London, staying only long enough to depart in 1863 at the age of 33, with a group of boys, to found his own school, "The Cedars" at Rickmansworth. However, Alfred Carter, School Captain from 1859 to 1862, wrote that he *used to invite the boys who had lost no 'conduct marks'... to a pleasant evening at his private house after 'Character Day'; they were also granted leave to go out alone with a chosen companion for walks on half holidays.* Rev. Philip Barker, one more Congregational Minister, from Spring Hill College, Birmingham (the future Mansfield), aged 35, lasted a year. His successor, Rev. George Bartlet, was a Scottish Presbyterian, a Congregational Minister and a Head with experience – at his own school at Scarborough; doubling the Roll during those last years, 1865-9, he was yet described as *weak, inefficient.*

Life under these regimes was loosening up, overcompensating towards freedom: a slightly more relaxed timetable evolved. In 1855 the School divided into Divisions – e.g. Maths, A to H, differing from those for other subjects. The first bath arrived in the wash-room in 1856. Henry Seymour wrote in 1900 that in Philip Smith's time, *among the older boys, nothing delighted me more than to break bounds on half-holidays... the only source of excitement was dodging the Masters whom we frequently saw on such excursions.* Alfred Carter valued Rev. Hurndall's *quiet hour in the Hall for reading good books*, instead of previous Sunday half-hours with the delights of *reading and repeating the Assembly's Shorter New Proof Catechism.* Games started to regain momentum: Cricket displaced rounders once more in 1855, although George Whiteley noted that *it was hampered for want of a level field... and a full hit to leg went for ever!* Nevertheless, for an unknown boy of the mid-1860s, life was still *Very dull... the most lasting impression on my mind is that the school was in a rotten condition and well deserved the collapse that it soon fell into.*

There were two gleams of hope. Alfred Carter recalled that around 1863/4, *when the School needed a new start, my father as temporary Treasurer, called a meeting of Old Boys at Radleys Hotel. One result... was the enlistment of Thomas Scrutton...* Secondly, the dissonance caused by the 'dyarchy' was a thing of the past, and no separate Chaplain was appointed after 1852, following the departure of John Pye Smith's last imprint on Mill Hill, his former student at Homerton, Rev. Samuel England. However the adverse financial trend was now in its final phase. At a fateful meeting, Secretary Dr George Smith threw down the Minute Book, exclaiming, *It is perfectly useless to carry on any longer. Nobis* concluded: *The ineptitude of the Committee on which former pupils had some representation was only exceeded by the apathy of the Life Governors.* Apart from the presence for a single day in 1869 of Prof Wilkins (the fifth Head of this period, according to Brett James, although ignored by Hampden-Cook), these were the last incumbents of the old Foundation. Some of the new mid-Victorian Public Schools were also having their ups and downs; although most were nevertheless forging ahead in numbers and reputation, the newly comfortable Nonconformists did not seem to favour a School which had been set up specifically for them.

Nonconformity was also waxing stronger politically. By 1852, 40 Protestant Dissenter MPs were in the Commons. Lord John Russell commented: *I know the Dissenters. They carried the Reform Bill; they carried the abolition of Slavery; they carried Free Trade.* Lord Palmerston concluded: *In the long run, English politics will follow the conscience of the Dissenters.*

Non-discrimination: the legislative road

When the Committee had first formed itself, the climate for Dissent, religious liberty and education, was hostile. By the time of the failure of the first Foundation, many of the earlier bastions of establishment prejudice would have fallen. How was the milestone about to be revealed in the history of education, linked to the history of Mill Hill? Any account of a major dissenting foundation merits an overview of the key historic events in its evolution; Information Supplement No.3 will highlight some of these 19th-century dates. Only three years after the School opened, Lord Sidmouth had attempted to bring a Bill before Parliament which would have given wider discretionary powers to (Anglican) magistrates to grant, or withhold, licences to dissenting preachers. The Bill was defeated by the force of the growing 'liberal' sentiment in the country: 'Liberal' had slowly come into vogue during the last quarter of the 18th century to denote this distinctive new political viewpoint. Two years later the libertarian trend was further strengthened by the Little Toleration Act: this abolished two of the remaining pillars of the Clarendon Code, the Five Mile Act of 1665, and the Conventicle Act of 1664. However in the following year, 17 leaders of the Luddite actions of 1811 were executed for doing what would later be seen as legitimate Trade Union work in defence of their jobs, in the spirit of the mythical 'General Ludd': six of them were sons of Methodists. Liberty was still a long way off, and Dissent was prominent in its defence.

By the end of the 1820s, the simmering cause of Catholic emancipation had taken over the political limelight from the issues of Protestant Dissent. Some narrow-minded Dissenters, including John Clayton of the Congregationalist King's Weigh House Chapel in Eastcheap, (brother of Mill Hill's William), were reluctant to back any further moves to repeal the other repressive anti-Dissenter legislation of Charles II, lest this might lead to claims for equal treatment for Catholics. Such views were manifestly out of touch with events and opinion; in 1828, the 'Old Whig' Lord John Russell, with the support of the Tory Sir Robert Peel, brought in a Declaration that would enable Dissenters, for the first time since Cromwell's day, to obtain public office without having to take the Anglican sacrament, and without fear of prosecution: two remaining pillars of the Code – the 1673/8 Test Act and the Corporation Act of 1661 had gone. At a consequential Banquet on 18 June 1828, a Toast was raised to *The Protestant Dissenting Ministers, the worthy successors of the ever memorable 2000 who sacrificed interest to conscience on St Bartholomew's Day, 1662.* In 1834, in the wake of the political Reform Act of 1832, a Bill was sponsored by Mr Wood, a Unitarian MP, to admit Dissenters to study at Oxford, and to degrees at Cambridge; it passed the Commons but was thrown out by the House of Lords.

That year also brought the historic case of the Tolpuddle Martyrs: four out of the six were Wesleyan Methodists. In 1841 Melbourne's lazy failure to abolish University Tests led to widespread Dissenting disillusion with the Whigs, even though Dissenters were *the bond and muscle of the Liberal party*. A further step forward came in 1844 with the Dissenters Chapels Act, which gave legal title if a chapel had been in occupation for 25 years. At last in 1854, an amendment was carried against the Government, to allow Dissenters to enter and to take first degrees at Oxford. Two years later, in 1856, Dissenters were admitted to all non-theological degrees at

Cambridge, but the individual Colleges were still able to frustrate the intention of this University Act by imposing their own religious tests.

Following Charles Darwin's earlier work on fossils, in 1859 a major cloud would appear over the horizon of religion, whether Catholic, Anglican or Nonconformist: this was the publication of his *The Origin of Species*. Some 20 years previously, in 1839, when Darwin's work as a zoologist was already known, John Pye Smith had published a praiseworthy attempt to prove that black was white with regard to the formation of the planet, with his observations on Theology and Geology – *On the relationship between the holy scriptures and some points of geological science*. Hopefully his Yorkshire spirit would have been honest enough to realise that here was a vision of truth that would far outshine his own thinking.

His death in 1851 precluded his seeing that shocking event. Nor did he see the final passing of the legislation in 1870 which would at last open up the Universities to all, without taint of religious discrimination. It cannot be a coincidence that the old battle for which he and his fellow-Dissenters had founded their Grammar School would now at last be won, at the very time that the original Foundation of 1807 foundered: both events were symptomatic of the same cause – the secularisation of Dissent, and the clear preference of a target-market now more middle-class than Dissenting, for educating their sons in the socially acceptable 'mainstream' of the Establishment.

Prospectus for second ('New') Foundation 1869: covered Playground connects Schoolhouse with second Chapel (l.); Top Field fenced but still unlevelled. 3.1

Unusual later-19C 'Hall Chair' with Coat of Arms No.2, bearing Dr Weymouth's invented motto (with the School monogram in the centre), one of a pair once guarding the Head's Study. *3.m*

A further feature of these years was that by the 1860s, there were the glimmerings – in today's terms – of a 'corporate management' model. The History will unfold several different versions, balancing the key 'power centres': firstly, the current central function within the Governing Body, however titled; secondly, the Head Master (the putative late 20th-century 'Chief Executive'); in the third place, but of central importance, the Governors in their own right; and fourthly, never to be ignored, the caucus of academic staff, whose views are represented by the Chair of the CR. The ideal 'model' is, of course, one in which the Court Chairman and Head are in harmonious, mutually confident partnership, each carrying with him or her the support of their respective constituencies – Governors and academic staff.

'The Scheme'

Mill Hill was not alone among the 'Public Schools' in discovering that an original foundation, conceived in earlier times for other purposes, needed to be re-fashioned for the new era of Victorian enterprise and imperial might. No fewer than 24 such schools, ranging from Dulwich, Caterham and Aldenham, to Grammar Schools such as Portsmouth, were, in J.A. Banks' phrase *re-established, rebuilt or reorganized in some important way*, during the 50 years from 1840 to 1890. As if to underline the need, and the opportunity, for such changes, during that same revolutionary period for education, both 'public' and 'Public', following Cheltenham's militarily-motivated lead of 1841, 48 completely new schools for boys were founded; perhaps even more importantly, between 1840 and 1900, 93 new girls' schools entered the public domain, future members of the Girls 'Public Schools' sector. These included several names that would have some future interrelationship with Mill Hill – North London Collegiate in 1851, Roedean in 1885, and Wycombe Abbey in 1896.

The first of the key men of Mill Hill's moment of destiny was Thomas Urquhart Scrutton, the Treasurer.

Despite the efforts of all the Head Masters and Governors over the preceding decades, the Roll numbers continued to fall, and by the mid '60s it was clear that things could not go on as they were. The School was closed formally after the second 'Half' of 1868, with a mere three pupils entering in September, and the boys were sent home: some, like Nathaniel ("Nath.") Micklem, then re-entered the School with 33 others in September 1869 upon the re-opening under the new dispensation.

The essence of the changes of what became known as "The Scheme" of 12 June 1869, was financial; it was necessarily effected through the then statutorily responsible body, the Charity Commission, in the Court of Chancery, under Vice-Chancellor Malins. New capital of £9,365 was raised (for present-day value, see Appendix G), negotiated by the Treasurer, who himself put up £175, through loans from names that would recur in the mortgage documents for years to come – Charlotte Boycotte, Stephen Olding, the School's current bankers – Consolidated Bank, and nine other prominent Millhillians. The whole of *the real and personal property* was vested in 10 new Trustees, including Samuel Morley MP, Alexander Scrutton,

'Ship Owner', and E.R.Cook, 'Gentleman'. The control of the Charity and the School was confirmed in the hands of between 15 and 18 Governors, among whom stood out the names of Benjamin Scott of the City Corporation, the ubiquitous Thomas Scrutton, an eminent medical luminary from the historic Pye Smith family – Dr Philip Henry, and Thomas Micklem, 'Gentleman'.

The peculiar system whereby those Governors had to organise the mechanism (the 'Life Governors') through which they themselves had to be validated, was re-enacted. The restrictive phrase was introduced that *as far as possible, at least one-half of the Governors shall always be Life Governors* – restrictive because there would only be five narrow categories from which they could be drawn: surviving Life Governors from the regulations of 1823; contributors of £20 to the new 'capital fund'; 'ministers of the Congregational-Independent, Baptist, or Presbyterian denominations'; and 'Old pupils' paying £20, or with a degree from a British University. Those Governors had to appoint, and could remove, Bankers, a Secretary, a Treasurer (but officially no Chairman), as well as a 'Head Master' and, significantly, appoint a Chaplain but *with the concurrence of the Head Master*. Formally laid upon the Governors was an ambiguous remit (s.20 [3]), sometimes honoured more in the breach than in the observance, that *they shall not interfere ... in the internal management of the School*.

It will be convenient here to anticipate the two minor changes that were effected in the Scheme during the ensuing century: the first through the Minister of Education of 6 September 1949, and the second through the Secretary of State for Education and Science of 25 March 1969. It was only fully superseded by Incorporation in 1998, when its time-bombs as to 'permanent endowment' and Governors' liability were exposed.

Unlike its successor 'governing document' of 1998, in this version of 1869 it was seen as important to confirm the curriculum: *the general principles of the Christian Religion, Biblical literature, such Ancient and Modern Languages as ... may be normally taught in Grammar Schools* [sic], *Mathematics, Natural Science, English Literature and Composition, Sacred and* [sic] *Profane History, Drawing, Music, Geography, Reading and Writing*. Above all, the second most important rule in the 'Preliminary', and an ongoing, fundamental precept for the future, the institution, henceforth confirmed through the usage of 'The Mill Hill School', *shall be open to the sons of parents professing other religious tenets*.

Such was the in many ways brilliant yet tenuous document, cradle for much later difficulty of interpretation, through which the Charity would be governed until today's single Incorporated status was effected for the whole 'third Foundation' in 1998. It took the ensuing 129 years before the confusion inherent in its drafting was finally resolved; if the Foundation were to have been judged by the Charity Commission to have a 'permanent endowment' of land and property, this would have debarred eventual Incorporation as a Company by Guarantee, since the assets could not then have been used to offset debts; also clarified were the confusion of 'Capital' and 'Revenue' Account expenditure, and the difference between 'policy' and 'implementation'. (This would be achieved, despite byzantine difficulties and setbacks, through the ingenuity of the protagonist who emerged to fill the central co-ordinating role in the School's corporate affairs in the 1990s, Lt Col Beverley

Morgan, Director of Administration and Finance – the DAF. By that time, school governance would be a very different matter, requiring its own handbook of over 500 pages, explaining a vast array of legal restrictions (see Chs.XI, XII, Information Supplement No.3).

The first Foundation of 1807-1869 had yielded 2,149 Old Boys. The Head Master chosen to implement its successor regime, first in a wide field, was Dr Richard Weymouth. His potential imprint on Mill Hill's fortunes and reputation was now to be tested – almost, in the language of that steadily-increasing body of professional men to emerge from Mill Hill, the engineers – tested to destruction.

Sources for Ch.III include: # 'Address on Public Day', 1845, by Rev. A Wells [1836-9]; H/C Mins 1829-1835, 1835-44, 1853-66; Ldgr – MHS A/Cs [Tradesmen, parents]; MHS Boys' Ldgrs 1839-41, 1844-51, 1857-8, 1859-60; MHS Parents Ldgr 1835-42; Farm A/C 1867-8; Ebbs/Carter 'Treasury, Biographical & Geographical Information' (1858); pre-*MHM* publctns, *"Liberty"*, *"Herald"*, *"Mill Hill Chronicle"* – see MHM 2000. P.Smith [1829-34?], 'Letter to the Committee in Reply to their Resolution making a Change in the Headmastership' (pte circ, 28.iv.1860): [whilst a pupil he determined to become HM & drew a picture of the HM's study, with the initials 'PS' over it]. Of the 'Research Cards' sent by Brett James to *OM* survivors, early in 20th century, 7 turned up in McClure House, 1996, thanks to its HS/M, Berinda Banks. Dscns with P.Rumball, ggs of Rev. P.Smith, 1.iii.2002.

Background: Congregational Year Books, advertisements, courtesy Dr Williams's Library, via T.J.Wright [1934-9]; 1851 Census; R.B.Pugh, op cit; PRO HO 129/135/4/1/5; Guardian, 'Who wants to be a Millionaire', 29.ix.1999; C.Binfield, *So Down to Prayers: Studies in English Nonconformity 1780-1920* (1977) (incl Baines family); J.A.Banks, *Prosperity and Parenthood, A Study of Family Planning among the Victorian Middle Class* (1954); Schofield, op cit; M.R.Watts *The Dissenters* (O.U.P., 1995); Horne, op cit; Channel 4 TV, 'Tempting Faith', 13.xi.99; Research, *'Papers of Robert Morrison'*, by Prof J.Barton Starr, Lingnan U, Hong Kong, (1999+): (caveat – mistakes in BJI, 45, 66, 127, 194); Newman Hall, op cit; Guardian, 13.i.2000; R.Boyd, *Independent Schools – Law Custom & Practice* (1998).

Other *OM* references: W.R.D.Adkins [1875-80]; T.A.Baines [1845-7]; A.H.Bamfield [1844-6]; J.H.Best [1871]; E.N.Binney [1846-50]; R.N.Binney [1847-50]; M.D.Bishop [1955-7]; W.S.Brough [1854-6]; W.Butler [1847-50]; A.M.Carter [1855-62]; P.R.Clifford [1926-32]; E.H-Cook [1874-7]; S.W.Devenish [1841-3]; S.Ebbs [1854-8]; H.W.Eve [1848-52]; W.A.Hankey [1817-9];

G.Harper-King [1933-9]; J.E.Gething [1843-7]; F.Helmore [1834-6]; H.Hinds [1848-9]; W.C.Hood [1834-7]; W.H.Medhurst [1835-6]; Micklem family – J.H. [1840-1] – "Nath." [1866-8,'70-1] – "Sam" A.M. [1946-51]; J.R.Morrison [1825]; Prince O.Nikkanochee [1842-4]; A.P.Perry [1845-8]; T.Piper [1811-7]; Pye-Smith family – Ebenezer [1814-22] – P.H. [1854-6]; C.Sabine [1809]; C.Sabine [1826]; family of Sir Titus Salt MP 1859-61, (see Ch.IV: transferred, Huddersfield Coll, to 'the more prestigious Mill Hill'):- William H. later Bt. [1847-8] at aet. 16 – George [1847-9] – Edward [1847-54] – Herbert [1849-55], aet.9 – Titus [1853-5]; B.Scott [1822-3]; Scrutton family – T.U. [1840-2] – A. [1844-9] – T.E. [1870-3]; H.Seymour [1855-60]; Smith family:- P.B. [1854-6], C.T. [1854-60]; Spicer family – R. [1854-60] – A. [1858-63] – E.[1862-5]; J.O.Spong [1851-4]; G.F.H.Sykes [1838-44]; H.A.Thomas [1861-2]; T.D.Walker [1926-9]; E.White [1829-32]; G.C.Whiteley [1857-60]; W.H.Wills – Henry (Lord Winterstoke) [1842-7]; T.McK.Wood [1871-2]; P.M.Woodroffe [1942-5].

170-year evolution of 'The Large', still used today for Assembly, lectures and large-scale drama productions, despite constraint of having Classroom 'B' on stage: (i) (top l.) Old Chapel facing The Ridgeway, pre-Marnham Block extension of 1905; (ii) (top r.) Tite Second Chapel of 1832; (iii) (centre l.) As "The Large Schoolroom"-cum-Chapel: note Honours Boards, gas lighting; (iv) Post-third Chapel of 1896, "Big School" with new Gallery, after first fire, 1909, Marnham extension, chairs and desks; (v) (bottom) As Assembly Hall, c.1921: benches, electric lighting, windows fronting The Ridgeway. (See also The Large in new contexts: Chs. VII (ii), XII). *3.n*

Dr Richard Weymouth, DLitt, Head Master MHS, 1869-86;
group once described as 'monitors' but more probably including five Assistant Masters;
School House, 1873. *4.a*

Phoenix: Entry to the world of
the Victorian Public School

Scrutton, Morley, Weymouth and Murray to the rescue

"An Institution strikingly alive":
Gladstone's Diary entry, 11th June 1879, following a visit to
Mill Hill as guest of honour, New Foundation Day.

At least three dates were crucial to Mill Hill's late 19th-century history – 1869, 1871 and 1872: consideration of a fourth year, 1891, will be the province of the next chapter. The first year is traditionally the most obvious – that of the New Foundation. This was brought about by the determination and generosity of two men. Thomas Scrutton, *OM*, chairman of the eponymous shipowners of Gracechurch Street (albeit a line with its roots in slaving), was both a Governor and the Treasurer, then the key role in the School's corporate management. The second was the senior Trustee, the great Victorian entrepreneur and Chairman of the still very active Dissenters' Parliamentary Committee, Samuel Morley: the largest textile employer in the world, founder of the 'Old Vic', and, in historian Manning's phrase, *indefatigable in all philanthropic work*. The next of the three epochs of Mill Hill's legal existence had thereby been ushered in, the start of the 'new beginning', the re-birth of the Phoenix from the ashes of the Foundation of 1807: (it also saw the change from a two-Term to a three-Term calendar).

To those figures of stature must be added two more: first, the new Baptist Head Master, and disciplinarian product of a naval upbringing, Dr Richard Weymouth MA, London University's first DLitt, *an imposing man, courteous and dignified*, who at last gave Mill Hill 'status'. The second was the Congregationalist master whom he soon appointed, then an obscure FEIS, but later BA, LL D – James Murray of the red beard, who might therefore justify description as the School's *éminence rouge* – later to make Mill Hill coincidentally world-famous as 'Mr Editor'. He was also, in 1887, the first former master (of what Simon Winchester has described as *one of the country's finer schools*) to become President of the OMC. It will remain to be seen whether honour is also due to Rev. Robert Harley MA, FRS, FRAS, *an energetic little man with a hearty laugh*, who performed from 1873 the divisive role of Chaplain, with the potentially threatening title of 'Vice-Master'.

The second date, 19 January 1871, marks a moment critical to Britain's educational history. This was the 17th and most triumphant of over 20 petitions or meetings of those watchful Dissenting Deputies with a Head of Government, pressing yet again for abolition of the anachronistic Oath still required of all students at Oxford and Cambridge: that of subscription to the Church of England's 39 Articles. At last it was Prime Minister Gladstone, now *their ally, so recently their bitter foe*, who in a surprising but politically sensitive *volte-face*, promised these representatives of the rising majority in the electorate *an Act by Easter*. Although the Headships of Colleges, Divinity Professorships, and certain other offices were still

Anglican preserves, the main obstacle to equality for Nonconformist students at the Universities (still, as late as 1854, being confused by the Dissenting Deputies as the nation's 'public schools') was henceforth removed. Mill Hill's new Head Master, although a son of the university which had welcomed Nonconformists from 1828, could now at least aim his academic sights at the Ancient 'Schools', as well as at London and the other non-denominational universities, although the first Oxbridge award did not materialise until 1884.

The third date, 1872, linked indirectly to that New Foundation, and also to the ending of the University Tests, and is at least equally significant; it was a date unheralded in the Governors' Minutes. The gifted editor of the *Mill Hill Magazine* would go on to UCL and St John's, Cambridge: yet even if he had started a year earlier than its opening issue of 1873, it is doubtful if this inevitably inward-looking young man would in his turn have grasped exactly what the events of that year portended. The very existence of the date was ignored in the School's first History. Its importance lay in this simple, but from any historical perspective, astounding fact: 1872 marked the first recorded attendance of a grand, territorially synonymous 'Mill Hill', through her newly appointed Head Master, at the annual meeting of what came to be the embodiment, in all its majesty, of the Victorian Public School – The Headmasters' Conference.

First impression on the HMC

What was originally simply 'The School Conference' arose out of the Clarendon Commission on the Public Schools of 1861-4. Although the brainchild of J.Mitchinson, of King's Canterbury, it was driven forward by Rev. E.Thring, Head of Uppingham, in 1869, whose indirect influence on Mill Hill lay also in his making games and exercises *a very conspicuous feature* of his school. Its purposes were firstly to *discuss the state of things* – a networking function which endures – but really to set up a Society whereby the masters of *the University Schools*, whose Heads saw themselves as *the most important profession in England*, could speak with *a common voice*.

Scarcely existing as a corporate entity in her transition year of 1869, Mill Hill was therefore understandably not among the 13 Heads attending (as individuals not corporately) the first meeting at Uppingham in 1869, nor at the second meeting at Sherborne in 1870. Yet within two short years, by 1872, Mill Hill found herself invited to be represented at the fourth meeting at Rev. A.R.Vardy's venue of King Edward VI Grammar School, Birmingham, in its own inaugural year of membership. Alicia Percival and J.W.Roche have chronicled the evolution of that body which eventually became known as the HMC. However, the published record leaves the impression that Mill Hill was only represented subsequently in 1886, under Rev. Wm. Haig-Brown's Presidency at Charterhouse, and then in 1890 at Oxford, under Warre. In fact Dr Weymouth was not only invited, in the phrase then used, 'as settled', and attended every year except 1874 (he sent regrets): but through and beyond his time, almost to the end of Charles Vince's increasingly troubled years, up to 1890, Mill Hill was there. More saliently, through Dr Weymouth, the School began to make her own distinctively 'Millhillian' contribution to its affairs, a tradition renewed nearly a century ahead by two Head Masters, Roy Moore, and later, Alastair

Graham. The initial 13 who had actually accepted Thring's first invitation are of interest both by presence and absence: 'exclusion' was never the word to use.

Those attending were the Heads of Bromsgrove, Bury St Edmunds, King's Canterbury, Felsted, Lancing, Liverpool College, Norwich, Oakham, Repton, Richmond (York), Sherborne, Tonbridge and of course Uppingham. The guiding committee at the start of that new decade which was to prove so vital for Mill Hill's re-fashioned reputation, was composed of some of the Heads of the nine so-called 'Great Schools', together with some of the now publicly understood Public Schools: one of the original role-models, the ever-recurrent Harrow, alongside Winchester, Eton, Cheltenham, Clifton, City of London, Repton and Sherborne again, and once more Uppingham. The 'Taunton' Commission of 1868 divisively defined these as the 'higher' or 'first Grade' schools – for the sons, up to 18 or 19, of *professional and independent gentlemen*; many of their Heads, such as T. Jex-Blake of Rugby, and Thring himself, are now seen as leaders of the post-Arnold phase of what the authoritative Gathorne-Hardy has rightly described as 'The Public School Phenomenon'.

Upon this very self-aware gathering – Thring spoke of a *profession so noble, so intricate, where personal experience is called into play every hour* – Dr Weymouth made his own impact at his very first appearance, immediately becoming something of a London thorn in the Oxbridge flesh. To quote Shrosbree, *the classics, supposed to be a substitute for English… fulfilled the same sociological function in Victorian England as calligraphy in Ancient China – a device to regulate and limit entry into a governing elite*; Mill Hill's new Head Master upstaged that elitism, questioning the already agreed move to demote Greek. *Is it to be understood that all the Headmasters are so ready to have done with Greek? I am astonished to hear it… Are schools to be first Grade Schools at all from which Greek is excluded?* Within the forum of what the Earl of Clarendon himself had privately described as the *stick-in-the-mud system of our great public schools*, he went on to raise a point of view which up to then had been marginalised: *in the University of London the rejection of Greek was negatived by 12 to 7…* He would come back to this theme the following year: *I think I have the right of complaining on the part of the University of London, that these resolutions have been sent first to Oxford and Cambridge, and that the younger University has been totally ignored…*

When it came to language in that first 'Mill Hill' year, at a time when many, like Dr Kennedy, believed that languages 'had to be learnt in early childhood', Mill Hill's great philologist was in his element, giving *some practical illustrations*: "*the new [German] style would be taught viva voce… anyone could… modify his English pronunciation… as he found out himself last year in Spain, though 'bithere' for 'videre' was not easy…*".

The Weymouthian sensitivity to meaning enabled him frequently to offer the *mot juste* which got a contentious motion agreed. He spoke about the recruitent of Assistant Masters, about 'good books', and the value of the deliberations of the Conference, which were demanded by some 2,500 members of the public.

Of particular interest from the point of view of Mill Hill's History was his intervention in 1873, with its quintessentially Victorian tone, and its tangential introduction: *As a Roman Catholic view of Sunday has been alluded to, I may allude to the Jewish view, which regards the Sabbath as a day of physical rest… As to such physical rest, this is a point on which we probably we are all practically agreed... allowing boys to lie in bed a little longer in the morning. We have Chapel Service at eleven, and at seven in the evening. Three quarters of an hour before the morning Service the boys are assembled to read the Greek Testament with myself and others... What they read then they are not required to prepare. In the afternoon I assemble the whole school... and that is the time of which I avail myself in reference to luxuries and vicious or doubtful habits, to endeavour to give Scriptural instruction, combined with some appeal to the feelings. I find the time thus spent very serviceable and apparently [sic] interesting to the boys, and I have reason to believe that the day is not felt to be over-burdened with services of any kind. After tea, some twenty or thirty boys are in the habit of assembling for further reading of the Scriptures... Another point, to which I attach some importance, is the setting apart some definite portion of the library as a Sunday library...*

Other, and to many of the attendant Heads unpalatable, but nevertheless significant Mill Hill themes come through. In 1877 he inveighed against corporal punishment, having *listened with considerable disbelief to much of what he had just heard. His own practice was to do without punishment as much as possible. He could only speak of a school comparatively small, containing 170 boys, but his impression was strong and daily strengthening, that it was quite possible to govern boys with very little punishment indeed. Where boys looked forward to severe punishment, nothing but [that] would do... short impositions would produce the effect desired. They should appeal to the animal part of a boy's constitution when it was as an animal that he sinned, as when a big boy bullied a smaller boy; but in ninety-nine cases out of a hundred the result could be obtained in other ways. In the last two and a half years corporal punishment had only twice been inflicted in his school, once upon a boy who was particularly active and effervescent in disposition, and was always breaking rules, and the other time for petty theft (applause).*

In the following year, 1878, perhaps prompted by his increasingly powerful mathematician colleague, Robert Harley, he complained *that only one mathematical discussion had been held since the Conference came into existence...* In 1879 his lone voice expressed a warning on behalf of the 'public schools' as a whole, and one with great meaning for the future competitiveness of Britain in the decades, and indeed centuries ahead. He cautioned against relinquishing mathematics and the classics, quoting the then German experience that *the technical schools [Realschulen] were sinking in public estimation in Germany in consequence.* Foreshadowing a comparison that Mill Hill's Governors would be drawing in 1940, in contemplation of their famous 'Middlesex Scheme' (see Ch.VIII), we should not *reduce the character of the education given in the public schools... below the level of the German Gymnasium...*

The significance of these events for the erstwhile Protestant Dissenters Grammar School cannot be overemphasised. From being on the outside of the Establishment tent looking in, for the previous 65 years of a decreasingly dissenting existence, 'Mill Hill School' had now graduated, through the eminent Dr Weymouth, to the inside track: the School was accepted, and on occasion applauded, by this new Conference of her established peers. The ancient, prejudiced barriers of Anglican exclusivity had been lowered, breached by the cumulative pressure of a steadily widening Victorian parental patronage. They had also been negated through Thring's drive for 'inclusivity' for *all schools of the higher grade, whether called Public Schools, Endowed schools, Proprietary Schools.* One other of those denominationally based schools which had followed Mill Hill's pioneering lead, Bishop's Stortford, was also part of this newly widened 'Establishment' from the same year, 1872. The records of first HMC attendance reveal that other good schools of particular interest to Mill Hill would have to wait for membership: St Bees (1895), The Leys (1905), Taunton (1911), Cranleigh (1916), Caterham (1924), Kingswood (1925), and two 'post-Fleming' – (1944 onwards) – Silcoates, and Tettenhall.

The phoenix had not only arisen, and been welcomed by the rest of the many-hued flock, but by the end of Weymouth's years it would academically outshine many larger members, not least Manchester Grammar School and St Paul's. Gladstone's impact on Mill Hill will be considered below; (he was, coincidentally, like quite a few other upright Victorians, a 19th-century family beneficiary of 18th-century slave-trading interests). Some immediate criticism could be levelled at him for his later imperious assertion, in 1879, with what André Maurois called *his love of indefinable shades of difference*, as guest of honour on what was now called 'New Foundation Day': that Mill Hill would perhaps not become a 'real' Public School until she reached the talismanic total of 200 (even though the total on the Roll was certainly one of Thring's 'HMC entry' criteria).

Re-defining the 'Public School'

In an important address on Public Day, 1845, which prefaced Ch.III, two further assertions had been made by the School Secretary (this was to be Richard Buckland's key role from 1899, fulfilling a role now more akin to an administrative director): *When Mill Hill was launched in 1807, it was designed to be just as much a 'public' school as the nine 'Great' or 'Ancient' Schools – that is, in the sense that it was manifestly not a form of aristocratic, private, domestic instruction.* Indeed in the education offered, the aspiration was to be superior to many of those 'Ancients'. The Prospectus had also made it clear that Mill Hill would embrace the other sense of the word 'public': *the provision of places at reduced fees for deserving individuals.* Yet there was no trace of an ambition to be counted as 'one of them', and that idea would also then have seemed unthinkable to 'them'. Even Shrewsbury had been excluded from this historically defined front rank, when in 1821 Lord Brougham produced his list of schools which would be outside the scope of his would-be educational reforms: the agonised Head of Shrewsbury, Dr Butler, pointed out that by any rating of having a national catchment area, his long-established, and Establishment, Grammar School surely qualified for similar exclusion as a superior 'public' school. Although Boarding status was not an automatic ground for inclusion in this evolving club, nevertheless it was assuredly one criterion.

On three counts – national catchment, free public places, and Boarding ethos – the Mill Hill Grammar School compared with the Public Schools as they were now becoming known – the capital letters mark an important evolutionary stage. Dr Weymouth adduced a fourth criterion in his HMC papers: the provision of a classically-based education that prepared boys for the Universities – the 'first-Grade Schools' of the Taunton Report.

The Public School games cult was already taking hold at MHS, despite Dr Weymouth's focus on academic prowess. *4.b*

THE NEW TYRANNY

"Of course you needn't *Work*, Fitzmilksoppe; but *Play* you must and shall."

Yet in fact the new middle-class market-orientated schools of the 1840s to 1860s, such as Cheltenham (1841), Marlborough (1843), Rossall (1844), Radley (1847), Wellington College (1856), Clifton or Haileybury (1862), had not merely soared swiftly into numerical ascendancy over their Nonconformist predecessor of 1807; they had from the start sought, and had quickly come to be associated with, 'Public Schooldom' before ever the idea of the HMC was invented. Whilst the Mill Hill of the first Foundation was still sticking proudly to her dissenting guns, her latter-day rivals were already directing their aim at the real commercial target of the age – the increasingly affluent, upwardly mobile, respectability-seeking middle classes of Victorian England – or more correctly 'Great Britain'.

Moreover, respectability was acquiring an increasingly strong scent of Anglicanism: George Eliot's comments had made their point (see Ch.II). Mill Hill's failure to grasp the commercial nettle had also meant that the School did not catch the flood-tide that the newer foundations were now exploiting so successfully, and thus those impressive numerical Rolls of 200, let alone 300 or more, were still eluding Dr Weymouth, even after his invitation to join the ranks of the insiders of 'the first Grade'.

Changes in perception would follow, but after a time-lag: the imperially Anglican Disraeli, in literary mode through his novel of 1878, *Endymion*, still preferred to type-cast Mill Hill: *it is a Non-conformist school... I do not much admire dogmas... I am a Churchman, as my father was...* That factor apart, the early invitation to join the HMC meant that the penultimate hurdle had been crossed, and willingly, by the Mill Hill Governors of the New Foundation: the final of the three fundamental questions posed earlier about the School's 19th-century evolution had now been resolved. The realistic, corporate aim was to be no longer anti-establishment – that way had spelt disaster, and times had moved on. As historian Alan Argent perceptively pointed out, *Mill Hill [and her fellows] sprang from a sense of moral outrage at the injustice and exclusiveness of the public schools; yet, once this outrage softened, they were absorbed into the system which originally they had opposed and sought to overthrow.* One further aspect of that absorption was sport: historian Hugh McLeod has shown how, by the 1870s, Nonconformity – and its educational outlets – increasingly embraced *religiously sanctioned recreation.*

Thus the earlier Brett James' viewpoint was at fault in several respects: at one extreme it over-claimed Public School status on that all too simplistic definition offered by A.F. Leach in his *History of Winchester College:An endowed Grammar School, which is wholly or almost wholly a Boarding School for the wealthier classes.* This could have meant that the Protestant Dissenters Grammar School had been a Public School, by definition a product of the Establishment, from inception. At the other extreme, Brett James echoed and seemed to endorse Gladstonian doubts with his phrase *at which figure [200] Mr Gladstone said we might consider ourselves a public school.* As Argent wrote, Brett James *apologised for the somewhat unfortunate title of Protestant Dissenters Grammar School, claiming that no school with so narrow a foundation could have been a public school in reality*: Argent rightly criticised *the snobbery of this denunciation... Mill Hill... need no more apologise than any Anglican or Roman Catholic foundation.*

Finally the first *History* left the question in the air when it stated that *at the end of 1908 ... [it was] possible to trace the [school's] growth ... into one of the public schools of the present-day type.* The trouble was not that there was any doubt in 1907 that the Headmasters' Conference acted as the seal of acceptance; indeed Brett James makes early reference to that fact. It was simply that in that first History the homework had not been done: the information was lying undisturbed in the HMC's archives.

Gladstone and Mill Hill

One small aspect of the legend of the great Sir John McClure – that in 1911 he was the first Head to be invited to join the HMC – now becomes a gratifying anachronism by a margin of some 39 years (see Ch.V). By 1872, admittedly long after many later Establishment Foundations had preceded her into the evolving magic circle, Mill Hill School had, at last, arrived. To put a stamp on that arrival, Dr Weymouth invited first the ageing Liberal Earl Russell that same year, then the Duke of Argyll two years later, and finally William Gladstone, to be the new Mill Hill's guest of honour on New Foundation Day: as he put it in his third, successful invitation of 31 March 1879, *failure of health* had prevented acceptance by the two earlier invitees.

Since a Gladstonian caveat has lain heavily upon Mill Hill for 120 years, the visit of 'the people's William' demands a closer look. Apart from God, writing, tree-felling, and helping fallen women, one of the greatest of the Grand Old Man's passions was the whole world of the classics, and in particular, Homer. It was this connection that had led to an ongoing correspondence between *one of the two most representative figures of the Victorian age*, the man whom Lord Salisbury, the Prime Minister of Empire, called *the most distinguished political name in this century*, and Mill Hill's learned Dr Weymouth. The 'G.O.M.' wrote to him (the famous Diary on 30 September 1878, notes him as 'Mr' R.F. Weymouth) and again on 9 October (one of 25 letters that day) on a work of his, now lost to posterity, *Obrinus*. On 31 March 1879 Weymouth wrote *in the name of the Governors of the School, as well as in my own*, both to invite him to *Luncheon*, and (surprisingly) to express his *great pleasure to accept your kind invitation to breakfast on the 24th prox'o* [April]; separately he sent a copy of the *Magazine*. On 10 June, showing great faith in the postal system, he sent a reminder about his attendance at Mill Hill next day.

As biographer Lord Jenkins wrote, Gladstone, the leader of the now-emergent Liberal Party, had been at Eton *well before the mania for the football field and the cricket pitch spread from Thomas Arnold's Rugby into the new "imperial" public schools ... Regency England... thought more of gaming than of games.* By 1896 the HMC would be debating a motion against 'The Worship of Athletics'. Thus a school with a classically inclined Head would stand well in Gladstone's eyes. However, Gladstone was also a staunch Anglican, and *an out-and-out inegalitarian.* Earlier, he had found the cause of Nonconformist equality *odious.* Although, as Roy Jenkins noted, he had deviated to the extent of listening to a prayer in a Dissenting Chapel doorway as early as 6 March

THE COLOSSUS OF WORDS
PUNCH, December 13, 1879

The eloquent Rt Hon
W.E.Gladstone MP,
four times reforming British
PM, Guest of Honour,
MHS New Foundation Day
1879: *Punch* cartoon,
'The Colossus of Words'. *4.c*

1831, Macaulay had written in 1839 that he should *'say in plain language that he would like to see Dissenters roasted in front of slow fires.'* He had spoken and voted against the matriculation and admission of Dissenters to the two ancient Universities in 1854. He had also earlier upheld *the full rigour of church rates on Dissenting parishioners.* Even though by the time of the great Education Act of 1870, his views had evolved to the extent that *he no longer believed that Anglicanism should be imposed on everybody,* he was still very much an Establishment figure.

However Gladstone's other passion, politics, was now finding a wider electorate: he needed Nonconformist support in the House of Commons. His visit to Mill Hill, in his 70th year, came in 'a year of waiting': Disraeli was in office, but a general election was looming, as was Gladstone's electoral tour, with the thunderous speeches that would make his name. By good fortune, this year of preparation for the Midlothian campaign was relatively a fallow period, if that word could ever legitimately be applied to a man of what his biographer calls his *pulsating energy.* It had at least the benefit that the statesman whom Queen Victoria described privately as *that half-mad firebrand* had a strong motive, and a window of time, to spare for the core of his future vote; Weymouth did not need to add that at Nonconformist Mill Hill *the religious education is undenominational.* W.E.G. came as a loyal – yet critical – Old Etonian, and with previous speaking engagements at Harrow in 1867, and Marlborough in 1877, behind him; a Governor of Charterhouse, and Lancing, he had been an examiner at Haileybury, as well as having at various times visited RNC Dartmouth, Fettes, Radley, Rugby and Westminster. Thus although *never a zealous educationist,* he arrived with a certain built-in perspective of his own as to when a School, not least an original Dissenting foundation, could be admitted into the notional club of the Public Schools. His Diary note for the day reads: *To Mill Hill. Went over the buildings, delivered an Address of perhaps 3/4 hour* [actually very short by Gladstonian standards] *after distributing the prizes. Read Mill Hill Magazines and worked on papers about the School.*

His remarks included the long remembered, indeed condescending observation, wrapped up as usual in what his biographer called his *convoluted obscurities and qualifying sub-clauses,* as to a School needing to reach 200 before it could become a Public School, although he also seemed to concede that Mill Hill had in certain respects already moved up into that category.

Although only one of more than 20,000 people mentioned in Gladstone's Diaries, Dr Weymouth nevertheless won a fulsome share of the Gladstonian oratory for the occasion, delivered in his rich, idiosyncratic Scots/ Liverpuddlian brogue: Mill Hill experienced what an earlier biographer, Philip Magnus, characterised as *the magic voice... the eagle eye... the superb gestures.* Gladstone was clearly impressed, for he added in his Diary this unequivocal commendation (any doubts as to a possibly pre-Freudian choice of words can be safely dismissed):

An Institution strikingly alive.

Among the many boys he shook hands with that day, on presenting him with a prize, was young Richard "Dickie" Buckland, later to become senior Partner in Vandercom, Solicitors, one of the great figures of the School and Scrutton's successor-but-one as a devoted Treasurer for 46 years, from 1899 (see Chs.VII, XII, and Appendix C). The pacific Gladstone closed with the Biblical commendation to think on *Whatsoever things are true, whatsoever things are lovely, whatsoever things are of good report.* As Dickie recalled, when in his turn presenting the prizes as guest of honour some 60 years later, on Foundation Day 1940 at St Bees, in the very different circumstances of the Second World War, these same values were the ones that he would also urge on the Mill Hill boys in Cumbria as worth upholding and fighting for in the conflict then unfolding.

Gladstone struck up a good relationship with both Dr Weymouth, and his firmly Dissenting, Liberal colleague, Dr Murray. On 19 June the following year, 1880, Gladstone, as was his wont, used the week-end hospitality of a wealthy acolyte, in this case the son of the 4th Earl of Aberdeen – and a School guest of honour a few years later – and stayed at Littlebury's, on Bittacy Hill – what he wrily termed his *temporary but historical abode, the house of Nell Gwynne*; he called on Dr Weymouth after Sunday church at St Paul's next day, and also wrote to Dr Murray. Clearly he found Mill Hill Village to his liking, as a rural retreat from a London *abandoned through fatigue*: he was there on five further weekends in 1881, from 25 June to 7 August, going to church on the Sunday, after walking along The Ridgeway past the School, which he had now got to know quite well. He called on Dr Murray on 31 July and wrote to him again on 6 August. It is surprising that no plaque exists which records the many visits of Mill Hill's world-famous visitor.

That original and somewhat daring invitation to Mill Hill had its sequels. On 1 October 1881, the G.O.M. wrote again to Dr Murray, on a typically Gladstonian point of precision – the pronunciation of "anthropophicism"; that same day Murray was put onto the civil list by the PM for a pension. (Later, on 7 February 1890, beyond this History's bounds, Gladstone visited Murray's new Scriptorium at Oxford). Meanwhile, on 29 October 1883, Dr Weymouth had sent him a Prospectus of his *Resultant Greek Testament*, prelude to his *Testament in Modern Speech*, a work still giving pleasure to many Millhillians – and Chaplains. Gladstone read and noted it in his Diary on 12 May 1887.

The Protestant work-ethic

At the start of his last decade in power, July 1891, Gladstone forged another link by staying at the country home at Lowestoft of one of Mill Hill's celebrated Nonconformist entrepreneurial families, the Colmans of the J.& J. Colman mustard empire. The Colman family hands were only one set of those already gripping the handles of Victorian influence and 'new money' during the early years of the school; their familiar household names crop up during the regimes of many Head Masters and Governors. Even if by the end of the century, a Governor would be writing somewhat cynically of the *Non Con Conscience*, a propos the School's dilemma about turning "The Three Hammers" into a laundry, it is important to highlight the

SIR TITUS SALT, BART.

Sir Titus Salt, textile manufacturer, founder of Saltaire Mill, *a palace of industry to equal the palaces of the Caesars*; like many 19C Noncomformist entrepreneurs, he naturally sent all his five sons to Mill Hill. *4.d*

peculiarly valuable connection between the Nonconformity of Mill Hill's origins, and the business strength of her families. The phrase 'Protestant work-ethic' is often bandied about, regardless of its roots; the German sociologist, Max Weber, coined it, to explain the extraordinary financial force behind the Protestant countries of Northern Europe. Later research on the Dissenters suggests that it was their general custom of leaving school early, not having access at least to Oxbridge – to then become indentured into a family or connected 'counting house' – which, combined with their basic pragmatic nature, led on in its turn to the business success of so many sons of Nonconformity.

Of many Mill Hill examples, several household names stand out: the Wills of the tobacco giant; the Spicer paper empire; the fast-growing Thomas Cook travel business; the Salter Rex property agency, and at one remove (the sole father of five *OM*s to merit an entry in *The Companion to British History*), Titus Salt of the woollen industry. With the support of families such as these, the first 'definitional' step towards the School's entry into the world of the Victorian Public School had already been taken, probably unknown to Gladstone, seven years before he came to speak. Mill Hill fulfilled the other criteria of not being privately owned, of being dedicated to Boarding, and of being open to all. The Gladstonian criterion of having over 200 boys on the Roll was only the icing on the Public School cake. Even if it cannot be considered to have justified his verbal withholding of Public School status, it would be the role of the great John McClure to apply that crowning numerical touch.

Fig.I MHS TERRITORIAL ERAS, START DATES: [1807]/1824-[2005/6]

1 Favell/ Tite							
	2 Weymouth/ Scrutton						
		3 McClure/ Wills					
			4 Jacks				
				5 Moore			
					6 Hart/ Sellars		
						7 Graham	
							8 The Millennium Development Plan

[1807] 1824	1874	1896	1907	1920	1957	1970	1983	1995	[2005/6]

1870s Mill Hill

The entry of Mill Hill into the New Foundation is a fitting moment to re-examine the topographical Mill Hill that Dr Weymouth, with Robert Harley, inherited and made his own. The map opposite reflects features identified in the OS map drawn in 1862/3, and revised in 1895; they depict what can be defined as the first two – '**1**' and '**2**' – of the eight main building (and equally important, re-modelling) eras from 1807 to the present, **Fig.I**. The work of the six subsequent eras will be described below (leading up to the Millennium Plan of the current Court and Headmaster, William Winfield – 'Era **8**').

Growing to 32 acres by 1886, the School at this time was small [**Fig.D(iii)**]. However the Village itself was extensive, full of life. It was also well-served with alcohol; in 1843 out of seven pubs, and two ale-houses, seven were still extant. These included, in Hammers Lane, *The Three Hammers*, bought by MHS in 1848, protectively if questionably, for £725 (*The Hammer* or *The Hammers* in the

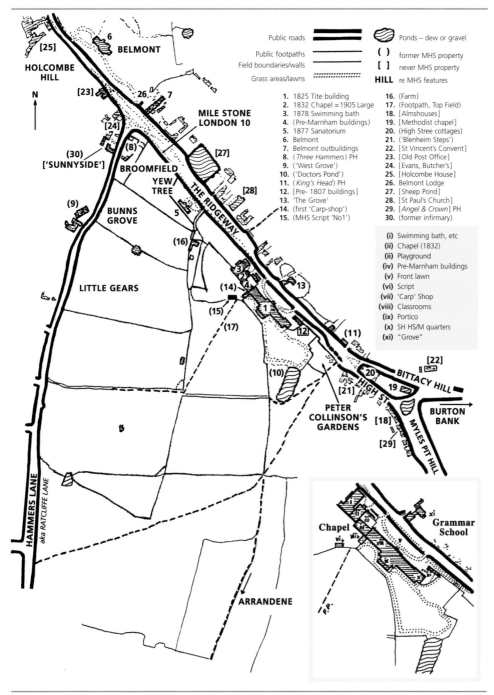

Public roads		Ponds – dew or gravel
Public footpaths		( ) former MHS property
Field boundaries/walls		[ ] never MHS property
Grass areas/lawns		**HILL** re MHS features

1. 1825 Tite building
2. 1832 Chapel = 1905 Large
3. 1878 Swimming bath
4. (Pre-Marnham buildings)
5. 1877 Sanatorium
6. Belmont
7. Belmont outbuildings
8. (*Three Hammers*) PH
9. ('West Grove')
10. ('Doctors Pond')
11. (*King's Head*) PH
12. [Pre- 1807 buildings]
13. 'The Grove'
14. (first 'Carp-shop')
15. (MHS Script 'No1')

16. (Farm)
17. (Footpath, Top Field)
18. [Almshouses]
19. [Methodist chapel]
20. (High Stree cottages)
21. ('Blenheim Steps')
22. [St Vincent's Convent]
23. [Old Post Office]
24. [Evans, Butcher's]
25. [Holcombe House]
26. Belmont Lodge
27. [Sheep Pond]
28. [St Paul's Church]
29. [*Angel & Crown*] PH
30. (former infirmary)

(i) Swimming bath, etc
(ii) Chapel (1832)
(iii) Playground
(iv) Pre-Marnham buildings
(v) Front lawn
(vi) Script
(vii) 'Carp' Shop
(viii) Classrooms
(ix) Portico
(x) SH HS/M quarters
(xi) "Grove"

Fig.D(iii) MILL HILL TOPOGRAPHY 1870s

17th century), with Alma Cottage and the old butcher's shop beside it; *The King's Head* of c.1709, closed in 1937, bought by MHS, and pulled down in 1949, after illicit help from a CCF grenade practice of 1947 (see Ch.IX); and – with no known MHS connection – *The Angel & Crown* (the former *Angel*) at the top of 'Myles Pit' Hill, closed in 1908, and demolished by the architect-owner, Col R.Seifert, making way for a row of award-winning town houses from 1964 to 1968.

One footpath foreshadowed the line of the future Wills Grove; another climbed up past the 'Monitors' Garden' to the wooden steps to Top Field, and continued its ancient way right up to the edge of the rough path which then swept down from the edge of Top Terrace, having formerly led on across The Ridgeway. It was a Mill Hill of quiet lawns, one impossibly angled and as yet untamed 'football play-field', many clumps of trees, and fenced farmland and pasture (see Ch.II). There were several ponds in the clay, some due to past gravel extraction, notably "Doctor's Pond" (aka "The Hollow") on the site of the later Collinson House, and smaller ponds in natural hollows on Farm Field, and the future "Fishing Net", in addition to the Village's historic Sheepdip on The Ridgeway (see Appendix D). A vegetable garden and pasture stretched along The Ridgeway across the tautologous Pyghtle Field (aka "Yew Tree") and part of Broomfield (aka "Gravel Field"), site of the Old Sanatorium of 1877 (now Cedars House), towards Hammers Lane. This led down to Orchard Terrace, purchased in 1847; Bunns Grove; and the six acres of Little Gears (Mill Hill's Upper and Lower Gears).

The inset map (overleaf) shows what constituted the main buildings; it omits the new, pioneering 1¼-acre Out-House, founded and funded by Rev. Harley in 1874 – "Burton Bank", a weary four-times daily, ¾ mile-long slog to the south-east, in Burtonhole Lane, purchased from him by MHS in 1882: (**i**) reputedly Britain's first indoor swimming pool, of 1878; (**ii**) Second (1832) Chapel, separated, as today, by a visible gap, from the Baths, and having then its own path and front lawn, curving up from The Ridgeway – (today's "Large"); (**iii**) the original enclosed play-ground, where Singlehanded (see Appendix E) was first played, flanked on The Ridgeway side by two lines of outbuildings (purpose unknown); (**iv**) building housing a first primitive gym, Murray's Natural History Museum, and also linking Tite's school-house to the Chapel (precursor of the Loggia, and the Marnham Block); (**v**) curved main entrance drive, as today; (**vi**) site of original wood-lined Scriptorium [No.1], reassembled in 1885 from "Sunnyside", to be moved c.1901 to its *shady position... under the trees at the top of the Choir Gardens*; (today's Script [No.2] replaced it in 1902: 'No.3' reinvented at Belmont; 'No.4' at St Bees, Cumbria); (**vii**) First 'Carp Shop' of 1888/9 (Vince's idea); (**viii**) 1825 building (including Dr Murray's 'Classroom 1'); (**ix**) Portico; (**x**) remnant of the pre-1825 building, following a different line at the front and at the rear – (site of the 1928 School House extension); (**xi**) original stables, the piggeries adjacent to the old Tite building (later located offensively near the San), other outbuildings, and the start of the brick wall of the old Peter Collinson mansion, 'Ridge Way House'; (**xii**) "Mussons", second of the four School shops (later "The Grove"), replacing "Skippers" at "Rosebank"; (Miss Skipper, and five other masters, would later help Murray on the *OED*).

Murray: 'The Arcadian time'

If Dr Weymouth was the full-time corporate figurehead, as well as the austere, disciplinary captain at the helm for Mill Hill at this time, the popular focal point on the main deck for all but two of his 17 years, from 1870 to 1885, was indubitably the 33-year-old tailor's son, born simply James Murray, without the 'Augustus Henry' – one of his first but riskiest appointments. Those risks lay first in Murray's disapproval of Boarding schools: unlike the many Ruthven-Murray descendants who boarded at either Belmont or the School over the ensuing 100 years, his three eldest sons were Day Boys, and none of his own brilliant children 'went away', even if that meant depriving his youngest son of a Winchester Scholarship; also in the fact that his only recent teaching job before having to go into commerce (at the Chartered Bank of India, Australia & China in 1864), had been as Head of Hawick Subscription Academy. The further risk element lay in the fact that the love of philology was what primarily drove him (Elisabeth Murray wrote that he hesitated before deciding to go to Mill Hill): that same intellectual enthusiasm had brought Weymouth and Murray together initially, even if it clearly did not make them blood-brothers.

'The Mill Hill Magazine', first edition 1873, inside facing page, featuring MHS Coat of Arms and monogram No.2. *4.e*

The pre-Chipsean – and the literary – "Mr Chipses" (Information Supplement No.2) each started their teaching in 1870; with his flowing beard, he was dubbed *Father Christmas* – but that was not until he moved to Oxford. He was quirky, irascible, idiosyncratic, yet lovable and hospitable, ready to enter into all aspects of his pupils' lives, whether the junior Third Form, which he ran, or the boys he coached privately. Betraying an athleticism bred on his native Cheviot foothills, he could vault a six-barred gate in middle age, and his long raking stride regularly won him the Masters' race on Sports Day). With unceasing curiosity, he was endlessly inventive, encouraging Tom Gurney, a fellow 'new boy' – one of his in-Boarders – to launch at last the substantive *Mill Hill Magazine*; the chocolate hue of the eventual School 'colour' was chosen independently of the *MHM*. He also founded the Natural History Society and Museum (lasting from 17 May 1876 to July 1939). His humour was abundant, evidenced in his spoof ballad, 'Mylne-hyll', purportedly an Elizabethan reference to 'the Hill'.

Coupled with this array of time-honoured teachers' attributes, and a by now characteristic Millhillian lighter touch, he was also destined to become the first of the two unquestioned world figures that Mill Hill's academic staff have generated over the 200 years (see Ch.VIII); Prof F.J.Child of Harvard was said by Sir Herbert Warren to order colleagues to visit three places in England – Westminster Abbey, The Tower of London, *and the Scriptorium at Mill Hill, where the Big Dictionary was being made*. No MHS History is complete without focusing on the creator of that legendary *Web of Words*, his grand-daughter's title for her best-selling biography. Often unsung by later media, the fact is that without Weymouth and the School, the *OED* would not then have become possible. (By one of the rounded coincidences of this History, which that father of 11 would have enjoyed, with his love of small children, Betty Murray's career culminated as Principal of the establishment which would become

Sir James Augustus Henry Murray, MA, LLD, DLitt, PhD, in court dress, prior to investiture by King Edward VII, 1908. *4.f*

coeducational, and launch the first Head of Mill Hill's Pre-Prep – Bishop Otter College at Chichester; see Appendix B).

However, it will not be possible to evaluate the contribution made by Dr Weymouth as Head Master, unless there is included later one piece of surprising post-hoc Murray testimony, evidence of the mutually stressful, sad cloud which hung over what Murray still regarded as his 'Arcadian time'. That time is well depicted in the biography, and in the Bodleian, *OED*, and local history archives on "Sunnyside" (now "Murray House"), as well as in Betty Murray's 1970s correspondence with Mill Hill:

A visit to Sunnyside was always interesting. He would invite a whole class ... to tea ... They might begin with a game of carpet bowls ... then James would begin to talk, perhaps on logic, or he would tell them about his books ... The evening would end with one of his famous recitations, or in summer they might adjourn to the honeysuckle and clematis covered porch overlooking the garden. There as dusk fell, he would tell them hair-raising Border tales of the occult or uncanny: (he had the gift of 'second sight', and believed his life was being directed from on high to some great purpose). Initially he found the life there rather arid; It was the deliberate policy of James and his colleagues to change the ethos of the school by introducing ... something of the atmosphere which was at that time transforming the public schools ...

One of his boys wrote: "His classes were always interesting. You never knew where you might arrive before the lesson was done. A nominal geography class might easily develop into a lecture on Icelandic roots, and we often tried to bring him back to the days when the Finnish landed on the shores of the Baltic, on occasions when we had not given adequate time to the preparation of our set lesson .... James understood boys and he was always prepared to support the monitors' requests for changes if he felt them to be reasonable and especially if they would give the boys the freedom to acquire self-discipline and opportunities for more self education ... He gave every year prizes to encourage serious collectors.

The precious rurality of Mill Hill in the 1870s did not, however, help his crowded schedule. After his fortnightly meeting of the Philological Society in London, he would have to take a long adventurous late night walk across the intervening fields and up the pitch-dark Hammers Lane from the Mill Hill [Broadway] station, like so many of the boys had to do at the beginning and end of every term. For family holidays in his favoured Lake District, they would have to take the School wagonette at 7 p.m. to the same station, to start the overnight 14-hour train journey from Euston: (a journey of similar length would carry the School to that remote landscape, under very different circumstances, over 60 years later). It was an exhausting work-load: fathering his own large family and acting *in loco parentis*; writing text-books and marking proofs; applying book-keeping skills gleaned from his banking career to the boys' accounts, book sales, and issuing pocket money; selecting speakers for Chapel and very often giving dramatic Elijah-like addresses himself – all this quite apart from doing the still requisite teaching. Notwithstanding, he had studied for and passed the London BA in 1873, and had been awarded an Honorary doctorate by Edinburgh, in 1874; this enabled him at last to order his coveted mark of status: a *full-dress gown of extra Saxony light scarlet cloth, faced with rich blue silk, price eight pounds ten shillings, with a black bonetta cap for fifteen shillings ... of the pattern that would have been worn by his hero John Knox.* He donned this cap on all occasions.

From 1879 he concentrated, in Simon Winchester's telling phrase, on *the lonely drudgery of lexicography.* A four-page appeal to all the papers brought in millions of 'slips' from the School, and all over the world, including, in the early 1880s, the extraordinarily learned fellow-bibliophile, Dr Minor, whom he soon realised must be Broadmoor's homicidal patient 742, the *surgeon of Crowthorne.* Focusing became critical: *Hoc unum facio* had to be his watchword. Yet he still liked boys to drop in at Sunnyside; *half the pleasure of an afternoon's walk was the prospect of a talk with Dr Murray ...*

The historic blue plaque records that he built there the first of his two Scripts (Mill Hill's four have been identified): *a Scriptorium as James jokingly called it, "Scrippy" to the family; it was of a portable corrugated-iron type which had recently come out. On the side of the house nearest to the village there was a small front garden, large enough to take a building thirty by fifteen feet ... approval of the 'shed' was obtained from the owners of the property and the school Governors, and the tentative arrangements with Dr Weymouth for release from part of his school work were formalised. James did not anticipate having to ask for more time than seven hours a week, which it was agreed should be Wednesdays, Saturdays and the last period on Fridays ... The ugly little iron room with its skylights, painted grey with a brown roof, looked rather like a chapel.* In Betty Murray's phraseology, *the gas light shining out of the Scriptorium skylights late at night became familiar to Mill Hillians;* (a century later the lights would be on well into the evening for a different reason – to enable Millhillian buffs of the 1980s to work on their equally beloved computers). The original pigeon-holes were later changed to shelves. His biographer went on to observe that *perhaps in memory of descriptions of Dr Johnson at work (on what Murray always spoke of as 'the' Dictionary) seated at the end of a table supervising his assistants, James constructed a foot-high dais for his own table.* The sepia photograph adorning today's facsimile beside the Quad (Script No.2) shows him thus benignly enthroned, wearing of course his stylish bonetta.

When he decided to move to Oxford in 1885, *reconciled to his servitude to [his] Dictionary ... he was sad to leave Mill Hill and to cut himself off from the society of school boys ... He felt deeply the loss of the wide views from his garden.* His *original workroom was presented to Mill Hill School and the cost of its removal to the school grounds was paid for by an appeal to Old Boys. Dr Murray wished it to be a place where all boys who wanted to read, study or pursue any quiet occupation, especially on Sundays, could do so without distraction. He expressed the hope that it would one day be viewed with interest as the original home of the Dictionary.* Again beyond the scope of this History, knighted in 1908, he instigated the intervention of Winston Churchill as Home Secretary in the release of Dr Minor back to America on 16 April 1910. He died at 78, in 1915, 13 years before Vol X, the last fascicule of his 414,825 definitions – culminating in the ultimate Scrabble-word 'zyxt' – finally astonished the world. In 1979, his great-grandson, Peter Ruthven-Murray, obtained a posthumous Grant of Arms: the motto was the belief by which he was driven, and which he shared with Dr Weymouth: *Deo Soli Gloria*.

Legacy to the 21st century

That first decade and a half of the New Foundation still reaches out to the Mill Hill of this new century, despite the passage of 130 years. Two more of the present Houses were named after the big figures of this period, Weymouth and Murray – and the colours of the recently closed Scrutton are those of today's reinterpreted School House. The oil paintings of Scrutton, Weymouth, Murray and also Vince, together with that of Richard Buckland (see Appendix C) still grace the School walls; the portraitist of Sir James Murray, and of Thomas Scrutton, was another of Weymouth's boys, Frank Ogilvie. As has already been noted, the Murray Scriptorium, today housing a far different mode of communication to that ever envisaged by the great Dictionary Editor, provides further linkage. But for the building of Collinson House in 1903, 'Doctor's Pond' would be offering one more reminder of the OMC's first Life Member of 1880, that seemingly accident-prone Head Master, Dr Weymouth.

The real legacy, whilst more short-term, must nevertheless lie in the influence that Richard Weymouth exercised on the three generations that he served and on those succeeding them. Four questions arise: what kinds of families and backgrounds became attracted to his revitalised school? – what was the academic record of the new team? – what overall effect did he have on Mill Hill's 'culture'? – and how did all this translate into that vital and inescapable bottom line, the size of the Roll? A further area could well be pursued in the fact that Britain was now approaching the heyday of Empire: that phenomenon was reflected in what Weymouth's boys went on to do, either in the six conflicts that erupted during that last quarter century – in Afghanistan, Matabeleland, Sudan, the Zulu wars, the Boxer Rebellion in China, or finally the Boer Wars in South Africa. More peacefully, some 25 per cent of the 915 boys who entered Mill Hill during those years went out to that imperial territory (India, Australia, Canada, New Zealand, South Africa, Ceylon [Sri Lanka], the West Indies) – the real story of Empire – or to lands where trade could not follow the flag, such as China, Java, or Peru. They did so either permanently, or in careers as doctors, missionaries, farmers, traders, politicians, or as the far-flung administrators of the *Pax Britannica*.

The quality of the 16 annual intakes benefiting from the regime of Dr Weymouth was high. It broke new ground: a further IPD Analysis – **Fig.F** – could have shown a sixth category, 'South-West England', the result of Dr Weymouth's standing in the West Country; some 19 boys were identifiable as coming in under his introduction, right up to 1884, from his own Portland area, as well as Devon and even Cornwall. The immediate London catchment continued, and the Nonconformist strongholds of East Anglia, as well as the newly popular constituency created by the Wills influence in Bristol, and the 'work-ethic' territory of the industrial Midlands and the north-west. The global outreach widened: the Americas; Bombay, Madras, Calcutta, Bengal; South Australia, Victoria, New South Wales and Tasmania; Rhodesia, Natal, the Cape; Tenerife, Buenos Ayres [*sic*], Ecuador, Chile, Mexico, Panama; Porto Rico [*sic*] and Jamaica; France, Guernsey and Roumania, and several from families working in Russia's great capital, titled then, as now again, St Petersburg.

In addition to nine sons of masters, who, like Mill Hill's two most recent Heads, did not share the misgivings of some later Heads about their offspring attending during their own time (four Weymouths, three Murrays, two Harleys), many other celebrated Mill Hill names now enter the annals, some to re-appear in the sombre context of the First World War (see Ch.V). These included both Atkin and Adkins; two separate Cook families; Dore; Crompton (designer of the original Gears cricket pavilion); Gunn; Gundry (today echoed through his son in the Gundry Music prize); Hart (Chinese missionary); Kemp; Lapthorn; Leonard; Marnham (the benefactor of the classroom Block bearing his name); the better-known branch of the first generation of Micklems (who married into the Curwens); Millard; Nimmo; a new era of Pye-Smiths; Rook; Salter of Kentish Town; Van Someren; the vast Spicer and Wills clans; the first three Bucklands; four more Scruttons; and a new Spong. (By the 1980s Spong and Wills would be the only ones of these names still on the School Roll.) Most notably Herbert Ward – the colourful explorer of the North Pole and the Congo, with the longest entry in any *Register* – is now commemorated in the Ward Art Bursary of 1999. J.E.C.Bodley, among Weymouth's first intake, became the Francophile historian and writer who entertained Lloyd George at his French château, during that famous statesman's visits to France before the First World War.

Immediate destinations varied as widely as ever. Of the mere 91 new boys who had entered under the declining four years of the Old Foundation's last Head, Rev. George Bartlet, 15 (but 16 per cent) would go on to a University: five to London, two to Oxford, four to Cambridge, and four to other universities. Although the

First Out-House, Burton Bank, in Burtonhole Lane, 1874, to house 35 boys: pioneered study-bedrooms for V-Formers. *4.g*

percentage of the 915 from Dr Weymouth's 16 years stays surprisingly the same (16 per cent), there is one marked change: the majority – 65 – would now go on to Oxbridge, 43 to other tertiary institutions, and only 38 to the two colleges of London (UC, or King's), or a medical school.

It is worth recording how different were the educational paths that were then pursued by Mill Hill's boys, who might enter as young as eight or as old as 16, for anything from one to ten years, as well as for the standard span of five (13-18). Four academic options then beckoned: (a) move on to another like establishment for the remaining school years (Eton, Shrewsbury, or even, somewhat hurtfully, the erstwhile breakaway school of Rev. William Hurndall at Rickmansworth); (b) into what would nowadays be called a 'Gap'; (c) to London or a similar College – Durham, Manchester, Birmingham, Edinburgh, Aberdeen, Dublin (or, for the Nonconformist ministry, New College, London), either in its own right, or, via a Scholarship, on to Oxbridge, like Tom Gurney; or (d) straight to Oxford and/or Cambridge, like the talented Ruthven-Murrays, through a Scholarship, or by paying the fees. As late as Inglis Gundry's time, from the 1920s onwards, 'the right type of boy' could still get to Oxbridge through parental influence and affluence, without academic qualifications (see Ch.VI).

It is valid to ask what benefit the former Protestant Dissenters Grammar School derived from 1871 onwards, through that hard-won Dissenters' exemption from the Anglican Oaths. The figures suggest that potential talent did indeed divert to Oxbridge, although Millhillians had gone on to the Ancient Universities from the earliest days; they would also continue to attend one of the non-denominational universities or colleges, if that was the right course for them – whether scientists, medics or even lawyers, like "Nath." Micklem.

As to Weymouth's wider cultural influence, it is noteworthy how many boys now seemed to go on to pursue the kinds of artistic or even 'multi-media' careers which would be very familiar to Millhillians of the 21st-century world: Harold Harley under the stage name "Mark Ambient", writer of – among many other hits – the West End musical, "The Arcadians"; two further noted historians of their day, H.Waylen, and J.R.Tanner, the world-wide authority on Pepys; that first *MHM* Editor, Rev. Tom Gurney, author of many religious works, including *The Church of the First Three Centuries*; artist Graham Petrie, member of the Royal Institutes of Oil Painters and of Painters in Water Colours; Arthur Ropes ("Adrian Ross") actor, and also composer, both of "Lilac Time", and of one of the many MHS School Songs that became the fashion up to the First World War. Not least was Sir Owen Seaman, one of Weymouth's classically grounded literary geniuses – writer, poet, humorist, and sole *OM* to have his initials carved (twice) on the *Punch* Editors' Table (see Ch.X). (He was also later to be connected with Mill Hill in another way, as one of the 150 distinguished guests at the City dinner given on 6 June 1928 to celebrate the publication of the *Oxford English Dictionary*.)

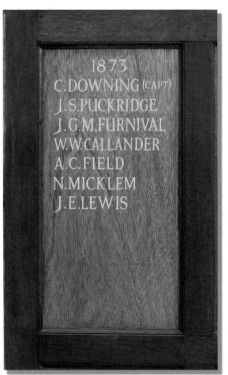

Honours Boards: (i) Cricket Pavillion – 1st XI from 1873; (ii) (r. opposite), Gym Champions, from 1885 (formerly on walls of second Gym, until Studio Theatre conversion). *4.h*

Although only eight subjects were taken by the Middle school under the Cambridge Local Board, results outstripped the country average. Prizes were awarded for Geography, Natural Philosophy, 'Structural Botany', and Chemistry. The School's regime was refreshingly wide, compared with the narrowness that still characterised the Oxbridge curricula. Science flourished, and produced inventors: William Watson with the first batting machine, and the physicist Thomas Dallmeyer, FRAS, FRHS, FRPS, with, among many other lenses, the creation of the first telephoto lens. Dr Weymouth invited Alexander Graham Bell to demonstrate his new invention, the telephone, in 1876, with boys listening through a jumble of wires in the classroom.

Forgotten lifestyle

The recently unearthed 'Mill Hill School Printed Papers' yield an invaluable insight into the day-to-day lifestyle of boys during this time. The fact that Dr Weymouth was the first Head to realise the significance of the newly reincarnated School's inner life (and to codify in December 1874 the unwritten Rules by which Mill Hill was run, binding those documents in a permanent form) in itself says much about him. Public Schools were now coming into the literary phase to be characterised by such classics as *Vice-Versa*, *The Fifth Form at St Dominic's*, *Stalky & Co* and *The Hill*: the girls' equivalents, in the Angela Brazil mode, would be a much later development. Many 20th-century writers would luxuriate in analysing this world of the Victorian Public School (see Sources data). 'Life within' was becoming valued in its own right: ephemera would need to be recorded for a future – unimaginable, yet confidently assumed.

Important too is the emergence here in its full sense of Mill Hill's use of the term monitor ('Mon.' in the first *Register*): the booklet later produced by Maurice Jacks (see Ch.VI) rightly assumed that monitors had long been part of the Mill Hill tradition. Previously, the first reference to any form of boy-leadership had been when future Head Master, Philip Smith, entered the School in 1829 at age 13, to become 'Head Boy' some time thereafter; later the role was associated with another distinguished *OM* name, Algernon Wells (son of the eponymous father already mentioned) who became, under the classical Priestley, a Silver Medallist, and a *Dux* of the School. By 1844, there was a School Captain, Henry Wills, as well as a Head Boy, Michael Underhill; thereafter the term 'School Captain' prevailed, with such names as Ibotson, Carter, and Satow among its holders. Weymouth's first appointee as a monitor was one of the trusted seniors he brought with him in September 1869 from Portland Grammar School, Eustace Kitts, age 18, who left the following year to become in due course a Judge in the North West Province, and one more of Weymouth's eminent writers, but now monitoring, in the title of one of his books, *Serious Crime in an Indian Province*. Significantly, he was also noted in the *Register* as a member of the rugby 'XV': *mens sana in corpore sano* was already becoming a powerful linkage (see Ch.XII).

The Rules that boys had to follow, and which the monitors now had to enforce, had both piety and pettiness about them, but the tone was benign, with an undertone of organisation: there was no hint of beating as a sanction (to become enshrined in monitorial power by the later Jacks' era, see Ch.VI). For a start, there were three sets of such Rules; (for some of the now obscure terms, see Appendix E). Of the 19 points in the 1878 School- (or Boarding-) House Rules, seven catch the eye: *3. Each Monitor is to conduct upstairs the Boys of his bedroom, and remain in order to ensure silence till all have risen from their knees... 9. The four Senior Monitors may have a private Study. 10. Scholars sup with the Masters and Monitors on Sunday nights... 13. After Evening Prayers no Boys but Monitors are allowed on the School side of the barrier, or may stay downstairs without special leave... 16. Boots must not be worn in dormitories... 18. The* [single!] *hot water tap in the* [one] *Bath-room may not be turned by the Boys, the penalty being a fine of Sixpence. 19. No Boy may stay up after ten o'clock'.*

Britain's first reputed indoor pool of 1878/9, with characteristic roof girders, (i); still in use up to the re-design of (ii) Buckland Pool opened 2005. *4.i*

There were 24 General Rules, including: *4. No Boy, when off the premises, may go into any shop or dwelling-house without special leave, except for a few minutes only, to the Post-Office or the shop opposite the School ... 8. No permission to go home or to a cricket or football match, is to be interpreted as setting aside gating or detention... 11. The avenue* [sic] *and choir gardens are out of bounds, and no boy is allowed in the chapel without special leave, or in the farm or gardens. 13. Catapults and slings and stone-throwing are forbidden. 15. All cutting and injuring of the desks and other school property is strictly interdicted.* **Every Boy is required to have a small weekly allowance of 6d., from which allowance damages ... (including cutting or scratching or writing upon the oak desks or tables) must be paid within a week by the offenders, or, in default, by the whole School...** *16. Every boy must keep to his own Class-room in play-hours, unless it is absolutely necessary to enter another... 18. One Penny fine is inflicted on the owner of any book, slate, hat, or garment found lying about, doubled in the case of a book from the School Library... 21. Every Boy is required to wear gloves during morning and evening service on Sundays ....*

Monitors, Scholars, Choristers, and even the whole School had separately listed privileges, for example: *2. Monitors may go out without an Exeant* [sic] *two or more together between breakfast-time and dusk; and are allowed to wear tall hats instead of the School cap. 4. There is also a Monitor's Supper at the School-House every Term... Scholars may sit next below the monitors at meals ... Choir-boys may go out two or more together between breakfast-time and dusk, but may take no other Boy without an Exeant ... There is a whole Holiday every Term for the whole School ... 3. When any Boy or Boys pass the Matriculation Examination of the University of London in the Honours Division, the School gains a whole Holiday ... 5. After dinner any Boy, if not gated, may go to the shop opposite the School House, wearing his play-cap, and without an Exeant ... 7. When Boys have leave to visit their friends from a Saturday to the Monday following, they may wear tall hats instead of the school cap ... fines are paid to the Games Fund or School Library.*

Other publications thought worthy of printing were: a 19-point <u>Particulars of Information</u>, including such questions as: **16**. *Is he destined for any Profession in particular?* **17**. *Is it desired that he should learn any subject or accomplishment not included in the school curriculum?*; a <u>Regulation List of School Requisites</u>, covering eight pocket handkerchiefs, six shirts, pairs of socks, towels with loops, three pairs of boots, night shirts, two hair-brushes and combs; one play-box, pair of slippers, clothes-brush, portmanteau, small leather bag, College [sic] cap, Mill Hill pattern ... of Messrs Cox & Son, Strand; (no mention of any need for swimming trunks for the Indoor Bath – opened, again with much proud printed communication to parents, on 4 December 1878); a <u>Monthly Report</u>, identifying seven headings: Conduct, Punctuality, Diligence in Evening Preparation, Classics, Mathematics, Modern Languages and English. The green, mauve or purple-coloured <u>Official Lists</u> for each New Foundation Day, recorded the recipients of the *Gold and Silver Medals, given by Old Mill Hill Boys [sic], for the best English Essays*, since their inception in 1834/5; the current 26 holders of senior or junior Scholarships (including the 1853 Bousfield leaving award of £50 p.a. for three years), started with John Lewis in 1869: of the winners of Prizes, only two – the Edward Sheffield (classics) and Walter Knox (chemistry) – survived into the 21st century. There was also a complete <u>List</u> of all 169 boys and nine forms, highlighting, for example, in Lent Term 1878: five Seniors (all among 12 in Form VI) out of 10 monitors (one in Form V Sen.), one in Form V Jun., and two in Modern Remove; the other forms were the IV, Upper III, as well as the then equivalent Forms of both the earlier and the later Mill Hill Preparatory School – Lower III, II, and I.

There were careful communications, either printed on behalf of both Dr Weymouth and his Vice-Master, or cyclostyled from the Head's handwriting, about that dreaded 19th-century Boarding-school incubus – the outbreak of any infectious disease that occurred – chicken-pox, scarlet fever, measles, mumps, or scarlatina. Also included were the weekday five-times-a-term public lectures, with a strong scientific or practical bias, starting at 'Seven o'Clock': 'Paris and the beginning of the Insurrection in March 1871'; 'Cryptogramic Botany'; 'The Constitution of the Sun'; 'The Philosophy [sic] of Heat and Cold'; 'Waves of the Sea'; 'Fermentation, with Experiments'; 'The Moon'; or 'The Telephone and its Ally, the Microphone'.

Three other documents provide insights into the Weymouth years. A <u>Visitors Book</u> now recorded the presence of visitors at various functions; two noteworthy attenders were the plain 'Mr W.H.Wills, with Miss Stancomb' (the later benefactress, as Dame Janet Stancomb-Wills, both of Sir Ernest Shackleton's 1914 Antarctic Expedition, and of Mill Hill School – see Chs.II, V).

The <u>Boys Journal</u> (1874) identified Mill Hill's earliest link with Cumbria (another would be the address at 'St Bees, Carnforth' – one of Murray's *Dictionary* contributors): the 1st XV Captain's widowed mother, Mrs Burnyeat, of Whitehaven, paid £33 10s. 6d. for the Lent Term, including 'Meat for Breakfast 31s./6d, Hair-cutting 1s./0d, Pocket-money 5s./6d'. Neither Miles Burnyeat, nor new boy and future monitor Herbert Marnham, availed themselves of 'Piano, Violin, Italian, a Separate Bedroom', or even 'Dancing'; (1870 had seen off Mill Hill's first and only Dancing Master, M. Eugene Coulon.) Young Herbert was however allowed 14s.-worth of ale, a Play-cap at 2s. 6d., a 9d slate, and tailor's bills at 18s. 6d.

Even more illuminating was Dr Weymouth's <u>Petty Cash Book</u>, kept meticulously in his neat sloping hand, offsetting with a 'Contra' column the monthly input of £50 'Cash' from the Treasurer, which also included income from Fines ('July 13 1882: Boys of Bedroom 5 for Counterpane torn, 11s.0d'), or Sales ('1881 Apr 28: Pony-cart & harness Sold, £7'). The entries not only indicate contemporary values, but also give a flavour of the School's and the Head's daily activity:

1879	Jly 24:	Items in Skipper's bill [school shop]	£1	14s.	6d.
	25:	Swimmers to Alex. Pal. [not the Bath!]	6	1s.	0d.
1880	Mar 19:	Hendon Fire B'de subscrptn	1	0s.	0d.
	22:	To Town, Ct. of Gov. [rail & cab fares]		2s.	4d.
	May 20:	Tracts for Sunday afternoon reading		1s.	0d.
	30:	Mr Erlebach: 1st Eleven to Cambridge	4	1s.	3d.
	Oct 30:	Lopping Elms	3	2s.	3d.
	Dec 17:	Handbell Ringers	3	18s.	0d.
1881	Apr 12:	Hire of Piano (Concert)	2	2s.	0d.
	Aug 27:	N.Bell, 1 ld. Hay [for school horses]	7	0s.	0d.
1882	Jan 22:	Extra labour, clearing snow from roof	3	10s.	0d.
	Jly 22:	Lawn Tennis Bats [*sic*]	1	2s.	0d.
	Dec 27:	Spong, Fire Extinguishers	1	9s.	9d.
1883	Feb 26:	Boys to S.Ken Mus.	3	14s	6d.
	Apr 12:	Choir & Others to Cryst.Pal [Sydenham]	3	0s.	0d.
	May 31:	Illstr'td papers for invalids		5s.	2d.
	Jly 17:	Harveyson, Horse [purchase]	£40	0s.	0d.
1884	Oct 18:	F.M.W. [his son Francis], tulip tree	1	1s.	0d.
	Dec 18:	H.M.Conference Subscript'n	1	1s.	0d.

"A great school..."

Weymouth's era presents a burgeoning self-image. He was seeking comparability with the established Public Schools, not least with advances made in physical education by the Eton-educated Rev. Thring at Uppingham; these sprang from a Prussian schools' model, but also from the nation-wide shock at the ill-health of men in the Crimean War. The Cricket Pavilion walls emblazon the first recorded team of 1873; later came the start of 'colours'. June 1873 saw the first official journal – an ambitious six issues a year for 3s. 3d. – *The Mill Hill Magazine*: even *The Wykehamist* had only been launched in 1866.

A third step, the formation on 2 December 1878 of the OMC, has been nobly covered in *Nobis*. Although the relationship between the School and her alumni dated back to the 1820s, the idea of the latter as a separate organisation was germinating by the time of the fourth issue of the *MHM* in December 1873: alternative terms – 'Old Mill Hill Boys', 'Mill Hill Rovers', or just 'Old Boys', were canvassed. Five years later the final formula was proposed in collusion by 'Quarter-Back' and 'Half-Back' (C.W.Cunnington, and the Head's younger son, Edward). That first *MHM* editorial was triumphalist: *we are no longer... a school unknown among the great educational institutions of England. We have already outrun not a few that went before us.*

In July 1874, its instigator, Dr Murray, was expressing the motivation for what he and the staff were striving for – *their aim to make this ... a great school.* Dr Weymouth himself had encapsulated this new self-confidence by inviting the author of the classic of classics, *Tom Brown's Schooldays* – Thomas Hughes MP – to present the prizes on New Foundation Day, 1 June 1873. His own speech claimed that *The Mill Hill boys have something of a Tom Brown spirit...* His guest, in a nice foreshadowing of the School's status a century later, challenged the assembled gathering to an awareness of the spirit of their times: *The boys – and the girls too – of England have succeeded to a great inheritance...* In October 1874, the same tone of eager emulation surfaced in regard to the background of C.F. Hayward, the architect of Burton Bank, Rev. Harley's new – and Mill Hill's first – Out-House (for 30-35 boys) in 1½ acres of J.Pawson's estate: *He had created boarding-houses at Harrow, Charterhouse, etc...*

"Doctor's Pond", gravel pool on site of present Collinson House, named 1880s, ref Dr Weymouth – he fell in, skating. *4.j*

A year later, December 1875, Vice-Master Harley wrote that his venture would embody *the best of the best* of *other Public schools*.

Yet as with Disraeli, perceptions still lagged behind the reality. To the fury of the *MHM*, on 3 December, *The Globe*, a highly respectable Conservative penny paper, included Mill Hill among the 'Middle Class Schools'. The phrase then meant *one which does not as its ultimate purpose aim at sending its pupils to the Universities...*; whereas *the aim of a first-grade school [ie Mill Hill] is to ... train its "boys" in the exercise of the powers and practice of the virtues, intellectual and moral [et virtutem et musas] which will be called for when they take their position as University "men"*: (Weymouth's motto of 1870 ushered in Mill Hill's second Coat of Arms).

Public Schools were now beset with what writer Rupert Wilkinson called a *comical exclusivity*: it was probably the painter F.S.Ogilvie who recounted to his writer-nephew Vivian, (following a similar snub to Shrewsbury from Westminster in 1866) the reply from Harrow to a Mill Hill post-card of the 1870s, requesting a cricket fixture: *Eton we know, and Rugby we know but who are ye?*" Nothing daunted, in July 1877 the *MHM* could quote the Headmaster's triumphant claim: *First place in Honours at London University in two successive years – no other school had done so*. The Chairman on Foundation Day declared that *an institution of this kind is a power in the country...*.

The *MHM* also reflected the day-to-day pattern. In 1879 Fives Courts were completed, and in 1885 subscriptions were sought for a £720 Chemistry Lab. Bowls and croquet were played, overseen along with all other sports, through a by now well-established 'GC' (see Appendix E), who considered the call, in April 1874, for *Big-Side at football twice a week...*. The Games Fund also had to cover *the want of seats on the Playfield, and the rent of the Ten-Acre ... Mr Bishop's Field*, later to be converted (December 1877) into a cricket field. Masters played in the teams. The GC's purview was extended to the new craze of bicycling in April 1877, when a team of 10, including two Old Boys, was formed, with safe excursions – no British motor cars appeared before 1893 – proposed as far as St Alban's, Hatfield, Aylesbury and Reading. Paperchases also enjoyed this freedom – reaching to Barnet and Neasden.

During 1876, a revived Debating Society discussed 'Women's Rights'; a similar debate a decade later, "That Woman has had more influence on Mankind than Man", produced equal voting, tipped only by the Presidential casting vote. Also later that year "Fagging" was described by J.B.Ritchie – hopefully, but prematurely to the tune of 90 years – as *one of the relics of the barbarous age of school life*. The long-lasting Mill Hill theatrical tradition was started that same year with the formation of a *Corps Dramatique* ('Scenes from Pickwick'). Many now belonged to the Natural History Society, roaming the Totteridge fields with the same apparent easy freedom as the paperchasers and cyclists. That broadening of horizons also engendered Mill Hill's first overseas visit: Dr Weymouth took eight boys on a tour of France for 21 days in 1877, culminating in an overnight return journey of 14 hours from Paris to Holborn. All-pervasive was a characteristic Mill Hill humour, perhaps an aspect of that quality of 'aliveness' remarked by Gladstone.

The impression is of care, variety, discipline, thoroughness, and high standards. Well might Lloyd Tayler write in 1875: *Of Dr Weymouth it must be recorded that he has amply proved his ability for the position he holds, by the high state of prosperity to which he has brought the School...* By these criteria, Dr Weymouth was surely running a well-ordered ship.

The Case of Dr Weymouth

For Conan Doyle addicts, this was the England of Sherlock Holmes. True to that spirit, below the surface of events at Mill Hill there was a Murray-Weymouth puzzle to compare with Winchester's 'Murray-Minor' mystery. Its causation could have been allowed to lie in Weymouth's 'Greek meeting Greek' confrontation with the ambitious Rev. Harley, owner of 'BB' – a ready-made political power-base – but for an astonishing letter.

The definitive but affectionate biography of Sir James Murray by his granddaughter has set down for posterity the strong, religiously rigid character and necessarily obsessive personality of her great subject. She defines their roots as lying in *his concealed but deep feeling of inferiority because he was self-taught.* The phrases she uses to pinpoint the temperamental effects of his self-imposed task are consistent over time: *bitterness... very great stress... chip on his shoulder... near breakdown... overwork at times made him very touchy... he enjoyed a certain sense of martyrdom.* James himself wrote frequently of his *sacrifices.* He had *legitimate grievances* [about the lack of appreciation of his lexicographical labours] *and in his overwrought condition he made the most of it.* (Great-grandson Dr Oswyn Murray has also conjectured: *perhaps Murray felt his own contribution to the school was underestimated...*). With *excitability and bouts of depression alternating with exhilaration,* today's jargon would categorise him as a uniquely gifted manic-depressive.

In her otherwise superlatively researched work, Betty Murray has nevertheless been shown by the author of *The Surgeon of Crowthorne* to have accepted a received idea in at least one respect – James was not 'surprised' but became quite aware of the status of this Dr Minor at Broadmoor. A comparable though understandable misreading led the eminent biographer to include in her text a quotation which is critical to Mill Hill's story – albeit incidental to hers – and with which issue must here be taken, if an abiding measure of Dr Weymouth's importance to the School's progress is to be gained. She relied unquestioningly on the Brett James' account of the Head Master, whereby he selectively but unattributably quoted from a sole *OM: if only he had been of a more sympathetic disposition and had possessed keener insight into human nature's little weaknesses... he would have been nearer to the ideal Headmaster.* She comments: *This account gives the clue to Murray's role ...*

Brett James did not exercise the historian's responsibility to balance this with other data, and did not offer an overall judgement of his subject. Betty Murray postulated an ongoing 'crisis' at Mill Hill as deriving predominantly from a facet of Weymouth's character, rather than from three other contributory factors: the UK's 'Great Depression', in the face of German and American industrial and agricultural competition; the personality clash with Murray's friend, Harley; and the inevitable tensions arising from Weymouth's strict discipline, manifestly needed in his successful campaign to revive the School after the collapse of 1869; (Head Master Dr Whale incurred similar reactions 75 years later: see Ch.VIII).

The key had seemed to lie in a letter – from a so-called (but at that time sketchy) 'Mill Hill Archive' – now no longer traceable either there or in the Murray papers at the Bodleian, nor discovered by Brett James in 1907. In it Murray apparently wrote from Oxford in 1886 to Treasurer Thomas Scrutton, in what Betty Murray would elsewhere describe as typically 'scathing' language, after Weymouth's resignation (other correspondence with Scrutton is sporadic, and never so fulsome): *Dr Weymouth has been a failure... the school has been sustained in spite of him by the enthusiastic devotion of those who gave it their* disinterested *services, whose efforts were constantly directed to supplying and concealing his deficiencies... What has happened now would have happened 12 years ago, if Dr Weymouth had been left to himself. When it was eventually decided that Harley must leave the School... for the remainder of his plight... it was James who held it together.*

She asserts that *this then was the background to James' work.* Contrasting Murray with Weymouth, greatly his senior and a man loaded with the kind of academic honours that Murray craved, she had written that *he was known to be able to forgive and forget,* yet it is clear that this was not true of his attitude for much of the time towards the publishers of the *OED: he nursed a lasting grievance.* Under the influence of that well-known 'halo-effect' with which biographers invariably endow their subjects, the loyal biographer even stated, without foundation but in the light of his equivocal applications for other Headships, the implausible thesis that the perfectionist, unbusinesslike Murray would have succeeded Weymouth as Head.

Most telling, however, is the question of the date of the letter. Murray repeatedly threatened to resign from the *OED* Editorship: *he was often tempted to give up, and the effect on his personality was lasting.* By 1886 Murray was entering the middle and most pressured phase of his work on the 'Dict'y'. Betty Murray herself records that *James had by 1885 lost his sense of humour, and his serenity; he bothered over trifles and took offence easily.* Complementing this is a trait which his biographer cleverly identifies: *when he had pen in hand he was always apt to get carried away... As so often he was dramatising and exaggerating his plight... He enjoyed a crisis and he enjoyed even more writing it up as a good story.*

Mutual stress

There is little question from the anguished references in the Court Minutes but that the stress was mutual. From the outset, the lines of demarcation were blurred between the Head Master, who had been promised that he would be 'supreme in the internal management of the school', and this first (and last) nomination of a 'Vice-Master'; it turned ostensibly on the rights of BB boys to share the box-room in the Head Master's domain, the School House, and on the Head's jurisdiction in the classrooms. The Vice-Master abrogated to himself the right to direct access to the Court; in 1877 both were asked to 'give ground'. By 1880 Harley went so far as to write to the Court: "I have lost confidence in him", but then 'decided to remain'. Weymouth finally thought to end the threat to his authority by writing to Harley, about 8 April 1881, ceasing his employment at the end of that Summer Term, only to have to apologise forthwith on 6 May: *I was wrong in dismissing him without the agreement of the Court.* Counsel's opinion was sought. There were six Court resolutions critical of Weymouth. In a distraught four-page letter, composed at 3.00 a.m. on 25 May, he wrote heart-rendingly to each Governor personally of *the hardest and darkest enigma of all my life ... you were afraid of the consequences of my action, while my mind was totally devoid of such* fear ...

In the second place, as a corollary, it is now equally clear that the span of 'management years' for Head Masters, in this case 17, can be too long, save in the best circumstances. The Weymouth of the 1880s was no longer the Weymouth of the 1870s. There were other minor 'errors of judgement' which cropped up concerning treatment of boys and parents – all resolvable, just as was the appointment of a new BB Housemaster, Dr Stock, and the arbitrated buy-back from Rev. Harley – for £10,500.

Above all – money talks. From 1869, the new Court needed to pursue every route to solvency, including debentures; in 1874 the opinion of counsel, J.B.Braithwaite QC, had been sought as to the very legitimacy of 'authorizing mortgages of Church Estates'. Yet by 1885 the 'profit' margin had disappeared. Under this multiple pressure, the 'forbidding' Weymouth suffered some kind of breakdown, brought on first of all by the undermining machinations of his Vice-Master, who finishes up as no hero in this story. In March 1886, Dr Weymouth's contrived 'letter of resignation' was read to the Court. A 'package' was proposed: in the event the Court went back on it, in the light of subsequent financial difficulties, causing Dr Weymouth further distress, and impoverishment in his later years.

Dr Richard Weymouth MA DLit, HM MHS 1869-86, in full academic robes, painted after the unhappy latter days of the Harley controversy, but representing him as in his disciplinarian prime. *4.k*

How then to explain that caustic example of what Winchester perceived as Murray's *detachment*, amidst a scene of seeming geniality? Allusion was made earlier to Vaughan Williams' "Wasps" overture: here, in a musical metaphor, it is as if a fiery Scots Murray, with his *Calvinist asperity*, had been buzzing away waspishly within his adopted English setting. Despite Dr Weymouth's negative side, Mill Hill's History has to question the legitimacy of Murray's uncorroborated post-hoc comments of 1886, not least in view of Weymouth's solicitude for Murray's evidently overworked state as early as 1880.

Those now unverifiable sentiments seem to fly in the face of their friendly letters that continued after the Mill Hill period, and of the farewell ceremony, *2 June 1885: I have enjoyed his friendship now for 15 years*, said the Head, to which Murray responded in terms of his *debt of gratitude to Dr Weymouth*. The overwhelming internal evidence for Weymouth is of capability, not over-dependence on Murray or Harley. Murray did not 'blow the whistle' on his Head Master *in situ*. Those acid comments from his Oxford fastness after the event must not be allowed to obscure the host of good things accomplished by Dr Weymouth for the benefit of the new Mill Hill: they stand

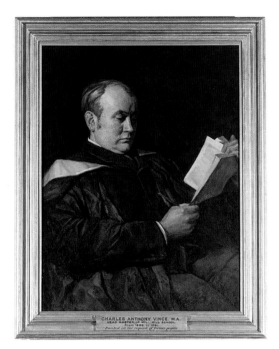

MHS Head Master
Charles Vince,
1886-91. *4.1*

the scrutiny of time. He had in good measure achieved that step-change in reputation and positioning which the 1869 Scheme devoutly postulated.

Of the man who *would make all the difference* [to the *OED*], Simon Winchester further observed that *the two best-known works about him were... written... by his son... and his grand-daughter Elisabeth, who might be suspected of having rather less than disinterested views of him.* Both the Editor of what Winchester describes as *the world's unrivalled* über-*dictionary for what in time might well become the world's* über-*language*, under the pressure of Murray's own self-appointed destiny – and his admiring, dutiful, single-minded biographer – could get things out of proportion.

Unconvincing Vince

Quantitatively, Weymouth's time had failed to live up to the promise: 34 new boys had entered in September 1869, 70 for the whole of 1870, 49 (1871), 30 (1872), 51 (1873), 63 (1874), 70 (1875), 56 (1876), 61 (1877), 51 (1878), 60 (1879), rising to a mini-peak of 70 (1880). Thereafter, a background of falling profits, whether or not due to the still-debated 'Great Depression' of 1873-96, had been eating away at the School's vitals; the entry declined from 57 (1881), 38 (1882), 62 (1883), and 43 (1884), to 35 (1885), and finally to a mere 15 at the start of 1886. The Court concluded it had to intervene.

A Fellow of Christ's, Cambridge, Charles Vince had been recruited from Repton in September 1886, when 21 new boys were enrolled. The Court had in mind the 19th-century convention, exemplified twice in the School's later story, whereby Public School Headmasters/ Head Masters or senior Dons of Oxbridge Colleges were deemed to be virtually interchangeable. The doctrine was easily flawed, as Vince's kindly but unconvincing regime underlined. The History has to focus on regimes that were allowed to last at least seven years. The five years 1886-1891 did, however, have the glamour of Mill Hill's first rugby 'cap': (George Heron had earlier played seven times for a soccer International XI, once as captain); Cambridge Blue and medic John Dewhurst won five England caps, 1887-90; and the School's second Cambridge cricket Blue, Cecil Fitch (later Lt Col) in 1888, emulated the later Lord Rochdale. Despite Vince's great character-forming sermons, already by 1888, a group of Northern Millhillians were driven to send an eight-page 'Memorial' to the Governors, complaining about "the condition of the School": where were the new Chapel, and the promised 'Workshops'? The Rolls plummeted.

The New Foundation's first 22 years had not proved a financial success. For a school to be scholastic, athletic or virtuous, let alone happy, was not enough. As the 'Incorporation' saga of the 1990s would underline (see Ch.XI), the legal position was actually that the money was not even the responsibility of the Trustees: in the event of a collapse, the ultimate risk lay with the individual Governors themselves. Books must balance.

Sources for Ch.IV include: *MHM*s – 'Per Annos' article in 1939, & 1939 Fndtn Day Note; 'Prntd Pprs' v.s 2 & 3, 1875-8, 1879-82; Boys' Jnl, Lent Term, 1874; Cash BK 1869-76; Petty Cash BK (Dr Weymouth) 1874-84; Visitors' BK 1879-93; Loan Certs BK 1870; Weymouth ltr to parents, ll.i.1886 "We are doing good work"; *Globe*, 3.xii.1876; Memorial, *OM*s to Govnrs 1888; Weymouth ltr to Buckland, 14.x.1892; Chris Sutcliffe, *History of BB* (OMC, pte circ, 2000) see also Appendix D. For Scrutton slave trading, see corr, G.Vero [1960-5]/G.Huntly, Mar 2001 'Shackleton', C4TV, 2.i.2002.

HMC: Records, Headmasters' Conference; A.Percival, *The Origins of the Headmasters Conference* (1969), *Very Superior Men* (1973); J.W.Roche, 'The First Half-Century of the Headmasters' Conference 1869-1919, Sheffield U, PhD thesis, 1969; *Jnl of the Untd Rfrm Church Hist Soc* v.6/2 1998, 72-96; Gathorne-Hardy, *op cit*, (HMC origination, 99).

19th C. Nonconformity/ work-ethic: B.L.Manning, *The Protestant Dissenting Deputies* (1952); J.Kitson Clark, *The Making of Victorian England* (1962); Lord Beaconsfield/Benjamin Disraeli, *Endymion* (1878), 70, [all characters based on public figures of the day]; J.Reynolds, *The Great Paternalist – Titus Salt and the Growth of 19th Century Bradford* (Bradford, 1983); J.Gardner & N.Wenborn (eds), *The History Today Companion to British History* (1995); corr, 1997/8 with Prof S.C.Holt [1948-54].

Murray: K.M.E.Murray, *op cit* [passim & Ch.VI, 112, n.46, 'JAHM to T.Scrutton Apr 1886' – not extant in MHS Archvs]; *Oxford English Dictionary: 1884-1928* (OED), & corr with Donald Hall, 1972/3; W.G.Ruthven Murray, *The Dictionary Maker* (Wynberg, RSA, 1943); P.Ruthven Murray, *The Murrays of Rulewater* (Penguin Books 1986); Murray Papers, Archvs, Bodleian Library, Oxford, & of the *OED*, corr, Dr Oswyn Murray (Praefectus, Graduate Centre, Balliol Coll, Oxford), Maj Colin Ruthven Murray [1933-7], 1998-2001; G.F.Timpson [1906-10], *Kings & Commoners* (1936), *Sir James Murray*; R.McCrum, W.Cran, R.MacNeil, *The Story of English* (NY, USA, 1986); *The Periodical*, v.XIII, 143, Feb 1928 (*Punch* cartoon); *Saturday Review* [Prof Child story]; S.Winchester, *Surgeon of Crowthorne* (Viking & Penguin Books, 1998); (thanks to Dr A.H.Pickering [1947-54], A.Bell [1948-52]; also *The Meaning of Everything – Story of the [OED]* (OUP, Oxford 2003) xx, 37, 71, 75, 86, 8811 208, 228 (thanks to P. Lloyd [1935-40]); 'Swallowing the Dictionary', BBC R4, July 2003; BBC TV ONE, A.Yentob, *Murray and the OED* 18.xii.2003. Five MHS A/Ms wrkng on *OED*, see corr, P.Gilliver, OUP,

12.xi.2003 #: G.F.H.Sykes the klepto-maniacal Sidney Herrtage, the pigeon-hole-building Alfred Erlebach & his brother H.A., F.E.Bumby; (some also attended the dinner at the Queen's Coll., OU, in 1897 to mark the Queen's acceptance of the *OED* in her Diamond Jubilee Year.

Political background: Gladstone Pprs, BL Add MSS v.374, 44,459 ff.215-6: 44,483 v.398, ff.296-306; P.Magnus, *Gladstone* (John Murray 1954), 203, 208, 263, 278, also q. in T.B.Macaulay, *Edinburgh Revw*, 1839 (ref. Gladstone's *The State in its Relationship with the Church*, 1838); R.Jenkins, *Gladstone* (Macmillan, 1995); H.C.Matthew & M.R.D.Foot, eds, *Gladstone Diaries* (Oxfd, 1994); [v.ix, x, & Index]; *Papers of W.E.Gladstone* (Reading, Engl. 1998), Weymouth corr. 1878, 1896; Andrew Roberts, *Salisbury...* (Weidenfield & Nicholson 1999); J.Grigg, *Lloyd George...* (1978), ref J.E.C.Bodley [1869-701; S.B.Saul, *Myth of the Great Depression 1873-1896* (1985); A.Maurois, *Disraeli* (1925).

Public School Literature: N.Carlisle, *Concise Description of the Endowed Grammar Schools in England & Wales* (1818); H.Staunton, *Great Public Schools of England* (1865); J.C.Minchin, *Our Public Schools: Their Influence on English History* (1901); Graham Greene, *The Old School* (1934); R.Graves, *Goodbye to All That* (1957); I.Weinberg, *English Public Schools: the Sociology of Elite Education* (1967); J.Wakeford, *Cloistered Elite* (1969); J.R.de S.Honey, *Tom Brown's Universe, Development of the Victorian Public School* (1977); D.Newsome, *Godliness and Good Learning* (1961); J.McConnell, *English Public Schools* (1985); Gillian Freeman, *Schoolgirl Ethic: Life and Works of Angela Brazil* (1976); Christine Heward, *Making a Man of Him* (1988); I.Quigly, *Heirs of Tom Brown* (1982); J.Rae, *Public School Revolution: Britain's Independent Schools 1964-79* (Collins, 1981); B.Simon & I.Bradley, *Victorian Public School...* (pp 11,180: Gill & Macmillan, Dublin, 1975); G.Walford, *Life in Public Schools* (1986); A.F.Leach, *History of Winchester College* (1899); Ogilvie, *op cit*, also q. in Wilkinson, *op cit*.

Fiction: D.Bussey & B.Robson, *Public School Fiction Show* (York, 1994); T.Hughes, *Tom Brown's Schooldays* (1870); F.Anstey, *Vice Versa* (1882); Talbot Baines Reed, *Fifth Form at St Dominic's* (1888); R.Kipling, *Stalky & Co* (1899); H.A.Vachell, *The Hill* (1905); J.Hilton, *Goodbye, Mr Chips* (1934); A.Waugh, *Loom of Youth* (1984); R.F.Delderfield, *To Serve Them All My Days* (1987).

Sport in Schools: *Schools Inquiry Commission* v5, pt2 (1868); A.Maclaren, *A*

System of Physical Education (1869); P.C.McIntosh, *Physical Education in England since 1800* (1952/68); M.Tozer, *Physical Education at Thring's Uppingham* (Uppingham, 1976); H.McLeod, [paper for *Festschrift* for Prof C.Binfield, Cambridge U, July 2001: 'Thews & Sinews: Nonconformity & Sport', & dscn, 26.vi.2001].

Customs: BMT Archvs (G.Smith); Bewsher, *op cit* (NB 29-33), OMC: [collusion between the two anonymous *OM*s was a fact, see 'Reminiscences" E.S.Weymouth [1869-74], *MHM* Feb 1906.

Topography: B.Cherry & N.Pevsner, *op cit*; Barnet Local Studies Archive – R.Calder, 'Mill Hill's Older Houses' (1992); T.D.Walker [1926-30], Mill Hill School Properties... (pte circ, 1990).

Other *OM* (& OB*) references: H.T.Atkin [1872-4]; W.R.D.Adkins [1875-80]; J.E.C.Bodley [1869-70]; R.Bousfield [1831-4]; R.W.B.Buckland [1878-84]; F.W.Buckland [1878-81]; S.C.Buckland [1879-87]; M.Burnyeat [1871-5]; A.M.Carter [1855-62]; F.E.Colman [1856-7]; F.H.Cook [1875-8]; E.H-Cook [1874-7]; W.E.V.Crompton [1882-3]; C.W.Cunnington [1873]; E.Curwen [1869-70]; T.R.Dallmeyer [1872-6]; J.H.Dewhurst [1878-81]; J.A.L.Dore [1885-8]; C.E.Fitch [1883-8]; E.W.Gundry [1879-82]; I.Gundry [1918-23]; J.H.Gunn [1870-6]; T.Gurney [1870-4]; H.Harley & A.Harley [1872-8]; S.L.Hart [1876]; G.Heron [1863-4]; H.P.Ibotson [1850-6]; G.Kemp, Lord Rochdale [1877-81]; E.J.Kitts [1869-70]; G.W.Knox [1853-6]; E.W.Lapthorn [1875-6]; E.Leonard [1870-6]; J.Lewis [1873]; E.Manning (b.1796, d.Aug 1874 - [1809-14] – oldest surviving *OM* in Dr Weymouth's time); H.Marnham [1874-80]; N.Micklem [1866-8, '70-1]; B.A.Millard [1876-8]; A.Nimmo [1880-3]; F.S.Ogilvie [1874-6]; G.Petrie [1871-6]; J.B.Ritchie [1870-6]; A.Ropes [1874-5]; A.E.Rook [1875-7]; T.Salt [1853-5]; A.J.Salter [1875-6]; E.W.Satow [1856-9]; T.U.Scrutton [1840-2]; T.E.Scrutton [1870-3]; Frederic Scrutton [1871-6]; J.P.Scrutton [1872-4]; F.Scrutton [1875-80]; O.Seaman [1874-8]; E.Sheffield [1823-7]; P.Smith [1829-34?]; A.Spicer [1858-63]; J.W.Spong [1879-84]; J.R.Tanner [1874-81]; E.R.Tanner [1875-80]; L.Tayler [1840-6]; M.W.Underhill [1843-4]; G.G.B.Van Someren [1869-70]; H.F.Ward [1877]; W.D.Watson [1880-2]; H.Waylen [1883]; A.Wells [1836-9]; F.M.Weymouth [1869-72]; W.H.Wills (Ld Winterstoke) [1842-7]; G.A.Wills [1870-2]; H.H.Wills [1871-2]; J.H.Wills [1873-7]. Ruthven Murrays – Harold [1879-85]; Ethelbert [1881-5]; Wilfred [1882-5]; Paul* [1974-9]; David* [1979-84]; Ann Caroline [1981-6].

1892: a new school family for what was still a 'family school':
the young McClures on Top Terrace. 5.*a*

Centennial and War: The Golden Age?

Sir John McClure: 'The Maker of Mill Hill School'

'He was persistently good to me...'
Kingsley Martin: *Father Figures.*

'It was a Golden Age': even if philosophically no single era of Mill Hill should stand out as more golden than any other, the School's 200-year History has to reserve a very special place for the Head Master of whose tenure that sentiment was so often, and so fervently, expressed. It would still resonate a century later, through the 1999 extension of the Music School (where Martin Briggs had 'Latinised' the prefix to '*Mac*'). The first History appeared in what was almost the 'reign' of Mr, later Dr, to become Sir John McClure – Head Master from 1891 to 18 February 1922. That work, by one of his 2,237 Old Boys and also one of his masters, planned for the first centennial, did not appear until 1909. By that time "The Bird" (aka "Crash", see Supplement 2) had already enfolded Mill Hill under the increasingly ample wings of his swirling scarlet hood and gown for 18 halcyon years: his remaining 13 years would be of a character tragically different from those which had preceded them. The epithet 'golden' was to acquire dark undertones.

Man of legend

With no Head Master do the constrictions of a History impact more harshly than with the years of John McClure and the community he built up at Mill Hill, and also at Belmont, thanks to another former pupil, future colleague A.J.Rooker Roberts. The task here is to etch in the key features in their parallel and closely-interconnected stories. By a strange stroke of fate, the 1922 issue of the *MHM* which was first to announce Sir John's death, had already been set up for printing when the news came through; it could not be changed, save for a brief tablet on the inside front cover. A generous memorial issue was to follow in April that year, the only one of its kind in the School's history: it must have gratified that great spirit, who more than any other of Mill Hill's Head Masters seems to permeate and watch over the destinies of his cherished creation to this day. Yet this gifted polymath, who was also a poet, born in the *murky, vigorous town of Wigan* and – like Thomas Priestley – with a good helping of *north country common sense*, had one supreme characteristic: he was a very simple man at heart. He would have liked the feeling of rebirth and continuance inherent in the unrelated title of the leader of that March issue: it was, simply, "Spring".

The embrace within which McClure secured the School for half of his 62 years, was, as *OM* Kingsley Martin later recalled in his autobiography, *Father Figures*, warm, fatherly, and vast. (It might only have been 11, if his 1901 resignation, for stress, had been sustained; he had to apologise for informing his MCR before the Court.) That indeed was the start of his many records: by the time of the publication of the first History, he had been Head for longer than his most long-serving predecessors, Thomas Priestley, and Dr Richard Weymouth. He was thereby to go on to create another record: no Head has yet served Mill Hill longer, nor is likely to, nor perhaps even want to, given the almost exponential rate of change in educational affairs, and the exposed position of all Heads – the so-called 'Football Manager syndrome' – in today's competitive world (see Ch.XI). Not for nothing does John Rae, in his book *Delusions of Grandeur,* utter the warning that *the ever-present fact of life for the head is that he or she is vulnerable, a condition not conducive to peace of mind...*

It may always have been so; trust is all. McClure won that trust early and in abundance; as a result, he became the very stuff of legend, and of anecdote. His appointment at 31, in an era long before the mare's nest of 'league tables', when a school succeeded through the leadership of its Head, was meant by the Governors to invite comparison with some inspiring 19th-century precedents: Arnold to Rugby at 33, Thring at 32 to Uppingham. He was recalled by one of his former mathematicians and later Fellow of the Institute of Actuaries, Owen Griffin, then in his 91st year, as *a 'big' man in every sense of the word, whom I regarded with awe.* For a new boy, the writer Andrew McGeoch, he looked like *an enormous bull-frog.* He is the only Head to achieve a dedicated biography, appropriately called *McClure of Mill Hill,* notwithstanding that it was written by a dutiful daughter, Mrs Kathleen Ousey; she was married to a staunch Millhillian, and thus perhaps entitled to be forgiven for viewing her father through an affectionately tinted lens. The Introduction by McClure's Varsity friend of 40 years before, Rev. T.H.Darlow, from which extracts have been quoted here, concluded: *Mill Hill School is his monument.*

He was the second Head to present that monument significantly on the stage of his peers, the HMC: he topped the poll in election to the HMC Committee for 1911, 39 years after the School's first presence on that prestige-giving body. The *DNB's* tribute to him – *he transformed (an) unknown Nonconformist school to public school status with 300 boy* – is a little generous in two respects: as the History's research has shown, Mill Hill became 'known' under Dr Weymouth, whose accession to the HMC provided the essential step to 'public school status'.

Two years later, on 3 June 1913, came the event recorded laconically in the standard-issue 'Mill Hill School Diary' of Jere Brierley, an "Erlesmere" boy – see Appendix D – from the Nonconformist heartland, Huddersfield: *Bird is made a Knight – we get a Half for it.* This honour, the first to fall to an HMC Head, was all the more remarkable when considered in the context of the many illustrious names of other Heads of that era and earlier, with their own particular niches in the Public School Valhalla. In the whole history of the HMC, only five other Heads have been so elevated for services to education; Mill Hill was one of an even more exclusive quartet to have a Head actually honoured during his incumbency – with Lord James of Rusholme (The Manchester Grammar School), Sir Desmond Lee (Winchester College), and Sir Roger Young (George Watson's).

Sir John's accolade was won primarily for his work in the public sector of education, not simply *qua* Head of Mill Hill. That fact in itself is also appropriately Millhillian: Mill Hill has consistently sought to bridge the divide between the two sectors – 'Public' and public; Brierley's entry for 18 February 1912 reads: *Bird gives us a jaw in Evg Chapel on snobbishness.* McClure had by this time graced the Senate of London University, the Corporation of Trinity College of Music, and the Council of Mansfield College, Oxford, that great source of support for Mill Hill, and guardian, through its stonework, of many meaningful Mill Hill names. In 1914, McClure became President of the Incorporated Association of Head Masters. The two educational worlds were interlinked; his experience of each sector reinforced the other. Uniquely, he was proposed as a nominee for Parliament, in 1921, an honour which, on the advice of the Governors, he wisely turned down. He is also the only Head to be visually represented in the heart of the City of London, where Mill Hill was conceived: in 1919 he was at St Paul's Cathedral, invited by King George V, for a Thanksgiving Service at the deliverance from the First World War [see Introduction.*o*].

Not least of his worlds was his devout Congregationalism; at a time when half the Church school population was Nonconformist this faith – never exclusive – infused both his school and his community life; he helped to create the first Union Church in Mill Hill Broadway, in 1908. (The only University Professor yet to be retained for a full MHS term, he is beyond comparison with the single day of Prof Wilkins' technical occupancy in 1869, or that of Rev. P.Smith: see Ch.III). He held the seat for Astronomy at Queen's College, London through to 1894, three years after his appointment. His abiding love of the heavens, in a scientific as well as a religious sense, was the source of countless lectures to the School and facilitated rather than weakened his faith: it demanded an acceptance that what Rev. Dr Nathaniel Micklem, Principal of Mansfield, later called the "Ultimate Questions", both spiritual and physical, were unanswerable. His restless intellect drove him towards another 'first'. He is the only Head to have found the time, and the energy, to study for a further degree during his period of service, following his LLD from Cambridge in 1897: the London University MusB in 1903, leading to a DMus six years later. The only comparison is with Dr Weymouth's award of a DLitt from that same institution in 1868. For a contemporary Headmaster such a nice diversion of effort is unimaginable.

He was the first in an array of Heads whose own musical talents served to enhance one of Mill Hill's most enduring traditions: the practice of music. Maurice Jacks would make concert appearances as a pianist, Dr John Whale would lead communal hymn-singing, and the present Head, William Winfield, and his talented wife, Margaret, would participate in school music as violinist and cellist respectively: McClure paved the way as a cello and double-bass player, and as an occasional conductor. Above all he played the role of music-writer, albeit under a characteristically whimsical *nom-de-baton*. School Concert programmes of the late 1890s/early 1900s refer to a certain Charlie Chaplin-inspired umlauted Teutonic composer, 'E.Düno Währiah', a pseudonym remembered by many an *OM* when lost in a foreign city. This *Herr Doktor*, highlighting the leaning that many of his contemporaries then had towards German culture, was the creator of "The Sailors of Bristol City"; a fugue for string quartet on the theme of "Yankee Doodle Dandy"; a canon for three female voices, "Mary Had a Little Lamb"; a piano trio on "Three Blind Mice", in the styles of Wagner, Beethoven and Puccini; and finally that celebrated overture, *Geliebt und Verloren* (Loved and Lost); it was conducted by someone else called McClure. Its score, now lost to posterity, must have had the same kind of musical charm as Dudley Moore's virtuoso Schubertesque and nonsense-German song, *Die Flabbergast*, from the "Beyond the Fringe" show of the 'Satirical Sixties'.

That endearing characteristic crops up continually; as Kingsley Martin recalled, *"The Bird" had a sense of humour all his own. He would explain a point to a blank-faced youth and then add, "You say you understand? Well, in that case I would sue my face for libel if I were you".* His re-written nursery rhymes were recorded in many a *MHM*: 'Those of the feathered tribe that show/ A close approximation/ Invariably coalesce/ In densest congregation.' This wittiest of Head Masters, with a face that F.O.Wills in 1929 likened to *a benevolent hippopotamus*, personified an enduring Mill Hill characteristic almost worth a book on its own – a penchant for the lighter side of life. It calmed the spirit of that Millhillian world of a century ago.

McClure never lost his touch for that world – the world of the school. He could sense the mood for all occasions, and all his different audiences. This was not a unique gift, but few have had it in so rich a measure. Some Mill Hill Heads have had excellent relations with their pupils, but could not quite get themselves across to, or 'recruit', their parents; others would run a well-organised teaching staff, but fail to carry with them the hearts and minds of 'the GC' as a whole (see Appendix E). Some may keep their Governing Body quiet, or at least at relative ease for a time, whilst other areas of that 'Octagon of Accountability' postulated in Chapter II, would be missed. McClure won them all to his side. Almost from the start this big looming presence was beloved by the Court, his staff, and the OMC, and at least his senior boys – and by many a tolerated and grateful 'maverick'. Of his presence on School visits abroad, Herbert Marnham recalled in 1912: *If you want to see McClure at his best, you must stand in the large central hall of one of the great Italian railway stations.* His effect on parents was described by one of Mill Hill's most independent *OM* Governors, Sir Ryland Adkins, as *almost mesmeric*; he could poke fun publicly at them on Foundation Days in his rich, mellifluous Lancastrian tones, and get away with it, witness two of his best-reported witticisms: *It is by a merciful dispensation of Providence that the average boy has but one Mother*, and *The more I see of the average parent, the more I admire the average boy.* From early on, the star had been born.

"Hurrah for the Worth of Mill Hill!"

With the 1891 Roll at 61, a compassionate Court had intervened; the cultivated Charles Vince could not redress it. As Rev. T.H.Darlow commented, the School at that time, like many Public Schools, was *"a curious amalgam of medievalism and modernism."* Six monitors supervised full and weekly Boarders, as well as Day boys, in a daily Assembly in The Large, a life dominated by what even Brett James called *"the votaries of muscle"*. The new Head, secure in what could still be legitimately termed, up to 1920, the Nonconformist mould, had luckily hit an upward economic trend: numbers rose again, reaching 99 in 1893. By the start of McClure's wars

Schoolhouse from Top Field, levelled 1902; 1832 Chapel visible beyond second Script (c/r.) and displaced Carp Shop (c/l.), at south-east and south-west edges of Quad respectively. *5.b*

(there were in fact two against 'the Boer'), it was up to 193. War did not have to be inimical to Public Schools: numbers were up again to 205 by the end of the second 'Boer War'. The era was driven by the dream of Empire: one of the earliest Speakers on (New) Foundation Day, in 1892, Dr Kenny, issued a challenge: *You are born into an age of transition ... Currents are hurrying this country forward into a new civilisation, new social orders; it is a great thing to die for England, it is a greater thing to live for England.*

As the clock rushed towards 1900, new things started happening. A second School song emerged (the score only re-discovered in 2000): *Hurrah for the Worth of Mill Hill.* McClure wrote to the monitors, accepting the call for a Tuck Shop, to replace "Mussons" (later "The Grove"), despite the charms of Misses Jane and Tilly. In 1894, the link between sports and 'moral character' was preached: *our immediate forefathers forgot this although the Greeks and Romans knew it full well.* The 1st XV had an unbeaten season; T.W.Pearson was rugby-capped for Wales. A debate asked whether "Professionalism in Cricket should be Permissible". There were now 'halves' on Monday, Wednesday and Saturday, with afternoon school on Tuesday and Thursday from 2.30 to 4.30 p.m. Fags earned 7s. 6d. a term. In 1897, the year the football pitch yielded, miraculously, to the building of a Vicarage (later Winterstoke House, later still the Pre-Prep), the playfield was 'levelled', ending the great toboggan run on the ancient 'Bus', terminating in the pond at the bottom. The Owls Club gave way to the Cambridge *OMs* Club. Trips were made with the Head Master from Holborn Viaduct to that unknown territory, 'the Continent'. The English Lake District was visited – for the *Magazine, a part of England which for many dwellers in the South remains for too long a closed book* – a comment full of unconscious irony for the 1939-1945 generations (see Ch.VII).

On 31 October 1896, Sir Henry Wills laid the first stone for a new Chapel. First sought in 1888 it was designed as a basilica, to fit between existing buildings, by a

Sir Basil Champneys FRIBA, architect of third Chapel of 1896 (i), with (ii) (l.) elevation drawings, ignoring existing Classrooms NOPQ (l.) and second Gym (r.). 5.*c*

THE NEW CHAPEL (EXTERIOR).

leading architect, Basil Champneys. Its severe but status-giving Anglican-collegiate, inward facing pews were relieved by baroque decorational touches. The germ of his ideas lay in the florid 'Queen Anne' brickwork of his work for Newnham College, Cambridge; it was not in the stonework for his Nonconformist Mansfield, Oxford – *pace* his *DNB* entry – or his later Rylands Library at Manchester, which in 1912 would win him the profession's highest honour. After Tite, he was Mill Hill's second RIBA Gold Medallist. *The Builder* wrote: *he has built at Winchester and Harrow, and with equal success at Mill Hill.* There was a McClurean flavour to the window marking the deaths at the school in 1899 of Henry Robinson, and Allen Whipp: as the 1998 centenary booklet noted, many a *pupil over the years was helped ... by its inscription* – 'Weeping may *endure for a night, but joy cometh in the morning.* Ventilation was inhibited by two 1903 stained glass windows, one to Dr Weymouth and one dedicated by Sir Henry Wills to Priestley.

With the lead of *OM* Sir Ernest Satow, Ambassador to Peking, and expert calligrapher, China's world power role was foreseen; at the School level, the only response was to admit two Chinese boys in 1906. Yet all eyes were on 'The Cape'. As many a Millhillian hurried to sign up in the Imperial Yeomanry, and in irregulars like Carrington's Horse, and Roberts' Horse, back at Mill Hill a debate voted that "The Boer War is justified". According to "Nath." Micklem QC, the Chairman of the Court, Millhillian – and indubitably male – corporate pride was such that during Jameson's raid, on the night before Krugersdorp, an *OM* was found cutting "*Et virtutem et musas*" on the stock of his rifle. This was also a time when McClure personally would set General Knowledge papers for the whole school, often producing hilarious howlers. Thus 'Mr Rhodes had a great deal to do in the Afghanistan war'. Other gems included: 'Equinox are a wild race living in the icy north'; and *L' ouragon s'augmentait* was translated as 'the orang-outang was growing fatter'.

While these Mill Hill boys were disporting themselves, on Foundation Day 1897 the Radical MP, the Hon A.J.Mundella, no doubt after a careful McClure briefing, disturbed the audience with a prophecy about a key new factor on the distaff side that would not see fruition at Mill Hill for another eight decades: "the future wives and mothers of England have opportunities... not presented to them till the last 30 or 40 years ... the Girls' High Schools ... Girton and Newnham ... are all doing noble work ... women are more conscientious generally than men, they are not accustomed to see Football and Cricket as the *ne plus ultra* of their education... Beware, young gentlemen, or you will have sisters who will surpass you ..." It was significant that one of the tributes to McClure in the special issue of the *MHM* was by the redoubtable Miss Tanner, AHM President, and soon to become Head of Roedean; Sir John was also a Governor of NLCS.

Following the would-be levelling of Top Field in 1898, the turn of the century brought an elevation. Three *OM* MPs entered the Commons: Alfred Davies – Radical, Alfred Hutton, and Colonel Sir George Kemp, later Lord Rochdale – both Liberals. By the Election of 1906, there would be seven: Sir Albert Spicer, "Nath." Micklem, Thomas McKinnon Wood, William Adkins, Sidney Robinson – Radical, Thomas Herbert – (with Rev. E.Hampden-Cook, one of two *OMs* to have nominated

McClure as Head) – and once again Alfred Hutton. The School was on her way to a very prestigious, public celebration of her first one hundred years.

An Imperial PM for the Centenary

If by 1901 that arbiter of Public Schooldom, *Boys Own*, was already ranking Mill Hill's cricket captain, Harold Wright, amongst a top dozen famed schools such as Eton, Harrow, Rugby and Winchester, 1907 marked the real milestone for the School's rising status. Not least of the achievements in that centennial year was a visit by a second Prime Minister, and thus the political leader of the British Empire, to speak on Foundation Day. This second successor to Mill Hill's first prime ministerial visitor of 1879, the Gladstonian Nonconformist Sir Henry Campbell-Bannerman had entered politics from partnership in a family firm, J. & W. Campbell, warehousemen and drapers, a background that accorded well with the solid middle-class callings of a good many Mill Hill parents of that time. As might be seen as appropriate for a School that would ultimately go co-educational – and here again he would have been in sympathy with a Head Master always concerned with women's education – he was the first Prime Minister to propose a woman, Florence Nightingale, for the Order of Merit – that original and venerable meaning of those familiar initials, 'OM'.

1907: (c.) Sir Henry Campbell-Bannerman MP, second Liberal PM as MHS Guest of Honour, First Centenary Foundation Day. 5.d

The later Sir John won his brief and officially unrecorded place in the PM's over-crowded diary at a time when, as Sir Henry's biographer puts it, 'he was riding high' in popular esteem. 'CB', as he was known to his friends, had only recently been returned, in December 1905, in the famous Liberal landslide, after 20 years in the wilderness. CB's immediate, personal and abiding achievement, far too neglected in the history of 20th-century Britain, was his magnanimity in reconciling the defeated Boer Republic in South Africa. He thereby brought Botha and Smuts into the still limited 'Colonial Conference' of self-governing nations within the Empire, the forerunner of today's doggedly surviving Commonwealth. As a consequence he gained the vital support of the new South Africa, then still 'Cape Colony', in the ensuing two world wars, the first of which was both to transform McClure's experience, and shorten his life. In terms of principle, CB has been well described as the 'last of the Victorians', an epithet which in a Mill Hill context could as easily have fitted McClure. This was the period of the *entente cordiale* with France, brought back into play once more in 1904, and moreover at a time when a Channel Tunnel was yet again under discussion; nevertheless, Britain was still desperately trying to keep Prussian Germany sweet, and in Mill Hill's 100th year, 1907, would have the experience of entertaining Kaiser Wilhelm for a State Visit, held, portentously, on 11 November.

The PM had been and was still that summer heavily involved in educational affairs, which would of course have further endeared him to John McClure's heart. Politically, educationally and socially, he was well-designed to mark the School's first 100 years. As a speaker, however, at least in the House of Commons, he was less

1902: Tuck Shop,
before additions of
Winterstoke Library (1907);
third Chapel (r.). 5.*e*

distinguished. He was by now in his 71st year; a description of him said that *he was not brilliant in debate.* Another had written of a *voice thick and muffled, his speech halting and unready, and the copious notes of his admirably constructed sentences ... held by a tremulous hand within smelling distance of his nose.* The *MHM* is respectfully silent on any aspect of his delivery on the day. Although of Scots blood like McClure, his guest of honour had to put on an act to speak with a Scots accent. Perhaps he did so speak on the day, no doubt to Dr James Murray's delight who was there to grace the occasion from his Oxford fastness. One more of those tiny strands of coincidence which mark the Mill Hill story: his birthplace and real home, as opposed to his London home in Grosvenor Place, or No 10 Downing Street – *that rotten barrack of a House* – was the village to which he would return whenever he could. It was called Belmont. (The young Rooker Roberts needed no such reminder: 'Spectator's' letter to the *MHM* in April 1905 had already put the idea of buying the empty 'Belmont House' into his mind).

Speakers at school speech days rarely treat them as occasions for major oratory – the sole exception had of course been Gladstone – nor do those oft-occurring occasions figure in the biographies. However, Campbell-Bannerman's words on the day went down very well: he clearly felt strongly about the causes for which Mill Hill seemed to stand. These were the days before heavy briefings and speech-writers, when even PMs would write their own letters, and often their own speeches too. Speaking of the need *to teach to think,* and *to form our own judgment,* he praised *this School which is free to the winds of heaven, which has no exclusiveness, and no desire for it.*

A time to build

All Head Masters would like to be builders. In the past it was only given to a privileged few to achieve that ambition, by virtue of their being in office at a time where a majority of the School's support among its Old Pupils was economically strong and willing, and when Appeal Funds could be pitched around a particular anniversary, or worthy cause. The presence of a well-disposed major donor also helped. Two complementary elements are, however, ongoing constants: the confidence of the Governors in the incumbent Head, and an upward financial trend.

It was McClure's destiny to fulfill these criteria, although the post-war Memorial Fund was an additional money-raising pretext he would have infinitely preferred not to have. His was the time not only of Mill Hill's second major, and most enduring, building period across the 200 years, but also of a triumphant extension to 80 acres of freehold newly-levelled hillside, a vital complement to any new building ('Territorial Era **3**'). Such was the Governors' belief in him, and such was the prosperity of the group of mainly Nonconformist owner-manager *OMs* who were to help fund these projects, that no fewer than 13 major buildings had arisen by the time of the outbreak of war. Rev. John Newton Holder, one of only nine Millhillians still able to recall this beloved Head, before his own death in 1997, detailed many famous commodity-enterprises then represented: Hartleys – marmalade, Foster Clarks – jellies, Strakers – stationers, and Austin Reed. (Holder fagged for *OM* [Sir] Norman Hartnell, later Queen Elizabeth II's dressmaker at the time of the 1957 royal visit; John McClure's benevolent and all-encompassing regime encouraged Hartnell *to concentrate on my sketching.*)

The name of the first 'Chairman' of the Court of Governors (who described himself simply as a tobacconist) is here pre-eminent. As Treasurer Dick Walker has written: *From 1897 the pace quickened, largely due to the support of Mr [William Henry] Wills (later Lord Winterstoke) ... He made sums available for various purposes, although mainly on mortgage at low rates of interest*; the day of his death, 29 January 1911, however, has *also been referred to as Black Friday for Mill Hill, because it had been expected that his Will would release the School from the mortgages, but it did not do so.* With a century's perspective on the Nonconformist work-ethic this is perhaps not so surprising: like Taunton School and the City of Bristol and the many other objects of Lord Winterstoke's generosity, Mill Hill would have to work for her benefactions.

Several Public Schools developed their own form of early hockey: MHS's unique 'Singlehanded', a major though introspective sport, preceded Double-Handed Hockey proper, with 1st, 2nd, 3rd IX colours caps and shirts; note ash sticks (made in the 'Carp' Shop); informal game on Quad. *5.f*

As the ailing PM spoke, looking out over the Quad that day in 1907, there were already within his audience's field of vision many 'McClure' buildings familiar to today's world – all still gas-lit. They included that third Chapel; the converted second Chapel, today's 'Large', of 1898; the 1900 Tuck Shop; Scriptorium No 2 with the Murray portrait (the facsimile, re-opened 18 December 1903, of the hut first re-located by the Terrace, but burnt down on 19 November 1902); the 1905/6 block of classrooms, named after the second major *OM* benefactor, gentle stockbroker Herbert Marnham; and beyond, Gymnasium No.2 of 1905 (today's Studio Theatre). There had been several much-lamented trees on the site of the original Winterstoke Library of 1907. Instead of the 1913 Music School, built to honour Sir John's 21st year as Head in 1912 (with Winterstoke Gardens, the last pre-war buildings) there was the old Choir Garden, while the timbered Carp Shop (No.2) used the wooded site of the future Science School. The Quad was used for 'winter cricket' and hard-court tennis in summer, interspersed from morn to eve by the fascinatingly dangerous game of 'Singlehanded' dating back to the mid-19th century. Not formally recorded until 1890, nor given Rules before 1891, it was characterised, like Eton Fives, by its use of odd elements in the brickwork; it flourished despite the advent of 'Double-Handed' in 1901/2.

The next six years would bring all but one of the facades that up to 2007, despite the ugly Fives Courts of 1908, constituted what was well described by Fabian Watkinson, a lecturer for the Victorian Society, as *a very pleasing ensemble.* In addition to Champneys, this would reflect the talents of Martin Briggs, and the School's consulting architects, Thomas Collcutt (the second PRIBA and Gold Medallist to be retained) with Stanley Hamp: see Appendix C. The valuable West Grove Estate,

1903: an early treeless Collinson House, Wills Grove, with top of Cinder Path right-of-way (r.): note duty constable. 5.g

south-east of Hammers Lane, would be acquired from the School MO, Dr Martin, in 1911/2, making, with the 'Fishing Net', Buckland Pool, Car Park, and land off Farm Road, the last pre-1914 land purchase. Although never a 'federal' school on the Harrow lines, the Court had launched Collinson, the first Out-House within the School's terrain, in 1903, on the old Rectory Field: this land, bought by W.H.Wills in 1896/7, was made over to the School in 1900 – site of the old "Peacock's" (now a Pre-Prep playground). Within another four years the first House beyond Wills Grove, Ridgeway, would be built on part of 27 acres of Park Lands bought by Lord Winterstoke in 1910 (Long Field, Park, Burton Bank, "Garth", and Winterstoke Gardens). Dick Walker has recorded: *When land on Wills Grove* [the former private Wills Road] *was purchased, the School entered into a covenant to maintain the road*; ownership – transferred c.1910 – was not ratified until 2001. Apart from the Gate of Honour (1920), the Science School and Winterstoke House (1924), there would be no more major building at Mill Hill for another 50 years, when the sesquicentennial of 1957 launched a new round of work under the partnership of Sir Frederic Sellers and Roy Moore.

Demand was the driving force: reputation grew, and applications kept on coming in, necessitating the use of three Hostels 'on the Birkbeck' – "Erlesmere", "Christowell", and "Haslemere"/ "Opawa". No fewer than 207 boys knew only these converted houses as their 'Mill Hill'. Collinson and Ridgeway were formed by the transfer of boys of all ages from existing houses; Winterstoke too would gain immediate solidity in this way; this necessitated moving its first Head of House, Roland Wade, from School House.

The long summer

First World War literature highlights the flavour of the decade that preceded it: a genial, other-worldly inevitability lay over these islands. Something of that elusive atmosphere can be discerned in Mill Hill's affairs, in common with other Public Schools of that time; it was epitomised in the strange fact that neither the outbreak nor the cessation of hostilities were referred to in the Minutes of the Court. Parochial matters came foremost: the replacement of earth closets in 1902; coping with the breakages which were carefully bewailed in the 'Breakages Book'; the perennial question whether the indoor swimming bath should be heated (Mill Hill's equivalent of what management gurus would now call 'the bicycle shed syndrome'); and the sad death of a boy in the Cross-Country run. (Despite resistance to replacing gas lighting with electricity, the Chapel would 'go over' in 1919: hence the phrase 'taking the spills' – it being a prefectorial duty to light the gas mantles with 'spills': monitors 'took the tails', and Harrowesque top hats – see Appendix E.) As the century's first decade drew to a close, and King Edward VII approached the end of the summer that was to bear his name, this was nevertheless a school unlike that of the post-war era: no landscaping of the Terrace below the Portico; an Aviary in the Choir Garden, but no terrazzo yet to floor the Octagon; nor any giant oil painting of Sir John to look down effulgently on the Dining Hall. 'School Cert' had not yet come into use; the pace of teaching was what the Board of Education Report of 1919 would still describe as 'full of old methods'.

The start of the second decade brought a perceptible change of style, and direction. Ivor Nicholson might roundly declare, in *The Captain* in 1909, that *there is no cadet corps at Mill Hill – one could almost say with a tolerable amount of certainty there never will be*; (a comparable misunderstanding in 1948, in a review of OM D.E.Morris's book on his path from conscientious objector to combatant, would term this a *pacifist school*). Yet a Rifle Club, formed in 1905, was followed in January 1911, despite vows to the contrary, by an OTC under the Bursar, Lt Col Gluenicke and the pressure of masters Cane, Andrews and Brett James (see Information Supplement No.2). It was created by James and K.T.Gemmell, not to anticipate war, but to emulate other Public Schools; Mill Hill had to 'compete', and did so, coming second in the Schools of the Empire Competition of 1913.

Governor Sir Ryland Adkins MP, would assert in 1918 that Mill Hill *was not a Seminary like Beaumont, Lancing, or The Leys*, yet that latter long-standing Nonconformist rival, together with Rugby, Shrewsbury, Oundle and Gresham's Holt, would be picked out by the Court as schools against which Mill Hill should now measure herself. There was a belated tightening up; two sons of the manse, and outstanding monitors, were reported in the Brierley Diary for 29 February 1912 (the fact is not to be inferred from the official *Register*): *Bentley & Snell expelled for gambling.* He also noted: *Dieser [Hallifax] degrades all BB monitors & prefects and twanks 17 chaps for having a gut at 2.00 at night. All monitors & prefects resign. No "Stop Talking"* – (sung by monitors since the 1880s). Even a master was fired, unprecedentedly, for bad language, and in 1910 another moved on, the story-laden Frank Gilbert. Gilbert's inability to control classes created a Mill Hill phenomenon: *Have a good Gillie roar with Mr Treleaven*, wrote Brierley on 19 September: (see Appendix E). Foundation Day

Ridgeway House opened in 1911, second Out-House within MHS grounds: (i) (l.) later aerial view showing Long Field; (ii) contemporary view of the House garden. 5.h

The Gym.   A.J.Rooker Roberts

First Gym replaced by south-
east wing of Marnham Block
(1905), with far door leading
into Large (second Chapel).*5.i*

Guests continued to reflect the increasing esteem in which the School was held externally, however, ranging from the *OM* Rt Hon T.McKinnon Wood MP, in 1912 (*Sec for Scotland & a member of the Cabinet. Half*, as Brierley recorded) to the Provost of Eton in 1920.

Belmont and the Main School

In 1912, a further reorganisation of forms ensued, now with a Lower School of Forms III A and B; a new Middle School with Removes A and B and an Upper IV A and B; an Upper School of V A and B, and a still under-filled VI Form. This was caused by a fundamental strategic development, whose success is a feature of the greater Foundation of the 21st century: the formation by Arthur J.Rooker Roberts, with the Court's full endorsement, of a new integral Junior House, seven years after "Spectator's" proposal. It opened that September with a record all-time ratio of two teaching staff to one boy – the nephew of the Lady Resident, Annie Pearse. This brought overall numbers to 232; Belmont then grew slowly – 1914 (30 est.), 1915 (30), 1916 (30), 1917 (28) and by 1918 (65 est.) Belmont would evolve into a separate Junior School, starting that new stage the next year. McClure was still its 'Head Master', as Master 'AJ' was proud to proclaim. Mrs Rona Bagnall, younger sister to his son and successor, Arthur ('AE'), recalled in her 89th year her family's connections with Mill Hill, back to the beginnings with Pye Smith's student, Lavington Rooker, the brother of her grandmother, Marianne Rooker (see Chs.II, VII and XI).

This diversion of boys below 13 to Belmont, deprived the School of revenue, and the Head of 'capitation' income: (annual 'boy'-fees of £7 10s. 0d. for Schoolhouse, £5 non-Schoolhouse, Boarders; Day Boys £3 15s. 0d.). By 1915 a boy's average career worked out at 3⅔ years, with 17 the leaving age. This situation was made worse by the judgement, formally expressed in 1917, that of the many Entrance Scholars that Mill Hill prided herself on, *half fail to justify their selection*. By 1915 there was *unrest among the older Boys*. There was unrest, too, over salaries and pensions, among the academic staff; this category included the Head of French and first female CR member, Mrs Constance Payne (a 1916 appointee, as was Belmont's first similarly isolated 'Lady Teacher', Miss May Goddard), whom McClure had constantly praised to his all-male Court. In due course a compromise solution was found for their quite natural concerns: Assistant Masters, like the young appointee Walter Hannaford Brown, were underpaid: in 1908/9 "Buster" Brown's starting salary was a bare £140 p.a., comparing with the Head's 1919 salary of £1,708.

Health matters

Health dogged the School, and Head, over these years: if a boy did not attend, the capitation reduced. *Have to wear coats in Chapel. Freezing hard*, wrote Brierley on 4 February 1912. McClure, too, had his *ups and downs, his times of real depression, his ordeals of personal health*, as Rev. E.P. Powell vouchsafed in his valedictory address. Brierley noticed on 13 February that *Bird gets ragged slightly in the lecture*, and on 1 March: *Bird very sick*. The equally watchful guardian of Mill Hill's interests, Treasurer Richard Buckland, reported that the Head was *overtired*, and *had in fact aged very fast recently*. He consulted J.L.Paton, High Master of Manchester Grammar School – the first occasion when that great fellow-HMC School provided an input to Mill Hill's well-being; (Donald Hall, Director of Science 1945-1969, and John Hawkins, Master of Belmont 1991-2004, were both 'OM's – Old Mancunians). While the McClures repaired to his favoured Grindelwald to recover, the eminent classical scholar Dr Arthur Way became Acting Head for two terms in 1913; (he had been Headmaster of Wesley College in an Imperial City, Melbourne, whose previous links with Mill Hill reached back to the early 19th century, with Rev. Evans, of the *Melbourne Herald*: see Ch.II).

When the newly titled Sir John returned that summer, he faced the prospect of being the first Head to have to contemplate the provisional closure of one or more Houses, if war should endanger Boarding numbers: in the event, in contrast to the situation that faced Mill Hill in the 1990s (with the Day trend overtaking that for Boarding), all was well. McClure had a Second Master in Ernest Hallifax, but he was not the strong support that a Head needed in these circumstances; he was eventually counselled by his chief to resign, resentfully, from that role. Belatedly, the value of what the Court had seen as a 'sinecure' was rediscovered. A.J.Williams was appointed (see Appendix C), a vital move. At Sir John's death he had to take over as Acting Head for two terms in 1922, with the loyal backing of boys and monitors, before Maurice Jacks arrived.

A rare *OM child of two centuries* was the controversial French film-maker, Claude Autant-Lara; he died at 98 in February 2000. A true child of one century was Dudley Tennet: in the height of the summer of 1996, despite the rug wrapped around him, he felt the cold. In his 96th year, Dudley was the first, and oldest, Millhillian to be interviewed for the History: as it transpired, that summer would be his last. His circulation was far from what it was when playing as a six-foot fellow-forward with a much smaller W.C.Ramsay in 1917. In his sunny sitting room in Edgware, with his wife Joy, he recalled that he had won all his three 'caps' in that single season – 3rd XV, 2nd XV, and finally the crowning glory, his 1st XV cap. He is still the only boy to have achieved this rare distinction; he overtook some who could not jump in the line-out as high as he could, but also stepped into the breach for older boys who had left early, sometimes in mid-term, to join up in this fourth year of the war. Those caps (see 5.*o*), donated by his daughter Mary, are part of the memorabilia used by the Headmaster to introduce new pupils to the traditions of Mill Hill; after Dudley's death on the last day of 1996, his family funded two chairs for the Terrace, and the restoration of the oil paintings, including that of his former Head. McClure would surely have valued these touches.

Dark classroom in
Marnham Block c1920:
note integral oak chair-desks
with inkwells, and
brown-tiled walls. *5.j*

A lost world

Other witnesses to that time were Roland Wade, Bill Bundey, Bill Crebbin, Tom Wardill as well as composer Inglis Gundry (son of *OM* and Governor, Ernest Gundry, honoured by a Concert and an annual Gundry Composition Prize in 2000). They also underlined one of the downsides to the McClure period – the slackness of the Housemasters. Inglis's autobiography recalled the sadism of a dormy prefect who could get away with hauling boys out of bed after lights out to run races in the dark, with beatings for the losers; he also bore witness to criminal sexual practices, including *le vice anglais* – larger boys against smaller, often good-looking boys, held face-down on the floor, against their will – practices hinted at in the Prospectus as *still graver evils.* Yet if McClure discovered any such abuse, a public beating in The Large would be the sanction, as it was for one Lister major, who had bullied a smaller German Jewish boy.

Such stories contrasted with the 'dear old *alma mater*' glow of the memories of Old Boys who died before the History could appear, such as Rev. J.Newton Holder, George B.Norton and the later Eric Dangerfield. Holder remembered Sir John's first words when being introduced to him – "A normal boy": the first time that anyone had paid him that gentle compliment. *He was a great Christian ... the strong connection with nonconformity led to the school being spoken of as the Nonconformist Eton;* (Bishop's Stortford thought of itself as the Nonconformist Rugby). *As he passed through the school, doors would be opened for him by the boys as if it were a free tribute to a man they held in high regard.* Another occasion exemplified once more the famous sense of humour: The GC donkey had been annoyed by one of the boys and in assembly one morning Sir John said: *Some boy or boys have been disturbing the patience of the donkey. I will say no more about it except, let brotherly love continue.* The humour was infectious: Holder recalled the story of one of the great Mill Hill masters, Vic Elliott (see Ch.VII). There was a boy called Ball, but everyone refrained from making the obvious pun – except Vic. Handing back an essay, he said in a voice down in his boots, as was his habit, *I only had one decent essay this week and that was Ball's!*

Eric Dangerfield was another cameo of the early 20th century: as Gowen Bewsher described him in the Chapel Commemoration Service on 21 June 1997, he had *that natural style of courtesy which instantly commands respect.* He regarded his generation of Millhillians – self-deprecatingly, but with tongue in cheek – as "unruly ruffians". Like Dudley Tennet, he was one of only 40 Day Boys. He recalled his daily school route for his daughter Sarah: *For the whole of my four years ... I rode there and back (by bicycle). There was no M1 ... or Watford By-Pass and the road from Hendon was a winding country lane on which I frequently met no one from the point of the parish church at the top of Greyhound Hill until I reached the bottom of the cinder path in Hammers Lane.* The young Dangerfield had the same fineness of features as the young "Steve" Norton, projecting a kind of serene innocence: their horizons had not been challenged by war or by social change.

Whilst Steve went into the family engineering firm of Nortons-Tividale in Dudley, where he eventually became mayor, Eric had to find his own way in the City: *A Public School education did not of itself open many doors.* Eric's love was gym: *I spent more time upside down in the Gym than right way up elsewhere.* He caught the attention of the PT instructor, Sgt Maj Peters, *who had been sabre champion of the Army at Aldershot, at which occasion HRH The Prince of Wales had been present, a fact which the latter had not forgotten when he visited the school in 1924 … he at once recognised Peters who was on parade with the 100 of us who formed the OTC Guard of Honour.* Two other, nationally-known names of this time were the sons of William Britain, a then-famous toy car manufacturer.

Further insights are provided by a second surviving diary, that of future Cambridge Scholar and technical author, Alec Eason (not least about the freedom then still being enjoyed by Millhillian cyclists on the open road; only in 1899, in Harrow, had England's first fatal car accident occurred): *Sunday 30 Sept 1901 – Used hot water to wash my hands … 23 Jan 1902 – got into my study [second term as 14-year old Scholar] … 1 June 1903 – Whole hol, Cycled to Chenies, Beaconsfield, Slough, Windsor, Uxbridge … 20 June 1904 – Cycled to London, 3 hrs 30 mins … 17 Dec 1904 – this year read c.50 books, baths 68 … 29 March 1905 – Memo for study tea: tongue 2/-, potted meat 5d, sandwiches 6d, Cadbury's cocoa 7d, Nestle's milk 5d, Cake 4d, Biscuits 7d, methylated spirit 6d.* Where the witnesses leave off, the *MHM* and unofficial ephemera like *The Brickbat*, or *No. 3 Red, A magazine for monitors, prefects and gentlemen*, take over. Many of the sharp features of that lost world can still be clearly discerned in such pages, most importantly those that related to the war. These were also the declining years of John McClure; there were signs of this in a falling-off of the academic performance of the School.

(i) 1912: Natural History Society excursion, all boys wearing brown velvet caps except (6'7") monitor; his monitor's Badge was based on a McClure innovation, as was (ii) 'Annie Pearse's', later OMC Vice-President's, badge. 5.*k*

Large slices of the timetable were now given over to the OTC. Although not every boy gained or even wanted a commission, nevertheless, of 120 'joining the colours' in 1915, some 80 were aiming for officer training; where tertiary education was mentioned it was clearly going to have to wait for the outcome of the war. There was little doubt about the objective in most minds from Lords Roberts and Kitchener downwards (though not in those of Basil Kingsley Martin and his fellow and often reviled conscientious objectors, who would serve out their war in the equally hazardous Ambulance Brigades): the mission of the nation's Public Schools was to provide its leaders 'over the top', its officers. That same concept of leadership was to be one of Winston Churchill's contributions to public thinking, part of what he called the *irresistible tides* that would sweep the British Empire forward to its glorious future. He would reiterate this theme later, in 1944, when the 'Butler' Education Bill was in draft, at the end of the Second World War, leading to Mill Hill's 'Middlesex Scheme' (see Ch.VIII).

Design for McClure
'Memorial Music School',
to marry with Script No.3,
and (r.) Library: note tree
on Quad.*5.l*

There is no questioning the patriotism, and the striving after a new kind of 'colours', of this generation of Millhillians, by far outweighing the priorities of education. Of a School in 1915 (now including 32 Belmontians in the totals, with any concern about the magical 'Gladstonian' mark of 200 way in the past), practically everyone was in the Corps – some 257 out of 289; this included at Belmont an astonishing 30 probationary cadets from the young 11- to 13-year-olds five minutes' marching away. By 1917, there were 10 hours of military service a week for all boys over seventeen. The two hours taken from prep time each week enabled three sessions of drill, trench work, and physical exercises, three lectures, and – a gruesome foretaste for those young men – one period of bayonet practice. Monday 'halves' were given over to field work for two to three hours; there was a weekly route march of up to five miles, carrying arms and packs. Under the supervision of its OC, Capt James himself, there were joint field exercises with other schools – UCS, Aldenham, Highgate, St Paul's – and annual camps at Henley and elsewhere. 'Bulling' boots, and polishing 'brasses' by fags for fagmasters, and for themselves, and the blancoing of 'webbing'– a dreaded feature of the post-1945 world, was even more in evidence as the war ground wearily onwards. Shooting had become by now one of the most popular sports; high spot of Foundation Day was undoubtedly not the speeches, but the annual Corps Inspections on Top Field, and the distribution of prizes, not those for academic work, but for the military competitions. There was no school orchestra yet, but there were, audibly to all within painful earshot, bugle and drum sections; the band would accompany batches of recruits from the Village, marching from the Hartley Memorial Hall to enlist at the Middlesex Regiment's barracks (renamed 'Inglis' in 1930) on Bittacy Hill.

Unlike her banished reincarnation during the Second World War, this Mill Hill felt close to the front line, somewhat like a rear echelon. Flanders guns could be heard on Top Terrace; a piece of the airship shot down at Cuffley was given to McClure for "The Bug" (the Natural History Museum); a "dogfight" was seen overhead. Their experience was immediate, sensory, almost tactile. Young men in uniform, sporting moustaches and suddenly looking years older, would come back on leave. In the trenches, the *Magazine* would be gratefully commented on. Twice-termly lists of the dead, wounded or missing, decorated, 'POWs', and 'Mentions' would appear, with ever-growing totals of men serving. One monitor went out to his unit, to find his former Mill Hill master, Lt Gemmell, now a junior officer, reporting to him. Parcels were sent under McClure's direction to the Belgian refugees; funds were raised for Serbian relief. Two refugee boys were taken in from besieged Antwerp in 1915; ten Belgians were accepted as Day Boys 'free of all charges'. The Debating Society constantly focused on the war, including the lateness of Britain's allies, the Americans, in arriving. Unmilitaristic ethos or no, this was a school at war.

The way it was

The regime of that lost world was highly regimented and over-stratified; Eric Dangerfield recalled that *all the monitors had 'swaggers'* (see Appendix E) *in their studies and permission to use them.* Fagging was in full swing: *at the age of 13 I still had in mind the senior position I had held in my Prep School but this was very soon forgotten when I was shouted at by some 'man' of about 16 or 17 and told either to collect his rugger boots from the 'Boot-Hole' in the basement, or to put his very dirty boots in his locker, having first cleaned off all the mud. It was an excellent levelling lesson for me...* As just tolerated Day Boys, wriggling inside stiff white collars, wearing, by order, the brown velvet School cap, 'Tennet, D.', like 'Dangerfield, E.', escaped some of the rigours of the monitorial system, but Boarders in the School proper felt its full force. Although undocumented, there were now three 'Out-Houses' – Burton Bank, Collinson, and Ridgeway, there being no House Notes at all in the *MHM* until 1922. Bill Crebbin conjured up the hierarchy of the School House corridor at this time, not very different from that still prevailing after the Second World War. *Leading from the classroom building, down the LH side were 3 common rooms for the junior boys – the first and lowest was the 'Art Room';* (Tom Wardill wrote in 1987: *position in the pecking order was determined by physical combat). Down the right hand side were studies, the first was the Senior Monitors', then Monitors, followed by Prefects and then senior boys... we passed for roll call en route for the dining hall under the portico. Beyond this was the Headmaster's study and at the far end of the Hall was a door leading to the domestic quarters... presided over by Miss Pearse, the Lady Resident.*

Most had to suffer the initial indignities of new-boy indoctrination, singing songs in the Art Room, while objects were shied at them; although taught "Willow Tit Willow" by his experienced father, Inglis Gundry escaped because as a Scholar, he

Combined School Houses by Portico, with Dr Way, (Acting HM during Sir John McClure's 6-month sick leave) and 104 boys: note 1st and 2nd colour ties, wide Eton collars for 1st-Year 'fags', waistcoats, two bow ties. *5.m*

went straight into Common Room 4. New boys also had to 'run the gauntlet', in "Tom Brown" and "Flashman" fashion, down the length of School House Corridor. This further piece of undoubted sadism was to last until one day in the late '20s under McClure's successor, M.L.Jacks; the eye of another elderly witness for the History was badly damaged in one such furious series of mass assaults on his fleeing person, and one more outdated tradition was at last stopped. McClure, Elliott, James, and their fellow-Masters must have known of these and other savage practices, but Nelsonian eyes were conveniently, and negligently, closed. For Wardill, *the Head was an object of fear, which of course could not be admitted... he made no attempt at motivating the lower forms of life.* Such aspects of the 'golden' years serve as a necessary antidote to the rosy view that all was well in that lost McClurian world.

Journalist Ivor Nicholson summed up the day: *The bell for getting up rings at 6.30 a.m. in the summer, 7.15 in the winter... After prep come prayers and breakfast [in the Houses, served by servants]. From 8.45 until 9.5 there is chapel, and then "Assembly" in the big school-room ["Stop Talking!"] ... School begins directly afterwards and finishes at 12.50 [no Tuck Shop food at Break] ... After dinner comes school (at 2.30 p.m.) followed by cricket/football, followed by school (at 3.40). After tea... prep, after prep, prayers.* The long gap until 'tea' at 6 p.m. was filled with buns, cakes, fruit and "Meltis" at Mr & Mrs 'Krug's', the Tuck Shop, which was then next to the new Winterstoke Library, on the 'Parade ground', the militaristic name by which the former play-ground was now known. There was that by now familiar complaint about the litter of orange peel all over the grounds, resulting from this vital additional sustenance, yet there was no thought at first by the much-maligned school 'authorities' of providing litter bins. Nicholson described the day's end: *All Lower School boys then go to bed, while those in the Middle and Upper school may obtain permission... to stay up till 9.45 to work.*

In war, there were of course privations, including the scarcity of marmalade, but just as 25 years later the hardships of St Bees were endurable because a greater overriding necessity was visible to one and all, so now, in the correspondence columns of the *Magazine*, the phrase, *There is, after all, a war on* could justify and offset all manner of unpleasantness. There were enthusiastic economy drives, with some extravagant suggestions coming forward: one was firmly resisted – the closing of the School Magazine. Games went on much as usual, although scarcely ever reported by the Head to the Governors – the only change being the introduction of more military opponents, such as the nearby Middlesex Regimental Barracks.

Mill Hill's 'warlike paradox'

As the war gripped everyday life, properly partisan articles and poems against 'the Hun' appeared more and more regularly, with only occasionally an attempt to see the war in broader historic terms. A frightful German, 'Herr Gumboilbusch', was invented in the pages of the *MHM*. "Thanks to William" became a common phrase to account for the supposed effect of Kaiser Wilhelm on practically every aspect of life: a very different connotation, compared with the constitutional implications of 'William' for Samuel Favell, John Pye Smith and their fellow-founders.

What were called 'Zeppelin Nights' were the greatest thrill of the week, when enemy airships would throb overhead, despite the efforts of the sole anti-aircraft gun sited in the village, and probably regardless of the blackout strips which were painted or stuck to the windows of the Chapel, and over the sky-lights of the Octagon. Once bombs were dropped nearby, although never in this war on the School itself; Dudley Tennet watched with great excitement as an airship burst into flames and crashed over by 'Holy Joe's' in the Mill Field, opposite Belmont. Most boys went straight from Mill Hill into the forces; some, like Dudley, found themselves in protected work, in his case in a local engineering firm, making tools for the war effort, although they took regular part in military training. The cumulative effect of the war on Sir John and his academic staff was onerous and heartbreaking. The historian Andrew Roberts records a telling contrast: more British troops fell in the first 31 minutes of the Somme offensive than in the entire 31 months of that earlier war with the Boers. From the photographed groups of monitors and teams in the years through to 1917, all too many would reappear as individuals among the 194 War Dead, or as names in the ever-lengthening lists of wounded, in the increasingly heavy issues of the *MHM*. The full toll would, of course, only be revealed when the fighting finally ended, and the data was gathered in, and eventually inscribed, in 1920, on the Chapel Roll and the newly-built Gate of Honour. This was the prime commitment of the War Memorial Fund, initiated by the Head Master, the Court, and the OMC.

How militaristic was Mill Hill then? Colonel General Hellmuth Graf von Moltke was the nephew of another more famous von Moltke, the chief architect of the increasingly feared Prussian military threat to European security from the 1890s onwards; he was the first of Kaiser Wilhelm's Chiefs of the German General Staff. When asked what he thought of the *Engländer*, the word the Germans always used to describe the British – and Imperial – Expeditionary Force: were they a military nation? Von Moltke replied: *No, but very warlike*. A similar distinction was made in relation to Mill Hill by one of her small band of latter-day professional servicemen, Lt Col Maxwell Macfarlane: *Mill Hill has never had any reputation for producing military giants yet, when it came to the crunch in two World Wars, I do not think that anyone could say*

Established era of colours and teams photographs:
(i) (l.) only picture of ill-fated 1914 1st XI Hockey: sole unscathed member was C.S.Anton;
(ii) snowbound 1917 1st XV. Note fully-evolved 'athletic millinery' for both sports – blazer, scarf, socks – and rugby caps. 5.n

HOCKEY, 1914.

I. M. CAMPBELL.   K. V. HOOPER.   W. M. JAMES.

I. E. OWEN.   L. WHITTOME.   W. M. WILLIAMS (CAPT.)   C. S. ANTON.   R. THEOBALD.
H. TURNER.   J. W. H. TRENCHARD.

MILL HILL SCHOOL 1ST XV. FOOTBALL, 1917.

C. P. M. WRIGHT.   L. W. BUTCHER.   J. G. ANTON.   H. S. SLY.   J. A. EDWARDS.   D. TENNET.   I. K. FURLONG.

W. C. RAMSAY.   K. McLENNAN.   R. H. DUMMETT (CAPT.).   E. S. BURNS.   A. S. BUCKLEY.
V. OWEN-JONES.   W. D. GIBBS.   J. F. MORRIS.

that the contribution by OMs was lacking in any way. Brett James wrote, in the first of Mill Hill's two – and hopefully final – *Books of Remembrance*, which was not published until 1920: *Mill Hill has never been a military school, and the ... foundation, perhaps, discouraged pupils in peace time from entering the Army.* Great meaning lies in the effect of the blast of war on an otherwise peaceful people: this 'warlike paradox' was to be revealed, as the History will reveal it, in all the four major 20th-century wars that Britain – and Millhillians – engaged in, as well as in the dozen or so localised conflicts, or wars by another name, that ensued during the Cold War period from 1948 onwards. (There was also some truth in that distinction as far as the immediately preceding Boer Wars in South Africa were concerned).

The roots of the Briton's preparedness to fight tenaciously for what he believed in, but only ultimately when he had to, lay far back across the centuries, with names like Agincourt, Crécy, Blenheim and Waterloo to commemorate it in the folklore. Many other place-names with special overtones for Millhillians were to be added to that list by the dawn of this 21st century, including Northern Ireland and the Falklands campaign.

The grim numbers

The statistics offer some measure of the 'warlike' disposition of Mill Hill's sons, translated from the capacity of countless generations to be *in the scrum*, as Reginald Pound puts it in his haunting tribute *The Lost Generation*. The First World War was in fact Britain's Second 'Great War'; the phrase was coined to describe the first major national struggle to occur within Mill Hill's existence, the Napoleonic Wars of the early 19th century, which coincided with Mill Hill's foundation. The time-span for the effects of this battle against the combined forces of Germany, Austro-Hungary, Turkey and Bulgaria, runs from the four years of what Harold Nicolson called *trench deadlock*, 1914-1918 through to 1920: a few battles and many wounds and disabilities lasted beyond the official end of hostilities at the November 1918 Armistice. During these six years, at least 1101 *OMs*, men and officers, were involved in the war, most on active service. Among those who died, the vast majority, over 80 per cent, were volunteers, a few, c.6 per cent, were Reserve men or 'Terriers' – Territorials, peacetime officers – and a handful were career regulars from R.M.C. Sandhurst; the remainder were conscripts, drawn in by Asquith's two Military Service Acts of 1916.

This force amounted to some 55 per cent of the total intake of well over 2,000 boys entering the School between 1877 and 1914: 1877 is perhaps the extreme edge, since that was the entry date of the oldest of Mill Hill's sons to die as the result of the war. This, at the advanced age of 56, was the intrepid explorer, and holder of the *Légion d'honneur* and the *Croix de Guerre*, that most original of Dr Weymouth's boys, Herbert Ward. If the only slightly less extreme comparison date of 1883 is taken, the entry-year of William Sommerville of Nairobi, who was also the first *OM* to fall in the war on 25 September 1914, the figure increases to 59 per cent. Perhaps the most startling comparison, however, is to consider those boys who entered at age 13 from 1896 onwards, within McClure's own time, and memory: the figure then suddenly reaches no less than 83 per cent. *Nobis* rightly details many individual stories: the youngest to die, at the age of 18, was Lt Noel Bishop on 16 September 1918. The last death in the field before the 6 November Armistice was that of 19-year-old Guards Officer Lt Geoffrey Lamont (of the Lamont Shield); *OM* Leslie Millard told Gowen Bewsher that Lamont was at once awarded the DSO, although he had been formally recommended for the VC.

The Official War Record also lists 16 members of staff; they included one who died as a result of active service in France, Prof Edward Milner-Barry, a committed *Germanist*, one of McClure's first appointments in 1891, a former Housemaster of School House, and the first Housemaster of Collinson, until he moved on in 1907 to take up a University seat at Bangor. One master was wounded, Lt G.A.Riding. Nine others served in France or the Gallipoli affair: Capt R.W.Harre, Lt K.T.Gemmell MC, 2Lt C.J.Jones, Lt Col Lee Harrison, R.M.Rayner, Cpl S.C.Rowland, RT Officer W.E.Weber and Pte G.M.R.Willis. The ninth, Maj F.R.H.McLellan, was to continue to serve Mill Hill as Modern Languages master throughout the St Bees time, and briefly on the return from exile in 1945. Four other Mill Hill masters are included in the Record by James as Officers in the MHS OTC: James himself finally as a Major, Lt W.H.Brown, 2Lt L.A.Cane, and 2Lt Victor Elliott. Lt A.J.Rooker Roberts is also included, as an officer in the OTC, although he was not, unlike the others, on the so-called 'unattached T.F. list'. The total of 'deaths due to active service' (= the 'K.i.a.'s) is 194:

Roll of Honour	OM deaths 193*	Estimate of
(as evidenced by biographies):	Master 1*)	all serving:
(Book total):	OMs serving 909)	1118
	Masters: full-time service 10)	
	OTC Officers, MHS 5)	

The three rugby caps of Dudley Tennet, sole achiever of all awards in single season, from 3rd XV, through 2nd XV to 1st XV, as elders left for war: WWI. Now forms part of Headmaster's history induction talk for new pupils. *5.0*

No less than 17 per cent of the 1,118 suffered death as a result of the war, 'paying the supreme sacrifice', in the language preferred in both wars. It is matter of note that the lists of names in the Book total 190; this is also the total on the Roll of Honour in the Chapel lectern dedicated to Capt A.F.Todd, one of *Mitchell's Famous Footballers*, who was to be further commemorated in 1998 through the School's first Sports Bursary. The Book's biographies – boys and one master – total 191, although the Introduction to the Record talks of 192 deaths; originally the Gate of Honour (inaugurated in 1920) recorded 193 deaths for the First World War. Excluded from its scheme of refurbishment in 2001 was the *OM* exporter Evan Leigh, who drowned when the *Lusitania* was torpedoed by a U-Boat on 7 May 1915: the overall total of 'deaths due to war' is thus 195.

The analyses of Public Schools and their role in this Second Great War do not usually highlight Mill Hill amongst the stories of the bravery of that 'Lost Generation'. Other schools that Mill Hill has competed with feature more frequently and more expectedly, or more grievously, such as the larger Day schools – Bedford at 21 per cent, and Dulwich with 515 deaths, or military Cheltenham with 690 deaths. The comparable figure of war dead, by way of example, for Eton – 1,157, out of a total of 5,650 men serving, was 20 per cent. A few other relevant comparisons among Nonconformist schools include: Taunton, with over 300 boys, where some 165 were killed out of 1,004 serving (16 per cent); Bishop's Stortford, where only 55 were killed out of only 600 serving (9 per cent), in a school just below the 300 level. In two smaller schools, Tettenhall and Eltham each lost 24 out of serving totals of 200 and 120 respectively.

In terms of impact on the School, the peak year for this slaughter was 1917, with some 56 deaths, one for every week in the year, and more than one for every Sunday Chapel service, with the preceding year, 1916, the second worst, and the last year of the war, 1918, third in the tally of deaths. No History can do justice to the poignancy of those 193 *OM* 'K.i.a.'s; indeed there could be some among the new generations of pupils, despite the participation of both sexes in the CCF well into the 21st century, who might not think that at this distance of time it should even try. Yet war in Europe has been a feature of the present world of Millhillians and Millhilliennes, most unforgettably in the conflicts in the former Yugoslavia and the Gulf: a hushed Mill Hill Assembly of the 1980s listened with renewed respect as Peter McDonough (then Belmont history master and future MHS Registrar) showed the *Nobis* photograph of the 1914 Hockey XI, of whom seven were to die, with three wounded, and only one surviving, A/Capt Charles Anton MC (and a 'Mention'). The 1913 1st XV, and the Gym VIII of 1908 revealed a similar toll; one member was E.Hinrichs, one of three brothers retained in the Register, despite Germanophobia. The History has to pay its tribute in its own way, whilst respecting the proper desire of every new generation to live for the future: unmindful of a similar saying of Nietzsche's, Sir John McClure himself suggested the right balance – *we should be thinking backwards, but living forwards.*

An honourable record

The *MHM*s from the 1880s onwards, with the hindsight of that War Record, still make grim reading. So much youthful achievement, often brilliance, in sport and in the academic field, at the 'GC' and for many thereafter at 'the Varsity' – all this was to be snuffed out. Whether it could in any sense be said to be wasted in what *Nobis* called a *monumental stupidity*, in the light of subsequent events, is a deeper debate than a School History should engage in. Perhaps the only relevant point has to be that many of those young, and not-so-young men, judging by their letters and statements, did not seem to think so.

Mill Hill's *Book of Remembrance* marks the villages, hillsides, woods and rivers of Northern France and Belgian Flanders, a recital of even some of whose names by itself conjures up a war which, 90 years on, forms a study for historians and for the School's own current 'PHSE' Programme. Notwithstanding its terrible successor-war of 1939-45, the First World War still presents a never-ceasing focus for television writers, for example, "The Unknown Soldier" of 1998: names like Ypres and Hill 60, Armentières, Arras, Bapaume, Beaumont Hamel, Cambrai, Le Câteau, Loos, Messines, Passchendaele, Thiepval, Vimy Ridge, and that fearsome umbrella-word for all those mutual killing-fields, the Somme, and its tributary, the Ancre (see

Chs.VI, XI). Every night at 8 p.m. the buglers ring out "The Last Post" in the one place that prevents those deaths from fading into oblivion, the world's first Gate of Honour, the Menin Gate at Ypres. No such daily reminder recalls the areas of the high seas where *OMs* also served and died: The Atlantic Convoy, the Irish Sea, China, the Black Sea, Scapa Flow, the Mediterranean and the Dover Patrol.

At least there is, in the RAF Chapel in the Strand, an ongoing remembrance of those first of the future 'Few', who chose the Royal Flying Corps or the Royal Naval Air Service (to become the RAF), or were attached to it. Through the fascinatingly exciting noise of the annual pageants at Hendon, 'the Aerial Ascot', some 120 Millhillians joined the new service, including two Haslemere *OMs* (see Appendix D): Lt Taunton Viney DSO, featured in *War Illustrated* in 1916 as one of 'The 100 Heroes of the War', for sinking a U-Boat singlehanded; and RFC Capt. Cyril ("Billy") Marconi Crowe MC, DFC, destroyer of 15 enemy planes. For many years, there hung in the classroom Block, funded by Herbert Marnham, a famous portrait of another pilot, Flt Sub-Lt Frederick Stafford RFC (SR). It was painted by his uncle, Frank Salisbury, RA, and exhibited at the 1917 Exhibition. (Through the efforts of the author and Peter McDonough, it was traced via its original loan to the RAF Museum, Hendon, to the Officers Mess at RAF Ouseley; a colour copy was obtained by the School in 2005.) The Mill Hill Roll of Honour also includes 21 deaths from four other battle areas of that war: Austrian Italy; Palestine, Syria and Arabia; as well as the Dardanelles and Gallipoli, where Harry Bishop, as Lt-Col, The Lancashire Fusiliers, would be part of the first unit to land in 1915, aged 47, winning a Mention in Dispatches. Involved too was the area of Mesopotamia (now Iraq), oil creating then as later, not least in Britain's first 21st-century war – the Iraq War in the same territory – a critical strategic theatre. The Roll lists one other strand of Mill Hill commitment which has characterised the School from early on: the medical world. Five *OM* doctors died, invariably tending their patients in hastily improvised conditions, and at extreme risk to their own lives: there are many such stories among the hundreds who survived the war.

There was no award either for one of the Erlesmere boys (see Appendix D), Lt Robert Kingsley Steel, 5th Bn Northumberland Fusiliers, who joined up on 5 August, the day after war was declared. His family produced a moving printed tribute to a son *killed whilst trying to rescue one of his men, who was gassed and wounded, near Ypres, 24 May 1915. I have earned the name 'Cucumber' from some of my men – (fellow 'lads' from the NE) –* wrote 'King' Steel

"Mussons", then the MHS shop, "The Grove", The Ridgeway: (purchased 1908). Note post-box, grass verge (r.), gas lighting, horse and cart: MHS Schoolhouse (extreme r.). 5.*p*

1097. The Grove, Mill Hill.

to his parents. According to the *War Record* that body of 193 *OMs* fallen, taken together with the larger group of 909 – all those who served full-time – accounted for some 191 awards for valour or distinguished service: 107 MCs, and eight bars to MCs; 21 DSOs, two with bar; 13 Military OBEs; 10 *Croix de Guerres* – French or Belgian, one with palm; nine DFCs, two AFCs; six MBEs, two KBEs; two CMGs; two TDs, and one class-distinguished MM for an NCO. In addition there were awards for outstanding conduct from some unusual donors: three *Légions d'honneur*, an Order of St Sava, and a *Croix de St Anne*; from the allied Italians an *Assiego* medal, a Red Cross Medal, a Silver Medal *della Saluta publica*, and a *Croce al Merito de Guerra*; from the Belgians a Chevalier of the Order of the Crown of Belgium, and four 1915 Egyptian Orders of the Nile.

There were at least 272 reports of wounds – one man received five separate woundings – as well as gassing and 'invalided out' cases; there were in all 173 'Mentions in Despatches', the next step to an actual award, one officer being 'mentioned' in seven different encounters. There was at least one recommendation for a DSO, which in the often arbitrary lottery of these matters did not quite make it to a citation. Surprisingly, despite this shattering and humbling mixture of bravery and concern for their fellow human beings under fire by those several distant generations of Millhillians, often, as the citations bear out, of the most reckless and self-disregarding kind, there was no VC. Apart from Lt Lamont, one of the nearest Mill Hill appeared to come to that honour was Lt Robert Lloyd, former Senior monitor and member of most of the school teams – as were many but by no means all those young heroes – and an Entrance Scholar to a then St Peter's College, Cambridge. He was described in a letter from a fellow-officer in an action on the final Ypres salient in April 1918. This tribute is typical of the hundreds of comments quoted in the Record from Official Reports, Commanding Officers, and Platoon Officers. Although, characteristically, again no award was made, it must stand, within the confines of these pages, to represent all those other sentiments and judgments: *His magnificent courage in leading his men in the charge after being wounded was fully worthy of the VC.*

The McClures share the sorrow

Whether these deaths were near or far, there was one man who unfailingly wrote to every mourning parent, and who deeply grieved at the loss of each of 'his' boys: McClure himself. It is believed of him, just as it was to be believed of another Mill Hill Head 30 years later, whom McClure had taught and influenced, Rooker Roberts, that his own death was precipitated by the presence of death amongst his charges. Many Mill Hill families, including some that bore witness for the author during his researches around the country, still retain in their treasured family possessions the letter that he wrote to a mother, father, guardian, brother or sister at the death of yet another *OM*. *McClure of Mill Hill* reproduced some of these.

The Battys, latterly living near Bristol, were typical of those families. Charles Batty, born in 1896, was a member of one of the large and loyal Mill Hill-oriented clans of that era, who would in due course be able to count six *OMs* among their number. From McClure's School House he became a Classical Scholar of University

College, Oxford. He was commissioned, after the OU OTC, into the 19th Durham Light Infantry, the DLI, as a lieutenant. After service in Flanders, he was killed, on 19 January 1916, at Ypres, one of more than a third – (15) – to die, from his entry of 43 in April 1909. The Head's letter, written only five days later, 24 January, reveals the strength of the feelings that he had to experience and express afresh so many times: *Words are powerless in the face of such a sorrow; but many tears were shed this morning when the sad news came... I thank God humbly and heartily that it was my privilege to teach and train such boys and I pray that I may be made more worthy of such pupils... May God give to you his parents and all his dear ones the consolation of His grace!* There were many other names that would resonate for Mill Hill beyond McClure's time and the next war: Pye-Smith, Lord, Viney, Pigott, Lapthorn, Sargood, Macfarlane, Compston, Hawes, Hubbard, Boardman, Farrow, Spicer, Stafford, Meggitt, Lackie, Elles-Hill. There would be two rooms in the Science Block for Lt Hugh Marnham and Lt Henry Brice; the Pusch Shield; and many scholarships.

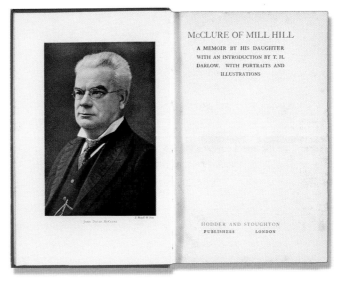

McCLURE OF MILL HILL

A MEMOIR BY HIS DAUGHTER
WITH AN INTRODUCTION BY T. H.
DARLOW. WITH PORTRAITS AND
ILLUSTRATIONS

HODDER AND STOUGHTON
PUBLISHERS   LONDON

JOHN DAVID McCLURE

Retrospective:
Sir John McClure, Head
Master MHS, 1891-1922:
biography flyleaf,
McClure of Mill Hill.
5.q

One other person to be commemorated beside Sir John is his wife. If anyone can be said to have established a yardstick by which the role of all later First Ladies of the School might be judged, it would be Lady McClure. She quietly backed her husband in everything – publicly, and privately, in peace and war, in sickness and in health – at the School, and Belmont. A typical gesture was to meet and congratulate the young John Wright on his Choral Clerkship to Sir John's old College, Trinity, in 1939, nine years before her death at 88, in 1948. Uniquely, she was given an annuity, and possession of the Briggs-designed "Vineries" on Milespit Hill, purchased by Ernest Figgis of Highwood House, for her lifetime. The School and the OMC were able to express through her their indebtedness for the work wrought by her consort, one of Mill Hill's five greatest Head Masters, who had guided the School into the 20th century. Her ashes lie with his, under the McClure window.

Sir John also carried some disappointments with him. As was said at the OMC Dinner of 1912: a Head *often has to be content to be misjudged and mis-read.* Even if true for many *OMs* of that time, he must have found too simplistic and complacent the sentiment offered in the School's first History: *what really gauges a school's success is the affection which is borne to it by the rank and file of former pupils.* For him *the best praise is that which one's soul whispers to one's intellect, not that which the world shouts in one's ear.* By the time of the 1918 Armistice, when an airborne leaflet proclaiming it fell onto the grounds, to new boys like Roland Wade, *McClure seemed a rather remote figure... there was a clear reluctance to go inside for normal classes: I would not put it as far as a strike.* Edward Higham wrote: *The whole school went literally mad*; there were processions round the village, everyone equipped with anything that would make a noise. Inglis Gundry recalled seeing McClure *with his white hair billowing in the wind*, personally ringing the school bell (then on the wall by the Loggia); John Wright believed that he had said *We must not rejoice*. This seemed to frighten the school into submission – they had called for a half-holiday – and all came in quietly. Later, boys' anger was vented by ditching a spoil of war, a German field gun, in the Sheepdip.

The most symbolic event identifying McClure with Mill Hill – top priority in the War Memorial Fund –– was the building of the Gate of Honour, opened by Gen Horne in 1920. Its site, fronting the main entrance, was where the great elms had stood until the 1917 storms made them unsafe. Wade wrote: *I watched it from one of the School House common rooms. When the names had been carved men came and painted gold leaf into the letters. When it was windy we often saw bits of gold leaf* [the 'skewings'] *being blown away and after five years of wartime austerity plus my north-country thriftiness I was horrified to see such waste.* Much else had been blown away by the war. In two short years, Sir John's own life was also to be borne off; in the sentiments of the Memorial Service of 22 February 1922, he 'crossed the bar', but his contribution to Mill Hill's future would be visible to all. A later, correct but surprising letter from Dickie Buckland, warned that a Head's *capitation contract* did not make him *a partner with the Governors in conducting the School*, yet partner Sir John surely was. At that same OMC Dinner, answering the unasked question as to why he had written no books about his time, he had said simply: *My writings are happily more lasting and they are round about me.*

Sources for Ch.V include: # Record Bk 1902-24, incl ltr, 28.iv.1923, Buckland to Regan at 27 Tothill St ref capitation; MHS Genl Analysis of A/Cs 1911-22; Prospectuses 1899-1903; Boys' Ldgr 1903-5; MHS Fees Ldgr 1895-04; Ousey, *op cit*; CH Inventory 1915; Archv, A.Eason [1901-5] (incl. *The Captain*, v.XXII, 21, 161-5) kind permssn of his dtr, Mrs I.Penny; Diaries of J.Brierley [1908-13] kind permssn of his family; reminiscences of T.J.Wright [1934-9]; H.C.Carter [1889-94] (father-in-law of Dr J.S.Whale, see Ch.VIII), score by L.A.Cane (see Ch.VI), "Hurrah for the Worth of Mill Hill!" (libretto in BJI); Oak, (*op cit*).

Background: A.J.P.Taylor, *English History 1914-1945* (Oxfd. 1965) (ref lst Military Service Act, Jan 1916); C.Binfield, *op cit* (for dating of 'Nonconformity'); E.Hobsbawm, *Age of Extremes, The Short 20th Century 1914-1991* (1994); D.Judd, *Empire* (Harper Collins, 1996); J.Rae, *Delusions of Grandeur* (Harper Collins, 1993); de S.Honey, *op cit*; K.Robbins, *Protestant Evangelicanism... c.1750-l950*, (0xfd, 1990); C. Binfield, 'We Claim Our Part in the Great Inheritance'; J.Grigg, *Lloyd George...* (1978), 31.

MHS & war: M.Gilbert, *First World War* (Weidenfeld & Nicholson, 1994); Andrew Roberts, *op cit* 845; R.Pound, *Lost Generation* (1964); P.Gibbs, *Pageant of the Years* (1946); H.Nicholson, *King George V...* (1952), 259, 274; N.G.B.James, [1894-8] *Book of Remembrance & War Record of Mill Hill School 1914-1919*, (NB 134, & opp. 109), (1920); C.Binfield, *"Church History"*, v.20, (1977), 'The Church & War', for Ecclesiastical Hist. Soc., Ch: 'Et Virtutem Et Musas: Mill Hill School and the Great War'; J.T.Steel, *Robert Kingsley Steel* (pte circ, Newcastle, 1916), [1902-5]; D.E.Morris, [1933-9] *China Changed My Mind* (1948) & review in *John O'London's Weekly*, 6.viii.1948; Computer Research project on MHS Records of WWI dead, by Berinda Banks, HS/M McC House, July 1997.

SirJ.McClure: M.L.Jacks/McCurthoys, *D.N.B.* (Oxford U.Press, 2004); R.Braithwaite,

Biographical Dictionary... Significant Figures (20C) Br. Congregational Churches... (U.A.L. Hist. Soc., 2006). Sir J.McClure, 'Preparation for Practical life: *Cambridge Essays on Education* (Ed. A.C.Benson, 1917). *Times*, obit 3.ii.1922; B.Kingsley Martin [1914-6], *Father Figures* (1935); I.Gundry [1918-23], *The Last Boy of the Family* (1999); A.J.McGeoch [1916-8], *Evocations* (1985); recollections for G.Bewsher by R.W.Atchley [1902-8] and of R.Gilchrist [1918-23] to his son, R.M.R.Gilchrist [1950-3]; corr with W.L.Bundey [1923-7]; W.L.Crebbin [1921-4]; Mrs J.Roberts, dtr of E.T.Dangerfield [1920-4]; O.P.Griffin [1920-2]; family of J.N.Holder [1918-21]; family of G.B.Norton [1915-9]; family of D.Tennet [1913-7]; R.H.Wade [1918-25]; T.E.M.Wardill [1915-7]; T.J.Wright [1934-9]. C.Chaplin, *My Autobiography* (Bodley Head, 1964) 10-11: Chaplin's first Music Hall performance, 1894, in F.Eplett's 'Jack Jones' ballad – "Well, 'e don't know where 'e are"...Ref MHV Free Church links, see J.V.Wright [1936-40], 'The "Tin Tabernacle" and other MH Chapels and Churches', MHHS Newsletter, (2004). *Heritage Today*, Sept 2004 #. Archival 'Pathé News'' films of opening ceremony, Oct 1920 #.

HMC: special thanks to Sarah Steuart-Feilding, & Gordon Millar.

Campbell-Bannerman: J.B.Mackie, *Model Member: Sir Henry Campbell-Bannerman, 50 Years Representative of the Sterling Boroughs* (1914); C.Binfield, *A Congregational Formation: An Edwardian Prime Minister's Victorian Education* (1996); J.Wilson, *CB – Life, Sir Henry Campbell-Bannerman* (Constable, 1973).

MHS/ Belmont architecture: B.Champneys:-obit, *Times* 6.iv.1935; *Builder* 28.vi.1912, *DNB*; *Journal of RIBA* 1912, Nov 1924; *AJ* 22, 29.x.1924; *Architectural History*, v.27 (1984); *Builder*, 17.x.1924; *Country Life* 21.v.1981; Briggs *op cit*; A.S.Gray [1916-22], *Edwardian Architecture* (1985); A.E.Richardson, *Monumental Classical Architecture* (1914); C.Stell, *Architects of*

Dissent: Some Nonconformist Patrons & their Architects (1976).

Other *OM* references: W.R.D.Adkins [1875-80]; C.S.Anton [1910-4]; C.Autant-Lara [1914-5] (obit, *Independent*, 9.ii.2000; films included *Le Diable au Corps, Le Rouge et le Noir*); C.F.Batty [1909-14]; N.D.Ball [1909-14]; H.K.Bentley [1897-8, 1900-3]; J.G.Bewsher [1948-52]; H.O.Bishop [1880-3]; N.F.Bishop [1913-5]; J.W.Boardman [1909-13]; H.C.Brice [1907-12]; Britain bros. – F.E. [1916-20] & L.D. [1916-9]; R.W.B.Buckland [1878-84]; E.Foster Clark [1908-14]; J.M.Compston [1912-6]; E.H-Cook [1874-7]; C.Marconi Crowe [1907-11]; A.Davies [1861-3]; W.Elles-Hill [1905-8]; E.T.Farrow [1910-3]; J.C.L..Fox [1983-8]; E.W.Gundry [1879-82]; B.Hartley [1908-10]; N.B.Hartnell [1914-9]; A.W.Hawes [1907-9]; T.A.Herbert [1878-81]; E.Higham [1915-91]; E.Hinrichs (later Herrick) [1902-8]; R.E.Hubbard [1913-6]; A.E.Hutton [1878-84]; G.Kemp – Lord Rochdale [1877-81]; D.W.Lackie [1913-8]; J.N.Lamont [1907-13]; G.S.Lamont [1912-7]; A.R.Lapthorn [1904-7]; E.A.Leigh [1859-61]; R.A.Lloyd [1911-3]; R.Lord [1905-9]; Macfarlane family – W.A. [1910-5] - A.M [1944-8]; H.Marnham [1874-80]; A.Meggitt [1910-2]; "Nath." Micklem [1866/8, '70-1]; I.P.Nicholson [1904-9]; T.W.Pearson [1886-9]; C.D.Pigott [1907-9]; E.P.Powell [1871-9]; F.L.Pusch [1908-10]; T.E.B.Pye-Smith [1901-5]; W.C.Ramsay [1912-8]; D.Austin Reed [1916-20]; H.Robinson [1898-9]; S.,Robinson [1878-9]; A.J.Rooker Roberts [1893-1900]; A.E.R.Roberts [1921-6]; C.R.Sargood [1909-10]; E.M.Satow [1856-9]; P.Smith [1829-34?]; H.E.Snell [1898, 1904-6]. W.F.Sommerville [1883-8]; Spicer family – A. [1858-63] – M.A. [1897-9] – C.W. [1897] – R. [1900-4] – F.R. [1901-5] – G.E. [1905-9]; F.J.E.Stafford [1912-6]; D.Straker [1893-5]; A.F.Todd [1885-92]; Taunton E.Viney [1906-9]; T.D.Walker [1926-9]; H.F.Ward [1877]; A.Whipp [1899]; Wills family – F.O. [1897-9]; W.H. (Lord Winterstoke of Blagdon) [1842-7]; T.McK.Wood [1971-2], H.Wright [1898-1901].

October 1920: dedicatory opening ceremony, Gate of Honour, previously 'The Artistic Memorial':
no MHS qualms in blocking traffic! Note wing collars, trilby hats. The ceremony was filmed for 'Pathé News'.
In 2004, the Gate received a £5,000 grant from English Heritage. 5.r

Pre-1924 aerial view, MHS grounds; note unroofed Fives Courts,
and (bottom r.) a tree-enclosed "Carp Shop". *6.a*

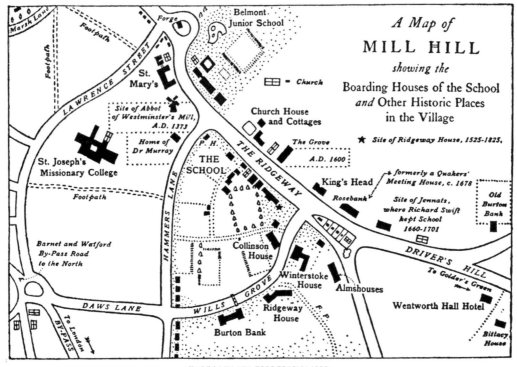

Fig.D(iv) MILL HILL TOPOGRAPHY 1930s

144

The Jacks Inheritance

Recovery, expansion, preparation

"Boys should hear what is going on round them …
to form their own opinions …"
Maurice Jacks to Court of Governors, 28 May 1935.

The year was 1922: the apparent high point of the British Empire. For the proving ground of that extraordinary Empire – the Public School 'empire' – the task facing it mirrored the challenge facing the country as a whole: to rediscover the momentum lost during the war just past, to build afresh in the ensuing fragile, febrile peace, and, ultimately, to come to terms with the fact that this longed-for peace was not going to last. In Maurice Jacks, the brilliant son of Dr L.P. Jacks, Principal of Manchester College, Oxford, Mill Hill's Governors chose, from a highly competitive field, a man whom many came to regard as the greatest of the School's Head Masters. Had co-education been on the agenda, his writings made clear that he would have been its first protagonist: his portrait rightly dominates the Visitors Room. For a later Governor, Rev. Paul Clifford, he was 'something of an enigma'; others, like the guest of honour on Foundation Day, 1987, John Garnett, revered enthusiastically, in his father's words, *the wonders of Maurice Jacks*. Such wonders as they were had both an inheritance and a 'shadow'.

The territorial aspect of the forward shadow cast by Jacks is shown in **Fig.D(iv)**; (for the 'shadow' concept see Ch.VIII). The period from 1922 onwards could as well be entitled "The McClure Heritage"; no one could ignore the effect of Sir John's reign on that of his successor, previously Dean and Classics Tutor of Wadham College, Oxford – 28 on 4 January that year, youngest Public School Head of his day. If McClure was Mill Hill's 'Maker', it was to be Jacks' role to be the 'Moderniser', and to re-equip her boys to deal with a very different, ever more threatening world. One of McClure's gifts had been that priceless asset for any Head Master, an abiding interest in, and insight into, all his boys, from the academic, to the less intellectually-endowed, as they moved up through the School. Kathleen Ousey's book about her father is full of the records of the gratitude that such interventions in the careers of 'his' boys generated. So, for example, he had advised Ernest Grear, a boy hostelling in Erlesmere (see Appendix D), not to accept the first Exhibition he was awarded, at Magdalene, Cambridge, in March 1909, because he felt that the boy was then too young to make full use of the University: true to prediction, Grear won a second Exhibition at St John's the following January and progressed, via war service in France and Italy, to a successful schoolmastering career. Sheer longevity made Sir John's a very hard act to follow: this personal bonding with his boys made "The Dean's" task even harder.

Goals to aim at

Spiritually, there was common ground; the historic Free Church background held firm. One of their greatest mutual continuities from the School's Dissenting and indeed Enlightenment origins, as Jacks would later explain to an OMC Dinner in

1934, was a *belief in freedom of thought*. Yet 1922 was a turning point. Kenneth Childs recalled: *there was a good deal of insecurity after Sir John*; out of some adverse trends, there were new goals to aim at. Grear's successes were part of the best season for awards then achieved; this was also, sadly, one of the high points of McClure's 31 years: a Classics Scholarship at Hertford, Oxford, in December 1909, another at Cambridge in 1910; two Maths Exhibitions to Clare and Sidney Sussex; and two more History Exhibitions at Jesus.

Surprisingly, awards had continued to be won during the war, including a mini-peak in 1916, firstly with Classics awards at two of the same Colleges, Clare and Hertford; a next step in Kingsley Martin's brilliant career, his Exhibition in Modern History at Magdalene, Cambridge; and an unusual Scholarship at City & Guilds Institute, London. Overall, however, the war took its toll academically as in other spheres. Over McClure's last 14 years, 43 awards were recorded at Universities, seen at that time as a modest average of three a year, against a combined Senior/ Junior Roll rising from 79 in 1893, through 259 in 1909, to a total of 282 and an ever-rising Belmont roll of 83 by 1922. Of the faculties, History had topped the list at 14 awards, with Classics now second at 10, followed by the other erstwhile major 'Public School' subject, Maths, at seven; Modern Languages, especially German, was coming into contention at six awards, despite having no official Head of Department, whilst Science still trailed, at a mere two. A more relevant yardstick by which to identify the baseline for Jacks as educationist might well have been to compare awards with the still modest VI Form numbers, but the data are not available.

By modern standards unthinkable numbers below the VI Form but still within the Upper School, or even in the 'Shell' – for those failing 'School Cert' (SC) at 16 – could gain places at Oxbridge, as favoured Public Schoolboys, not always with even the minimum of five SC 'credits': the *MHM* records many who found this easy route over the 31 years. Noltingk's *Dissenting Conformist* tells of *the disproportionate numbers from the Shell... in school teams and indeed in the aristocracy of the monitors*. Three boys even got into Cambridge from the 'Upper' Remove. At levels below this, too, prowess had not been overwhelming, nor was it in English Schools as a whole. The 14-year period 1909-22 may be taken as a reasonably balanced period for comparison, embracing five wholly peacetime years, five years directly affected by war, 1914-18, and four post-war years; (results are not available for 1913/4). Taking averages, only nine boys were allowed to enter for Higher Certificate (HC); of those only six passed, with three distinctions a year; in 1909 Mill Hill's pass at 77 per cent exceeded the country's as a whole (53 per cent). By 1922, when MLJ first reported the figures to the Governors, the School, at 53 per cent, had fallen below even the country's low of 66 per cent.

At SC level, the picture was much the same – an average entry of 21.5 boys, with only 15 passing, and a similar pattern of country-wide comparison. Sir John had not hidden the facts from the Court: on 26 June 1918 he warned the Governors that *the standard of work... has deteriorated, is deteriorating, and ought not to suffer further lowering*. He added forlornly: *Under present circumstances, I do not see how to prevent it*. Sociological factors were at work, too, with many ex-Public School fathers believing that school was basically there for boys to enjoy themselves, and play games, before getting down to the serious work of real life: as Sir Rennell Rodd complained to the School in 1921: *It does not entail any social disadvantage to leave school with a nebulous brain.* Sir John had even resorted to 'superannuation' – asking parents to remove their sons, if they were not up to scratch. With great quantitative pressure on places he could afford to, although Mill Hill's increase in Roll numbers, fair in itself, had not been as good as other schools', for example that other comparable erstwhile Dissenters Grammar School, Bishop's Stortford College, where numbers rose from 135 in 1910 to 279 in 1919. McClure's great achievements in so many fields should not conceal this Parthian posthumous shot to his successor on the numerical and scholastic fronts, notwithstanding his esteem in the eyes of *OMs*, of which the further £4,000 raised for the McClure Scholarships and Music Prizes is one more example.

Recovering scholastic respectability

Jacks had *gifts of leadership quite out of the common.* Peter Calderara summed up this transition period: *Jacks worked a kind of miracle after Sir John.* The new Head wrote to George Timpson: *My job was to be accessible to everybody.* It took him a decade to raise standards to a level fit for what he claimed at the 1931 OMC Dinner to be the *ninth oldest public school in the country.* (In fact mere antiquity had never been a prime Mill Hill reason for respect: there were 100 older schools in England and Wales in the HMC listing before Mill Hill came to impact on the scene.) When 24 Public Schools combined to co-ordinate their Entrance Scholarships, Mill Hill was offered a place in the second group of eight, alongside Rugby, Repton, Oundle, Marlborough, Rossall, St Edward's Oxford, and Sedbergh; if this period was a peak for Mill Hill in purely Public School terms, the School was certainly among the more expensive – tenth in the 1927 Public School Year Book.

Mill Hill's internationalism at work: group of *OMs* at Anglo-Chinese College, Tientsin, North China, 24.ii.1925. The Principal borrowed the MHS motto. *6.b*

Although he made it clear from the start, in 1922, that *in a school the dead traditions must be thrown out*, there were, in Kenneth Childs' judgement, *no violent changes straight away*. George Goyder wrote, however, in *Signs of Grace* that one custom was to bait masters whenever possible, and that it was said that Jacks had to beat half the School before order returned. Another custom – hands out of pockets and doffing caps when passing the Gate of Honour – was preserved throughout Jacks' time in office. What Dr Peter Trier describes as *'the rigid year system'* stayed in being: at one extreme, First-Year boys could not actually have their hands in their pockets at all. At the other loftier end of the hierarchy, school prefects could sport coloured pullovers; monitors marched down the Corridor at Line-Up, singing "Stop Talking!" (see Appendix E) – with of course their hands in their pockets – and the two or three senior monitors each year could and did sport moustaches. So too for Maurice Jacks *a well-controlled system of fagging* was a vital part of character training, he being the first of Mill Hill's two Head Masters to have experienced the value of such training in the context of war. Bernard Noltingk, one of an outstanding crop of mathematicians and scientists, described *the bogey activity of fagging... as a useful introduction to the realities of the social ladder*. Sport was now to be seen, in MLJ's words, primarily as a *means to an end*. To reinforce the need for industriousness, he was having to warn his still strongly sport-orientated constituency on Foundation Day, 1931: *these things matter more and more*.

Since scholastic standards are one area of contention about the Jacks time, the first remotely recognisable 'modern' era for comparisons, they are the initial focus. The 'MHS Destination' record, **Fig.J(i)**, is explained in Ch.VIII. It shows: (A) Oxbridge Awards and (B) 'Commoner' Places; (C) Medical/ Veterinary College entrances; (D) Places and Awards at other establishments (Architecture, Agriculture, Engineering, etc); and (E) Places at the Service Colleges: Sandhurst (then RMC); RAF Cranwell; Royal Navy/ Merchant Navy Training Schools. By these markers, MLJ's best years came at the start and finish of his regime, for 34 boys went

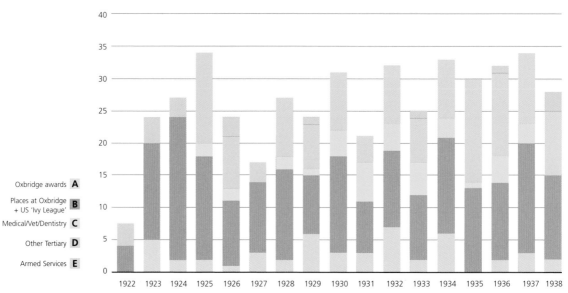

Fig.J(i) MHS LEAVERS' TERTIARY EDUCATIONAL DESTINATIONS 1922 – 1938

Oxbridge awards **A**
Places at Oxbridge + US 'Ivy League' **B**
Medical/Vet/Dentistry **C**
Other Tertiary **D**
Armed Services **E**

on to further education in both 1924/5, and 1936/7. However the Oxbridge awards, at two and three respectively, were low in both these academic years. That was what counted publicly, even though informed critics such as *OM* Francis Cammaerts, later a schoolmaster himself, regarded Mill Hill's Public School/ Oxbridge bias as "profoundly harmful", supporting *the inferiority of science studies or indeed any studies which had an occupational direction.* *OM* Paul Clifford held Jacks responsible for *the Philistine nature of the School*, despite the Classics (*a bright light* for Cammaerts, under Alan Whitehorn), or Maths for the mathematicians. Cammaerts with his 2½ years French and History in the VI Form of the 1930s, commented: *the four teachers involved were by any subsequent standard I have encountered unspeakably bad ... the French* 'Grand Siècle' *had no lead up to the eventual Revolution, nor anything on Art, Music or Design ....* Others, like *OM* Peter Parr, have refuted these judgements: as ever, the quality of results fluctuated from year to year.

Yet just before the economic depression struck, MLJ was able to declare 1929/30 to be *the School's best year ever*, with a Roll of 348, which with Belmont's 122 produced a 'Foundation' of 470. There were 21 HCs, 63 SCs. Despite only three Oxbridge open awards, there were 15 Commoner places and nine at other tertiary institutions. However by 1933/4 a new record of six Oxbridge awards, 15 places, and nine other tertiary places, was to be reached. Three Hospital places made this total of 33 places, 10 per cent of a School Roll, which had fallen down to 332, notwithstanding initiatives to assist parents over fee-paying. The Head tried at one brief stage in 1933 to support this trend by re-introducing the 19th-century custom of highlighting the two intellectually most gifted boys; there suddenly appeared on the '*Et virtutem et musas*' listing in the *MHM*, albeit unheralded in the Governors' Minutes, two 'Heads of the School' – one for the Classical and Modern side, and one for Maths and Science, ranked only just below the school prefects in precedence. He cannot have achieved whatever 'political' aim he had, for this idea ended the following year; perhaps he did not need to, for by 1934-5 there were 44 *OM*s up at Cambridge, and 25 at Oxford.

MLJ – man and achievements

However this record may be viewed, who was this absurdly young-looking ex-'Greenjacket' captain (King's Royal Rifle Corps), severely wounded early in the war, 1914, who was now to tread in McClure's well-worn path, and who would lift the school's reputation, in the words of refugee scientist *OM* Peter Trier, to *an all-time high*? The time of this grandson of the Irish and Grammar School-educated Rev. Stopford Brooke, and also a Classics 'First', saw a trebling of both the SC and HC scores; a stream of newspaper articles reporting his sought-after speeches on educational occasions up and down the country; flying the flag for Mill Hill from Canada to Geneva; and appointment to the HMC Executive, succeeding his friend Cyril Norwood, Headmaster of Harrow. The School would be selected as one of 36 in

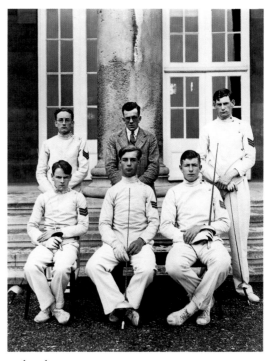

Later MHS Fencing V: future WWII SOE hero Francis Cammaerts DSO, captain: (see Ch.VII). *6.c*

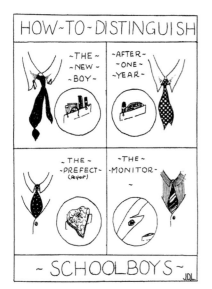

HOW~TO~DISTINGUISH

~THE~ ~NEW~ ~BOY~

~AFTER~ ~ONE~ ~YEAR~

~THE~ ~PREFECT~ (*Ayear*)

~THE~ ~MONITOR~

~ SCHOOLBOYS ~

The tie as status symbol:
(i) *MHM* cartoon: four stages
of 1920s MHS hierarchy;
(ii) CUOMC (l.) and
OUOMC colours *6.d*

an acclaimed work of 1937, *Our Great Public Schools*, and in an analysis in *Winchester and the Public School Elite* would be classed in a second group of 17 *'most expensive public schools'* producing Cabinet Ministers from 1886 to 1936.

At Jacks' death on 24 January 1964, A.D.C.Peterson spoke in *Nature* of the *warmth of his personality, only half-concealed by a surface austerity.* HM Roy Moore would write: *his was a frank and generous nature ... his pleasure in life communicated itself to all who knew him ... a man of courage and integrity ...* The later Professor Jacks had *gravitas*, was shrewd, popular and ubiquitous. Returning from his Public Schools Canada visit in 1930 – among a 'School' of Headmasters – a *colossal burst of cheering* greeted his first Assembly in The Large. He gave piano solos in Concerts; sustained a black eye through attempting to join in a rugby XXX practice, and kicked off in 1924 in the first match to be played on the re-levelled playing field; joined in on cross-country runs; and batted – modestly – in matches against the 1st XI; and that on top of a teaching load including Scripture. Photographs of him (with "Lobo", one more in a long line of popular Head Masters' dogs), and the James Gunn portrait, show a dignified figure, trimly-suited with waistcoat and watch-and-chain, a centre parting to his thick dark brown hair. He often affected formal grey spats; *OM* Dr Kenneth Childs observed him as *c.5' 11"*, *spare, eyes rather sunken, heavily lined on his face ...* (these were the effects of diabetes – he was saved by insulin), *... and stood very upright ... a great stickler for protocol.* He had distinction as the only Head to feature in a Physics formula '$I2BT=MLJ$', a calculation for water melted down by electricity.

For *OM* Lewis Wild, *he was always clearly in charge.* In 1937, the Chairman of the Court highlighted his *singularly accurate, clear and well-disciplined mind, a humorous tenacity – a scholar, and man of affairs, strong, sensitive.* Teaching was in the blood: his brother went on to become Head of Bedales. MLJ's Second Master, A.J.Williams, who had stood in as Acting Head for two terms after Sir John's death, wrote equivocally that *the industry of the school was probably never better* than during his time. He also ascribed to him the quotation – without translation (not needed in those classical days): *grates persevere dignas non opis est nostrae* (see Appendix F).

Oxford *OM*s, like those at Cambridge, had their own colours, and a termly Newsletter: they wrote of *that well-known and ready laugh*; the *MHM* Editor called it *friendly and infectious.* His pet expressions were legion: boys could be *cuckoos, cows* or *owls*; notebook-less boys were *Ninnies*; pencil-less boys were *pointless.* Roland Wade told a nice story of his earlier time in School House: *He had a sense of fun ... coming with the housemaster into my dormitory one evening before lights out, a boy who was good at drawing silhouettes ... was showing them on a wall with a torch. Eventually it came to one of him. Jacks had four features, a strong, strangely-matured head, a loud laugh and bushy eyebrows, and he could not easily pronounce his Rs. When he saw the silhouette he gave a top-grade example of his laugh and said 'terwific eyebwows' to the delight of all.* At the fast-proliferating OMC dinners around the country he became as welcome a speaker as Sir John had been, gaining an equal reputation for humour, and his *fine, jousting form.*

He quickly achieved the confidence of all; financial benefits duly followed, from the Court, and within the OMC. In his time the School's 'look' was formed well into the successor century. Electricity superseded gas from 1924, starting with the

Chapel. By the year end, Mill Hill at last had a Science Block, replacing cramped labs in old classrooms by the Chapel; also "Park" cricket ground in "New Field", the pavilion a gift by *OM* James McGowan. (Park Cottage's first Head Groundsman was Augustus Chase, grandfather to later Governor, Graham Chase.) There was a third new House, designed by *OM* architect Martin Briggs; plans show 'Servants Quarters' among additions to old St Paul's Vicarage, facing the Village's High Street.

From a choice of "Wills Grove House", "Vicarage House", "Up Field", or "Home Field", it was named "Winterstoke" after the School's great benefactor; it was then given a new frontage as today at Mill Hill Pre-Prep, now to face the School. (The only House sharing a name with a locomotive, its nameplate hung on the House wall until 1995; this GWR 'Saint' Class was withdrawn in 1934.) Mill Hill's sentinel at the other end of Wills Grove would be "Garth", built on a ground lease by L.A.Cane (Head of Music) in 1934.

The year 1926 saw the start of the labour-intensive levelling by the boys themselves (aided later by mechanical means) of yet another terrace, out of the slope that Wilf Sobey had called "The Fishing Net" (see Appendix E); by 1933 the task would at last be completed with an additional widening for a cinder track. In 1927 the Loggia Notice-Board was built, and next year Hamp's well-executed extension south-eastwards of the Tite School-House, today indistinguishable from the original brickwork: only from inside the first floor-well is the demarcation between old and new visible. That year fulfilled one of Jack' firmest requests, a School shop, on the model – where else – of Harrow. The Court's Business Committee listed the items the modern boy needed: 'photographic plates, wireless equipment, ping-pong balls, decorations for studies, etc'. The School's clothing supplier since the 1900s, "Blenheim Steps" in the High Street was bought with the OMC's new purchasing arm, Rosebank Ltd, formed in 1923 as the vehicle for many defensive lease-back acquisitions of property in the Village over the ensuing years. With this new shop 'in bounds', Jacks' tighter policy was enshrined in the detailed new Rules of 1928, later eulogised by Buster Brown as *your strong and generous government*. Excluded were the nearby Hill Top Café – what *OM* Lewis Collison noted, mysteriously, as the *shop just past The King's Head on the way to BB, on the left-hand side*; and Farm Road, another part of today's ordinary world which was then 'out of bounds'.

By 1933 the buildings opposite the Marnham, and the fields from the then Masters' Hostel, "The Grove" (purchased in 1908), to *The Kings Head*, had also been acquired. The niece and adopted daughter of Lord Winterstoke – Janet, later Dame Stancomb-Wills – was responsible for the oak panelling in the Dining Hall and the eponymous Gate by the bus-stop of 1928: she helped Nonconformist Taunton too – a 'sister' school, still calling on Mill Hill help 70 years later, over 'Incorporation'. She also

1924: OTC CSM raises customary "Three Cheers for HRH The Prince of Wales!", as Prince opens Science School (delayed due to royal arm injury): Maurice Jacks (l.). *6.e*

THE BUCKLAND POOL
Opened June 19ᵗʰ 1937.

Former open-air Buckland
Pool, opened 19.vi.1937.
"West Grove" (former
overflow Boarding House)
visible in Hammers Lane,
beyond trees, pre-Todd
Garden and Drapers'
Homes. 6.f

financed most of Top Terrace, completing the north-western steps donated by Herbert Marnham. With her sister, Mrs Richardson, she had been appointed a Vice-President in 1912 (see Appendix C). A Chapel plaque commemorates her generosity.

Despite the Thirties' Depression Mill Hill now re-invested for the future, keen to avoid any taint of unprogressiveness. By 1934 came new squash courts (mooted in 1908 – to be the Piper Library by 2000) and an extension to the adjacent Gym of 1905. The year 1935 saw the closing of the first 'Out-House', the old dilapidated Burton Bank. It was re-opened by Jacks' fellow-educationist Sir Walter Moberly on 5 October, at the edge of the Park, one of six possible sites – twice the cost, for nine extra 'places': the Medical Research Council's successor block still stands. Mill Hill was now news – Moberly's speech on the need to be more open to all classes, a marker for the School's future, was well reported. Carrying forward the School's traditions, a copy of *The Times*, a Sports programme, a crested silver spoon, and silver coins had been buried at the Foundation stone Ceremony in March, by Dr Cyril Norwood (see Ch.XII).

Concern for the environment was symbolised by Brett James' founding of the MHHS in January 1929, and also by the School's care for the arborial setting. Although two elms in Peter Collinson's garden were pollarded in 1928, and one of his cedars lopped, due to its dangerous overhang above the Top Field path, there were enhancements. In 1935 there was a subscription planting of "Jubilee Alley" on the car park crest, leading from Farm Road – (as the 'Hornbeam Arch' it still survives above the Sports Hall); Jacks' personal 'Coronation Oak' of 1937 is still perched today – unmarked – above the slope between that road and "Fishing Net"). That year too an OMC-School project for an open-air Pool, honouring Richard Buckland, was commissioned. The wisteria round the Winterstoke Library were preserved, despite the need for light in that self-defeatingly dark spot; and there was satisfaction in being able to maintain a line of oaks below the new BB garden: (see 'Spirit of Place', Ch.XII).

The Dimbleby-biographer of one celebrated *OM* father made a retrospective accusation of the 'social myopia' of the Mill Hill of the late 1920s, with a *blinkered view of society*. In fact, whilst in internal matters Jacks was a reformer, he had his own sense of the pace of change that this still traditional institution could take. From 1923 he started to revise the curriculum – with the results encapsulated in **Fig.J(i)**. He brought about a 'Medical VI', and a Special VI aimed at 'Commerce', but abolished Book-Keeping and Shorthand. Another decade would pass before he could reintroduce 'School Medallists'; he innovated briefly the academic 'Head of School' award, starting in 1933 with the future celebrated Christian Arabist, Albert Hourani, but ending with three further recipients in 1934. Slowly, career lectures – on Medicine, Mining, Shipping, the Services, "Becoming a Vet" – came into being. The Public School Hymn Book replaced McClure's preferred Congregational version; the

Head read from Anatole France in Sunday evening Chapel; Masters read the daily Lesson. Girls from The Mount School acted in the plays. In 1925/6 Jacks overhauled on scientific lines a still predominantly House-based 'Dietary', including later, in 1934, the revolutionary idea of a mid-afternoon bun and compulsory glass of milk. This needed a special roll-call, and a new task for the monitors, whose duties he had modernised as a priority, in a confidential booklet, still relevant today.

In 1928 he spearheaded, ahead of other Public Schools, an idea increasingly popular in Germany, on which he had written in one of his books: 'Physical Education' came under an HoD, Hedley, as opposed to mere 'PT', with the Austrian, Fritz Stampl as coach. His most newsworthy reform was the 1931 clothing 'experiment'. A 'Man of the Week' feature in *Everyman* declared that against *the cast-iron nature of public-school conventions... Mill Hill is to set the example*: all boys now had the 'choice' of wearing grey shorts, open-neck grey Clydella shirts and grey socks, or long grey trousers. Jacks presented this move, like the option of joining the Scouts, as 'non-compulsory', but neither boys nor parents ignored who was offering the option. The *MHM* remarked that its virtue lay in having longer in bed in the morning, there now being fewer clothes to put on. According to Bernard Noltingk, *School caps should be worn to and from school... trilby hats were correct wear at other times.* From that same year of enforced economy, boys were for the first time required – incredibly to the contemporary eye – to share domestic chores by making their own beds, and serving at table, in place of "skivvies" like Letty Tales, in their brown and white uniforms. There was also a simplification of the array of expensive 'colours' – the "athletic millinery": the Public School 'empire' at its 1920s-40s zenith exhibited an endemic taste for display, in common with so many of history's empires.

"Day Bugs", as *OM* Richard Graves recalled, were "looked on as lesser mortals, a trodden-down minority." At long last in 1933 they were were given much-needed dignity through a globally-distinguished name, 'Murray', and some exclusive accommodation. This included by 1935 senior studies, and plans were laid to provide chairs for them in the Chapel aisle (see Appendix D). Noltingk wrote that for years afterwards buses on the Golders Green to Mill Hill route bore witness to one team of unusually badly behaved Day-boys: *[G.A.] Holmes and [A.] L.Milligan... had the endearing habit of taking with them a small screwdriver and occupying... the conductor's absence by progressively removing the screws that held the seat upholstery together.*

From 1930 onwards, Jacks ushered in the concept – despite some martially-conditioned *OM* opposition – of Scouting as an equally manly and socially worthy prelude to the OTC. In 1933, based on the prompting of his Bedales-educated wife Emily, he brought in the idea introduced there 20 years previously, the sensible but at first sight somewhat unmanly half-hour 'siesta' after lunch. Through his influence, the School MO, Dr E.B.Morley, carried out a thorough and objective review of the School's health between 1922 and 1936. This highlighted the progress made through good Matron appointments (such as those of the

Ancient "Sanny Cab" outside the "San", to take invalids to hospital or home, one aspect of M.L.Jacks' inheritance. 6.g

Sole Millhillian memorial
plaque in Westminster
Abbey: wartime and
ceremonial broadcaster,
Richard Dimbleby CBE. *6.h*

delightfully named Sister Love, and Miss Timewell at Belmont), as well as through sharper detection, across the 33 categories of illness which had so plagued, and undermined, the life and reputation of the School in the previous century: from Colds, Influenza, Measles and Conjunctivitis, to Typhoid, Polio and TB. Not for nothing did 'Health' take historical pride of place in the reports that the Heads of both the School and Belmont made regularly to the Court. A lax regime under McClure had allowed a paralysed, chairbound Captain Markham at the "Sanny", with his wife, to diagnose under such entertainingly misleading headings as 'spots', 'podache' and 'bad funk'. Significantly, with that flavour once more of a Mill Hill unafraid to take an individual line, Dr Morley commented, against the trend, that although not encouraging 'invalidism', *we try to avoid the tendency, prevalent in some Schools, that it was "not good form" [to be ill]... no boy is rebuked for reporting sick.*

Living to the full

Both the establishments within Mill Hill in those two all-too fleeting inter-war decades led a full life. In the School, there was a still highly committed Corps, and three 30-strong troops of Scouts evolved – Picts, Vikings and Hottentots. Jacks believed *every boy should have a hobby.* There were more than 25 different Clubs and Societies on the go, some waxing, some waning, some no longer familiar: Christian youth Crusaders, Wireless, Photography, Aeronautical, Philatelic, Gramophone. Film shows in The Large had grown from the 1920s time of future film-maker 'Baynham Honrie' onwards: *Kinematograph Weekly* acclaimed *the first public school to possess a Kinema of its own and a specialist journal, The Mill Hill Animated News.*

Music flourished, mainly under the hand of yet another master remembered on the Chapel walls, Laurie Cane, who served the cause of this longest-established Mill Hill Muse up to and beyond his retirement, after a near-record 40 years' tenure, in 1935. He petitioned the Court that Music was no longer *an elegant extra*, but *an integral part* of a Public School's provision. There was a Choir reducing from 70 (possibly due to the custom of Choir feasts and whole day holidays) to a later core of 30; a Choral Society of 40; and an Orchestra of 20, to which were donated McClure's double-bass, and Inglis Gundry's cello; as well as a Dance Band known for its *syncopated cacophany.* Under an initially enthusiastic Music Circle of 50, there were recitals by the great English cellist, W.H.Squire, and the violinist C.Morland Braithwaite. Visits to the Albert and Queen's Halls, and to the Greek play at MLJ's alma mater, Bradfield, became regular events. J.P.Howard, who also started to produce plays at "The Grove", put on gramophone concerts for all who cared to come: for Roland Wade as for many others, they *opened my eyes to a whole world of music I had never known.*

In 1924 E.M.Forster had castigated a pervasive athleticism: *ignorance of the Arts was notable... it was the Public School attitude...;* yet at the 1928 HMC conference, as appointee on the Board of Architectural Education, Jacks insisted that they were *not quite such philistines* as had been suggested. Mill Hill's Art and Architecture vied on Sundays with the historic Natural History Museum, Model Railways and Aeroplanes, Chess and Printing (managed in 1931 by one Thatcher, D. – see Ch.XI). There were

Science, Classical (The 'Interpretes'), and French (later to be the Modern Languages) Societies. A Peace Pledge Union ran parallel with a League of Nations Society, with over 100 LNS members, fighting for pride of place with a more parochial Debating Society and with the self-styled 'thinkers' group, the Informal Discussion Circle. Committees thrived – for Script, Games, Tuck Shop, Informal Lectures, the Magazine, the Young Farmers Club, and the new in-bounds "Blenheim Steps" – to be run for the next 31 years by a redoubtable Miss Gillies, up to her retirement in 1959. Drama flourished at School level, with both a Dramatic Society and a shadowy body that only appeared in Valete slips and photo albums, the Shakespeare Society; the range was narrow, from "Ambrose Applejohn's Adventure" to "The Tempest". At House level, School House led the way with its Informal Concerts, under the aegis of a role-model of a Housemaster's wife, Mrs "Vic" Elliott. Identified there was a new Compere and *magnificent touch pianist*, a name already introduced: although not even a prefect, the young *OM* Richard Dimbleby enjoyed a warm senior study *filled with thick cushions to lounge on'* and a fag who *prepared his food and cleaned his shoes*. A well-thumbed Elliott "Gilbert & Sullivan" score bore the inscription – *In memory of the Savoyards and with grateful thanks for the hospitality you gave someone who was pleased to help you*. Come the Coronation of King George VI in 1937 (a MHS holiday), this was the name that would gain world fame as one of the BBC's first Outside Broadcasters. Those initiations, minus the comforts, were later to stand the future war correspondent in good stead in some much less salubrious situations in the Western Desert, well portrayed in one of his early books, *The Frontiers Are Green*.

One of MHS' most notable cricketing "Blues", Bill Murray-Wood, School Captain 1935, playing for OUCC at the Varsity Match, 1936, seen here in fashionable company. *6.i*

For many, played five times a week, *rugger was really the school religion*; *OM* John McGavin wrote that *matches on Top Field were great occasions – the whole school and masters were there*. New boys had to get the signatures of every one of the School 1st XV. The glorious seasons – and the names – of '22 to '31 on the school and international field are still bathed in a nostalgic glow: "Joe" Hume, Roger Spong, Wilf Sobey (later a master at Belmont), "Kloot" Lawther, Joe Auty, Harold Carris, and future "Blue", Lewis Collison. The first unbeaten season since 1909 was 1926; but the headlines would later be stolen by Peter Howard – pictured by MLJ as *the inkiest, untidiest scrap of small boyhood that I have ever known, and one of the most active and irrepressible*. This former Head of Winterstoke and Oxford "Blue", went on to captain England against Ireland at the age of 22 in February 1931, and later to become, with his wife Döe Metaxa, the Wimbledon Doubles Champion, something like icons of the period. Döe recalled in 1997 that *rugby football simply was Mill Hill at that time*. However, by 1933 cricket had caught up, and under the prolific future "Blue", Bill Murray-Wood, there was a match of two centuries against Highgate, and an unbeaten season on the Park in 1935. The role of Mill Hill sport – 'Sparta' v. 'Athens', as Sir Walter Moberly put it – is examined in Information Supplement No.6: everything was played – tennis on Top Terrace, and 11 other sports, including hockey proper and the unique Singlehanded hockey (filmed in 1933). Squash racquets, intended at first for recreation, remained so up to 1950, reverting from competitive status in the 1990s; rounders stayed that way. Millhillian skiing was confined to Saalbach, in

1930: England v. Ireland:
all-time record of three *OM*
rugby caps: Peter Howard,
Roger Spong & Wilf Sobey
(see Appendix J). *6.j*

Austria. Golf and even a Mill Hill Yacht Club were catered for. Lacrosse and rowing enthusiasts had to wait until their University days, but this did not prevent the achievement of Oxbridge "Blues" in both, and of a sculls competitor, H.L.Warren, at the 1936 Olympiad in Hitler's Berlin. It sometimes seems a wonder that any work was done at all, yet there are many examples, including the mathematician C.J.Cross-Brown, or the lawyer David Morris, of senior monitors and busy all-rounders who still managed to win major awards to their 'next stage'.

Status

These years are also noteworthy for four defining moments in the style and status of Mill Hill. The first came in 1932 when a nearby Prep School Head, Mr Seaton, announced that he was going to open a new private School, and call it the 'Mill Hill Grammar School'. Under Jacks, Mill Hill had been co-operating happily on many common matters with local state-sector schools, including Watford Grammar School, Queen Elizabeth's Barnet, and Hackney County School, although the focus remained firmly on the Public School movement. Notwithstanding this, the Court was necessarily swift in defence of Mill Hill's historic right to the name of the 'Mill Hill Grammar School'. It prevailed without needing to go to court, and in 1933 accepted the rival's alternative formula – 'The Highwood Grammar School'. (A similar threat arose in 1947 when a proposal to found a 'Mill Hill School of Salesmanship' was averted; however, the Court would not be so successful vis-a-vis a new and future academic rival, Mill Hill County High School, in 1986.)

The second moment came towards the end of Jacks' time, sparked off by a letter from W.E.Vernon Crompton FRIBA, one of three *OM* architects who tendered for the McClure Music School design; in it he refuted the School's right to own what was in effect Mill Hill's unmonogrammed 'Coat of Arms No.4'. Garter King-of-Arms at the College of Arms was consulted; as a result new armorial bearings were formally sanctioned for 'Coat of Arms No.5'. Since the meaning of the elements within this shield has often been the subject of latter-day speculation, the unearthing in 1997 in the Barnet Archives at Hendon of a belated and somewhat rueful letter from the writer of the School's first History, merits noting. On 25 June 1957, he wrote from his retirement:

When Philip Smith was headmaster... 1853-60... he got to know Lord Teynham, who was rather an eccentric... and did... a lot of preaching. He seems to have come down to Mill Hill and offered... his own coat of arms for the use of the school. Philip Smith accepted them, and they went on being used for many years. Then Col Mitchell, who was bursar, asked the College of Heralds [sic] if we might vary the arms of the school to satisfy the old boys with a slight variant. He was told that Mill Hill School had no coat-of-arms; and when he showed the coat-of-arms in use... they... found that these belonged to Lord Teynham. At the school we had to do something about this contretemps, and the existing arms were slightly modified. The cross... was changed ... and in the space was a book, open, presumably the bible. When I wrote my history ... just after its centenary ... I had done my best to interpret the arms ... but you will see that there was really no justification for it at all ...: N.G.Brett James.

Today's College of Arms definition is: 'Argent, on a Cross quadrate in the centre Gules, an open Book proper, a Chief Azure thereon three Martlets Or'. Many followed Brett James' path of imaginative exegesis, including even Maurice Jacks himself in 1936, yet the post-hoc apologia appeared to be ill-founded. While wrongly ascribing 'Public School' status only to 1895, heraldic writer Christie-Murray later commented: *Guillim says that martlets, depicted without feet, are ... "also given for a difference of younger brethren, to... trust to their wings of virtue and merit, to raise themselves ... having little land to put their feet on".* (Only once, in 1999, for Cedars' entrance gates, did the martlets ever mistakenly acquire feet.)

Thirdly, in 1938, after MLJ's retirement, *OM* Col J.D.Mitchell, veteran soldier and School Bursar-cum-Secretary, identified the origins of the phrase coined by Dr Weymouth for the School's second and final motto: *Et virtutem et musas*. The 2nd Epistle to St Peter, ch.1, v.5, reads: *And besides this and giving all diligence, add to your faith virtue, and to virtue knowledge.* This motto had even been adopted for *OM* Lavington Hart's Anglo-Chinese College in Tientsin in 1902 (visited by *OM* Sir Albert Spicer in 1925). A fourth aspect of Mill Hill's style was the installation in 1938, with the local authority, of the Martin Briggs-designed Windmill signposts on Milespit and Highwood Hills, marking boundaries to that ancient Village which still ensures the School's *rus in urbe* character.

Both schools evolve

For Belmont, too, this was a time of both expansion and proper conservation. Early in 1922, Rooker Roberts was deploring the loss of 100 trees over the preceding 10 years, and the need to cull one more ancient elm. However, in addition to the planting of a sapling by every boy, he masterminded the purchase of 54 acres of Mill Field, in *terrestrial alliance* with Ernest Figgis; (he was the benefactor to Lady McClure – City broker, conservationist, father of Rev. Peter (School Chaplain, 1951-7) and grandfather of *OM* Alan Figgis). AJRR levelled the grounds, to form playing fields comparable with those of his 'old school'; Gordon Smith's *Belmont* also details the enthusiastic building plan which then took shape under the architect J.C.S.Soutar.

By coincidence of timing the richness of recall of the daily pattern of life under Jacks is comparable to that under Thomas Priestley

1935: grant of MHS Coat-of-Arms: the inclusion of Bible in the centre of the cross is crucial new element. *6.k*

Mill Hill Village sign by the pond on Milespit Hill, one of the two created by MHS in 1938 for the local authority, designed by *OM* architect, Martin Briggs. *6.l*

and Rev. Philip Smith, which Brett James researched in the 1900s; in the mid-1990s, contemporary oral history was able to re-capture the whole period back to the end of the McClure time. One aspect was prudery: *OM* Norman Yates recalled that *the more salacious adverts were cut out from the daily papers on display in the Scriptorium, and a Monitor (selected as above temptation) was appointed to put his hand over the lens of the cine projector in The Large in the kissing and love scenes during film shows.* Some very modern notes were struck too: of William Morrison, who died at school in 1936, it was said that he *believed that a monitor should be a friend to those under him ... more could be done by kindness than by anything else.*

OM Donald Overy recalled that he only met MLJ in 1927, *when I went to receive the 'moral lecture' [the "bog"] which he gave to each new boy: (sex and hygiene – well ahead of its time).* OM Oswald Pedder's memory was that boys only went to the Head's study to receive an 'O' ('Optime'), or a caning. *OM* journalist Rupert Cherry related that he caned very hard, as a man in the prime of life, yet *the only exercise he seemed to take... was to hit a tennis ball across Top Field for his Alsatian dog to retrieve.* Pedder also recalled a startling feature of that time: Mill Hill as the sole Public School apart from Eton to have MPs in all the three parties. *OM* Dr Kenneth Lloyd recalled the *fixed places at the Dining Table.* OM Donald Hailey valued *quiet hour* with no talking, after Sunday evening chapel. Cherry also wrote of *Sunday afternoons, the whole house ... went for a walk, marching six or seven abreast in a solid rectangle;* weekdays began *with a bell to wake us at 7 a.m., then a warning bell before we were due at breakfast at 7.30.* At Assembly, *the monitor taking the roll call would say your name, and you answered 'Adsum'.* OM Huw Pool conjured up images of the support staff at that time – *Capt Harding of the OTC, "Quart" ex-RN, who looked after the (indoor) swimming pool, and "Vesti", our Italian butler, in School House.* John McGavin remembered *pea souper fogs ... the Sunday gut ... and lectures by the WWI padre, "Woodbine Willie", Howard Somerville the Everest climber, and "Tubby" Clayton who founded Toc H.*

King Gustav of Sweden congratulates *OM* Francis Crick on award of Nobel prize, Medicine, 1962, for DNA discovery. *6.m*

The all-embracing Science School, opened on 27 October 1924 by that tireless celebrator of Public School buildings, the Prince of Wales and future King Edward VIII, had heralded a notable era for Mill Hill Science. Half a century after Rugby's lead in 1857, it was nevertheless among the first modern multi-faculty Blocks: many indeed followed – one or two preceded it. Some Millhillians move out into the wider world with a clashing of cymbals; others, many of them modest 'late-developers', do so without school honours. Cecil Goyder, member of a distinguished family already introduced, was one of many examples of the latter; Mill Hill's Science made world news through his 'G2SZ' wireless experiments, and won princely praise on the day. The School Science Archive, lovingly

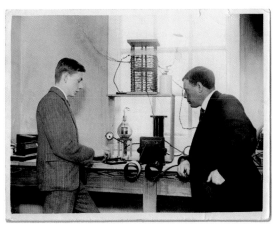

Under watchful eye of Buster Brown, 18-year-old Cecil Goyder operates his brave, primitive wireless set in unheated basement of the uncompleted Science Block. *6.n*

prepared by his mentor, Buster Brown, complemented by the world-wide press reports kept by his brother Claude, in Canada, record the full story of his achievements, 1920-4. Although today, in the words of a later expert, Peter Duck (builder of Mill Hill's first amateur TV set in 1950) a *footnote in the history of communications*, this break-through was *driven by the same passions as those in the race to space*, to quote *The Star's* commentary of 18 October 1999 (the anniversary of the New Zealand link-up, 75 years on). Despite his Housemaster's disapproval, in 1923 from the School House roof (the aerials appear on contemporary photographs) and then in the still unfinished Science Block – Room Y – Goyder pioneered short-wave two-way radio, first with the far west USA and the Byrd Arctic expedition, and then nine days before the Royal visit, with Z-4AA in Otago. Ranked in the annals with the names of Edison, Hertz, Fleming and Baird, *England's Marconi* went on to equip India with radio, advise UNO and win the CBE.

Mill Hill's greatest son

Harrow claims Churchill among her greatest sons. In Mill Hill's context, one *MHM* article argued for P.D.Howard; or, if bravery in war were the criterion, Chs.V and VII pay due tribute. Yet by 1934, one name stands out: the emergence from Northampton Grammar School and then from Mill Hill's Science VI to research at UCL and Cambridge, of Francis Crick OM, unraveller, with Watson, of DNA, the greatest scientific discovery of the 20th century and joint Nobel prize-winner: he *provided most of the bright ideas*. In a panel of intellectuals in 1997, Mill Hill's only holder of the Order of Merit was voted third among the century's greatest contributors to European civilisation, after Churchill and Einstein. The sole tribute Mill Hill paid at the time was the joint award to this thrice HC-winner of a Walter Knox Chemistry Prize, apart from membership of the Tennis VI. Like Goyder earlier, there was no prefectorial dignity for this son of an *OM*, not even inclusion in that Jacks innovation, a "Head of the School (Maths and Science)": the title went to C.H.B.Priestley. Congratulating B.Noltingk on First Class Honours at Oxford, Herbert Coates lamented that Crick *had not so done*. (Only later would plaques be erected in the Science School to these two outstanding alumni: see Chs.XI and XII.) A compliment paid to Mill Hill in *Double Helix* was repeated on 25 October 2000 from the by now 'J.W.Kieckhefer Distinguished Professor' Crick at San Diego's Salk

Institute: *My whole scientific career was grounded in the excellent science teaching I had at Mill Hill ... I am extremely grateful to the school for pioneering science reading in this way.* Prof Steve Jones, in the 1998 Prestige Lecture, would observe that geneticists now divided time into 'BC' (before Crick), and after him. On the death in 2004 of this 1975 winner of the Royal Society's premier scientific award, the Copley medal, David Giachardi, the chief executive of the Royal Society of Chemistry, spoke of *his gigantic service for humanity'*; Dr Roger Penderson, from Cambridge University, said *His legacy will be remembered for centuries.* His story is recorded here less with borrowed pride – the pride lay after all in the possession of those evolved cerebral genes whose molecular structure Prof Crick was later to decode – but rather in simple gratitude that a world-class intellect, *one of the grand men of science*, as the *New York Times* declared, was launched from Mill Hill.

A Public School aware

Some assume that the privileged status of the Public School also implied a cosy outlook on the world outside: yet Mill Hill's choice of "Merrie England" as a school play in 1935 was not symptomatic of any ostrich attitude – more of a last look at an era already past. The quotation heading this chapter was part of an explanation to the Court of an event in 1935 which gained much publicity, a last-minute substitute League of Nations Society lecture by a Mr Entwhistle, a pacifist exponent of the "No War Movement". Jacks defended the action while rejecting its thesis, contrasting Mill Hill with Wellington, where there had actually been an outbreak of Communism: Mill Hill boys *were more than capable of looking after themselves in such matters.* An outward awareness was one of his most formative contributions to boys at the School during his time; it had several manifestations.

Boys with Peace Movement sympathies were allowed off OTC, for community service. In Chapel collections, 'Save the Children' benefited for European Relief, as did the Russian Relief and Reconstruction Fund; also the Seaside Camps for London Working Boys. Rooted in the Social Settlement Movement of the 1880s (e.g. Harrow's work at Nottingdale), today's Community Service was foreshadowed in the work for Roland House, Stepney, and, from 1927, with the involvement of dedicated *OMs* such as George Goyder, Dick Walker and later Nigel Baker and Andrew Welch, in Lambeth's Alford House – "one of the finest enterprises of the OMC". From 1926 the School worked for the League of Nations cause, with all the idealism of her liberal origins, jointly winning the Shermon Award for the LoN Branch making the best use of its opportunities. For those using the Library there was an informed reading list: *Red China*, by Mao-Tse Tung; *Fascists at Olympia*; even Stalin's *Second Five-Year Plan*. There was a call to take the *Daily Worker*, to counterbalance the *Daily Mail*.

Reinforcing this orientation, through contacts with the Association for German Refugee Professional Workers, the 25-year-old Herr von Sendemann was given hospitality to teach at Mill Hill, having had to leave his homeland because his mother was half-Jewish. David Morris recalled that MLJ also brought about, while there was still time, the admittance of many Jews emigrating from Nazi Europe. Three of that group of 18, which included Ebstein, Block, Katzenstein and Michelsohn, attended the reunion of "39-ers" in 1999, (two became future Mill Hill parents): they were

Theo Marx, Norman Mirsky, and Peter Trier, who came over from Darmstadt in 1935. Dr Trier proved to be one of Harry Coates' star Maths brains, as well as a national investment – he went on to work for the Admiralty Radar Establishment, and later to head Research for Mullard, winning the CBE. Maurice Jacks maintained contact with him after the war, and wrote on 18 December 1946, to congratulate him on his naturalisation. Trier wrote: *there was no discrimination at all against foreign boys ... this relaxed tolerance did not spring up by accident, but was initiated and fostered by M.L.Jacks.* "Bill" Oppenheimer (later Owen) from Wiesbaden, making a properly Millhillian record by winning 1st XI hockey colours from his first term to 1938, went on to be the only *OM* to become a Lt Col in the US Army. Most importantly, there was an initially reluctant focus on world affairs, including events in the Far East and in Spain, as the clouds steadily gathered over an increasingly Fascist world. One *OM*, Arthur Street, was said to have left Oxford to take part in the Spanish Civil War. There was a family strain of bravery: it was his younger brother Denys who with fellow OB and *OM*, Cyril Swain, was among the 50 Allied airmen shot by the SS after "The Great Escape" of March 1944 from Stalag Luft III – now commemorated in a sombre panel at the RAF Museum, Hendon: (see Ch.VII).

Although at first Mosley's apparently pro-Christian right-wing Movement, as in the country at large, won over a few adherents, mostly in Brett James' Ridgeway (*We happen to harbour the more virulent members of that Society*), its 'Party' withdrew from a School Mock Election, and never gained ground. Non-partisan debates and topics included; "The League ... is doomed to failure as a means of preventing war" (won by a heavy majority as early as 1931); "Austria" in Spring 1933 – *pessimistically convincing*; and "The Challenge of Hitlerism" (as early as December that same year); and "The Probable Character of the Next War", which left a 1934 audience *feeling thoroughly optimistic*. A League of Nations Society Debate – "This House deprecates the suppression of individual liberty in Germany by the National Socialist Party" – was won in 1935, but by only 26 to 17 votes. Other talks were John Strachey on "Communism"; "Mussolini"; "Danzig"; "The Troubles in Spain"; and "Poland". Commenting on the 'Hitler Olympics' of 1936, the *Magazine* Editor wrote sardonically: *Thousands marvelled at the achievements of National Socialism, lapped up the propaganda, and went home to spread the greatness of the new Germany.*

There were a few straws in the wind – a 1938 *MHM* article about a German in Nuremberg getting irate at some Millhillian's whistling (headed *Furor Teutonicus*); nevertheless boys still went on to study at Vienna, Freiburg, and Frankfurt. *The more ... travel abroad, the better*, said MLJ in 1934. For many senior boys, masters and *OMs*, the most memorable examples of this process of preserving a window to the world outside were the International Summer Schools, starting in the 1932 Long Vac with the *Oberrealschule der Frankischen Stiftungen* in Halle; a few Germans, and some Frenchmen, but predominantly young Swedes and Danes, came to Mill Hill, shared the work and the rules, and laid wreaths on the Gate of Honour – Millhillians, some in plus-fours and checked

Start of Millhillian commitment to voluntary social work, and 'public benefit' (see Ch. XII): (i) appeal stamp for Roland House, in parallel with continuing work for (ii) Alford House, Lambeth. *6.0*

ALFORD HOUSE

An artist's impression of the new Club

INTERNATIONAL SUMMER SCHOOL, 1932.

THE WELCOME TO THE GERMAN PARTY.

IN THE KITCHEN.
(Reproduced by kind permission of the *Daily Express*.)

The first International Summer School ('ISS') group, 1932, main entrance: *MHM* caption: 'Welcome to the German party'. 6.p

stockings, being received back in their homes in return. The years 1914-1918 had not been forgotten in 1936: *the two minutes silence still means something very real to us.*

The pre-war interaction with Germany merits the attention of this History; at issue is a school's duty of care. Above all it showed how the Boarding school concept could be subverted politically: Nazism called for imagination, unhelped by Public School "fair play". *How Public School Boys Live* was translated into German and read widely; Vivian Ogilvie, working as a schoolmaster in Germany, wrote: *the Nazis... made a study of our public schools in the hope of learning the secret of these successful* Führer-schulen.' At Mill Hill in 1932, Otto Püster could declare at a Gate of Honour ceremony, *We Germans are free from any hatred;* 1935 brought a hockey tour with Rugby to the Bremen *Club zur Wahr,* and in the Olympics Year, 1936, joining with them, Cranleigh, Wellington and Tonbridge, in a tournament in Hanover.

Ted Heath, visiting the Nuremberg Rally in 1937, wrote: *Everybody... could recognise with perfect clarity the expansionist nature of Nazi intentions.* This was still the time of what Alan Bullock called *The Counterfeit Peace,* and of relative political naivety for Mill Hill as for Britain – democracies had not yet grasped totalitarianism. Bullock's judgement was: *Anyone who visited Germany in 1936/7 needed to be singularly blind not to see the ends to which all this activity was directed.* The Nazi salute, publicly forced upon England's football team in 1938, was replayed on Collinson Piece by a German hockey team representing what by now Mill Hill acknowledged as "fanatical National Socialists".

Yet J.E.Whitehead (already assailed by a war-induced breakdown while Winterstoke Housemaster in 1924) made a surprising choice for the ISS exchange – a *N.S.D. Oberschule* at Feldafing, Bavaria. Led by this 'enthusiastic European', German Masters Sam Segger and Martin Forrest took parties there up to 1937. Of four *OM* survivors by 2002, Norman Yates wrote: *even before my visit in 1935* [sic, recte 1936] *most people, including my parents, expected an eventual war if the Germans were not restrained... It was like taking part in a comic opera, with all the boys swaggering about dressed all the time as soldiers, with bayonets at their hips and steel-shod boots on their feet... they took me to all the sites of notoriety, the burning of the books, Woolworths with* Jude *painted in large white letters on all its shop windows.* 'Triple colour' Peter Parr, *took a surreptitious photograph* [at Friedrichshaven] *of the Zeppelin that later crashed in America.* Yates was told: *It will never come out because our Führer has installed magic rays.* He was asked: *I hear you have a Jew in your party; although we had Moss (of Moss Bros) I said 'no', fearing for his safety – that was the end of the honeymoon period for me.*

The School brochure merely commented that they visited *a number of Labour Camps, in which men of all classes live and work together for six months.* (Philip Gibbs, had observed: *In the evenings they had lectures ... a side of those Labour Camps which we did not see or hear*). For *OM* Arthur Downer, the Germans' behaviour was *impeccable*. While a Mill Hill party sailed to Sweden on 11 August 1937, Feldafing made its second visit to Mill Hill, with two Masters and eight boys; (one was the son of Goering's Adjutant, Gen K.Bodenschatz, Deputy Chief of Staff, *Luftwaffe*, and a witness at the Nuremberg Trials). The Germans wrote later: *the English and the Germans are tall and blonde and have blue eyes ... anyone who knows history is aware of their common racial origin.*

Those Millhillians would still have been shocked to learn that Feldafing was well on the way to being seen as the 'top school of the Third Reich' – 'State School of the Nazi Party' – and the first private selective *Internat*, re-founded in 1933/4 by Hitler''s deputy, Rudolf Hess, and by his 'Brown Eminence' and *Chef de Cabinet*, Martin Bormann, where the Nazi *Prominenz*, including Bormann himself, sent its sons for special training. The Leader of its re-formation was *Standartenführer* Goerlitz, photographed in Feldafing's first annual report in full SA uniform. Director of Studies Hans Simons, one of those masters and a former *Reichswehroffizier*, was already a *SA-Sturmführer*, and an enthusiast for the ideas on education made public in *Mein Kampf*. His colleague, Gustav Stoehr, was in charge of 'national-political instruction'. Most periods, 14 a week, were devoted to exercise and sport, the next most, five, to English, one to Religion; History was limited to 'contemporary History' post-1914. Even in 1937, those eight *Jungmannen* belonged to the SA, leaving school as *SA-Truppführer*, with a third of the pre-war leavers going on to a political career. Chosen staff lectured this elite of Britain's – and Mill Hill's – future and well-indoctrinated opponents on the "Racial" and "Jewish" Questions, wearing not merely *Lederhosen* but even brown shirts like their pupils, who wrote observant essays, clearly after visiting Mill Hill, on "Thoughts on my impressions of England".

Jacks was not naive about the implications. His speeches from 1935 onwards proclaim an increasing awareness of 'The Danger of Neutrality'; the *MHM* comment seemed to sum it up: *We attained a better understanding of the character and spirit of modern Germany.* (Michael Hart later compared this event with the parties which he took in the 1970s to Russia: 'we met many ardent communists, but then our pupils were prepared.' He surmised that Whitehead might have had to accept whatever exchange the German Embassy, later under Ribbentrop, no doubt eagerly offered to Mill Hill.) Yet the belief in *Körper, Seele und Geist* was deceptively close to Jacks' publicised admiration for Physical Education; boys – and masters – came from all over Germany; 282 boys – the Roll for 1937 – lived under strict internal discipline in *Villen* (Boarding Houses). They played games with Salem (already met by Mill Hill in the Public School Games, the cradle for the future Gordonstoun, whose Head, Kurt Hahn, had nevertheless been imprisoned the day after the Nazis came to power), and even with liberal schools such as *Landerziehungsheim Schondorf* (see Ch.X). The parents paid fees, and – no doubt appealing to gullible English eyes – in 1937 Feldafing still claimed independence from an overriding Hitler Youth system under Ley. In one context, it might even have seemed a reasonable 'fit' to a Mill Hill where in Francis Cammaerts' criticism, *nothing was as important as team games.*

HOMEWARD B.P.

"Homeward": later *MHM* woodcut symbolises, equivocally, the
first retirement of
Maurice Jacks, 1937. 6.q

To this issue there is one more aspect: many within *the psychology of island immunity* simply could not take Nazism seriously. Arthur Downer, at 16, *never gave a thought to the possibility of war... in two years time.* Visiting the Passion Play, Jacks wrote to Buster: *We were lucky* [sic] *in seeing Hitler himself on our second day in Oberammergau – not so like Charlie Chaplin as you'ld think, but more dignified. We 'Heil-ed' with the crowd, & so avoided a concentration camp! I was impressed with what I saw of the League of Nations.*

That German exchange was the last before such vain attempts to keep open the bridges of dialogue were overtaken. For the final Swedish visit in August 1939, Donald Hall had to bring his party back, a week earlier than planned, on the very brink of war. Despite this aspect of the ISS, much was learned from these pre-war activities. Single-sex Public School life at that time, demanding what one *OM* has described as "total divorce from the home", certainly had its faults; yet most of this generation of Millhillians went into an eventually inevitable war with a better sense of the realities of the world than McClure's equally idealistic sons, whose memory they still honoured every Armistice Day. They had indeed heard what was going on round about them and formed 'their own opinions', as Maurice Jacks broadly intended. Insofar as lay in him, and in his time, he had prepared Mill Hill for what was to come.

In his last letter to parents of December 1937, MLJ wrote: *I put down my pen with a sad heart – how sad, nobody knows but myself.* The Court now needed to dust down its selection procedures once more. There was a job to be done: in fact staff standards had lapsed, as the Jacks years ran on. (Later, Martin Meade-King recalled for Terry Allan how CR attitudes were exemplified in the custom of 'new boy' staff not being allowed to talk to senior masters until spoken to.) Here was an opportunity to try anew to make as bold an appointment as they had made 15 years before.

Alfred Goldman recalled that as the Head came in for his last Chapel, to a dignified voluntary, Peter Hawker at the organ jumped to a jazzy rendering of "Where's that Tiger". Although MLJ kept a straight face at this mark of popularity, what Paul Clifford saw as this *introverted, cold, aloof personality* had *fallen in love* with Mill Hill. Duty now called him back to Oxford, as a 'Prof' – Director of the Department of Education – a period which friends believed was not altogether happy. He took with him his 'museum': home-made master keys, catapults, and "the apparatus" – trousers, jacket, shirt-front, collar and tie, fixed to pyjamas by a bicycle clip, to make monitors think the wearer was fully-dressed at breakfast Line-up. He thought he was saying good-bye, but it was only *au revoir*, for he would prove to be one of Mill Hill's most warmly welcomed 'returnee'-Heads to school functions over the years until his death at 70, on 24 January 1964.

'TKD': study in governance

A *prie-dieu* in the Chapel, currently not in use as being too socially discriminatory, was presented when the Archbishop of York came to visit in 1938. It is the sole reminder of the School's only Wesleyan Methodist Head Master, Dr T. Kingston Derry. Notwithstanding that he served less than what this History has taken as a 'norm' of seven years, there is a place for a short reconsideration of his time. Other career evidence lies in *Who's Who* and his *Times* obituary of 30 July 2001: a Tabarder at the Queen's College, Oxford and a Double First, his wartime work with the Foreign Office (including secret service in Vichy France) was followed by a further 50 years as an outstandingly dedicated educator. He could have had an alternative career as an historian; his writing culminated in his *History of Scandinavia* in 1979, three years after the award of his OBE. He spent the later years of his life in Norway, with his Norwegian wife, where in 1981 he was made a Knight in the Order of St Olav for services to Anglo-Norwegian relations, an honour for a foreigner and no longer so awarded.

There have been a number of short tenures among Mill Hill's Headmasters; Dr Derry's was among the shortest, lasting from his appointment in January 1938, through March to May 1940. At his final Assembly, there was to be no jocular farewell on the St Bees chapel organ: an earlier attempt to break down barriers by playing "Teddy Bear's Picnic' in time with Dr Derry's rather deliberate gait, at the end of one organ scholar's last term, July 1939, had been severely frowned upon. Brevity need not automatically equate to a lack of personal success: a short tenure does betoken, however, a shared failure in the mutual relationship between a Head and the Governors in that complex constituency, the "Octagon of Accountability" (see Ch.II). It is only when, as later, a governing body engenders a sequence of such faults that the outside observer may be tempted to rephrase Oscar Wilde's Lady Bracknell's immortal words: *To lose one Head may be regarded as a misfortune, to lose* [two] *looks like carelessness.* Yet prior to the Second World War only this one Head Master was 'lost' to Mill Hill. If the five years of Charles Vince up to 1891 were less than successful, the all-but 70 years since the New Foundation of 1869 were nevertheless a period in which Mill Hill's Court in its appointments arguably 'got it right'. That perspective has to be preserved, when considering the case, or more correctly the tragedy, in the true classical sense, of 'TKD': 'The Tick', from the acronym of his initials. Many boys, like Vladimir Raitz, hated him. Early on, TKD asked his senior monitor, Peter Parr, whether he had yet been given a nickname: Parr, with the tact he would later need as a dentist, said *Not yet, Sir.*

There are several unusual aspects to the incumbency of Dr Derry, a man of widely respected integrity. From 1946 to his retirement in 1965, his subsequent career concluded with the successful Headship of History at a significant Grammar School, St Marylebone ('SMGS'), an even older foundation than Mill Hill; from those colleagues and pupils there is thus a longer line of testimony to qualify Mill Hill's perceptions of him. Second, there was a willing postal communication between him and the author in his mid-90s in Oslo, looking back, *qua* reasonably objective historian, on a short painful episode in a many-faceted career. Third, in *Nobis*, by a later Mill Hill Governor, there is an unprecedented criticism of the opposition to him. In the *MHM* which reviewed the previous term's School play, "Julius Caesar", the caption was, prophetically, *Et tu, Brute.*

Dr Derry's case exemplifies an endemic problem – the difficulty in reaching any absolute viewpoint, given a Head's multiple accountabilities: hence all attributes can appear both positive and negative. It is also a sad fact that there was no love lost between the successor and his predecessor. What lessons can the Mill Hill of 2007 nevertheless draw from those distant events?

Pupils from SMGS as well as Mill Hill were aware, to quote an Old Philologian, James Bidwell, of *a certain inflexibility*. Dr Derry believed in the value of sticking to principles; this trait had been inculcated in him at his own strict Public School, Kingswood, where he recalled having to write out 250 times: *Manners makyth man is the motto of Winchester College, but good manners need not be confined to Winchester*. The 'GC' would have called this a 'copy line' (see Appendix E). An SMGS colleague's later comment was widely endorsed at Mill Hill: *he was clearly a strict disciplinarian – saw things very much in black and white*. He was seen as seeking *laws and rules set in stone*. It is but a small step to another shared SMGS/ MHS perception: *he was fairly intolerant of even minor misdemeanours*. Much later, in a speech at the opening in 1995 of Oslo's International School, Dr Derry observed how in a comparable institution with over 400 pupils, no school games and no prefect system, there was a perfect orderliness: *it makes one think*, was his wry comment. Much would need to change in those intervening years. In this context a second, very positive attribute, his high academic standard, could not be expected to get a fair hearing at the Mill Hill of 1938/9, which to quote *Nobis* was now *in a rut*, needing *a shake-up*.

Another SMGS colleague, E.McNeal, commented: *his students were very much aware of his scholarship*. A former pupil wrote that he was *the nearest thing to a don on the staff*. In TKD's own eyes the combination of these two aspects in his make-up, and his incoming view of Mill Hill, were to give him the self-imposed objective of making himself "a reforming Headmaster". In itself this was not only a perfectly laudable aim, but one which at least four other subsequent Heads would also espouse.

R.H.Hodgkin, the Provost of Balliol, wrote to Buster Brown in retrospect, in 1943, that Derry *was trying to carry out the reforms he thought were necessary in too great a hurry*. The trouble was that the Mill Hill of 1938/9 did not feel the need to be reformed, at that exact moment in her history. The sequence of events provides a classic case-history about the delicacy of trust that needs to exist between a Head and his Governors. The Chairman of Governors of another Protestant Public School, Silcoates, has said that usually it will be clear within the first year whether a new Head is going to last, and be effective. Kitson Clark, a Cambridge Tutor, wrote that there had been *storms all round* following Dr Derry's arrival. There were interventions of many kinds; the father of one boy in Collinson requested that the School achieve better results with his younger son, and the mother, unaware of this, took exception to the Head's resultant comment in the next Report, and took the boy away without notice; the Court, notably including Rooker Roberts, endorsed TKD's actions. A number of boys were removed, not by parents, but by TKD, one of them for writing *sneering remarks* in a textbook about the reforms he had begun to put in place. The stage was set. (That first year also revealed one other disturbing common attitude of the 'authorities', only incidental to Dr Derry's case, which to the eye of the 21st century must bear later comment.)

By 24 March 1939, the Court was reporting *rumours of unrest* and *an unsatisfactory state of things... for some time past*. There was a secret burning by the boys of Derry's excellent History books, which had been used in one year-group, and according to one boy, the school was "seething" with dissent of a kind that had nothing to do with Mill Hill's origins. Many just could not take his personal 'style': *that's how we did it at*

Repton, was a remembered but unforgiven phrase. The sole member of his staff still able to bear witness, at the distance of nearly 60 years, Donald Hall, merely relayed the later not exactly *bon mot* of one of the 'old school' of Housemasters who went up to St Bees with Dr Derry, "Tom" Jackson, who clearly had an axe to grind. In the line of many 19th-century Public School Heads – Keate of Eton, Thomas James of Rugby, or Mitchinson of King's School Canterbury – Dr Derry, at 33, was a short man, but with a strong presence and precise Oxford accent – he very rarely raised his voice; he was wont to place visitors to his study on a low chair, and appear to talk down to them, standing on the fender of his fireplace. He had been an ambitious young Head of History at Repton. Tom's topical but unfair witticism was: *Hitler, but littler*. It was clear by now, as *Nobis* expresses it, *that the School and the Headmaster were on completely different wavelengths.*

Yet the Derrys would also be recalled for their kindness by new boys such as David Turner, when under the Derrys' care in their temporarily shared House, "Fern Bank", at St Bees. He is described by one of his senior monitors, in a group that went with him on a hair-raisingly dangerous cross-country walking tour across the Norwegian glaciers, as having lots of *guts*. At SMGS after the war, he damaged his nose while organising an informal rugger practice. *St Bees Remembered* tells how he would take a group of his seniors on a similarly arduous walk up to Helvellyn and Striding Edge. The very clear implication is that he had virtues to be loyal to. Alan Elliott, the son of the then Second Master, Victor Elliott, recounted how his father remained faithful to the Head, believing that his duty lay with whoever was '*on the bridge*' at any given time. One of the Governors rooted for Dr Derry, declaring he was worth two of any master at the School; two Governors were to resign over the whole affair. The *Nobis* judgment was that *not all the unhappiness was of his making... the undoubted administrative ability which Derry possessed has never been fully acknowledged... although his objectives were sound, his means of achieving them simply did not suit Mill Hill.*

Certainly TKD achieved one major project, for which the School should remain grateful: by dint of what the Court did pay tribute to as *his initiative and energetic action*, he brought the School through the successive shocks of Munich and the outbreak of war. He found St Bees, not as was thought for the ensuing 50 years, through some unknown process of networking within the HMC, but simply because his mother had heard on

Dr Kingston Derry, MHS Head Master 1938-40, looks after the last MHS President, The Earl of Athlone (l.) and former Governor Jack Todd: Cranleigh match, Top Field 1938. 6.r

the radio that St Bees School was liable to close through lack of numbers. Dr Derry organised the two departures – the September 1938 false alarm – and the real thing of September 1939. Having got the School into her exile, and indeed having created good sterling 'backs-to-the-wall' PR out of it in both *Illustrated Sporting & Dramatic News*, and in the *News Chronicle* that autumn, "The Tick" did actually live up to his nickname; he kept things ticking for a further seven months. Events finally overtook him, with the inevitability of true tragedy, for there was that rigidity in his own make-up which he later accepted might, in this phase of his life, have led to his undoing.

Elements in the situation

There are a dozen salient points in 'The Case of Dr Derry'. Jacks' personal act was a hard one to follow anyway – as hard as McClure's had been for Jacks himself in 1922. A familiar landmark had gone; schools collectively are conservative, and do not take kindly to change, unless they have already become aware of the need for it. Jacks was tall, urbane, with a good head of dark brown hair, and with the stature of one more in the line of Millhillian public figures; although an eminent DPhil, Dr Derry was none of these. However, as revealed by a Board of Education Inspectors' Report, discussed on 2 June 1939 (no surprise to critics such as Francis Cammaerts), Derry inherited a *really lamentable state of work in the school ... the standard was deplorable in the lower forms ... a lot of poor material ... and quite poor teaching ... the masters were not making efforts ... The Head was facing a really difficult task ...* Reversing such trends would be even more arduous in a school where, as Dr Pickard-Cambridge would later complain to the Court on 14 December 1940, *both masters and boys had a sub-conscious feeling that games counted even more than work.* The Governors sensed moreover in 1938 that tough times lay ahead; they needed a new Head incisive enough to make the hard decisions. The diagnosis was correct; in this respect the selection process was on target. Though there was a very human side to him, realised more at SMGS than at Mill Hill, Dr Derry could project a very determined *persona*. He needed to, for the Housemasters were then at their most baronial – jealously guarding the drawbridges to their fiefdoms: an entrenched force on the look-out for what Harrow's historian has called a 'Runnymede' with their new Head. Tom Jackson's Burton Bank, the original Out-House, only recently moved from Burtonhole Lane, still had some of the character of being 'apart'. Any Head would have had problems, let alone amidst the looming challenges of 1938-40.

(i) School Housemaster's house, sitting room during era of Mr and Mrs Vic Elliott, extension of 1928; (ii) (opposite) – today the Crick Room for formal meetings. Bronze by *OM* Herbert Ward, 'Grief', in far right corner. *6.s*

TKD had already been tasked with continuing the confidential negotiations with Middlesex County Council (see Ch.VIII): he had no reason to suppose that the Court would not back him in problems that might arise in all other areas. Yet the whole organisation was by now in a state of apprehension about things in Europe. The barbarians were not merely at the gates, but, after the Guernica attack in the Spanish Civil War, could be imagined up there above them all, raining bombs down from the sky. Everything would be tested to breaking, from nerves, stomachs, health and bedsprings, to loyalty and trust.

By November 1939, the Court in London would actually give Dr Derry the remit for economies, made necessary by, as it were, the triple pincer movement of increased costs due to the move, the uncertainties of compensation for their usurped territory, and the reduced numbers due to parents who would not join them in that move, despite the prospect of increased safety from the dreaded air-raids. The scope for such economies was made more difficult by virtue of the fact that, as with McClure in the First World War, no wartime Head can control the composition of his CR. There were at least two good young men whom he had already appointed, and who would return to lend distinction to Dr Whale's post-war staff: Mervyn Wigram was being called up, and Donald Hall (his organisational skills instrumental in getting the School more or less bedded down at St Bees) would shortly be called to secret services for ICI, vital to the war effort. The remainder were at the upper end of the salary scales, with only Percy McAllister getting a good 'chit' from the BoE inspectors.

Once up at St Bees, distance militated against communication and understanding between Head and Court: it took a Head four days out of School to attend Governors' Meetings at the OMC Town Club at Whitehall Court, SW1, and return to Cumberland: some Governors did make the trip, but no Court was ever held up there for the convenience of any Head who, as usual, had a teaching load on top of everything else. Any absence further strained the scarce resources. Already, by the time of their arrival in exile, TKD had had to report that *one Housemaster had seemed unwilling to shoulder his fair share of the burdens... it was not what a Headmaster had the right to expect.* Underneath everything, time was running out as fast as money from the coffers, and boys from the Roll: the loss of the School's 52 Day boys had reduced numbers to 255.

Then there was the issue of 'Out-House senior monitor' David Morris, which had surfaced at Easter 1939. David Morris himself made available his clear recall of this aspect of the affair. He was asked by Dr Derry to write him a letter saying why he had opted to leave early, after the Head had fought hard to get him a further scholarship to stay on. Dr Derry only quoted parts of that letter to the Court, not in itself a heinous offence, but one which acted as a fuse in the bad atmosphere that by now existed. Amid accusations of concealment, some *OM* Governors invited a few senior masters (and Morris) to a covert dinner, unknown to the Head, to find out what was going on: (a dubious move – if others were to have inferred malice, it might have cost these Governors their jobs). If the Head had got wind of it, he could rightly have accused them of undermining him.

A master diplomat, with full powers, might conceivably have squared this circle of difficulty, with time, and the right atmosphere among the CR. He might have brought the Treasurer and/or the Chairman of the Court with him, so that they could have steered the ship ahead in partnership. It is possible that the Court might have realised that their man was was only doing what they had asked him to do, to make savings on the pay-roll, albeit in a manner that was not calculated to win friends. However events did not happen that way. Dr Derry had set about changing things from the moment of arrival. His recipe for savings fell in due course on two senior 'barons' – Jackson and Morrison – men of some ability, who had been, rightly or wrongly, thorns in his flesh from the outset, questioning his changes. Some, like Derry's request for the wearing of academic gowns at St Bees, were not intrinsically wrong, and could well have raised self-respect and morale. *What, in war-time, Head Master?* was JPM's apparently mocking riposte in the *CR*. Moreover, both men had shown unquestioned commitment to the School, had a firm constituency among the boys and the monitors, and, the crowning touch in Mill Hill's case in those days, the confidence of the OMC. Even so, on 19 March, the Court agreed *that the interests of the School would best be served by terminating* [their] *contracts.*

Dr Derry should nevertheless – metaphorically – have picked opponents his own size: his chosen targets were too well-stockaded in the Mill Hill heartland. If it comes to the crunch, any Head in any school is bound to lose out against a nearly united CR. Here was a certain inbuilt blindness to realities, a fault of political *nous*, in a new culture that he may mistakenly have thought was like his previous conditioning at Repton: after all had not a previous Head, C.A.Vince, also been a master there too? Like other subsequent Heads, he was to discover that Mill Hill was indeed *sui generis*, and that this difference had a whole world of meaning.

Had the Court and TKD made a mutually wrong choice on 27 July 1937? Many good schoolmasters eventually make a private, commonsense judgement about themselves, and settle for a House as the entirely satisfying acme of their ambition. Yet this was not a case of an outstandingly gifted Departmental Head rising above his 'level of competence' – what is today called the 'Peter Principle'; UCS were simultaneously considering Derry for their next Head. Could this all have been foreseen? These are ultimately quite unanswerable questions. There was perhaps one lesson to be drawn. There is a dubious convention that a casting vote makes decisions unanimous – ranks close; in the Chair was "Nath." Micklem KC (taking Silk first under Queen Victoria, then later to be QC again under Queen Elizabeth). *Nobis* tells the story: *The Selection Committee* [actually an enlarged Governors' group] *of 16 then voted – and split right down the middle.* In other words, there were enough doubters at the selection to cause the Court to stop in its tracks, and ask itself: should we proceed? This is what would surely happen in today's world in an industrial/commercial context, where the effects of a less than well-endorsed top appointment are so well understood that expediency is rarely allowed to prevail in cases of doubt: the selection committee has to go back to the drawing board. Had it done so in this case, the all-round tragedy would have been avoided: the School would have had a temporary hiatus, not the first, and one not insuperable (as the events of 1978 and 1995 would later prove); the disharmony in the *CR* would have been kept under control; Dr Derry's administrative career would not have had its temporary shock.

Anticipating the next chapter, would a less forceful man have got the reluctant school to its wartime exile at St Bees quite as expeditiously? Would the lessons of the Inspectors' Report have been applied as relevantly? The announcement of Hitler's invasion of Norway on 9 April 1940 came as a *deus ex machina*; the Derrys put their special knowledge at the BBC's disposal. Dr Derry spent his war in political intelligence, including a spell with SHAEF. On his departure he wished Mill Hill well in a gnomic, cryptic message, hoping that *the future of the school would be worthy of the best of its past traditions.*

After a brief stand-in by the loyal Victor Elliott over Easter 1940, Rooker Roberts, an almost mystically committed *OM* and Governor, and the first Master of Belmont, who played a somewhat equivocal role in the Derry matter, would step into the breach. Fences would start to be mended, notices to the key but resistant Jackson and Morrison withdrawn, and somehow, with a recalculation of natural wastage, the immediate cost problem would be resolved. The sigh of relief would be audible from St Bees to Whitehall Court. The corporate entity survived – just.

Pre-war insular attitudes

The one disturbing point in the concerns of the Court at this period was the attitude to what it called 'foreigners'. To the surprised eye of the wholly non-discriminatory Mill Hill of 2006/7 there was evidence then of a degree of a national vein of insularity, which sits oddly with the School's earlier code of religious and racial tolerance. There had been a generous welcome to many boys from Europe, for example Norman Mirsky, a German Jewish refugee, finding himself *astonishingly – accepted*, on arrival in Dr Derry's Mill Hill in Autumn 1938: *I had got used to looking before turning a corner: no need for that any more!* Although there was also an acceptance of the rightness of taking in some refugee teachers, there was still a lingering concern about what should be the right 'proportion' of boys from non-Christian homes and backgrounds. Both the pre-war incumbents were caused to enter into such discussions, and Derry had an informal instruction to initiate a *numerus clausus* of 10 per cent of admissions. In the flurry of events, this thread was lost to view; no action was taken. One educationist *OM* recalled some anti-semitism both at St Bees, and post-war; a 1950s insistence on daily Chapel and Saturday classes did in effect exclude strictly observant Jews. Roland Wade was one of two positive *OM* witnesses: *I do not remember racism or anti-semitism*; Donald Salinger, from an Anglo-Jewish family, found *that the school was pretty tolerant – I know we were excused school for the major Jewish festivals.* Nevertheless, there is food for thought here; even a School with a long belief in tolerance could have its blind spots, from which to draw lessons. The correctness of Mill Hill's actions in all matters of equality from the latter part of the 20th century onwards make these earlier *lacunae* in the record the more puzzling.

With his resignation, Dr Derry would pass out of Mill Hill's annals, although not out of touch: he and Buster corresponded genially for many years. Those tricky problems in corporate governance remain on the record as a reminder for the future.

Meanwhile sterner things were at stake: Hitler had already secretly signified through one of his few written papers, the Berchtesgaden document of August 1936, his decision that Soviet Communism must be destroyed through war; all Soviet War Games assumed Germany as the aggressor. Following the next stage of expansion – Austria in 1938 – Hitler had summoned his Generals to plan the dismemberment of Czechoslovakia, and Poland, as preludes to that strategy. War with the West had not yet crystallised in a mind that, like Stalin's, saw the world solely in terms of struggle: indeed the Munich capitulation confirmed that belief, and led directly to the Russo-German Pact of 1939. The two dictatorships could be forgiven for thinking, on the basis of the evidence then, that Britain had no stomach for another war. Many *OMs*, and MHS Assistant Masters, were due to take part in the removal of that serious misreading of the British character, which was to find its reflection in Mill Hill attitudes of the wartime and post-war periods.

Sources for Ch.VI include: # *MHM* March 1964; 1977 (No 496), ref J.E.Whitehead; MHS Trsr's 'Agenda Record Bk' for CoG 1935-44, & for B/C 1932-9; Jacks' Newsletter, Dec 1937; MHS Press Cuttings 1932-8; "Buster" Brown Archv; HM's Notice Bk, 1939-40; Jacks 1964 obits – *Times* 1.ii, *Nature* 14.iii; R.M.R.Gilchrist [1950-3] to Ed, *MHM*, 18.ii.1993 ref R.Gilchrist [1918-23]; Sutcliffe, *op cit*; *Kinematograph Weekly*, S.viii.1920; corr Donald Hall – Dr E.Murray 1972; *Everyman*, 30.iv.1930; dscns, Gov. G.Chase, 2003, re Crckt Coach/ Hd Groundsmn, gdfr Augustus Chase.

F.H.C.Crick [1930-4]: Crick, *What Mad Pursuit, A Personal View of Scientific Discovery* (1973); J.D.Watson, *Double Helix* (1968) #; *Daedalus*, Jnl, Amer.Acad. Arts & Sciences 'Francis Crick DNA & the Central Dogma' (1989); Ltr, Crick to Winfield, 25.x.2000; *Guardian*, rprt, *Europe Quarterly* poll, 16.vii.1997, & 11.viii.1998, ref F.H.C.Crick, Order of Merit; Prestige Lecture 19.xi.1998, Prof S.Jones, 'Evolution', comment in dscn; J.Gribben, *Science, A History…* (Allen Lane, 2002), comparison, Crick & Watson,, pp 63-8; C4TV 7.iii.03: 'DNA, The Story of Life'; BBC R4 programme, 'DNA…', 12.iv.03; *obit, The Independent*, 30.vii.04 and *obit* by author and John Shilston, *MHM* 2004. Also *'Neue Zürcher Zeitung'*, 13.x.04, 'Francis Crick – ein Leben für die Wissenschaft': (thanks to T.Allan [1945-9].#)

Background: Barnet Archvs, Hendon, (L373.42), 25.vi.1957; Judd, *op cit*; F.A.M.Webster, *Our Great Public Schools* (Ward Lock, 1937)#; T.J.M.Bishop & R.Wilkinson, *op cit*; Hope Simpson, *op cit*; J.Morley & N.Monk-Jones, *Bishop's Stortford College 1868-1968: A Centenary Chronicle* (1969); Dr L.P.Jacks, *Faith of a Worker* (1925), *Life and Letters of Stopford Brooke* (1917); M.L.Jacks, *Education as a Social Factor* (1937), *Physical Education* (1938); J.Dimbleby, *Richard Dimbleby* (Hodder Headline, 1975) #; F.R.Dimbleby [1927-31], *Frontiers are Green* (Hodder & Stoughton, 1943;) Noltingk, *op cit* #; Rev. Paul Rowntree Clifford [W.Ham Cntl Mission, 1926-32], *An Ecumenical Pilgrimage* (1994) #; E.M.Forster, *A Passage to India* (1924); D.Christie-Murray, *Arms of Mill Hill School* (Harrow, 1962) #; Corr/ dscns with OMs of 1922-58: P.Calderara [1927-9]; F.C.A.Cammaerts [1930-4]; R.Cherry [1923-6]; A.D.V.Elliott [1937-42]; N.S.Farrow [1927-30]; A.P.B.Figgis [1953-7]; H.Fry [1924-8]; A.I.F.Goldman [1934-7]; R.W.Graves [1919-

24]; I.Gundry [1918-23]; D.C.Hailey [1928-32]; Mrs D. Howard, widow of P.D.Howard [1922-8]; K.N.Lloyd [1928-31]; J.McAdam [1945-8]; J.S.McGavin [1925-9]; N.Mirsky [1938-42]; D.E.Morris [1933-9], D.D.Overy [1927-30], O.S.Peddar [1928-32], H.H.Pool [1919-26], D.P.Salinger [1928-31]; T.Springer [1921-5]; P.E.Trier [1935-8]; D.J.Turner [1939-43]; R.Wade [1918-25]; T.D.Walker [1926-9]; G.L.E.Wild [1927-30]; P.M.Woodroffe [1942-5]), (later Sec. to CoG until 'Incorporation', 1998); also with Katharine Whitehorn [1939]. Dscn, A.Ereira, 14.iii.2003, ref 1950s. C.M.Meade-King, HS/M SH, 1946-55. Lord Rennell of Rodd GCB, GCMG, GRVO, PC – poet, diplomat, statesman (1846-1941). G.Gorodetsky, *Grand Delusion…* (Yale UP, 1999).

International Summer Schools & WWII: R.Overy, *Russia's War* (1998); recall by M.Sellers [1936-41], A.C.Downer [1934-9], N.D.Yates [1933-6] & P.T.Parr [1933-9]; MHS Brochure 1937 #; Institut für Zeitgeschichte, Munich: *Feldafinger Beobachter – Reichsschule der NSDAP*, Jan-Marz 1944 #; H.Scholtz, *NS-Ausleseschulen, Internatsschulen als Herrschaftsmittel des Führerstaates*, 299-325 (Göttingen, 1973) #; Wiener Library: *Der erste Jahresbericht: NS-Deutsche Oberschule Starnbergersee 1934/5*; A.Bullock, *Hitler…* rev edn (1962), Ch 6 'The Counterfeit Peace, 1933-71*; E.Heath, *The Course of my Life…* (1998); R.Wistrich, *Who's Who in Nazi Germany* (1982); E. Stockhorst, *Fünftausend Köpfe…* (Bild und Blick Verlag, 1967); Sir Philip Gibbs, *The Pageant of the Years* (1946) 387-8; Wilkinson, *op cit* 89, q. Lord Salter; Ogilvie, *op cit*; corr, M.Hart, 1998; C.Wilmot, *Struggle for Europe* (1954), 412; P.L.Delaney, *How Public School Boys Live* (trans, Leipzig, 1934); R.Griffith, *Fellow Travellers of the Right…* (1980); R.Overy, *Interrogations, The Nazi Elite in Allied Hands, 1945*, 82 (2001). M.Pugh, *Hurrah for the Blackshirts – Fascists & Fascism in Britain between the Wars*, 2005; (see also sermon by Rev.P.Hunt, MHS 3.x.05): *The BUF had organisations in at least 11 major public schools including…Mill Hill….*

Dr Derry: corr, Dr T.K.Derry, OBE, Oslo, 1997-2001 #; *News Chronicle* 3.xi.1939 #; *Illustrated Sporting & Dramatic News* 10.xi.1939: 'Famous Schools in a New Setting: Mill Hill Boys in Cumberland' #; *Times* obit, 30.vii.2001 & *MHM* obit 2003; Archvs, Bedales S; City, Westminster (St Marylebone GS GMs) E.McNeal, Dep. HM, St Marylebone GS; Old Philologians R.Berger,

J.Bidwell; corr MLJ & RWBB to AJRR, May 1940 #; dscns 1996-9, A/M Donald Hall; E.ap G.Lewis [1939-44]: V.Raitz [1937-9].

Goyder family: access to MHS Science Library's Archvs #; dscns & corr with the Goyder family, & range of press & Archv material on C.W. Goyder CBE, [1920-4] suplied by his brother Claude [1925-30] (including: GPO Cablegram Nr 18, 19.x.1924, "World at Their Fingertips: RSGB History", 101-2; International Press Bureau, *News Chronicle* 12.viii.1924, *Nat. Geographical Soc* ltr 24.x.1925, *New York Herald Tribune* 2.iii.1924 #; Goyder, *op cit* #; *Independent* 3.iii.1997, & *RSA Journal* CXLV No 5477, Mar 1997; obits of G.A.Goyder; commentary on modern radio commctns, P.M.Z.Duck [1945-50], 11.i.1997, *Star*, Dunedin, 17.x.1999, courtesy of J.E.C.Dicks [1944-7]; lttr to author by Dr.G.Howat, 20.vi.05: fellow-member with TKD of OU and CU Schools' Exam Bd.

UK Nameplate: Great Western Archive, 'Saint' class: 2976 'Winterstoke', built 1905 as 4-6-0, named 1907, withdrawn 1934. * John Daniel. Internet 2000; * data, Roderick Shelford, 2003.

Other *OM* references: W.R.D.Adkins [1875-80]; J.R.Auty [1924-7]; N.Baker [1955-61]; P.A.Block [1936-9]; M.S.Briggs [1896-9]; R.W.B.Buckland [1878-84]; D.E.Buckley [1923-7]; H.E.Carris [1923-7]; H.K.Childs [1922-6]; L.H.Collison [1921-7]; W.E.Vernon Crompton [1882-3]; C.J.Cross-Brown [1931-6]; J.R.Easonsmith [1923-8]; P.Ebstein [1936-8]; A.P.B.Figgis [1953-7]; E.L.J.Grear [1906-10]; R.L.Grimsdell [1927-31]; S.Lavington Hart [1876]; P.N.Hawker [1932-8]; G.A.Holmes [1930-4]; 'Baynham Honrie'/ P.B.H.Thompson [1919-21]; A.H.Hourani [1928-33]; J.W.G.Hume [1919-25]; N.G.Brett James [1894-8]; K.Katzenstein [1936-8]; G.W.Knox [1853-6]; T.H.B.Lawther [1922-8]; J.McGowan [1887-91]; H.Marnham [1874-80]; B.K.Martin [1914-6]; K.T.Marx [1934-7]; P.L.Michelsohn [1936-9]; A.L.Milligan [1930-4]; J.D.Mitchell [1895-9]; W.B.Morrison [1931-6]; G.B.Moss [1934-7]; W.Murray-Wood [1931-5]; W.J.Owen aka Oppenheimer [1936-8]; C.H.B.Priestley [1929-34]; A.J.Rooker Roberts [1893-1900]; J.Shilston, [1930-3]; P.Smith [1829-34?]; W.H.Sobey [1918-24]; C.Southwell [1869-74]; A.Spicer [1858-63]; R.S.Spong [1918-24]; Street family – A.D.M. [1929-34] – D.O. [1935-40]; C.Swain [1926-9]; D.Thatcher [1928-32]; H.L.Warren [1924-8]; W.H.Wills [1842-7].

The Great Divide

"Mill Hill on Sea": Wartime in Cumbria

Semper memores opis datae:
(memorial window of the St Bees Old Millhillians Association,
St Bees School Chapel, dedicated 18 May 1997).

As the School pianos were at last offloaded from an advance train-load at St Bees station yard, late one evening in early September 1939, a novel sound rang out in the cold clear Cumbrian air. Donald Hall, then Collinson House Tutor, recalled seeing Katharine, the 11-year-old daughter of his boss – Housemaster Alan Whitehorn – suddenly strike up the tune of "Chopsticks" on the freezing keys; she was immediately accompanied by the new, buxom House Matron, the eponymous Miss Bigg. This cheerful impromptu by a celebrated future journalist and author of *Whitehorn's Social Survival* (and also the first "Old Millhillienne" – see Ch.XI) was in a way symbolic: it seemed to invoke an ancient Mill Hill quality – the spirit of improvisation – now needed for Katharine and others to survive at all, in these traumatically unfamiliar surroundings.

Although the second of the two World Wars to cut through the Mill Hill ranks was in many ways – paradoxically – less of an event in the life of what was still the 'GC', it radically altered the process of education, in a way that its 1914-18 forerunner did not. If, economically, the Thirties depression was a 'Great Divide', this third Great War that Britain and the School had undergone was the 'Great Divide' in educational terms: the universe of the Public Schools was about to lock on to a new orbit that would reach out into the next century. As **Fig.F(iii)** showed (Ch.II), the homogeneity of Mill Hill's intake, and accents, was about to become one facet of this long slow process of change; nothing would be quite the same again.

A small incident, vouchsafed casually one day in 1998 at Walker House, by Bill Burton, a long-standing member of the Mill Hill contracting staff, highlights the incongruities of this strange chasm that was soon to open up in the whole ethos of the buildings and grounds. His elder brother, Tim, had been one of the local workforce drafted in to prepare the School in August 1939 for the imminent takeover by the Emergency Hospital, including the provision of lavatories for the army of nurses that would be arriving. One of the more draconian decisions of that frenetic time was to burn, on Top Terrace, any School clothing or other items that were still left around in lockers and studies from the previous term. Tim spotted a tasseled brown velvet Rugby cap lying on the ground near the bonfire, missed by the sacrificial flames. In a wild moment he put it on and started to lark about with it. Dr Derry was due to leave on the night of the day that war was declared, Sunday 3 September, for an overnight car drive, with Col Mitchell, the School Bursar-cum-Secretary, to join the forward party temporarily occupying the guest

WWII evacuation to St Bees, Cumbria, to avoid anticipated German saturation bombing of London: first departure of Belmont boys, 'Munich' 1938; (note use of MHS School cap). 7.*a*

rooms at the *Seacote Hotel*: (that same day an Inventory had been made of the contents of the whole School). Dr Derry, spotting the luckless Tim from his study, charged out immediately to tick him off, for *letting the School down*: in the very act of destroying part of the Mill Hill's tradition, there was also an attempt to celebrate it, however forlornly.

Outwardly, that historic divide in time, and the contradictions it exacted upon Mill Hill, are marked by two parallel aspects of the School's story, which thus form the two sections of the History's central chapter: the enforced exile of both schools to Cumberland; and the unimaginable occupation of their hallowed territory, those intrinsic frameworks for school life, as part of the war effort. Belmont had the better of the deal: in September 1938 a would-be 'recce' contingent of some 30 boys (out of a future 55) from the Junior School, led by Arthur Roberts ("A.E."), his mother-in-law Mrs "Tiggi" Clark, and Bertie Ricks, had actually decamped, for the temporary occupation of a former girls' school, St Helens, at Cockermouth which Mrs Pattie Roberts is believed to have 'found': in Ronnie Aye Maung's words, *a huge and sombre house ... like something out of a Mervyn Peake ghost story*. It was far enough away from the Main School's future base for A.E. to preserve jealously what Dr Derry later described as the young Master's desire for *the maximum independence for the junior school*. Those 1938 dates compare with the pathetic flights of Neville Chamberlain from Heston Airport (the later Heathrow) to Germany, in his foredoomed endeavour to placate Hitler on Czechoslovakia, which are now believed to have made the Second World War finally inevitable:

c.Monday 15 Sept: Belmont assembles; decision to evacuate finalised.	(Neville Chamberlain): *22 Sept*: flight to Bad Godesberg, return 24th;
c.28 Sept: train-party to St Helen's, Cockermouth.	*29 Sept*: flight to Munich: return with 'piece of paper' – "peace" 20 Sept;
c.Sun 1 Oct: party back to Belmont.	

Exile to the 'safety zone'

West Cumberland was a 'safety zone'. The text for Rev. Michael Whitehorn's sermon at the SBOMA 1989 service was: *the stranger who sojourns with you shall be ... as the native among you;* for those Belmont strangers, after Mrs Brenda Roberts went up with the new Cook, Miss Hardwick, on 27 August 1939, the ground had been cleared, with the benefit of a woman's eye, for their two-part arrival. The first was on 7 September, the second late on Friday the 22nd, with the bulk of the southern party, as the Cockermouth-Penrith coach in a LMS prototype 'Schools Special' – for Roedean and Sedbergh as well. (The Mill Hill print in St Bees' *Queen's Hotel* misleadingly records 3 September). 'Mill Hill on Sea' absorbed its new 'natives' – somehow. Despite a plan of 12 January 1939 to take over Mrs Chance's Workington Hall for 'the School', as one boy wrote, *we first arrivals, most with parents, helped the masters and their wives clean up houses ... which had not been occupied for years.* Other 'evacuees' included: Felsted, to the Wye; Leys, to Pitlochry; Malvern, to Blenheim

Palace, and thence to much-bombed stay-put Harrow in 1942, whilst, according to legend, the Army barred the Head's entry to his own study. Some had happy experiences: Kingswood to Uppingham to share a location, like Mill Hill; The Mount, a local girls' school already featured, to a country house at Amberley, Gloucester. Roedean, the school to which the Whitehorns tried to send their spirited daughter (she 'cycled away', back to St Bees almost at once) found themselves at the *Keswick Hotel*. (While they spent the war there, their own buildings in Brighton were, like Mill Hill's, taken over for the war effort. An *OM* officer, Graham Patterson, training at what was now HMS *Vernon*, the Navy's Torpedo School, was much comforted by the famous notice left on his dormitory wall: *if you require a mistress during the night, ring bell*.)

Rooker Roberts ("A.J.") wrote that the School's task was like that of Sisyphus, ever rolling his boulder 'up the hill'. That metaphor was not accidental: this was the recurring archetypal 'Hill' of this History. He added: *We are now embarked on a journey where to struggle is even better than to succeed*. Characteristic of Mill Hill, with a now ingrained habit of surviving against the odds, her exile seems to have been tougher than most. One representative of this moment of change was the young Katharine's father, self-styled "The Baron" while at Mill Hill, a revered Head of Classics, when Classics Departments still set the tone for a whole school. With a heavy 'Baronial' pair of eyebrows, he was – as the letters received on his death in 1981 make clear – the educator, in the widest sense, of generations of Millhillians. It may appear ironical that the only classical quotation to grace the chapter-headings of this History should introduce this surely unrepeatable era in Mill Hill's story, so apparently inimical to all academic tradition, including the classical (see Appendix F). For if ever there were a time when the *musae* had to battle for survival with *virtutem*, it was the six years to 26 July 1945.

At first sight it seems extraordinary that any education was achieved at all, in the broader sense that Alan Whitehorn's beleaguered colleagues would have understood: writing to him on 9 February 1940, Jacks' former scholar, now Oxford's Prof Albert Hourani, sympathised with *that wretched institution on its nomadic course. Scholarship by all means*, conceded A.J. in September 1941, *to the limit of our capacity*. By December 1940, that capacity was demonstrated: (at Cambridge, Maths and Classics Scholarships for Geoff Sears at St John's and John Henderson at Trinity, with John Campsie's Classics Exhibition at Merton, Oxford); a year later Ian Wright equalled that Trinity triumph, coupled with Michael Kempster's Brasenose History Scholarship: for the future Deputy Editor of *The Economist* and first *OM* to merit a full-page 'bio' in a newspaper, Norman Macrae, a Languages Exhibition at Corpus, CU. Foundation Day 1944 would record five Oxbridge awards, including a Cambridge Maths Major. Less extraordinary was it that the monitorial ranks of that era bred two future Governors (Judge Michael Kempster and Rev. Michael Whitehorn), and two OMC Presidents (Judge Esyr Lewis QC, and Roy Mills).

Five men were to lead 'the good fight' for Mill Hill in exile under the Chair of Governors, "Nath." Micklem KC (not to be confused with his son, Rev. Dr Nathaniel Micklem). For all of them, the Christian spirit of that great hymn was significant: Dr Derry up to *c*.18 April 1940; then Rooker Roberts, the third *OM* and sole Rugger

KATHARINE WHITEHORN

THE Mr Chips of Mill Hill School, Buster Brown, used to explain why he stayed away from auctions. He often liked to pick up wireless parts in job lots with the odd basket-chair or incomplete encyclopedia thrown in; but one day he was bidding for a lot which included a parrot. 'Thirty bob,' he said. 'Thirty-five.' said someone else. Buster stopped; but the parrot said, 'Two pounds!' and he became its astonished owner.

Even without the hazards of parrots, it's odd to realise how much can get auctioned. Railway lost-property auctions are always full of absurd things like boxes of bedroom slippers, a barrel, organ, a stuffed ape; the

Head of Classics' daughter, Katharine Whitehorn (later journalist on *The Observer*) attended MHS, 1940; technically, first Old Millhillienne. *7.b*

THE NEW LIBRARY.
Book Plate:
A VIEW OF THE PRIORY CHURCH.

Mill Hill adapts:
(i) September 1939:
change-of-address
note for parents;
(ii) St Bees Priory as
book-plate;
(iii) Tomlin Head on book
prize-label. *7.c*

"Blue" as Head, the man who feared being seen as 'ousting' him – from 9 May 1940 to his sudden death in the Summer of 1943 (echoing another death in harness, that of his idol, Sir John McClure); next, for a holding operation up to Spring 1944, Maurice Jacks once more, already a 'Lakesman' through his Trusteeship of Wordsworth's Dove Cottage – ready, if asked, to stand in, in 1940. He told A.J.R.R., *I envy you.* He described his friend, Dr John Whale, who would see the School back home in autumn 1945, as occupying *a distinguished place in the life of this country.* A vital fifth wheel on what might easily have become a very shaky coach was provided by Victor Elliott, Second Master, who, as his wife told their son, Alan, *had a lot on his shoulders* from late 1939 onwards, and who loyally manned the bridge as Acting Head for the second half of an illness-riddled Spring Term, delayed after the worst snows for 50 years – from at least 18 April to 8 May; he was one of those senior teachers who are always the backbone of a school. That frequency of change at the top would demote the epicentre of power down the School's 'system'; it had several effects, not least the relationship with those who left to join up, in contrast to the continuity embodied in John McClure in 1914-18.

Getting the bearings

The wider definition of 'Mill Hill' demands a seven-year time-span, to July 1946; only then did the Junior School return – from Cockermouth to a cockroach-infested Belmont. The unequal battle waged by both staffs against the odds did have lighter aspects; yet to the Main School's drive to 'come through', there was a darker side – initially irreconcilable – which will need examining. Its special setting was elsewhere described by author Graham Sutton: *Saint Bees School lies in a dale which curves round behind the headlands; moonshaped, five miles through, nowhere very wide, its green sides too steep to plough …* This became for the boys a *romanticised Northland* – to borrow a phrase from one of Dr Derry's fine later war-histories, *The Campaign in Norway* (being waged during his last months at St Bees); in the words of *The Herries Chronicle, a land at once so bare in its nakedness and so rich in its luxury.* At one level, it was a gloriously schoolboyish, Arthur Ransome time – Mill Hill's wartime romance. For those of a different literary bent it also had a flavour of that supreme comedy which would be re-visited in the 1980s as a House Play – Evelyn Waugh's *Decline and Fall.* Notwithstanding the fuller account conveyed in the 60 unrestricted, poetically-licensed pages of *St Bees Remembered,* this chapter has to reflect a mainly schoolboy's-eye-view of this phase of Mill Hill's story.

For 128 MHS boys out of the 486 who experienced St Bees at all (plus up to *c.*50 non-MHS Belmontians) and a few locally-hired staff, it was their only experience of 'Mill Hill' School. The SBOMA still rated 155 members on 29 April 2000 (54 had attended the 60-year AGM – 9 July 1999). They could espy 10 'memorials': the Sturgeon print of Top Terrace on the wall of *"The Queen's"*; an extant former classroom block at "Seacote"; Mill Hill-funded seats in Main Street and West's Field; the St Bees School chapel window; the 1999 Priory Paddock project; entrance gates and stables on the "Seacroft" site; a "Dr Clitterhouse" poster and Visitors Book at Richard Stout's garage; and perhaps a few surviving initials on the St Bees Head mine shaft. The witnesses to this time grew fewer with the years: encapsulated in these pages is a pen-picture of that remote terrain, for the guidance of those many thousands who might never have got any nearer that fiercely beautiful corner of England than through the Dent Field Centre or a family holiday in the Lakes – no less gaunt yet exhilarating today than it looked to Millhillians in 1939.

What *St Bees Magazine* called the *bicycling legions*, and the *MHM* the '*band of pilgrims*', had to find their bearings quickly around the village. To the uninitiated, the mere names confuse. Only the fact that "Seacroft" contains an 'r' would remind one that it was the House for Ridgeway (owned by an unforgettable local fisherman-artist, John D.Kenworthy RA), where initially, as Esyr Lewis recalled, the privileged and soon unaffordable pre-war infrastructure was re-enacted, with a Housemaid and a Boot-Boy on the payroll. Mr West's *Seacote* Hotel at the other end of the village was the social hub, with central catering – novel for Mill Hill – and where morning Assembly was staged, before breakfast in "The Devil's Kitchen", complete with "Stop Talking!". *The School in a Pub*, was the *Daily Mirror* headline. Here, until re-merged as School House in September 1942, Weymouth and Scrutton resided, and most teaching took place – or was valiantly attempted. Perhaps the 'c' located at the heart of that name harked back to those traditional Public School classical studies, rating on average three staff, and still the largest department. "Seacroft" to "Seacote" mark the south-eastern and western outposts of the territory (and later also Harry Coates' lodgings, No.3 The Crescent, bought by *OM* owner of *Whitehaven News*, Liberal James McGowan JP, former Governor and benefactor for the 1926 Park pavilion). Bicycle-driven impacts with those narrow winding drystone-walled roads, in black-out or blizzard conditions, would leave lasting imprints on many an *OM* chin or shin. A map is essential: the best model for the village, **Fig.K**, is to imagine the three initials of one of the School's legendary figures – Tom F Jackson – the only Housemaster ever to be awarded a House Scarf for stoking the boilers, and the only master to extend those fire-making propensities to the sacred confines of the Chapel, when his hastily stowed-away pipe, a constant companion, started to ignite in his pocket, in the middle of his lesson-reading. The 'T', 'F', and 'J', when superimposed, provide a rough skeleton.

Mill Hill quickly acquired landmarks, strung out along the spindly arms of this resultant figure: the *Abbot's Court Hotel*, and two of the three 'ready-made' ex-St Bees Boarder Houses: "Eaglesfield" (after "Grindal", part of Burton Bank, known as the 'Nomads' – and later Collinson) and "Tomlin" (Winterstoke: curiously, also the name of a 1960s Head of House). The coast road at the bottom of the 'J' curled south eastwards up and over the brow of the hills to Lancashire, and, as it must often have seemed, to civilisation too. The map identifies the key, nostalgic features. The Tuck Shop had four phases: (i) sharing Mrs Hale's village and St Bees School shop; then solo at (ii) "Grindal"; (iii) at Ashley House; and finally (iv) at "Mrs Midd's", 38 Main Street. There were improvised rugger pitches on Tomlin Field, while West's Field was for cricket ("Away" matches to St Bees); tennis courts, a grenade range, parade grounds for the OTC (from late 1940 evolving nationally as a JTC, also a first Air Training Section); an Assault Course by Pow Beck; and huts for the Scouts, and Young Farmers; also a hut for the Band – still today integral to School life – replete, as now, with mace, drums, sash and proud Drum-Major).

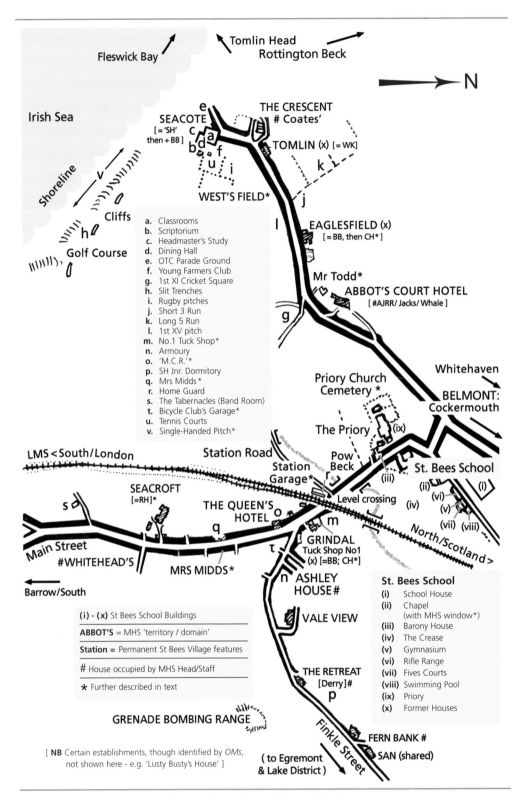

Irish Sea

Fleswick Bay

Tomlin Head
Rottington Beck

N

SEACOTE
[= 'SH'
then + BB]

THE CRESCENT
Coates'

e
c a
b d f
u i

TOMLIN (x) [= WK]

k

WEST'S FIELD*

Shoreline

v

Cliffs

h

Golf Course

j

l

EAGLESFIELD (x)
[= BB, then CH*]

Mr Todd*

ABBOT'S COURT HOTEL
[#AJRR/ Jacks/ Whale]

g

a. Classrooms
b. Scriptorium
c. Headmaster's Study
d. Dining Hall
e. OTC Parade Ground
f. Young Farmers Club
g. 1st XI Cricket Square
h. Slit Trenches
i. Rugby pitches
j. Short 3 Run
k. Long 5 Run
l. 1st XV pitch
m. No.1 Tuck Shop*
n. Armoury
o. 'M.C.R.'*
p. SH Jnr. Dormitory
q. Mrs Midds *
r. Home Guard
s. The Tabernacles (Band Room)
t. Bicycle Club's Garage*
u. Tennis Courts
v. Single-Handed Pitch*

**Priory Church
Cemetery ***

Whitehaven

**BELMONT:
Cockermouth**

The Priory
(ix)

LMS < South/London

Station Road

SEACROFT
[=RH]*

s

**Pow
Beck**

**Station
Garage***

r

(iii)

St. Bees School

(ii) (vi)
(iv) (v)

(i)

**THE QUEEN'S
HOTEL**

o

m

Level crossing

North/Scotland >

(vii) (viii)

Main Street

#WHITEHEAD'S

q

MRS MIDDS *

t

GRINDAL
Tuck Shop No1
(x) [=BB; CH*]

Barrow/South

n **ASHLEY
HOUSE #**

VALE VIEW

St. Bees School
(i) School House
(ii) Chapel
(with MHS window*)
(iii) Barony House
(iv) The Crease
(v) Gymnasium
(vi) Rifle Range
(vii) Fives Courts
(viii) Swimming Pool
(ix) Priory
(x) Former Houses

(i) - (x) St Bees School Buildings

ABBOT'S = MHS 'territory / domain'

Station = Permanent St Bees Village features

House occupied by MHS Head/Staff

* Further described in text

THE RETREAT
[Derry]#
p

GRENADE BOMBING RANGE

[**NB** Certain establishments, though identified by *OMs*,
not shown here - e.g. 'Lusty Busty's House']

FERN BANK #

SAN (shared)

Finkle Street

(to Egremont
& Lake District)

Fig.K MILL HILL ON SEA: ST BEES, CUMBRIA 1939-45

At the central junction, where the horizontal of the 'F' marks the level-crossing from the south – and the *al fresco* concert hall for that rendering of "Chopsticks" – lay the third St Bees former House, "Grindal"; it was shared, unthinkably, to begin with, between two Houses, Burton Bank and Collinson, until reclaimed, as St Bees' numbers recovered from a nadir of 81, in January 1943. An east-facing side road off Main Street up a steep hill is Finkle Street. After *The Queen's Hotel* to the west (the unofficial MCR), it was the location of seven key points: *The Albert* pub, abode and solace for Bertie Ricks; "Ashley House"/ YHA (with the Bursar's team); tucked away, a later dorm, No.1 Vale View; opposite, the Orderly Room of the OTC/JTC, under Maj Bee, and Sgt Maj Crouch, taken over as the Armoury. Next was "The Retreat", at first occupied by Dr Derry, and an escape for 13- to 14-year-olds, many of whom remembered the kindness of the Norwegian Mrs Derry as a female presence on duty; it bore its name more in hope than actuality, since it had to cope with over a dozen boys up to Spring 1940, to deal with the health-hazardous overcrowding of such dorms as could be contrived elsewhere – some with 40 or more boys. Later the Elliotts were joined there by their relations by marriage, the Milligans, from "Fern Bank", next in line up the hill to High Walton. The final staging post was a house which doubled up as a joint and friendly "San" for the host and guest schools.

1940: first of four 'MHS' Tuck Shops, Main Street: mixed wartime 'uniform' – open-neck shirts and bicycle clips. *7.d*

The St Bees factor

Although Dr Derry told an *OM* lunch on 28 October 1939 that there would be no 'fusion' of the schools, from the outset a two-way co-operation prevailed, typified on 12 November when the St Bees Head Master, John Boulter, delivered an 11th-hour Sunday sermon; later instances were debating, plane-spotting "Bees", shows by the MHS Sub-Cinema Society, and the loan of MHS JTC rifles after the Armoury fire on 17 January 1940. Mill Hill had use of the San, Chapel and Library, classrooms and Science Labs, Swimming Pool, Golf Course, Gym, Rifle Range and Fives Courts – on calculations of 'boy-terms' and 'boy-days'. *They were a source of constant fascination to us in their smart grey suits and carrying umbrellas* wrote a St Beghian, yet rivalry was endemic. Derby matches on the Village fields – no Mill Hill slope – later saw their 1st XV lose to the "Softies from the South", as George McNeil ironically dubbed his fellow-enthusiasts for *Rugby, lovely Rugby!*

Attitudes to emotional matters were primitive; through to 1945, talking to girls was forbidden. When Dr Whale arrived in 1944, his daughter, Margaret, found it all very lonely; at one stage she attracted admiration from a St Beghian, only to find that his would-be friendship was rebuffed, on her behalf, by a group of over-protective Millhillians. At School dances, the local teenage female population, and a few young WAAFs attending, may well have shared their affections impartially between these two young male communities. A twinkle comes into many an *OM* eye when this aspect of their youth is mentioned; a lady nick-named "Lusty Busty", whom Pat Scarf *accidentally ran down* on his bicycle, was promptly co-opted for the weekly dancing classes, held – to the 78s of Victor Sylvester – in the ground floor of The Priory.

Dedicated *OM* A.J.Rooker
Roberts, founder and
Master of Belmont 1912-37;
MHS Governor, and
Head Master 1940-3. *7.e*

Legend tells of Ivy; a dancer called Betty; and the so-called "House of the Scarlet Harlots", where two red-haired domestics lived. One *OM* wrote: *Of course the hormones raged then, long before we knew we had them ... there was much talk, but precious little action.* Although relatively near, neither Hunmanby Hall School (at Armathwaite Hall) on the odd boating trip across Bassenthwaite, nor the adjacent Roedean, despite the "Welcome" on their doormat, appear to have promised much comfort to Millhillians (not counting once having to spend a communal night in the shared train, snowed up, in a tunnel). There was one discreet forced marriage to a girl on the staff; and a monitor was caught *in flagrante delicto* with "an imported girl" at 2.00 a.m. in the Tomlin Head LDV Hut, no doubt with thoughts of the joys that a 'K.i.a.' might deny him. He submitted himself to an *in camera* 'monitorial' – a sanction that is shocking in 21st-century eyes; a fellow-monitor thought it was *a very glamorous way to leave school and go to war!* (See Appendix E).

"Your leader in the North"

Survival demands unity, and a particular kind of leadership that Mill Hill's Governors have tended to understand well – one of body and soul. After Dr Derry's departure, for three and a half years, with the Rooker Roberts family, Mill Hill found the old-style leadership she needed, exercised now from the "dark and dreary" premises of the *Abbot's Court Hotel*. In the words of Alan Elliott, AJ's *over-religioned* approach now had its moment. In his first sermon on 26 May, he preached on *the spiritual forces behind Mill Hill ... I have come to be your leader in the North.* The two men ran their schools in tandem: a sobersides, Cromwellian father, and – Cavalier yet never cavalier – the equally kind but sparky son (he sat in on Court Meetings with pet squirrel "Hansi" in his pocket). Some 20 miles separated them, A.J. at the St Bees of medieval Archbishop Grindal, and A.E. at Wordsworth's historic Cockermouth – a cycle ride away, as John Gould found when taking his younger brother for a meal at *The Pheasant* on Bassenthwaite. One Lavington Rooker had been a Homerton student of Pye Smith's; Dr William Rooker of Tavistock was envisaged as the School's third Head, and later the Chaplaincy; and there were five ejected Ministers among the Roberts' forebears: their spirits must have blessed the way their descendants held both forts of a still markedly Nonconformist institution at this most critical time. For those with a long perspective, the railway company carrying the School north and south would hark back once more to the 19th century: it was the London Missionary Society, still a beneficiary of Chapel collections in 1945, that had first made the initials 'LMS' important for Mill Hill.

For David Turner, A.J. was *a really loveable character who got on well with Staff and boys alike ... everybody rallied round and the school held together through a very difficult time.* Whilst not gainsaying the emotional rapport that he could engender, he could also appear to some VI Formers as a little out of touch intellectually, even an *old buffer*, for boys who might one day be sitting their Oxbridge scholarship papers at St Bees, and whose reading, in Hugh Gauntlett's phrase, was now ranging *from Lenin to T.S.Eliot.* This might seem a harsh verdict on a Governor of 58, who had come out of retirement at short notice, worrying about the effect of such a decision on a wife 12 years his senior, and who had for most of his working life beamed his mind to the interests of Prep school boys under 13; but schoolboys of that era had no reason to be too understanding of any masters, let alone Head Masters, even when they were performing manifestly superhuman roles.

Rooker took over, as he was proud to say, in the same month that Churchill was appointed PM; he sought to parallel that famous touch. It can be observed in the 29 Letters to "Dear Parents", modelled on the Christmas missives started in 1926 by his former colleague, Maurice Jacks (to be unexpectedly resumed in 1943). They perform many functions, then and now, explaining the difficulties of life at St Bees, communicating his love of nature, and his optimism, but also the conditioning of his very traditional upbringing, much social comment, and some unconscious humour. His first epistle of May 1940 declared: *Mill Hill School means the boys who compose it, and my aim is to get the best from the School for each boy and from each boy for the School.* The theme of August 1942 had entertaining overtones for the co-educational School of 50 years later: *A Dance was held in Seacote... Masters' wives and the ladies of the community generally partnered some two dozen of the senior boys... it was educational in the best sense... another side of the boys was revealed, and it was well worth revealing. I felt it was a most effective way of extending the refining influence of Ladies' society into our somewhat* [sic] *monastic austerity.* One of his last letters conjured up Foundation Day, June 1943: *the wind was from the south-west, the horizon blurred with rain-squalls and the sea breaking into white-topped waves which hurled themselves spitefully against Tomlin Head... we should have despaired, but at St Bees the weather is a quick-change artist... No one ventured out without a mackintosh, and hats had to be held on or discarded altogether. Yet I saw sunshine on the faces of everyone I met...*

That sunshine was also an inner quality. Donald Hall recounts being complimented back in 1939, before leaving for top secret munitions work for ICI, when Dr Derry told him, *You've done yeoman service here, Hall,* without actually knowing how he and other masters had done it. 'Yeoman service' was indeed the term for all the members of a still unequivocal *masters'* CR, despite the later part-time presence of two female teachers.

In his last *Newsletter* of June 1943, following a visit to war-torn Mill Hill, A.J. wrote, prophetically: *Journey's end for me was the School Chapel...* By the time that journey did finally end, a month later, A.J. had forged a great spirit to bind the staff together. Lifelong friendships were made. In his address on the deaths in retirement of both Tom Jackson and Percy McAllister, within eight days of each other in 1970, Mog Morrison would recall how Tom had *mended boilers, radiators, leaking roofs, cooking cauldrons, knife-cleaning machines, electric circuits, sewing machines... wearily emerging from the 'Ramp' [a concrete incline] at Seacote after unblocking the drains, making his tired way to a bath before starting his marking.* Mog cited William Cory's famous

'Mens sana in corpore sano': St Bees firm sands at low tide, used for cycling, running and Singlehanded.*7.f*

words: *They told me Heraclitus, they told me you were dead ... I wept as I remembered, how often you and I, Had tired the sun with talking and sent him down the sky.* This St Bees factor would reach far into the Mill Hill annals, as one by one the names from those days were no more: young "Dougie" Sim's family; Jimmy Irving, returning with the School as Cricket Coach/ groundsman, who died on 9 February 1970; and Mrs Middleton, the unwitting cause of an outburst of democracy in 1943, when the threat to sack her from her role as Tuck-Shop provider was stymied by a passive resistance movement of the whole school. On 13 April 1944 her loyalty was rewarded with a rise of 5s. to 36s. p.w., and "Mrs Midd" remained on her native soil, to die on 28 August 1967. Millhillians and staff apart, these were the last adult survivors, although local figures such as Florence Smith of Stone House Farm, and Sissie Spencer of "Quietways", in Keswick, remained in touch with Buster Brown up to the 1950s.

The bare statistics

An assessment of the St Bees years might have started with the bare statistics – and bare was a seminal word, governing knees, cupboards, necessities and essentials, and one extremely fast run through the village early one morning by a nearly-naked senior monitor, as well as the often daunting bareness of the surrounding scenery. All this was in total contrast to the abandoned life in Mill Hill Village – any perambulation by anyone along The Ridgeway, dressed in virtually nothing, even for the most worthwhile of bets, is not quite imaginable.

Fig.L shows some of the interrelated factors, of which the most basic was the MHS Roll, which fell steadily from the 256 (208 ex-London, plus 48 new boys) who arrived in September 1939 [80 more to Belmont] to the 133/[52] of March 1943 – the size of a pre-war Prep School, and rock-bottom turning point for financial viability; later, two Day Boys brought the Roll up to 187/[57]. Belmont's lowest point, mathematically at least, was the third term of 1942, down to a Dickensian "Dotheboys Hall" level of a mere 44 boys. Against rumours of closure, Rooker, with the OMC, made an unprecedented appeal for support in December 1942, but despite his perception of a shift of the tide, with an upturn in enquiries – "it may be in the hope of a speedier return..." – only 150 made the return to London by 2 October 1945 (99 new boys entering on 1 October), 60 per cent of a 1945 Roll of 249/[est. 67]; this included 21 boys from the Bursary scheme organised by Dick Auty's group of Yorkshire OMs. 'Boarding Houses'* signifies the separate buildings, plus various small units in lofts and attics rented in friendly private houses; <x> = the total of traditional MHS

Fig.L WWII: EVENTS IN EXILE: 1939-1945

Heads @	>.........TKD....] [AJRR..] [MLJ....] [JSW..............>						
Terms at St Bees		[10T]				[2T]	[4T]
	[Sept	[Jan	[Jan	[Jan	[Jan	[Jan	[Jan
Calendar years	1939	1940	1941	1942	1943	1944	1945
Numbers							
MHS/[BMT]	256/[80]		187/[57]	165/[49]	133/[52]	171/[59]	249/[67]
Boarding Houses*	5 <6>	(+small units)			4 <5>		
A/Ms (av)	23		15	16	15.5		16.5
Monitors	9	11	10	12	14	8 5 4	7
The tide of war		June 40+: Blitz Enigma Code broken					
		June 40+ Dunkirk October: Alamein					
				January: Stalingrad			
						June 4: D-Day	
						May '45 VE Day	

'Houses'. From the original 5+ <6> in 1939, this reduced to 4 <5> by January 1943 (see Appendix D).

Some of those negative factors had a positive side. Compared with post-war pupils-to-staff ratios among other Public Schools of 11.4 to 12.87, (today it is 10:1), the ratio then in 1943, normally 15:1, was 11:6; A.J. even claimed it as 10:1. This had obvious benefits in the quality of teaching. However, whilst a school such as Harrow, staying on in London, could postpone staff lay-offs until 1942, of 23 A/Ms (plus the Head) including two PE staff, and Maj McLellan, who went up to St Bees, only 15 remained a year later, among them Percy McAllister and S.W.Segger, with ubiquitous Science Master Buster Brown. He had joined McClure's staff in 1908, had served and supported three successive Head Masters – Maurice Jacks, Kingston Derry, and Rooker Roberts – forming enduring friendships with each, corresponding with the first two, and later with Dr John Whale, as well as with many hundreds of *OMs*; from retirement in 1938, he was recalled in 1939, to teach up to November 1941, later to return once more to join the Belmont staff from September 1942 to April 1943. The Modern Languages torch, in addition to J.E.Whitehead, was handed on through the succession of Col. de Watteville, Mr Prinzheim, a raggable Mr Levy, Friedrich Cronheim and, once more in 1945, de Watteville. When G.Dudley Page, the Art Master (maker of a film about St Bees life) was called up by the end of 1941, Art ended as a formal subject, until, under Dr Whale, Mrs Coates later took one class a week; by 1943 Maurice Jacks would bewail the decline in PE. Some boys in the Upper Remove were allowed to take SC a year early. The history-laden Shell Form was disbanded in October 1942.

The arrival of Bertie Ricks (the second "Mr Chips") in 1941, kept the CR at 16. The Music staff consisted of Donald Dalley to July 1941, C. de Ville to late 1943, and Myra Hess's sister up to 1944, when Dr Whale recruited two brilliant men – Alan Rusbridge and Hans Berge. The obligations of "law, custom and decency" towards conscripted masters' post-war rights to their jobs needed to be proclaimed by Governor Sir Henry Richards in February 1944, (yet Dalley would still be forced to claim compensation for loss of office, in August 1947). The 16 becomes 16½ if attendance at Miss Satterthwaite's (part-time Science teacher at Whitehaven Secondary School) is counted. A decreasing Roll meant that many boys gained an experience of the school hierarchy, which they might not otherwise have enjoyed. The all-time minimum of four monitors in early 1944 also had its advantages, from the point of view of 'the rest': the amount of overview of all that went on was very limited.

The chronology brings out three other important facts of life which earlier descriptions omitted. Whilst Maurice Jacks set himself up explicitly to pave the way for a successor such as John Whale, his necessarily short tenure partakes more of the preceding reign than of his successor's: like Rooker Roberts, and Dr Whale, he answered what he saw as Mill Hill's 'call'. His two terms, with Rooker's 10, constituted two-thirds of the total St Bees years; for all the year-entries from September 1939 to 1943, there were at the helm two Heads who gloried in the spiritual qualities of a Mill Hill which both knew intimately. Framing them on either side were two very different

A School House dormitory, Seacote: note tightly-squashed beds, and variety of vital home-provided bed coverings. 7.g

younger men, questing for new standards there and then, and who each attempted to impose the academic disciplines of a peacetime teaching establishment upon a somewhat unmalleable community of war-exiled men, women, boys, and servants. There is also the grim fact that for most of Rooker's time, until the Enigma Codes were broken, and up to Montgomery's offensive at El Alamein (October 1942) and the Russian pincer movement at Stalingrad (January 1943), there was little but bad news from the war, and no glimmer of a good outcome at the end of it all.

Buckland's insight

Many loyal men, and women, watched events at faraway St Bees, and wrote continually, anxiously and vicariously about them. For these insights, the History is indebted to Buster Brown's vast correspondence, ranging from the former Lady Resident, Annie Pearse, to William, the father of the three distinguished Goyder brothers, already encountered in this story. It is, however, through the letters from the ever-watchful School Treasurer, Dickie Buckland, that the best perspective can be formed. The adverse external conditions – there were two inches of snow on 10 May 1943 – mirrored what Dickie himself relayed, in the premature judgments of some critical *OMs*, as the inner *disaster of St Bees*. He conceded privately on 21 March that year that *the real fault, as I see it, is not that that we were mistaken in going to St Bees, but that we adopted a plan which has proved too rigid for the circumstances;* there was a single path of hope, foreshadowing the 'Middlesex Scheme' with stark directness – *One great remedy is to buy boys, who have promise enough to do us credit, and we are willing enough to do this…* On 2 June that same year, Dickie confided his dismay at the aggressiveness being displayed towards the Governors by *OMs* "who so deliberately attack Roberts".

Suddenly the mood changed. By *22 June*, after Foundation Day, Dickie bore witness to it in words ringing with the heroic spirit of the School's Dissenting Fathers: *I've never felt that strange assurance of a finely going concern more certainly than I felt it this past week-end…* Out of Rooker Roberts' untimely death that August came Maurice Jacks' unexpected return. Dickie was moved by both men's example of what the latter had described as the "sense of duty" which drove him to resign in order to serve at Oxford in 1938: *Never did anyone give up his life more nobly for a cause than Roberts for Mill Hill, and never did anyone with greater courage step into the breach than Jacks, who without counting the cost is putting on his battle-harness and bringing us the time we need to gather strength for victory. We are passing through an epoch of momentous import and it behoves us all to rally round the standard we have fought beneath.* On 17 October 1939 Maurice Jacks had written despondently to Buster Brown about the School's future: *I wonder sadly whether there will be a Mill Hill in the new world: this uprooting detachment from many of her best assets, snapping of so many links… may well have a shattering effect.* He could not have imagined that he himself would have the opportunity to rebuild those links, and help restore that future place in the world of education.

The downside

With so many changes, there was no single St Bees experience: some boys encountered four different Heads, and most came under two. That lack of continuity was part of the downside, one of a dozen unpropitious elements making life difficult. Some stemmed from the sheer fact of war and the flood of depressing news on 'the wireless'; for all boys from 1939 onwards, as in the First World War, the OTC/JTC (an ATC was formed in Whitehaven on 10 July 1941) was not just a diversion for Fridays (and Tuesdays too up to 19 November 1940), it was for real: lessons about camouflage or covering fire on Corps Day, or the increasingly frequent 24-hour Exercises over the fells, might well save one's own skin in the not too distant future. Rooker pronounced his innate belief that *games are a mirror which reflects very faithfully the spirit that is a school.* Even though rugby, cricket, tennis and fives were played competitively from as early as 21 October 1939 onwards, and hockey from Spring 1941, war also meant problems such as a dearth of materials for 'colours', or of sticks for 'Singlehanded' (played in autumn 1939 on the firm sand at low tide and reincarnated by 1944/5). The *MHM* in March 1941 worked out that '*in a 77-day term, 32 days were spent in bed, 16 working, 5 in games, 1 shaving, 3 on a bike ... ¼ day in that commodity of short supply, a bath.*'

Revolutionary central catering, Seacote Dining Hall. *7.h*

Food was a constant gripe. Peter Lloyd told his parents of the 1939 menu: Breakfast: *1 sort of fish or tinned meat, 1 spoonful of marmalade ...* Tea: *fish or sausage or tinned meat, spoonful of jam, cheese, Bread and Margarine ... Why not butter? Perhaps when rationing comes in [8 January 1940] we shall get our 4 oz per week.* Even in late 1943, new boy Michael Berry had begged his mother to *send me some dried egg or anything in tins (except SARDINES);* Tom Teale wrote of his first meal, *I had rarely tasted anything so unpalatable in all my life.* Some of the additional pressure derived from these shortages. In 1943/4 the cutlery and crockery were still inadequate, so fags had to get over to Seacote dining hall earlier and earlier each dark, freezing morning in order to 'bag' such items for their House and their personal fagmaster: some 17-year-olds who after June 1940 were in the Mill Hill platoon of the Joint St Bees LDV (Home Guard) used their bayonets as eating knives, and jamjars served as cups for those unlucky enough to come at the end of the queues. There was an exchange rate as between jam and butter; fags were sent out in summer time for blackberries to make up what the school fare lacked. Other tensions arose from the mere fact of being evacuees, having to 'mark out' a recognisable if unavoidably diffused Mill Hill space, despite the absence of the familiar chocolate and white signposting, in someone else's territory – one of the basic aspects of alienation in every animal kingdom. From a secure, enclosed world where all problems had been foreseen and solutions prescribed, they had moved into an environment of first-time questions, whose answers had to be

'The cycling legions': boys returning to Seacote after day's tour on the fells; (c.top) Tomlin (Winterstoke).7.i

invented afresh. Initially all was makeshift: rules, timing, sleeping accommodation, beds, washing facilities and classrooms. Only School House, inured pre-war to a spartan existence, was "molly-coddled" with central heating; elsewhere heating (if at all) fought ventilation (if unavoidable), *pace* Bertie Ricks' mania for fresh air: *You're all going to die!* was his favourite diatribe against the supposed danger of suffocation, on entering his classroom at Seacote, where the windows were closed by the inmates to keep in whatever warmth there was.

To a 21st-century eye, there was a darker side to this life, a throwback to Victorian images of the schoolboy 'republics'. A minor intimation for Tom Teale would come at Leeds, before even the start of the long journey over Settle and via the Cumbrian coast; an older boy threw his brand new cap onto the platform, saying *You only polish your shoes with them.* The *vanity and arrogance of puerile power*, stemming from the tradition of the Ancient Schools where boys reigned as *a self-governing tribe*, was in full spate during these years. In a Record which senior monitor Tony Blair kept in February 1943, he contended: *I have yet to hear of a better system...* adding revealingly, *Junior boys are just as willing to obey and be punished...* One example of this 'tribal system' was the expectation even of prefects such as "Kin" Coombe that a fag, John Sievers, would clean his shoes, like a shoe-black, while he was sitting down, wearing them; even in Collinson House post-war, a form of *running the gauntlet* was still practised in one dormitory after lights out. It was aspects such as these that caused a brilliant *OM* scholar, Dr Denis Witcombe, later to become Head Master of a major HMC school, Nottingham High, to ensure that in his school he put *control back into the hands of adults.*

That vanity was displayed to the indigenous hosts by *those strange folk from Mill Hill who wore long trousers, collars and ties* (at first, blazers too – succeeded in 1943 by grey tweed jackets). *Relations with the St Bees boys were strained... but improved,* continued George McNeil. Although seen by the locals as a *much more open society,* many *OMs* have written of the GC's initial attitude as *condescending.* Things changed, *vide* the *MHM* of March 1945: *The generous hospitality of the people of St Bees bears out the truth of Pericles' dictum that it is the men who make the city, not the walls... the interest and concern which the villagers have shown in our activities have been comforting and encouraging.* Psychologically, what some early ex-urban Millhillians, in their capacity as 'all-Boarders', saw as their superiority in 'tone' to the open-necked culture of the St Beghians, expressed an enforced underlying sense of inferiority in physical status: many of St Bees' fine red sandstone buildings were off-bounds to the GC, who remained based as *foreigners* as one *OM* has put it. To make it worse, St Bees, whose numbers – once facing closure – began to recover as soon as the deal with Mill Hill had been struck, were very sport-competitive, despite victories by the 1st XV (Dec. '40), and 1st XI (July '40, '41). One year, when Ridgeway House could have provided both a first and second School XV, Mill Hill's senior House competition was called off.

Of the internal aspects of this darker side, one *OM*, who spent his life in the Human Resource field, wrote: *bullying was rife at St Bees...* and of *the enormous significance of a punishment process managed and applied by an all-male peer group of boys.* 'Copy' was the standard penalty; a would-be variant line "Life without a woman is like a pipe without tobacco" was not allowed. Lateness for meals or from a bath, talking after lights out, skipping a game or a run – all led to a load of lines or a beating. The Head of Morrison's House in 1944 was apparently allowed to beat boys with a cricket bat or a hockey stick, hitting, as David Clifford wrote, *various strokes – off-cuts, drives, etc on the luckless victim's posterior.* David Turner got 'eight of the best' for breaking bounds from the San. Although A.J. only imposed *pedestrianism* for cycling *to the annoyance of St Bees inhabitants,* up to the advent of Dr Whale, said by Adrian Stanley to be *almost alone in his liberal attitude,* there were few signs of that earlier ideal – *the Arnoldian accountability by the monitors to the Head.* Scholarship-boy Neil Wilson, unfortunate enough to be elevated prestigiously into the V Form on arrival, had to kow-tow to boys of the Second Year who were two forms below him. Although he had a benign fagmaster, who never beat him, nevertheless his summing-up was: *the place ran on Fear.* For one boy, it was *an almost wholly hostile environment.*

The cloistered Boarding tradition – and transient custom – defy generalisation. Educational historian John Chandos put it well: *conditions could vary sharply not only between different houses in the same school at different times ... but between different bedrooms in the same house at the same time.* In parallel, *an innovation once successfully imposed, quickly ... graduated into a tradition, for in a very few years after its appearance there would be no member of the "republic" who had known life without it.* Tony Blair wrote: *Customs peculiar to the great school [at Mill Hill] ... have necessarily been dropped;* (see Appendix E for the decline of the pre-war 'Gilly Roar', after a final two-minute airing to welcome Mrs Roberts off the 8.40 p.m. train on 30 May 1940). The very House where the regime of the Housemaster forced a future OMC President in the autumn of 1943 to cycle as far as Millom, would become transformed under an enlightened Head of House, John Visser, and after 1945 a benign Housemaster, Percy McAllister, into an oasis of humanity. Some 'old-school' masters beat as a routine, like T.F.J. with *Rupert, his amiable artefact.* Not surprisingly in his House, BB, Blair proclaimed that *the distinction of years has always been very sharp... the fags learn (chiefly from 2nd Year) to respect their seniors and keep their place.* One senior monitor wrote: *BB operated a much harsher regime ... it was certainly carried on by John Methven ... I never understood how such an avuncular* [sic] *figure as Tom Jackson allowed it.*

A life of Reilly?

Yet this dwindling community emerged triumphant. Expeditions were organised, for example, to Peter Howard's Suffolk farm or the Broads. One small instance of the 'good fun' spirit were the 'mouse-races' on West's Field, recalled by Roger Thorne.

An early manifestation of this spirit came in the first term, on Sunday 19 November, in a celebrated incident, well described by its modest hero, Peter Lloyd (later to display heroism of a different kind on 'Gold' beach, Normandy at H-Hour+12, D-Day+1, and indefatigable photographer for this History). His verbatim account to his brother reads: *Your daily [sic] Mirror is in error. First there were 11 boys (not 10) ... after diner [sic] we went for the usual house walk every Sunday, this time along the rocks at the bottom of the Cliffs on St Bees Head, we reached Fleswick Bay: a roll was taken and we proceeded back, but we got as far and no further because the sea had come in*

Drama flourished, despite unpropitious conditions: poster for "The Amazing Dr Clitterhouse", 1944, Seacote Hotel. *7.j*

quickly and cut us off from the other rocks, so we ... tried to get back the other way; we then found that we were cut off there ... we were on dry land between two pieces of sea about 50 yards long and about 5 feet deep. So myself and Bacon volunteered to wade through and get help. We did this and walked all the way back over the cliffs ... reporting to Mr Bush, Meade-King and Tom F. The time was then about 4 o'clock; they organised a search party which went on top of the cliffs, and Mr Warr and Mr Coates climbed down the cliffs about 300 feet high with the aid of mountaineering ropes. They found Hutton etc at about 8.30 just as the tide was going out and they were starting back over the rocks ... Luckily we had changed from Sunday clothes to ordinary ones before the walk ... needless to say we got wet through. According to the Daily Telegraph, I swam a mile in the icy raging torrent. Actually the water was quite warm ...

While boys were noticed going round singing, the wider musical tradition was upheld: among the artists invited up were Denis Matthews, the Boyd Neel orchestra, and Ida Haendel; (Stephen Dreyfuss crashed his bicycle into her large car, to earn the unmusical rebuke – *You bloody fool!*). Films were seen legally at Seacote – or illicitly and more enjoyably at 'the flicks' at Whitehaven. With Bertie's arrival, Mill Hill's customary drama was revived, with charity shows of "The Three Musketeers" (using a third of the School), "The Amazing Dr Clitterhouse", and "The Pirates of Penzance"; Mrs Elliott revitalised the pre-war "Savoyards". Difficulties became challenges to ingenuity. Bleak mountains acted as the threshold to an exciting seascape and countryside, facilitating fishing, riding, hill-climbing, canoeing, golf and, after 3 June 1940, sea-bathing. Ornithology flourished as in the days of Dr Murray; aircraft recognition and trainspotting came into their own. Three successful future entrepreneurs, John Gould, Ben Jakober and Michael Berry (the last boy to leave St Bees in July 1945), honed their commercial arts through their MHS Bicycle Club (free repairs, via salvaged spare parts, for 1s. 6d. a head per term) – a boon to the whole School when cycling was allowed post-Chapel on Sundays after 23 May 1940. Despite the lack of air raids, National Registration Cards and gas masks had to be taken on formal excursions. A war flavour was also provided through Blitz stories from the holidays; they were enhanced on the long train journeys – lasting sometimes nearly a whole day, with soldiers guarding each station, and occasional incidents such as the company of captive U-Boat sailors. There were many sights across the Bay – where boys were surprised to glimpse the Isle of Man, with its complement of interned aliens (some benighted Dutchmen tried to escape to the mainland): also German bombers overhead en route for Glasgow; cruisers on patrol; naval firing practices, and even another school out there – of porpoises. Despite a lack of resources, it was a rich freedom – in the words of one *OM a life of Reilly* – with bounds that were liberally wide, and usually viewed anyway with Nelsonian eyes.

Whatever the official diet, there were unofficial compensations that would have been inconceivable back in NW7. Gardens were 'Dug for Victory', yielding, despite the elements, potatoes, lettuce, radishes, beetroot, carrots, dwarf peas, french beans, marrow, tomatoes and even currant bushes. Mrs Midd's speciality was pink ice-cream, unheard-of in wartime. Clifford Johnstone would still describe with relish, 50 years on, the cream teas, and what in 2006 parlance would be 'All-Day Breakfasts' at Mrs Batey's farm, at Calder Bridge, consisting of two fried eggs, two slices of ham, fried potatoes and a mug of tea – all for 2s. 6d., as if rationing did not exist; rumour had it that a 'Man from the Ministry' arrived one day and banned it. A local worthy was reputed to nip over the fence at the *Abbot's Court Hotel* and remove some of the owner's hens and eggs with a long walking stick, and make this contraband available to eager Millhillian black marketeers at a market price. Farm fare partly explained why boys opted for the Youth Service Corps, an agricultural alternative to the JTC or 'ATC' permitted by A.J. The Young Farmers Club had a field day, including the story of the gaggle of geese entering the French windows of an enraged Dr Whale's study, and relieving themselves on his carpet; from Rottington Farm, near "The Three Sisters" – three cottages that marked the end of one of the school runs – YFC members once collared 100 surplus roosting pigeons, to be handed in, dead or alive, but definitively plucked, for pigeon pie that night.

Comic war- and Waugh-worthy incidents abound, truth proving better even than that great fiction. The habit of the rustic gardener at Seacroft of urinating loudly against the external corrugated-iron wall was ended when Freddie Steele, practising his future skills as Chief Engineer of the ITA, connected the sheeting to an electric current – a result not for thinking. At Tomlin the House Matron suddenly found a stream of sooty toilet-paper cascading into her bath: it had been forced up the chimney next door by two boys anxious to assess the length of a roll, after a Whale edict that paper had to be rationed. The unexpected return of the Housemaster caused them to panic, hastily stuffing the coils up the nearby chimney, whence it was wafted up and then down by the force of the draught. The coast was a camera-forbidden area; a virtual military incident arose when a mock-up – by Bertie Ricks of course – of a JU 52 parachutist transport plane was placed in a hedge as part of a Corps exercise, from whose belly at the right moment a group of grey-uniformed Millhillians emerged. The Coastguard, who could not see the waiting JTC capture platoon due to dead ground, immediately called out the defence forces: laughter, and red faces, all round. Two flares were lit over a stove in the Common Room, excused under the pretext 'preparing for November 5th'; in that same room, the discovery of how to make live rounds from blanks led to the explosion of a round that went through two walls, lodging in the blackboard at the end of the next classroom. In neither case were any retributions remembered. Due punishment was, however, wreaked upon the luckless BB boys at "Eaglesfield" who poured down a jerry of water on the head of Tom Jackson, mistaking him for one of the members of the 1st XV, coming round to serenade everyone after a celebratory Dinner. Less comic but mostly more enjoyable were the treks into the countryside. One 27-hour footslog, equal to any later generations' Lyke Wake Walk over the North Yorkshire Moors, was entitled "2,661,120 painful inches". Peter Lloyd averaged 130 cycling miles a week; David Turner recalled a 90-mile ride to Keswick, over the Whinlatter, Wrynose, and Hardknott Passes.

Survival 1945: heroic group of MHS MCR masters, by St Bees beach: (see also Supplement No.2 – "Characters"). *7.k*

Such *pro's* outweighed the *con's*: there was one outstanding benefit – an *esprit de corps,* unique in the history of the School, a binding force of deprivation, but also of shared fun and excitement, to which the annual Reunions of the SBOMA bore eloquent testimony. This camaraderie paralleled the experiences of those who left that distant outpost, each to play his special role in other distant outposts in the war itself. Call-up was brought down to age 18 in November 1942: an Air Ministry official told the School, in language redolent of the previous Great War: "The country's great need is for officers of the right type, and the Public Schools are supplying this type."

'Sleep still, thou warrior...'

A poem in the *MHM,* 'To the Dead', underlined that although war brings many kinds of separation, death is the one absolute. No History can do justice to the loss of siblings, parents, friends, teachers or pupils. Yet the Second World War, fought, in Churchill's words, *for simple and honourable purposes,* has been well commemorated over the years: a Service in the Chapel on 29 June 1947, in which, appropriately, M.L.Jacks read the lesson; in the Dedication of the Memorial plaque in the Chapel, and the inscriptions on the Gate of Honour, at a Service on 29 October 1947 – both conducted by Dr Whale. Not least was Brett James' most poignant *Book of Remembrance:* one of four *OM* names on the Village's Second World War Memorial on The Ridgeway (out of 124 *OM* deaths – 42 were OBs), his elder son, a young Lieutenant, led a platoon attack on Riposto, in Sicily, on 9 August 1943. A group of *OMs* laid wreaths on the Gate of Honour throughout the war, helping to perpetuate into this succeeding century the unbroken tradition of the 'November silences'. On Remembrance Day 1976, C.D.L.Smith (an *OM* who on his own death 15 years later was to be buried near his beloved St Bees, at St Katharine's, Eskdale) recalled the deaths of three of his friends who did not return. Three days before the 50th Anniversary of VE-Day – 5 May 1995 – Belmont laid out the Slynn Garden of 42 shrubs, commemorating its own dead (see Ch.XI).

While MHS comes back in 1945, Belmont remains in exile, at former St Helen's Prep School, Cockermouth, until 1946. *7.1*

There were 11 'St Bees' Millhillian 'K.i.a.s', including Lt Charles Dutton –– survivor of the Anzio landing, and Sgt Peter Collinson Wilson – with the 'Pathfinders'. Brett James' death might have made it 12, had his father not declined Dr Derry's pressure to decamp with the *keen staff of veterans*: the son went on to Aldenham in 1939, whilst the father taught at St George's, Harpenden. In one sense, the 1939-45 conflict belongs mainly to Maurice Jacks' era: 104 of the 124 were 'his', notably the sole *OM* to feature in Martin Gilbert's monumental *Second World War,* Capt Donald Knight, shot after parachuting into Yugoslavia to assist Tito. Two deaths echoed the School's history: outstanding sportsman 2Lt Brian Piper, great-grandson of that early *OM* and 19th-century Hon Treasurer, Thomas Piper; and P/O Christopher Bradley Payne, son of Constance Payne, and grandson of Dr H.Bradley, James Murray's great co-Editor; a third echo was Capt Roger Pye-Smith, great-great-grandson of John Pye Smith, who survived (see Chs.III, IV, V, and XI).

The remaining nine of those 124 had been McClure's boys, six of whom had the cruel fate to survive one war, only to fall in the next; (a latter-day analogy would be if a survivor of 1939-45 had died in some Third World War arising from the Cuba Missile Crisis of 1963). They included: Capt Philip Batty, a former Cambridge rugger "Blue"; Surg-Cdr Alfred Cocking; one of the oldest campaigners, Sqn Ldr Thomas Lloyd DSO, and holder of the Order of St Sava – he had left after the first centenary, in 1908; and two whose brothers had been killed in that first World War, Capt Ronald Bentley, and Lt Col William Macfarlane MC, TD, the only father with a son who would go on to fight in yet another 20th-century war (see Ch.IX). Nine brothers fell: three Clanceys, two Strachans, two Williams, two Duttons. The youngest to die was 19-year-old P/O Ian Fyfe; the oldest, Col John Bain, aged 45. Four representatives of that historic race which Nazi Germany sought to exterminate also lost their lives in the struggle: Pte Kurt Katzenstein, ILH (The Imperial Light Horse) from Munich; Pte Peter Dreyfuss, of the RAF Parachute Div.; P/O Basil Bloom; and Pte Gordon Strauss.

Mill Hill seems prone to anomalies in the matter of her war dead: in 2001 there were only 120 deaths in the chronological Roll of Honour, and on the Chapel plaque (minus Lionel Lester); 122 on the marble Gate. These lists cover nine years from the first death, Fl Lt Richard Allin, in a storm off Hong Kong, 18 October 1939, to that of the 44-year-old conscript, Maj Walter Longley James, who died 10 January 1948, from the protracted effect of 'war strain', the one *OM* pictured in the Record but missing from the 120/1 lists. With the First World War figure of 194 (and David Tinker: see Ch.XI), these 124 make the 'K.i.a.' total 319 deaths.

That small total of 11 from 'St Bees' explains the difference between Mill Hill's muted perception of WWII, as compared with WWI, when, in Brett James' words, *'the School and the Old Boys seemed so much closer together.'* No death notices percolated through after that of Edgar Knowles, still a Lance-Corporal, prior to commissioning, in Ireland, in December 1944. Many deaths were not known until after the war, including five deaths in captivity: through illness – former RFA Lt Charles Howell, at Changi Camp, Singapore, and finally on Formosa; or from wounds – Lt Eric Beart, after the 1942 St Nazaire raid; or like W/O Peter Thorne, one of 11 *OM* or OB escapees from prison camps, meeting death on his last attempt, in February 1945.

Most atrocious was the Hitler-directed shooting of 50 out of 76 POWs on 24 March 1944, after 'The Great Escape' – a notorious war crime; the murdered men included *OMs* Fl Lt Cyril Swain and Fl Lt Denys Street. (*OM* John Nunn was actually waiting in the same tunnel, and – albeit omitted in the *Record* – P/O J.P.Lloyd was also imprisoned there.) Posthumously, three of these victims were in the 128 *OM* 'Mentions in Dispatches'. Millhillian graves still lie in many a corner of a foreign field – at Stavangar, Faenza, Granville and Bréviaires (near Versailles), Neu-Ruppin and Lingen am Ems, and at three Dutch sites – Issum, Nederweeterdijk, and Bergen op Zoom, and perhaps still at Tobruk. Many sites lie closer to home – the Airborne Cemetery; RAF Brookwood; the Jewish Cemetery at Brighton; and at Enfield, and Surbiton. Jane Austen's home at Chawton was secured for the nation by the father of Lt Philip Carpenter in his son's memory. For them all, in David Smith's moving words, *the days of their youth were the only days they would have.*

POW life was described by Lt Michael Witlet, inmate of *Schloss Colditz* as *masses and masses of boredom, occasionally enlightened by flashes of adventure*. It was the fate of some 40 *OMs* – in Germany, Italy, Tunis, Japan, Malaya, and Formosa. There were also two in Burma: Philip Stibbe, who became one of what Brett James would call – oddly – the four *OM* 'song-birds' to write formally of their experiences – *Return From Rangoon;* and, thanks to the persistence of Edward Fiddy, after an omission of 60 years, George Brockman, who died on the 'Railway of Death'. Others did put their thoughts to paper, including one typical example of the stiff upper lip of British and Public School fable: for Sqn Ldr Charles Waterman the war was *an interesting experience (with some unpleasant incidents)*. FO Brian Attwood DFC wrote from Iraq in 1940: *We here hope for one thing... that is that England will never give in.*

One perspective came, before his death in March 1941, from the other son of Belgian Prof Emile Cammaerts, Francis' brother, Sgt Obs Pieter Cammaerts. His mother copied his words in a letter to Buster of 15 July 1941 – he forwarded it to the *War Record: The war seems very far away and very inappropriate. It has not affected the yearly return of life, has it? The Eternal Spirit, the guide of our destiny, who looks down pityingly upon our foolishness, gives us this grain of comfort... I have had 20 such happy years that the rest does not matter...* Of the 21st-century survivors, Gordon Stannard, wrote of *my acute awareness of the price to be paid in war. My own brother had been lost at sea, and now names were being read out in Chapel and posted on the Notice Boards. It was even worse for the masters and their wives, who had known even greater numbers of the casualties, and their parents as well.* Colin Stannard was an Acting Leading Seaman, one of many presumed killed, whose death could not be confirmed until the summer of 1942.

Over 1,300 *OMs* served in various capacities and survived, compared with some 1,100 in the First World War: most were officers, ranging up to Commander RNVR, Brigadier and Air Vice Marshal rank; 101 were non-commissioned, from Privates, LACs, and ABs, to WOs. Gp Capt Joseph Redding, served eight years, volunteering for Barrage Balloon duty in 1938, closely followed by the seven-years' service of Maj Denis Thatcher, MBE. Most of the epic actions, battles and theatres of war were represented: Norway, Dunkirk, Dieppe, Greece, Crete, Yugoslavia, St Nazaire, Dakar, El Alamein, Tobruk, Malta, Tunis, Sicily, Salerno, Anzio, D-Day and the invasions of the South of France and the Channel Islands, Arnhem and the River Ems. *OMs* were in the Atlantic and North Russian convoys, Singapore, Hong Kong, Malaya, the Burma Road, Kohima, Okinawa and the Phillipines. There were Submariners, Gliders, Night-Fighters, Paras, Commandos, Chindits, Phantoms, *Maquis*. The famous "Ark Royal" was but one of the ships in which *OMs* sailed. RAF *OMs* flew Liberators, Hampdens, Mosquitos, Lancasters, Wellingtons, Stirlings and Typhoons, as well as the legendary Hurricanes and 'Spits'. Three *OMs* served on distinguished war HQs: Maj David Rees with "Monty"; Lt Col Alexander Monteith with "Ike"; and Paymaster-Lt David Mungavin on the PM's staff in Washington. At least 166 were wounded. Of 80 serving 'medics', Surgeon Nigel Kinnear (to become Regius Professor at Dublin), attended Belsen (as did the BBC's Richard Dimbleby), after that Concentration Camp was overrun on 15 April 1945; (that experience was also the lot of a later Mill Hill master, then Sgt Ted Winter, at nearby San Bostel Camp).

In wartime everyone does what they have to do. Over 200 served as non-combatants in the AFS, Police, ARP, Royal Observer Corps (ROC) or Home Guard (including 31 boys with the School's Cumbrian unit); none were among the 760 deaths on the 'Home Front'. The oldest volunteer was 76-year-old Eustace Sowter, a pupil of Dr Weymouth. Two served in the Friends Ambulance Units. There were *OM* scientists behind the scenes, too, working for the MAP, Atomic Energy, Radar or, like Francis Crick, Mine development. Six Carters served, five Catesbys and four Briggs. Sgt Hans Panofsky, and, as already recorded, 1st Lt Wolfgang Oppenheimer, were two Millhillians with particular reasons to fight for the Europe of their birth. The service of Cambridge zoologist Prof William Thorpe, later President of Jesus College, took a different form: he championed the preservation of the famous Wicken Fen wetlands, saving them from being used as a bombing practice range.

As his Imperial War Museum recording and a C4 TV series in year 2000 relate, one of the quietest heroes was initially one of England's 58,000 conscientious objectors (a further facet of the 'Non-con' provenance), Lt Col Francis Cammaerts, with the DSO, a *Croix de Guerre* with two palms, *Officier de la Légion d'honneur*, and the American Medal of Freedom (Silver Palm). In 2005 he was living quietly in France, not far from the scene of his SOE resistance work as agent *Roger* (covering St Etienne/ Nice/ Albertville/ Marseille) and where his escape from prison and a firing squad was achieved at the eleventh hour. In such a context, Lt Col John Easonsmith must be remembered too, with a DSO and MC, also operating behind enemy lines – portrayed by W.B.Kennedy Shaw as *the finest man we ever had in* [the Long-Range Desert Group] – and killed on Leros in 1943. Others to be highlighted include: Sqn Ldr Nigel Walker, DSO, DFC, Bomber Command, for consistent courage in European skies; *OB* Wg Cmdr "Bob" Braham – triple DSO, triple DFC, AFC, CD, *the most decorated fighter pilot of WWII*; Maj John McGavin MC, for his exploits in Italian East Africa; W/O H.K.Rich; Sgt T.A.Warren: and Maj Donald Salinger with SOE's China equivalent, Force 136, 1941-5 (for two honours available for one 'bridge-blowing', two officers 'tossed', Donald lost, winning only a 'Mention').

Pace the shortcomings of the *War Record, OM* honours totalled: eight DSOs, eight DSCs (Navy), 15 DFCs (RAF), 24 MCs (Army), two MMs (still the socially-loaded version of the MC, for non-officers, abolished later in the century), two AFCs (for gallantry not on active service), and Fl Lt John Haviland's two French awards – the AEC and AEF. There were also two Knighthoods, a CB, five CBEs, 18 OBEs, 25 MBEs, at least six GSMs, many Territorial and Volunteer Decorations, and other awards – a Periodic Award for Gallantry, a Certificate of Merit for Meritorious Service, a CiC's Citation for Gallantry, a King's Medal (Disabled), a Special Constabulary Medal, and a Royal Humane Society Certificate. As in the First World War, there were no VCs, yet the proof of Millhillian qualities is further reflected in the variety of awards made by foreign governments: from the USA two Bronze Stars, three Legions of Merit, and an Army Commendation Ribbon; from France six *Croix de Guerre,* and for Lt Harry Whiting DSC (RNVR) an *Etoile Vermeil*; Belgium created two Chevaliers of the Order of King Leopold II, and two *Croix de Guerre*; there was a Chinese 'Cloud and Banner' Medal for Air Commodore Eric Burns; a Royal Order of

Orange-Nassau from Holland; an Albanian Red Star; and from Norway an Order of St Olaf (the same award made later to Dr Derry); from Norway too a *Kommandue*, War Medal, and to Lt Joe Fox a Decoration for Services to their Navy.

Among 11 Masters listed, Maj Alan Bush won an 'immediate MC' at Arnhem in September 1944; he was wounded, captured, escaped, was wounded again but fought on. His citation read of an *example ... at all times heartening and inspiring*. Others were: Capt I.V.Balfour-Paul, MC; Capt G.Baxter; J.Blackburn DFC (RAF); Capt C.M.T.Bowring; Sqn Ldr D.Dalley; Lt Col G.W.Hedley; Sgt C.M.Meade-King; Sqn Ldr G.W.Murray; A/Maj A.L.Warr; and Capt M.R.Wigram. *The Record* missed the service of Maj Harold Pegrum, MC, and should have included the names of Donald Hall (war-work for ICI) and Norman Brett James himself, in his ROC role. (For the value of the war-service staff, see Ch.VIII.)

As a sociological comment on the nation-wide catchment from which Mill Hill drew her pupils at that time, 60 different territorially-based Regiments were listed, most of which would still be familiar to National Servicemen of 1947-60. This long list included: The Beds. & Herts., Black Watch, Royal Berkshires, Border Regt., Buffs (East Kents), Cameronians, Cameron Highlanders, Cheshires, The Dukes of Wellington's and Cornwall's Regts., Devonshires, Durham Light Infantry (DLI), Essex, Gloucesters, Gordon Highlanders, Green Howards, Hampshires, King's Own Scottish Borderers, King's Own Yorkshire LI, Lancs Fusiliers, Lincolnshires, City of London Yeomanry, The Loyals (North Lancs), Leicestershires, Duke of Lancaster's Yeomanry, North Staffs, Middlesex Regt, Royal Norfolks, Royal Northumbrian Fusiliers, Ox. & Bucks. LI, Seaforth Highlanders, South Wales Borderers, Staffordshires, Somerset LI, Sherwood Foresters, Royal Scots, Royal Warwicks, Royal Welch Fusiliers, Royal West Kent, Wiltshires, Worcestershires, and the West Yorkshire Regt.

The ambivalent experience

Despite the slaughter, or even because of it, for many *OMs* it was the serendipitous happenings that stayed in the memory: Maj Curtis Dudman – survivor of the Tobruk siege – landing up in a Western Desert dug-out with Capt Neville Jones; or the posting of Sqn Ldr Norman McMichael's *MHM* by a not-quite express camel; or other chance meetings – three *OM* RNVR Sub-Lts in Taranto, or Howard Walker MC waking up in casualty to see former study-mate, MO Morus Lloyd Owen, bending over him. Service life re-enacted the strange ambivalence of life at St Bees.

With a similar ambivalence, the deaths that were of immediate impact on the exiled community were inevitably those of the four boys who died there accidentally. Two are commemorated in school prizes to this day: David Needham died of septicaemia in Carlisle Hospital on 19 February 1942; in the *sad summer* of 1943, Hamilton Bailey, a promising young bowler, was killed at Preston Station on *29 July*, when an open train door caught him as he leaned out of the window – it is thought to have brought on Rooker's heart attack on 8 August. As A.J. had written, *such happenings leave their mark*; the funeral service was taken by Rev. Paul Clifford in Mill Hill Chapel; (he was later asked by W.C.Ramsay if he was interested in the Headship now sadly vacant, but he was not available).

The third death was one of the Yorkshire Bursary group which, with others from the North, became an important non-'SE Triangle' element in the future constituency. Witnessed by Tom Teale, Donald Leath went out on a seemingly unsanctioned walk on Tomlin Head on the first day, 2 September 1943; only after 'Lights out' did the Housemaster realise that a boy was missing – 'he was found at the foot of the cliffs next morning'. The death of a fourth boy, from a heart defect – John Jefferiss, in March 1945 – is recalled in the Chapel Collection Plate.

That wider 'foolishness' of which Pieter Cammaerts wrote, brought about separations from home and family, too, as the letters home illustrate most touchingly, yet the predominant character of St Bees was positive. If despite the downside, for most of the boys, the St Bees saga provided *the time of their lives*, and for the staff a challenge to character, corporately too it has an ambivalence. It can be seen as either an inspired example of resource and flexibility, or as possibly the most damaging policy decision Mill Hill ever took, albeit for the best of motives, and on the best available thinking about the nature of aerial warfare, with financial consequences reaching far into the future. The national Emergency Medical Service was a *fait accompli*: whether Mill Hill could have held on 'on the Hill' can only be a matter for conjecture. The Government knew of the School's plans to evacuate and lease; probably the pass had been sold, and the die cast. Later eras would do well to remember that there was nothing inevitable about Mill Hill's survival: the craft was afloat, but subject to all the frailties of a man-made construct. At the time, and without the benefit of hindsight, it was not grand strategy but the daily tactics of coping that were uppermost in the mind.

Underneath it all lay another more widely-felt separation: the severance of the School from her roots and homeland, and a sense of the loss of ongoing values. Rooker had forecast in March 1943, more in hope than expectation, that *the first*

Headingley RFC ground; Rooker Roberts'-inspired input of Yorkshire Bursary boys to "Mill Hill on Sea", with *OM* project organiser Dick Auty; a one-off broadening input to the post-war MHS pupil pattern. *7.m*

generation to return will not commit the error of taking everything for granted. Wistful stories had appeared in the *MHM* from May 1940, headed 'Three Hundred Miles Away', personifying much-loved features of the landscape back at the 'other' GC (that entity too now suffering an ambivalence, even a schizophrenia). Some, like this musing by the 'bell-pull', are now unidentifiable after the passage of the years: *I was right in the middle of things. I can remember quite well that boy who used to come and call for Corlins* [call-ins?] *just next to me, every day.* The Magazine writer wondered if the stones and trees had forgotten their departed occupants, feeling the need to give them a voice. Tony Blair, a nostalgic senior monitor, compiled a unique record of the customs still remembered as a 1939-er, after four years of banishment.

In that sense, these young Millhillian writers need not have worried: whilst Mill Hill was surviving 'on Sea', those buildings and fields back in that other Village, with their ground staff, were 'doing their bit' for the war effort too.

Sources for part (i) of Ch.VII include: # *MHM* 1944-5; C/TCs Mins 1944-51; *Book of Remembrance... 1939-1945*; W.H.Brown Archv; Bewsher, *op cit* (incl Howard Walker [1921-5] story); "The St Bees Magazine", 1939-45, courtesy S.R.Samuels [1943-8]; # *Times*, 30.x.1940, Dr Derry to OMC lunch, *vice* Annual Dinner.

Background: H.Macmillan, *Winds of Change...* (1966), Ch 9; Wilmot, *op cit*: Churchill speech, 13.v.1945,1954 edtn, 787; M.Gilbert, *Second World War* (Weidenfeld & Nicholson, 1989), 456, 510,& *Holocaust* (Weidenfeld & Nicholson, 1989); A.J.P.Taylor, *English History 1914-1945* (1970 edn), 558; P.Brickhill, *The Great Escape* (1979); *The Guardian* 10.i.1999. obit, Marcel Zillesen (survivor of Stalag Luft III). Ref F.Cammaerts [1930-4]: M.R.D.Foot, *(SOE in France: an account of the work of the British Special Operations Executive in France 1940-1944* (HMSO, 1966); Impl War Museum Archv; C4 TV, 27.i-10.ii.2000, 'Churchill's Secret Army'; & corr, 1998-2000; BBC 2, 30.xi.2000, 'The War Behind the Wire'; CRYPTOS Soc, Reform Club. 4.iii.2002: Graf von Thun Hohenstein: 'Why Chamberlain's flight to Munich made war inevitable'; M.Smith & R.Erskine, *Action This Day, Bletchley Park...* (2001); A.Spooner, *Night Fighter Ace* (1997) [ref Bob Braham]. J.Chandos, *Boys Together* (1945).

St Bees: A.Cotes & J.Bell, Hon Secs, St Beghian Soc; St Beghian Newsletter, Jan 2001, courtesy Editor, D.E.Lyall; "Occasional Jottings", Newsletters of SBOMA & continuous help from the late Editor, M.R.W.Berry [1943-7], indebtedness to late C.D.L.Smith [1938-43]; Newsletters to parents by A.J.Rooker Roberts, HM 1940-3 [1893-1900]; *St Bees Remembered* & help from author, D.J.H.Clifford [1943-7]; *Daily Telegraph* obit for A/M Maj. A.Bush MC, 24 June 1998; K.Whitehorn *Pick of Punch*, 'Walking out of Roedean' (1998); *Wisden* (1942); J.Wilson, *West Cumberland at War* (Distington, 1999); H.Walpole, *Rogue Herries* (1930); E.Waugh, *Decline and Fall* (1928); A.Ransome, *Swallows and Amazons* (1933) etc; G.Sutton, *Shepherd's Warning* (1946); *A Sermon preached at the Gravel Pit Meeting House in Hackney, April 11th 1824, on the decease of Mr Lavington Rooker, late Student in the Protestant Dissenting Academy at Homerton* by J.P.Smith DD (1824). J.R.Williams, *The Whitehaven News, Centenary 1852-1952...* (1952) [ref J.McGowan, fmr Hon. Sec & Pres, OMC]. Letters home by M.R.W.Berry, M.P.Lloyd [1936-40], & A.H.Gray [1942-6]#.

Dscns with A/M Donald Hall; Mrs Gavin Lyall (née Katharine Whitehorn [1939]); Lady Elliot (née Margaret Whale); Mrs Rona Bagnall (daughter of A.J.Rooker Roberts); Hon Mrs Richard Robbins (formerly Mrs Brenda Roberts); Bill Burton; corr – A.E.R.Roberts [1921-26] > P.Hodgson, 1983; discn, G.Smith, Aug 1999 (ref author's est. 50 non-MHS Cockermouth OBs, basis 8%). Corr/ Dscns/ Memorabilia:- R.Aye Maung [1945-50]; R.Bee [1949-54]; J.P.Bolton [1936-40]; P.S.Burns [1937-42]; C.Campbell [1938-42]; S.A.Dreyfuss [1942-5]; J.Eatough [1937-41]; A.D.V.Elliott [1937-42]; H.Gauntlett [1939-44]; M.I.Gee [1942-6]; P.E.Gill [1937-41]; J.B.Gould [1944-6]; B.J.S.Harley [1937-42]; M.A.Hastilow [1936-40]; J.S.Henderson [1935-41]; W.T.Jackson [1941-4]; F.C.Johnston [1943-7]; M.E.I.Kempster [1936-42]; S.C.Kinnersley [1937-41]; E.ap G.Lewis [1939-44]; A.M.Macfarlane [1944-8]; G.H.McNeil [1938-42]; D.I.Marks [1943-8]; T.C.Micklem [1939-43]; W.R.Mills [1937-40]; N.Mirsky [1938-42]; D.G.Morgan [1946-51]; A.G.Patterson [1929-34]; E.P.Payne [1936-40]; D.M.Petrie, A.L.Poole [1942-6]; L.Phillips [1941-2]; G.T.Risdon [1936-40]; G.E.Rowland [1938-41]; P.Scarf [1940-4]; J.D.Sievers [1942-6]; J.Addison Smith [1940-5]; A.R.Stanley [1944-8]; M.C.Sweetman [1943-8]; G.Stannard [1940-5]; R.Thorne [1939-43]; D.J.Turner [1939-43]; J.B.Visser [1941-6]; B.Warmington [1938-42]; I.R.White [1943-8]; M.D.Whitehorn [1936-41]; D.R.Wilson [1940-4]; F.N.Wilson [1944-9]; D.T.Witcombe [1943-8]; P.M.Woodroffe [1942-5]; G.Wren [1940-4]; I.M.Wright [1937-42]; R.A.Wyld [1940-4]; F.P.Zimmerman [1939-43].

Other *OM* references & WWII: R.S.Allin [1924-6]; B.A.B.Attwood [1932-5]; J.R.Auty [1924-7]; E.W.Bacon [1937-40]; Hamilton Bailey [1941-3]; J.E.Bain [1913-7]; P.A.Batty [1912-7]; E.H.Beart [1916-23]; R.C.Bentley [1906-10]; J.A.Blair [1938-43]; B.J.B.Bloom [1931-3]; J.Brett-James, J.S.Campsie, P.J.Carpenter [1935-9]; Briggs family – A.H. [1937-41] – D.H. [1930-4] – J.L. [1930-4]; R.W.B.Buckland [1878-84]; E.S.Burns [1912-17]; P.E.G.Cammaerts [1933-6]; Carter family – D.H.N. [1933-7] – D.W.N. [1924-9] – G.S.N. [1893-7] – H.D. [1919-25] – L.H.N. [1936-41] – J.M.N. [1930-5]; Catesby family – E.A. [1921-5] – M.W. [1928-33] – P.A. [1933-6]; Clancey family – R.W. [1930-3] – D.A. [1931-4] – K.C. [1935-9]; N.J.Clarke [1935-40]; P.R.Clifford [1926-32]; A.W.Cocking [1905-10]; J.K.Coombe [1939-43]; F.H.C.Crick [1930-4]; P.K.Dreyfuss [1936-9]; H.C.Dudman [1913-20]; Dutton family – D.A. [1933-7] – C.L. [1936-40]; J.R.Easonsmith [1923-6]; J.B.Fox [1924-6]; I.R.Fyfe [1935-9]; J.M.Haviland [1934-6]; G.F.Hourani [1927-32]; C.G.Howell [1910-3]; C.Hutton [1936-9]; B.Jakober [1944-8]; M.Lloyd Owen [1921-6]; W.Longley James [1917-22]; J.F.Jefferiss [1941-5]; N.D.Jones [1928-32]; K.Katzenstein [1936-8]; N.Kinnear [1919-25]; D.E.Knight [1932-6]; E.I.Knowles [1939-42]; D.D.H.Leath [1943]; L.H.Lester [1925-7]; T.W.Lloyd [1906-8]; J.P.Lloyd [1929-34]; P.J.Longley [1928-32]; N.A.D.Macrae [1937-42]; W.A.Macfarlane [1910-5]; J.S.McGavin [1925-9]; J.McGowan [1887-91]; N.F.McMichael [1918-22]; M.Methven [1939-44]; "Nath." Micklem [1866-8, '70-1]; J.D.Mitchell [1895-9]; A.Monteith [1920-4]; D.M.Mungavin [1931-5]; D.F.Needham [1940-2]; W.J.Owen/ (Oppenheimer) [1936-8]; H.E.Palmer/ Panofsky [1939-43]; C.B.Payne [1928-33]; T.Piper [1811-7]; B.I.Piper [1938-42]; R.E.S.Pye-Smith [1935-9]; W.C.Ramsay [1912-8]; J.E.Redding [1901-4]; D.H.Rees [1915-22]; H.V.Rich [1919-25]; A.E.R.Roberts [1921-6]; D.P.Salinger [1928-32]; G.W.Sears [1936-41]; E.T.Sowter [1880-1]; M.Stannard [1933-8]; F.H.Steele [1942-7]; P.G.Stibbe [1935-9]; Strachan family – A.M. [1929-33] – I.M. [1931-5]; D.O.Street [1935-40]; G.Strauss [1928-31]; C.D.Swain [1926-9]; D.Thatcher [1928-32]; P.S.C.Thorne [1937-40]; W.H.Thorpe [1917-20]; S.Tomlin [1966-7]; N.F.Walker [1928-32]; T.A.Warren [1925-8]; C.E.Waterman [1930-4]; W.R.G.Whiting [1897-1903]; Williams family – O.L. [1931-4] – R.S. [1934-5]; P.C.Wilson [1937-41]; M.Wittet [1932-6] – a Colditz prisoner.

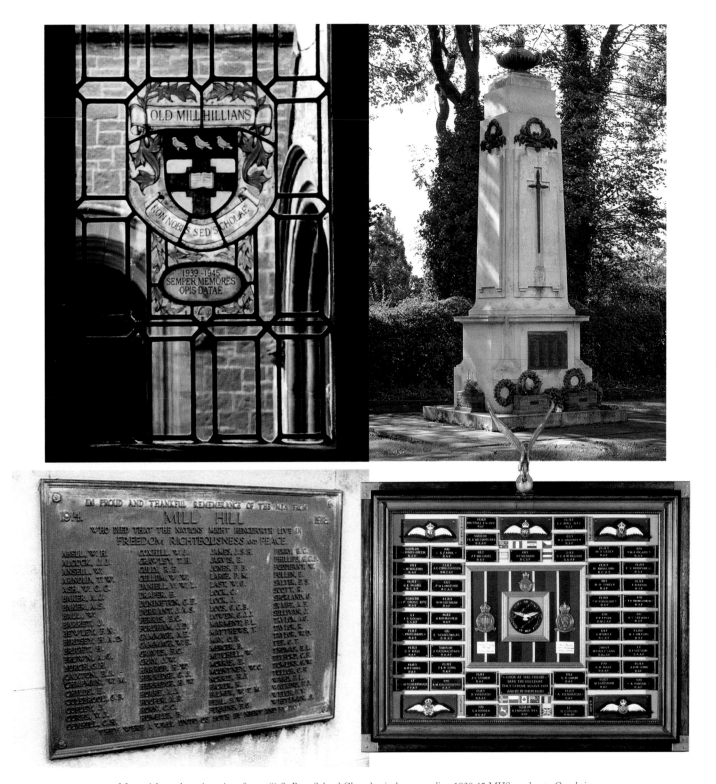

Memorials to the exigencies of war: (i) St Bees School Chapel: window recording 1939-45 MHS exodus to Cumbria, funded by SBOMA through *OM* M.R.W.Berry; (ii) Mill Hill Village obelisk, on The Ridgeway; (iii) its panel marks Millhillian deaths from both World Wars; (iv) plaque at RAF Museum Hendon, pays homage to the 50 allied airmen shot after "The Great Escape" from Stalag Luft III, including *OM*s Swain and Street. 7.*n*

1940s, Mill Hill Emergency Hospital: military multi-national patients and nurses
on the Quad; Marnham Block in background, with Fives Court
(serving as a Mortuary). 7.o

"They Also Served": A History in Parallel
Emergency Hospital in WWII – the unknown story

"The Mill Hill School was selected because of the natural geographical
and topographical advantages which it possessed."
(Dr W.S.Maclay, Medical Superintendent,
Mill Hill Emergency Hospital: Report, December 1940).

Twelve years before the 300-mile exodus of Mill Hill School and Belmont had set off from Euston on that early day in the Second World War, there had been set in train another long 'journey' of a very different nature, yet one which was to be intimately linked both with it, and with the history of Mill Hill Village, including the nearby Mount School – and of two famous London hospitals. This wartime story is now told for the first time.

Unlike that public scene of confusion, the journey of 1927 had begun in precision and secrecy: it was the start of an extended process of government thinking which was to mark out an important parallel element in Mill Hill's saga. This was the role to be played by two other vital strands in the School's history – hitherto only touched on briefly in the School records: the Houses, buildings, laboratories, and even the treasured grounds themselves; and the role of the ground staff and servants. (Their chapter would also be the first to play an unintentional part in fundraising for the School: see Ch.XII.)

It was a nice coincidence that government policy not only gave the School, including some of her official representatives, a substantive role in the prosecution of the war, but also that this should centre round a field of achievement which had been a constant in the School's history: the practice of medicine. Apart from providing a vitally needed therapeutic facility for thousands of war-damaged service personnel and civilians, male and female, young and old, Mill Hill's peaceful hilltop was about to become the setting for two series of experiments, conducted by some of the world's most eminent psychologists. They would not only transform understanding of personality, and give rise to a new technique for the measurement of vocabulary, but would also enshrine the name of Mill Hill in the annals of two related but still relatively unproven disciplines, psychology and psychiatry; one vehicle for this association would be a new treatment or technique, offering creative alternatives to the contentious field of psycho-analysis. Many of those young Millhillian future doctors, marooned in St Bees, or away at war, would have given their eye teeth merely to have been flies on the wall during these fascinating researches.

Yet this experience is barely touched on in the official records. An Institute of Psychiatry review baldly says that its staff were *transferred to emergency hospitals at Mill Hill and Sutton* where *teaching and research were efficiently organised.* An account of the Child Psychiatry unit at the Maudsley adds that to treat children there from 1940 to 1942 *staff came from Mill Hill and Belmont* [Sutton!] *Hospitals.*

The Belmont which is of interest to Mill Hill also played its part, but in a complementary field, another aspect of the Foundation's historic focus; this was the world of science and industry, through one of its most prestigious exponents – the giant chemical conglomerate ICI – which was about to lease Mill Hill's Junior School. In fact the whole community of "The Ridgeway", by which name Mill Hill Village was often better known locally, became involved in this 'occupation'.

As another aspect of the School's story, the Mill Hill Emergency Hospital – 'MHEH' – would also require inputs from the local population to staff its work, on the payroll or, like the mother of local resident Gordon Wallis, for voluntary duty; (a friend of the Brett James family, he was a frequent visitor to Ridgeway House, in Wills Grove, where they kept a sophisticated household, including a French *'Mam'selle'*). The MHEH would enlist the facilities of two successive Vicars of St Paul's for services in Chapel, and engage in co-operative activities with the Middlesex Regiment down at the Barracks. Moreover, quite apart from the School's buildings, the medical world would need to take over, as further nursing accommodation, the Sanctuary on The Ridgeway; a private house, No.4 Holmdene Avenue; and the evacuated Mount School, on Bittacy Rise, as a 12-bed in-patient child psychiatry unit. ICI too was to lease an additional building, Berkeley House, in Wise Lane, for five years from 1942 onwards.

Leased or commandeered?

Initially, through one of a long line of loyal Secretary-cum-Bursars, Lt Col Douglas Mitchell CMG DSO – whose 10-year career was ended sadly in 1945 by an accident at St Bees – the Court had planned to lease the School at commercial rates to various large City companies, and the buildings had been allocated to provisional occupants, such as the National Provincial Bank, and ICI itself. Col Mitchell wrote to ICI on 30 January 1939 pointing out that *the price for the option... already operated with various Banks and Insurance Companies, was 10% of the rent.*

Unknown to him, ICI Central Staff Department had already, on the 23rd of that month, reported internally that *a large number of other firms have... been in search of similar accommodation, and any delay in signing an agreement... might result in our falling between stools.* In that same memo, ICI noted that although the Bank was in negotiation for the *Administrative School Block... the Dining Hall... kitchens,* and *two private Houses, the Head Master's, and the [School] Secretary's, the [ICI] Secretary feels that I.C.I. would be entitled to make a counter offer:* they were already considering the availability of over 50,000 square feet of space for *350 people, and sleeping accommodation for about 170,* in the Science Block, Music School, Library, Reading Room, Gymnasium, and Sanitorium. Of the two Houses on offer, Collinson and Winterstoke, ICI were still considering on 6 February, whether to lease Winterstoke House from the School; BB and Ridgeway House were marked off for two other would-be tenants; only the Tuck Shop was *of no value as an office.*

However by 28 February, the position had radically changed, with disastrous financial consequences for Mill Hill which would reverberate right the way through into the post-war period. It now became clear with the escalation of tension in Czech Sudetenland that the Ministry of Health saw Mill Hill as a future Hospital in the event of a now increasingly likely war; however there would be 'no help with transport'. 'MoH' officials visited on 11 March. On 25 April, the School was notified that it would be *commandeered:* Blenheim Steps and the Science Labs would be needed too; and the Loggia would have to be glazed and bricked up for an Operating Theatre between the wards planned for School House, and the Marnham Block.

Fortunately this plan did not come to pass. Also, the stage in The Large would need to be removed. Two hospital huts arrived on 23 May, followed by a solitary bath chair. On 27 June even though the position was still not officially clear, a senior official from the LCC Hospitals Department made another visit. On 25 July, the 'proposals' came through at last: for an ARP measure, £1,000-worth of trenches were to be dug in the 'Hay Field', as ICI were already planning at Belmont (perhaps as a defence against paratroopers?). All windows were to be darkened, with the School to pay one third of the costs. Burton Bank, now also abstracted from the proposed 'commercial' deals, was to be evacuated, with a special future role in view, immediately upon the announcement of a National Emergency. The MoH was in possession from the beginning of August, even while the Governors were still trying to establish some kind of post-hoc understanding with the MoH Compensation Officer: that buck was later neatly passed to the Department of Works.

The Governors' Minutes do not actually record the declaration of war on 3 September: everyone was too busy with the frantic work under way for St Bees. Two days later, the Ministry's Hospital moved in. Only on 14 December 1939, would the 'duration' – "de facto T.of H.", termination of hostilities – be defined as *during the present war between England [sic] and Germany and any other country hereafter joining actively with Germany in such war*. ICI's seven-year lease of an eventual 1,750 square feet at Belmont, from 24 August, would carry an initial notice period of 10 weeks after "T. of H.", with the ominous marginal comment: *Negotiations in hand for longer notice*. Both clauses were to have financial and practical implications for Mill Hill during the summer of 1945.

Barts, The Maudsley, and national policy

The two world-famous medical establishments whose paths crossed with Mill Hill School's for the ensuing six years – St Bartholomew's from the heart of the City, and The Maudsley from Denmark Hill – were no strangers to countless Millhillians before and indeed after this momentous period. There is a nice symmetry about the wartime conjunction with Mill Hill, the services to be provided by these two noble hospitals contrasting with their long-standing relationship to the School as trainers of aspiring medics. Given what Correlli Barnett has called *the historian's priceless gift of hindsight*, this hitherto unknown aspect of Mill Hill's history is interesting in more ways than one. It is an astonishing fact that the planning for Britain's emergency medical services in the event of war had been started as early as 1927. Although Barts' official History surprisingly makes no mention of it, the Archives of the Hospital record a 'Highly Confidential' memorandum (HO 16/5/3) of 27 October 1927, sent from Guys Hospital, in association with the MoH Sub-Committee of the Committee for Imperial Defence, to the Secretaries of all the London Hospitals, asking for *estimates of the numbers of beds and casualties in the next war [sic] during air raids in the first few days of war*.

Preparing for war, September 1939: (i) Sandbags against Marnham (later Priestley) windows; (ii) digging air-raid shelters, Top Field: post-war use – damp Hobbies Rooms. 7.p

That first memorandum of 1927 was written a mere nine years after the end of the 'war to end all wars', in a Britain now apparently at peace, and trying to make the League of Nations do the job of preserving it. This was the task which some 20 years later would at last be started in earnest by its successor-body, the United Nations. In contrast with what turned out to be an uncannily prescient piece of governmental thinking, the only outward sign of the future enemy power which it had in its sights was the first of Hitler's Nazi Party Days at Nuremberg that same year; this followed the publication of volume two of a turgid new book, 12 months before, *Mein Kampf*, which sold few copies even in Germany. To all appearances, Germany under Stresemann was treading the long path back to peace, within that still fragile League. (In fact, it is clear from published documents that from 1923 onwards, in the utmost secrecy, the German High Command was planning how to recover her military strength for a point some 13 years ahead – 1936.) However, as if to underline the outward supremacy of the Weimar regime, the Nazis would only poll 810,000 votes in the German Elections of May 1928, winning 12 seats out of 491 in the *Reichstag*. To all except a few far-sighted senior civil servants in Whitehall, there seemed to be no threat there: fascist Italy under Mussolini seemed far more menacing.)

This anachronistic British thinking focused on the exaggerated but widespread fear of what author Uri Bialer called *the shadow of the bomber* and the casualties this would bring to densely populated cities, enhanced later by Churchill's warnings in the 'Wilderness Years' on German aircraft production. This was the well-spring for the Report about the Hospital, drawn up by the MHEH Medical Superintendent after the first 16 months of war: *The experience gained in the Great War 1914-18, where it was shown that for success neurotic casualties must be treated near the front line, has by this location been put into practice.* Mill Hill's peaceful hillside, a bare nine-plus miles from Trafalgar Square, was in due course to present a perfect solution to this problem.

Planning meetings continued throughout the pre-war years, while in other areas, such as armaments, Britain appeared to be dragging her feet: not so, as far as C.C.Carus-Wilson MC, Clerk to the Governors of Barts, was concerned, with his Fellow Hospital Secretaries and their opposite numbers in the MoH; perhaps the Military Cross had sharpened his awareness of war's medical implications. By the summer of 1939, the plans of the nation's EMS – the Emergency Medical Service – were ready for implementation, later to be the blueprint for the post-war NHS.

To that tranquil island, from the outbreak of war, under Dr the Hon Walter Maclay as medical superintendent (later to become a Principal Medical Officer in the MoH), were to come some 40 clinicians, and hundreds of nurses and auxiliaries. These included major figures from the academic research community, some of whom would train later generations of Millhillians to follow in their footsteps at their respective institutions.

Dr Aubrey Lewis, the leading British psychiatrist, who later, as *OM* Prof Robert Kendell put it, *... built the Maudsley, and the Institute of Psychiatry, into the world-famous teaching centre it became*, was Director of Research. He was *the guiding spirit*, in the words of one of his appointees, Dr Hans Eysenck, who later wrote, at the end of a spectacular life, an illuminating autobiography, *Rebel With A Cause*, which contains much Mill Hill background. Eysenck was joined by Hilde Himmelweit as co-researcher (herself to become the Professor of Social Psychology at LSE, and a renowned psychologist, with her studies of the effects of TV on children); and by two soon-to-be famous psychiatrists Dr Linford Rees and Dr Maxwell Jones, from the Maudsley. (That time was recalled by his then secretary, Mrs Glenda Baim, from the Mill Hill District WVS – future grandmother of *OMs* Spencer and Miles Baim and mother-in-law of Heather Baim, MHS Registration Secretary from 1984, and thereafter the Belmont Master's Secretary until 2003.) This new "Mill Hill community" also included Dr Girling Ball, the venerated Dean of Barts, with Lady Ball, living at "The Grove"; two frequent visitors, Dr J.C.Raven, soon to become the author of *The Mill Hill Vocabulary Test*, and Desmond Furneaux – in Eysenck's words, '*an outstanding psychologist whose work on intelligence has had revolutionary consequences*'; Dr R.Scarisbrook, involved in fatigue tests for what will shortly be identified as 'Effort Syndrome'; and F.C.W.Capps, the Sub-Dean of Barts.

As far as Eysenck was concerned, *there was no laboratory, no apparatus of any kind.* Avoiding what he called *psychiatric gobbledegook*, he would *sit peacefully on a bench in the parklands surrounding Mill Hill, trying to think out a research programme that would combine practical usefulness and scientific rectitude.* The result, for him, was that his days at Mill Hill *were some of the most interesting and fruitful of my life, and it was there that I laid the foundations of much of my future work.* While the School's family was enduring its privations and hardships in the wild terrain of Cumbria, the *alma mater* relinquished on the London home ground was about to make her own unique contribution to the war effort, under the impulse of this extraordinary concentration of medical talent.

'Therapeutic Communities'

Two experiments evolved under Lewis, set within the context of what was now designated as the Mill Hill EMS Hospital Class 1, No.M 9377, Sector 3, London Region. It may be convenient for the work of Maxwell Jones to be considered first in this process of re-discovery, since it followed on directly from developments at the Maudsley in 1938/9 by an *émigré* Viennese doctor, Joshua Bierer: he was engaged at the Runwell Hospital, London, on work of no ordinary kind. Some sense of its importance lies in the fact that it, and the subsequent work at Mill Hill, rate three full pages in Edward Shorter's *History of Psychiatry*; in another of those linguistic coincidences with which Mill Hill's story abounds, the building at Runwell where it took place was called "Sunnyside House".

Bierer was exploring how a new approach, later to be termed 'group psychotherapy', might work instead of psycho-analysis, with its perceived tendency to make the patient dependent on an analyst; he saw his patients becoming *independent, active, and self-deciding.* Although such groups are now practised widely – (for example in the Anti-Addictive programmes developed by *OM* Dr Robert Lefever) – the first to be assembled anywhere in Europe were at the Runwell, on 8 December 1939, three months after Barts as an EMH had already opened at Mill Hill. With the first phase of the war in 1939-40 taking an unexpectedly quieter turn in the West, the original plan for the Mill Hill site would need to be flexible.

Writing from a Maudsley, not a Barts, standpoint, Shorter goes on to describe what happened next: the fact that he describes the new site as a *former Public School* can perhaps be forgiven – the circumstances of Mill Hill's absolute departure could well have looked fairly permanent to the casual observer. Even the newspaper story immediately following the evacuation of servicemen to Mill Hill from Dunkirk, of 5 June 1940 – all carefully preserved by Red Cross Nurse Mrs A. Rayner, sister-in-law of *OM* Richard Graves – described Mill Hill as *a once-famous Public School which has been turned into a hospital.*

In Shorter's words, *Now the scene shifts ... to a northern suburb of London, where at the outbreak of war the Ministry of Health set up the Mill Hill Emergency Hospital, a psychiatric center [sic] ... for the treatment of military and civilian shell-shock cases ... it was staffed by members of the Maudsley Hospital, and included an Effort Syndrome Unit, so named because much psychosomatic illness among troops, presented itself in the form of shortness of breath and the like, following exercise (so-called soldier's heart). Heading this ... unit was a cardiologist and a psychiatry resident, Maxwell Jones, a young Scottish physician ... who had graduated seven years previously from ... Edinburgh, and was at the Maudsley at the time the war broke out. It was under Jones at Mill Hill that the notion of "therapeutic community" truly germinated; and it germinated almost by accident. Many of the war nurses were not old-fashioned authoritarian ward-sisters, but mature professional women who had chosen nursing as their war-work.* (This is also clear through the evidence of Audrey Rayner, and her sister Helen, the future wife of *OM* Dr M.E.Moore, and also an SRN, Mrs Alice Bond, who have helped to uncover further this unknown chapter in the history of Mill Hill.)

Shorter goes on: *These women were accustomed to free communication, not giving orders to patients and receiving them from doctors ... at Mill Hill, the doctors would bring the patients together in a group to explain, in a nice way, that what they really had was a form of hysteria ... They began by ... having the nurses act out little skits in front of the patients.* They invented a family, with a *normal father, an hysterical mother ... and three daughters ...*

This work continued steadily while other equally interesting Maudsley work was going on, led by the later Prof Eysenck, another *émigré* from Hitler's Europe. Several books have been written about the escape to England of this small but important band of first-class professional minds; some of them, such as Hans Berge and Friedrich Cronheim, were also to bring to the School herself under John Whale, both at St Bees and later back in Mill Hill, the benefits of their fine intelligence, the product of generations of central European and Jewish culture. One book's title was: *Hitler's Loss ...* That loss to Europe was also an immeasurable 'Mill Hill' gain then and for years after the war – for the Emergency Hospital in medicine, and for the School in the fields of language, literature, art and music.

Looking ahead, by 1944, under Maxwell Jones at the MHEH, *the patients themselves had begun to participate in the psychodramas, though as yet they did not use that word ... Early in 1945 the therapeutic community was tested on a larger scale;* it thereby moves beyond the strict confines of Millhillian interest. *The Mill Hill group was asked to take over a unit ... at [a] hospital at Dartford ... [treating] returning POWs with combat fatigue.* Shorter later relates that Eysenck had been *the director of the psychological department of the Maudsley Hospital,* and the first to compare the outcomes of psychoanalysis with other therapies. The outcome was his celebrated book, *Dimensions of Personality.* In it he pays tribute to those by this time installed in the school's premises who made his work possible: *The Hospital authorities, particularly Dr*

W.S.Maclay, and Dr A.B.Stokes, did everything in their power to further our efforts. The psychiatrists... helped us in every conceivable way... The Assistant Matron, Miss Goodyear, gave invaluable help in... arranging for group tests. Mr J.C.Raven allowed us to use his standardization data, and to reproduce in this book parts of his... Mill Hill Vocabulary Test.

Eysenck himself lived in one of the Houses – he does not say which one. (The Matron lived in the same House, on the floor above, a co-location as inhibiting for Eysenck as it would have been to generations of Millhillians before and after him.) *Once a week all the staff were required to stay the night at the hospital, firewatching, keeping a look-out for incendiary bombs dropped by enemy planes. This was a nationwide practice...* Photographs at the Maudsley Archives and those provided during 1997/8 by Audrey Rayner and Alice Bond show the staff, both military and civilian, going about their business at Mill Hill during this strange, uprooted period.

Army of occupation

The original purpose envisaged for Mill Hill in 1939 had been simply as the MHEH, anticipating much clinical trauma from immediate bombing, including children's cases. When this did not materialise, a revised approach made possible the introduction of the Maudsley staff, causing the disposition of resources to change. From being originally a 400 surgical-bed general hospital, plus 200 neuro-psychiatric beds, as at September 1939, the segregated buildings were ideal for the flexibility now required: it was transformed by late 1940 into a 610 bed hospital (360 neurological beds, 150 'Effort Syndrome' beds, and a mere 100 for surgery cases). This would change further by January 1943, as the course of the war itself changed for the better: 425 neurological beds, 100 for Effort Syndrome, and a mere 25 for surgical, some 20 beds having been denied them through two of the many bombing raids to hit the District. (These may well have been aimed at the Middlesex Regiment's barracks at Mill Hill East, not at the Hospital.)

If some of the Maudsley research may seem a little specialised for those who do not have a medical turn of mind, the general Barts role, and the role of the actual buildings of the School during this period, will have a somewhat greater immediacy; they contrast with the more sedate office plans envisaged by ICI. Audrey Rayner provided an excellent description: *Barts patients were civilian, the Maudsley patients were civilian at first, then servicemen. In 1940 (June), Barts patients were evacuated and the wards cleared for the men from Dunkirk. We had the French*

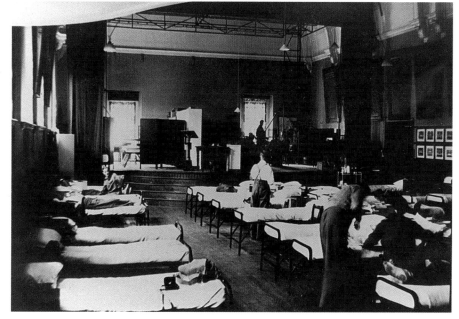

The Large as Casualty Ward, before the first air-raid, 1940. Note oil paintings, Honours Boards, team photos. 7.*q*

contingent who were given beds all over the school. I was in Marnham (The Large) where there were approx. 70 beds and 6 in the small classroom opposite. The men were general wounded... straight off the Beaches. As they were lousy, they were, if not too badly wounded, stripped and sent to bathe in the swimming pool. Their clothes were destroyed and they were issued with pyjamas; fortunately it was very hot.

The 80-year old Alice Bond also had very clear memories in 1998; *Taking over the school was a very hurried affair. Patients were arriving before things were organised, Eight of us nurses... were accommodated in the Museum. The first night was a bit scary for us. I think we slept with one eye open – watching the shelves above our beds hoping desperately for no air raids. We did not fancy waking up to find a dead snake coiled round our necks... Some of our patients were... French, Dutch, Belgian... There was great excitement in the worst days of the Battle of Britain... the paper boys chalked up how many German planes had been shot down by our Spitfire pilots. There were some nasty cases from the London Dock fires – Firemen, Policemen, ARP Wardens.* Gordon Wallis recalled climbing up to Evans the Butcher, opposite *The Three Hammers* one such night, and seeing the sky a solid red glow all over East London.

The School Houses were each allocated a different form of case-load: only those with a malign sense of humour would seek any parallels with the psychological state of mind of their subsequent and rightful owners. Burton Bank was to receive depressive and obsessional cases; Ridgeway took in cases of acute anxiety. Winterstoke catered for cases of 'acute conversion hysteria'. Chris Sutcliffe, House-master from 1973 to 1983, remembered the former School physician, Dr Morley, who stayed on with his Mill Hill Village practice during the war, telling him how one day, when he was calling at the House, one of these same patients suddenly threw a glass at him, breaking it against the wall: (perhaps a case of hysteria not yet converted).

Glenda Baim recalled "the very depressing chaps" sitting around the grounds; she told a story of a malingerer professing a limp, which she noticed had switched from one leg to the other between surgery visits. Collinson was the place set aside for the women patients, both civilian and military. An Army officer once said to Donald Hall after the war, having learned where his Mill Hill allegiances lay: *Ah, Collinson, that's where we kept the batty ATS!*: (nerve-damaged members of the Women's Auxiliary Territorial Service). The Gymnasium had an extraordinary role – almost a kind of 'isolation' ward for *cases of hopeless prognosis*, to prevent them *endangering the optimistic therapeutic atmosphere* among the other patients. The peacetime Gym fanatics, however fanatical, had luckily never had this kind of effect on the rest of the School.

The Head Master's Study was used by Dr Maclay *where he would show his visitors a cupboard still containing a number of canes, facetiously remarking that it would probably be regarded as imprudent if he used them on one or two of the recalcitrant members of his staff.* His Deputy, Dr Stokes, was to prove a most co-operative friend when the School at last came to re-occupy her lost home, in summer 1945. The last patients were not to depart until just after the agreed definitional date for de-requisitioning: this was 'the end of hostilities', the cessation of the Japanese war – 22 August. It was at least an improvement on the six-month delay originally threatened.

Miss Goodyear, when not striding out purposefully, as Matrons were wont to do, along the paths to the various units and buildings, or talking with male patients resting on the Portico or sitting in the Square, is shown in the photographs at work in one of the School House rooms; her office seemed to be looking out, through windows criss-crossed with anti-blast sticky tape, onto Top Terrace. The windows of the whole of the Marnham Block were similarly 'criss-crossed'.

The Science School performed many roles. It was an HQ for the Area EMS Director, Sir Girling Ball; an Old Merchant Taylor's boy, he no doubt sympathised with the fate depriving his old rival school of her home; (he was then Dean of the Barts pre-clinical Medical College – transposed in September 1939 to Queens' College, Cambridge). It also served as the telephone exchange, down in the basement, safe from the anticipated air-raids. Pathology and biochemical labs, and a lecture theatre for the various medical students who came there in the early days – these were the two roles most similar to any of the buildings' peacetime purposes. The then Squash Courts housed a Clothing store, and also provided a temporary Mortuary with the Fives Courts (shelved for the bodies), where a notice on the wall pointed the way to one part of the Air Raid shelter provision, the Marnham basement. Seven other bunkers were gouged out of the grounds; by 2006 only those on the Top Field slope and below Collinson Field would still be there, having served as damp and makeshift Hobbies Rooms post-war. The X-Ray Theatre was in the Marnham Block. The McClure Music School was taken over by the Military Registrar. The Cricket Pavilion on the Park became the porters' living quarters, requiring it to be connected in November 1940, for the first time, into the internal telephone system, as was The Mount Girls School nearby, a month later. Maurice Jacks wrote to Buster Brown on 17 October 1939: *I cannot bear to think of the old place in the hands of the medical vandals. The Art Room is an Operating Theatre – Ye Gods!*

Every spare foot of School space was utilised for wards, divided into 'Central', 'East' and 'West'. Glenda Baim recalled that *it felt exactly like some historic hospital, with nurses scurrying about everywhere, and soldiers in the grounds.* The Maudsley Archives still contain photographs of many of these locations which to a Millhillian eye are a priceless part of the School's heritage, and should all by rights appear in these pages. There are a few precious photographs from Audrey Rayner and Alice Bond; several show two rows of seven beds down the length of The Large, with the pre-war double rows of Oxbridge Honours Boards on the walls. From articles in the *Mill Hill Magazines* of the Second World War era it is clear that they were lettered in white on a dark green background; below them were another double row of 30 or more MHS team photographs, still in place and intact at that time – *c.*1940 – albeit unnoticed by their then unseeing, and indeed sometimes very ill or badly wounded inhabitants. All the Maudsley photographs lay unidentified and undiscovered until the research carried out for this History.

French Wounded from Dunkirk

In spite of his wounds, a French Algerian soldier brought back from Dunkirk has a good joke with his nurse. He is one of a number of French wounded who are recovering in a once-famous English public school which has been turned into a hospital.

1940 press cutting about a 'once-famous Public School': 'French wounded from Dunkirk': Algerian soldier and nurse. 7.r

Other photographs show soldiers in trousers, gym shoes, vests and thick-strapped army braces, enjoying games of volleyball, and soccer, on fields hallowed for the 'oval ball'; one of the fields was lent to the Mill Hill Barracks. There was much PT under a Sgt Instructor Harris, and a PTI team, imported to provide exercises *specially suited for neuroses patients*. There were mass exercise sessions on Top Field, on the Quad, and on the 'Fishing Net'. There are also shots of swimming and diving competitions at the Buckland Pool. Dickie Buckland must have been as pleased to know that his contribution to the School from 1937 was being put to such valuable use during the war – however much this eminently peace-loving man detested its necessity – as he would have been to know of its new role in the 21st century.)

Dunkirk spirits

All nationalities benefited from Mill Hill's pleasant terraces and restorative air, not least the survivors from the Dunkirk 'miracle'. The spirit of that extraordinary Victorian and Edwardian Millhillian writer, Herbert Ward, would have delighted to see that there were some of his *'Poilus'* among them, with the distinctive ridged oval 'Adrian' helmets which had not altered since his days when he ferried the wounded in the First World War. The photographs show many of them still wearing the only uniform they had left after getting across the Channel – somehow or other – in that mighty little Armada of June 1940. One of them, in Audrey Rayner's words, was a *young Algerian ... with nearly every medal in the French Army for bravery. In his pyjamas he went 'A.W.O.L.' down to Mill Hill Broadway and shopped for his friends.* Many of these soldiers recounted to the nurses, in Audrey's telling phrase, *the horrifying, sad, transfixing and humorous stories ... of their experiences in the War*: none of this precious first-hand material now survives, and may well later have died with some of its tellers.

The Scriptorium (the 'Reading Room' for ICI) was used as a recreation room, under the eye of a kindly Sir James Murray (his ghost no doubt working out some clever semantic game based on the wording of the soldiers' various shoulder-flashes). Lord Winterstoke too would have been glad to know that his Library was being put to an extension of its original use as *a reading and writing room* by so many ordinary 'Tommies', now for the moment, or permanently, out of action. The Tuck-Shop, of course, in Army usage, did have a vital purpose: it became the Canteen. Other shots of June 1940 show groups of men working away at various stools and chairs in the School "Carp Shop", with that legendary bright summer sunshine of 1940 streaming in through the open doorway. Another therapy was pottery, and there are several rather staged scenes of soldiers, aided and abetted by uniformed Barts nurses, and therapists in 'civvies', fashioning clay pots and bowls for the benefit of the *Sport & General's* cameraman. It was all part of a news feature at a cataclysmic moment in the war, much-needed to boost the nation's morale.

Later that summer and early autumn, sitting in wheel-chairs on Burton Bank's quiet lawn, there were reputed to be dozens of nerve-shattered Battle of Britain pilots, out of the camera's gaze, including some crazily courageous Poles. There is no record of any pilot having crashed his plane and getting killed nearby, and thereafter haunting the grounds as 'the BB ghost' – a story recorded in the BB House Book, and half-believed by many generations of Burton Bankers, right up to the 1990s (see below). The relatively intimate, un-wardlike – and un-warlike – dormitories of BB and the other Mill Hill Boarding Houses could readily be imagined as providing an ideal environment for the individual care that many of these serious cases demanded; the photographs only show the smiling walking-wounded, a familiar sight along The Ridgeway, kitted-out with their striking 'Hospital Blues'. The "San", perversely, defied its erstwhile role, while perhaps foreshadowing its later destiny, by becoming the main 'Boarding house' for the female section of the establishment, in this case the nurses. By 1942, the emergency phase was over, for the time being; D-Day was to revive that situation two years later. Despite the abundance of coincidence in Mill Hill's story, there is no known instance of an *OM* serviceman finishing up at his old School for treatment.

From being at the start the domicile of a single female resident – the future Mrs Moore (a Barts' Secretary) – Winterstoke remained thereafter a full house. Ridgeway took on a new additional life as a staging post for trainee members of the Women's Royal Naval Service. "Wren" Diane 'Molly' Temperley was drafted to MHS in September 1942:

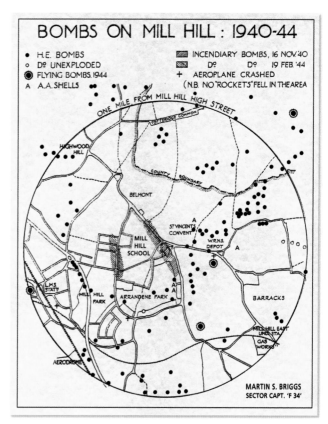

Fig.M BOMBS ON MILL HILL 1940-44

My recollections were of a large building with endless concrete stairs: (this sounds like Ridgeway). *The assembly Hall, known as the fo'csle, was used for lectures, PT, Divisions etc. This floor was also made of concrete, as I remember clearly going on watch at 05.30 to scrub the floor. We slept in large dormitories in bunks ... We were all in civvies, as the W.R.N.S. were not kitted out until they had been in the service for 2 weeks. I was there for seven days before being drafted to Greenwich Naval College ...*

Most of the central school buildings were put to uses entirely unimaginable to all save the handful of ex-St Bees senior boys, prefects and monitors, who were asked to come back a few days earlier than the planned date of 1 October 1945. Together with the teaching staff and the Housemasters – a valiant effort, no Effort Syndrome here – they removed the vestiges of the hastily departing Hospital, although many painted wall-signs remained. Some after-effects were still noticeable years later: research chemist Neil Wilson recalled the radioactivity in the Science Block, due to X-rays, affecting gold-leaf electroscope tests. School House corridor apparently led down to the Operating Theatre; Mrs Hazel Wallis could still picture vividly, as a girl at St Mary's Abbey school opposite Belmont, going along The Ridgeway for voluntary work in the Theatre, and seeing some very gory sights in the waste-bins. *OM* Chris Ousey remembered that surplus X-Ray equipment was piled high in the Car Park. An upstairs room in the Marnham Block behind the gallery was still decorated with the kind of 'Patient-Art' which features in the Maudsley Archive itself – another form of therapy, still remembered by a few boys. *OM Michael Gee recalled clearing Top Field by hand, discovering syringes and needles still lying around, from no one knows what previous event:* the photographs only show the PT classes taking place there. The writer, as a small new boy of 1945, noticed the concreting of the steps leading up to the Loggia passage, a necessary desecration from 1939, to enable trolleys to be trundled up to 'Ops'.

Fires were started

Although **Fig.M**, the map by Millhillian architect Martin Briggs, as Sector Capt F 34, only includes two incidents, Mill Hill's buildings sustained three incendiary raids while 'the School' was enjoying the safety of St Bees: 16 November 1940, 31 November 1942 and 18 February 1944. The map shows that the land opposite *Old BB* also received a crashed plane (source of the legend?) and a V1. Rooker Roberts reported to parents in his St Bees Newsletter of March 1941: *The classroom where I had taught for seven years was open to the sky... the Large was roofless too, and its naked walls, charred beams and twisted girders stood gaunt and stark... The stately Dining Hall was a ruin, all the more pathetic because of its association with the convivial side of human nature. One expected to hear the howl of jackals, echoing amongst the deserted pillars.*

Audrey Rayner remembered clearly: *Later... we were bombed by incendiaries, and the Hospital was very badly damaged by fire. The patients were dispersed and salvage work began. The roof was mostly burnt off; Marnham and the dining hall were completely exposed to the elements and as it poured with rain, it was not easy to rescue property in swirling water! The wards... upstairs were also seriously damaged... When the temporary repairs were finished, the whole Hospital was turned over to the Maudsley... School Houses were relatively unscathed.* Alice Bond recalled it too: "*One nasty drizzly cold dark night down came a Molotov Basket which sprayed 150 incendiaries all over the buildings and grounds. When the emergency passed, some RAMC lads went round counting them, and collected a few pieces of the bomb. I was offered a small... souvenir... So much damage was done but the one and only casualty was an RAMC lad who climbed a ladder to tackle an incendiary on the chapel roof... over went the ladder... the lad fell to the ground and broke his ankle... At least... the Op. Theatre [was] undamaged.*

This was not the first 'air attack': a 1970 *MHM* article – "Confessions of an Old Boy" – recalled *a shower of shrapnel on Collinson House roof, after a WWI Zeppelin was shot down over Barnet.*

The unwelcome burning of Tite's School Roof made a change from its saga of inundations over the centuries. The damage was repaired, the effects no more to be seen. However, the charred timbers under the north-east section of the angled School House roof still clearly register the German attack of 1940, Tite's 100-year-old solid oak beams proving too thick and obstinate to bow to Goering's best efforts and burn through completely. No doubt somewhere up there, apart from Alice Bond's solitary piece of shrapnel, some fragments still remain of those raids, as yet undiscovered by the generations of boys who once climbed there defiantly after hours, for that fell purpose, over the intervening years. The third raid of 1944 merely caused minor damage to "Garth" and four houses in Winterstoke Gardens.

ICI at Belmont

Nothing so dramatic happened at Belmont under ICI's occupation, lasting until 1946, necessitating an extra year at Cockermouth, whilst the Main School was back in Mill Hill; (the C/T Minutes show that Arthur Rooker Roberts was in fact happy to postpone the task of recruiting scarce domestic staff post-war). ICI wanted to extend the lease, but Arthur had *committed himself to the parents*. ICI's Millbank and other Head Office properties in Central London had been required for war purposes, and were in the thick of the potential bombing. The Publicity Department, the Africa Department and the Lime Division all came out to Mill Hill. By 1944 an ICI letterhead read: 'Southern Region, Belmont, the Ridgeway'.

The original requirement had been for space at Mill Hill for 400 people, with the possibility for separate sleeping accommodation for 200. By the end of the war this had translated into a total of over 5,000 square feet solely at Belmont, using 20 rooms for just under 40 staff, with increasing pressure on space as the war progressed, and other units moved in and out. The contracts of 3 May and 15 December 1939 were for a rental of £1,750 p.a., based on the costings that the Main School had worked out in the early days when it had hoped to get a commercial deal out of the evacuation.

Many ICI staff recorded their memories of their various evacuations to different parts of the country. Surprisingly, none were set down about Belmont's beautiful acres. Jumping ahead in time, no great damage was done, and the return in the Long Vac of 1946 was relatively painless, all managed with skill and efficiency by Arthur Rooker Roberts and his hard-pressed, and by now understandably impatient, team.

The old MHS Natural History Museum, now to be used as a nurses dormitory: occupants lay awake, fearing pickled wildlife falling on them due to the reverberations of the bombing. (The tattered remnants of its ornithological exhibits were discovered in the roof of the Music School in 1999, undisturbed, other than by microbes, since the hasty departure for St Bees, in September 1939: see Ch.VII (i).) *7.s*

The view from St Bees

These events were not entirely unnoticed by the *MHM* at St Bees. The first, heavily nostalgic, issue in December 1939, reported that the traditional November 11th service had been conducted in the Chapel and at the Gate of Honour by a friendly Vicar of St Paul's Church on The Ridgeway, with a few *OMs* present, and that Medical Superintendent Dr Maclay had then taken them round the grounds to show what transformations had been wrought.

A Bart's man wrote in the *St Bartholomew's Hospital Journal* War Bulletin: *On arrival we were immediately enshrouded in a not unpleasant school atmosphere. Portraits of past Mill Hill headmasters frowned on us severely, busts of Virgil and Dante* [later rediscovered in the Music School roof] *gazed at us with jaundiced eye at our first meal in the school Hall... we slept in the Murray Scriptorium... many words not to be found in that dictionary were to be heard as we staggered about in the black-out seeking some sort of bed...* There was an accompanying article by one of those *OMs: The Marnham Block is heaped with sandbags... the boot-hole has been dismantled... concrete air-raid shelters have been built behind the Music School, now filled*

millhill School. - The Museum.

with Medical Students... Coming to the School House we see iron steps leading direct to Nos. 1 and 2 Dormies from the Loggia... The corridor is even darker, and the Octagon is painted blue, giving everywhere a "dim religious light"... In Nos 2 and 3 Studies the victims are prepared for the slaughter and anaesthetised... only the Portico remains untouched.

'The Fire at Mill Hill', in the *MHM* March 1941 issue, was the evocative account by the opera composer, Inglis Gundry, of *one of those nights in the Autumn blitz when planes had been humming over the North-West of London with the persistence of mosquitoes... The first shower of incendiaries fell largely on the grounds. The Rifle Range... was soon sending flames 50 feet into the air. Horses, hay, cars and other inflammable material was hurriedly removed... another shower had fallen with more deadly aim, and most of the school buildings were hit... "bread baskets" of two or three hundred had fallen on the Ridgeway. Men had been sent to the School House roof [where] the bombs had already penetrated the slates above the dining-hall... if only Mr Brown [Buster] and Westmore [the Butler] had been sleeping in their old bedrooms and had been supplied with sand and shovels, the damage to the dining hall could have been avoided... The Chapel was saved... The Library was luckiest of all... a bomb had landed on one of the rafters, it had exploded but remained perched on a beam, where in the airless enclosure it burnt out harmlessly. So the books were saved!*

As a lighter reminder, *OM* Mark Sellers recalled that a Mill Hill XI went down to play the Emergency Hospital on the Park (tea back in the Tuck Shop) on 10 September 1941. Of 155 for 9, Dr Stokes scored 22, Dr Jones 12; Brian Piper took three wickets, and scored 26 out of 128 for 6, Geoff Sears 31, and Ian Wright 27. The resulting honourable draw seemed an apt conclusion.

Looking after the shop

Meanwhile, Mill Hill had not quite written off 'Mill Hill' for the duration, and the patrol of three *OM* fire-watchers now became nine. A History faces the invidious task of mentioning some names to the exclusion of others; the criteria have to be those of the interests and development of the School itself.

For many reasons, the name of Sir William Ramsay CBE, *Légion d'honneur* – the initials W.C.R. would have been familiar to many – crops up usually in the context of that mainstream Millhillian game to which he devoted so much of his life and enormous energy, from captaining the 1st XV at the end of the First World War, to presiding over the fortunes of the game worldwide, as RFU President in 1954/5 and 1979/80. Whether he was performing small unchronicled acts of kindness, as he did for one small boy trudging wearily along The Ridgeway after a Sunday exeat, offering him a lift back to Winterstoke in his capacious car, or bringing his genial presence to bear on what was then the Annual Dinner of the Cambridge Old Millhillians Club, as the author's guest in 1953, or whether he was taking the public lead in some new initiative, "Bill" was a quintessential Mill Hill figure of his time. He embodied many of those virtues which his father, Rev. Alexander Ramsay, Moderator of the Presbyterian Church of England, carried down from the family's Nonconformist Scottish past, to the benefit of Mill Hill's British but then still Nonconformist present. (There was even a moment in McClure's time when all three of the School's constituent Nonconformist strands – Baptist, Congregationalist, and Presbyterian – were represented at their topmost level by Millhillians). Bill seemed to be the very best advertisement for Mill Hill, never sentimental or rosy-eyed about the School, but practical, down to earth, and, as will be clear in the context of the 'Middlesex Scheme', always forward-looking.

Mill Hill was fortunate in having Bill around when the School was away in Cumbria; he it was who primarily 'looked after the shop' throughout the war, ideally placed for this role, as the Area Director of the ARP/Civil Defence operations; Col Oscar Viney also assisted. When the fire-bomb raid took place, Bill was immediately over to the School, surveying the damage, and ensuring that any things of value were preserved from further loss. Others connected with the School would make periodic visits, including the former Winterstoke Matron, and Science HoD Donald Hall's future wife, Enid Stancliffe; she remembered going into a devastated Large, with her umbrella up. Even when the School returned in September 1945, Donald recalled that there was only a temporary roof, and that *the tiered benches on the balcony were covered over by a floor, level with the rooms at the back.*

It is evident from the Governors' Minutes of 9 January 1941 that Bill Ramsay was the official means of keeping the governing body aware of how things were, 'back at the ranch', while they were trying to keep their fingers on the pulse of Mill Hill in exile. He reported initially that at least £5,000-worth of damage had been done to School House, Marnham Block, Chapel, Library, Tuck Shop, Script, Rifle Range, San, and Winterstoke. The final bill went far higher; a first tranche of £5,258 was received by 11 September 1941. More damage was done to Wills Grove, but by the military authorities not the Germans. (The fear that the Local Authority might even take over this private road was only finally resolved in 2001.)

A loyalty of groundstaff

Dr Morley too may well have helped by keeping his eye on things. At a much less commanding but still invaluable level, however, Governor Bill Ramsay was not the only custodian of Mill Hill's relinquished *terra firma* for those six years of banishment. Apart from the 'tasselled-cap' incident, the School support staff rarely get a mention among the crowded pages of a School History, yet their records of service, in the 21st century as ever, were long and loyal. They have only surfaced in connection with the sociological background to Thomas Priestley's time, and later in Dr Weymouth's era, when Servants' Races were a regular part of Sports Day. During the Second World War a small group of the team of groundsmen was kept on, to look after the grounds, the produce, and the farm, primarily for the sake of the new occupants, not with any concern for the School's residual interest.

The Maudsley Record has 12 men on the books in July 1940 (compared with today's combined team of 23): C.Shaylor, J.V.Dias, C.F.Raynor, F.Burfoot (in Alan Elliott's memory he had only one tooth), W.Cook, J.Raynor, W.Rayne, L.H.Shaylor, J.Lock, J.F.Eltham, and P.Hope. Under a Leading Assistant Gardener were six assistant gardeners, one Head Pigman, and four men looking after the farm and kitchen garden. Donald Hall remembered that one of the two Shaylor brothers – called "Frank" – had hidden away quite a bit of equipment and chemicals when the hospital was clearing out because he thought they could be of use "post-war"! His brother "Lett" was also a gardener after 1945; "Bill" Cook was still with the School at the Sesquicentennial in 1957, and appears in the photograph of the Queen planting a tree; F.Burfoot was in charge of the Head's Garden at the Grove, and "Jack" Rayner looked after the boilers (retiring in 1967 after 47 years' service). "Ernie" Baker – his death reported in 1973 – had been the 'Carp' since 1924; during the war he built the sheds along the BB path.

They were all transferred to the payroll of the MHEH, just as their stock, above all their horses, were also transferred to the new books. Much went by the board of course, and the scene facing the School when returning in 1945 was pretty barren and neglected. However, these representatives of the School did what they could to keep the place in order, despite the proper priority demands of the wartime occupants. (Not all members of 'the Team' survived: the Maudsley archives show that on 20 January 1941, 'an aged chestnut mare', and again on 30 June 1944, another 'aged mare, unfit for useful work', had to be finally 'superannuated' after life-times of faithful service as *GC gee-gees*.) None of the men who could have observed so much of interest ever thought to put words onto paper; it would not have seemed important at the time. 'Coping' was once more the name of the game, as elsewhere; but even if the memories did not endure for later ears, Mill Hill's pleasant acres, under the ministrations of this small unsung team, did survive, for the enjoyment of those who returned, and their successors.

Back to the 'eldorado-island'

Mill Hill's war was now technically over at last, and the peace was about to be waged; however, as the records show, the final compensation for war damage would still not be completed, five years later, by 1950, and wider effects continued into the longer-term. The Treasurer Dickie Buckland wrote to the Ministry of Works that it had been *a fine war work*. Apart from the Maudsley photographs and documents, the ICI papers, and the memories of the few that surfaced at the time of the writing of this History, nothing else is left, save for those last remaining, and now unnoticed, air-raid shelters on Top Field, to conjure up the story of the wartime life of the buildings and grounds of the School and Belmont. That is unless the new firing range which was necessitated by the destruction of its predecessor – used as occupational huts, or the space created by the disembowelling of other bunkers to facilitate the Music School extension of 1999 – may be counted on the positive side. The soldiery are now untraceable, likewise most of the staff, and the ICI HQ personnel. Prof Hans Eysenck would have been the only professional clinician to add his personal memories to this story but a second brain tumour intervened, followed by his death in the late summer of 1997.

The sole literary testimony, and one more of those strange Millhillian coincidences, is to be found in the biography of the *émigré* Jewish-Hungarian writer, Arthur Koestler, author of the critique of Stalinism, *Darkness at Noon* (his masterpiece), who as an alien could only serve in the Pioneer Corps; falling sick, he became a patient at the MHEH. It was the *OM*, Kingsley Martin, who having previously, on 2 April 1941, as Editor of the *New Statesman*, offered him a job, later wrote to him at Mill Hill: *Don't forget that you have masses of friends in this country, and that we treasure you as one of the people we are most proud to know*... From 'Ward 6, Central

West' (probably one of the former School House studies) Koestler wrote to his girl-friend on 27 December: *it is so nicely and efficiently run that one would think it is in a different country... The hospital is a former public school, with lawns and playgrounds on the top of Mill Hill.* His biographer noted that he *was allowed to work in a room put aside specially for his use...* although dressed, in Koestler's words, *immer noch in Blau*, he could not visit any pubs or restaurants. Writing of his recovery, in the setting of Mill Hill's greenery, he was to create a phrase with a symbolic value for Millhillians that he could never have conceived: *It was in short a minor miracle – an eldorado-island in the midst of the general army-muddle.*

To the hundreds who contributed to the well-being of this 'eldorado-island' by simply being at their post, and not doing any irreparable damage while they were there, the School and Belmont must remain ever-grateful. Some indication of the good relations achieved between the School and her wartime occupants must lie in the nomination as a Governor, a year later, on 5 December 1946, of the Medical Superintendent, Dr W.S.Maclay, on the resignation of Sir Walter Moberly.

John Visser, the senior monitor who had to supervise the improvised clearing-up operation in September 1945, one of only seven of his year-group to make the return, judged that *the buildings at Mill Hill were not in as bad a state as might have been expected after six years except for the Murray Scriptorium, which... looked in danger of falling down. Of course everywhere needed substantial redecoration...;* School House corridor and the studies off it were *particularly dingy with their yellow and brown paint.* Yet there were compensations: *we all ate in Main Hall... much to be preferred to the draughty and sometimes damp Seacote. The Parks were a wonderful improvement on West's Field for cricket.* Alice Bond's final comment conjures up those sterling days: *Anyone... can be proud of having any connections with such a school. It really did a marvellous wartime job, and... proved that the true British spirit will always be there when needed.*

OM Kingsley Martin, Editor, New Statesman: befriender of Hungarian émigré novelist Arthur Koestler, MHEH patient. In the ideologically challenging 1930s, he was accused of being deeply involved in the alliance between communism and socialism, despite his espousal of Koestler, and snubbed by the Eton-educated George Orwell. 7.t

Sources for pt (ii) of Ch.VII include: 'Inventory' 3.ix.1939 C/T's Cmtee Mins 1946 (see Appendix E) #; dscns with P.M.Woodroffe [1942-5] ref fund-raising, Dec 2000.

WWII background: C.Barnett, *Collapse of British Power...* (Sutton, 1997); A.L.Bullock, *Hitler: A Study in Tyranny* (rev.ed. 1962); O.Lehmann-Russbueldt, *Aggression – The Origin of Germany's War Machine* (1942); *Observer*, 9.iii.1997, quoting article by C.Dirks, in *Die Zeit*; U.Bialer, *The Shadow of the Bomber* (1980), 130; *Trans. of the Ryl Historical Soc* 6th ser. v.XI, (2001), 234; ICI Publicity Dept.

MHEH: corr, 1997 with Prof H.J.Eysenck, Emeritus Prof, LU, Inst of Psychiatry; with Prof Robert Kendell CBE [1948-53], Pres, Ryl Coll. of Psychiatrists 1996-9; & A/Ms Donald Hall, Chris Sutcliffe; Archvs of the Maudsley, & St Bartholomew's Hospitals; *History of the*

Institute of Psychiatry 1924-1974 (1974); H.J.Eysenck, *Rebel With A Cause* (W.H.Allen, 1990), *Dimensions of Personality* (1947); E.Shorter, *A History of Psychiatry* (Wiley, 1997); M.Jones, *Social Psychiatry: A Study of Therapeutic Communities* (1952); V.C.Medvei & J.C.Thornton eds, *The Royal Hospital of St Bartholomew 1123-1973* (1974); *BMJ*, 9.v.1964, obit of Dr W.S.Maclay CB, OBE, MD, FRCP, DTM&H, DPM; D.Cesarani, *Arthur Koestler, The Homeless Mind* (Heinemann/Harcourt Education, 1998), 181-2; Koestler Archv, Edinburgh U, MS 2301/3, 2372/1; A.Koestler, *Darkness at Noon*, trans D.Hardy (1940); recollections of service at the MHEH from Mrs Moore, wife of Dr M.E.Moore [1928-32], & their friend, Mrs Temperley; Mrs Audrey Rayner, sister-in-law of R.Graves [1919-24]; Mrs Alice Bond, SRN; Mrs Glenda Baim, 5.ii. & 18.ii.1999; also A.D.V.Elliott [1937-42]; Mr & Mrs Gordon Wallis, Mill Hill; H.Barnes, HS/M, BB, for access to 'BB House Bk', & legend of

wartime 'BB Ghost' (crash at 'old' BB); J.Hawkins, Master of BMT, & Mrs Rona Bagnall, sister of A.E.R.Roberts [1921-6]; ICI Archv, Millbank, for BMT occupancy 1939-46; Barnet (Hendon) Archvs; dscns, F.N.Wilson [1944-9]; Record, Queens' College, Cambridge 1991 (ref Barts' Medical College); W.J.Braithwaite, *Lloyd George's Ambulance Waggon* (1957), ref NHS origins. G.Smith, *The English Companion...* (Penguin, 1984) 180.

Other *OM* references: S.Baim [1988-93]; M.Baim [1992-5]; M.S.Briggs [1896-9]; R.W.B.Buckland [1878-84]; M.Gee [1942-6]; I.Gundry [1918-23]; N.G.B.James [1894-8]; B.Kingsley Martin [1914-6]; R.M.H.Lefever [1950-5]; J.D.Mitchell [1895-9]; C.E.R.Ousey [1942-7]; B.L.Piper [1938-42]; W.C.Ramsay [1912-8]; A.J.Rooker Roberts [1893-1900]; M.M.Sellers [1936-41]; G.W.Sears [1936-41]; O.V.Viney [1900-3]; J.B.Visser [1941-6]; H.Ward [1877]; I.M.Wright [1937-42].

Dr J.S.Whale, in academic gown, with group of parents on Top Terrace, Foundation Day, 1948. *8.a*

The Long Shadow of "The Whale"

Out of exile: rediscovering the roots: the fight for reputation

"I hope you thought that what I did was of some value":
Rev. Dr J.S. Whale, at his portrait presentation,
Mill Hill School Octagon, 29 October 1983.

Commentators on schools sometimes fall into the trap of asking: when was the place at its best? If a purely academic perspective were to be taken of Mill Hill's first 200 years, then unquestionably the decade influenced by Rev. Dr John Seldon Whale would represent the zenith. This is not, however, to suggest that, taken in the round, Mill Hill was then necessarily at her 'best'. Indeed it has been argued by some that certain Head Masters have done more for the individual, the mass of less scholastic pupils, both before and after this time: it was said of McClure, for example, that 'he saw perfection where imperfection strove'. A counter argument might easily pick out such boys who in the 'Whale' years graduated from the then IV Form to the equivalent of today's top universities, including Oxbridge, surely evidence of the permeating effect of a high academic 'tone'. Yet there can be no ranking order between 'reigns' on this complex issue: many unique factors, internal and external – (witness Dr Whale's one-off scholastic bonus, the Middlesex scheme) – embracing staff and pupils, across both the maintained and private sectors, combined to mark out this particular, even unrepeatable, 'peak' era – but a peak it remains. For this reason, this chapter has a special focus on the academic infrastructure to that time.

For John Visser, the senior monitor and future civil service 'mandarin', already encountered in the setting of St Bees, who helped bring the School back from exile, *1945/6 was a difficult year, but it was also exciting ... one was conscious of laying the foundations for a new era.* That third post-war era in Mill Hill's story would witness the sombre fulfilment of a concept first invented by H.G.Wells and soon to be made world-famous by Churchill, the *iron curtain* cutting off the western world from the east: for one small part of that western world, Mill Hill, it was an austere, hierarchical time, imbued with purpose, and earnest – yet not entirely grey. The principled visionary at the helm was Rev. Dr J.S.Whale.

Rarely will a Head's purpose be defined by the appointing Governors. This is a blurred, multi-faceted world far removed from the precise 'Mission Statements' craved by armies and management experts. All Heads live with the sure knowledge that their achievements will only be truly assessable, if at all, after the passage of time, and certainly well after their actual span of years in post. However, the unique point that distinguishes teachers of pupils at any level from the manager of a business is that their market is people; finding their own identity through such institutions, those pupils actually need to discover what, and who, first set them on their road. In the case of a select few Heads, that process of self-discovery is made easier by virtue of the fact that the Head has made a special impression, as did Dr Whale from 1944 – an impression which casts its own beneficial forward shadow over the school.

In terms of academic results it is particularly difficult to pinpoint responsibility and achievement; yet Heads do announce, without caveats, the academic results for 'their' years, leaving their parental audiences to draw their own inferences about who was really to be credited. In most schools, the Heads of Department stand first in line for praise, yet the Head sets the standards for those Departmental Heads during his or her tenure; in Dr Whale's case, a spiritual tone was also set, in his capacity as Chaplain. Even if the 'buck' may not be stopped over any one desk at any one time, it can at least be shown to be hovering over the desks of both the departing Head and his successor for some undefined period of years. It is an area that teaching staff are uncomfortable about, and yet an outside observer needs some kind of theoretical basis for comparison, however different the underlying circumstances.

John Whale is to be counted, with Dr Weymouth, Sir John McClure and Prof Maurice Jacks, at the forefront of Mill Hill's 'Famous Four' in terms of his contemporary external standing; as with Weymouth, theology was his field, but the intellect was his goal. An experienced Housemaster, Edward Stanham, later Second Master to the next Head, Roy Moore, wrote that ... *the consequent results should not lie solely with his successor since it was the former's groundwork which laid the foundation for them*. The concept of a 'forward shadow' period, after the formal end of a term of office, is relevant to the very nature of the sowing of intellectual seeds – their slow germination and blossoming. The achievements of Dr John Whale covered many fields. However, as has been suggested, his chief claim to fame must lie, in Edward Stanham's words, in his *drive towards academic standards throughout the school*. He did this at one of the most traumatic – and dramatic – times in her history.

The model is advanced in this History that a minimum of two additional years be taken as a period of credit, at least for Heads, before a successor starts to feel encroached on. However much of a change-agent the new Head is asked or aspires to be, there are time-lags – and 'old' lags – inheritances both of masters and pupils, let alone of previous attitudes and practices, which cannot, and some would argue should not, all be revolutionised in the short term. Thus all Heads will have to accept (they may even sometimes be glad to avoid that responsibility) that the academic output for an ensuing period – be it two or even more years – ought in some degree to be partially credited to their predecessor.

The post-war impact of "The Whale"

Taking over in the Summer term of 1944, Dr Whale told the Court that he intended to make Mill Hill his *life's work*, albeit that his senior monitor, Esyr Lewis, recalls his saying that he only reckoned to carry out the role for some eight years. He brought the School physically back home, and spiritually back to her Nonconformist roots. His uncompromising realism about the future post-war role of the Public Schools, of which he was, as a former Head Boy of Caterham, a fervent advocate, made him the tough man for the hour. Even his chosen Second Master, John Morrison, told Brett James that he found him *difficult to work with*. He was equally uncompromising, even at times brusque, with parents; a later English master, Ted Winter, related how he invited parents in to his study, to dial TIM, if they brought their boys back to the School entrance hall after the 6.00 p.m. deadline for Sunday exeats. His reforming zeal coincided with one of the most decisive periods of change not merely in Mill Hill's history and the history of British education, but more widely in that of Great Britain itself.

The corollary to his record was the famous Middlesex ('MxCC') Scheme. This also met the School's immediate financial task – to secure more Boarding fees, to address an endemic Mill Hill need – a better 'return' on those beautiful but expensive fixed assets, 'fixed' or unquestioned since the Jacks era: the Quad with its Library and "Script", Church Cottages on The Ridgeway, the ancient "Grove", and rest of the estate. However since his imprint on academe would be the most lasting, it is opportune to examine the 'output' of one particular Head at a vital era, using the 'Two Year Forward Shadow' model. An assessment of "The Whale's" regime would therefore start with the Foundation Day successes of 1946 (not 1944) and go on to include the results announced by his successor in summer 1953; it affected accession to the whole range of tertiary campuses. Although the cohort leaving in July 1946 had some two years under his influence, those leaving at the end of Roy Moore's second

"Nath." Micklem QC/KC/QC, *OM* Chairman of Governors, 1922-44, member of a typically large MHS Nonconformist family: took silk under three sovereigns; one of four 1869 boys to attend twice through MHS closure-to-reopening. *8.b*

full year would have had their first three formative years, into the Lower VI, under the spell of 'JSW'. The forward shadow of this especial Head Master among all those 27 substantive incumbents that have graced Mill Hill over her first 200 years, could well be seen as extending even longer than that simple period of two years, even though successor-Heads and their Governing Bodies will naturally assume the burdens of their own day. (A comparison could be drawn with the ongoing influence of what *Nobis* called *the sheet anchor of the Mill Hill community*, another *little bespectacled man* – Governor Dickie Buckland, whose death on 17 December 1947 was honoured by a commemoration service taken reverentially by Dr Whale.) He lived throughout the incumbencies of seven of his eight 20th-century successors, becoming the only centenarian among Mill Hill's Heads. Celebrating his 100th birthday on 19 December 1996, he died, peacefully, on 17 September 1997, in his 101st year. His death echoed the death of that other Mill Hill centenarian, Chair of Governors, "Nath." Micklem QC (father of John Whale's life-long friend Rev. Dr Nathaniel Micklem, Principal of Mansfield) in 1954.

All Mill Hill's Head Masters could claim some particular strength; their 'management styles' range, in the jargon, from 'Consolidator' to 'Enabler'. Several were also, like "The Whale", 'Shakers of the tree' – 'Change-makers'. None, however, has quite won the particular status that JSW acquired in his seven years as leader. One of his most outstanding successors has described him as unique, in terms both of his time, and his mark upon the School and his staff. Even though the word 'spell' might well apply only to those – mostly VI Form humanists – who actually experienced "The Whale"'s teaching during his time, that spell lasted for boys and masters for the rest of their lives, witness the wording of many of the messages that were sent to the family on the occasion of the 100th birthday. For example, Dirck Gunning (the gifted nephew of the equally clever Hubert Phillips, the gloriously funny columnist "Dogberry", of the *News Chronicle*) and one of JSW's favoured Scholars, and State Scholars, wrote on 9 December 1996: *I loved my time at Mill Hill under your guidance – how we stood in awe of you! ... I am proud to know that I was at school under one of the great Public School headmasters.*

Of Dr Whale's seven years in 'the hot seat', what they lacked in longevity they made up in intellectual intensity, innovation and personal energy: his Thursday morning Current Affairs talks; History of Architecture on Friday evenings; the Philosophy of Religion lectures; the revival of drama. Some Heads never look back; yet many successors in office, even if they had not met JSW in person, were conscious of a special aura about this most globally renowned of Mill Hill Head Masters. The concept holds good, despite his lesser direct impact on the science side. The geographical derivation of what can now be seen as an academic high-water mark for the School, also merits analysis. By 1950 this came from London – 259 (101 + 158 MxCC 'bursary holders'); Southern/ Home Counties 22; Herts 15; Ox/ Bucks/ Berks six; E. Anglia eight; Midlands 14; Yorks/ Lancs/ Cheshire 32; Cumberland five; Scotland four; Wales 14; Devon three; Channel Is. two; and all overseas four.

"Get me Oxbridge!"

Fig.J(ii) sets out key aspects of the results for the 1945-49 'Cohorts', showing seven sets of figures, the first five of which were the main criteria; (State Scholarships and Open Awards ceased by the 1980s to give a comparison basis). These factors make comprehensible to later generations the driving forces behind Mill Hill's teaching staff and a central core of her pupils at this time:

1. Awards at 'Oxbridge' ['**A1**'] (pink): these were the Major, and Minor, Entrance Scholarships and Exhibitions, usually 'Open' to all, offered by joint groups of the individual Colleges of Cambridge and Oxford Universities. Here was the – admittedly snobbishly divisive – fiercely fought-for measure of any School's academic prowess, from the easy late 19th-century Varsity days, through to the late 20th. After the Second World War, they were predominantly open to men only, and still heavily 'Public School'; there were only two colleges in Cambridge, and five within Oxford that admitted women. Few of the Colleges had begun to expand after the deprivations of war; boys were tutored at schools whose Heads and staff were still overwhelmingly Oxbridge themselves (see Ch.XII); boys were steered towards Colleges where the School had had some previous success and thus reputation; however much it might be publicly denied, family connections still mattered.

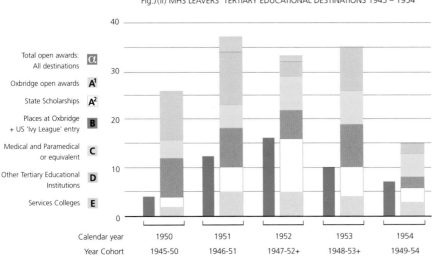

Fig.J(ii) MHS LEAVERS' TERTIARY EDUCATIONAL DESTINATIONS 1945 – 1954

Total open awards: All destinations	α	
Oxbridge open awards	A¹	
State Scholarships	A²	
Places at Oxbridge + US 'Ivy League' entry	B	
Medical and Paramedical or equivalent	C	
Other Tertiary Educational Institutions	D	
Services Colleges	E	

Calendar year	1950	1951	1952	1953	1954
Year Cohort	1945-50	1946-51	1947-52+	1948-53+	1949-54

When John Whale said, as he is reputed to have done, to his loyal but burdened Second Master, once he had weighed up the problem facing him at Mill Hill in 1944: "Get me Oxbridge!", this is what he meant. Oxbridge Scholarship Entry was decided at highly competitive written and *viva voce* examinations over three days in December or in the following January or March, in the intoxicating atmosphere of rooms in one's chosen College. By the 1960s the initial exams were moved back to the schools themselves, with only a '*viva*' if the papers had warranted it. Boys would be enticed by the School – with much parental arm-twisting – to stay on an extra term, if there was a reasonable chance of their winning such an ultimately prestigious prize, worth on paper from £100 to £40, according to excellence, which was, however, deducted from any other State or County award that might be given. The successful, though narrowly Public School, rivalry of these years was exemplified in the 1950 HC results: in terms of Distinctions Mill Hill (at 26) came third highest after Clifton (29) and Shrewsbury (27), and, in the total of 75 HCs, fifth highest after Marlborough, Downside, Clifton and St Paul's. The skewing of the following year's potential cohort through such extra terms beyond their five-year span was considered worthwhile, given the mileage that could then be made at next summer's prize-giving. It was a self-justifying system understood by all; democratic it was not. Unlike what a later Head, Michael Hart, described as *the big academic schools*, Mill Hill could only rarely afford dedicated post-Higher/ 'A' Level Scholarship Groups. Morrison's Classical VI was one contrived exception; he seldom taught more than 30 boys in a year. Some linguists and historians also benefited from individual tuition. John Whale's personal interventions in boys' careers included a weekly English essay session for one gifted mathematician, who went on to achieve a distinguished life in Industry.

2. State Scholarships ['**A2**']; these were awarded on the results of the Higher – or later A-/S-levels – the normal minimum being two distinctions: they were means-tested, unlike the Opens. A formal application was needed. In one case in 1950 a boy won three distinctions but had not been entered: the award was initially proudly placarded by JSW on the Marnham Block noticeboard during the vacation; a shamefaced later reference was made to the possibility of six awards if only they had been entered. The unfortunate boy had to take his excellent case to the County Council in order to gain his funding for Bart's.

3. Oxbridge 'Commoner' Entry ['**B**'] (grey): despite the ancient title (paying for their 'Commons'), non-award 'Place'-acceptance by an Oxbridge College was even more keenly striven for than its equivalent today, qualifying also for fees through a County Council bursary, plus a lodging allowance. It could be achieved on the basis of a State Scholarship, or on the decision of the College in question. Wily experienced 'old Oxbridge Hands' at Mill Hill, like Mog Morrison or "Scailes" McAllister would recommend boys who had not yet got a 'place', to sail off with a letter of introduction into the lion's den of a given College, and try to make their number with the Admissions Tutor, or indeed any Tutor known to Mill Hill. As late as the 1970s, new Oxbridge entrants to the CR – riling some non-Oxbridge men – were ticked against a master-chart of College crests so as to ascertain who among the staff knew whom, or had been at which College; it was an extended form of that inter-Public School

competitiveness. A boy's strong Games record counted too – Colleges were keen to add to their tally of "Blues". This blatantly 'old-boy-network' method succeeded in those days in a surprising number of cases, according to the PA, Betty Dove, who served John Whale's successor, Roy Moore, and later Michael Hart; she also served Morrison in his post-Bursarial/ Second Master role as Acting Head in 1961.

This was not the level of Oxbridge entry that JSW primarily sought, to offset the tradition of "effortless superiority"; it could not be presented with the same 'PR' force, 'presentation' being one of his *fortes*. Nevertheless, for boys who did not want to stay an extra term, but go straight into National Service, for demob in July or August in two years' time, ready for the opening of the October university term, this form of entry was entirely satisfactory; it was no more costly – (or no less cost-efficient, depending on the parents' means). At least two future Heads of Academic Institutions entered Oxbridge this way during this period. All it lacked was that much-needed element: glamour for the School. This also rubbed off briefly on the Scholar or Exhibitioner himself: he had a lasting *Magazine* record of his Prize '*Honoris Causa*', although usually *in absentia* and thus not tangible to him, at the next Foundation Day; later he might well enjoy a much-prized room in College throughout his time (as opposed to 'digs' of varying quality).

4. Entry from Science or Medical VIs to Medical/ Paramedical/ Dental/ Veterinary Schools (separated here from Medics at Oxbridge) ['**C**'] (orange): these were more or less self-selecting, and exemplified what has already been established as a specialty of Mill Hill over the centuries. This Medical group included a few actual Open Scholarships to those Hospitals. John Morrison's favoured alternative route – study classics at school, and then go on to read Medicine – was by this time starting to decline in popularity, in favour of the more vocational course.

5. Other campuses ['**D**'] (pale blue): although not yet valued equally with Oxbridge, if there were special curricular reasons, likely boys would be steered to other tertiary destinations: Agriculture at Reading; aeronautical or engineering high-fliers to the then City & Guilds, or the then Imperial College, London, or other centres of scientific excellence, well in evidence prior to the Robbins report into Higher Education.

This Oxbridge emphasis might well appear to later generations as too exclusive. A certain intellectual assertiveness, that could easily look like establishment arrogance, could be absorbed, by osmosis, from the time of Dr Whale: it went down well in High Table talk, or in civil service/FCO interviews. It would not be reactivated until the era of Alastair Graham. Foreigners did not understand this very British, anachronistic approach. It was embedded in the still class- and history-bound context for British education at this time; it followed a war that Britain had, to all intents and purposes, won – had she not? – thereby underlining her nationally-held belief that all was well in the British way of doing practically everything. This generation of post-war Millhillians would discover how fallacious this belief was to prove. By the 1960s, JSW's successor, Roy Moore, would be warning parents of the limitations in the assumed Oxbridge avenue to success in later life, and pointing out the virtues of other universities.

6. The Services, involving further education ['**E**'] (brown): not that the service life held attractions for most Millhillians, but a career via Sandhurst, Cranwell, Dartmouth, Plympton or King Edward's Naval School was still an honourable option for a few boys, even if not figuring high on JSW's own scale of preference. He had served in Ambulance Units and Hospital Ships in the First World War, although he made clear when appointing a talented conscientious objector as Music Master in 1944 that he *did not sympathise with Mr Rusbridge's views as a pacifist.*

It should be emphasised that none of this selection of the data should imply any superiority for these career-entry points over others: indeed many of those of "The Whale's" boys who opted for what would undoubtedly have appeared to him to be the less academically prestigious, less public-service areas of life as actuaries, accountants, surveyors or farmers, to pick four equally valuable professional paths at random, could well be said, with '20:20 hindsight', to have done just as well, or better, in their subsequent careers. Nevertheless, the fact remains that the first four of these five options were what drove Mill Hill forward up the long painful path of renascence, after the happy romantic years at St Bees. Their pursuit is indissolubly linked with the leadership of Dr John Whale.

Another analysis could as easily have shown the July Higher Certificates (and Distinctions) gained over these Whale years:- 1946: 20 (9), in a School numbering 311; 1947: 26 (7); 1948: 36 (9), in a School of 390; 1949: 53 (9). However important to the individual boys concerned, these results alone were not what counted: it was where the School 'got' boys to after that. Prof Stephen Holt recalled how the whole school was given a day's celebratory holiday when Roger Phillips won the Major Maths Scholarship to Trinity College, Cambridge, in 1948 – *the world's greatest* as JSW had put it; as boys queued up at the bus stop to get down to *the fleshpots of London*, they all made way for Phillips as he turned up to join the throng. However, as **Fig.J(ii)** showed, the full effect of "The Whale's" influence on his staff and on the academic standards they achieved with the material before them, only started to emerge during the years 1950-53. A further 'block' is developed here for comparison. The '**α**' List comprises all the Awards that could be the subject of the Honoris Causa

(i) Wall fitment to Schoolhouse wall (below) reveals where (ii) the 1914 School Bell still hung, opposite the Loggia, until replaced by an all-school electric system. *8.c*

Prizes: Open Scholarships or Exhibitions to Oxbridge, or any University/ Medical School, (dark blue), as well as State Scholarships, (for methods of calculation see Sources).

The '**α**' (dark blue) block, the highly visible tip of the iceberg, reaches its peak with the star 1947-52+ cohort, winning 16 Awards at Oxbridge, rising from 12 for the 1946-51+ cohort, and starting to fall away again, to 10 for the 1948-53+ cohort. It is still 7 by the time the 1949-54 cohort comes through, although this must be treated here as beyond the attributable influence of "The Whale", and now within the span to which his successor, Roy Moore, could legitimately lay claim. What is most interesting however is that the final fifth year of the post-war return, the 1945-50+

cohort, only wins four Awards: two Opens, one Scholarship in Modern Languages at Cambridge, the other at Oxford for History; no Classicists, Scientists or Mathematicians. One of the two State Scholarships went to the same Linguist, the other to a Chemist, the most brilliant boy in that cohort, who went on to take a Double First, and later led a distinguished academic career. This is merely on a par with the comparable totals for the preceding years: 1946/7 (four), 1947/8 (four), 1948/9 (three), and only one in 1949/50. This was the second successive Trinity Maths Scholar, Kurt Metzer, one of two Jewish refugees from Europe via India, studying later under the Nobel Prize-winning Pauli. Characteristic for that first post-St Bees generation, the effects of the "Whale" regime came through more slowly than is generally thought.

The main block shows a more optimistic and more significant picture. The three cohorts for 1946, 1947, and 1948 are virtually equal in their high achievement, at 37, 33, and 35 entries respectively. Again, the 1945 cohort achieves at a slightly lower level, 26 entries, compared with the final year in this five-year analysis, that for the 1949-54+ cohort, when only some 15 entries were gained to tertiary education. The main block must be seen as a truer reflection of the impact of any Head Master – the wider spread of influence and standard-setting across the whole VI Form and all departments. The levels of non-Award Oxbridge entry (Category **B**) for these 'Whale-attributable' years were good and steady too, at eight, eight, six, and nine boys, only to fall off to two with the 1949-54+ cohort. The first-destination Medics to Medical Schools (**C**), that historically important Mill Hill category, achieved a steady level of four, five, seven, seven, and five entrants across these years; these were a source of great satisfaction to the Head of Department, Donald Hall, himself an ex-Manchester Grammar Double-First from Trinity, Cambridge, who knew quality when he saw it, and also knew that quiet hard work and self-discipline were implicit in any achievement, scholastic no less than sporting. The levels of non-Oxbridge entry (**D**) fluctuated from year to year. In Chapter XI it will be necessary to look at the way these results formed trends during the succeeding years.

A Common Room of standing

The teaching staff must of course take their proper share of credit for such results, in any era. The national policy switch from School and Higher Certificate exams to the first 'GCEs' at the end of this period makes absolute judgement impossible, just as do changes in outside circumstances over the succeeding years. These can only be highly qualified, relative pointers, but despite those reservations, the overall academic outcome of "The Whale's" years is impressive by any standard; its memory trace lasted well into the rest of the century, in turn to

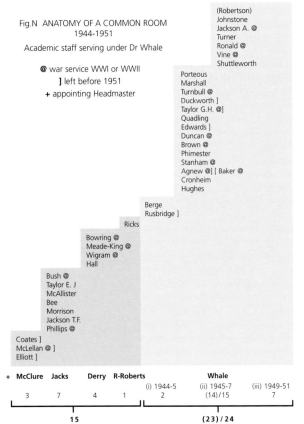

Fig.N ANATOMY OF A COMMON ROOM
1944-1951
Academic staff serving under Dr Whale

@ war service WWI or WWII
] left before 1951
+ appointing Headmaster

inspire or depress succeeding generations of staff, who had to face many problems differing from and in some ways even greater than those that confronted Dr Whale and his hard-pressed team of colleagues in the autumn of 1945. At least it can be said that the majority of the two decades of that post-war generation wanted to learn, to compete and to succeed; the raw material was workable. Only by the turn of the century was this vast 'post-Robbins' effort towards the tertiary sector starting to be questioned, with the Governmental Report publicised on 6 February 1997, which first raised publicly what many had already suspected: that graduate supply was exceeding demand on a continuing basis, and that the nation's notional return on money expended on graduate education was about to fall below the required '9%' level. This doom-laden Kingsley Amis *more means worse* scenario was, however, not there to trouble either Dr John Whale, for whom it would have been an unthinkable denial of all he believed in, or his immediate successor.

Illicit snaps could be taken in post-war Marnham Block classrooms, of one of Dr Whale's outstanding, but not-too observant, academic appointments, Dr "Fritz" Cronheim. *8.d*

A claim was made in "Martlet", 1997, that JSW *made a number of outstanding appointments, and... produced a Common Room which... is unlikely ever to have been surpassed [in Public School history].* The record bears closer examination: **Fig.N** shows the scope, and the limitations, of a Head's power to change through appointments – including that already noted of another Music Master while still at St Bees – Hans Berge, "to get the arts going again". In 1945-47, he was able to make 15 new appointments, including another distinguished refugee, the Heidelberg-educated Dr Frederick Cronheim, as well as Edward Stanham, Geoffrey Hughes (who went on to become Head of St George's, Harpenden), Allan Phimester, Douglas Quadling, Michael Brown, and later Christopher Porteous, Tony Turnbull, and Cliff Baker. In the last three years, with numbers still rising but levelling off, he made seven more appointments, including Guy Shuttleworth, making the total 24 in all. Two-thirds of his appointments were Oxbridge. Nine of his CR had war service; by 1949, 14 masters, *c.*50 per cent of a staff of 31, had served in the world wars. This was a new, once-for-all input of broader experience in the School's make-up, which carried forward to JSW's successor, and which many of those generations believed gave them a very special kind of training for life.

Of the masters who came back in 1945/6 to serve under JSW, no fewer than 15 had been appointed by his predecessors: four by Dr Derry – Donald Hall, Thurston Bowring, Mervyn Wigram and Martin Meade-King. In addition there were still seven survivors through the war from Jacks' choice – John Morrison, Lyle Bee, Percy McAllister, Tom Jackson, Edward Taylor, Warren Phillips and Alan Bush MC. There were even three masters appointed by McClure – Victor Elliott (1911), F.R.H.McLellan (1911) and Herbert Coates (1916), Second Master up to his 1948 retirement.

JSW himself felt that some of his appointments were among the best things he did for Mill Hill, not least Douglas Quadling, who went on to grace the CR of Marlborough as Senior maths master, and also to write *Mathematical Analysis*.

Mill Hill's second "Mr Chips", Bertie Ricks, was foremost in establishing the (all-male) drama tradition, here with first of three MHS productions of 'The Dream', Feb 1949. *MHM* woodcut by MHS Head of Art, artist/cricketer/former WWII commando Cliff ("Massacre") Baker. *8.e*

Although the majority were excellent schoolmasters, a broad judgement might be that only five of those previous appointments could be regarded as 'outstanding', and at least another five of JSW's own choice. This is not to detract from his CR, but to offer some kind of comparison with the pre-war selections. The one omission from this analysis was of course Bertie Ricks, one in a long line of enthusiastic theatrical impresarios at Mill Hill, who was appointed in 1941 at St Bees, by that wise old bird with an understanding of the kind of teacher with whom boys flourished, Rooker Roberts; this appointment was one that JSW, deeply-ingrained Public School man that he was, wholeheartedly valued, just as he cherished his warm, vicarious friendship with the first "Mr Chips", Buster Brown.

If the forward shadow concept has relevance to pupils and their academic performance, it is even more apposite for a Head Master's staff; 29 of JSW's masters continued to serve Mill Hill after he resigned in April 1951, three to act in their turn as Second Masters, one an Acting Head, and seven to become Housemasters, in addition to the five serving from 1945/6 onwards.

Three of his appointees went on to lead other fortunate institutions. Compared with what could have been described as the 'Jacks inheritance' after the First World War, "The Whale's" CR constituted 'a goodly heritage'.

Middlesex Scheme: the 'Middle Way' at its best

The salient feature of those uphill years was that much misreported phenomenon, the Mill Hill/ Middlesex ('MxCC') Scheme. The prime example of the School's self-appointed 'Middle Way', bridging the two educational sectors, public and 'Public', this was the underchronicled trail-blazer for a key but still undervalued section of the 'Butler' Education Act; had it succeeded more widely, it might well have transformed British society. The Pygmalion undertones of the MxCC scheme echoed earlier policies, and resonated elsewhere in the 21st century, through the BBC2-sponsored 'Second Chance' experiment; unlike that one-off project however, most of these boys were already scholastic achievers. The School's mould-breaking role in this phase of educational, and social, history, set out here publicly for the first time, commands close consideration.

Here was a policy which John Whale inherited in 1944, but thereafter so wholeheartedly championed as to make it his own. This scheme was a much earlier, extraordinarily far-sighted initiative of the Court, and of its Treasurer, R.W.B.Buckland, in full co-operation with the Middlesex County Council. It envisaged the sponsorship of boys at the School; in return the School would potentially be able to make use of the Enginering Workshops at the new Hendon Technical College. Unknown to anyone outside, it actually dated from 8 June 1939 and not, as elsewhere reported, as late as 1942, when the Chairman of the MxCC, Alderman Fuller, and his Director of Education, visited the School for exploratory talks. On 27 June, two Governors, Col Viney, and the educationist, Sir Walter Moberly, proposed that the Head, then Dr Derry, should carry on negotiations. To many other Public Schools, this might have appeared a threat to that proud 'independence', for so long a battle-cry; yet Mill Hill's trail was first blazed in 1920. That same far-seeing Treasurer, supported then as in 1939, by the inveterate Governor from the McClure time (also a Governor of Harrow and Stowe) Arthur Pickard-Cambridge, had first mooted the idea of a 4 per cent intake of boys from other schools, with parents or a nominating Authority paying the fees. The idea was introduced of having three Board of Education Governors on the Court, one drawn from the MxCC; (part of 'Recognition', in the context of the 1918 School Teachers Superannuation Act); as a proviso, 10 per cent of pupils should come from 'the immediate neighbourhood'. There had been another torchbearer: the writings garnered by Emily Jacks for a potential 'Life' in 1964, manifest Maurice Jacks' passionate interest, before and after the 1938 Spens Report on Secondary Education. Jacks proclaimed: *there is a great future for these schools in association with the national system.*

In the dark days of 1939, the Court's renewed exploration of this input to its Roll would be in principle very similar. It maintained its awareness of the merits of the State system, Pickard-Cambridge pointing out on 14 December 1939 that *English was better in Secondary Schools*; on 30 January 1940, with the School now ensconced at St

(i) *OM Dickie Buckland, Secretary to the Governors for many years, b1865, d1947;*
(ii) *Chapel Window. 8.f*

Bees, the Court was already discussing *the contingencies of State intervention after the war*. On 28 May 1940, the saviour from retirement, A.J.Rooker Roberts, reported that the HMC had met on 10 May to review the possible appointment of a Royal Commission on the future of the Public Schools. By March 1941, the three Governors who constituted the temporary device called the "Composite Treasurer", reported on The Public and Other Schools (War Conditions) Bill then going through the Lords, welcoming this *legal correctitude to our adventure*. On 24 June 1941, Mr H.M.Walton, Secretary of the MxCC Education Committee, made his genial presence felt for the first time as a Governor.

On 23 December, the Court debated with deadly seriousness the School's *chance of survival after the war* under the phrase *Mending or Ending*. As neighbouring Harrow School, sometimes competing with Mill Hill for a potential bursary holder, would also appreciate, *we have a Local Authority who possess not only wealth but a generous conception of its responsibilities*. On 9 April 1942, the Court discussed the report of Governor Sir Henry Richards' 'Special Committee on the Future of Mill Hill': *we have got to give something material... it is not enough to say, here is a Public School... with a fine spirit and... the home of leadership... Our hill-top... might become the centre of a great Gymnasium in the wider sense of that word*. At the Annual Court of Life Governors at Mansion House, with that scion of Mill Hill's first Founders, Arnold S.Pye-Smith, symbolically present, as well as the two liberal-thinking Goyder brothers, George and Claude, it was announced that the Court would welcome three Governors from the MxCC in *a great national undertaking – the entry of a Public School into the National System*. A meeting with the MxCC Education Committee was held at Mill Hill on 24 July in the Head's Study, by permission – ironically – of Dr Maclay (already met as the genial Medical Officer of the occupying 'MHEH'); it was adjudged by MxCC's H.M.Walton as an *unqualified success*. Pickard-Cambridge foresaw *an experiment likely to be of very great value not only to Mill Hill but as an example that other Public Schools might like to follow*. By 16 February 1943, *the negotiations were proceeding satisfactorily...* On 22 June, Buckland reported that in *the suggested experiment* the MxCC might fund 20 boys a year for five years, to reach 100 at the end of that time, several as Boarders; however they realised they now had to await what the present, or future, Government might say, and matters were held in suspense.

Churchill, 'Rab' Butler, and the Fleming Report

Even in the depths of wartime, many visionaries were bravely, and idealistically, looking ahead to the post-war world. A Committee of the HMC (but by no means every Public School) and, within that body, Mill Hill, had been one such group. It was a moment when the School led the way in trying to make history.

Unknown to Mill Hill, this aspect of educational history was being influenced by the statesman whom Mill Hill had first contacted in the First World War (as Secretary of State for War), Old Harrovian Winston Churchill, working now in uneasy conjunction with "Rab" Butler, President of the Board of Education, and his Labour Parliamentary Under-Secretary, James Chuter Ede. Rab himself, in his autobiography, *The Art of the Possible*, declares that Churchill's *interest in education was slight, intermittent and decidedly idiosyncratic*. Anthony Howard in his biography of Rab details how Ede's diary records as early as 4 February 1942 just such an intermittent moment, aside from the cares of waging war – a meeting where a grand idiosyncratic Churchillian vision was laid out for the very process that Mill Hill was pursuing: *The PM was glad to know that the public schools were receiving our [the Board's] attention. He wanted 60-70% places to be filled by bursaries – not by examination alone but on the recommendation of the counties and the great cities...* (In very different circumstances, Christ's Hospital and Rendcomb could have provided precedents for this policy.)

The PM then continued with one of his imaginative oratorical flourishes; even if his memory of that first contact with Mill Hill did not bring her name immediately to mind, nevertheless he expressed the very spirit in which the School was already actively engaged with the MxCC. It needs to be read with care, since his underlying democratic sense belies the words, which ring a little awkwardly to 21st-century ears: *We must reinforce the ruling class – though he disliked the word 'class' – We must not choose by the mere accident of birth and wealth but by the accident – for it was equally accident – of ability. The great cities would be pleased to search for able youths to send to Haileybury, to Harrow, and to Eton.*

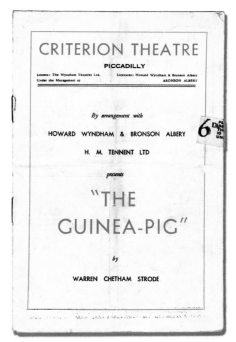

Programme for "The Guinea Pig", Warren Chetham Strode's play, later a film, about the scholarship boys entering Public School under the 'Butler' Education Act, 1944. *8.g*

It is pity that he could not have added – 'as Mill Hill has pointed the way', for that in fact was the case. Churchill had a sense of the potential of the Boarding school life for the formation of character, essential for him in the future leadership of the nation, and his beloved Empire, which Butler, despite his own upbringing and his governorship of Felsted, did not: as Howard observes, he was *never a worshipper at the public school shrine.* Butler was far more concerned with the broader implications of his future Education Bill for the cohesion of the nation and for social justice, and with the attendant problems of welding the Church schools into the whole. Because these problems now threatened progress on his intended legislation, the President, in Howard's unequivocally 'rugger' and impliedly Public School metaphor, announced in the House of Commons, on 16 June 1942, that he was appointing a Committee of Enquiry into the whole question of the Public Schools – the standard politician's 'kick for touch' at times of difficulty; Rab wrote in his autobiography that *the first-class carriage has been shunted into an immense siding.*

Behind the scenes, as early as 20 October 1941, as Howard reports, referring to the Ede Diaries, an internal Note from a civil servant, G.G.Williams, on 'The Financial Position of the Public Schools' had recorded a surprisingly alarmist view about the future of some of those schools, dividing them roughly into four categories, from *future almost assured*, through *suffered a decline but still... healthy*, to Group C – *future doubtful* and Group D – *danger of extinction*. Schools as apparently safe as Cranleigh, Haileybury, Malvern, Cheltenham, Lancing, Tonbridge, Bromsgrove, Repton, Bryanston, Dean Close, Eastbourne, as well as Mill Hill, and even Harrow, made up Category 'C': Mill Hill was not alone in her problems.

The famous Fleming Committee would outline two Schemes – 'A' for financing the Direct Grant schools, and 'B' for places at the Independent Schools. As the MxCC noted, its Report of 1944, appearing one week before (but not part of) the

Coalition's Education Act achieved Royal Assent, spoke of the Public Schools being the custodians of *a very high educational value*, and of the need neither to destroy them, (as many 'Old Labour' diehards wanted) nor to refuse to associate with them, but to work with them to achieve *a much greater measure of social and educational unity in the nation*. It was a grand vision, with overtones that still resonated, still unfulfilled, 50 years later. Under Scheme B, one of the statutory duties, not just an enabling power, imposed by a Conservatively-reformist but unquestioningly Boarding-educated Government upon Local Education Authorities through the resulting Education Act of 1944, lay in its Section 8 (2) (d): to provide Boarding *accommodation* and/or education where education as Boarders *is considered by the parents and by the Authority as desirable*. This new jurisprudential 'right' on the part of parents was to be one aspect of a new system to secure *the spiritual, moral, mental and physical development of the community, and to afford variety of instruction and training to meet the differing ages, abilities, and expectations of the nation*; (as a philosophy it could equally well be applied to the Mill Hill vision of the 21st century). It needs emphasis that the 1945 Labour Government did not enact but inherited this legislation, being part of its inception through the Deputy Leadership of the Haileybury-educated Clem Attlee.

"Guinea Pigs" or Gold Mine? The Middlesex Scheme

This was the grand national backdrop. Through a question in the House on 12 May 1945 by Sir Edward Campbell – "Shall we not call it the Butler Act?" – the enabling legislation for the Mill Hill/ MxCC scheme was – confusingly – to carry the name of a Minister whose heart was not as fully behind this Section of its contents, as was that of his PM. This aspect of the 'Butler Act' has suffered through the later criticism of the Public Schools Commission of 1966: *it is clear that as an instrument of national policy the Fleming Report rapidly became a dead letter*. There were other echoes: John Rae wrote that *the hope was not fulfilled. Neither the LEAs nor the schools themselves showed much inclination to put the schemes into practice*; he quoted the idealistic Robert Birley's conclusion that *the schemes were doomed*. Howard dismissed them as *a smattering of Council-financed pupils totally overwhelmed by a vast array of traditional public schoolboys*, and an Eton writer has declared that its beneficiaries would not have filled more than a few rugger teams. Mill Hill's Middlesex/'BBS' bursary-holders for the next 35 years would give the lie to these gloomy judgements.

If Mill Hill has here a part in history, the origination by the Court was one of its most forward-looking and statesmanlike acts. In the language of her highly respected LEA – the MxCC – (which would eventually meet its sad demise in 1965) – this was its own much-prized 'Mill Hill Scheme'. On 22 March 1945, it singles out *the willing co-operation of [Mill Hill's] Governing Body, which was sympathetic to the ideals embodied in the Education Act and the Fleming Report... the cordial spirit shown throughout the negotiations*. The timing is critical to an evaluation of the significance of the scheme. The County Council received a report that it was *not without a sense of gratification for your Committee that while the... Fleming Report* [was] *not published until June 1944... consultations and negotiations have been in progress since 1942 with the Governors of Mill Hill...*; this led to *a scheme of co-operation being reached independently which reflected the main recommendations of the Fleming Committee.* One historian, Vivian Ogilvie, would at least pay tribute to Mill Hill's pioneering role, writing of *the only important independent school to take considerable numbers of these* ['Scheme B'] *boys,* and in 1963 a reforming HMC Headmaster, John Dancy, praised *a most satisfactory arrangement,* whilst assuming that only 20 per cent of places, not the original 40 per cent, were ever taken up. Yet John Wakeford would later exclude Mill Hill – perhaps it was a reverse compliment – from his *Cloistered Elite,* since its *25 per cent intake of boys directly sponsored by the [MxCC] significantly affects its character,* quoting the Head of Christ's Hospital that such boys *caused more behavioural problems than average.* James McConnell only cited 'The Dulwich Experiment' of 1946, and George Snow derided *a few Local Authorities who sent a few special cases to a few selected schools.* Misunderstood, and relatively unsung, Mill Hill actually led the way in this noble if politically-constrained post-war process: as now transpires, this is a story of which the School can be justifiably proud.

The Middlesex Scheme threatened to be an extraordinary event in the life of Mill Hill. (The transition in 1997 to co-educational status might compare with it in terms of 'shock to the system', but this current new status had had its path cleared for it over the preceding 25 years. The exodus to St Bees in 1939 had also been a shock, of a different kind, but the School's texture, the sociological background of the boys, was still constant, indeed comforting – Yorkshire notwithstanding – despite the external discomforts.) There were manifold doubts, ranging from a Governor who perceptively wondered whether these boys would find it *difficult to adjust themselves to home life in the holidays,* to the ex-Belmont boys about to encounter this supposedly alien force. Yet as John Dancy later judged overall, the two putatively discordant cultures at Mill Hill, quickly became a seamless garment, fulfilling Maurice Jacks'

The MHS grounds have provided location shots for many films and TV series: part of "Mr Perrin and Mr Traill" was filmed on Top Field, 1949; whole School had half-holiday. *8.h*

prediction that *the boys imported ... would in a very short time be indistinguishable from the rest*. The over-written shock of a new 'presenting culture' became a non-event, overlaid, as it was, with other more pressing factors: the demolition of the Script and the Library was mooted, for the building of a new Dining Hall over the car park but the 20 tons of steel required were not obtainable; there was no linoleum for the bathrooms; compressed asbestos boards [!] covered the dining tables. Beyond the memory of all but four of the staff there stood one surprising statistic from the days of the First World War. When Sir John McClure had analysed the origins of his 1917-18 intake, in his final but fundamentally important Educational Report of 1919, more than a third were discovered to have come from exactly the same backgrounds as those now emerging through the Middlesex scheme. Messrs Buster Brown, Coates, McLellan and Elliott might have been aware of the fact that no less than 35 per cent of the boys of that era had come, in McClure's words, *from Local Grammar Schools and Municipal Secondary Schools*; Mill Hill had in one, albeit forgotten sense, been here before.

The cost framework, and the composition, of the Council's team should have reassured them: the Secretary of the Education Committee was H.M.Walton, Clerk to the Governors of the Stationers' Company School from 1929, and already proving as faithful a servant to Mill Hill, as he had been to that respected Grammar School. On the basis of per capita payments from the MxCC to the School of a £50 tuition plus £110 Boarding fee, the Mill Hill scheme would cost MxCC £6,400 for c.40 boys in the first full year, and £32,000 for a budgeted 200 pupils in a school of 500 boys by July 1950 – this out of budget of £8.5 million, for the Council's Roll of 250,000 pupils. At one stage the point was made that the 1944 Act would cover such a Scheme out of tax-payers' as opposed to Middlesex ratepayers' money, but Rab advised that the deal should not be disturbed. A Governor had also questioned whether it would be wiser to run a parallel scheme with other LEAs, to *"keep a foot in both camps"*. Today, the scheme seems eminently affordable; it offers pause for thought for the comparable national affordability of the abolished Assisted Places Scheme of the 1980s-late 1990s.

The Head Master himself had personally interviewed, with representatives of the six new proposed Middlesex-nominated Governors, every one of the initial short-list of sixty. From them emerged those first 40 equally apprehensive 12-year-old boys, together with their even more apprehensive parents or guardians, to be met with a scholastic, not sociological, concern on Dr Whale's part: would they, for example, in the

Script (No.3) on the Quad, as it was post-WWII, angled central reading shelf replacing flat tables; a beaming Dr Murray over fireplace continues to survey his handiwork. *8.i*

words of the great humorist, Peter Cook, "have the Latin"? To "The Whale's" surprise, many of them did. Language did not help; officially, for a start it was labelled, both by the School and the LEA, as a five-year 'experiment'. Experiments partake of the physical, not of social engineering; they go wrong as often as they succeed: their connotations are of explosion, damage, and the cutting of losses if they result in failure. Fifty years before 'estuary English' would gain acceptance as the language of the television age, there were other linguistic fears: boys were privately described by some as coming from 'Council' schools, and would no doubt speak like 'oiks', in that exaggerated cockney to be caricatured on stage and film in the parents of a young Richard Attenborough. This was in Warren Chetham Strode's success of 1948, "The Guinea Pig", which would set the Fleming Report Scheme in dramatic context; (the film of the play was partly shot on Longfield in 1948, though less well remembered than the later Top Field location for the film "Mr Perrin and Mr Traill").

Secondly, that experiment with the Middlesex "Guinea Pigs" was thought by some *OMs* to be carried out not for idealistic reasons, but primarily on short-term expedient financial grounds, at the expense of the School's traditions, and 'against the grain' of the School's natural – even God-given – middle-class constituency. As a final insult to Mill Hill's other 'secular' religion, these boys could not conceivably have been taught to play rugger, but were presumably wedded to that other then unspeakable variant. These insiders were not to know that for the MxCC Education Committee, as emphasised in its March 1945 Report, the very fact that they had 'had placed at their disposal excellent buildings, ample playing fields and a School with fine traditions' was the essence of a Scheme that even the film's 'Lloyd Hartley' would have valued. Welcoming, appreciative hands were about to touch the Mill Hill tiller. The later presence of *OM* Sir Graham Rowlandson as MxCC Chairman no doubt assisted this process.

In 1944, the Court had identified four areas of advantage: the authority of the MxCC would now be 'behind' the School, making it an important centre in the County... and one of the foremost 'Government Schools' – (Harrow thought the same way about its own more modest intake); there would be a guarantee of *the very best boys from the best schools*, but with the Head Master ultimately having the HMC-protected rights of selection, and 'superannuation'; the use of Technical Colleges if needed; and last, probably mistakenly, better priority in getting back to Mill Hill in 1945. Yet at least one of the still mightily 'baronial' Housemasters was doubtful and condescending in his attitude; other members of the staff, several from good Grammar School backgrounds themselves, were calm, pragmatic, and non-discriminatory in their approach. However, many senior boys, replete with their St Bees conditioning, must have quietly made up their minds to teach this new, defensive minority how Mill Hill did, and said, things. There were after all precedents in the Public School system for teaching 'new bugs' at any level the way to behave, whether those doing the teaching were old staff in the CR welcoming a new Head, or established monitorial Heads of House explaining to an incoming Housemaster the meaning, and the inviolability, of 'the green baize door' that separated 'the House' from the Housemaster's quarters. In any case, there was now rapidly evolving a strident class-consciousness in Britain, contrasting with the unity of the wartime era, and Mill Hill inevitably reflected that divisive spirit. These 'lower-class' boys would be a problem, a threat to the status quo; would they not have to be dealt with?

The first wave of Middlesex boys themselves came with no such common attitudes. Parents of likely boys in given schools got together in the spring of 1945, deciding between them that this newly advertised scheme, with what was then a revolutionary social flavour, was worth exploring; most of them had little idea of the challenging step-change they were letting their offspring – and themselves – 'in for'. There was no mental preparation process; the Day-to-Boarding gulf was either unimaginable, or romanticised by fathers brought up on a vicarious diet of Thomas Hughes, Talbot Baines Reed, or *"Greyfriars"* – many of them, unknown to Mill Hill, actually ardent rugger fans. Within a common bond of black market clothing coupons, these special new boys arrived in their Houses, segregated from boys of their previous school, after weeks of feverish activity, having to cope with the unfamiliar world of Tuck Boxes, Cash's Name Tabs, and 'overnight cases', somewhat like lonely lambs to the collective slaughter.

The 'LFs'

One widespread belief, still alive at the time of the research for this History, was that these lucky fellows – 'LFs' as Old Belmontians called them – all came absolutely 'free': the myth needs exploding. Every parent was severely means-tested, taking the Council's existing paradigm, the County awards for tertiary education. The father of one later boy had to repay his grant, as his small family-business profits turned out to exceed the qualifying level, thus forcing his gifted son to forego a certain but costly place at Christ Church, Oxford. Evidence as to the finances of this first 'wave' lies in the analysis of the categories of parental income, and of additional expenses grants, published by Middlesex in 25 July 1945. These apparently unforeseen items included: *music tuition, books, stationery, Linen Room articles, clothing, JTC fee, excursions/ entertainments, medical fee/ medicine ... art and drawing materials, hire of games equipment, increased cost of laundry, and pocket money.* The previously costed level of £20 would clearly not cover this list; the Council agreed to cover them where *financial circumstances warrant such payments.*

Of that first cadre of 40, parental salaries range, by inference, from £450 to £700, since the highest contribution level towards expenses is £120 pa, the amount to be levied against a parental salary of £700: (see Appendix G for conversion into present-day values). There were three parents in this category; more than half the incomes were in fact at the lower end – 23 homes being shown as required to make no contributions to these additional costs ("Nil + E", in the analysis), i.e. with parental incomes in the range £450 to £550, depending on the number of children. Would this financial factor reproduce as a divisive social and behavioural factor?

The reality, as against the fears, was very different. Whilst in terms of a given House the majority of boys were obviously non-Middlesex, from the St Bees 'freemasonry', or already friends at Belmont, Middlesex boys in the School's first intake formed an equal or even in some cases a larger element, given the low numbers entering in the last year at St Bees. The School had envisaged receiving boys of all types, from all social backgrounds: in reality many of the Middlesex Schools, as their

Heads soon discovered, despite the 1944 non-scholastic criterion of selection being *ability to take advantage of a public-school education*, were being creamed of their brightest, albeit along with some of lesser academic potential possessing other attributes. For the County Council this was simply a switch of resources: to the providing Grammar Schools, they were handing talent to a potentially competitive school 'on a plate'. Not surprisingly, these Heads began to be more chary of allowing names to go forward, not unassisted by a tiny handful of boys who turned out to be unable to 'take' Mill Hill, and either ran away, or caused their parents to renege on their contract with the school. In one historic North London Grammar School, the two top boys from the Q fast stream got in, together with two boys from their lower A and B forms: a fifth boy from the B Form got in at the last minute, when another family belatedly declined a place that had been offered. By the 1950s, the intake would fall to *c*.20 p.a., by agreement, due to the failure of the MHS Roll to reach 500, but also because from 1947 the quality of intake showed a temporary decline.

That cohort of 40 was concentrated in Mill Hill's own fast stream; some 15 were placed in 'Remove A', and 10 in 'B', nearly two-thirds of their whole intake. Private fears that their linguistic knowledge would not match up to a classically-based Prep School education proved groundless, at least as far as Latin was concerned, within the space of the first term. The 'Remove A' Middlesex boys in particular showed themselves excellent Latinists and French-speakers, as well as superlative in practically everything else, achieving places in form where only a few of the brighter ex-Belmontians achieved parity. One 'Middlesex' mother sought to enquire whether her very bright boy, later to become an outstanding senior monitor, a CBE and a pillar of the medical profession, could apply at the same time for one of the School's Entrance Scholarships. *But Madam, he hasn't the Greek!*, was "The Whale's" disdainful reply.

A misconception by the Head Master himself, proclaimed proudly on several public occasions, was that Mill Hill enabled these boys to proceed one year faster to their School Certificate: for many of them this was manifestly not so. They had already been programmed to jump in their third 11+ year to a pre-Matric form, the same level as Mill Hill's Removes. Whatever else the School may have done, Mill Hill did not do this for them; they themselves did it, with distinction, for Mill Hill. They had come, in the main, from first-rate, long-established, old-style Grammar Schools, many with comparable Oxbridge Heads and teachers, men and women, not from the feared stereotype, the 'Secondary Modern'. In social, if not quite yet in financial terms, they came from a similar broad-swathe 'middle-class' background; that final stage of social equalisation would only come when some of these boys themselves progressed sufficiently in their own careers to afford the option of sending their own sons – and later their daughters – to their new 'old School'.

In the Houses inevitably there were ructions, as the two worlds started to size each other up, and settle down to co-exist. Some of these relationships erupted into transgressions, resentments, punishments and outright bullying with a 'class' edge to it: even, in one case, *speaking Cockney, after warning* – sanction awarded, one 'Copy'. As the History will examine, under the regimes of both post-war Heads, some Houses were worse than others in this respect, partly depending on their varying

The most-capped *OM* rugby player, Jim Roberts, flying down the wing at the Lansdowne Road ground, Dublin; (later all four of his children followed him to the 1980s co-ed MHS). *8.j*

'House spirit' and traditions, which seemed to have travelled remarkably well from the St Bees existence. On the games field, the neophytes soon picked up this new and to most (as to Thomas Hughes) far more thrilling version of football, not needing to care about the 19th-century class-ridden origins of the game, (at least as far as England was concerned); they were by no means the narrow-track 'swots' of the popular, and fictional, image. Many were already budding games stars in their own right at their Grammar Schools. Of the five examples already cited, one went on to become Captain of Gym, another Hon Sec. of Athletics and a member of the 1st XV, and a third a member of the 1st Squash V. Within a year, Middlesex boys made up a third of the U15 XV, helping to form the dominant 1st XVs from 1948 onwards, one to become a "Blue" and an International (see Supplement No. 6). Whatever misgivings anyone at the School might have had were soon dispelled. Members of staff agreed that the behaviour of most Middlesex boys was indistinguishable from that of any other boy from the North London catchment area. Even for the Housemasters, it was not important who was what: only a red 'M' in the Bursar's confidential 'Boys Account Book' marked them out. Although each Middlesex boy developed his own individual view, they all became, in varying degree, assimilated post-war Millhillians, conforming to the abundant rules, but entering into the life of the school. The only real, and life-long, difference was that, deep down, this new form of schooling felt like a bonus, not an unquestioned birthright.

By the end of the first year, prizes on Foundation Day were already starting to wear a strong, though by no means exclusive, 'Middlesex' flavour. By the end of Year Two, for many the SC Year, the pattern was becoming very clear: the best Middlesex boy won eight distinctions, and many others achieved five or four. One would be described by the Court as *the best linguist we have had since the war*. Looking solely at the 'traditional' areas, by the end of this first five-year cohort, the 'Guinea-Pigs' had belied their 'experimental' image in every sphere of the School's life: the group of 40 would yield seven Heads of House, two seniors and eight other monitors, six members of the 1st XV, three each of the Hockey and Cricket XIs and Fives VI, five of both the Athletics and the Singlehanded teams, two of the Gym VIII, 10 Secretaries of School Societies, and in that least 'Grammar School' of all activities, Corps, a Senior CSM. Of those who went on to do their National Service, most would win Commissions. The picture would be enhanced by the results of the tertiary stage of their education, bringing many professorial and PhD honours to the credit of Mill Hill.

A final stage would lie with the Court, and of that typical extension of Mill Hill life, the OMC: that single cohort would yield successively a Town Club Secretary, an Hon. Sec., one Chairman, the first of several Presidents and Governors, one the Vice-Chairman. Some 10 per cent (including three from that earlier, well-bonded U15 XV) would in their turn finance the education of their own sons, and daughters, at the Mill Hill of the 1970s/1980s, creating eight new *OMs*. Mill Hill's completely self-financing investment in these 'Guinea Pigs' – not only then but even into the 21st century, through four contemporary members of the Court of Governors – was on the way to becoming a continuously productive Gold Mine.

Success story?

In all other schools (e.g. Brighton) where post-Fleming schemes were adopted, the intake was much smaller. In some cases, the entry point was even then at the age of 11. Mill Hill and MxCC had initially opted for age 13, Boarding only, and just in sufficient numbers to achieve a significant effect; also under the 'Nine Boroughs' scheme, post 1965, some places were created for 11-year-olds at Belmont. Where the intake was so small, bursary holders presented no threat to 'the system', and all kinds of prejudices could run amok. In one such school not so very far away from Mill Hill, one bright historian was not allowed to do history, because the Head of History would not suffer any bursary boy into his 'domain'; there is no record of such exclusiveness taking place at an ever-tolerant Mill Hill.

It is impossible to assess the true effect on the pupils of what a later BBC R4 programme described as *the good-natured scheme which changed their lives*; there could not be any control sample with which to compare them. Each boy or girl, each generation, each receiving school itself was different. Not that the thinking behind the schemes was aimed primarily at re-engineering: their 'social engineering' was more concerned with providing 'opportunities', of a somewhat undefined order, to deserving individuals. Some believe they would have done equally 'well' by remaining at their mixed Day Grammar Schools, others that Mill Hill made them more competitively successful. Whether Mill Hill enabled them to cope better with the social pyramid then presented by British society is a more difficult question. Were they more 'rounded' by virtue of having boarded? Did they make better sense of National Service thereby? Did they become better physical specimens? Or did the absurd privileges and year system do more harm than good, leaving lasting resentments? These still remain open questions, which only a detailed programme of research could have answered.

As the above analysis indicates, from the School's viewpoint, the Middlesex stream won the right to be treated, not as a sub-group for preferential treatment, but simply *pari passu* with boys from the former traditional backgrounds. Their attitudes and views had to be taken into account in the way the School thereafter developed. Over the ensuing 20 years, Mill Hill's commitment to the original scheme was as whole-hearted, and as broadly-based within the School community, as had been the commitment of those early Founding Fathers to their initial piece of social – or rather socio-religious – re-engineering for quite other ends, in 1807. The Middlesex scheme was firmly in line with that bundle of differentiating points, which can be rightly called 'The Mill Hill Tradition'.

H.M.Walton had said at a meeting of the Court on 21 June 1945, that Mill Hill had made *the first gesture of this kind, which he was sure would give the lead to the country... the new Minister of Education... was quite as keen and enthusiastic about the scheme... and they were delighted at the Ministry at the co-operation between Mill Hill and Middlesex*. MxCC used this prototype to found its

The derelict 18C *King's Head* pub on The Ridgeway, across from Wills Grove: its use by MHS CCF for grenade-throwing practice hastened its end by the 1950s. *8.k*

subsequent 'experiments' for 10 boys at Merchant Taylor's from 1946 onwards, and for 15 (more expensive) places for girls at Wycombe Abbey, also from 1946 onwards. The Scheme was carried on just as committedly by the successors to JSW's selection team, with Middlesex and then with their successors, the constituent Education Authorities. Some boroughs, with a differing political motivation, were less willing, reinforced by what Roy Moore's later Second Master, Edward Stanham, calls *the understandable reluctance of some headmasters to release their best pupils*. For Mill Hill, as opposed to Dulwich, there was a longer-term effect: the funding of the Scheme enabled the School to remain for so long essentially a Boarding school for boys.

Next phase

In July 1950, the Court heard *in silence* John Whale's report that he was *feeling the strain* of the increasingly arduous task of running a cash-strapped Boarding Public School, with few endowments, still suffering from the effects of its wartime exile, and at a Roll of 390, well short of the 1951 target of 500 so bravely planned in Col Oscar Viney's 'Seven Year Plan' of 19 September 1944. He had changed his mind, now wanting to resume from April 1951 the literary career which he had always managed to maintain in parallel, to the great benefit of Mill Hill's external reputation as well as his own. On Foundation Day 1951 a comment escaped from the Court Chairman – that he had perhaps retired *before his task was completely finished*. One fact weighing with Dr Whale was undoubtedly the threat of the Russian-induced Korean crisis, from June 1950 onwards, with the real menace of a third world war, (see Ch.IX), yet the agonising question of the re-evacuation of London schools in the event of an emergency did not cross the bows of the C/T's Committee until 28 September 1950; it was at its meeting of 21 July that the Chairman reported Dr Whale's letter to him, giving two months more than the contractual six months' notice. Like Harrow's Rev. Ford, this was Mill Hill's last ordained Head; however difficult some of the Court's earlier dealings with this strong-minded leader may have been, it was shocked, as was the whole Mill Hill community, on learning the news.

Although in terms of dress, *Nobis* could term it *the end of the traditional Headmaster at Mill Hill*, at least two successors might deserve that epithet; JSW's sense of 'theatre', which his Secretary, Sonia West, remembers as one of his striking characteristics – (*Everything had to be just so*) – might have had something to do with it. The timing was perfect: he was going out, as they say in show business, 'at the top'. Every school's story is peopled with might-have-beens: the composer Sir Malcolm Arnold is said to have spent four brief hours as a Millhillian in the 1930s before deciding to return home with the family chauffeur: even if Dr Whale did not secure the entry of *OM* Roy Dexter's son Ted, future England cricket captain (he then went to Radley), there had been those notable rugger seasons, with names like Ramsay, Williams and Roberts to evoke the great Collison, Spong, Sobey, Howard days of the 1920s. Also the first fruits of the intellectual revolution were now coming through; many boys, including two subsequent professors, Robert Kendell and Stephen Holt, had their careers enhanced significantly through JSW's watchful intervention at a critical moment. Margaret Whale, now Lady Elliot, recalled in 1998 the organisational skills which had enabled him to leave a school well-disciplined for his successor, despite the fact that it was still urgently in need of funds and new buildings.

Before he decided to move on, the Court was pleased to agree two precedents. On 9 February 1950 he gained permission for that elder daughter Margaret to be married that September in the Chapel. This necessitated its becoming registered for the solemnisation of marriages: an application had to be signed by 20 householders that for a year they had used it as a place of worship. Secondly, in response to a letter from Dr Whale of 7 July, the Court agreed to his son, Roger, entering Winterstoke in autumn 1951, free of entrance, tuition and Boarding fees.

Among many innovations, Dr Whale ended the 50-year use of the somewhat gaunt McClurean "Head Master's House" (prefering "The Grove"); "St Bees" then used as a single masters' hostel, (now as Collinson House bedsits). *8.1*

The Whales had done the School proud as a family: Mary Whale, with her Millhillian family connections, had graced so many public, and private, occasions with her gentle charm, from participation in the Sunday evening Playreadings to the teas at "The Grove"; Margaret and Helen had either studied or taught at Belmont or the School; and finally a Whale was about to become a Millhillian on his own account. Even John, the eldest – and a Wykehamist – had been involved in bringing in a glamorous show business friend, the American Betty Jo Jones, to help judge one of the Reading and Speech competitions; what Oliver Holt has recalled as this great teacher's *marvellous feel for the written and spoken word* was an area ever close to his heart. There was one field where "The Whale" did not fully achieve his goal: the School's outmoded traditions. A wish to broaden the monitorial appointments had been frustrated at St Bees in 1945 by the senior monitor: when he wanted to make an 'intellectual' a monitor, *You can't, Sir*, replied this power-base leader of 18 to his 'new boy'; (this goal was achieved later through such monitorial appointments as that of his much-prized Jeremy Gibbon). His typed edicts on punishments were circumvented in the tougher Houses, forcing one Housemaster to write to his Head of House on 24 November 1949, in an attempt to soften the impact of the 'colours tests', 'voluntary' Sunday games, and fagging. This area of reform would remain for his successors.

The modesty of John Whale's sentiments as he spoke to a circle of well-wishers at the belated unveiling of Ken Jackson's portrait of him, in the Octagon of School House, that sunny October afternoon in 1983, contrasts with the firm-focused and often uncompromising leadership which he had given to the affairs of Mill Hill for those seven hard but fruitful years. Yet the toughness was directed to the good of this still Free-Church institution, in which he so instinctively believed, and which he was determined to restore to greatness as a national school. *Nobis* called John Whale *one of the greatest Head Masters the School has ever had*. It was appropriate that he spoke in that echoing chamber of Mill Hill's first Dissenting Heads of 1825.

If a school might be judged by the staff he selected, this Head Master, like Harrow's earlier Weldon, must stand high. He had striven above all in the field he most espoused, the intellectual; the fact that his time also coincided with the ushering in of a new phase of social blending, which well anticipated the later years of his century, is a theme to be taken up at a later stage of the History. *I have done what I came here to do*, he said at the end to Donald Hall. Although he went on to lead a fourth career of equal distinction, which is set out in detail in the *MHM* of 1997/8, what he did for Mill Hill cannot be overrated: it was indeed *of some value*.

One subsidiary aspect of that value was the choice as his new official home, after the privations of the St Bees exile, of the ancient "Grove", claimed by local historians as *The oldest continuously inhabited house in Middlesex.* (The real family home, that vital haven from the equally continuous stresses of the job, which many of his fellow incumbents have sought and needed, would be "Wild Goose" on Dartmoor, close to his native Cornwall.) Apart from a brief sojourn in Park Cottages, while overdue renovation work was carried out in 1947, that tradition was handed on to future generations, while the former Head Master's House was re-named "St Bees", to commemorate the School's long wartime evacuation.

For a select group of Millhillians, a quiet event in Oxford on 20 March 1998 set the penultimate seal on the life of this remarkable Head Master. Appropriately for the last of Mill Hill's own ordained Minister-Head Masters, an engraving was unveiled on a column of the Chapel of the same College, Mansfield, where the architect of Mill Hill's own Chapel, Basil Champneys, had first risen to fame.

A wider gathering witnessed the commemoration of the School's own plaque on 24 April 1999: (a second tablet refers to the *OMs* who contributed to a set of blue-covered choir chairs, to match the then blue of the Apse). The wordings were

Despite Dr Whale's academic and doctrinal influence, rugby football was still the real MHS religion and power centre: six members of the successful 1949 1st XV included three successive senior monitors. 'Colours' unchanged from 19C. *8.m*

complementary: 'John Seldon Whale, 1896-1997, Student and Tutor of this College, Eloquent Expositor of Christian Doctrine'. The School's plaque asserted two key points: ... International Scholar... Head Master, Mill Hill School, 1944-1951. In his tribute to this *Renaissance Man ... one of Mill Hill's greatest Head Masters*, Prof Stephen Holt, then Rector of what was to become Roehampton University, London, and a member of one of Mill Hill's traditional large and loyal families, offered this message: *His years here provided the opportunity to put many of his educational ideas into practice – humanist ideas which placed the development of the individual at the very centre of his educational objectives ... the development of skills and training ... should not be at the expense of developing the things Dr Whale really believed in ... 'intellectual honesty, the scientific temper, the historical sense'. These are not skills, they are attributes – the product of a successful liberal education.* Mill Hill has cause to be grateful for her own share in the process of education which both these locations, in the company of other names from Mill Hill's Nonconformist past, so simply but movingly enshrined.

All was not grey

If a focus on the two strategic issues of this post-war period has emphasised the serious, top-driven character of John Whale's Mill Hill, this is not too surprising. A war-torn Europe was evolving rapidly into a Cold War world; the Nazi tribunals at Nuremberg were being displaced in the headlines by the show trials 'behind the Curtain' in Communist East Europe; rationing and austerity continued relentlessly to colour – or rather de-colour – daily existence; the British economy, and parental incomes, were slow to regain momentum.

Yet this should not leave the impression of a monotone era. Puritanical maybe: yet if the underlying spiritual code was Nonconformity, the outward behavioural code was conformist – tight Rules were posted up in every House Common Room. All conformed to a sometimes brutal year-system, said to have been reinforced by Maurice Jacks in the 1920s in an attempt to reduce communication between older and younger boys, and thereby, supposedly, to minimise 'pashes' and homosexuality. The resultant bullying eventuated in retributions by tormented fags against tormenting 'Second Years', evocative of *Tom Brown's Schooldays*. In one house, in the summer of 1946, a bully was encircled by the 'First Years' and forced to box with the toughest of their group until knocked out; another was tied to a tree and the grass around his feet was set alight. Normal life resumed next term as if nothing had happened – but of course it had, things were changing. The sub-theme of toughness is explored in Ch.IX; the two post-war decades were comparable.

It was also a time of commitments: to King and Country, and to Britain's still-leading role in international affairs; to traditional institutions and thus to Mill Hill, and to success within the School's hierarchy, each level of which – monitors, school prefects, house prefects – got its celebratory photograph. By extension, there was commitment to the alternative society driven from within, the cult of games – replete with the revived peacock-like 'athletic millinery' of the Jacks era, whose details had to be learned by fags from gestetnered 'Colours Lists' for regular Tests. Every House had to amass athletic points; boys with legs, but no eye for any ball, would be seen trudging round the Park at week-ends, each round scoring one House Point. Michael

Berry *bust his gut* to try to win the Schools' Life-Saving Award for a third year running, in 1946. The figure-head of this rugger-led athleticism was the ex-Paratroop hero (and also a product of the Jacks era), Maj Alan Bush; but nearly all the staff also believed, as pre-war, in the value of games as a short-cut to a Mill Hill – and a House-identity, regardless of whether as individuals they could still, as Alan did, take part in person.

Scrum-half Ray Wyeth was awarded an apple by the well-advanced Housemaster of Ridgeway (though not his House) for getting stuck-in to a scrum better than his forwards. Hockey wizard John Cranwell, won an ice-cream from an admiring Tom Jackson (umpiring, and again not his Housemaster) when he had scored 63 in the House Cricket final: when he was finally out for 80, his own Housemaster, Percy McAllister, awarded him not one but three free teas at Blenheim Steps. For School matches on Top Field, attendance, and the sustained two-tone, nationally-renowned 'Chant' of "Mill ... Hill" were mandatory; with the unbeaten XV of 1950 (there was a draw with Cranleigh) the customary clapping in supper Line-up featured throughout the term (see Appendix E). Transatlantic games became the rage, introduced by boys like "Nat" Micklem, Michael Henderson and Pat Mulvaney, who had been educated during the war in the States or Canada – basketball, and for the first and last time, in the severe winter of 1947, ice-hockey on The Ridgeway pond.

The blue School-crested blazer continued, successor to the 'MHS' red-monogrammed blazer of pre-war; team 'patches' (eg 'XV') could adorn the top pocket. Two *OM* ties evolved, yet there was no School Tie, just a 'Utility' blue affair; as a new boy you had to win the right to boast membership of Mill Hill's particularly strong version of an 'OBN' by winning the House Tie, a first step onto the rungs of the highly-prized political ladder. When the first Tie was awarded other than for games – in fact to one of the Middlesex 'intellectuals' for leading a House Choir to success in the then annual Music Competitions, there was an outcry – whereas in terms of the management skills needed to weld reluctant players into a team, despite manifold distractions, it probably deserved recognition even more than, say, the CCF Newcastle competitions that dominated every summer term. The 'silverware' was kept on permanent display in the Houses, and polished to obliteration by generations of 'Copy' boys. The accolade for a Housemaster too was to be awarded a Tie, or a Scarf, by his House. John Whale himself is the only non-former House Tutoring Head Master known to have been so honoured: Gordon Hawes presented him with a Winterstoke House Tie when he came to visit during his final, and at long last slightly more relaxed, Spring Term – prior to the entry of his youngest son, Roger; to everyone's delight, he immediately took off his own severely clerical neckwear and donned his hosts' gift. The idea that 50 years later a Winterstoke House Tie, by then obsolete (due to its translation into "Grimsdell"), could just be bought, not hard-fought for, would have been anathema to 'House Spirit'.

There was also an equal and opposite force, and equally colourful, at work from the ground upwards, glimpsed through the pages of the House punishment books. Boys did not meekly submit to the system; the more adventurous, the less they conformed, and the more they incurred retribution, whether in the form of beatings, Copies, or 'Pound' (see Appendix E). Thus 'B' got 2 Copies for 'Clambering over the roof of the swimming baths'; 'H', a future Champion, got *2* for 'Showing off his gymnastic capabilities in dormy...'; 'C' – 1 copy for 'Blowing a bugle in the precincts of the House'; 'P' – *2* for 'Wearing corduroys in chapel'; for a future monitor and Governor, six with a swag for 'direct unprecedented cheek...'; a future *OM* Hon. Sec is rumoured to have had one of the last "monitorials".

Yet despite initial youthful resistance, underlying everything to a passionate degree that would seem strange to many who knew later, less centripetal, more individualistic regimes, there was an equally unquestionable commitment to the idea of School as a part of life, and thus of Mill Hill's intrinsic worth as an embodiment of history, nationhood, and manhood. This sense would motivate many Millhillians into acts of fealty extending out to the end of the century and beyond, whether expressed through the four Governorships stemming from that generation, or through contributions to the work of the OMC, or in a myriad of activities. The long 'Shadow' of The Whale's years reached forward in many ways that would not only have surprised him, but still surprise many of his former pupils as well.

Sources for Ch.VIII include: # MHS Record Bk 1902-26; # C/T's Mins 1944-50; 'MHS Boys A/C Bk 1945-501; House Punishment/Pound Bks, 1945-50; ltr L.R.Bee to A.M.Flutter, 24.xi.1949; M.L.Jacks pprs, incl ltr, *Times*, 6.iv.1935; interviews/ corr/ dscns with: J.B.Visser [1941-6]; "Nat" Micklem [1944-7]; K.R.Calder, [1945-9]; T.Allan, R.M.Aye Maung, J.Roberts, B.P.Stark, R.A.Stroud, A.K.Woollaston [1945-50]; M.D.Henderson [1946-50]; R.C.Hubbard, R.W.Wyeth [1946-51]; W.G.Hawes [1945-51]; S.C.Holt [1948-54]; R.E.Kendell [1948-53]; A.P.B.Figgis [1953-7]; A/Ms Donald Hall, Edward Stanham, Tony Turnbull, Ted Winter, Rev. H.Starkey; Mrs Peggy Phimester; Dr Lena Brown.

Background: M.Gilbert, *Winston S.Churchill* (Heineman, 1986+), v.s VII,VIII; J.Charmley, *Churchill, The End of Glory* (1993); "Cold War", BBC2, 17.x.98; T.Heald, *Networks* (1983) [analysis of 'OBNs' – Old Boy Networks]; BBC2, 22.viii.99, "The Union Game ..."; H.G.Wells, *The Food of the Gods* (1904).

'Butler' Act: BL Add MSS, 'Diaries of J.Chuter Ede; A.Howard, *RAB* (Copyright © Anthony Howard 1987, by permission of PFD on behalf of Anthony Howard, 1971); R.A.Butler, *The Art of the Possible* (Penguin, 1971), 120; MxCC Edctn Cttee Rprts 1942-

6+; MoEd pprs, PRO; J.Dancy, *Public Schools & the Future* (Faber & Faber, 1963); Ogilvie, *op cit*; Rae, *op cit*; J.Wakeford, *The Cloistered Elite* (1969); J.McConnell, *English Public Schools* (1985); G.Snow, *The Public Schools in the New Age* (1959); Wilkinson, *op cit*; M.D.W.Jones, *Brighton College 1845-1995* (Chichester, 1995) & C.Tyerman, *op cit*; *passim*; BBC R4, S.vii.94, Sonia Beesley, 'The Guinea Pigs', (author as consultant); BBC2 TV, Mar/ Apr 2003, 'Second Chance' series.

J.S.Whale: *Who's Who* 1997; pprs ex John H.Whale, incl address at Dr Whale's funeral service, 24.ix.1997; obits in *Times & Guardian*, 19.ix.1997, & *Daily Telegraph*, 20.ix.97; *Cambridge Review*, 1.xi.1940; *MHM*, Dec. 1997, with School's obit, as well as other *MHMs* 1944-87; *MHM*, Spring 1978, Autumn 1999; *Nobis*, 64; "Martlet", Dec 1996; address by Prof S.C.Holt, 24.iv.1999; Brett James' Wartime Diary v. xii #; dscns/corr, P.Harris, ref Sir M.Arnold, Aug 2003: #. Jewish refugees fleeing Hitler's Europe via India [K.Metzer, F.E.Loeffler]: Voigt J.H., *Wechsel Wirkungen Jahrbuch*. 'Emigration von Juden aus Mitteleuropa nach Indien...' (1991).

[* **Calculation of Fig. J.** The complication is that a selected entry will include pupils from perhaps 3 different entry Cohorts. This gives a confused picture of the performance of a

particular 'year of influence' of a given HM. Here, the raw data has been allocated both forwards and retrospectively to what is described as the Cohort for a given Entry-Year, giving the start year (e.g. 1945), and allowing that some pupils' results might extend beyond the 5-year span into the next December/ early Spring. The totals add up to the same figures as in the *MHMs*, merely appearing under slightly different year labels: overall trends are not changed. The main block totals the nett number of individual boys gaining entry to tertiary education, eliminating duplication between Categories **A-D**. Any future Medics total will be slightly undercounted by virtue of the fact that some pupils won Oxbridge Opens on the basis of Science, but then switched to Medicine.]

Other *OM* references: R.W.B.Buckland [1878-84]; L.E.Collison [1921-7]; J.H.Cranwell [1948-53]; G.A.Goyder [1922-5]; C.S.Goyder [1925-30]; A.H.D.Gunning [1945-9]; P.D.Howard [1922-8]; K.Metzer [1946-50]; "Nath." Micklem [1866-8, '70-1]; P.G.Mulvaney [1945-8]; R.J.N.Phillips [1946-9]; A.S.Pye-Smith [1893-7]; A.W.Ramsay [1944-9]; A.J.Rooker Roberts [1893-1900]; S.G.Rowlandson [1922-26]; R.S.Spong [1918-24]; W.H.Sobey [1918-24]; G.A.Stannard [1940-5]; O.V.Viney [1900-3]; G.R.S.Whale [1951-5]; J.E.Williams [1945-9].

Highpoint of the 1950s: a radiant young Queen Elizabeth II was
Guest of Honour for the Sesquicentennial festivities in 1957, here with Roy Moore,
MHS Head Master, 1951-67, en route to the Chapel, past classrooms NOPQ. *9.a*

Sesquicentennial and All's Well

A world at peace?: the semblance of stability

"Mill Hill was to produce men of decided Christian character.
There could be no better aim."
Roy Moore: Foundation Day 1957.

The decade of the 1950s opened under the threat of a third world war, with the resultant secret planning of a renewed evacuation for Mill Hill and Belmont; its climacteric, after Suez and the Hungarian uprising of 1956, was the visit of the new young Queen in the following year to mark the School's 150-year celebrations. Evolution into the 1960s revealed it as a time of underlying change for society and for the Public Schools, beneath an outward shell of stability and continuity. As the global economy started to grow ever stronger, the nation that still prided itself on winning the preceding war would be admonished by 1959, with perhaps more insight than was realised at the time, that *we had never had it so good*. Academically, was that famous Macmillan phrase also to be true of Mill Hill?

This period could be seen as an 'Age of Transition'; in the words of the Head of English, Ted Winter, scholastically and sportively *the School was doing nicely… the Governors wanted a Head Master who would keep things ticking*. Yet if a school's history were primarily denoted by the 'imprint' of its Heads, and the prior conditioning that they brought to bear upon the School, then the time that followed the years of "The Whale", could equally well be styled an 'Age of Contrasts'.

At the opening of this new decade, it was the differences, not the similarities, between Mill Hill's first two post-war Head Masters that were most strongly perceived. Indeed, superficially, what could be more different? A tall urbane, informal and relaxed figure started to stroll with long leisurely strides through Mill Hill's corridors, terraces and pathways; a man with brown eyes and smooth features, and a serene and welcoming smile always lurking at the corners of his mouth, where his predecessor had been small and intense, with sharp blue eyes that challenged you, always looking purposefully ahead to the next problem to be tackled. For Ted Winter, while John Whale *kept everyone on their toes, including parents*, Roy Moore was *courteous, kindly, sociable and concerned with maintaining standards of manners and behaviour… an excellent communicator*. Yet he was fully capable of facing down a Housemaster just after the end of the decade, who insisted that either a certain boy left or he did: the Housemaster duly retired the following Christmas. His then secretary, Betty Dove, recalled his being closeted with this outraged senior staff member for a whole day during this mini-power crisis, only to appear calmly that evening at a social function as if nothing untoward had happened.

Here was a man with a broad experience of life, an ex-Squadron Leader with a 'good war' record in Bomber Command, organising escape routes through Occupied France: a leader who had grieved to send young pilots to their almost certain deaths, and had commanded men a good deal more intractable than Housemasters. He described himself, with mock modesty, as a *former, merely temporary member of the junior service.* He was a rounded character who could laugh with other equally broad-minded war-service masters such as Michael Brown, at some of the more outrageous stunts that would be pulled during his time, such as the flying of the Winterstoke House Matron's corsets from the School flagpole, or – shocking to many – placing a bed atop the Gate of Honour. This new Head, who could be tentative – even at times, in the eyes of one of his staff, Alec Robertson, *an exasperating procrastinator* – had a favourite but actually commonsensical phrase: *give me 24 hours to think it over.* He succeeded a man of the cloth, imbued with a highly focused academic background, a believer in the traditional classical Public School system, and who always appeared sharply certain.

Even with an Anglican Chairman in Prof Sir Arthur Pickard-Cambridge, the prospect of Mill Hill's first modern Anglican Head Master appeared so much of a differentiating point to Dr Whale's and Mill Hill's Free Churchmanship, that it was felt vital to appoint a Free Church Chaplain, the fives-playing Rev. P.H.Figgis. Taking due pride in his 'AKC' (Associate of King's College, the non-theological version of its Diploma of Divinity), Roy Moore was the product of The Judd School, the sister school to Tonbridge; not of Oxbridge but of the once-Anglican College within England's third oldest University (and the background of Dr Weymouth); the only Head in over 80 years to arrive with what was termed 'technical experience' (the Headship of Lawrence Sheriff School, Rugby) but limited to Day schools, a bias he offset by not questioning the traditional Day-Boarder balance. A lecturer to graduates, and a powerful combination of classicist, historian, theologian and world-class writer, gave way to a *very good classroom teacher*, and author of a fine though unpublished English text-book.

To crown it all, despite his Rugby connection (of which he used to speak in the same breath as 'Tonbridge") and his enjoyment of their game, the new man's prime sporting love was cricket. The differences in personalities and conditioning resulted in the appearance of great contrasts of style and manner, accentuated by the fact that the predecessor never met the successor. Some thought these also reflected differences in intellect – and the Whale mind could indeed seem daunting – yet Roy Moore's own capacities in the field of literature were very considerable, witness their respective and equally deeply-argued reviews of the annual School Plays; according to Alec Robertson, *he had a deep understanding of the metaphysical poets.* Perhaps "R.M." displayed his strengths less strongly, although both were, in their dissimilar ways, good 'showmen' for Mill Hill: he was a charmer – of women and most parents, although not easily accessible to all his boys – whereas one more of Dr Whale's *fortes* was not necessarily to rely on placating anyone, but on the force of authoritative argument.

Inevitably too, the contrasts in their respective lengths of tenure would in due course add to this perception of difference, Roy Moore's spacious 16 years more than doubling John Whale's anxious seven. However, as this History has shown many times, there are problems in trying to parcel out the phases of a school's story neatly in line with the reigns of its Head Masters, as the change of leader to and from Roy Moore – April 1951 to September 1967 – illustrates. Accidental 'handover' dates can be deceptive. The era of Roy Moore can now be seen to have two distinct phases, the first and longer part of which forms the present focus. A shorter second phase from 1964 up to the arrival of Michael Hart in 1967, falls more naturally into a succeeding chapter. The very geniality of R.M. and indeed of his long first era has often been allowed to stand for the whole of his time – *wasting the fat years ... living in the very nice past*, as one of the more outspoken members of that moving spirit within his MCR, the cricketing team "The Millers", expressed it. As will now unfold, two powerful punches were waiting to be unleashed, however genially, during his last three years. In cricketing parlance, he aimed for a 'safe knock'; he took time to play himself in, learn the strengths of his experienced team, and get used to this new wicket: googlies could still come at you at any moment. Having mastered the bowling, the final years of his innings produced some well-crafted, if leisurely, stroke play.

Continuity

In many respects both the regimes and the outlooks of John Whale and Roy Moore actually had much in common. First and foremost each had the backing of the same trio of senior staff; (this could even be counted a septet, if the long-serving and highly traditional Tom Jackson as *'Eminence Grise'*, Lyle Bee at BB, Warren Phillips, and even for a time once more, Herbert Coates, were to be added into the equation). This loyal supporting trio of other pre-war masters consisted of John Morrison, Percy McAllister, and Donald Hall – Housemasters of Ridgeway, Winterstoke, and Collinson: the firm, coeval bridge- and tennis-playing alliance of the first two, and the close working combination of all three, was the cement that bound things together. The two senior stalwarts were also, as the *MHM* later put it, the *Arachnoid brothers spinning the web of the Timetable*. Both had looked down the barrel of the same gun at St Bees, during the short reign of Dr Derry: Mog had actually been given notice, as had Tom Jackson: McAllister knew that it could even happen to him too if numbers got any worse. Roy Moore, and John Whale, were fortunate in being well served by a group of successful survivors who appreciated a Head who appreciated them, and responded with appropriate commitment: both they, and as in a different sense their ex-war-service colleagues, had been tested in battle.

Both men benefited from the service of the same self-effacing archetypal Head Master's Secretary, the slim, observant and perceptive Sonia West, a figure in the School's life in her own right – like many of her successors, helping "Heady" as she called JS, ("Whaley" to his MCR) to run his day with meticulous efficiency, and likewise Roy Moore for his first six years. This History has gained not only from her memories, in her nineties, of her two Head Masters, but also from those of Betty Dove, the equally effective Secretary who succeeded Sonia in 1960, who was to continue to service Mill Hill in this role until 1969, after Michael Hart's arrival. The two men also enjoyed that extra ingredient, not always the case in later eras – the vital presence of a wife and consort: Roy Moore's wife, Muriel, was soon entering into the life of the School, and also of Belmont – as wholeheartedly as had Mary Whale.

Despite their denominational differences, the obituary on Roy Moore's death on 1 January 1992 applied to both: *a devoted Christian*. As H.M.Louderback, a US exchange teacher with the insight of a spectator, would write in 1963, *chapel here is still so much part of a boy's life*. Roy's son, John, himself a later Head Master at The King's

School, Worcester, passed on a collection of his father's sermons: they compare in seriousness of thinking, and – at the time of delivery – in sonority, with those of John Whale himself, at his renowned pulpit best. (Both Heads decided not to send their sons to Mill Hill during their incumbency, unlike the sons of Weymouth, McClure and Rooker Roberts before them and both the Winfields later; the eldest and younger Whales had gone to Winchester and John Moore was sent to Rugby). Roy Moore also shared with Dr Whale the realisation that the world outside was changing faster than those around Mill Hill's comfortable hilltop fastness could really envisage. Each spent much energy, whilst endorsing the principles of the past, propounding Mill Hill's need to adapt to the incipient competitiveness of the State sector; while the Whalean solution lay in 'more Oxbridge', Roy Moore would be advocating a greater openness to the virtues of the other institutions developing in the tertiary system – 'Redbrick', and those that would become, generically, the 'Polys'.

As to the Middlesex Scheme, operating at a decreased level (even by 1953, only 23 applicants were selected), R.M. praised it as an acknowledged success, no longer an experiment; celebrated fully-fledged *OMs*, such as the year 2000 'Prestige Lecturer', Tony Fitzjohn, leader of the Kora Wildlife Reserve in Kenya, would often openly endorse a kind of dual debt both to Mill Hill and to their preceding Middlesex 'launch-pad'. In a 1953 analysis of the 237 boys who had entered during the Scheme's first eight years, 121 of whom were in the School at the time, R.M. showed the all-round contribution that the Scheme had made: one or two each year now came from Secondary Modern Schools; 18 had become monitors or, like Fitzjohn, been in the 1st XV or XI; one had been Head of the School. Although 4.3 per cent left pre-SC, and 16.4 per cent at SC, 94 per cent gained 5+ passes at O-Level; 81 per cent left at HC but 71 per cent gained 2+ passes at A or S Level, 31 per cent went on to University, nine won State Scholarships, eight won Open Scholarships to 'Oxbridge'. Some 25 per cent of the 1963 Roll would enter under the scheme, 46 per cent having won university places during the preceding five years. The major criticism of the Court at this time which evokes the Macmillan quotation is this: it was at fault in not preparing for the vacuum in purely 'conformist' academic standing which the Scheme's demise in 1965 would reveal.

Roy Moore could not at that stage have foreseen the less happy experiences that a few Middlesex Day boys would have during an initial 12+ year at Belmont in the later 1950s, then dominated by two 'old school' bachelor Assistant Masters, Alston and Gee, under an increasingly troubled Master. With unconscious irony, the savagely brilliant Belmont production of 1998, *The Lord of the Flies*, conjured up the Junior School's robust culture of 40 years before, all too well: the unquestionably equally robust later monitor, 1st XV member, QC, MP and author, Robert Marshall-Andrews, nevertheless remembers his vulnerability in his pre-MHS year to duckings in the pond, and being beaten-up in the vaunted 'freedom' of the Belmont woods.

The new Head Master's attitudes to people and things also came from the same socially-conservative mould as those of his predecessor. It was a mould that valued dignity, conformity and orderliness, hierarchies and seniorities: the conditioning of a generation that had survived and been shaped by a war of moral values. Initially there was a continuity running in a direct line from pre-war, through 1951, to at least 1964. Profound changes were going on under the surface of society at this time, however. (William Winfield would quote in his first substantive Foundation Day speech in 1996 the comment by the Chief Rabbi, Dr Jonathan Sacks; *it's as if in the 1950s and 1960s we set a time bomb ticking, which would eventually explode the moral framework into fragments*). Even if for most of Roy Moore's time those shifts both in pupils' attitudes and parental expectation moved faster than he felt able to respond to, in his last three years he would not only pave the way for a radical change in the curriculum but would be the first Head to take at last a tentative step towards internal reform of Mill Hill's version of the Public School 'system', a reform that had eluded his predecessor, and was to be carried forward more significantly by Michael Hart. This was to be the final abolition of the medieval foundation stone of it all – personal fagging. By the end of his 'Age of Transition', Roy Moore emerges as a would-be reforming Head Master.

OM Sir Norman Hartnell, pupil of McClure, appointed royal dressmaker to both Queen Elizabeth II and the Queen Mother. *9.b*

'The system'

At the start however, in spring 1951, all that lay unimaginably in the future. In 1951 the 'GC', like Belmont, still aimed predominantly at Boarders, a Christian School yet with no anti-semitism, and at least one Jewish senior monitor. The School was basically run by the monitors, with some Houses largely shut off even from the eye of the Housemaster himself. Beating was the *lingua franca* – by several Housemasters, by monitors, and by some older boys; beyond this era, one master, O.J.Wait, was still recalled by Paul Goldman as laying *a slipper on his desk at the beginning of every class*. Arcane 'colours' tests ("What is the name of the Headmaster's dog?"); year privileges; petty punishments – these were still the order of the day.

Much of that tribal overhang from earlier ages, bullying, inextricably interwoven with the 'year system' yet remained (see Appendix E). It was no worse during the 1950s than in the late 1940s: it was sporadic, not widespread; at a whole School Assembly in The Large early in his reign, Roy Moore issued an edict against it. It might be incomprehensible to the Mill Hill of 2006/7, with an Anti-Bullying Council, and a Pastoral Care policy, but for the fact that, as late as 1997, research showed that across the country 81 per cent of children still feared bullying at school. At 1950s Mill Hill its incidence varied according to the personality and strength or weakness of character of the Housemaster, and of the Head of House; or the fortuitous combination of a group of case-hardened boys usually from the then more traditional Boarding prep schools, in the upper years of a House. It could be offset by common decency or by the relative physical prowess of a House's first year 'cadre'. (Maxwell Macfarlane remembered his 1944 School House intake, having had to endure "Fags' singing" at St Bees, deciding "by common consent" not to perpetuate the ordeal on the next year, down at Mill Hill; Michael Henderson and Ronnie Aye Maung described the "Fags' Revolts" at the end of July 1946, when the 'First Years' of their Houses decided that they could no longer 'take it'. In 1945, in some Houses, it had been reinforced as a reaction to the restrictions of NW7, compared with the relative licence of St Bees; Oliver Holt called it a *Bully's Charter*.) The view has been advanced that the sheer fact of wartime inhumanity engendered this schoolboy imitation.

For goodly portions of this time, First Years were not allowed to talk to the years above them – that was "Guff" (see Appendix E); it even made an otherwise caring elder brother not dare to talk to his sibling at school – a replica of *The Fifth Form at St Dominic's*. Tony Turnbull, Housemaster of Collinson 1960-74, recalled the incident of two boys returning from successful joint participation in the same BB House cricket game: for talking to the Second-Year boy on the way back, the First Year boy was beaten. There were two other factors in the equation: tradition was more deeply entrenched in the older Houses, and although several perfectly normal Heads of House were reluctant to accept it, there seemed to many boys that there had grown up, almost in the very woodwork, a belief that being 'tough' made for a 'strong' House. In the early 1950s, one tough Head of House awarded no Ties at all to his victorious House Team, a fact still resented half a century later by 14 keen non-recipients.

Beating must be distinguished from bullying, yet both these manifestations of 'toughness' ran in parallel; they converged if beating got out of control. In the time immediately preceding the war, BB's then pacifist but popular Head of House once resorted to beating the entire House, for reasons that seemed totally justified to him, due to one miscreant not owning-up to a particular offence. One sporting senior monitor of the later JSW years was renowned as a sadistic beater. One Housemaster was called by some "The Slipper". In RM's era, on one occasion a senior monitor threatened to beat the entire school if there was repeated vandalism at the end of term.

Perceptions of toughness vary widely: those at the top of a House's hierarchy naturally played down the disadvantages, claiming, as Maurice Jacks did, that a good year-system provided the necessary character-formation that a Public School was designed for: *It never did me any harm, old boy*, would be the standard private comment by successful 'survivors', with assurances that the erstwhile tormented were now on the best of terms with their one-time tormentors. Even self-confessed 'victims' of that system who have been honest enough to speak out, such as Dr Alan Stroud, can be in two minds about the whole subject, observing wryly, as many others have done before and since, that *anyone who can survive five years at a Public School can survive anything*, yet one 1950s Middlesex boy was ostracised by his own year for retaliating against a beating by a Second Year. Moreover, these generations of Millhillians were not going out to fight any single war against a commonly recognised foe, unlike their respected seniors of the pre-war and 1939-45 vintage; they would nevertheless all, or nearly all, have 18 months to two years taken out of their lives for 'National Service' at the end of their time at the GC. Many OMs discovered that Mill Hill had indeed prepared them well for the institutional bullying and toughness of the parade ground and barrack room variety, which all had to endure.

However, with the more enlightened perspective of the 21st century, it is not enough to fall back on the accidental pay-offs of 'the system' – of the patriotic ends justifying the means, nor on the explanation that such boys were not 'suited' to a Boarding school. For some less resilient boys who suffered from the extremes of bullying, physical or mental – (You're not at home now, X!) – the memories not only lasted throughout their lives, leaving a residue of antipathy to the School which could easily outweigh the benefits, but could go on working against the School's interests in all sorts of unseen ways. Dr Stroud provided a striking example of this process. He found himself in conversation with Philip Stibbe – as the History has already noted, one of Mill Hill's undoubted wartime heroes – during the 1970s, when he and his wife were considering how best to educate their son. Alan recounted something of his own post-war experiences at the School, to find to his surprise that Philip was not only also an *OM*, but was able to cap those stories with his own pre-war experiences at the same House. As a result the Strouds sent their son to Bradfield, where Philip was then teaching, on the guarantee that there was and would be no bullying in the Stibbe House.

The admittedly overstated epithet, "Belsen Bank", was coined by Burton Bank boys and others in the 1945-50 era, even if at the same time they could – ambivalently – describe other Houses as "tame"; it was still recalled by former Burton Bankers and others during the research for this History, but BB was not alone; if its citation here needs justification, it lies in the fact that, by 1958, the BB House Notes would record that *the year system has almost vanished and in its place an improved system of respect has gradually arisen.* By 1960, in another House, Winterstoke, there was even one member of the House Staff – "a rebellious spirit" – who *refused to avail himself of a hired servant* (i.e. a fag), a sign of things to come. Yet for many boys, in all the Houses, the 'system' was seen as necessary, good for 'house spirit', and (in the title of the book about Ellesmere College) all part of the process of *Making a Man of Him.* Of the bullying and unofficial beating still in being in any of the Houses in any of Britain's Public Schools at this time it would seem that either the Housemaster was unaware of what went on beyond the green baize door, or that he was aware, but condoned it as either unimportant, or even beneficial; or simply that he felt powerless to intervene, against monitorial prerogative and House custom.

A very few boys left prematurely, not necessarily due to bullying; at least two more ran away from Winterstoke, by common agreement a notably civilised House, to the dismay of its kindly Housemaster (two had run away home to Whitehaven in 1946). Some came back; most survived; many passed through their time without even registering what might be going on to 'others' in other Houses: no one could be expected to see the problem in the round. Either way, at Mill Hill as no doubt still at many other Boarding schools during those war-conditioned post-war decades, a degree of criticism must lie with those who turned a blind eye to the more flagrant instances of this redundant aspect of 'the system'.

Dr Whale had made a small step forward by instituting House Punishment Books in 1945, presented to each Housemaster and titled and signed in his own hand, an unprecedented incursion into the baronial fiefdoms. The *Monitors' Punishment Book* was inspected and countersigned by JSW (and his successor), with regular admonishments in neat red ink; thus all punishments were officially recordable on paper. The trouble seems to be that House *Punishment Books* became the object of rivalry among pupil-'staff' for witticisms – a boy throwing pencils about was indicted for "Propelling Pencils"; also these measures were not followed up and 'monitored' as efficiently as in the better-managed regimes of the late 1990s – one of the basic lessons of good management in any enterprise. Dr Whale once noticed bruises on a boy's back in the changing rooms, and enquired how they got there; after the boy's would-be true-blue reply, *I don't know, sir,* he inspected the House in question but the only tangible outcome was that the boy was winkled out by 'the House' and punished – unjustly: he had 'let the House down'. In this same House, first years could be beaten by anyone 'above' them, with no records kept. There is a verifiable case of a boy being about to be beaten by one such rebarbative older tyrant (not even a house prefect) with a shoe so worn down that the nails were showing: the boy had to plead for mercy like some 19th-century literary hero. It was anachronistic, even then; it happened; fortunately it passed.

A number of parents, like the Pye-Smiths who appeared in the Introduction, found even by the 1960s, to their disappointment, that things had not changed within Mill Hill to the extent that they had expected. The long Pye-Smith connection with Mill Hill ended in favour of the Quaker Leighton Park, with its more modern reliance on self-discipline, rather than the externally-imposed monitorial regime that still held sway at Mill Hill.

The eye of the Court

This substratum to life at the School was not unseen on high. In Mr Justice Sellers MC, LLD, the new Chairman of Governors who succeeded the ailing Sir Arthur Pickard-Cambridge in 1951, Mill Hill's Court was to enjoy at its helm one of its most devoted, and appropriately 'hands-on', Chairmen; his was even a 'saddles-on' role – he was to be seen on horseback at various times around the School, keeping his eyes open for what was happening 'on the ground'. He inherited and built round him an outstanding Court, including, by 1962: Lord Brain, Lord Ogmore, "Nats" Garrett and Millard, Oscar Viney, Stanley Farrow, the two Walkers – Philip and "Dick", Alfred Hawes, Bill Ramsay, and Dr C.S.Darke, as well as H.W.Walton, a MxCC Governor, to be described as "almost an Old Millhillian"; the choice of his successor, the 'distingushed airman' Sir Dermot Boyle, was an idea of R.M.'s. Albeit that the agonising reappraisals of later in the century were not then there to divide them, the fact that *OMs* constituted no fewer than 16 out of 19 Governors, and even one of the six MxCC nominees (Sir Graham Rowlandson, of the City of London's Court of Common Council), did not appear to bias decisions; as George Goyder wrote later, they formed *a happy band of brothers.* Roy Moore was able to establish the kind of satisfying partnership with his newly appointed Chairman that some other Heads before and since would only have been able to admire or even envy (see Appendix C).

Sir Frederic, as he later became, took the Housemasters to Dinner at Gray's Inn and entertained senior boys at his historic home, Highwood House. He had sent two sons to the School; the elder, Mark, going on to lead a successful career in industry, made a major contribution to this History. Lord Justice Sellers was raised to the Supreme Court in 1959. He could be compared with four other *OM* members of the Law's high places – Alfred Lawrence; Thomas E. Scrutton; another eminent Governor, Sir Cyril Salmon; or Justice of Common Pleas, Noon Talfourd: the compliment bestowed on Governor H.W.Walton could have fitted Judge Sellers himself. He is commemorated at Mill Hill through the plaque on the wall of the SFC, which he opened three years after his own retirement, on 31 October 1970. However, from the point of view of the School's sociological evolution one of the most significant things that Sir Frederic did during Roy Moore's time – the only Chairman ever to have had both the need and insight to do so publicly – was to warn the School in 1957, from his vantage point as Chairman of a comparable school, Silcoates, that some of Mill Hill's age-old customs were due for review. As Donald Hall recalled, *At the Speech Day held three days before the Queen's visit when there no visitors except parents ... [he] spoke quite forcefully about intolerance between year groups.* Judge Sellers' very modern words on the day bear quoting:

> *You boys chance to be here at this 150th Anniversary. May you too not take stock – look back, then look ahead. What is your tradition of the relationship between boy and boy? Does an injunction to 'snitch off' show any warmth of heart, any ... comradeship between boy and boy, or, may I add, any sense of justice? Does a year or two's difference in age, or a term or two longer at school justify any superiority or the flouting of ordinary human understanding and friendship?*

Would that R.M. had felt able to brave Millhillian conservatism on this issue there and then, and act upon that opening. Some things had started to change, but in the main the reforms that both he and John Whale had contemplated, and which he at last did begin to tackle, would remain for Michael Hart to take up, a decade – and countless potential parents – later.

One in a long and sustained line of eminent *OM* lawyers: The Rt Hon the Lord Salmon (a Lord of Appeal), MHS Governor. *9.c*

Supplying the "Army of Innocents"

One other element that both 'post-war' Heads had in common was an involvement with the National Service generation. Military service for *OMs*, voluntary or compulsory, reaches back – if not quite, as *Nobis* put it *to the very beginning* – certainly to the Regency period, when Francis Dalton was Surgeon-Major in the Royal East Middlesex Militia. A century or so later, from 1947 to and beyond the Duncan Sandys' post-Suez legislation, with the last NS man leaving the forces in 1963, two million young men aged 18 (and upwards if deferred for University) spent from 12 months to two years in the three services; two-thirds went into the Army, notwithstanding that Friday afternoons at Mill Hill were now apportioned between four equal 'arms' – Army, RAF, Navy, and Scouts. On 2 April 1997 BBC 1 TV celebrated the 50th anniversary of the inception of this 'peace-time' conscript force – the "Army of Innocents"; an ITV series in 2002 simulated their experience as the "Lads' Army".

For most of the 'Lads', civilian innocence was lost early on in the eight to ten weeks of 'Basic Training', the common initiating ritual. Very quickly anyone who had not learned the art of survival and self-reliance in his previous life made up for that deficiency, and the streets of London or Glasgow were as good a preparation as a Boarding school – and both social extremes would now meet and work side by side. Coping with the absurd regulations of an inflexible hierarchy and arbitrary injustices was no surprise to these *OMs*; a new language had to be learned, to supersede the 'Millhillisms' of the preceding years, and the highly refined arts of 'skiving' became the lot of many. One *OM*, having reached the dizzy rank of Sergeant in the Education

Corps, and wishing to sunbathe within his office, simply put up an official notice outside his door saying 'No Education Today': so much for the work ethic so carefully inculcated at Nonconformist Mill Hill. For many there then followed a 'POC' (Potential Officer Cadet) course for those passing 'USB' (Unit Selection Board), leading on to a full-scale physical and leadership test – 'WOSB' (War Office Selection Board), and passing-out as a subaltern; some were 'Deferred Watch', or were 'RTUd' (returned to unit) to work out their weary 'Days to Do' on their personal 'Demob Chart'.

Everyone at Mill Hill knew of this odd experience lying ahead: newly minted Officer Cadets with white gorget patches on their uniform lapels would appear in the visitors' pew in the Chapel on Sundays, or, after commissioning, attend OMC Dinners in the tight-fitting splendour of their 'Blues', or visit their old Houses on leave, just as they had done in the First World War. Stories were passed along the grape-vine and further embellished *en route*: of the legendary RSM "Freddie" Brittain at Mons OTC, Aldershot; or of pre-breakfast parades, and suicides, at Eaton Hall OTC, in the Duke of Westminster's stately home outside Chester.

The real point for the Mill Hill authorities, however, was that despite occasional Interim Society Debates about the uselessness of National Service, all this military discipline – reinforced, as it still is, every Friday – was accepted as the natural order of things, or at least up until the late 1950s when a questioning of the *status quo* emerged. National Service was indeed a cut-price 'continuation of war by other

KOREA 1952-1953
Chain of Command - February 1953

National Service blooded many 'post-war' *OMs*: (i) (above) some won honours, like the 1952-3 Korean Campaign Medal(l.) and the UN Medal, awarded to *OM* 2/Lt "Tom" Rothery, seen here (r.) (ii) as o/c 5 Platoon, sixth in chain of command of 1st Duke of Wellington Regiment.

9.d

Left to right: Lieutenant General P. Kendall, Commander US Corps. Major General M. M. A. R. West, Commander 1st Commonwealth Division Brigadier D. A. Kendrew, Commander 29 British Infantry Brigade. Lieutenant Colonel F. R. St P. Bunbury, Commanding Officer 1 DWR. Major R. H. Ince, Officer Commanding B Company, 1 DWR. Second Lieutenant T. M. Rothery, Officer Commanding 5 Platoon, 1 DWR. Corporal J. Clark, B Company, 1 DWR. Private J. Goodall, B Company, 1 DWR

means': wherever the inexorably diminishing British world presence needed military force, NS men and their young officers went. At the OMC Town Club in Whitehall Court in London, one of the Stewards, Jack Young, who had done 'Boy Service' in the First World War, was a willing listener to tales from young *OMs* passing through or staying the night – about epic deeds in all the theatres where the Union Jack was still being flown, defended or invited – in: Kenya, Aden, Honduras (Belize), the Russian Border in (Western) Germany and Berlin, Vienna, Cyprus, even Jordan, and the longest scene, Malaya, where 100 conscripts were killed in 12 years of fighting against the Chinese-led communist guerrillas. One *OM* of the 1945 intake, Denis Chamberlain, an outstanding all-round athlete, attained the almost unheard-of heights of captain, but contracted polio in the jungle, losing the use of both legs. The revised 18-months' stint of 1948 was increased to two years in 1950 when the North Koreans invaded South Korea, incited by China and, as is now known post-*glasnost*, encouraged initially by Russia; the 1938 evacuation scare was re-enacted in 1950/1 (see below) – a ghastly prospect first for John Whale and then Roy Moore and their colleagues, the collective memory still far from forgetting the tribulations of St Bees.

Some 200 NS men lie in the Pusan Military Cemetery, out of 700 all ranks and kinds of service. The Korean War embroiled several *OMs*, earning the Korea Medal and the coveted UN Medal; the brilliant pianist (also, incidentally, one of Mill Hill's wasted musical talents) 2Lt Alan Fenner, experienced action under fire, winning a 'Mention in Despatches'; Maxwell Macfarlane, by now a Lt 'Gunner', was wounded. What many of these 'peace-time' soldiers experienced was touched on in two articles. In "An *OM* in Korea", in 1951, 2Lt Alec Ramsay wrote: *The kit we carry is simply colossal, and it is over country much worse than the Lake District, as the hills are steeper, and we go up 2000 feet, and come down and then go up again. Sweat simply pours off, as we need the warm clothes, and can only carry them, by wearing them ... The last 48 hours have been very hectic. We moved from our rest area at less than two hours' notice, right up to the front line, where the 6th R.O.K.s [Korean militia] had crumpled up and were in full flight ... We fought our way up the road and had just occupied a small feature when we became involved at close quarters with a heavy force of Chinese ... eventually they worked all the way round us and a couple of men got shot from the back, so we withdrew under fire ... carrying our wounded with us ...*

2Lt Tom Rothery saw nine months' active service in his family regiment, the Duke of Wellington's, soon after leaving as Head of Murray in 1951. He later described, in 'The Iron Duke', serving with *OM* Capt James Selway, a "regimental honours" hill battle, "The Hook": *Under constant shell and mortar fire, in our deep bunkers we were only aware of those close by ... though we had all witnessed death, it was something we could not really comprehend ... I do not think that any of the [NS] subalterns or soldiers realised what a significant action we had been involved in.* Most *OMs* settled for a pip on the shoulder and survival intact. Postings ranged from Alasdair Breeze's and Stephen Holt's Royal Marine Commandos, and another *OM*'s hush-hush job in MI8, to the posting of former Chess Champion, solicitor Matthew Baldwin, as a privileged Clerk to the Commandant, Sandhurst, and to Capt M.A. Melsom's task in the Congo in 1962, where he gained the MBE. 2Lt Ronnie Samuels guarded Nazis Rudolf Hess,

Albert Speer and Admiral Doenitz as allied prisoners in Berlin's Spandau prison. There were a few 'regulars' too: Michael Wilkins rose from Corporal, CCF, to become one of Mill Hill's most distinguished soldiers, finishing his career as Lieutenant-General and Commandant-General of the Royal Marines. O/C Joe Milburn, The Border Regiment, passed out among the first 20 at the RMA, Sandhurst, and was later, as Brigadier, Deputy Lieutenant of Cumbria. Col J.Michael Phillips became Defence Adviser to the British High Commission in Bangladesh; Lt, later Lt Col John Hewson, one of many *OM*s in the now merged but illustrious Middlesex Regiment, won his MC for bravery under fire in the EOKA conflict in Cyprus in 1958; the then Lt A.B.Cowing (see Ch.XII) also joined that very *OM* regiment in 1959, having been Under Officer at the RMA. Maj A.M.Flutter went on to lead the All-Arms Junior Leaders Regiment; 2Lt F.J.Hardie served with the South Staffs, also in Cyprus; John Holmes, later Brigadier, Scots Guards, would later win his MC in Northern Ireland and head up the SAS.

The year 1956 brought Suez, an event marked in a special address in The Large by Roy Moore. It is as misleading to think of these as merely 'post'-war years, as it would be to think of the post-World Trade Centre catastrophe era as a time of peace. One external global threat had succeeded another; for many the toughness of the Mill Hill of this era could be seen, at least retrospectively, as justified by the outside conditions, and the need to cope with the testing times ahead.

Academic patterns

The academic 'carry-over' from the era of Dr Whale has already been explored. His theme – Mill Hill's need to place academic standards before other competing goals – was stressed by Roy Moore from the outset. However, this was tempered with his perception of the need to cater for the whole man: *Games too have their place*, although later he would qualify this with the caveat: *We do not make a god of games here*. The new GCE system was now in force, nullifying comparisons with previous HC and SC results. One of "The Whale's" legacies was the 30 *OM*s then 'up' at Cambridge, and almost as many at Oxford.

There are three notable features: the usual 'good years and bad years' pattern about which Roy Moore always appeared to his secretaries to be more philosophical than his predecessor; the number of boys now finding it expedient to seek further formal training at all; and the number who now sought or were fully prepared to accept this training outside the increasingly competitive but still elitist Latin-based confines of Oxbridge, where consequently even as late as 1958, 85 per cent of places were still going to products of the Public Schools (compared with 53 per cent in 2000). By 1961, one insular outcome of this trend was the breaking of the traditional mould of University Letters to the *MHM*: London, Manchester, Birmingham, Durham, Nottingham, Queen's Belfast, and Queen's College, Dundee, at last started to gain their place in the sun, and on the printed page. The last year of State Scholarships, 1962, saw nine won, with six Oxbridge awards, 25 A-L distinctions, and 159 O-L passes in 739 subjects, from a School Roll of 432. By 1964 it was still possible for Mill Hill to be ranked among the top 20 Public Schools.

Girls!

Older critics of the 'beat' generations of the 1960s were later at pains to point out that sex had actually been discovered before the flower-power decade. Certainly, girls had been invented at Mill Hill before the 1950s; 'pen pals' and actual girl friends had come and gone throughout the generations, as the pages of the *MHM* and the reminiscences of *OM*s can testify, even if most of this normal healthy activity had been a thing of the holidays, remembered fleetingly once the monastic seclusion was resumed each term. St Bees was something else (see Ch.VII); its freedom was still recalled with a sigh by many a now elderly *OM*. At Mill Hill both before and after the war, not a few romances, and marriages, began with the arrival of someone else's sister on the Saturday visiting day. The unofficial species, 'Old Millhillienne', had already been launched in late 1939 (see Ch.XI).

It was, however, during this new decade that what was then termed by men the 'opposite' sex started to loom ever-larger in the ongoing life of the School. The first squash match against a Ladies team, organised by the former champion Susan Noel, was played in 1951. Debates were held with Queenswood that same year and subsequently. After a successful debate against North London Collegiate (NLCS) the *MHM* later expressed mock horror at the event: *Hey man, I am disillusioned, like. I never knew women could talk! It ain't natural*. The bastions of prejudice were not charged all at once, however: even in 1953, the year of the Coronation, there was a closed debate – perhaps an appropriate phrase – on "The Female Mind". In 1957, the year of the visit of Her Majesty, The Interim was still able to debate the motion that "This House deplores the education of women".

THE NEW NEEDLEWORK ROOMS

Combining the best qualities of both traditional and modernistic schools in its gracious and dignified design.

Architect : LE CORPBAKIER.

Sculptor (Reclining Figures) : HENROY MOORE.

'Things to come': (i) 1952 CCF Band Inspection on Top Field: (back row) opera impresario Peter Hemmings (choir manager); Bill Skinner (later drum major, and Governor); following Gen Sir Brian Horrocks, RSC actor/film star – David Buck, CSM; (ii) (above) *MHM* cartoon forecasts, if chauvinistically, 'New Needlework Rooms'. *9.e*

In the sedate late 1940s, dancing classes had been re-started (their first appearance was in 1870): a suitably restrained dancing teacher from the Ada Foster School of Dancing arrived on Tuesday afternoons in the Music School, accompanied by her two only slightly less restrained potential dancing partners: a nice but inaccurate rumour suggested that going up to Mill Hill constituted a punishment for misbehaviour. To shellac records of the quick-step, the waltz, the fox-trot, the tango, the samba and the rumba, and, yes, even the polka, VI-formers would take it in turns to complete a tour of the room with this strange person called a girl, trying to work in as many newly-learned steps as possible before the gramophone stopped, and it was someone else's turn. It was fairly arm's length, and not exactly cheek to cheek: there were after all plenty of chaps from other Houses watching. Dancing across a ballroom in those days required as much tactical pre-planning as a 'Newcastle' platoon movement on the Parade ground the following Friday.

Painfully-learned steps would be gingerly put into practice, and a new set of toes trodden on, at occasional dances – home or away fixtures – with Queenswood or NLCS, wearing either your own, or your father's, or even your grandfather's dinner jacket, a stiff shirt, and wing-collar and, if you were lucky, black 'pumps'. Away 'matches' were better: various pranks could be tried, to impress one's impressionable partner, such as ringing the bells at Queenswood. Housemasters with teenage daughters would occasionally entrust them to the more sober of their senior boys at dances at the girls' school, on the reasonable assumption that not much could go wrong under the circumstances: there is no known record of a Copy being awarded for lack of dancing spirit. What the fond parents, and quite probably the boys too, did not know was that some of those daughters already had their eyes on various attractive members of 'their' House (as the daughters of Winterstoke HS/M Percy McAllister explained in 1995 at the nostalgic 'Wake' for its passing as a House, prior to its start-up as the Pre-Prep).

"Sam" Micklem remembered how everyone noticed the evening at a 1950 end-of-term Ridgeway House supper when one of the seniors, a handsome blond boy, finally plucked up courage to put his arm round Mog Morrison's daughter, and steal a furtive kiss. It was all decorous, 'good fun' and vicarious. With the 1950s, things began to gather pace. By the end of the decade, every House was starting to have its own House Dances, again on a reciprocal basis – with The Mount School, St Helen's at Northwood, and St Margaret's, Bushey, added to the list of potential collaborators. School dances continued in what came to be identified as "the Dancing Season", held on the still far from even floor of The Large. Sentimental writings started to appear in the *MHM*, allowed in by the ever-present Censor of the day: "A Parting Kiss" headed the literary Section in April 1958. There was a proposal to create a new society – The Neck-Romancers – in 1958. Comments appeared about the respective success of members of the monitorial fraternity, and the academic staff, with their fleeting partners of the evening. The floor was always first taken by the master i/c Drama.

Following the lead of The Interim, other School groups such as the Modern Language Society would start to open their doors to girls from nearby schools, such as NLCS: not of course co-education proper, but the first timorous, shaky steps had at last been taken (or – historically – resumed, see Ch.II), rather like those in the Music School, towards joint corporate activity with those future equal members of the Mill Hill School Foundation. There was still room for enjoyable confusion: at the 1960 Queenswood Dance, one of the *31 elegant young ladies* mistook a master for the Head Boy, and another asked one of the older boys what he taught. At one school play, "School for Scandal", in 1957, one boy was so well made-up, and the expectation of seeing a real woman was so impressed on the mind of one courteous boy at the back of The Large, that he immediately offered his seat to 'her'. The *MHM*'s comment was that they hoped *that "she" was man enough to refuse*.

Outside events

These were some of the broad background themes to Mill Hill in the 1950s. How did these next 13 years unfold up to 1964, and what other sub-themes emerged?

Some events, only associated indirectly, were external to what Roy Moore at one of his first Foundation Days could still refer to as a "family school". The 1951 Festival of Britain brought into prominence the *OM* architect Ralph Tubbs OBE, who was responsible for the Dome of Discovery, among other projects: in 1956 he was asked to address his skills to a somewhat lesser task, the conversion of "Cleveland" on The Ridgeway as the School's MCR. Also in 1951, the General Election had returned four *OMs* to the House of Commons, once more representing, as in the 1900s, all three political parties: Arthur Holt and Donald Wade (Liberal), Donald Scott (Conservative), and Percy Holman (Labour); their number was enhanced in 1955 by Sir Eric Errington and J.A.Leavey. The premature death the following year of King George VI would usher in the 'new Elizabethan Age', and the Coronation Year of 1953, with happy consequences for Mill Hill five years later.

Re-evacuation scare

However, the immediate dire prospect facing Roy Moore, and Arthur Roberts at Belmont, had first been brought before the Court on 28 September 1950: the decisions of a Conference arising from the Korean conflict, held in the utmost seriousness in April 1950, under the auspices of the Ministries of Education and Health, to concert the evacuation of all London Schools 'in the event of war' with the Communist powers. Some of these documents, reading like a re-run of 1938/9, were classified "Top Secret"; many were not released by the PRO until 1981/2. The despair that attended this news is reflected in the C/T's Minutes: *if Mill Hill is closed down altogether, it might prove impossible to start all over again.* The Court's actions would be camouflaged in the Accounts under the heading 'Special Deferred Expenditure': parents were not to be told at this stage, and boys were kept totally unaware of what might be impending. Under the governmental plans for 'Independent Schools' in the 'Civil Defence Zones' (*areas of concentration ... liable to heavy attack*), 'Hendon, The Mill Hill School' would be 'allocated' to the vicinity of Oundle.

A task force consisting of the then Bursar, Captain Horne, Belmont's Arthur (once more) and Brenda Roberts drove up to Northants to look over a former hospital, Lilford Hall, owned by the Bristol Merchant Venturers; Brenda Roberts was well-equipped for this role, possessing the temperament that could take such a

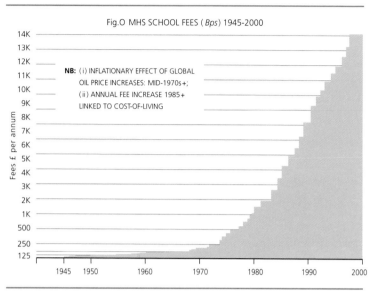

Fig.O MHS SCHOOL FEES (*Bps*) 1945-2000

NB: (i) INFLATIONARY EFFECT OF GLOBAL
OIL PRICE INCREASES: MID-1970s+;
(ii) ANNUAL FEE INCREASE 1985+
LINKED TO COST-OF-LIVING

renewed dislocation in her youthful stride; she had had the job of supervising the actual 1939 evacuation to Cockermouth. An empty Remand Home was also inspected at Apethorp; Belmont was earmarked for Wadenhoe Manor nearby. One month after Roy Moore's arrival, two ex-wartime masters, Paul Duncan and Arthur Vine, were being called up for training under the 'Z' Reservists scheme.

Leases were signed at Oundle looking to 1954, but actually covering the next seven years up to 1958; despite the heavy pressures on the School's budget, an expenditure of £2,750 was sanctioned. (Lilford Hall was sub-let, in March 1953, when the international situation had calmed down, to the Committee for the Education of Poles in Great Britain.) Those last still visible relics of the Second World War, the air-raid shelters above Top Field and behind the Music School. might still be needed again, even if not for the community of Mill Hill. In fact it was not until October 1955, with the news that there would be no further official pronouncement by the MoE, that the leases could be ended, from 6 April 1956, and £2.000 worth of stock realised.

Nor was this the only impact of war on a Mill Hill now technically at peace. Rationing of most things, from food to fuel and paper, all affected the school at the opening of the decade, although by September 1952 Roy Moore could claim that *the worst of the shortages due to war are over*. An incendiary bomb was found as late as 1956 on the roof of the chapel. War Damage was still being repaid, to enable the floor of The Large to be replaced; of course the state of much of the fabric continued to reflect wartime and post-war stringency.

Diversity within traditionality

This was still a very tradition-based Mill Hill. The strange Millhillism of calling monitors and school prefects 'the School Staff' continued in being, and, as Keith Armistead recalled, monitors still 'stood in' for academic staff when absent. The initial entry to that hierarchy still lay with the Houses, their 'Staff' invariably choosing new members on grounds of 'togetherness'; capable 'loners', who would shine in later careers, would often be excluded. In a decade when other boys' Boarding schools were taking the plunge as co-educational Day schools, Mill Hill did not even contemplate change: the demand still seemed to be there.

Annual fees for this unchallenged regime were raised again in March 1951: Boarders up from £240 to £255, and thereafter at two- to three-year intervals. Later in the decade, (1956, 1957) some interesting comparisons were drawn with the competition, the shifting focus of that competition varying all the time. Belmont fees were then £225 for Boarders. With the gradual decrease in the Middlesex element, the School's reliance on her feeder prep schools became once more a vital factor, and with it the policy problems of Belmont's role vis-à-vis the main School, a topic to be examined later.

Fig.O charts Mill Hill fee increases for the post-war period. In May 1952, in line with HMC caveats about 'No changes in Year One', the new Head presented the customary assessment – 'The Present Position of the School and Future Policy', highlighting the fact that with 375 Boarders and 45 Day boys, the School, although in other respects at a desirable level, was now full. A ratio of 14.8 boys per 27 full-time masters was seen as 'rather large for a school of this type'. There seemed to be no particular pressure (yet) for more Day places, and there was a healthy overall demand. Nevertheless, Roy Moore was 'a little concerned' about the early specialisation now in place, and the consequent need for some 150 individual VI-Form timetables.

By 1950, the Memorial Fund had extended Collinson Field, creating a new field and tennis courts above Gears; a planned Martin Briggs commemorative signpost never took off, however. Games began to rate higher in the HM's reports, in the wake of the 1950 record-breaking 1st XV, and also in line with his shrewd awareness of the OMC constituency's value within his audience. By 1952, Alec Ramsay (later Oxford Captain) and Jim Roberts at Cambridge (going on to win an unequalled 18 England caps) were gaining "Blues", the first since the late 1920s; nearly the whole School attended that year's Varsity match. In 1954 John Williams became the first international for 23 years, since Peter Howard in 1931, with nine caps for England as well as participation in a British Lions tour. By the end of the decade, another game, golf, became available (begun in 1901, it revived at St Bees); it was re-initiated by Tony Turnbull for boys who declined to play cricket in the summer term; a golf pro was retained at Finchley Golf Club, and soon an informal team was created and playing matches. Boxing also received Turnbull's attention: one of his unlikely stars was the slightly built mathematics and chess 'king', John Borgars, who went on to box at bantam-weight for Oxford, and gain the ABA Featherweight Championship for Oxon, Berks and Bucks in 1968.

The racket and the stick emerged, however, as the main sporting symbols of this epoch, and also of three outstanding MHS individual sportsmen. Mike Corby, and Warren Phillips' son, Tim, made headlines well into the 21st century – (with future Scottish Squash cap and cricket "Blue", Tony Dyer) – for hockey, squash and tennis. They were 'in' nearly everything. Following the win by Tim Phillips and Mike Corby of the Public School U16 tennis event (the Thomas Bowl), a Mill Hill team of four, completed by Peter Worrell and Bob Hudgell, won the Youll Cup in 1958. Phillips also won the Evans Cup (Public School Squash Championship) in 1958 and 1959. Corby won the Drysdale and Lonsdale Cups in 1959, led both England and GB

Late 1950s flowering of the racquet and the stick: future UK's most-capped international (squash and hockey) – and future Olympic hockey Captain, *OM* Mike Corby; (std, 3rd l.) 1st XI(H) 1958. *9.f*

OM all-round sportsman, multiple "Blue" and Wimbledon competitor, Tim Phillips, in his later role as Chairman of the All England Lawn Tennis and Croquet Club. *9.g*

OM Sculptor Prof Phillip King CBE, PRA, President of the Royal Acadamy of Arts, at work in 1981 in his Dunstable studio. *9.h*

Squash teams in 1967, 1969 and 1971, and the England and GB Hockey teams, playing in the 1964 and 1972 Olympics. He became the most-capped British sportsman on record, voted as the best British Amateur Sportsman. Crowning his playing career with the Real Tennis Mixed Doubles trophy in his mid-50s, he oversaw his two fields as President of the England Hockey Association and the SRA. Phillips won a triple "Blue" at Merton, Oxford, (in tennis, squash and hockey), played in three of the tennis Grand Slams (including Wimbledon) and reached the USA Open Men's Doubles semi-final in 1964, later becoming All-England Club Chairman. He rebutted the commonly-held false antithesis – the 'either sport or work/ culture' idea. (For full details of these two outstanding careers, see Information Supplement No.6.).

'Singlehanded' was still in vogue, but "Terrified" wrote to the Magazine in 1956 protesting against its dangers: it stayed, for the time being. An attempt was made to amend its unique rules (see Appendix E); the *MHM* recorded that in 1908 they had even entered the realm of English grammar; 'any person making a fair catch is entitled to a throw at goal, his opponents being at liberty to *impede* him': this exemplified an unusual figure of speech – *'Litotes'*– intentional understatement. The year 1962 was memorable for sport: in rugby, the best year since 1950, with only one

school match lost; in Roy's first love, cricket, there was registered at least a best post-war season in Mill Hill terms, winning seven matches and only losing four.

On the cultural side, all the Arts flourished, from the increasingly literary, satirical and graphic *oeuvres* in the *MHM*, to the annual plays – still predominantly Shakespearean – "The Tempest", "Macbeth", "Othello", but also pushing out the boundaries with Shaw's "Major Barbara", and "Captain Brassbound's Conversion" (successors to his "St Joan" of 1947) as well as "School for Scandal", "Murder in the Cathedral", "The Importance of Being Earnest", and "A Man for All Seasons". The distinguished line of producers moved on from Bertie Ricks to Ted Winter, and thence to Tim Stringer. A celebrated *OM* TV actor, one of the "Dr Who"s, Patrick Troughton, adjudicated at a Reading and Speech Competition; (in 1963, due to the snow outside, a now established area of Inter-House competition, the House Plays, made their appearance). Perhaps inspired by this *OM*'s thespian example, David Buck was launched from his Mill Hill debut to an acting – and writing – career at Cambridge, the Royal Court and the RSC, crowned by a 'roistering' Cyrano de Bergerac at the Regent's Park Open Air Theatre, and a one-man Falstaff at the Fortune, winning two BAFTA nominations for "1984" and "The Idiot": the 1989 *Times* obituary praised his *quintessential Englishness, huge humour and great tenderness*.

Although Mill Hill never sought to be a 'musical school', at this time music led the way. At one end of the spectrum, several jazz bands evolved – The GC Dixie Six, The Flat Four Stompers, and The Cool Four. At the more traditional end, Peter Hemmings had started a Choir Book in 1948, noting annual cycle tours to attend some of the country's great cathedrals; his initiation in conductorship was the first step along an impresario's career which led on from the Scottish National Opera to the LSO, the Los Angeles Opera, and the Boards of the Royal Opera and the Royal Academy of Music; he was one of Mill Hill's two 'Arts' Commanders of the Order of the British Empire, from a single year-group, 1947, in a single House, Winterstoke. There were School Choir performances at St Paul's Cathedral and the Festival Hall, initially under the cultured Hans Berge, and a revived orchestra in 1955.

Berge's death in 1956, with a Chapel service accompanied by the Amadeus Quartet, was one of the School's most moving occasions for many years. It had undertones for the wider input by the intellectual Jewish community out of Nazi oppression in pre-war Europe, described by art critic Brian Sewell in terms of particular relevance for Mill Hill: *They were, in their own way, part of the last manifestation of the Enlightenment.* Hans Berge was succeeded by the sensitive Sydney Barlow.

The other cultural field being cultivated at the same time was that of Phillip King, later Henry Moore-trained Professor of Sculpture at the Royal College of Art and from 1999 24th President of the Royal Academy of Arts; sole Millhillian mentioned in the *Oxford Companion to 20th Century Art*, he made his career through such august events as the Venice *Biennale* of 1968. (His appointment as CBE came in 1975, followed by a Retrospective at the Hayward Gallery in 1981.) Meanwhile another gap, that between the Arts and the Sciences – the 'Two Cultures' thesis – was being bridged nationally; from 1957 every Arts boy had to take an O level in General Science. A special society was later formed, under Donald Hall's aegis and at his new home in Winterstoke Gardens, for scientists to make their own crossing of that gap: he named it after the Innominate artery. The cause of the sciences had appeared to suffer a severe blow in 1955, when a fire gutted part of the Science School: out of this nettle, however, was plucked the flower of the new Biology Wing to the rear of the older building, erected in 1956 and aided by a grant of £12,000 from the Independent Fund for the Advancement of Scientific Education in Schools. As a first sign of things to come, an *OM*, Roger Coleman, gave a talk in Current Affairs in 1961, on 'Computers' or rather as it was still being spelt then, 'Computors'.

Bridging the cultural-sporting divide in a less serious way, one of the increasingly encouraging examples of Millhillian creative talent, set out in a *MHM* of 1960 to prove, under the title "Scrum-Half Shakespeare", that the great bard must have been a rugger player. Proof lay in such key quotations as those of Launcelot in "Merchant of Venice" (*Do I look like a prop?*); *The centre is not big enough* (Leontes in "A Winter's Tale"); Marina's *I never hurt a fly half as much*, in "Pericles"; or Hamlet's *I should convert on the instant*. Travel too expanded as an aspect of this broadening culture: trips to Italy in 1952, Austria in 1954, and Poland in 1961. The skiing party to Kleine Scheidegg in Switzerland in 1953 was colourfully reported, including the overheard cry of agony from one of the group, possibly not a linguist: *Oh mon leg! Mon leg! C'est broken – c'est broken!* OM Lewis Van Moppes instituted his Travel Grants in 1961, and many subsequent exploratory visits, usually by two Millhillians in tandem, were recorded.

Territorially and conceptually the most important step was the acquisition of Belmont by the Foundation in 1963 (see Appendix H), yet the focus was still mainly on the Senior School. Roy Moore retained a special love for the grounds; first of all Ridgeway Field was levelled and Memorial Field was given its layer of topsoil. At the end of 1952 there had been some tree-thinning in the copse below Top Field, to 'open up the vista of Harrow and the Hills'; in Spring the following year, the gift of J.H.Todd enabled two Blue Spruce and three Cedars to be planted by the Buckland Garden. In 1954, a 21-year lease of "Well's Field", 1.805 acres at the rear of Arrandene Paddock – a former 1st XI ground – was agreed, whilst on the other hand it was decided to sell some of the Hammers Lane field to the Linen and Woollen Drapers Cottage Homes. The "Trees" booklet was produced in 1957. The famous 'Kissing Gate' by Ridgeway was removed in 1961; in the hard winter of 1962, a limb fell off the Collinson Cedar – an ill omen for the future of the School's historic arboreal heritage: by 1998 the last of Collinson's cedars would disappear from the School's grounds.

Royal Visit and Sesquicentennial

The setting of the school was celebrated publicly with the reproduction of Dennis Flanders' drawings in November 1956 in *The Illustrated London News*, and G.F.Timpson's *"Et Virtutem"* was produced the following year. With the making of a 35mm film about life at the School, and a commentary recorded by Richard Dimbleby, now CBE, this was all part of a concerted effort aimed at the School's impending 150-year Anniversary. In the centre of this activity both temporally and symbolically, the twin events of the summer of 1957 stand out; an ILN photographic spread was devoted to Mill Hill's second royal visit, that of Her Majesty Queen Elizabeth II; it achieved international coverage. Roy Moore's eloquent description on Foundation Day, 1958, embodies the uncomplicated optimism of that time: *a day of sunshine and happiness – a young day whose tone was set by the youth and grace of the Queen.*

The occasion had been masterminded by a patient, knowledgable, but ever-anxious triumvirate of the Head Master, the Chairman of the Court, and an often underrated Mill Hill luminary, her President, the Earl of Athlone. Tortuous correspondence, guided by the School's two lines of communication with the Palace, eventuated on the day, 1 July, in a brilliant success. It was a triumph for Roy Moore, his magisterial and duly resplendent monitorial team ('tails' were still 'in', fortunately), and Mill Hill's customary behind-the-scenes staff work. A cedar was formally planted on Top Terrace, the first in a new cedar tradition. One of the monitors on the day, later a Governor himself, Roger Graham OBE, remembered the highlights with due pride, and, as a keen photographer, the School's feat of being able to present Her Majesty with Robin Watts' finished print of her arrival by the time she entered the Science Block, some 20 minutes later. The congratulatory royal comment was recalled: *It is nearly as fast as a photo-finish!*

A serious strategic purpose underlay these outward events: the vital need to launch the School's 150-year Anniversary Appeal, and at the same time to signal the fact of change and to reassert Mill Hill's pole position in the world of education, after nearly two decades of desperate struggle. It was a key moment in the School's long history, to be later emulated in the 200-year celebrations to be staged in the publication year of this History, 2006/7. £62,000 of the appeal's target of £75,000 was reached by 1959, the year which witnessed the opening of **'Era 4'** with the building of the new Art School.

The order changeth

The decade then moving to its close and the new one hard on its heels also brought with them change of another sadder kind, the passing of familiar faces. Some, like Percy McAllister, Lyle Bee and Donald Hall from their Houses, ending their long stint; only in 1959 would this be restricted to lasting 15 years or age 55, whichever was the longer. Some, like Alan Bush and Martin Meade-King, from the Housemaster to the Head Master phase in their teaching careers, Christopher Porteous via an appointment to the Civil Service Commission, or Paul Duncan to a similar role in the University system, at Loughborough; yet another –

MHS Common Room at "Cleveland", The Ridgeway, first redesign of 1956, through *OM* Ralph Tubbs CBE, architect of Festival of Britain centrepiece, Dome of Discovery, 1951. *9.i*

Mervyn Wigram – through the Housemaster mode to that related field, Her Majesty' Inspectorate. For yet others, all still members of the pre-St Bees fraternity, retirement came at last: Bertie Ricks, Warren Phillips, Tom Jackson, Frederick Cronheim, Thurston Bowring, and, at the age of 76, the CCF's extraordinary focal point, with his glass eye – RQMS "Dasher" Crouch BEM. John Morrison would also retire (temporarily) after his valiant two-term stand-in for Roy Moore. For a few this time also marked life's end; legendary figures (see **Fig.T**, Ch.XII) who spanned nearly a century – "Dieser" Hallifax, A.J.Williams, Mrs Constance Payne, (McClure's and the School's first woman teacher), "Nick" Brett James, "Hookey" Turner, Buster Brown, "Camel" McLellan, Vic Elliott. Not least were the deaths of Maurice Jacks, the Head who had returned again to open the new ATD Block; and a famous name already encountered, the longest-serving Chairman of the Governors, dying just after his 100th birthday – "Nath." Micklem QC (father of Rev. Dr Nathaniel Micklem, and grandfather of Caryl, "Nat", and "Sam").

Whilst Jacks' death early in 1964, at the age of 70, would profoundly affect the wider and older Mill Hill world, one other death had already touched not merely her family but the immediate community within both the School and the village: that of Mill Hill's 'First Lady', Muriel Moore, in September 1959. Tom Jackson wrote in the *MHM* that *her welcome to the Queen was as unpretentious as her welcome to the smallest new-boy invited to tea ... May her memory be green beside the buildings and among the grounds where she loved to walk. It was a pleasure to meet her anywhere and at any time.* Roy Moore was brought very low by this tragedy. The Court's decision to grant him a sabbatical in

Daily Herald headline– "Fire Chaps!" – fifth of Mill Hill's six conflagrations: "the vast column of smoke now towering above the building" (J.F.Adamson: Diary). Science School fire, 1957, (i) provided opportunity, with outside industrial funding, for (ii) (opposite) new Biology Wing. *9.j*

America, from January to September 1961, was compassionate and wise, and also providential, for the trip revived his spirits, and also enabled him to find a new companion to share his life, the future Mrs Lydia Moore.

Style

In any era, style is a matter both of the style of the person within, and the external style presented to the world; in this latter and lesser sense, Mill Hill styles at this time were mixed. While Reading and Speech competitions continued, and the new Queen's English dominated many activities, the vocabulary in the School was accused at one stage of verging on the gangsterish. The formality of dress for formal occasions, including the now standardised green tweed jacket, and the anomalous use of monitors' morning dress for the newly-innovated main Chapel on Sunday evenings, contrasted with a somewhat hectic informality. One monitor, secreted back into school for the morning of his appointed reading-duty in Chapel, found himself with no time other than to do so still dressed in the prized black corduroy suit and 'brothel creepers' which he had been wearing the night before during an illegal dinner in Soho – whither he and one other respected monitor had been driven by another monitor in his equally illicit, and illicitly parked, car. At the Easter Dances in 1962, a veritable harlequinade was sported: *brown checks, blue checks, chelseas, creepers, boots, tab-collars, button-down collars, thin stripes, pin stripes, coloured stripes, thick stripes, slim jeans, suede ties, ad nauseam...* as the *MHM* feelingly described the sartorial variety on show. Perhaps GC clothes were not so much making, as anticipating, the man to come.

OM Andy Mortimer recalled that behaviour during these middle to later Roy Moore years had the same uninhibited panache. A secret society was founded in the mid-1950s – RASBO, 'Royal Society for the Abolition of Bureaucratic Organisations': its activity manifested itself in the spreading of the duck-boards overnight on that holy of holies, Top Field, to form the letters of its acronym. An attempt to syphon off this surplus energy among the apparently irredeemables, 'the awkward squad', was the formation of "The Cadre", under the wing of a German master, Kirch, out of a dozen members of the Corps.

To the envy of many, this egregious group managed to win permission for a famous – indeed unique – Initiative and Endurance Test, the aim being to see which pair of boys could get furthest, and return, in 36 hours, on five shillings, whilst wearing Corps uniform. One pair finished up on Bournemouth beach, enjoying the local scene and scenery, under escort by the Military Police;

THE NEW BIOLOGY WING
(Drawn by B. Dunglinson)

another couple got down a coal mine in Wrexham, while another duo ascended Snowdon; another pair set sail on a trawler from Grimsby, and had to be searched for; another team got as far as Le Touquet; the winners, led by the Corps' Under Officer, got that much further and strode up to the sentry on duty at Edinburgh Castle, demanding his signature on their form to authenticate their arrival: he duly complied, impressed by military bearing when he saw it. It was a lovely romp; it was not repeated. However, 'The Cadre' evolved as a much envied super-Corps, with macho WOSB physical tests, into the 21st century.

Prelude to new ideas

The newly-returned Head Master's spirits needed some strengthening, to face the decade now unfolding. During his absence the Second Master, John Morrison, presided as Acting Head, supported by Secretary Betty Dove, knowing that he enjoyed those priceless assets – the backing of the School, the Governors, and the OMC. He also enjoyed another less official asset, a cynical, unerring insight into the mind of the eternal boy and the ability to inspire proper fear in consequence.

OM David Brown, later a successful Management Consultant in the US, recalled how the YFC in Farm Lane was the centre for all sorts of illegality by some of his fellow future entrepreneurs, ranging from smoking to selling the farm's eggs. Mog's apparent attempts to catch his villains red-handed would be foiled by his trusty, and fortunately noisy, dog, which would always precede him along the track, alerting the Young Farmers to approaching authority. There was no period in Morrison's long career in Mill Hill's service when he would benefit more from the reputation underlying the Latin tag which he had chalked over his door at St Bees and thereafter made his own, and which generations of boys remembered with affection: *"Oderint dum metuant"* – 'let them hate me as long as they fear me'. After several expulsions, Mog handed back the kind of tight ship that Roy Moore liked to think that he too had run. Mill Hill has been fortunate throughout her history in generating in the No. 2 role half a dozen senior Masters, from A.J.Williams in 1922 and Vic Elliott in 1940, to Allan Phimester and later William Winfield, who would be capable of stepping into the breech when circumstances required, holding the ship steady at its critical moments.

Not that the start of the 1960s was a time of crisis, so much as one of impending, pent-up challenge. With Roy Moore's resumption of the Head Master's chair, a number of forces both revolutionary and devolutionary were evolving at Mill Hill. Already in the late 1950s, the House Notes were reflecting some of these trends, showing that the words of Sir Frederic Sellers in 1957 had not fallen on stony ground. In 1958 a new area of privileges had been ushered in – more freedom for Upper VI Formers in terms of bounds, and visits to cinemas, regardless of prefectorial status. BB, by 1963 the reputed home of what were now *those anti-establishment types*, had already for at least seven years freed itself of its past; the Scrutton House Notes in 1962 claimed that *We no longer "persuade" unwary juniors to do boxing and cross-country.*

Fags were now doing work '*voluntarily*', not least in Murray, at last further re-located, via the former rifle-range, in its *"wooden shack"* on Farm Road. In this sole but increasingly important Day House, morning Chapel and 4 p.m. roll call had become mandatory in 1951. By the late 1950s – for the first time no longer the smallest House, a significant milestone – it could boast of its first full-term senior monitor, and its first Senior House rugger shield in 1960; House Debating and Playreading Societies and a House Magazine also evolved.

A new spirit seemed to be abroad, one which questioned established practice. A survey in 1959 (partly repeated in 1962) showed that if given freedom of choice, 72 per cent (64 per cent) would not regularly attend the CCF, or Scouts, whilst 23 per cent would not go to Chapel (even if a resolute 47 per cent would still opt to attend three times a week). Two questions in 1962 – (a) Do you agree with co-education in principle; (b) Would you agree with it at this school? produced predictably 'NIMBY' responses – 75 per cent said 'Yes' to Q(a), and 58 per cent 'No' to Q(b). This ambivalence was reflected in the *MHM* Editorial for December 1963, which commented that 'however rebellious we are in our behaviour, we tend to conform very strictly in our ideas'. Nevertheless views that would have appeared sacrilegious a generation earlier were now openly discussable, and cartoons and comments in the *MHM* reflected this growing anti-'Establishment' scepticism, perhaps a contemporary lay expression of the ancient 'nonconformity'.

"Well really, Roy! Since when has Buckingham Palace come before rugger?"

1959: traditional Team Card, at an end-of-term MHS sports dinner for Head Master Roy Moore, satirises his being made a CBE (awarded for his work for RAF benevolent causes). *9.k*

Externally this could well be perceived, in the Macmillan sense, as a 'good' epoch for what was now, from 1963 onwards, a single integrated Foundation. It had gained excellent publicity through an ATV programme in the autumn of 1960 on the Public Schools, which had brought the School much benefit; Mill Hill was featured with Winchester, Harrow, and Bloxham, and Roy Moore was interviewed. It had enjoyed the filming of "Now and Forever", featuring Jeanette Scott at 'Millingham School for Girls'; the Flanders drawings had appeared in the *ILN*; the Royal Visit had won international column inches; the film about Alford House, "We Are the Lambeth Boys", became a classic. Intellectually, albeit at one remove, as Roy Moore proclaimed it on Foundation Day 1963, came that *feather of the highest quality in any school's cap*, the award of a Nobel Prize – to Francis Crick. The *MHM* complained that whereas McClure's Knighthood had won an extra week's holiday in 1913, and Lord Brain's recent accession to the peerage an extra day, the School did not manage to celebrate this great moment; a further 36 years needed first to ensue (see Ch.XII).

There was one untoward media event: the publication of a Press story in the *Daily Mail* in June 1961 that insinuated that there was an anti-semitic aspect to Mill Hill. This was hotly contested and well refuted; with a wider 'PR' perspective, this potentially negative item was more than offset by the excellent publicity achieved through other events. Its untruth was daily demonstrable in the increasingly mixed and religiously tolerant life of the School, and in the wide range of beliefs that would be discussed, under the guiding hand of a new Lancastrian and Presbyterian chaplain, Rev. Henry Starkey. A theology student at Fitzwilliam House during the war (where he first encountered Dr Whale in declamatory mode at Cheshunt College), his unadvertised 'word-of-mouth' selection in 1957 was symptomatic of the historical sphere of influence still at that time asserted by the United Reform Church over the School's affairs. One of Mill Hill's 'characters' in his own right, Henry became, however, an important ecumenical force, and would even, two decades ahead of his time, favour the idea of an Anglican in-house chaplain succeeding him, when he decided to resume his wider ministry in 1981. Although also holding pacifist views, he nevertheless took a full part in the Remembrance Day services in November, unlike his predecessor.

He recalled several disparate events of this, the longest 20th-century chaplaincy – some straying into the time of later chapters: the welcoming of a new master under their roof at St Bees House in 1971, characterised as *"quiet, efficient and gracious"* – the young William Winfield; the growth under his leadership of the 17th Hendon Scout Troop from 30 to 100; the instigation of two mini-reforms – the widening of the steps leading up from the Quad to the Chapel precinct, to prevent the 'Line-up' bottle-neck by the Fives Courts, and the omission of potentially embarrassing middle names from the now annual Valedictory services; and on a lighter note, the

Deutschland und die Welt   Frkfrter Allg. Zeit   Mittwoch, 3. Juli 1957 / Nr. 150 / Seite 5

Im Cutaway eskortierten Schüler der Londoner Mill Hill School ihre Königin, als diese zur Feier der 150. Wiederkehr des Gründungstages der exklusiven Erziehungsanstalt einen Besuch abstattete und das Gelände der Schule besichtigte. (dpa)

The royal visit achieved worldwide coverage: rare cutting from Germany's leading paper , the *'FAZ'*, describes the *'Cutaway'* monitors of an *'exclusiven Erziehungsanstalt'*. 9.l

discovering, during standard pre-Chapel tours, of the Eagle Lectern perched on the Vestry roof and the disappearance of all hymn books from the pews – both pranks quickly solved before Chapel began.

In a wider management sense, the School had worries. The post-war population 'bulge' was pressurising beds and numbers. Academic entry standards were variable, and in particular those at Belmont, just celebrating its 50th anniversary in 1962 during what proved to be the concluding years of Arthur Roberts' tenure; Belmont boys were failing to get into the Main School at Common Entrance. There was a tension between the carefully constructed, conservative 'School Rules', and those for whom the rules were created. The balance between Day and Boarding numbers was beginning to create 40 years of polarity on this 'heartland' issue; Governor Lord Ogmore's visionary, and in hindsight modest, idea, '400 Boarders to 100 Day boys' made Roy Moore unhappy: the soon-to-be familiar argument was that it would mystically *change the character of the school*. Yet whether the Mill Hill heartland liked it or not, change was in the offing, for a now publicly dignified Roy Moore, Fellow of King's, appointed CBE in the Birthday Honours of 1962 by the monarch he had welcomed to Mill Hill five years before. There was a spate of critical literature about the Public Schools: they were now news, as was, once again, Mill Hill. The restored and re-energised Head Master and the School would have to respond to the challenges implicitly presented by Mill Hill's reacquired, hard-won, heightened prominence in the public eye.

Sources for Ch.IX include: C/Ts Mtngs 1950-1; Sutcliffe, *op cit*; H.Osborne, ed, *Oxford Companion, 20th Century Art* (Oxfd, 1981); B.Sewell, *Evening Standard* 2.vii.2002, 'Gift of the immigrants'.

Background – Korean War/ National Service/ Armed Forces/ Suez: PRO, Kew, London – PREM 8/11; ED 135/10, Memos. for Inspectors: NS 513; 522, 31.vii.50 (Emergency Feeding in Time of War); 523, 2.viii.50 (Civil Defence Zones); 527; 537 (School Shelters); 135/11, NS 556, 11.vii.51 (Civil Defence: Evacuation); NS 567; Fd Marshall Lord Carver, *Britain's Army in the 20th Century* (1998); T.Hopkinson ed, *Picture Post 1938-50*, (1970); *MHM*, 1951; T.M.Rothery [1946-51], 'Reminiscences of a NS Subaltern, 1952-3', *The Iron Duke', Regimental Magazine, The Duke of Wellington's*, (Spring 1998); K.Kyle, *Suez* (1991), 136, 240/1, 350; A.Gorst & L.Johnman, *The Suez Crisis* (1997); P.Cradock, *Know Your Enemy...* (2002), Ch.5 'Korean War'; corr/ dscns with Lt Col A.M.Macfarlane [1944-8]; Lt Col J.M.Hewson MC [1946-50]; Brig J.H.Milburn [1946-51]; Prof S.C.Holt [1948-54]; Capt P.J.E.Cheshire RN [1948-53]; Brig J.T.Holmes MC [1963-8].

Roy Moore era: *Times*, 6.i.1992; Heward, *op cit*; Survey by Opinion Leader Research for NCH Action for Children, 1997, *Guardian*, 22.ix.1997; *ILN* November 1956; *RA Journal*

Mar 2000; MHS Prestige Lecture, 7.iii.2000, A.M.Fitzjohn [1958-63]; *Trees* 1957 (jointly produced by MHS Art Club, & Natural History & Printing Societies) #; R.Moore pprs #, & dscns with Dr John Moore; dscns with A/Ms Donald Hall, Tony Turnbull Paul Hodgson, Alec Robertson, Ted Winter, Rev. Henry Starkey; HMs' Secretaries Mrs Sonia Gribble (née West) & Betty Dove; Hon Mrs Brenda Robbins; R.Aye Maung, D.W.Rodda, R.A.Stroud [1945-50]; M.D.Henderson [1946-50]; M.O.T.Baldwin [1947-52]; D.A.B.Brown [1956-61]; P.H.J.Goldman [1963-7]; G.M.R.Graham [1952-7]; R.Marshall-Andrews [1957-62]; A.S.Mortimer [1957-61]; J.M.Phillips [1959-64]; T.D.Phillips [1954-60]; W.Skinner [1949-55]; Obits, D.K.R.Buck [1947-52], d.27.i.1988. Excerpt from Adamson Diary, #, thanks to D.Compston [1952-5].

Prof.P.King PRA; see R.Berthoud, *The Life of Henry Moore* (Faber & Faber, 1987) 281-82: 'another young sculptor who was to achieve a brilliant career... (Philip King)'.

Sport: ref M.W.Corby [1953-8], *Sunday Times* '1000 Makers of [world's] Sport', and "Best All-round Amateur Sportsman", 1974; (59 Hockey caps, 98 Internationals for Britain & England; 34 Squash Internationals).

Other *OM* references: J.F.Adamson [1952-7]; Beth Baker [1973-5]; H.B.Bangham [1970-5]; J.A.L.Borgars [1959-63]; W.R.Brain

[1908-13]; A.J.Breeze [1947-53]; P.R.Clifford [1926-32]; D.A.Chamberlain, R.H.L.Coleman [1945-50]; A.B.Cowing [1951-6]; F.H.C.Crick [1930-4]; F.B.Dalton [1815-9]; C.S.Darke [1926-31]; F.R.Dimbleby [1927-31]; A.R.Dyer [1954-9]; E.Errington [1913-4]; N.S.Farrow [1927-30]; A.C.Fenner [1945-50]; A.M.Flutter [1946-50]; N.C.Garratt [1924-7]; G.A.Goyder [1922-5]; I.F.J.Hardie [1948-53]; A.W.Hawes [1907-9]; 'Times' obit, 7.i.2002, P.W.Hemmings [1947-52]; P.Holman [1906-9] ; A.F.Holt [1928-31]; O.C.Holt [1944-9] P.D.Howard [1922-8]; R.A.Hudgell [1954-9]; P.King [1947-52]; A.T.Lawrence [1854-9]; J.A.Leavey [1929-33]; M.A.Melsom [1948-53]; Micklem family 'Nath.' [1866-8, '70-1]; T.C. [1939-43]; "Nat" [1944-7]; "Sam" A.M. [1946-51]; N.L.Millard [1920-4]; T.D.Phillips [1954-60]; R.E.S.Pye-Smith [1935-9]; W.R.Ramsay [1912-8]; A.W.Ramsay [1944-9]; G.Rees-Williams, Lord Ogmore [1944-6]; A.E.R.Roberts [1921-6]; J.Roberts [1945-50]; S.G.Rowlandson [1919-26]; C.B.Salmon [1917-22]; R.D. Scott [1917-9]; T.E.Scrutton [1870-3]; Sellers – M.M. [1936-41], P.M. [1942-6]; J.A.Selway [1942-6]; P.G.Stibbe [1935-9]; T.N.Talfourd [1807-10]; G.F.Timpson [1906-10]; J.H.Todd []1960-4]; P.D.Troughton [1933-7]; R.S.Tubbs [1925-30]; L.Van Moppes [1914-22]; O.D.Viney [1900-3]; D.W.Wade [1918-20]; P.O.Walker [1916-20]; T.D.Walker [1926-9]; P.R.Warrall [1955-9]; R.Watts [1953-8]; M.C.L.Wilkins [1947-50]; J.E.Williams [1945-9].

Michael Hart CBE, MHS Head Master, 1967-74: presentation portrait set against background of his beloved Dent. *10.a*

The MHS south-west facade. *10.b*

"There Must be Change!"

Facing up to the problems of the sixties and seventies

"...far from the straight and narrow paths of our founders and predecessors ...
boys is just the same as ever":
Michael Hart's address, Foundation Day 1973.

If the Second World War was the major force for change in the evolution of the Public Schools, with seismic effects lasting far into the future, the decade from the mid-1960s through to the mid-1970s should be seen as one of the most decisive times for Mill Hill's own internal response to those changes. It is no coincidence that this phase of the History is all-but identical with the period characterised by Westminster's John Rae as the 'Public School Revolution'. Harking back to medieval times, Dr Rae sought a modern equivalent, when this revolution might be said to have started, to that turning point in British history, the day of the 'Tennis Court Oath'. Even if in Mill Hill's context too no one date can be identified, nevertheless there is a clear month of departure from the traditional way of doing things: it is, surprisingly, November 1963.

That was the month in which the Court of Governors received Roy Moore's announcement of two new committees of reform: one, with Edward Stanham, Donald Hall, Oliver Wait, and Tim Stringer, to investigate the organisation of the School; the second, with Allan Phimester, Keith Rutter, Chris Sutcliffe and, again, the MCR's veteran head, Donald Hall, to examine – hopefully with an equally fresh eye – the curriculum. Thus the three years 1964-1967 carried with them an unexpected leaving gift from the Head who was soon to announce his retirement: although this move may not have made overmuch immediate impact on some of the more critical members of the School's MCR, it was to prove the start of the process of change to bring Mill Hill, like her fellow schools, fully into the 'post-1945' world.

The Cuban Missile crisis, when President Kennedy and Chairman Krushchev stared into the face of a third, and nuclear, world war, and both 'blinked' sufficiently to avert it, was just receding – for the time being – from the public gaze; the Iron Curtain still divided Europe, with the Communist invasion of Czechoslovakia yet to come; Vietnam was about to emerge as the new East-West battleground, and a unifying cause for youth world-wide. It was certainly not a world at peace, but at least the British economy was beginning to recover from the cataclysm of 20 years before; people could start to think about making their world better, even if it could not yet be made safer.

At the Court in March 1964, the findings were presented. Other more significant changes would follow under subsequent regimes, but this was the turning point. 'Fagging', that formidable custom so deeply enmeshed in the whole Public School system, originating in a dearth of servants and redolent of the personalised service of medieval times, was to be replaced by 'House Duties'. The built-in *over-seriousness* about games, virtually unchallenged since its emergence into cult status in the late Victorian era, was henceforth to be *kept in the right proportion*, to achieve greater emphasis on *sportsmanship*; the valuable spirit of competitiveness would thereby be broadened to cover other fields of activity, such as drama, with wonderfully creative implications for the future. There was to be more Science and more English, and various other curricular changes that the times required. In October that year, Roy Moore also announced a new scheme for uniform. By way of perspective, although three years earlier Ellesmere College had already abolished the prefects' power to beat, some 75 per cent of the Boarding schools in the 1966 Kalton survey for the ISJC still allowed it, and in about 66 per cent, fagging still held sway.

The need for change and adaptation was predicated upon what Dr John Rae has well described as *the educational ferment of the sixties... a period of extraordinary restlessness... in the independent schools*. It was reinforced by the first of two major external factors: the return to power of Harold Wilson's Labour Party in the 1964 General Election, bringing with it in its electoral mandate a major threat to the future of the independent schools.

On 31 March 1965, after 20 successful, even crucial, years, the historic but much diminished Middlesex Scheme came to an end with the disbanding of Middlesex County Council, under the new Labour Government's reforms. It was to continue on an individual Council basis as the 'Borough Boarders' scheme, deprived of the leftward-facing Hounslow and Haringey, but keeping in Sudbury and Ashford (henceforth technically in Surrey), and also parts of Barnet's area which were now in Hertfordshire. Dr Butcher, of the Barnet LEA, took on the coordinating role for the nine boroughs, thus beginning a fruitful era of cooperation between the School and her own LEA. In truncated form, the Scheme would last 12 more years, until 1977, with Enfield the final participating Borough. The Scheme had its own impact on the visits to be paid by the Newsom Commission in the late 1960s.

At the Meeting of Life Governors on 24 June 1966, with regard to that Commission's newly-revealed Report, Roy Moore sent a warning salvo across the bows of his assembled audience: *I am sure there must be change, and that it must be to the advantage both of the independent schools, and of all education in England*. To the same audience at his farewell meeting, on 15 June 1967, he fired his parting shot, with characteristically humorous self-deprecation – *we must change our ideas from the days when we thought of Oxford and Cambridge, with the possible addition of London, as the only Universities of value*. One aspect of that change which he alluded to was highlighted in an article in *The Times* that year, about the advances that Mill Hill was making, under the guidance of Chris Wormell, in the teaching of the New Maths, and the building of the School's first computer, using 'punched card techniques'; later, a single 'state-of-the-art' Elliott 803 would be bought.

In October a Court Sub-Committee set about selecting a new Head, following Roy Moore's announced wish to retire a year earlier than the age which his contract suggested. In July 1967, the final Report on his 16 years was presented with *mixed feelings... Mill Hill has become part of my life*. On a sunny morning in August, unseen by the boys, but remembered by many staff, and by his Secretary, Betty Dove, a tearful group witnessed a final exodus from "The Grove", as Roy, with Lydia and their adored retriever, Bruce, set off for the new phase in his career, as a Lecturer at the University of California, Berkeley. A long, but royally blessed chapter was closing.

Producer of pearls

A British institution almost as conservative as a British Public School – the Foreign Office – was the subject of a BBC2 programme on 4 January 1998. It included an aphorism voiced by Lord Renwick: *The FO regards the arrival of each new minister as an oyster regards the arrival of a grain of sand... The intrusion of an irritant with a very low statistical probability of ever producing a pearl.* Although no member of the hitherto genial and congenial Mill Hill MCR had ever expressed such cynicism, most long-established staffs secretly harbour a similar sentiment about any new Head Master.

The advertisement was still concerned to make genuflection to Mill Hill's origins: *The School has a strong Nonconformist tradition, but is interdenominational* [the McClurean word] *and the Head need not be a Nonconformist.* By this stage in Mill Hill's evolution, however, the reference to 'Nonconformity' was in the nature of unconscious code for the ever-relevant need for the functions of 'questioning and challenging' – desirable, indeed enlightened, but in no way theological qualities. The Court selected a man of British birth and German blood (who still pronounced 'hundred' as *hundert*): 'and', not 'but', was a vital distinction. Boys spoke of Michael Hart's arrival in September 1967 as a *breath of fresh air*, that same priceless commodity which he later sought to breathe into the now predominantly urban lungs of Millhillians and Belmontians, through the Dent Field Study Centre in the Yorkshire Dales. In the words of Alec Robertson, *he went to work with a will*; to some stuffier members within the oyster of the Mill Hill MCR his advent would also prove a salutary internal irritant, as he began to introduce civilising touches to a still hierarchical community: in a sense, these matched the external irritants that were then assailing western society in general, and all institutions of education in particular.

The boys' compliment was no doubt in many ways unfair to his older predecessor, but it was timely: it was Michael Hart's destiny to win the first of his three Headmasterly posts in the decade of Lindsay Anderson's satirical film "If", written by two Old Tonbridgians. What fellow Head Master John Rae dubbed *the guerrilla war*, personified in "Danny the Red" (Daniel Cohn-Benditt) and Tariq Ali, seemed to threaten the whole basis of the West's educational establishment, especially in England and France. A new Head taking over any school at this time was either going to fail miserably, or work with the changing mood and succeed spectacularly. This was the era when the 'Generation Gap' was being discovered – or more correctly, rediscovered: it had always existed, but never quite so noticeably, or so internationally, as in the late 1960s.

His was also the decade that saw the start of a second, far more insidious, external event: the Saudi-led world oil price-rise of 1973, which as John Rae has written, *first doubled and then almost trebled the fees in independent schools*; costs (including heating oil itself) would all suddenly become 25 per cent dearer, at a time when under the prevailing difficult business conditions parental incomes were marking time. Macro-problems notwithstanding, there now stepped confidently onto the stage a 39-year-old exponent of what Michael Hart himself described as the *vice-roy's* role in the School, a modest if somewhat tongue-in-cheek portrayal of the Head's relationship with the Chairman of Governors. His fruitful partnership, first with Sir

Frederic Sellers, and then, from March 1968, with his equally celebrated successor, former Chief of the Air Staff at the time of Suez, Marshal of the Royal Air Force Sir Dermot Boyle, was to produce great things for Mill Hill over the succeeding seven fast-moving years. With an energetic spring in his step, Michael at 6ft 3ins was that much taller than Roy. According to Alec Robertson, his study door, like that of the famous Windmill Theatre, *never closed*. For Ted Winter, he was *hyperactive ... with the courage and imagination to face and execute the reforms he thought necessary*. This was a man of the new Europe, the first Head of non-British parentage and with an American wife, Dabney, to complete the new international flavour. (She was in fact the second successive American to assume the role of the School's first lady.)

Michael was a born teacher, who also regarded the job of Head Master as a natural avenue for his organisational skills. While respecting Mill Hill's older traditions where they matched the new age that now seemed to be dawning, in the wake of 'Flower Power', he did not preserve continuity for its own sake, in the way that had seemed right for many of his predecessors. He was unpompous, accessible, inclined to use christian names – initially to the MCR's amusement – and no respecter of persons, even, if necessary, of himself: what previous Head could have empowered and enjoyed such apparently comical but in reality affectionate cartoons of himself and his staff as those which appeared in the redesigned *MHM* shortly after his arrival? Although his 'new look' publication did carry Priestley's updated, elegantly nostalgic 1845 etching of the School (minus ducks on "Doctor's Pond"), Michael did not look backwards. He made no secret of not having studied the time of the previous leader at the helm – John Whale – who had first made a seven-year stint respectable: respectable in the sense of its being long enough to gain the confidence of the Governors and to see through the effects of his own changes of direction, whilst also reaching beyond the last of the five-year cohorts entered by the preceding regime – the 'Shadow' effect. In the view of a future fellow HMC Head, *there was a sense of direction and a wider view of the possibilities of education, and the experience pupils should be open to*. For his own successor, he was *an omniscient, indefatigable and good man*.

The war-conditioned years were behind him, even if they were not yet fully behind Mill Hill. By 1967, one third of the staff of 30, serving a School of about 450 boys (a ratio of 6.5 per cent), was still of the seasoned wartime vintage – two even of the pre-war time; for masters conditioned to fight Germany, such as Michael Brown, it was not easy. Many of the others had done National Service. Within his era such notable pre-war and post-war figures as Tom Jackson, Percy McAllister – and RQMS Dasher Crouch – would reach the end of their long, affectionately-remembered lives of service, and two loyal and long-serving stalwarts, Edward Stanham and Donald Hall, would be retiring. For Michael Hart, it had been a war with especially sombre overtones, giving a sharp edge to his historian's respect for freedom of thought. His father "unwisely" electing to take the family back to Germany in 1939, Michael had to grow up under the Nazi regime, surviving as best he could, with a liberal Protestant background, first in the former Huguenot *Collège Français* in Berlin, and then Boarding in the *Landerziehungsheim Schondorf*, near Augsburg, Bavaria, finally going 'underground' when a Nazi Head was appointed in 1944. His nickname, "Otto" – which he shared with an eminent British historian, and which came with him from his previous school – was used rather admiringly, ('and' not 'but'), in no way indicative of any perceived stereotyped 'teutonic' characteristics.

We came alive under his Headship, which was achieved with enthusiasm and courtesy, wrote Alec Robertson, who recalled Michael calling by at midnight outside his study window, *for a chat*: it lasted until 2.00 a.m. He was the first Head to bring to bear upon Mill Hill the perspective of two of the older 'Establishment' Public Schools, Sherborne, and then – one of the Ancients – Shrewsbury; there he had been a highly respected Housemaster of School House, and Head of History, having gained First Class Honours in History as an Exhibitioner at Keble, Oxford. When comparisons were made with a range of other Public Schools, they were not, however, drawn with these two but usually (and geographically) with Merchant Taylor's, St Paul's, Felsted, Haileybury, Aldenham, The Leys and Epsom. Belmont invariably looked to St Paul's Colet Court and UCS Junior School. Later, when 'The Friends of Mill Hill' was being set up, the model compared was not with a competing boys' school, but that operated by one of Mill Hill's familiar corresponding girls' schools, Queenswood, yet another sign of things to come.

Irreverent sign-of-the-times *MHM* cartoon of academic staff: Rev. Henry Starkey, Michael Hart, Paul Hodgson, (later Governor) and Alan ("Dylan") Prosser-Harries. *10.c*

Change-agent

The here and now were what mattered. As Roy Moore had warned, Mill Hill's future called for change: Michael Hart, with the more flexible of his older staff and the young graduates he started to appoint as new-style House Tutors, was the change-agent. The tributes to him in the Life Governors' 1975 Report would say that he had made an *outstanding contribution to almost every aspect of the School's activities*. He was able to do this with what he praised as the *generous, loyal and expert collaboration of so many colleagues*. One example of this lay in one of Mill Hill's traditionally strong areas: Maths master Chris Wormell had firmly positioned the School within the new age, through the creation of a Computer Room in the former Tuck Shop and through study-visits at the Computer Centre at Hatfield College, as well as by authorship: *Mathematics through Geometry* made an impact on maths teaching at that time.

Although deeper internal and external forces were now at work, challenging Mill Hill as never before, in terms of territorial changes Michael Hart's time was blessed as no other Head's had been since the days of McClure, (**Era 6**). This resulted from one of his earliest measures, a new funding Appeal, to offset one of the Dissenters Grammar School's chronic, and endemic, problems – under-endowment. On 19 March 1968, a mere six months after taking office, the new broom swept in the fund-raising firm of Hooker Craigmyle. When they had done their stint, the Appeal was grasped by Paul Hodgson (appointed to be a reforming Housemaster for a now too traditionalist Ridgeway, where a boy Head of House seemed to take precedence over an adult House Tutor). However, as a letter from a loyal *OM*, Dr John Mungavin, emphasised, it raised some major issues: surviving in the past by a *capacity to change*, should Mill Hill not *develop in the '70s as a big London day school like St Paul's, UCS, Dulwich etc…*? Would *OMs'* sons still get in on grounds other than CE scores?: *Mill Hill's strength… was her old boys. Plainly this depends for continuity on father-to-son connections.*

Notwithstanding realistic Millhillian fears about co-ed trends, and also about what was in effect the passing of 'the family school', the £180,000 fund created a first grass-covered Quad in the car park, centring on a VI Form Centre – a *transition to higher education* – with to the north-east the existing Art Block. Above all, whilst having devoted his life to Boarding schools, Michael Hart did have that perspicacity promoted by Mungavin – to create the first purpose-built Day House.

The new Quad also provided a more accessible site for a slab of Rennie's grey granite London Bridge of 1832 (see Ch.II), which a Millhillian member of the City of London Corporation, Ivan Luckin, had marketed, as the *'world's largest antique'*, to Lake Havasu City, USA, in 1968

1973: (i) VI Form Centre & new Day Houses framing second Quad, the future Stoa, product of the 1970 Appeal; (ii) (above) topically re-designed interior of 'Cafe 6', outcome of the appointment of two VI Form Directors (see Ch.XII). 10.d

for its new theme park; (Americans assumed it was the more famous cantilevered Tower Bridge). Funded too were a new Belmont classroom, and carrels and study-bedrooms in the main School. Even in 1968, some historically-minded Governors enquired whether the School's dissenting Founders could feature in the Appeal: the topical judgment was that it would be difficult to do so *in any concrete way*.

In Dentdale, built not of concrete or brick but stone, and five hours' drive beyond the School's less and less confining bounds, was an 18th-century cottage ("Batty's Grocery Store"). Funded by a group of Yorkshire *OMs*, after an initiative in Spring 1970 by David Franklin and David Bromehead, one of the Junior School's leading young masters, who also helped finance the scheme, the aim was to introduce boys, most of whose background was now entirely suburban, *to all aspects of country life*. For 32 years, 1972 to 2004, this was Mill Hill's Field Studies and Outdoor Pursuits centre, a project so close to his heart that it would form the background to the official Hart portrait. Thousands of Foundation pupils, staff, *OMs* and other invited groups went on to enjoy its tranquillity – despite cobblestones – for Scouting and CCF field exercises, scientific studies on Malham Moor, classical explorations of Hadrian's Wall, cricket and rugger fixtures, Lyke Wake Walks, or general relaxation. Dent also had the deliberate covert benefit of continuing to try to assert Mill Mill's historic national catchment area, whilst all trends were towards a narrower, locality-based intake. At one point, the project encountered some local environmentalist resistance, voiced through the *Yorkshire Post*. This elicited a typical Hart characteristic: he went up personally to make the School's 'PR' case, and won the local community over. The freehold would be bought in 1980. Dent's visitors, still by definition *off-comers*, were welcomed as no longer mere *'Erdwicks off the fells* by the indigenous *Dentonians*; (see later policy change: Ch.XII).

That same refreshing 'upfrontness' would surface in other contexts. Meetings were put in train with key 'constituencies': with parents of New Boys (leading to the first Parents Forum in 1971), and with all First Year Boys themselves. The successful Quinquennial Reunions with five-year cadres of *OMs* were also initiated. Likewise in 1974 the Head Master put the School's point of view about a set of proposed new houses in Wills Grove to a special meeting of the Mill Hill Preservation Society. This touch was applied notably to the School's underinvested relationship with its core market, the Prep School 'feeder' system. Michael organised visits to and from Prep School Heads, enabling them to run two of their annual conferences at Mill Hill. As he himself acknowledged, the results may only have been qualitative – many potential scholarship winners were still drifting to the London Day Schools which had by this time established a marked head of academic steam; there was as yet no repair to the intellectual gap widening with the continuing decline in boroughs subscribing for the 'BBP' Scheme.

Quantitatively, more boys started to opt for Mill Hill at age 12/13 from a wider range of Prep Schools, which became listed in the *Magazine's* Salvete notices, a nice 'PR' touch again, although Prep School provenance could also signify a Middlesex/ 'Nine Boroughs' Boarder. There was now entry at the transition ages of 11+ or 12+ as well, enabling worried parents to opt out of the patchy State comprehensive system, or boys like Tom Jenkins to transfer to Boarding status after a year at City of London. Some boys went to another of Michael's innovations – or rather, after a 50-year gap, reversions – a Form III, for some 13 to 20 boys; however, the shades of Rooker Roberts need not have worried. By now this was a more benign, small-boy-friendly Mill Hill than the bullying regime he had witnessed at the end of the previous century, and which was the motivation for his founding of Belmont in 1912. As a by-product, over the 15 years 1968 through 1982, some 125 boys like Tom did a six-year stint, 15 put in seven years. Others went to Belmont for two years. Tom Jenkins, like his elder brother Simon, was a son of the Presbyterian manse; he was enabled by the libertarian regime of these years to adopt a happily sceptical, radical stance while at Mill Hill, becoming Chairman of the School Council, albeit also No 2 in the relaxed Winterstoke of the Allan Phimester/ Chris Sutcliffe era: not quite as radical as the boy who turned down a prefectorial appointment on the ground that he had not been consulted. Another feature of the 1968-82 Rolls was the decline in the presence of children of *OM*s – 114 (6 per cent) out of 1,790 entries; some 16 of these were the offspring of erstwhile Middlesex boys. The Rolls also record six more of their shortest, and also some of their most distinguished, surnames – Ng, Yu, Lo, Ho, Ko, and the musician Winston Ku – harking back to pupils Lu and On of 60 years before.

This younger and, on his own admission, impatient Head displayed the same directness in relation to another of the issues of the time: drugs, principally then cannabis, which he saw as the top of the ladder, smoking being the bottom rung. Expelling two implicated pupils, he also managed to secure the co-operation of the editor of the local newspaper, the *Hendon, Finchley and Edgware Times*, ensuring minimal publicity. As opposed to the breaking of technical rules, such as Bounds, the worst behavioural deviations that his predecessors had had to confront were occasional outbreaks of theft, vandalism, lying and its counterpart – 'not owning up' – or the immemorial incidence of drinking. Of the isolated but well-nigh inevitable adolescent homosexual attractions – "pashes" in the language of Mill Hill and some other schools – which arise under certain conditions when a single sex is cooped up together for long stretches of time, he observed in 1968 in *Conference* on 'The Boarding House as a Community': *there are widespread and often intense sentimental attractions between boys*. In contrast to drugs, his views on sexual misdemeanours were *more elastic*.

'Mill Hill School Cottage',
Dent Country Activities
Centre, Cumbria, 1972-2004,
brainchild of Yorkshire *OMs*
Joe Fox, Philip Walker
and others. *10.e*

Caring for the total individual

This psychological understanding of the total individual, not just for a boy's position as defined by the School's system, was evidenced in Michael Hart's being the first Head to institute a counselling function, through a psychiatrist, Dr Murray Cox, a Belmont parent, at the London Hospital, who also served Christ's Hospital. He was the first to enunciate the concept of pastoral care, which has now matured into a major factor within the School's life. He sought to make more widely available the skills of his innovative Chaplain, Rev. Henry Starkey, famed for sermons such as one which Simon Long recalled: kicking over a bucket of water in the Chapel, which he had personally carried that morning round the grounds the same distance needed to obtain it in middle Africa. Reflecting this *person-based* orientation, boys would even seek audience with the Head himself, a practice which would sometimes cut across a previous ruling, e.g. on hair-length by the Ridgeway Housemaster and highly vocal member of the then 'politically' powerful 'Millers' cricket team, Michael Brown.

As another aspect of this theme, Career Counselling would be developed by 1968 as a 'major department within the School', serving all boys from entry to leaving. When the VI Form Centre was built, a room was set aside for Careers. The OMC played a pioneering role in this process: the Hon Secretary of the OMC Town Club had invented the idea of the *OMs'* Careers Forum during Roy Moore's time. Groups of VI Formers would come up to Whitehall Court for an evening's discussion with younger *OM* members of various professions and business fields, gaining the otherwise difficult sense of what such career paths actually 'felt' like. A dozen and – for a Public School then – rather unfashionable thematic areas were covered, from Selling to Engineering. Both R.M. and his successor were happy to praise this venture in speeches on Foundation Day and in Reports to the Court, and Michael Hart, true to form, attended the first meeting held during his time. They were abandoned in 1970 for a 'continuous assessment and advisory service', but they constituted one more example of the way the OMC has been able to play a relevant, proactive part in the School's evolution, whenever required.

A European 'USP'

Michael Hart's visionary, if – by 20 years – too optimistic European enthusiasm, aided by Michael Brown, now as Head of Modern Languages, and in due course also his no. 2, William Winfield, led to the creation of the first school exchanges, and in 1971/2 of one of Mill Hill's most notable educational 'USP's – a 'unique selling proposition'. This was the *Section Bilingue*, named after the wording of the *baccalauréat*, the scheme for the part teaching of Geography or History at IV/V Form level entirely in the French language. This was indeed an innovation, listened to quizzically by the Court, but which won much acclaim in HMC circles: it was not only 'unique' among that membership, but it was also a 'proposition' that seemed to make sense in an economic context that was now starting to look more and more European. 'Europe' also included a talk from Europhile MP Ted Heath, then Conservative Party leader. This prominence for the academic side of Mill Hill's reputation was well timed; the initiative lasted until timetable pressures forced it out of the increasingly crowded curriculum of the 1990s.

In the same vein, Michael Hart disbanded "The Bench", JP John Morrison's reincarnation of the old "Shell" V Form for two-year O-Level takers. However the real keynote of the Michael Hart years was internationalisation. A Language Lab was made possible in 1969 when the historic Tuck Shop function was merged (to the surprise of older generations, in the event it was *not much lamented*) with the Blenheim Steps shop in the High Street, reversing Maurice Jacks' 1920s innovation; its equipment was the gift of the Millhillian Walker family, and *OM* Dick Friedel. (Blenheim Steps would then be replaced in 1971, by arrangements for clothing with Broadway retailers.) Russian had been started up by 1968, through one of Michael Hart's inherited larger-than-life characters, "Willie" Gallagher. Above all the link was now instituted with the 1,000-strong *Institution Join-Lambert* in Rouen; its 30th birthday would be celebrated in 1998. There were also exchanges with Schondorf and Le Caousou, Toulouse (to be succeeded in the 1980s by the *Christian von Dohm Gymnasium* in Goslar), and at teacher level with both countries (also with Lakefield College School, Ontario). These trans-national activities also led to the expression of some challenging viewpoints about the host school, for example the *MHM* article by Gutts Reinhardt, in October 1973, where he questioned Britain's specialisation to only three subjects at VI-Form level. They also facilitated an invaluable look by Millhillians at themselves in relation to others, exemplified in the article by the *MHM* Editor, Mark Griggs-Smith, "The German Way", which rightly won the 1973 OMC Literary Prize, judged by a happily re-visiting Roy Moore.

Channelling endeavour

Games had always had, from the days of Mill Hill's emulation of Arnold's Rugby onwards, the covert function of channelling competitive teenage energy. Team sports continued, albeit with less glory than *OM* pundits sought. The historic rugby tradition was underlined by the 1969 RFU Centenary Match against W.C.Ramsay's XV, and by John Martin's Oxford Rugby "Blue" in 1973. In 1970, under coach Paul Hodgson, the Hockey XI was for the first time undefeated by any schools; Steven Roberts won a Hockey "Blue" at Oxford in 1974. However this period is more notable for the 'Minor', and more individualistic sports. Golf, fencing, judo, water polo, canoeing, sailing on the Welsh Harp, clay pigeon shooting and even lacrosse came into play; badminton was spearheaded with success at County and national level by the growing Malaysian contingent. In 1969/70 the Shooting VIII won the School's first Bisley event – the Cox Cup.

One of Hart's best moves was to ask Chemistry master Tim Jackson to re-start a School Orchestra. This also enhanced the choral tradition. The *MHM* wrote: *MHS is the only school in the country sufficiently rash ... to put on large-scale choral works with boys as soloists*; Sidney Barlow's Music Headship launched two such soloists onto a world stage – David James and Peter Jeffes. There followed the first-ever joint MHS-Belmont

Tim Jackson conducts pioneering MHS orchestral concert at the Queen Elizabeth Hall, London, 1973 (note future MHS HM William Winfield, violinist: stdg. l.). *10.f*

The silver Trophy, donated by actor John Slater in memory of his son Simon, awarded for the annual cultural highspot, the Inter-House Drama Competition. *10.g*

concert, at the Queen Elizabeth Hall in 1973. The Inter-House Music Competitions still kept their place in the calendar, despite 30 other activities, including as always some never covered in the *Magazine* write-ups: The League of Gentlemen XI, The Cotton Club, The Hammer Hounds. One article alluded to the 'Kinemania', with a membership of 450, a fraternity who apparently saw such 'educational' films as "Danish Blue": there is some reason to doubt the veracity of this report. New fashions formed: a Motor Car Club (1970), Societies for War Games, and Numismatics (1971); in the same year a School (as opposed to its hitherto popular 'House') activity, returned with The MHS Debating Society – the old "Interim Society".

Perhaps the greatest advance was in English, which continued the surge begun under Roy Moore, after the School's first 'pure' English award at Oxbridge – Robert Hillenbrand's Exhibition to Trinity, Cambridge in 1959 (emulating Hugh Gauntlett's Maths and English Exhibition to Balliol, Oxford, in 1944); English played a major part in the Exhibitions won at Oxbridge by John Landaw (1967), Christopher Thompson (1974) and Vir Sanghvi (1975). As Director Ted Winter wrote, the concomitant activity – drama – played *a formative as well as an aesthetic role in the life of the School*. An event in 1968 added a sad lustre to this development: the son of the Stratford and Whitehall Theatre actor, John Slater, had died of cancer; the Simon Slater Trophy was given in his memory.

The annual showpiece School plays continued. Choices branched out to Brecht, Arthur Miller, and "Zigger-Zagger"; this play gave rise to a nice example of what Tim Stringer would later describe as *good Headmastering*. The Head Master had voiced some doubts about this ambitious production: Tim offered him a copy of the text: by next morning, Michael Hart had read it, clarified the problem areas, and enabled his busy colleague to proceed with the production, with confidence in his own judgment, and in his Head, renewed. Shaun Sutton, father of pupils Simon and Lucy, and BBC Head of TV Drama, judged "An Enemy of the People" in 1970, and was guest of honour in 1972 at Belmont, where the plays too were of quality, ranging from "She Stoops to Conquer" to "The Italian Straw Hat". In 1970 the 50-year tradition of House plays, pioneered by School House, evolved under Ted Winter to replace the Reading and Speech Competitions, with pupils totally responsible; a cup was given by costumier Mary Adnams. This event would be later called by Head of Drama Michael Miller as much a 'Festival' as a competition. The Hart years saw the institution of three awards: the Ramsay Cup (part-financed by the US Ambassador, Mr Walter Annenberg) for the pupil embodying Bill's qualities of enthusiasm, integrity and tolerance; the Martin Woolf Memorial Prize for the Remove pupil exemplifying steady progress in House or School (Martin died in a climbing accident in the summer of 1973); and Murray House's own Peter Davies Award. The fillip now given to creative writing resulted in plays such as Guy Vinson's piece about Northern Ireland in 1974, as well as in the "Forum" of the McClure/Murray Houses, and "Hard-Up", one more in the long line of unofficial MHS *Samizdate*.

In what previous era would it have been possible to devote a double-page spread (in the Magazine of 1973) to opportunities for 'Poetry in London', and a review of *Double Flute*, a collection of the poems of a member of the 1st XV, Richard Burns?

This had just been presented to the Library, where Tim Stringer and William Winfield were doing their best as Patron and Custodian to keep things in order. The *MHM's* visual high-point was the set of very 'with-it' sketches, led by a design commissioned from Hardy Amies (would that Sir Norman Hartnell had lived to see it) for an imaginary new School uniform in 1968, complete with *de rigueur* flared trousers, and tight open-necked shirts of a suitable fancy cut and mode. They did not really seek approval, but they were a sign of the vitality now bubbling away within a School still self-evidently – indeed "strikingly" – alive: nostalgic viewing for the generations for whom the length of a boy's hair had been, in John Rae's phrase, the *casus belli* in the guerrilla war. The historical perspective, then unavailable, suggests no lasting revolution.

Energies were not merely turned inwards, in any narcissistic way. The tradition of community service, begun with the Alford House project in the 1920s, saw its expansion into many new avenues during this time: the cause of the charity "Shelter" was espoused; the Scouts, and – still going strong today – the Task Force, gave service to the residents of the Drapers Cottage Homes on Hammers Lane; help was also given to St Vincent's Orphanage along The Ridgeway. A period of service with 'VSO', prior to university, appeared on many Valete notices.

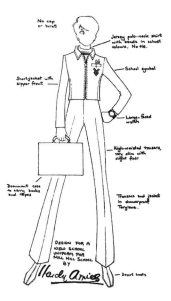

Hardy Amies' designs for a 'with-it' MHS uniform. *10.h*

Organisation man

Service even became self-service in 1968: lunchtimes in the ever-more crowded Dining Hall were thus made possible in two whole-School continuous sittings. The traditional Grace, *Benedictus, benedicat – Benedicto, benedicatur* thereby became obsolete; the old House dining rooms of 1945, in the far front School House corridor, were converted (now the Visitors WC, and other rooms); the external WCs (the 'thousand-pounders') below the Loggia achieved a more 'seemly' purpose – wholly rebuilt as the new Bursars's offices (see Appendix E). The Hart organisational broom reached into every corner of School life. What he termed *a powerful injection of new blood* introduced such names as Bickerdike, Brownlie, Comins, Knowles and Winfield to a staff which continued beyond the opening of the new century. A symbolic move was the replacement of one of the Classics posts with that for a new English master, Tim Corbett; Hartley Heard joined another cricket "Blue" on the Staff, John Wait. One of the main differences within the texture of the School's life, striking to older generations, was the creation in 1971 of a new joint Boys-Masters 'Council' of 21, with Tim Stringer as its first (Staff) Chair. It was elected by Houses and by Forms, to complement but also to act as a better communications channel than the monitorial body: photographs of that erstwhile all-powerful and often self-perpetuating entity now no longer dominated the *Magazine* pages. The 1970s generation did not seek this kind of power. Another significant change was the writing of a simpler set of School Rules in 1970, codifying the earlier R.M. measures. Thus Rule 12 defined the end of fagging; Rule 13 marked a long-overdue full stop to the power of any boy to inflict corporal punishment. Future generations of Millhillians would learn with incredulity of the barbaric practices of earlier, but not all that early, times – the 1940s at St Bees and the early 1950s (see Appendix E). A House play of the 1998 competition would portray such bullying as an occurrence of historical interest, not topical concern.

Another calendar item – Fridays – was also scrutinised, eventuating in the introduction of Orchestra and Community Service. The Head Master analysed the ways that the School spent this precious afternoon, speculating that there must be better ways than training for the "The Defence of the Realm". The Falklands War of a bare decade later, the 1990s Gulf War, and the World Trade Centre catastrophe of 2001 would give this optimistic questioning a sadly premature ring. What Michael Hart called "fancy dress" (morning suits) was ended. By 1975, "Stop Talking!" had finally withered away, its singers reduced to three by Roy Moore for Assembly in The Large *c*.1953. All these parochial changes were mirrored intelligently in the increasingly committed pages of the *MHM*, contrasting with a perception of general indifference. The March 1970 editorial commented on *the year system and an intricate web of rank, privilege and responsibility...*, pointing to a new approach where *everyone* [could have] *an opportunity of running the House... for 1 year* with *no one hurt at having failed to make the grade*. In May 1971, Howell James, a future Governor, wrote of *a somewhat dormant establishment, sinking into lethargic stupor...* yet now showing *hopeful signs...* [which] *may rebuild our former prowess*. The September issue argued that *gloom and continual recrimination* were becoming *boring*.

Political and economic time-bombs

Of the four apparent 'time-bombs' that would be fused, if not necessarily in an explosive state, by the end of the 1964-74 decade, one – national-political in nature – had been evident from the mid-1960s, whilst the larger geo-political problem of the Middle East oil crisis only impacted, at least on the man in the street, from 1973 onwards; this latter problem would be seen to underlie the later Gulf War. The former – the Labour Party's doctrinaire antagonism to private education – seemed to be more immediately threatening; although John Rae's judgement was that the threat remained real right up to James Callaghan's defeat at the polls in 1979, in the event it proved not a time-bomb, but a damp squib, at least for the ensuing 30 years.

The Newsom Report of 1966 had seemed to pose a major legal and economic threat to Public Schools. Investigative visits were paid to Mill Hill on behalf of Dr Royston Lambert, first by John Hipkin in spring 1967, and then in the autumn by Dame Kitty Anderson, on the basis that Mill Hill's 'Middlesex' Scheme might have something to tell them. In the event their findings were, erroneously, that Mill Hill did not appear to have done enough of a 'social engineering' job to act as a possible model for any future national scheme of alignment between the public and private sectors – no boys of working-class families being deemed to have benefited from it. Anyone acquainted with the scheme knows that from the very start this was not true, even though 'social engineering' had never been part of the original thinking. The second phase of the political process, the 1970 Report by David Donnison, Professor of Social Administration at LSE, took the public debate a stage further; it led the GBA and HMC to devise their Assisted Places Scheme of 1981, in which Mill Hill took part. Harking back to the lack of recognition which a too-modest Mill Hill had received from the educational world in respect of the School's shining role in the pioneering Fleming policy, it was not surprising that the GBA too appeared to be unaware of the Middlesex scheme. Mill Hill could initially only offer two subsidised potential Boarding places within this new scheme.

In 1973 Roy Hattersley addressed the IAPS Conference, and again alluded to the possibility of annulling the Public Schools' historic charity tax remission. In his report to the Court Michael Hart was bullish: any 'nationalisation' of the independent sector would cost taxpayers a cool £1,000 million over six years; loss of charitable status would have only cost Mill Hill of about six per cent of current revenue – damaging, but in no way crippling. This issue went dormant for the next 30 years, realism prevailed, politics moved on. By 1974, Mill Hill was simply able to deal with her own economic problems, uncomplicated by political pressures.

The academic results for Michael Hart's time, however calculated, maintained several positive trends: continuance of awards at Oxbridge – often four or five a year – and likewise a steady entry to the medical schools; a trickle to the Service Colleges – RMA Sandhurst; The College of Air Training, Hamble; and RNC Dartmouth. Some 80 per cent of those with the basic two A/Ls would get into a University, Poly or College. In one year 50 boys went on to 25 Universities – these now including new *OM* correspondents from Aberystwyth, Dundee, East Anglia, Keele, LSE, Sheffield and Southampton, as well as the Architectural Schools. Nevertheless, there was an underlying problem which went back to the weaker age-13 entries manifesting themselves five years previously, and to Mill Hill's apparent lack of attraction for the brighter boy, even despite the presence of reasonably generous Entrance Scholarships. Mill Hill was not getting what the School had previously come to regard as a fair and proper share of the intellectual market; it was a vicious circle, a 'Catch-22' situation. The Head Master did all that lay in his power, but time was what was needed. He developed a philosophy to try to come to terms with the situation: Mill Hill was right for *the all-rounder, the open-minded boy, who has talents not yet crystallized in any one direction*.

The decline of the BBP entry played its part. The loss of Brent Council in 1973 was *a further nail in the coffin..* As Michael Hart pointed out to the Court, there were now only some 30-40 former BBP boys in the school at any one time, compared with 70-90 even *three or four years ago*: the starker 1949-50 comparison would have been of about 180 out of a Roll of 350 boys.

The problem was on the way to a resolution by the end of the Hart years, with much better O- and A-level results announced for the years 1970/1 and 1971/2, but it was still basically 'unfinished business', and a great disappointment to the Head Master himself, as well as to many of his hard-worked staff.

Day v. Boarding

The 'Boarder v. Day' debate had been the subject of raging passions at Mill Hill, as elsewhere in the private educational spectrum, for 50 years or more; it too affected academic performance. An irrelevant but snobbish historical undertow also lingered on: in 1860, when Bristol Grammar School had petitioned for permission to take Boarders, the Master of the Rolls refused on the grounds that *Boarding schools were for one class of society, and Day schools for another.*

Sole extant picture of "Stop Talk-ing!", time-honoured monitorial chant, sung, in full stride, before formal occasions: enacted by *OMs* at Canadian Annual Dinner 1954. *10.i*

Familiar non-Millhillian occupants
of The Ridgeway: the daily gaggle
of Canada Geese en route from
the Sheep Dip. *10.j*

In contrast with other Boarding schools, such as Clifton, where the late-19th-century clerical Head, John Percival, founded two Town Houses early in his reign, ensuring they proceeded step by step with the Boarding Houses, at Mill Hill the Boarding issue had become a touchstone of corporate character, the very spirit of *the Hill-top fortress*. Although many eminent Day boys had emerged unscathed, nevertheless even after Maurice Jacks had formalised matters with the naming of the House as 'Murray' in 1933, until a decade after the Second World War, Mill Hill's Day boys remained in a different, if not exactly second-class, category (see Appendix D). The appointment of the first full-term Day boy, Bill Skinner, as senior monitor, in 1955, had been as much of a philosophical point of no return as any: at last, Day status had achieved parity, replete with all the monitorial pomp and circumstance of the time.

There was another sub-issue: Mill Hill has been accused by some of perpetuating a Governing Body that was too influenced by its *OM* corpus, and certainly the Day v. Boarder debate was sharpened by that factor, calling for all Michael Hart's most persuasive arguments. The accusation is hard to deal with accurately, and at the end of the day any judgement about a Governing Body must be as to the long-term quality of its judgments, not its individual short-term decisions. The list of the Governors who served in the Sellers and Boyle eras is an impressive one, given such names as Bill Ramsay, Alf Hawes, Dick Walker, Stanley Farrow or Dr C.S.Darke. They were all devoutly rooted in the 'Boarding ethos', and equally sincerely believed that an influx of too many Day boys would kill it, especially once the Head had warned in 1971 that the ratio of four Boarders to one Day boy might well evolve, on HMC nation-wide trends, to as few as 2:1 by 1975/6. Belmont, however, did not go along the path of 'Day overtaking Boarder' until 1989.

The language used was in itself interesting, and evolved from an initial tone of disaster as the problem edged nearer. On 20 July 1972, Michael Hart put it darkly: even at the 4:1 ratio, *the School could retain a strong Boarding school programme and character... but it would be difficult if not impossible to run the School on traditional Boarding school lines*. All depended on what exactly was meant by the 'Boarding ethos' – a strong, integrated constituent, or the sole overriding character? One compromise was what Ted Winter later termed Michael Hart's *sound-bite – fortnightly Boarding*: Saturday night at home, and return for the Sunday evening Hobbies Hour, and Chapel.

At the end of the day, of course, the trend in the market-place had to prevail: parental and pupil preferences; the growing influence of mothers as opposed to fathers in that choice; a new breed of Housemasters' wives, with careers; and above all, the economic consequences of ignoring the trend. A second Day House, McClure, had been informally opened in 1967. The traditional objections to Day boy status can be summed up under three headings, each carrying a counter-argument with it: 'softness' (humanising); a unified school 'Tone' (healthy diversity); preparation for the male dominant role (learning to balance the 'male' with the 'female' role). Michael Hart's task was to articulate this trend; the growing demand for Day places was the ace in the pack.

'Non-Christian' entry

The Day issue was further complicated by another matter. Increasingly Mill Hill, in line with other metropolitan schools, was learning to accept a greater dependence on her geographical locality, as parents increasingly disliked having to travel long distances in order to remain in touch with their Boarding offspring at weekends. In North West London this now embraced a growing, affluent and successful Asian community, just as socially ambitious and as committed to individual growth through education as the traditional Jewish community alongside which it had evolved. The success of the City of London for investors and exporters from the Pacific rim countries, later to be called the Tiger economies, also entered the equation, with many middle-class Japanese and Korean families settling in the Finchley area.

For a School rooted in a somewhat militantly Dissenting past, this was all becoming rather difficult to swallow at one gulp. Not surprisingly these were mostly highly intelligent boys, hard-working non-Protestant exponents of the 'Protestant' work-ethic, and their closer family cultures favoured Day boy status. Michael Hart warned of the danger of there emerging too strong a contrast between a highly academic Day element, and a less able, less distinguished but traditionally 'Christian' Boarding quota. The demand from overseas families in the former Empire, principally from Malaysia and Hong Kong, was also growing, although this conversely aided the Boarding lobby; Ridgeway was at one stage spoken of, affectionately, as "The House of the Rising Sun". Unfortunately all these highly differentiated strands of intake were often referred to in terms of the 'Non-Christian' entry, when under the surface the Boarding theme was uppermost in the Mill Hill mind. It was not religious or racial intolerance, nor xenophobic exclusiveness: there was a genuine concern to preserve within this small community that great Enlightenment virtue – 'balance'. Various target percentages were raised, under various definitions: no firm unyielding limit was ever formalised, but a watching brief was now maintained. These topics are re-examined in Chapter XI.

Michael Hart's last Foundation Day address referred to the *Punch* cartoon (i) of "Jock the Bootman" (here as a School Porter) inspired by the then *OM* Editor, Owen Seaman (ii) (below). His are the only initials carved twice on (iii) (l.) the famous *Punch* Editors' Table (top l. and r.). *10.k*

AT CENUS IMMORTALE MANET MULTOSQUE
PER ANNOS STAT FORTUNA DOMUS...

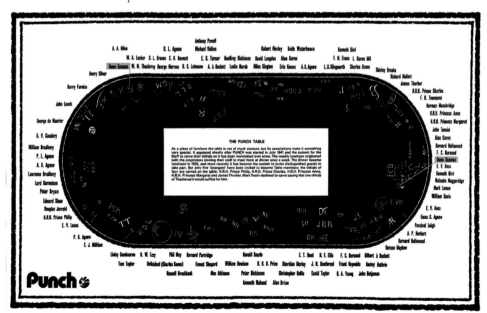

MR. OWEN SEAMAN

Co-education

In 1973, Michael Hart decided to change the course of his career by moving into educational administration, as one of Her Majesty's Inspectorate – at least that was the plan. The deep shock at this unexpected news was akin to that which greeted John Whale's comparable announcement in the summer of 1950.

Of the two other thematic time-bombs left ticking, over which the Head Master could and did exercise some control, with fuses well-lit by him in advance, the first, the Day v. Boarder issue, had already started to be addressed. The second, co-education, was still so radical that it was not really yet on Mill Hill's agenda, although as early as March 1968 an imaginative editorial sanctioned into the *Magazine* by the unseen 'authorities' (the behind-the-scenes 'Censors' – Tim Stringer and the Head) commented that co-education would fit in well with the system there being exposed for comment; a coat had been trailed. There was a co-operative Convention, "The Challenge of Industry", with 23 girls from Copthall County Grammar School in 1970 and a joint Chapel event with NLCS girls, "Green Pastures", in 1973. Joining the VI, at least on equal terms of finance if not automatically of classroom treatment, came some masters' daughters, and a few girls from The Mount School attended Computer Programming classes (see Ch.XI). As this History has shown, even if there was an element of misogyny amongst both masters and boys over the years, the distaff side had always, from the very start, been at least a familiar aspect of the School's life, from the 'Crumpites' of the early 19th century through to the first Old Millhillienne, up at St Bees; Housemasters' wives, Lady Residents and Matrons, female teachers, and at an earlier time school servants, had for long played important and much-loved roles. From the 1940s onwards, the School had allowed a female element into many formal activities, from dances to debates; from the 1950s, Houses held their own regular dances and discos, and generally the artificial barriers imposed by an all-boys Boarding system were being increasingly laid aside. Members of 'the fair sex' were never far from the Millhillian mind, indeed seemed to be getting ever closer, with mysterious *MHM* article references, as for example to a lady called "Loreley" in a 1970 Lacrosse match at The Mount School.

Behind the traditional opposition to co-education lay a more serious, unspoken, historically-based viewpoint: the all-male culture had bred men for war, companions for the trenches, self-denying leaders for the outposts of Empire. It was still a time when women at the School were expected to play second fiddle, and even Michael Hart did not seek to change that; wives of Housemasters were not allowed to have outside jobs – their role 'in the House' had to come first. A by-product of all this was an all-too male approach to managing people in industry: the possibility of a different 'female' approach to the problems of society had not yet dawned on the British mind. This was an age before female Prime Ministers or Presidents had come into their own, except in Israel; indirectly, through *OM* Denis Thatcher, Mill Hill would in due course have a vicarious *sub rosa* part to play in that world-famous evolution.

The gender-equality issue was now bubbling away merrily, and many Heads within the HMC's thinking circles (for example – and of later significance for Mill Hill – at Marlborough) quite apart from such equality-based schools as Bedales, had already recognised it. The topic was first raised in a Court Report of 25 November 1971, the Head Master hypothesising that although it was not yet a central aim, a "genuine co-educational School with one or two all-girl Boarding houses" needed to be thought about. It was presented in terms not so much of principle as of expediency and commercial competitiveness: if Mill Hill did not bite the bullet, others would, and even purely male numbers would suffer.

There was also the pragmatic short-term argument that a good infiltration of some bright young female minds, untainted by the fashionable late-1960s young male distaste for hard work, and seemingly unable to get good VI Form teaching at their own single-sex schools, would enhance the modest academic standards that Mill Hill was still suffering. It was clearly also the case that for many of the boys themselves the idea of learning, and enjoying their adolescence, in the same setting as girls, was a much more natural way of going on; it was also something the absence and denial of which was becoming increasingly irksome by comparison with that ever more relevant factor, the experience of their peer-groups elsewhere. Most of the Middlesex boys could have told them as much.

In 1972 the Court agreed to discuss the matter further. Despite Michael Hart's modest disclaimer that this was not one of his priorities, the line of thinking had been prepared for his successors, to reach its fruition with the formation of Mill Hill's first all-girl Boarding and Day House, Cedars, in 1997. Symbolically, and but for the potentially Dickensian sound of it, it could even have merited the name Hart House.

A myriad daily details

In a chapter focused on corporate change, it is also important to underline much that was constant in this decade, and where possible to reveal the 'non-corporate' details; there is all too good a chance that in a broad sweep school History, not all elements will receive their due place in the text of time. The unchanging importance of good teaching and good teachers can easily be one such casualty, even if some amends are offered in Information Supplement No.2 – "A Gallimaufry of Mill Hill Characters". Another element is the ongoing, but often undervalued, role of Governors. Fortuitously, these two strands come together in reviewing Michael Hart's years, through a letter that surfaced from a Millhillian who was to prove to be one of the longest-serving Governors, Gowen Bewsher, to Tony Turnbull, one of the longest-serving post-war Masters, Head of Chemistry, and successor to Donald Hall as Housemaster of Collinson; it dates from after the Hart years, but may nevertheless be appropriate here. The naturally modest reluctance of each man notwithstanding, one passage in particular, echoing Brett James' diary phrase *the rich reward of teaching*, may be taken to stand for the tributes to the army of teachers, and to the motivations of an almost equally long line of Governors, without whom no Head could function: *A School Master can only judge whether or not his career has been worthwhile by the effect that career has had on his pupils... You have taught things infinitely more valuable than academic subjects. You have taught boys to become men... I always instance you as being the very finest type of Schoolmaster which in doubting moments, makes all that* [we] *endeavour to do for the School, worthwhile.*

OMC-organised 'Career Forums' for VI-Formers were held at Whitehall Court, SW1, the unique OMC London Town Club. *10.1*

The actual flavour and detail of school life is another area where history's eye is often disappointed – not necessarily revealed from the official accounts, but rather from glimpses here and there, probably unintended at the time to be of any importance, and sometimes coming from outside observers, not Millhillians. Thus the exchange student, Michel Voute, wrote of his surprise in 1971 at a mere 10 minutes in Chapel before lessons began at 08.50, and the still-compulsory support for 1st XV matches. In a *MHM* 'Letter from St Paul's' in 1973, the writer, George Horvath, commented on the 'yobbish behaviour' of Paulines outside school, a phenomenon that had not surfaced at Mill Hill; he also wrote of the focus of academic effort at the top, not the broader emphasis that Mill Hill seemed to be achieving.

House Reports also allow brief flashes of insight that can easily be missed. At BB in 1971 *The Box* [TV] *reigns supreme. Nobody ran away;* two years later came complaints that *the phone is constantly out of order, the papers seldom arrive in time for breakfast.* At Ridgeway *for the first time in years* there were colours tests, (an event also reported for McClure in 1973); the Discussion Groups in Michael Brown's study were obviously a special feature. At Collinson in 1972 there was a surprising comment about *friction between older and younger members of the House*, yet the following year, *those in the House Drama Group enjoyed a good night out at "No Sex Please – We're British"*, whilst others watched "Dr Who", and "The Persuaders" on the new colour TV. Murray were relieved from *early Rolls on Saturday afternoons*; term closed *with a riotous Hog*, and winning the Chess Competition. Scrutton *had to adopt a "Sport is not all" policy.* An unofficial beer-making kit overflowed in the attic, now become a 'Smokeless Zone', and a trunk loft (the bedroom which first featured in the Introduction to this History) and the dormitory ceiling collapsed underneath; a fire at Winterstoke was put out by Mr Phimester, and his Head of House *forgave* him for squirting the liquid all over his shoes. These and a myriad other daily details would be the ones which individual pupils would be recalling for a future History, when all the grand strategies and noble sentiments had long since lapsed into oblivion.

'Far from the straight and narrow...'?

On Foundation Day 1973 – fittingly for his European beliefs, Bastille Day, 14 July – after the speeches and prizes, Michael Hart took his audience on a tour of the 'pavilions' awaiting their inspection. In a reference to the final pavilion, he offered a witty illustration of his own particular set of balanced values, of the modern mix of change within continuity – not at the expense of it – and an ever-conscious need to look to the individual pupil's interests: it was also his way of paying his own respect to the things that do not change, *the myriad daily details*, alongside those that do.

For those of you who feel that we have strayed far from the straight and narrow paths of our founders and predecessors, there will be much to confirm your fears in the pavilion marked 'School History', fully documenting the cold baths, short hair, and singlehanded hockey [see Appendix D] *of the good old days. For others there may be more comfort in the copy of the old Punch cartoon of an old boy commenting to the school porter that there had been many changes in the old place and eliciting this reply: "Yessir, the Head Master is changed, the Assistant Masters is changed, the Tuck Shop is changed, but, bless you, the boys is just the same as ever."*

Unknown to Michael Hart this was a singularly fortuitous illustration, not merely because of its appearance at the front of the first History, nor just because it was the first time that a Mill Hill character (Jock, the bootman) or setting (the Portico) had graced *Punch's* illustrious pages, of both of which facts Michael and members of his audience were well aware. What he did not realise was that the Editor who had engineered this tribute after his appointment in 1906, the great journalist and humourist, Sir Owen Seaman, had gone on from Mill Hill in 1878 to complete his education at Michael's previous school: he was in fact both an *OM*, and an Old Salopian. There was thus a nice symmetry and indeed a wider continuity in the story than appeared on the surface (see *10.k*).

CCF Inspection 1969: unusual double role of Marshal of the Royal Air Force Sir Dermot Boyle as Inspecting Officer (for second time) and Court Chairman, with first RAF CO of CCF, and CCF S.S.I. Maloney. *10.m*

Michael used Mussorgsky's "Promenade" round "Pictures at an Exhibition" as the thread of his speech. Ending with the closing of "The Great Gate of Kiev", he was thereby about to open two gateways: perhaps unconsciously – the School's own impending entry onto a new and tortuous path, and consciously – the gateway to his own respected 'promenade' away from Mill Hill a year later. It was a pleasant way of saying both 'beware' and '*au revoir*'. From Mill Hill, Michael Hart went out into the very different world of inspecting and standard-setting. However, after a short two years, headmastering would out, and he returned to be Head of the European Schools, first at Mol in Belgium from 1976, and in Luxembourg from 1980 to '89, when he became Director of Alden Biesen's European Classes in Belgium, and then to write, and lecture about European matters, and to win his *Conseilleur de l'Ordre de Mérite* (Luxembourg) and, like Roy Moore before him, to be appointed a CBE.

From the School's point of view the most important fact was that he remained a friend to his successors, including the present Headmaster, William Winfield, who, with the European Initiative, has taken the European dimension into the new century. The institution in 1998 of the Michael Hart European travel award, to complement those other important travel bursaries founded earlier by *OMs* Lewis van Moppes, and Ernest Shanks, is a further ongoing reminder of the freer, more open and international Mill Hill of this era.

Those early paths of the founders had not been entirely forsaken: rather, they had been meticulously inspected, revised where necessary, and made passable for future generations of not over-revolutionary Millhillian pupils, who deep down, obstinately, in "Jock the bootman"'s vernacular, would be much *the same as ever* – accepting the premise that boys and girls can be educated as equals. Some 24 years after Michael Hart enunciated the problem, and the solution, Mill Hill would be biting on that much debated co-educational bullet. He had carried forward the peaceful but irreversible reformation of what he had perhaps over-generously described in 1968, with at least a nice genuflection to the School's history, as one of the country's foremost "reforming schools".

Where is Belmont?

The main School, not Belmont, was Michael Hart's chief task. The evolution of the Junior School, set out in Gordon Smith's book, is summarised in Appendix H. The fact that this story has only been touched on so far, and even at this stage is still tantamount to a postscript, is simply a reflection of the then reality. That was how Mill Hill's Prep School had – seemingly inevitably – been seen at the level of the Court: a valued separate entity.

By the middle of Roy Moore's reign, in 1959, he had persuaded the Governors that it was time to change what had evolved over the two preceding decades into an 'arm's length' relationship. Rooker's tenure of 18 years as founding Master and proprietor – 1919-37 (from 1912 to 1919 it was the School's Junior House) – gave way to the two decades of his son Arthur Roberts *as a reasonably efficient Joshua to my father's Moses* (as he put it in a letter to Gordon Smith of 1987). This culminated in two counterpoised factors: the production of generations of happy boys, and a gradual fall-away in standards, both academic and internal. With the decline of the Middlesex Scheme by the mid-1960s, the senior School's reliance on the quality of the Junior School's product was once again central.

On 26 April 1963, a bargain buy-out for the School of £41,494 was concluded – "a strict contract price", as Arthur's lawyers called it – using his father's outdated but unamended valuation formula, without any top-up to reward Arthur for his qualitative contribution. Mill Hill, as a charity, had the justification of minimising costs, but this arrangement was not exactly charitable. An unhappy Master then at a stroke moved from ownership to salaried employee status, with all living expenses, but no pension, and reinforced by the demotivation which that abrupt change implies. Roy Moore, albeit his normal kindly self, now had the last word in all staff appointments, the root cause of the Governors' concern, despite the contractual phraseology *in the closest consultation with the Master of Belmont*. The timing was unkind to Belmont, in that Mill Hill's Head Master was looking to retirement. It could not last. In April 1966 Arthur retired; the family link ended.

The first of the seven years of his successor, James Burnet, were also the first years of the incoming Mill Hill Head of 1967, Michael Hart. To begin with, neither the Court nor its Heads had become seized of what the new relationship required of them; one Governor even had to ask where Belmont was. Burnet, a good choice, from a relevant background, nevertheless had what he later described as *a nightmarish first year*, coping with staff resignations, whether forced or voluntary, including among the Matrons, a constant headache. At Clifton College Preparatory School he had experienced a good close working understanding with his Senior School (of the kind that later Mastership lineages such as Brighton College, and Caterham Junior School would also presuppose): the traditional 'arm's length' was once more an example of that *sui generis* factor in Mill Hill's story; there was in fact nothing inevitable about it in any wider IAPS context. Thus there was no one to induct Burnet – he was all but alone at the deep end.

Burnet coped manfully; by the end of Michael Hart's time, and into that of his Classics successor from Marlborough, Alan Elliott, the situation improved. Despite the end of the 'family' there was once more a 'family atmosphere' at Belmont; regular meetings were instituted at Head and Bursar levels, and an ex-Belmont MHS Governor, Michael Kempster, had been dedicated to cover Belmont issues. This involvement, though not yet as close as Belmont sought, ran in parallel with that other reform of Michael Hart's, a revivification of the Main School's links with her chief feeder market, the Prep Schools. From the Hart-Burnet era onwards, the shape of the relationship moved on from that of an Addendum, however warmly welcomed, to that of a fully-integrated part of the Mill Hill agenda, bringing with it mutual benefits. Burnet's successor, Peter Foster, has been described by a Governor as *the archetypal good and reliable prep school head*. One outcome of this era would be the first consideration, in 1981 under Gordon Smith, of the idea of a Mill Hill Pre-Prep, the future third part of the Foundation's 'Trinity'; at the time, he did not feel it was necessary; it was not yet even a gleam in the Court's eye.

As the last quarter of the 20th century dawned in 1975, a challenging hare had already been set in motion by Michael Hart along its ultimately triumphant course: co-education. Although Susan, the younger daughter of Peggy and Second Master Allan Phimester, declined Michael Hart's offer to make history by becoming the School's first full-time Millhillienne (choosing to stay at NLCS), Beth, the talented artistic daughter of Jess and Art Master Cliff Baker, would pick up the gauntlet and enter the VI Form (see Chs.VIII, XI). The future would now be characterised by issues conceived in the sharply differentiated terms not only of 'Day v. Boarding', but also of 'Girls v. Boys', both at the Main School, and thus formally and necessarily, but far less gladiatorially, at her now legitimised Junior Partner, Belmont.

Much turbulence was to ensue before the trails of reform Michael Hart had laid down would finally be resolved; many forces would balance uneasily about the fulcrum of the next two decades.

GOODBYE SIXTIES

"Goodbye Sixties": *MHM* evocation of the spirit of the Public Schools' tradition-challenging decade. *10.n*

Sources for Ch.X include: BMT Archvs, corr, G.Smith with J.Burnet, 1998, & with A.E.Rooker Roberts [1921-26]; PRO Kew London, ED 148/14-37 (Public Schools Commssn 1965-70, Chair, Sir John Newsom, Pprs of Dr Royston Lambert, research unit visit); N.G.Brett James, 'War Diaries 1943-6], v.12, Oct '46# corr/ dscns with Michael Hart, and with AIMs Donald Hall, Tony Turnbull, Alec Robertson, Chris Sutcliffe, David Franklin, Ted Winter, "Tim" Stringer, 1996-9; Governors N.S.Farrow [1927-30], W.Skinner [1949-55], H.M.P.James [1967-72]; Sir S.Jenkins [1956-60]; T.Jenkins [1972-8]; D.J.Wright [1964-70]; ltr, J.M.Mungavin to Maj M.F.L.de Spon, 12.vii.1969.

Background: G.Kalton, *The Public Schools: A factual survey of Headmasters' Conference Schools in England and Wales* (1966): MHS, App 1; J.Rae, *PS Revolution op cit*; J.Dancy,

op cit; *Guardian* 5.i.1998; *Hendon, Finchley & Edgware Times*; 'section bilingue', W.R.Winfield, in *Centre for Information on Language Teaching & Research*, (1978), *Intensive Language Teaching* (1979); S.M.Hersh, *Dark Side of Camelot* (1997); BBC 2, "The Cold War", 26.xii.98 – "greatest crisis of the 20th Century"; Wakeford, *op cit*, q. *Conference* v.5 No.1, Feb 1968; M,Hart, *EEC and Secondary Education in the UK* (1975); *Who's Who* (1992); letter, J.G,Bewsher [1948-52] to A/M Tony Turnbull, 17 May 1978; *MHM* reports on OMC Careers Forum by the author.

Other *OM* references: B.Baker [1973-5]; R.S.Burns [1956-61]; C.S.Darke [1926-31]; P.Davies [1957-62]; R.W.Friedel [1929-33]; P.M.Griggs-Smith [1969-74]; N.B.Hartnell [1914-9]; A.W.Hawes [1907-9]; R.Hillenbrand [1954-9]; Yvonne S.W.Ho

[1977-9]; D.L.L.James [1964-8]; P.W.Jeffes [1964-9]; M.E.I.Kempster [1936-42]; A.T.T.Ko [1968-70]; W.Ku [1974-9]; J.N.Landaw [1963-7]; I.J.Lo [1976-80]; I.F.Luckin [1922-5]; C.L.Lu [1907-9]; J.K.W.Ng [1969-73]; T.M.On [1915-7]; W.C.Ramsey [1912-18]; A.J.Rooker Roberts [1893-1900]; K.Roberts [1979-81]; V.R.Sanghvi [1973-5]; Sir O.Seaman [1874-8]; E.P.Shanks [1924-30]; S.J.Slater [1962-7]; S.H.G.Sutton [1968-73]; Lucy Sutton [1981-3]; D.Thatcher [1928-32]; C.J.Thompson [1969-74]; E.M.Van Moppes [1921-6]; G.W.Vinson [1969-74]; P.O.Walker [1916-20]; T.D.Walker [1926-9]; Katharine Whitehorn [1939]; M.H.Woolf [1971-3]; A.Yu [1981-6].

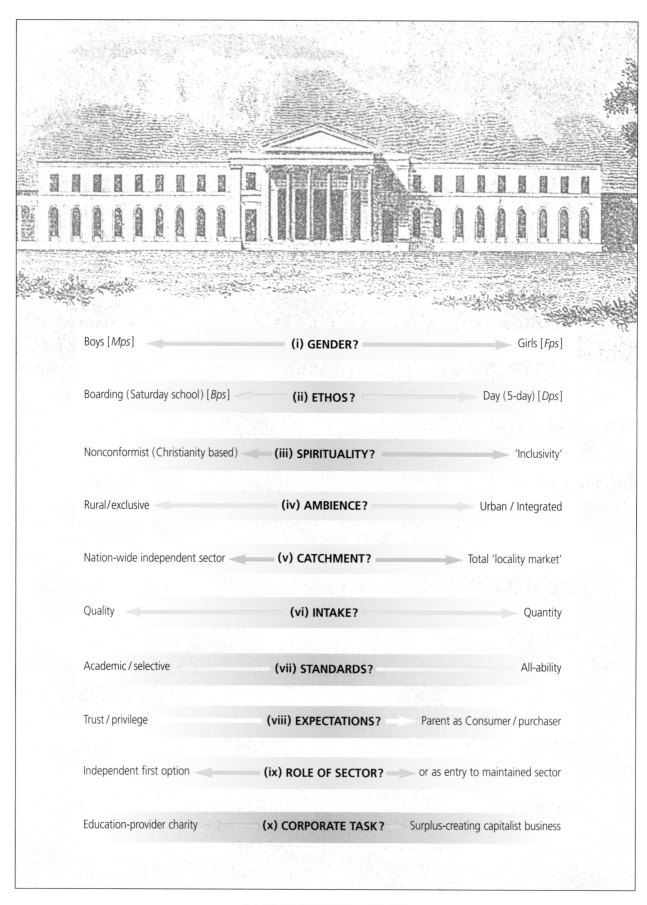

Boys [*Mps*] ⟵————— **(i) GENDER?** —————⟶ Girls [*Fps*]

Boarding (Saturday school) [*Bps*] ⟵———— **(ii) ETHOS?** ————⟶ Day (5-day) [*Dps*]

Nonconformist (Christianity based) ⟵———— **(iii) SPIRITUALITY?** ————⟶ 'Inclusivity'

Rural / exclusive ⟵———— **(iv) AMBIENCE?** ————⟶ Urban / Integrated

Nation-wide independent sector ⟵———— **(v) CATCHMENT?** ————⟶ Total 'locality market'

Quality ⟵———— **(vi) INTAKE?** ————⟶ Quantity

Academic / selective ⟵———— **(vii) STANDARDS?** ————⟶ All-ability

Trust / privilege ⟵———— **(viii) EXPECTATIONS?** ——⟶ Parent as Consumer / purchaser

Independent first option ⟵———— **(ix) ROLE OF SECTOR?** ——⟶ or as entry to maintained sector

Education-provider charity ⟵——— **(x) CORPORATE TASK?** —— Surplus-creating capitalist business

Fig.P POLICY DIMENSIONS: 1975-1999

A Very English Solution

From 'revolution' to evolution: Public School to Independent

"The time for decision has arrived":
Alastair Graham to Court of Governors,
7 March 1987.

One stormy, overcast midsummer afternoon in August 1987, a meeting was progressing in the Head Master's Study. In today's management-speak, this had been the 'operational centre' for all but one of Mill Hill's leaders over the preceding century. It was sited at the very heart of the ancient Tite building, the noble structure that had defied whatever could be pitted against it for more than 150 years. Suddenly there was a huge cloudburst directly overhead; within minutes the magenta-coloured wallpaper covering the inner north-east corner of that handsome mahogany-panelled room started to change colour; a dark brown stain made its way down from the ceiling. Instantly, the Head Master, Alastair Graham, sensing what had happened, tore out of the door, through the Octagon, up the School House staircase, and into the dormitory above – let out and in occupation at this time of the year for Camp Beaumont. A catastrophic scene met his gaze. The ceiling had caved in under the seemingly unstoppable weight of the downpour, at last overcoming the defence offered by that time-honoured but ever faulty Dining Hall roof: beds, clothing, hi-fi equipment – all lay under a mass of sodden plaster. The next two hours saw both Head and visitor – who happened to be an Old Millhillian – frenetically engaged in damage limitation, using buckets to catch the cascades, saving what could be salvaged.

The symbolism of this incident would only become apparent after the event, for the year 1987 was a significant one for the future Mill Hill School Foundation. The School had seemed to many observers to be 'losing the plot' as the last quarter of the 20th century edged forward; even that metaphor would seem to some to be controversial. A period of difficulty gradually acquired a sense of crisis. For the best of motives, a quiet, very English battle was in progress, not about any single issue nor between two constant protagonists, but nonetheless an ongoing battle about principle and process: about who runs a school, how fast things must change, in what direction, how to balance quantity of intake and income with cost-control, and with quality – whether defined academically, sociologically or in terms of gender. It was about an institution that to all involved appeared very much worth doing battle *for*.

Many initiatives in that process would follow, yet in many ways the year 1987 would indeed prove to be the key *time for decision* which set them in train. The elements outside, over which finally no human agency, however well-intended, could exercise control, had now invaded the School's heartland, rendering much that lay in their path at first sight unserviceable, possibly obsolete. Alastair Graham's successor would even crudely – but not wholly inaccurately – assert later that the school that some Millhillians had known *no longer existed*. Rescue efforts could only momentarily influence the situation: what was now at issue was the 'edifice' itself.

On 14 January of the previous year, at a meeting of the Court under Sir Cyril Philips' chairmanship, an *OM* Governor (its 'Vice-Chairman', a customary, not a constitutional title, which was later made official, then abandoned), had tabled a critical report which analysed the School's A-Level results for 1975-86. Still taking the role – in T.S.Eliot's phrase – of turbulent priest, he followed this on 7 March 1987 with a strong plea about the direction in which Mill Hill, and the Court, appeared, to his group of *OM* Governors, to be heading. This incursion into the day-to-day management of the School had eventuated two months later, on 7 May, in one of the Court's most momentous meetings, bringing in its wake years of debate; a Ten-Year Strategy Paper by a new Long-Term Finance and Policy Sub-Committee, followed by a practical Five Year Plan; and for the first (and hopefully last) time, an oligarchic Management Committee.

Here were symptoms of a wider national malaise. In the union-dominated 1970s, it seemed impossible to 'get inside the secret gardens' of the country's schools. Now the maintained sector was changing; the challenge of an evolving market-place had finally broken into the Mill Hill dream that had been dreamed in that distant originating century. At stake were the basic nature of the School, indeed the very soul of a still spiritually conscious establishment, with its hallowed beliefs and customs; its functioning as a business; the identity of the future 'operational centre' itself; and the roles played by its Heads. Even that hill-top location chosen by the Founders, and the then £½ million real estate of "The Grove", were questioned.

Dimensions of challenge

If the Governors' role in any school's history is invariably shrouded behind the Head's visible role, the next phase of Mill Hill's story requires a change of emphasis – a focus on the internal debate. Over the next 25 years, corporate governance of a high order, and an increasing professionalism, would be called for, outstanding being the tough measures spearheaded by *OM* Governors Stanley Farrow and Dick Walker to contain costs, against the pincer movement of exiguous resources and rampant inflation. As the Court steadily determined to face up to reality, 10 key dimensions, **Fig.P**, would emerge, varying in impact over time.

That assessment is certainly not to exclude Belmont from such considerations, since in most respects not only did the criteria apply to both schools, but henceforth developments within the 'Junior School' would start to have a more decisive feed-back effect than ever before on 'the School'. Mill Hill's positioning left or right along the first five of those dimensions had been taken for granted over the previous centuries, or had been ones which most staff and boys, and particularly what the Hooker Craigmyle fund-raising firm termed POBs – the inner core of a school's 'Professional Old Boys' – thought were crucial. Aside from a fee-threatening inflation, there were other parallel factors at work, implicit within those dimensions, common to many schools: the cost of property in the surrounding district; a gradual decline in the appeal of teaching as a profession; and the increasing multiplicity of the legislative framework within which schools would have to operate, resulting in an ever-growing bureaucracy. Those difficulties would be compounded by the introduction in 1988 of the General Certificate of Secondary Education, GCSE, replacing the GCE and CSE, and the evolution of A-Levels; these caused major changes in the provision of the educational programme, both then and into the turn of the new century (see Ch.XII).

The semantics of this time are interesting, with key words revealing the incipient shifting of positions: *primarily as a Boarding school... the character of a national school rather than a local school... founded on Christian principles*. Chapter XII will indicate the balance reached in each of these dimensions – some with trends that were unambiguous. Here only the key features can be highlighted, taking first of all, dimension **(ii) 'Ethos'** – Day numbers overtaking Boarding, as parents, above all mothers, increasingly prized a week-end home life. The national trend-data on the Boarding-Day issue, verifiable through the ISCis computerised censuses for most Independent Schools from 1983 onwards, showed a continuous increment of about 2,000 additional Day-boys, and an average decline of about 1,500 Boarding-boys each year, apart from a misreading of a brief 'bottoming-out' in 1987. The then Bursar, Ted Webb, a charming non-financial ex-Royal Marines officer, later to be exonerated by a Governor as *a child of his time*, had never attended a HMC Bursars meeting; thus despite the warnings of the Head Master, the Court's decisions were impaired by lack of knowledge of the wider market beyond Mill Hill. The Boarding-to-Day swing that took place at Belmont in 1975 hit the School in 1989: an educationalist Governor had to warn that *full Boarding was a total barrier to most parents*.

(iii) 'Spirituality' – the Nonconformist background broadening out to 'inclusivity' (the old HMC phrase in a new context): this reflected sociological change in NW London – never 'multi-faith' but *a family of many faiths and one faith*, as it would be later described by the new 'Foundation Chaplain', *OM* James Fields. **(iv) 'Ambience'** indicates a trend towards a more open, London-accessible, though still uniquely rural, environment.

Most importantly, however, the first dimension, which surfaced in 1971 – **'Gender'** – had no inevitable trend. The Foundation might theoretically have opted to remain single-sex, like that historical comparator – Harrow, or, up to 2004, rival Highgate. Presenting first as a major change, its resolution within two decades is examined below. The History has shown that the critical seventh dimension, **'(Academic) Standards'**, had fluctuated periodically from the high scholastic tone of, for example, the Dr Whale period, to the all-ability, more 'comprehensive' policy which had reappeared during Michael Hart's time. In the closely-related sixth dimension – **'Intake'** – Michael Hart had startled his still unequivocally MCR with a statement after arrival: *he took it that his first job was to fill the school*. As one of his chosen Housemasters, Alec Robertson, later put it, this was *a very early warning of the changing nature of the Head Master's role. It is a business: no pupils = no income = no school*. (The DfEE's *Guardian*-inspired 'League Table' initiatives of 1992/3 would later reverse this balance yet again, forcing a re-focus on quality – one aspect of government policy, affecting both **Dimensions (v)**, and **(ix)** – the evolving role of the Independent Sector itself).

The eighth element, **'(Parental) Expectations'** was the newest of the behavioural pressures, reflecting the growing strength of well-informed Day parents, and relatively unknown in earlier times: the trend from a traditional belief that parents could trust a school as an institution which by divine inspiration knew exactly where it was going (and which it was thus a privilege to be part of and pay for) to the new sense that education was purchasable, and therefore open to challenge (thus paid no sooner than any other domestic creditor). That element embraced a startling statistic: that by 1989 as many as 41% of ISC-pupils' parents were 'New School Tie' – new to the independent education field. The fifth dimension – **'Catchment'** – the trend from 'national' to 'locality/ area', became a fact, closely tied to **'Expectations'**: newly-affluent parents started to scrutinise educational performance across the Independent/ Maintained spectrum. (Only by the mid-1980s did the new 'pc' Independent label start to edge out the customary 'Public School'.)

The related ninth factor was also novel in the degree of its incidence – a two-way movement between the sectors, at various levels (including 11+ transfer). By the end of the period even that boundary was beginning to blur, with private-sector educational institutions bidding to take over public-sector failing schools. The tenth element, highly contentious – the surplus-making corporatism of a school – had always been implicit but never before so crucial. Short-term, low-profile muddling-through to better times was no longer an option; the new target mode was, in essence – make a surplus on fee income and be seen to succeed, or – eventually – fail.

These dimensions inevitably gave rise to various viewpoints about the course that the School should pursue; thus the two ensuing decades would offer no easy ride to any of the Heads required to 'deliver'. The corporate regime that would survive would be the one which from top to bottom positively embraced the imperative logic of these changes. Mill Hill was not alone in this process: it was the common HMC experience of this time – some schools, such as Royal Masonic, did fold. At the parental level, these incipient tensions could be sensed, although less immediately than at the level of the School's staff. At the pupil level, little of this underlying debate came through – nor should it have: the task was to teach, not to allow the underlying corporate problems and consequent erosion of available time to impinge on that teaching. This was a concept that Alastair Graham sought constantly to assert, although some Governors felt that his own presentation of issues sometimes itself complicated debate.

Tough at the top

Although the School's Founders would not have recognised any debt to Emperor Napoleon I, there is cause to be grateful that the first Foundation had to wait until the year 1807. But for the delays imposed upon reform by the impact of the French Revolution, a hypothetical Mill Hill Bi-Centenary could have come up for celebration in the early 1990s. Had that been so, instead of the beginning of the policy stabilisation and a tighter structure which is characteristic of the Mill Hill of the millennium, a different story would have presented itself.

Never would the representation of the School as a homogeneous, closely interwoven tapestry seem more questionable. For much of the period from 1975 to the 1990s, the image of a kaleidoscope would be more descriptive. Shake it one way, and there appear five generations of active – even sexually-liberated – pupils, enjoying their adolescence within a unified but liberal regime. Shake it another way, from a top-down perspective, and other, divisive vistas open up. Corporately, the 25 years form five phases, each with a distinct flavour; aficionados of Mill Hill's origins could ascribe Bunyanesque epithets to each of them. There were five initial inflation-beset years of *stasis*, 1975-79, with a School facing serious policy problems and where, up to Autumn 1979, indiscipline seemed unchallenged – witness the hissing of the Head in Chapel, the hoisting of a giant effigy to him, or the defacing of noticeboards. Then came six good Graham years, in the memory of one of his key choices, Tim Dingle, one more Mill Hill "golden" time, 1980-85; the short but crucial fulcrum passage from 1986 to 1988, to whose significance the History will return; a penultimate six-year transition of some tension, 1989-94; and a final period when what might easily have become a 'battle' began to achieve its step-by-step, very English solution, 1995-99. The apparent symmetry of those time-divisions around that central fulcrum should not imply any inbuilt balance in this complex, long drawn-out era: from a corporate point of view, it was an uneasy process, for which no quick ready-made policy evolved.

Although at least three heroic figures will be seen to stand out from this period (with two more from Belmont), the challenges inherent within those 10 key dimensions were reflected in discontinuities at the top of the School's governance. Many different pairs of hands were now to touch the Head's tiller, the success of one substantive appointment seeming uncannily – yet not without historical precedent over the preceding 100 years – to vitiate the choice of the next. First came Alan Elliott, from 1974 to 1978, a would-be liberalism coming across, perhaps unfairly, as too 'soft'. Second Master and Yorkshireman Allan Phimester, as Acting Head – 1978/9 – won what *Nobis* termed a *special place among the immortals*. Cambridge Languages 'First', Alastair Graham, served longest – 1979-92: Mill Hill's first Squash "Half-Blue" Head, member of CU's Hawks Club and a Wykehamist from Eton, he put MHS back on the HMC map, elected as Chairman of its London Division. He was the last 'Head Master', in one of the loneliest times in the hot seat. He was followed as a putative 'Foundation Chief Executive' – 1992-5 – by Mill Hill's second incumbent Head and now formal 'Headmaster', Euan MacAlpine, a man with his roots, and his heart, in the Highlands, but possessed of a vision of 21st-century education, based on his previous Bedales model. There was then one more year of an Acting Headship, this time for a newly-styled Deputy Head; thereafter, with a true

Icon of an era, David Tinker, Captain of record Shooting VIII 1974-5; later, as a Lt RN, to lose his life in 1982 Falklands War. (Of this late 20C sample of what would become a co-ed sport, however unrepresentative, three boys were sons of OMs, one a former 'Middlesex' boy). *11.a*

grasp of Mill Hill's geographical context, and – politically more significant, with a *Millhillian* consensus behind him – William Winfield was selected for the 'Headmastership' itself in 1996.

This fifth new Head had been a noted bowler of leg-breaks in his days as BB House Tutor, with all the attributes of 'keeping to a straight line' that the cricketing imagery might imply, yet it was the field of his first love, music, that would best depict him. To mix the metaphors, it would be as a safe pair of hands, wielding a firm baton, and as a manager of ensembles of staff, that his strength would emerge.

1977: long-haired monitors and 1974-8 MHS Head Master, Alan Elliott. *11.b*

Like his predecessor, he would make his mark as a tough picker of staff. The task was now a quadruple one, with this chief 'Executive' at that stage as first among equals, in close partnership with the farsighted Director of Administration and Finance, needing to oversee three schools as well as the overall finances. Chapter XII will suggest it to be a unifying, professional performance, by sheer complexity defying comparison with any previous Mill Hill 'reign'.

Given the recency of the time, the classical principle of 'say only good of the living' – enunciated in a comparable history, *Rugby Since Arnold* – is here preferred. Moreover, in view of the brevity of tenure of three of its exponents, the 25 years 1975-99 are best taken as an entity, rather than attempting to trace the short-term impact of each individual within it, although this underplays many of the considerable advances under Graham; local colour, the detail of the inner life of the School, will occupy the last part of this chapter. Indeed for this period only this one Head occupied the crease for more than the seven years, a period which up to now, in the light of the reigns of John Whale and Michael Hart, has seemed to be the minimum upon which an even-handed view can be taken. As a final recourse to the cricketing idiom, this is not to underplay the value of the two 'overnight batsmen' who were brought in to hold the crease at two critical junctures, Allan Phimester in 1978, and William Winfield from 1995 to 1996.

This atmosphere of uncertainty was also mirrored in the equally vital complementary strand in the central hub of governance, the Court Chairman. At a time when that function's normal steadying presence 'above the battle' was required, no fewer than six figures succeeded each other, all for their own or fate's good reasons, in this core role at a most taxing time. First came an outstanding Chairman – Marshal of the Royal Air Force Sir Dermot Boyle, representing the military element in the saga, succeeded after a seven-year term in 1976 by Sir Alan Orr, one-time Lord Justice of Appeal, who resigned through ill-health in 1979 (the first Chairman with a son who had served on the staff, Classics master G.R.Orr). An Old Millhillian, the lawyer Michael Kempster, then took on the task, most efficiently but reluctantly, not believing in *OM*s in this role; he resigned in 1981 upon appointment to the Bench in Hong Kong. An experienced public administrator, and Mill Hill resident, Prof Sir Cyril Philips, former Vice-Chancellor of London University, was then asked to join the Court; in his autobiography, *Beyond the Ivory Tower*, he made no reference to his time on the Court – perhaps it did not accord with that title. Resigning in 1989, he proposed to the Governors a successor-nominee of Judge Esyr Lewis QC, Sir Gordon Slynn, a distinguished Judge at the European Court. Many good things derived from this incumbency for all three parts of the 'Trinity', although Graham had some difficulty in accessing a busy lawyer's international diary. In January 1995, Mill Hill's 12th MP Governor, Dame Angela Rumbold, was asked to take over: Sir Gordon had identified her early on as a successor – Mill Hill's first female politician – after a firm tradition of lawyers, academics, and servicemen.

A move towards the future

By electing her, the Court had now made a decisive move towards today's Foundation. Dame Angela Rumbold PC DBE MP, her formal style by 1992, was steeped in the world of education, and not least in pre-school provision, a policy area that she had made her own. Educated at a top single-sex GPDST school, Notting Hill and Ealing High, with a First in law at King's, London, she had entered Parliament in 1982, representing Merton, Morden and Mitcham until 1997, achieving office successively in the Department for Education and Science from 1986 to 1990, and then the Home Office, under that other female political 'first', Margaret Thatcher. Both would have been pleasantly surprised if the future Mill Hill connection had been prophesied, at the time of the PM's successful informal visit – the fourth historic Prime Ministerial presence to honour Mill Hill – with her Millhillian consort, Denis, at the peak time of Mill Hill's painful heartsearchings, 1987. *A propos* the value of Dame Angela's 'experience as a former Chairman of a London Borough Education Committee' (in the carrying into effect of the Education Reform Bill of that same year), her senior colleague at both Ministries, the Rt Hon Kenneth Baker, wrote with understatement, in his autobiography, *The Turbulent Years... I had a lot of help from Angela Rumbold.*

Allan Phimester TD, Acting HM, 1978-9; one of the select few staff to reach '100 Club' status (100 terms). *11.c*

If the new Chairman's speeches in the Commons were any guide, she would now focus, as the daughter of a scientist, on the basic *logic* of situations; she would also be there to combat any possibly *negative factors* among colleagues. Opposing the *mediocrity of a blanket system*, she had consistently argued in public for the interests of parents – they were *the key to improvement, and if they are allowed to choose what they want for their children, they will choose academic standards.* The end-purpose was *a high quality, broad and balanced education*; this would be unashamedly grounded in *old-fashioned ideas of... standards, uniform, and good behaviour.* If that were to have been the 'programme' on which Mill Hill selected her to lead them, it would have been a timely one. The proceedings of *Hansard* for that time reveal one other attribute not easily inferrable from these quotations: a capacity for hard work. Professional politicians can bring two further gifts to the table of any institution: an awareness of timing, coupled with a capacity for toughness with the people they can work with, be they fellow-politicians or civil servants, Governors or especially, Headmasters. Her 'Art of the Possible', placing the School in a broader, relevant national context, was what Mill Hill now needed.

From the start, the new Chairman looked for the possibility of that partnership, initially with a Headmaster she inherited, which had typified the first three quarters of the century. She would also show a political touch in welding the Court's Millhillian caucus into a clear view of the Foundation's future; (although that element in the Court has sometimes been criticised, Mill Hill, unlike many schools, had only four times in the 20th century chosen an *alumnus* as Chairman). She grasped that the *OM* Governors, using the vantage point of their power-base – both via the constitution, and in practice by virtue of their loyal attendance – could bring a head of steam to bear on actuating policy, once they had been convinced of a line of thinking, however challenging to their conditioning. Causes could be championed by some of the *OM* Governors, backed initially by educationists such as Paul Hodgson

Cambridge Squash "Half-Blue" Alastair Graham, Head Master MHS, 1979-92, replete with CU Hawks Club tie. *11.d*

(a former MHS Housemaster and thereafter Head of Queen's, Taunton), Bob Stewart (a widely experienced former Prep School Head), Imperial's Prof Charles Phelps (up to his death in 1999), June Taylor (former Head of Sherborne Girls School) and the first in a new line of eminent science men, Prof Michael Proctor (Dean of Trinity College, Cambridge).

The fact that Dame Angela could count *OMs* among her relations (the Secretary to the Court, Peter Woodroffe, and the Zuppinger family), and so might share a putative Millhillian over-sensitivity, was fortunately irrelevant: this new Chairman would place Mill Hill, without prejudices, in the setting of an informed view of what *OM* Sir Michael Bishop, heading British Midland (later 'bmi'), and formerly Chairman of Channel 4, would describe in his speech on the millennium's final Foundation Day, 25 June 1999, as an *ultra-competitive* world: it was an appropriate note to strike.

Only in the third strand of the top management team would there be a discernible continuity. Immediately upon appointment in September 1987, Lt Col Beverley Morgan was launched on a fast learning curve as the School's first qualified Accountant, and first Director of Administration and Finance (and later first Company Secretary), a pathfinding new job-spec compared with the traditional 'Bursar'. The title, instigated by an accountant Governor, Roy Constantine, had meaning; the historic position of Treasurer would soon cease, giving the 'DAF' a pivotal role, which he proceeded to perform with distinction.

The fact that the School came through this period even as well as it did is also due to the constancy of that fourth element in the running of a school, the vital teaching staff – members of the emerging mixed CR, headed up initially by two new Directors of Studies, one of Alastair Graham's innovations, and including senior staff such as Second Master Chris Sutcliffe.

Choices and options

It has been clear in earlier generations how a governing body can get appointments wrong, despite vigilance. 'Good performers at interview' still get through; the provision of references from within an interviewee's previous establishments is still self-evidently flawed, prone to omission: referees apologise at HMC conferences about names whose cards they 'marked', when talking privately with later incumbents, after such 'mistakes' have worked their way through the system. Given the importance of 'getting the right fit', and the knowledge available today of the inherent fallibility of such processes, the traditional means whereby schools, and other professions and areas of public life, still choose their top person is open to question. There is no magic wand: today, a multi-million-pound turnover commercial enterprise may well select its Chief Executive after from 10 to 20 different interviews, over a period of six months or more, aided by consultants, indicators of managerial 'competences', and even WOSB-type Assessment Centres.

Schools' customary methods of enhancing this process – taking informal soundings along the grapevine – are only as good as the Chairman of a Governing Body chooses or has the time, to make them; a suitable Governor would covertly try to meet a representative from a candidate's current CR, to ascertain how they were seen on the ground. If added to this, major change is afoot, the selection determinants will reflect the inevitable underlying differences; in consequence an increasing degree of Governor intervention with the Head can result (a situation encountered in many previous regimes). There are too, as seen in relation to the pre-war case of Dr Derry, further pressures deriving from the educational world itself: not making a speedy appointment – a common situation in business – seeming to some insiders to be more damaging to reputation than precipitately making what actually turns out to be a wrong one. In Mill Hill's case, even the insider experience available in Governor Roger Griffiths, former Headmaster of Hurstpierpoint and HMC Secretary, was marginalised by some in one selection, on the strange grounds that he might be too close to the field. Provenance can also be critical to Head Master appointments, overweighting other more fundamental, more lasting *ad hominem* factors: whilst for the Mill Hill of the 1970s/1980s a Nonconformist element in a candidate's background might no longer be as decisive as it had been historically, it still mattered, and could tilt the balance when things otherwise seemed evenly weighted. High academic and intellectual capabilities, and co-educational track records at Marlborough and Bedales, ignoring the differing organisational characters of both those institutions, affected some judgments, perhaps understandably, about two of the potential Heads of this time.

Not surprisingly, the Court tended to polarise, although not in personalities. There were in effect two camps, and a specialist element in between. There were those arguing the primacy of the evolving consumer market-place – "What did Mill Hill's potential parents want to pay for?" – and the legitimacy of a Head's role in answering that fundamental question.

Counterbalancing them was a grouping that sought to maintain a traditional Boarding school for boys, combined with the 1980s business language – postulating a 'Chief Executive', who would answer to a company 'Board', coupled with the need for a new function – marketing. This group was at the same time following the example expressed in a different context, at another historic cross-roads, 1945, by that fervent guardian of Mill Hill, Dickie Buckland, believing intuitively like him, as he had put it, in the old Baconian wisdom that *we should walk in the old way till we can see clearly that the new way presents a solid line of advance*. With the eye of history, here were undertones of those power struggles of the early 19th century; education could not just be left to the educators. The purport of that *old way*, for the most understandable gut-reasons, was to seek to preserve Boarding – almost by a Cnut-like act of will; to continue to see a WASP-ish England as the catchment, both in concept and by locality; to keep girls in their – admittedly academically vital – place; to discriminate towards ancient but long-submerged Nonconformist roots; and to restore rugby to its erstwhile lead-status as Mill Hill's would-be unifying inner force and outer image. The problems raised by this dialogue only became clear in the 1990s: one free-thinking, American Governor criticised the Court's planning as being *defensive... the act of a well-intentioned ostrich*, when in fact they should be working on *the religious and social implications of the 21st century*.

1935 Jubilee aka "Hornbeam" Arch, prior to building of new Sports Hall, 1983. *11.e*

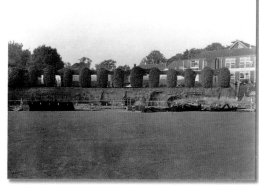

This then is a glimpse of the policy hinterland from 1975 to the opening of the third millennium; space precludes coverage of such Graham achievements as Prep School linkage, the new IT centre, or the tackling of Year 7 entry at age 11 at Belmont or through guarenteed places. Conceived in 1990, the embryonic structure would be reborn as the 'All-through School', now meeting all entry-ages, the 'Trinity' of the Mill Hill School Foundation. A Pre-Prep, headed by Pauline Bennett-Mills, would be created out of the Winterstoke Boarding House, under the courtesy label of its benefactor's name, Richard "Grimsdell". Midwives to the birth were Chris Kelly in his External Relations role; two successive Court Secretaries; the previous Master of Belmont; and as appointers of its first Head – John Hawkins and Bob Stewart.

Performance

A brief preliminary account of the key 'technical' theme – A-Levels and leavers' destinations – is given in **Fig.J(iii)**: the characteristics – an increasing diversity within the tertiary sector, but a reduced Oxbridge salience. Pupils, and parents, were becoming more campus-wise, selecting the right course for the future career, unmesmerised by ancient 'cachet', (and also avoiding further school fees). Allan Phimester cited a case in 1978 of a potential Oxbridge-entrant opting for the veterinary course at Glasgow University. In earlier days, he would have been pressured to do a 7th Term UVI Oxbridge Entrance – and in fact not without reason; despite the surmise of at least one Governor at this time, about employers taking on management trainees earlier than before, the prevailing practice among the mainstream graduate recruiters (members of AGR) was in precisely the opposite direction, and the major firms still restricted their search to 'good' degree graduates at a limited number of Universities and the post-1992 former Polys. Scholarship successes, such as William Bains' Open at Corpus, Oxford in 1975, or those of Clive Partridge and William Kennet at Cambridge in 1977, then later Darshan Mistry's RAF Scholarship, and the 11 Oxbridge places of 1987/8, were still duly feted. The abolition of Oxbridge Open Awards in 1985 demystified matters, but as a later Table will show, a very different picture would be emerging as the century closed. In the new A- and O-Level League Tables from 1993 onwards, Mill Hill's broad-ability population would move the ranking up and down from year to year, in the *Daily Telegraph* Divisions 2 to 4, with no pattern yet emerging.

The report delivered to the Court by its Vice-Chairman looked at the A-Level results for the 10 years 1975-86. This was the most painstaking analysis ever undertaken, let alone by a Governor: the mathematical skill of its compilation was a measure of the concern experienced by everyone, from the Head Master onwards, about the School's academic performance. The production of trend-lines, with three-year moving averages, made interesting reading to those familiar with Boards of Directors, baffled by results for single snapshot years, with their inbuilt capacity to mislead. Alastair Graham, the first Mill Hill Head to have worked in a City environment before teaching, was the first to appreciate such an approach – (his numerate successor would have welcomed it too), if – and it is a vital 'if' – it encompassed a school's inaptness to fast turn-round, and if a crucial often misunderstood distinction could be observed: as one Governor summed it up in 1990: *not running a school as a business, but running it in a business-like way.* As a rare picture of the educational bill-of-fare that Mill Hill was then offering, the detail merits attention.

The report quantified the perceived concern, using the Head Master's own raw data, giving points to each performance of the annual 90-100 A-Level candidates across some 14 recurring core subjects, and a further 11 one-off specialist ones. Five points went to an 'A' Grade, down to none for the fail Grades F and G. Nine subjects examined in detail were, in descending order of candidate popularity: first, Maths, both 'Maths for Scientists' (247 Candidates), and 'Modern' i.e. candidates mainly taking Modern subjects (163); Chemistry (330); Economics, the consistently least successful option of all (278); English Literature (261); Physics (253); French, showing a surprising downward trend, considering the emphasis placed on French exchanges (252); Biology (204); History (151); and German (80). The other five recurrent subjects were: Politics, Geography, Art, Latin and Further Maths. No fewer than 11 specialist, often one-off subjects were listed, to be seen as either a valiant Millhillian adherence to the historic pursuit of diversity, or as a potential diffusion of scarce, costly, academic resources. These (with brackets indicating the number of years in which candidates presented for them) were: History of Art (1); Physics with Maths (4); Business Studies (1) as distinct from Commercial Economics (1); Greek (2); Music (3); Computing / Computer Science/ Electronic Systems (4); and four additional languages, reflecting particular nationalities: Spanish (4); Italian (3); Turkish (2); and Japanese (1). Russian at this stage was not an option offered.

The predelictions of Head Masters, or senior figures of the CR, could be detected, both 'Greek' candidates occurring under Alan Elliott; the prevalence of History and Politics underlined the strength of the Department built up by Allan Phimester; the availability of language options emphasised the Modern Language backgrounds of both Michael Hart and Alastair Graham.

As always, administrative school-level morals could be taken from such an analysis, highlighting relative weaknesses in some departments, either of teaching or pupil option-takers. There were five upward trends (German, History, English, Chemistry, Biology); trends in other subjects analysed were disappointing. The gravamen of the analysis lay, however, in its revelation of the rough quartiles within these results: while the bottom 50 per cent showed a consistent if unexciting level performance over these years, the top 50 per cent and top 10 per cent showed marginal declines. The average 'points' per candidate were 6.4 in 1976; 6.0 in 1985.

This analysis was later supplemented by a further Report for the two years 1986 and 1987, showing a different picture, underlining the improvement now credited to the Head. In any case, attribution was not the immediate purpose: the task was to take action, and this the Head Master, watched anxiously by the Court, now proceeded to do. His *firm sense of direction* had been praised soon after his appointment; *the time for decision is now* was his equally firm demand at the Court of

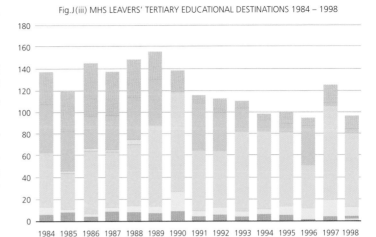

Fig.J(iii) MHS LEAVERS' TERTIARY EDUCATIONAL DESTINATIONS 1984 – 1998

A Oxbridge awards

B Places at Oxbridge + US 'Ivy League'

C Medical and Paramedical

D All Tertiary Educational Institutions

E Armed Services (all countries)

F Resits or unknown

G Tuition, Working, HNO, Gap, Re-pat, NQ

7 March 1987. He was aided in this process by the Master of Belmont, now attending all Court and FG&P Committee meetings; backed by IAPS and HMC statistics, he underlined the dangers of not grasping the cultural, and Day-trend educational nettles then apparent. Of the knock-on impact of such a policy, the dissociation of thought that characterised some of the thinking in this trying period was encapsulated at the Court meeting in 1985: *it was felt that [Belmont's] implementation would on balance not have any substantially... adverse effect upon Mill Hill School.*

The tide of events

The corporate story of the 1990s has been foreshadowed. By 1991 a new Master had been appointed to Belmont – John Hawkins, from Caterham Prep School, to succeed Alastair Graham's fellow-spirit in the process for evolutionary change, Gordon Smith, who decided after 11 years in post to retire two years early: Belmont's *History* of 1994 is testimony to their and their predecessors' inputs for the wider Mill Hill. For maintaining a sense of balance, the inputs of other Governors also deserve mention: on the seeming red herring of whether there should be an additional 'Chief Executive', while one member feared that this would undermine the Head, another was able to point out that the Head was already by virtue of his office the 'CE'. When a faction wanted both the fashionable US ideas of a Development Officer and also a Marketing Officer, a Governor asked the brave, unpopular question: "Can we afford all this?"

After an increasingly rough ride, yet with results reviving to an earlier 'high', 1992 saw the New Foundation's first true retirement, Alastair Graham moving on from his *13 years of challenge, change and opportunity* – Mill Hill's 'fulcrum' years. What he described as the *plughole* inherited in 1979 had become a *demand overflow*. He and Penelope, a model for a modern Head Master's wife, continued to offer a supportive presence in their favoured area of European school exchanges.

He had witnessed the passing of the post-war population bulge, and *remorseless inflation*, followed by the recession of the early 1990s. The Tuck Shop was relocated to the more secure former Armoury – inner fortification displacing the external; the Scouts evolved into CCF Adventure Training in 1985; some of the School's 38 staff houses were sold. For leavers a new tradition – valedictory services in the Chapel, resplendent with a new Organ; Sunday Chapel now ceased – Alastair Graham found the Chapel of the 1980s *the greatest challenge...* At his best, Alastair Graham will be remembered for an heroic grappling with an array of problems – personal and corporate, macro- and micro-educational, parental and environmental – and for espousal of a more flexible approach to Boarding. There were organisational advances too: the centrality of 'Seventh Termers' in a Third Year VI; the Director of Studies role; the system of Form Tutors; the introduction of Staff Appraisal; the concept of Faculty Blocks; the emphasis on Design studies and CDT; and the achievement of an insider, Chris Kelly, for the culturally-unnatural role of Sales and Marketing (re-styled as the Director of Educational Services). For some however, Graham's Wykehamist articulacy and forthrightness could be misconstrued or misunderstood.

He had consistently argued the case for a contemporary Head to divest himself of the tactical, in order to concentrate on the strategic; he had caused a focus on the paucity of bursaries, and, with Treasurer Roy Constantine, on the lack of a capital reserve. The School, Mill Hill Enterprises Ltd, and the Village look back to the fruits of this 'Building Era **7**' – the Sports Complex by the "Fishing Net", opened by commentator Brian Johnston in 1983. Few will now recall the failure to get past the planning stage of what some saw as a sound idea for a much-needed flagship – a Business Studies Centre, with an Industrial Fellow, such as had been built by many schools, including St Bees: this had involved the pursuit of seven sites, ranging from the Winterstoke Lawn to the lower Wills Grove Allotments.

The Mill Hill of this time had a full share of 'PR' – from the unwanted 1986 *Toffs on Hunger Strike* headline, over catering deficiencies, and the story, leaked by a master's wife, of the School's *Squirrel cull* of 1990 (Mill Hill's first example of whistle-blowing), to several positive media moments. On 29 January 1984, with John Julius Norwich as guest of honour, the centenary was celebrated of the publication of volume 1 of the Murray Dictionary at Mill Hill. The year 1987 brought the visit of a fourth Prime Minister to Mill Hill, with her consort, later Sir Denis Thatcher, whose destiny it was, over two decades, to be closer to the great affairs of state than any other *OM*. On 23 April 1988 Sir Robert Telford, President of Marconi, unveiled a plaque in the Science School to Cecil Goyder's epic radio-communications exploits of the 1920s (see Ch.VI). Prompted by Gowen Bewsher, in 1991, came the celebration of the centenary of McClure's appointment.

1986: the later Sir Denis Thatcher *OM* accompanied by his consort, the fourth incumbent or future PM to visit MHS:
(i) the later Lady Thatcher meets two *MHM* Editors;
(ii) Denis Thatcher (r.) talks to a monitor. *11.f*

"Football management is for wimps"

Since the choice of the next Head has been the subject of much *revisionism*, and also of national public press comment, the History has been at pains to try to present a true picture. Sensing that this was a critical moment, the Court followed the lead of its Chairman, Sir Gordon Slynn, then commuting between London and the European High Court in Luxembourg; yet a new, high £60K salary failed to attract the would-be 'business CEO' target. Finally biting on the bullet of co-education, they picked a man not merely with a record of Headship, in the Roy Moore vein, but from that co-ed field to which they were now looking. In 1992 Mill Hill welcomed the Head since 1981 of the doyen of the country's co-ed schools, Bedales.

Governors can sometimes forget that recruitment is a two-way process, yet in appraising their appraisers, many incoming Head Masters prefer to ignore the lessons of their potential school's previous history, relying instead on the buzz within the HMC. Angela Rumbold later ascribed Mill Hill's late 1980s *poor public image* in part to what seemed to the outside a reluctance to embrace change. Old Cranleighan and former maths don, Euan MacAlpine, was aware of what he might be taking on: he knew Mill Hill as a boyhood opponent on the ostensibly sacred field of rugby football; in 1968 he had turned down – in favour of Winchester (where he became a Housemaster) – an offer of a post by Michael Hart, whom he admired; and he knew Alastair Graham well and had empathised with him in his policy problems. What he could not know was that his own unconventional posture – for Angela Rumbold *he*

Science School plaque to Cecil Goyder's 1920s wireless feat, unveiled in 1983 by Marconi Chairman. *11.g*

was not an easy man to work with – itself fitted into a convention, one forged previously by two other first-class degree holders – Dr Derry and Dr Whale. He shared some of the characteristics of those archetypal predecessors: a sharp mind; an apparent respect for standards; and the often inevitable concomitant of these features – an impatience with those less well-informed. The steely blue-eyed glance, the crisp speech, the wiry frame – these were also common traits of these three self-motivated, historically recurrent, would-be shakers of the Mill Hill tree.

There were, however, differences: a greater height, a shock of unruly white hair; more overtly, a Bedalian disdain for formal suiting, preferring an old cardigan when in his study or during holidays, a blazer outside, or kilt and tweed jacket for CCF Inspections. An atheist coming to a school of spiritual values, he worshipped neither at the altar (nor at the shrine of Mill Hill's erstwhile alternate religion – rugger); the Anglican Rev. Paul Hunt, the Chaplain re-appointment of September 1993, needed all the more to be and was, in MacAlpine's words, *outstanding* in filling that gap. The question was raised whether Bedales' flat organisational matrix, different origins, and a freer approach to pupils, could blend with a more disciplined hierarchy (the kinds of 'cultural' factors for which headhunters in industry develop sensitive antennae): the Court was assured by the new Head that he would adapt to his new setting, as he had to Winchester's. He was told at interview that his analysis of Mill Hill's problems was *the best ever heard*; the challenges that needed to be espoused were in fact more fundamental than those encountered by any of his forerunners. It was as clear to him as it was both to the Chairman, Lord Slynn – and to the successor Chairman who later had to accept his eventual resignation, Dame Angela Rumbold – that ethnic trends in north-west London were changing the face of the School's world for ever: full co-education, a predominantly Day basis, and a significantly growing mass of pupils holding religious beliefs which debarred contact sports – these appeared to be the only realistic, viable outcome for an Independent competing in north-west London, looking to the opening of the 21st century.

The ensuing events have the subtle texture of a C.P. Snow novel. Euan MacAlpine's fate was to arrive before an *OM* majority on the Court had come round to this contradiction of their own schooling: psychologically, he was the well-defended messenger who is often sacrificed for the truth of his message. Early on at Mill Hill, he assumed the mantle of what politicians call a 'good butcher', declaring two posts redundant — even if they were subsequently reinstated when pupil numbers later increased. During what turned out to be his three-year span, from September 1992 to July 1995, he thought to carry with him what he called the *thinking section* of the staff and pupils. Although he oversaw a period of falling Rolls, he did not realise that he alienated some Prep School Heads when pupils were refused. He even suggested (prophetically) at an OMC Annual Dinner that the School should sport a soccer team. He would not try to persuade parents towards Boarding. He had been asked by the Court, without it being made explicit, to be the Head of the whole Foundation; he could not expect to make close ties with either semi-autonomous Belmont, nor with the third Executive, the DAF, although neither relationship was one of enmity; whilst intervening directly into the balance sheet, he gave free rein to John Hawkins in forming the Pre-Prep.

Three crucial moments ensued. The first was a Court meeting on 19 March 1994, held on the same day as the Twickenham Centenary RFU match; it had been agreed earlier in writing that the Agenda would be kept short; however, after the departure of key Governors, the Chairman nevertheless decided to continue the meeting. The accounting year was changed from the calendar model, vital to forward planning, to September-August, and full co-education was voted in. Later, the Head joked at an *OM* Dinner about the way this group of "rugger" Governors had left early. At the next meeting on 18 June, the year was reinstated, but trust in the dual management of the Agenda was shaken.

The second arose later in October at Belmont. Lord Slynn, who held to his own concept of the Chairman's role, had conceded to a vociferous minority of five out of a Belmont parents' meeting of 90, with the Master, that co-ed entry would only start at the 7+ stage. An F&DC Meeting confirmed the Court's September decision that a delayed Belmont co-ed entry would adversely affect Mill Hill's plans for co-education from September 1997. The School-Belmont relationship was still opaque at this time; even if it would impact on current Belmont parents, on 10 December the Court reinforced the F&DC view. As if on cue, Lord Slynn tendered his resignation, *as a matter of honour*. In the event, despite the reservations of some of the parents about the change, none withdrew their children. Euan MacAlpine, unfairly, was blamed for not fully briefing the Chairman in advance. Subsequently, Dame Angela Rumbold was asked to succeed Lord Slynn (who had retired from the European Court of Justice on appointment as a Law Lord). The third moment for the Head had thereby been created. His one-time sponsor had gone; he had already asked the new Chairman early on if he should resign.

The new Chairman inaugurated two Committees – the Academic, first under Charles Phelps and then, after his death, Bob Stewart. Pastoral Care came under former Day boy, Bill Skinner; a new Finance & General Purposes Committee (then under Gowen Bewsher) became the responsibility on his retirement in 1999 of Roger Graham, both new men ex-Cambridge *OMs* with corporate – albeit not educational – experience. There was, however, one radical conclusion – the Court's choice of a new Head was not working. The Bedales' way just could not become Mill Hill's – a disavowed informality of dress forming the outward pointer to a failure to achieve a supportive consensus within that ancient yet novel concept, Mill Hill's time-honoured 'Octagon of Accountability'. Withstanding his initial emotional temptation *to throw the whole lot in the air and start again*, Euan MacAlpine had made some advances: interestingly the most notable – the all-day co-ed Pre-Prep – had been made easier to push through due to the Court's fears about the fall in Boarding, and its higher fee-income. He also codified definitions of responsibility (in the 1990s baronial Housemasters could still arrive at differing solutions to identical problems, e.g. to smoking); he espoused the co-ed culture and language to suit it, and also a

Still-flourishing CCF at Annual Inspection, 1993, newly-badged to Royal Fusiliers; Col J.Gunnell; OMC President, Governor, and *Nobis* author, Gowen Bewsher; and Euan MacAlpine, first so-styled 'Headmaster' MHS, 1992-5. *11.h*

certain openness: for example, publishing an Annual School Record; albeit not in the most tactful way, he had effected changes to existing job-holders' responsibilities – a managerial task familiar in business, but often blurred in schools. However, in school politics, it's not what you do, it's the way you do it. Like the egregious Dr Derry of 50 years before, he was not winning the key constituency, the confidence of the Court.

Resignation was the only outcome, sensibly anticipated by its subject. As usual in such cases, a deal was struck. "Peterborough", in an article in the *Daily Telegraph* on the parallels being drawn with the turnover in soccer team-coaches, wrote (28 June 1995): *He is an unusual schoolmaster, said to be the only member of the* [HMC] *to wear a beard but not a tie* (he always wore one at Mill Hill). *His appointment by... [the] alma mater of Sir Denis Thatcher, generated surprise.* Ignoring the evolutionary processes preceding his arrival, the columnist continued: *Last year it seemed he had conquered the forces of tradition, with the announcement that Mill Hill would be going co-educational in 1997... MacAlpine's successor at Bedale's, Ian Newton, only lasted 15 months'* (actually 27 months, resigning in December 1994). *Two other new heads, eased out recently by their Governors, are John Rees at Edinburgh Academy, and Jennifer Smith at Harrogate Ladies. By comparison, football management is for wimps.* This phase of unpopular, uncomfortably rapid change caused some pain for all concerned; it can be compared to the legendary crises that many Public School histories have highlighted, for example, the famous case of Dr Hayman at Rugby. Its effects would colour the ensuing decade.

Eloquent of 1990s style pervading Mill Hill life – and architecture – awning-extension to Sports Hall, facing 'Astro' field (aka "Fishing Net"), provides new site for co-ed sports – hockey and tennis. *11.i*

The Executives

One of the departing Head's most sharply recalled actions had been to appoint the Third Master as Deputy Head, alongside the existing Second Master, Chris Sutcliffe, in 1992. Later to become one of the longest-serving masters, William Winfield had joined in September 1970, having had to begin to act as No 2 in the same way as Victor Elliott in 1938-40: to support 'the man on the bridge' even in those areas where his views differed. For example, he was jocularly questioned for wearing a suit on one occasion by the loosely-dressing Head (who had himself been ordered by his Chairman to wear one). When Euan MacAlpine resigned, William Winfield was asked by the Court to take on that most exacting of tasks performed only 17 years previously by Allan Phimester, and before that by A.J.Williams in 1922: the role of Acting Head, knowing that simultaneously the Court with which he regularly deliberated was also looking at the process of selecting a new substantive leader of the School.

MHM caricature of supposedly ferocious hockey-playing girls, as envisaged by quizzical MHS male population. 11.j

There are two ways for such an incumbent to play his hand: consciously to hold the fort, in effect presiding over a moratorium, desiring only to resume his duties after his stint in the limelight; or to seize the opportunity presented, and set about proving his mettle for the new job. "WRW" had taken part in practically every area of the School's life, except that of Housemaster, during one of Mill Hill's most taxing times: BB House Tutor; a significant player in the School's musical life; Library curator; Chess Patron; lively involvement in Dent; initially Joint Director of Studies under Alastair Graham, with John Veal, and sole Director upon the latter's untimely death in 1989; and not least an excellent teacher of Languages, with a fervent commitment to the School's European dimension. Here was not just a man who loved Mill Hill, with a sense of duty towards the School during a time of difficulty – as the History has revealed, the CR had a good pedigree in producing such people. For Lord Slynn he *looked the part*; Dame Angela Rumbold wrote that he *liked order, achievement, clarity of vision, and is totally committed*. He knew how things could be made to work, and was respected by his fellows, parents, and the pupils, male and female. As a rider of historical interest, he also happened to come from a broad Nonconformist background and, relevantly, before taking a Modern Languages degree at Clare, Cambridge, he had been Head Boy at an old-established North London Grammar School, William Ellis. The Court and Dame Angela had seen enough of this capability at work before his year of Acting Headship to be reasonably sure that, despite a wide field of excellent outsiders, here – historically a gamble and contrary to all precedents for nearly 150 years – was a man with the capacity for growth under responsibility: 'the man for the job' was only the second staff insider, after Thomas Priestley's auspicious example of 1834. Despite a natural concern about its impact on family life, he was at 48 still young enough to take on what was to become an even more complex management role – at the centre of the new Foundation's 'Trinity' of educational institutions. He declared his willingness *there and then*.

Just as crucial, like the equally committed Head who had first appointed him – Michael Hart – he brought with him a desire to tackle the backlog of decisions that he knew Mill Hill had not yet faced. The Court's decision was promulgated on

(i) New gates (with reinstated feetless Martlets) lead to car park, and (ii) "Cedars", first all-girls House created in 1997 out of former "San" on The Ridgeway. *11.k*

9 March 1996. The customary declaration of unanimity actually meant what it said: there was a broad sense that the Mill Hill Foundation was now in good care. One of the Acting Head's first decisions in May 1995 had been to invite the former rugger coach, Biology Head and successful Housemaster of McClure, Tim ("Thumper") Dingle, to take the job of 'running mate', Acting Deputy Headmaster; (the last insider to win that increasingly vital – but also increasingly transitory – role, the Court thereafter asserted a right to finalise that choice). This move might well have caused some reaction, given that several older men had now to accept a bold younger appointment, but the Mill Hill CR sensed that this was their hour for rallying round; it was ratified the following March. Within the space of months, an excellent fellow Deputy was chosen (effectively from outside, filling-in during the Acting Headmastership): Judith Herbertson, former Head of Modern Languages at the GDST South Hampstead High School, was the first woman to fill that office. Despite her popular sobriquet "Herbo-Cop", she introduced valuable consultative skills to that still-evolving role. The process of succession would be reversed, when Tim Dingle came to move on to the next step in his career, the Headship of Royal Grammar School, High Wycombe, in April 1999. In September that year it would be Judith Herbertson's turn to welcome a new outsider Joint Deputy, Julian Johnson-Munday; she could also co-ordinate policies requiring female insight, be they pastoral or sartorial, although the School was not splitting along sexist lines. Indeed her most recent extra-curricular activity had been to lead a mixed party to Ethiopia in the preceding spring – one to be triumphantly repeated: it was the most adventurous co-operative overseas project ever undertaken (involving not merely Upper VI boys and girls, but also attracting back Millhillians hardly yet 'Old', in their first or second years at university). It was however vital that the declared co-educational policy was seen to be endorsed at the top of the main School, as it already was up to age 13 at Belmont, and from the outset at the Pre-Prep.

Overseeing the Foundation at that inchoate stage were four 'Executives': the 'Headmaster' (superseding the term 'Head Master') had 'dotted lines' of consensual communication to the DAF (in effect a *secundus inter pares*), also to Belmont's then Master and the Pre-Prep Head. At the School, the Senior Management Team was the Headmaster, with two Deputies; the Director of Studies, Andrew Gaylor; 'Senior Housemaster' Trevor Chilton; and an ex-Belmont returnee to Mill Hill, the recently appointed Registrar, Peter McDonough. The Belmont SMT embraced what would prove to be the last 'Master'; his Deputy Head; Directors of Activities and Administration; and the Heads of the Upper and Lower Schools: at the Pre-Prep, the Head and Deputy Head. The senior members of the DAF's Foundation team at Walker House were the former master, Administrator Dr Roger Axworthy, making a mid-career switch, and the Foundation Accountant, Penny Hill.

The management task was strengthened by the Head's presentation of a comprehensive 'School Development Plan, Phase I, 1997-2001', of 22 March 1997, building on the DAF's paper 'The Way Ahead, 1991-7', and 'The Planned Marketing of Mill Hill School'. The thinking in these papers had already confirmed what would earlier have been unthinkable – ending School House boarding; it had made a critical Governor exclaim: *The Titanic has changed course!* The 'SDP' was the most holistic re-think in the School's history. Complementing it in 1998 came incorporation as 'The Mill Hill School Foundation Ltd', the third phase of Mill Hill's legal entity. This at last obviated the problem of the 1869 Scheme – personal liability for each Governor in an increasingly risky world. On the Internet the new Charity, No. 1064758, was classified by the DfEE as e-Mail 'www.Millhill.barnet.sch.uk.', Registration No. 302/6000. However, officialese did not clarify the corporate nature of what was now a company at law, no. 3404450, holding AGMs in October every year. **Fig.Q** depicts the complex integument of the 1990s: these lines of accountability would only work with the Executives' willing co-operation – they would need review.

Five generations of pupils passed through Mill Hill's portals during the course of these corporate events. What other factors affected their school careers? Four themes are treated here: co-education; interface with the world outside; the 'APS'; and 'value-added'. Other aspects – Day/Boarding ratios, the ethical and spiritual 'mix', and structural developments within the 'Trinity' and the Foundation – will be covered in Chapter XII; an overview of Belmont's history appears as Appendix H.

"Genderquake"

Co-education, like all reforms that embody the spirit of their age, appears in retrospect to be – quite simply – normal. The boys had voted as early as 1885 that *woman has had more influence on mankind than man*. The prophecy of Radical MP A.J.Mundella, at that distant McClure Foundation Day, had taken a century to fulfil, prompted by an *OM* at a 1971 Life Governors meeting, and emerging as a *ballon d'essai* under Michael Hart in 1973, four years after girls entered the first HMC VI Forms at Alan Elliott's Marlborough. Of the impact of girls (new) on boys (old) in 1977, Karen Roberts wrote that it could not be over-estimated: *It was a culture shock for them.* That shock merits mention here. Even two years later, as she and five other new VI Form Boarding girls entered the Dining Hall, *total silence fell upon the whole room while the girls were evaluated...*, yet she would soon recall having had *a whale of a time... despite a culture of mocking and teasing; all girls were bestowed with at least one nickname.* Expectations were shaken for some later 16-year old girl-entrants, like the School's first female *OM* Governor, lawyer Annie Williams: *I was expecting stripey blazers and the sound of Elgar drifting down the corridors, but what I got was a tough, unorthodox school in the middle of reinventing itself... nothing could have been a better preparation for a career in the City – an injection of iron into the soul was exactly what I needed.* For others, like Karen Roberts, there was little prejudice from either the masters or the

Fig.Q MILL HILL SCHOOL FOUNDATION LTD: 1990s CORPORATE ORGANIZATION

boys if the girls were prepared to 'muck in'... maybe the ethos of Mill Hill rubbed off on us. This benefit was mutual: *Mill Hill taught me and my contemporaries to be comfortable with members of the opposite sex and to consider them as friends;* somewhere along that path those friendships also blossomed privately into the first inevitable, but quite rightly unattributable, inter-Millhillian teenage love affair.

Co-education at Mill Hill illustrates above all how a trend evolves into dominance: significant stages can be traced along the 39 steps towards this goal of sexual equality, each in itself a milestone, to the eventual moment when an *OM* could say, *I was at school with your mother.* Some have already been flagged up: as Ruth Kearns wrote perceptively in 1985, *before girls were accepted into the Sixth Form, the contexts in which boys saw women at Mill Hill must have been predominantly domestic.* Apart from those first truly co-educated 19th-century young ladies from Miss Russell's Academy and Miss Crump's, the History has noted Miss Warr as the first Lady Matron in 1812, and her successors Hannah Cooke (the only lady to earn a commemorative window in the Chapel) and Annie Pearse (earliest Honorary Lady Member of the OMC, also commemorated in the Chapel, but with a plaque). Mrs Constance Payne was the first full-time teacher while Maj F.R.McLellan was 'at the Front'. Torches were re-lit in 1939-40, with Katharine Whitehorn – the first master's daughter as pupil – technically the first Old Millhillienne. The real break-through occurred in 1974/5: for *two rather unusual years* Beth Baker (although never formally honoured in the Register), daughter of Art HD Cliff Baker, became the first full-time girl pupil, after several girls from The Mount School had attended part-time. At that stage, *a minority of masters... felt that Mill Hill was not the place for girls...* yet *the responses of the boys helped me to integrate quickly.* These were brave early days: she recalled that, with characteristic dry humour, her affectionate father told the still strongly <u>masters</u>' Common Room as Beth left for Art School: *Thank you for turning my uncouth and uncivilised daughter into an uncouth and uncivilised boy.*

Beth was followed in 1976 by the first McClure House Day-girls, Diana Kirkwood, and Juliet Newport, the first *MHM* Editor and school prefect, and the first to demonstrate the benefits of bright girls in the seventh-term 'Oxbridge VI' – an Exhibition to Emmanuel, CU; also Nicola Moody and Jo Stanton, the first daughters of *OM*s. The first six VI Form Boarders entered Ridgeway; the quality of their new bed-sits caused some envy. 1978 saw the first Head of House, and thus *ex officio* the first monitor, in the resuscitated Priestley – Joanna Shannon. With 21 girls in the School by 1979, Kathleen Goodchild became the first captain of a 'Girls Sport' – netball. Two years later, Carole Alexander finally threw the gauntlet into the male camp, winning the first captaincy of a both-sexes sport, small-bore shooting. The first four Boarders joined Burton Bank in 1982. In School House in 1983 the first girl to carry the distinction of having School Roll 'No 1', became also the first to be sadly remembered in a Foundation Day memorial prize – Alison Hampton, killed in an accident at Hull, after leaving Mill Hill.

In the same entry year Tessa Kingsley would go on to win triple firsts – Head of House in McClure, a Duke of Edinburgh award, and the Slater drama cup: later there would be many cultural stars – the pianist Sheryl Lee, the actress and designer Joanna Potter, the "spine-chilling" singer Elli Mouskas, the model Ariane Moody.

Beth Baker and Humphrey Bangham became the first *OMs* to be married in the Chapel. From 1986 the "Bees" girls formed the "St Bees posse". In the next decade, the final 'school staff' height was climbed when Kathy Haering, Liz Kenefick, Cordula Nagel, Val Taylor and Katie Kaimakliotis became joint senior monitors (Heads of School), from 1994 to '99. The loop extended in 1997 with the arrival in McClure of the first IV Form girls, and the introduction of the Headmaster's proactive, comprehensive Equal Opportunities Policy (of course embracing religious and racial equality as well), and the re-conversion of School House for Day pupil co-education by September 1999. Penelope Graham was praised for getting 'Girls' Activities' going; there was a string of firsts, in hockey, netball, cross-country and tennis, culminating in the first-ever fives fixture at U14 level in 1998/9, and a victory. The "San" had first been suggested as a Boarding house 48 years earlier by Bill Ramsay; 1999 saw Cedars House in the converted San enter the first all-girls team in the annual Newcastle CCF competition; Anne-Marie Childs had already won "Best Cadet" in 1983. Anna-Lena Doerks became the first girl to enter the Navy. The girl-pupil target for the School's Roll, already 15 per cent by 1998-9, achieved 20 per cent by 1999, a year ahead of schedule, targeting 120 – 25 per cent – for the year 2001, with a Boarding target of 40 per cent posed for 2004.

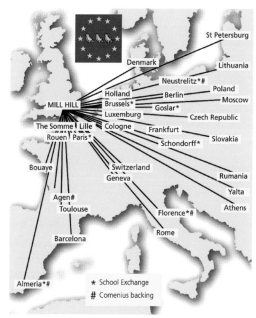

Fig.R MILL HILL IN EUROPE 1995-9

At the staff level, Dr Elizabeth Harle had emerged in 1977 as the first substantive female member of what the male editors of the 1983 Register still called 'Assistant Masters' – and the first to marry a colleague from the CR, Stephen Lovick. Lucy Sutton became the first female of 10 latter day *OM* Foundation staff, (with Rev. Stuart Gibbons, Austin Vince, James Orchard, Clive Greenhough, Andrew Phillips, James Fields, Richard Veal, Ian Wicks and Anjali Sicka). Lindsay Farrant (at Weymouth, then Ridgeway) and Berinda Banks (McClure) triggered some reactions by being picked for the male-'baronial' Housemasters' domain, causing some initial friction. The third of the then nine Houses to have a Housemistress welcomed Pauline Mills, at Cedars, in 1997; School House (using the former Scrutton colours), Burton Bank, Collinson, Priestley, Weymouth and Murray continued with male Housemasters. With Judith Herbertson's appointment – sealed by the Court – as the first Joint Deputy Head, there were by the turn of the century 16 women on a teaching staff of 60; she was able, however, to testify to the notable degree of co-operation with which her prominent role had been welcomed by a still mainly male CR. Pauline Bennett-Mills' selection as the first Head of the Pre-Prep in 1995 (and Lynn Duncan's as Belmont's first Head in the next century – the '39th step') would mean that there were now women at the Foundation Executive level. Women created their own similar landmarks within the Finance Directorate. The solution to Mill Hill's dilemma had in fact taken place quietly, in a carefully planned way, although Mill Hill had not yet taken the step exemplified by a friendly and now fully co-educational rival, St Bees School – the inclusion of a girl cricketer in the cricket first XI.

Taking an early overview of co-education in 1985, Ruth Kearns could claim that Mill Hill had *done a great deal to help women so far*. By the end of the century her goal could be said to have been achieved: *girls are treated as individuals and allowed to express themselves as such... on a level parallel to that of the boys*. This properly graduated revolution within Mill Hill's erstwhile male bastions was effected in common with 156 other HMC former boys-only schools in the UK, with a further 32 at least taking girls in the VI Form. In the Houses and in the hierarchy, in music, drama, sport and even in the CCF, and in the School's day-to-day life, aided by timely rules about relationships, hair, dress, jewellery and behaviour, co-education had succeeded.

The extent to which single-sex schools still showed up better in the media 'League Tables', however discredited, is an issue to be addressed in the final chapter.

International windows, peace dividends

Observers of the Octagon from former, more strait-laced eras would not have recognised its late 20th-century guise. From the Graham era onwards, visitors would discover an explosion of colour and activity, with artwork displays and news, and photographs – of all appointments, staff and 'staff', but especially as constant reminders of the internationalism that was now part of the School's policy. Some 150 overseas visits – 'VSO', linguistic and cultural, exploratory and sporting – were organised over the 25 years, by staff as well as pupils of many age-groups, to places as far apart as Israel, Egypt, Morocco, Hong Kong, Nicaragua, India, Turkey, Barbados, the RSA, Fiji, Singapore, Australia, Hawaii, New Zealand, Argentina, the USA, Canada, and even the Yukon, where Joe McCarron used the Bursary endowed by *OM* Lewis van Moppes. European destinations included Lithuania, St Petersburg, Moscow, Slovakia, Ukraine, Georgia, Denmark (a choir festival); Goslar, Cologne, Berlin, Schondorf, Frankfurt and Neustrelitz; Paris, Rouen, Bouaye, Agen, Toulouse, Lille, the Somme; Almeria and Malaga, Alden Biesen, Hasselt and Antwerp, Luxembourg, Geneva, Rome, Holland, and Switzerland (the first Eton fives tour). Many of these trips, such as the two to Ethiopia, yielded character-forming benefits far exceeding the expectations originally entertained about them, of the kind that National Service had once – threateningly – offered.

This factor was reflected on Foundation Days, with prizes for the European Initiative (won in 1999 by one of the two senior monitors, Rasheed Hassan) as well as through the Hermeville, Barcelona, Cologne and Rouen Prizes – this last celebrating its 30-year anniversary in 1998 for linkage with the *Institution Join-Lambert* in Normandy. At that time, internationalism also acquired salience in a different way: an increasing part of the Headmaster's array of competences was to be his ability to pronounce the names of worthy prizewinners from east of Vienna, introduced through private educational agencies, as a result of *détente*, as well as of the recruitment work of the Registrar, Peter McDonough. 'RoC' (China), Taiwan, Macau and Iran also entered the Register. After the first new Boarders from the Czech Republic, and a still recognisable 'USSR' and 'Yugoslavia' in 1991, pupils started arriving from Azerbaijan, Kazakhstan, Latvia, Macedonia, Romania and Ukraine. By the century's end, this trend saw 'International pupils' figuring in the school directories. The *OMs* Literary Prize – a sturdy survival from the 1920s – was awarded to Maria Hvorostovsky, and the Jubber Prize for Science to Gennady Ilyashenko. Less surprisingly, Ilia Belokriletski won an 'EFL' prize – a worthy part of the syllabus which was not highlighted in the League Tables. This activity had spin-offs: Hena Ahmad went on to read Medicine at Charles V University, Prague; in a European History lesson, pupils from Albania, Russia, Hungary and Bulgaria provided new insightful inputs in class.

Of the less peaceful interaction with the world, so familiar to earlier generations, the Mill Hill connection during the last quarter of the 20th century was mercifully limited; of the dozen or so areas of conflict in which the UK took part, before and after the so-called peace dividend yielded by the ending of the Cold War in 1989, regular officer *OM*s were involved in all except the UN/NATO operations in the former Yugoslavia.

Study of a study, 1990s. *11.l*

The most tragic theatre, suggested by Gowen Bewsher for inscription on the Gate of Honour, was the Falklands Campaign. Juxtaposed with Lt Gen Sir Michael Wilkins' role as Chief of Staff to the RM Commandant General, and Dr Richard Pine's service on HMS *Sir Galahad* for the RFA, a single incident – the death of Lt David Tinker RN on 12 June 1982, aged 25, on HMS *Glamorgan* – impacted beyond the conflict itself. This arose from the book by his father, Prof Hugh Tinker – later to be the Royal Court and BBC2 play, "Falkland Sound to Plymouth Sound". The modest memorial in the Music School's Tinker Room gives no hint that he was in fact a kind of archetypal Millhillian – in his father's later words, *a bright particular star... a strange mixture of conformity and nonconformity. When he was made a Prefect, he resigned... after about a month because he felt that [they] had too much power over other boys. And yet in the Corps he was a somewhat masterful head* (Under Officer, RN). With refreshing, uncynical enthusiasms for many aspects of his school time, including poetry (described in the *Observer* as *the nearest we are likely to get to a Falklands Wilfred Owen*), he was Joint Editor of the *MHM*. He was also Shooting VIII captain; master Ian Brownlie, wrote: *He held the ideals and manners of the most respected Public Schoolboys of 20 years ago, while holding unshakeable views about what was no longer relevant in the 1970s.* With Richard Dimbleby – for his radio broadcast from Belsen in 1945 (and the first Millhillian to have a dedicated memorial in Westminster Abbey) – his name may well be remembered more poignantly from that dark century than those of any other Millhillian: a sombre thought.

Another serving Millhillian, Lt James Fox, was commemorated by a tree on Top Field. (In 1988 Alastair Graham had asked a junior boy to fetch the senior monitor, to be met with the reply: *Oh, you mean James, Sir!*) The names of SAS Maj Gen John Holmes OBE DSO MC, and Lt Col Maxwell Macfarlane, would recur in the respective contexts of Dhofar, and Ulster, the Gulf and the Sierra Leone theatres; Capt R.G.Bewsher won a Gulf 'Theatre' medal. A "Gunner", Lt Col Ashley Manton, extended the coverage, serving in Hong Kong and South Korea; Brig Joe Milburn did tours of duty in Rhodesia and the Congo, as well as in Borneo and the Cameroons.

The Studio Theatre was converted in 1998 from former Gym: old climbing-rope fixtures still visible on roof-beams. *11.m*

This was also the time of the last echoes of war service: in the OMC Presidency – ex-Capt Roy Mills, RA, in 1998/9; and in the School's CR – with the retirement of Arthur Vine, Ted Winter and Alec Robertson in 1983. Tim Stringer was the last Short Service Officer; Austin Vince the last Regular, leaving Mill Hill CR in 1998, but doing a further stint at the School up to 2001. The sole former military presences were Lt Col Beverley Morgan (Walker House) and the ex-Sandhurst Head of Science at Belmont, Jinny Fisher. Despite many complaints at the School Council about the time absorbed, army (with a non-uniform 'Duke of Edinburgh's' squad), navy and RAF sections still engaged energies every Friday afternoon – mandatorily for the IV and Removes. Paul Bickerdike, too young for National Service, had to learn soldiering with other CCF COs at formal camps, setting a service record by 1999 (see Ch. XII), the increase in the 'establishment' creating the CCF's first Lt Col. Even if much of the well-battered martial 'silverware' of yesteryear now lay unused, the annual inter-House 'Newcastle' for drill and turn-out, dating from the First World War, was still keenly competed for, by the girls as well, looking equally smart in uniform. The CCF was re-badged from the former Middlesex Regt to the Royal Fusiliers in 1998, with an elegant candelabra (and later a new Drum Major's sash) to mark the new allegiance. Through the century's end, the Kosovo 'ethnic-cleansing' massacre and the US terrorist cataclysm of September 2001 would remind Mill Hill's new generations of the realities of a still dangerous world.

Value added, value repaid

The reciprocity of contribution between school and pupil, in Belmont as in the Senior School, has been a recurrent theme of this History. This chapter also embraces Mill Hill's participation in 'adding value' to a special sector of the educational market, the Assisted Places Scheme, first proposed by the GBA in 1970. In addition, a few pupils can be identified, regardless of provenance, who by their achievements over this time repaid particular 'value' to Mill Hill.

The 1980 Education Act ushered in the APS. It was the Thatcher Administration's echo of the 'Butler' Education Act of 1944. Unlike that Act, it was open to pupils at 11, but quantity was limited, and schools had to make a financial input; schools were assessed for qualification, and for numbers of places, parents paying contributory fees, as then. For Mill Hill, as Paul Bickerdike observed, it did not seek out the *intellectual cream* as the Middlesex scheme had formerly done. Politically, it offered risk for heavily participating ISJC schools since, if there were a change of government, they might be left with funding requirements for the school career of the 25,000 pupils included. This factor made some Governors suspicious as to whether Mill Hill should be involved, despite the fact that refusal might be at odds with the School's tradition. In the end, a fund of £100,000 was set aside over the first five years (equating to one per cent of total fees) to offset that possibility, with a total subsidy of £660,000. From 1981, the annual intake for the School rose from eight to a peak of 13, while at Belmont 21 were entering in its closing year, 1997; by the final entry of 2000, 322 APS had merged unexceptionally, like the Middlesex Boys before them, into the general stream. No separate analysis could be made of their record; if the Middlesex Scheme is a yardstick, the significant value they added to the School's life, and the School to theirs, can safely be assumed. There were two further aspects: participating schools had to conform to the State system for the publication of results, and to overarching legislation. Gordon Smith at Belmont felt he had to give up corporal punishment; although the Main School was more reluctant to do so, the Children Act of 1989 harmonised the two sectors anyway. The DAF was able to confirm that there was no financial 'blip' for the Foundation when 'New Labour' phased out the APS through the Education (Schools) Act of 1997; numbers were phased out completely by 2005.

There were many, including APS pupils, whose personal success added value to the success of the School during these 25 years. As always, selection of individuals is invidious; inevitably, in sport the emphasis at this stage was male. England rugby teams welcomed Ben Levenstein, the first *OM* to get into the England U16 XV. The first professional *OM* rugby players won U18 caps: Adrian Flavin in 1997/8 (later switching to the Ireland U21), and Gerald Arasa with three in 1997/8. The American role-icon of the scholar-sportsman could certainly be identified in the first Oxbridge "Blue" for this period – Tim Jones capped for Oxford (1978), playing later for Wales B. Ben Jordan won the first A.F.Todd Sports Award in 1997. The 1st XV won the Middlesex Schools Cup in 1993. That other major sport, cricket, had many star turns too: Justin Le Fort's third century in 1998; or the 133 n.o. for Steven Selwood (later in the Junior England XI); Ian Maciver (in England's U19 XI, 1978), and Paul Robin (164 n.o. v. Nottingham HS). David Goodwin (157 v. Highgate, 100s in three of his five 1st XI seasons, and Presentation Bat winner) challenged the Murray-Wood legend of 1935 for Mill Hill's best cricketer (see Ch.VI), whilst not yet beating Brian Piper's record for the fastest-ever century (136 v. Sedbergh at 2.4 runs per minute in 1942). Tim Dawson's Oxford "Blue" (1981) echoed S.R.Wright's (Exeter, 1973). Bowling talent included Charles Freeman, Windsor Roberts, Ehraz Rashid, Richard Peach, Mark Brandon and Vishal Bhimjiyani. The Middlesex Schools Cup was won in 1993, 1995 and 1999, the U15 and U19 Cups in 1995.

Looking to the new century, other competing sports were soccer (now daringly asserted as *the beautiful game* by new coach Peter Lawson), swimming, basketball, badminton, athletics and cross-country, tennis, croquet, judo, golf, and a renewed fives tradition – with a firm Belmont influence from Christian Arnold. Colours now came in jumpers, squares, umbrellas, and even an 'Old Weymouth Tie'. In the wake of Stephen Roberts' Cambridge "Half-Blue", hockey's triumphs – at last in 1998, after 36 years, on an Astro-Turf, included Basit Nasim (the Middlesex U18), Simon Bunyard (U16), and Simon Choudhury in the South England U18; a trophy honouring Mill Hill's and the UK's greatest world sportsman, Mike Corby, was awarded to the 'hockey player of the year' from 1997 onwards. Although fencing,

Music School Studios (opened in 1999 by *OM* Sir Michael Bishop, Chairman of **bmi** airline). Location was the site of old air-raid shelters, forming SW flank to evolving Stoa. *11.n*

like squash, faded as a School sport, Ellis Scott was All-England Epée Champion in 1999. Simon Ratzker was Middlesex Champion in the U17 400 metres in 1997. A win in the Middlesex Schools' Golf Championship (1992/3) rewarded Chris Sutcliffe (its re-inaugurator in 1979). The Rifle Range merit board honours the 1970s/80s full-bore shooting heyday: record marksman Neil Black won the Silver Jubilee at Bisley (second in three events, 900 competitors) – Adrian Harvey the Wellington Cup (best at 200 yards); Jamie Carswell shot for Scotland in 1996. A team snap-shooting win in *Country Life's* 1998 Competition provided a climax to Ian Brownlie's 29 years as coach.

In contrast, if a reminder were needed that this was an 'educational community', standing out academically were Pelham Barton's Maths Olympiad in 1975 (he took an Open Scholarship at Queen's College, Oxford) and Matthew Frise's top score in the UK Senior Maths Challenge, and his Biology Olympiad in 1998, first out of 400: he went on to take a first in Medicine at Emmanuel, Cambridge. Also in 1998 seven pupils got 'AAAA' or better, at A-level. As examples of individual scores, reflected on Foundation Days, Richard Corbett, Hidetaka Kobayashi, Andrey Kharlamov, and Vlad Gorobtsov each scored five 'A's over the years 1995-7, going on to Robinson and Girton (Cambridge), and LSE. Behind them at GCSE, David Borchard and Mark Simmonds were achieving 11 'A's, and Peter Thonemann 10 'A's in 1993/4, emulating Tim Kenefick from 1988. Oxbridge in-College scholarships after Year 1 included the names of Frise, Corbett and Thonemann; the latter became a Fellow of All Soul's, Oxford. Stephen Nunn went on to read Russian and Japanese at Leeds; Cedars even awarded a House Tie for Academic Achievement – to Michelle Dugan.

The 25-year period grounded in the 'Public School revolution' of the 1960s/70s nevertheless ended in a quandary; only now would that doggedly enduring 'Public School' nomenclature start to look a little passé. As the old century closed, the portents were that every area of Britain's now more recognisably Independent Schools' performance would need to be re-sharpened to meet the challenging reinvestment being mooted for the public sector. It looked as if, in the Mill Hill that would greet the new millennium, neither the 'hard factors' of male sporting achievement nor the much hoped-for co-educational academic prowess in the League Tables were on hand to restore the School to former prominence; a traditional solo empire had become embattled, but the tripartite successor entity did not so far appear to have a found a coherent new role.

Yet the world of work was changing rapidly, almost before the very eyes of pupils and staff. 'Softer' career qualifications were being demanded by an increasingly affluent, technology-based, communications- and leisure-driven workplace. Of the *cultural structure of the School*, Alastair Graham had asserted as far back as 1992 that theatre and music were now becoming its *central pillars*. Many House Reports would remark on the ever-increasing managerial and teamwork qualities required to stage the annual House Plays. Was there here a more balanced, more career-relevant, more life-formative concept of talent, achievement and transferable skills? Would this emerge as the keynote for the Foundation of the 21st century which would accord with the aspirations of the Foundation's multi-racial catchment area? Would this process endow Mill Hill with a new kind of winning reputation?

A 'battle for Mill Hill'?

Historical perspective needs time; a School History is always in danger of lapsing into a mere recital of events, without shape or priority. Yet just as the 'Battle of Britain' has only now, some 60 years after the event, proved to be the decisive turning point in the survival of Britain in the Second World War, so too a future historian may well judge to be just such a key moment the appointment of William Winfield to head up this third, and still evolving, new foundation. The survival of Mill Hill at the first 'New Foundation' in 1869 was clearly a significant make-or-break moment, yet the historical judgement has to be that the strongholds of Nonconformity would somehow have rallied to the flag: the residual religious forces, the supporting Millhillian funding sources, but above all a unified sense of purpose – all these factors underlying the School were too strong to have allowed such a collapse to last.

None of those factors, however, was behind the embattled Mill Hill of the 1980s/90s when, as has been described in this necessarily extended chapter, many elements were combining to threaten the long-term successful existence of the Independent schools. In the belief that the School will indeed survive, the single event of the unplanned emergence of this current most unassuming yet tenacious of Headmasters – and it has to be a hypothesis only at this stage – may prove to be a turning-point just as decisive for the Mill Hill of the 21st century, as was that national event of 1940 for the country as whole.

To whatever degree building carefully on the experiences of his two predecessors, William Winfield's vision does at last appear to have been able to combine the need for change, with an invigorating sense of the continuity that has been the inner strength and – to use Dr John Whale's telling phrase – the *raison d'être* of this

Court of Governors at time of Incorporation, with (top r.) the Director of Administration and Finance. *11.o*

strangely unique school; he will be shown to have the necessary stamina, and the opportunity – lasting well beyond a Headmaster's 'honeymoon period' with the Governors – to carry his complex constituency with him, and see through his wider 'cultural' reforms.

Those reforms will be seen to be set within what can be inferred as the four imperative, sequential but overlapping, priorities of the Millennial Court: first, financial viability; second, resource updating, leading thirdly to much-needed aesthetic improvement; but finally, the inescapable, longer-term educational bottom-line – academic performance. The resolution of what was never an outright oppositional battle, more a very English process of gradualism, now coming to fruition in the first decade of the new century, may well have started in 1995.

Sources for Ch.XI include: ISCis Censuses 1982-2000, & advice from Jt Dir, R.Davison, 2002; corr/dscns with Lord Slynn, Dame Angela Rumbold, Alastair Graham, Euan MacAlpine, Gordon Smith, John Hawkins, Pauline Bennett-Mills, Beverley Morgan, Rev. .Paul Hunt, P.W.Woodroffe [1941-5]; A/Ms Tony Turnbull, Rev. Henry Starkey, "Tim" Stringer, David Franklin, Chris Sutcliffe, Ian Brownlie, Tim Dingle, Judith Herbertson, Peter McDonough, Harry Barnes, Trevor Chilton, Tim Corbett, Paul Bickerdike, Andrew Gaylor, David Woodrow; Beth Bangham née Baker [1973-5]; J.G.Bewsher; R.G.G.Bewsher [1976-9]; G.N.Field [1975-7]; A.D.Halstead [1971-6]; J.T.Holmes [1963-8]; S.Long [1970-5]; A.M. Macfarlane [1944-8]; J.H.Milburn [1946-51]; Karen Roberts [1985-7]; W.Skinner [1949-55]; Annie Williams [1981-3].

Background: L.H.Tinker, *Message from the Falklands. The Life and Gallant Death of David Tinker, Lieut RN. From His Letters & Poems* (Junction Bks. 1982; Penguin, 1983); South Atlantic Medal Association, www.sama82.org.uk; K.Baker, *Turbulent Years...* (Faber & Faber, 1993); Hansard v.127, c1095, 17.ii.1988; v.145, c429, 18.i.1989; v.175, c911-3, 3.vii.1990; Hope Simpson, *op cit*; BBC2, Holocaust Memorial programme, ref R.Dimbleby broadcast, 27.i.2001; M.D.W.Jones, *op cit*; D.Tyerman, *op cit, passim*; Sir C.Philips, *Beyond the Ivory Tower...* (Radcliffe Press, 1995); S.Bungay, *The Most Dangerous Enemy, A History of the Battle of Britain* (Aurum, 2000); Carole Thatcher, *Below the Parapet, The Biography of Denis Thatcher,* (Harper Collins, 1996).

Other *OM* references: Hena Ahmad [1994-6]; Caroline Alexander [1981-3]; G.Arasa [1997-9]; W.A.Bains [1969-74]; H.B.Bangham [1970-5]; P.Barton [1969-76]; I.Belokriletski [1998-2001]; V.Bhimjiyani [1996-2000]; M.D.Bishop [1955-7]; N.D.Black [1973-8]; Svetlana Bogomolova [1998-2001]; D.Borchard [1990-5]; M.P.Brandon [1992-7]; R.W.B.Buckland [1878-84]; S.J.F.Bunyard [1993-8]; J.E.Carswell [1984-9]; T.R.Chapman [1968-72]; Anne-M.Childs [1981-3]; K.Chliaifchtein [1998-9]; S.Choudhury [1998-9]; R.Constantine [1950-3]; R.W.Corbett [1991-5]; M.Corby [1953-8]; M.J.Cuming [1951-6]; T.A.J.Dawson [1976-81]; F.R.Dimbleby [1927-31]; Anna-L.Doerks [1997-8]; Michelle Dugan [1997-9]; J.Evans [1983-7]; J.T.Fields [1973-8]; A.Flavin [1995-7]; J.C.J.Fox [1983-8]; C.Freeman [1970-5]; M.C.Frise [1992-7]; S.F.Gibbons [1947-52]; Kate Goodchild [1979-82]; D.L.Goodwin [1990-5]; V.Gorobtsov [1995-7]; C.W.Goyder [1920-4]; G.M.R.Graham [1952-7]; C.Greenough [1983-8]; R.L.Grimsdell [1927-31]; Kathryn Haering [1994-6]; Alison Hampton [1983-5]; A.N.Harvey [1973-9]; R.Hassan [1995-2000]; Yvonne Ho [1977-9]; Maria Hvorostovsky [1998-2000]; W.H.Ibotson [1810-5]; G.Ilyashenko [1997-9]; T.W.Jones [1970-5]; B.N.Jordan [1998-2000]; Katie Kaimakliotis [1998-2000]; Ruth Kearns [1984-6]; T.Kenefick [1985-90]; Elizabeth Kenefick [1996-8]; M.E.I.Kempster [1936-42]; W.F.N.Kennet [1975-7]; A.Kharlamov [1995-7]; Tessa Kingsley [1983-5]; S.Kiriliouk [1998-2002]; Diana Kirkwood [1976-7]; H.Kobayashi [1992-6]; Sheryl Lee [1995-7]; J.Le Fort [1995-6]; B.M.Levenstein [1991-6]; W.Lepard Smith [1807]; E.Lewis [1939-44]; Clare Lewis [1977-9]; I.Maciver [1972-9]; J.McCarron [1982-7]; A.R.Manton [1961-6]; Corinne Mellor [1977-9]; R.Mills [1937-40]; D.K.Mistry [1983-6]; Ariane Moody [1991-3]; E.C.Moody [1943-7]; Nicola Moody [1976-7]; L.van Moppes [1914-22]; Elli Mouskas [1995-7]; W.Murray-Wood [1931-5]; Cordula Nagel [1996-8]; B.R.Nasim [1992-7]; Juliet Newport [1976-8]; S.M.E.Nunn [1994-9]; J.Orchard [1988-93]; C.S.Partridge [1972-7]; .G.Patterson [1929-34]; R.J.Peach [1990-4]; A.R.B.Phillips [1968-73]; R.Pine [1954-9]; B.Piper [1938-42]; Joanna Potter [1991-3]; W.C.Ramsay [1912-8]; E.Rashid [1993-8]; S.C.Ratzker [1996-2001]; A.E.R.Roberts [1921-6]; A.J.Rooker Roberts [1893-1900]; R.S.W.Roberts [1979-84]; P.A.Robin [1977-82]; Anna Saroukhanova [1997-9]; E.Scott [1998-2003]; S.A.Selwood [1993-6]; Joanna Shannon [1977-9]; Anjali Sicka [1991-3]; M.A.C.Simmonds [1988-93]; P.H.Smith [1811-8]; Jo Stanton [1976-8]; M.O.A.Stanton [1943-8]; Lucy Sutton [1981-3]; Valentine Taylor [1997-9]; M.Thakur [1996-01]; D.Thatcher [1928-32]; P.J.Thonemann [1991-6]; D.H.R.Tinker [1970-5]; A.F.Todd [1885-92]; R.J.Veal [1982-7]; A.E.Vince [1978-83]; Katharine Whitehorn [1939]; I.M.Wicks [1976-80]; M.C.L.Wilkins [1947-50]; E.Williams [1808-14]; Tanya Woolf [1977-9]; S.R.Wright [1968-73]; J.A.Zuppinger [1929-33].

Lady Matrons: Hannah Cooke (1869-81); Annie Pearse (1899-1926).

At the end of 20th century, MHS's 'minor' competitive activities symbolised
the School's growing diversity: chess, athletics, sailing, croquet, badminton, karate,
squash, tennis, basketball, mountaineering and skiing; (later even hurling and riding). *11.p*

Mill Hill's 'secret weapon' –
the glorious territorial
setting: the land is Green
Belt, and every major tree
has a preservation order.
(i) (above) Top Terrace;
(ii) (l.) The Quad. *12.a*

Chapter XII

New Foundation for a New Century

The Mill Hill Trinity today

"We have become an international community in which country and class,
race and religion are all intertwined in a way which no other generation has known...
We live as one society of precious humans":
William Winfield, last Armistice Day sermon of the 20th century,
11 November 1999.

The deeper but as yet indiscernible patterns in Mill Hill's educational 'Middle Way' must await discovery by a future historian. Nevertheless, as this century has unfolded, one thing is clear: corporate governance is facing a new array of challenges 'extrinsic' to the School – for example the fact that some 40 per cent of UK 18-year-olds now go on to university. Against a backdrop of increasing uncertainty at the secondary and tertiary levels of the educational system, would the Court be able to plan a clear, robust, worthwhile role for the new Foundation?

A school history is not the forum for a study of educational politics, but there were at least six symptoms of this uncertainty: the ongoing debates about a new British-style *baccalauréat*; the ramifications of the 2002 Education Act; the university-funding polemics of 2003; the Office of Fair Trading initiative on admissions to universities – in 2004; the 'PQA' (Post-Qualification Application) system from 2005 onwards, and the Tomlinson Report on the long-term re-set of the 14-19 curriculum. Minds had to focus on the re-checking of the School's task in preparing pupils for future careers. The nature of the syllabus forming that preparation, and an insight into the lives of those taking part in it, have to be major themes in this final chapter.

The Court had already successfully resolved Mill Hill's 'intrinsic' dilemma – how to re-fashion the School to become a viable mixed Boarding and Day establishment, competing with both the independent and maintained sectors. Indeed, in a Report to parents that was part of this refocused thinking, the Headmaster, William Winfield, had encapsulated a crucial 'mission statement': *To make Mill Hill the finest boarding and day co-educational school in London.* Not having been fortuitously located in a 'Boarding-magnet' area, let alone enjoying national 'brand-name school' status as in the 1920s and 1930s, here was nevertheless an assertion of a recognisable 'Mill Hill brand' in realistic contemporary terms, with a target that was now geographically precise. With the fulcrum years of the late 20th century surmounted, the epithet *finest* was deliberate, according with the all-round policy which Mill Hill continued to espouse – educational, spiritual, cultural, social and physical: to equip future graduates for the career task predicted by the Association of Graduate Recruiters – 'cv enhancement' in a dynamic but ever more unstable work-place.

The assertion forming this chapter's heading echoed the words of the School's Founders: *We teach ... man to regard man as his brother, in every clime and of every colour.* These millennial statements, by the 'man on the bridge' of the Trinity's flagship, concentrated on the final part of its potential three-phase journey; the hope was that those young Millhillians coming on board at stages 1 or 2 – the Pre-Preparatory School at "Grimsdell" and the Preparatory School at "Belmont" – would graduate to

'Year 9' on merit, as did 'The Super Eight' – the first 'all-through' pupils, in September 2002, who were also the first cadre to start to enjoy the Foundation's 'Through Curriculum'.

Yet can precepts adequately convey the real life of a school? Before 11 September 2001, this uniquely 'European' generation might have been seen as growing up free from the threat of war. Today, however, as in the 1950s, the inner thinking of young people has still been shadowed: the new menace – global terrorism. The US-styled '9/11', and its dire consequences in the Middle East, recalled that other date when 'the world changed', 3 September 1939, etched indelibly on Millhillian minds of that time.

'The Super Eight': the first 'all-through' pupils, 2002 September – from Pre-Prep at "Grimsdell" through Preparatory School at "Belmont", and on to MHS. *12.b*

Is an historical perspective even possible, or must this History accept for its contemporary chapter the limitations of its 1909 predecessor, and confine itself to a *reportage* of events as they unfolded? If some parallels with preceding eras are helpful, how relevant are they to the 21st century? How to balance the hard facts – buildings, numbers, names – with the 'soft' data, those intangible continuities which are still a vital part of the Mill Hill experience, including the visual theme that introduced this chapter – the School's territorial setting?

s.i Reportage: 2000/1-2006/7

That hard data can certainly be reported. **Fig.A(ii)** charts this generation's' population – just short of 1,200 – for the School, Belmont, and the Pre-Prep, from 2000/1 through to 2004/5. As to 'Pupil Provenance', the earlier **Fig.F(vi)** (p.47) emphasised the reliance of 21st-century Mill Hill on a Greater London catchment area, buttressed by an ongoing international intake.

All these 21st-century pupils benefited from a carefully modulated regime of 'Pastoral Care' throughout their Mill Hill career, contrasting hugely with the lot of earlier cadres. Parents of new pupils were now inducted with a well-organised introductory evening in The Large which many found impressive, to help forge the necessary Contract with the Foundation. At one point the Octagon greeted those new pupils with a Welcome Board in nine languages. Mill Hill also facilitated 'inclusivity' for four observed creeds – Christianity, Judaism, Hinduism, and Islam – Thursday, Friday and Saturday Chapels still offering a focal point for a unifying corporate spirituality. Each faith had many different strands of belief recognised: in the words of Rev. James Fields' pioneering 'School Hymn', forming the start of a new Hymnal – *Our different faiths revealing one world*. This contrasted ecumenically, if optimistically, with the pre-1980s era of an ever-tolerant but core Christianity.

Houses: although 'School spirit' was proclaimed in annual staff-produced Mill Hill Magazines, its complement – 'House spirit' – was

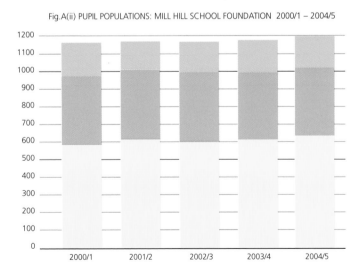

Fig.A(ii) PUPIL POPULATIONS: MILL HILL SCHOOL FOUNDATION 2000/1 – 2004/5

to be embodied eventually in the activities of ten Houses. One hundred years old in 2003, Collinson carried on a tradition vital to the enduring Boarding House ethos by marking House births (or deaths) with gatherings and Histories; Weymouth simultaneously celebrated the tenth anniversary of the third of its 'lives' – 1993-2003. The way had been paved by Burton Bank – deemed 125 in 2000, Ridgeway – 75 in 1986, and Winterstoke – a truncated 72 in 1996 (by then it had become the Pre-Prep), and later, in 2004, on the 80th anniversary of its founding in 1924. Boarders now occupied a mixed BB, Ridgeway, Collinson. Purely 'Day-pupil' and happily mixed were Priestley, School, McClure, Weymouth, and Atkinson, the newest of two planned Houses, after Mill Hill's first Head Master (see Appendices B and D); likewise Murray, Housemaster Tony Slade planning a 75th birthday for 2008. All-girl Cedars evolved as a mixed Day House in 2005.

Activity, 'Partnership' and travel: overseas sports tours continued; girls emulated the boys, starting with a netball visit to Barbados in 2001, and continuing with an unbeaten hockey tour to South Africa in 2004. Other tours included: to Italy, Fiji, Australia and Canada, for boys' rugby; to Venice, the Chamber Choir in 2002/ 2003; exchanges with *Lycée Montaigne*, Paris and the *Liebig Schule*, Frankfurt; the European Seminar Weeks; and visits for classicists to Greece and artists and economists to New York. Voluntary groups were involved with Partnership projects in Ethiopia, Nicaragua, and India, strongly supported by House Charity schemes. By 2003, more than 50 per cent of pupils would make an annual educational trip abroad during their school career. A 335-strong CCF covered RN, Army and Duke of Edinburgh's Scheme and a revived RAF section, with Gliding and Flying; Community Service provided a Friday alternative. The erstwhile Corps Band, traditional Mace restored, re-emerged thanks to a Mill Hill drummer parent, and a son from Belmont.

House anniversaries, 2003:
(i) Collinson centenary:
unique representation of
six generations of
Housemasters: first
'Old Millhillienne' and
"The Baron"'s daughter,
with his five successors;
(ii) new Weymouth's 10th-year
birthday, with Housemaster
and monitors: board shows
record of senior monitors. *12.c*

Timetable: to be outlined later, new classrooms will house what by 2005 had already become a mixed full-time CR of 65. On a generous teacher-pupil ratio of 1:10, staff were teaching some 1,380 'elements' over, in effect, six mini-terms, working to a timetable of inevitably increasing pressures, for staff and pupils alike, and now having to conform to the State's National Curriculum Years 9 to 13; its compilation now required its own software. From 2002 this embraced for the first time the 'Integrated Day' concept, whereby taught games were included in every pupil's weekly timetable. (By great ingenuity, a new non-examined Complementary Studies component, with its own HoD, Philip Thoneman, was introduced for the LVI from 2004, ranging from 'Slavery' to 'The History of Maths'.) A later section will examine the curricular implications of what the Millhillian Treasurer, Richard Buckland, was already berating way back in 1908 as the *steady and continual advance of centralisation.*

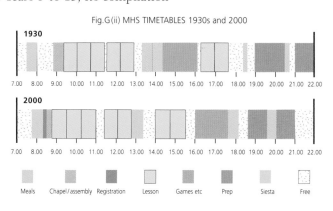

Drugs testing

Headmaster William Winfield must be applauded for his realistic and measured response to drug taking among pupils at Mill Hill School.

Four youngsters caught smoking cannabis have been allowed back into the school under a supportive regime of drugs testing. The school makes a clear distinction between experimentation and serious dealing. Three youngsters who supplied the drugs were expelled.

Statistically, around half of youngsters will come into contact with cannabis between the ages of seven and 16. For schools to pretend drugs are not an issue in simply not realistic. Nor is the ultimate sanction of expulsion the

MHS wins press eulogy for 1990s anti-drug policy. *12.d*

'Investors in People award of 1999: an unusual tribute to a school's management skills as a business. *12.e*

Discipline: the peculiarly Millhillian *School Staff* structure underlined further changes from the past. It was still headed by up to a dozen monitors, supported by prefects and house prefects, with signs of a revived aspiration to attain that transitory hierarchy, now elected under varying levels of democracy. However, unlike the 10 of the tiny Mill Hill of 1811, or the 15 serving the somewhat larger School of the 1919 era (when one monitor, Vivian Lloyd-Thomas, was actually still in the Upper IV Form), all had to be in the VI Form. There were still two Seniors – not, as pre-Second World War, one from School House and one from an Out-House, but one boy and one girl; they and other monitors became Emeritus after their stint was done, creating opportunity for others – no more that imbalance decried by Michael Hart as *10% trained to lead, 90% to be led.* However, overall discipline had mainly reverted to the charge of the staff proper, the academic, most noticeably in the Dining Hall, where Deputy Heads supervised the queues and the behaviour, with a monitor. The graded Detention sanctions for that 90 per cent, were still 'Activities', 'Defaulters' and 'School'. Going directly to the Headmaster were major breaches (alcohol, theft, sexual misconduct, and bullying); above all, that scourge of the century's teenage culture, from which no school could claim immunity – drugs. As early as 1995, the Headmaster had taken a consistently firm line with this problem, ranging from expulsion for actual dealing, or suspension, even, if unavoidable, at vital exam preparation times, to mandatory counselling. The national and local press commended Mill Hill as one of the first HMC schools to make use of a supportive regime, with compulsory tests, to give pupils a second chance.

Mill Hill as a Company: of the corporate themes highlighted for what was the £14 million turnover business of 2005, transparency and vulnerability in 'the outcomes society' necessitated retaining two dozen advisers – seven listed in the returns to Companies House, and 13 as 'competent persons' under Health and Safety rules. This was on top of the advice still provided by the HMC, the GBA, the London ISBA, and the 'Haileybury' regional Bursars Group. This ranged from Banking/ investment – NatWest, and Allied Irish Banks, and Solicitors – Reynolds Porter Chamberlain, to Planning – SPD Savills, and Chartered Surveyors – Maunder Taylor, and Wennington Associates. Architects included Stock Wolstencroft, and Barnsley, Hewitt and Mallinson, and for Insurance – HSBC Holmwoods. Health & Safety called for Owen David Risk Management; Auditing and Economic Forecasting brought in PricewaterhouseCoopers. Other sources were: Opinion Surveys – Mori, Warwicker Associates; Fire safety – Locke Carey, CF International, AF Controls and AVO International. Space Audits lay with Ove Arup; Catering/ Hygiene was the major concern for Sodexho and others. Also consulted were the Police Crime Prevention Unit, and the London Fire/Emergency Planning Authority.

The litigious forces bearing down upon all schools had been the trigger for this proliferation, not least the child-protecting Care Standards Commission of 2003 (see Information Supplement No.3). Most invasive to the Independent Schools' historically-prized independence had been the Human Rights Act. Veale Wasbrough offered the provisional view that *an independent school is to be a private, self-regulating community, largely outside the control of the State, but subject always to the laws of the land.* This left open the nice question whether the Foundation was *a private organisation exercising a public function,* a point that would soon take on political significance.

As another aspect of governance, a re-constituted Life Governors body maintained its right to propose Governors, in a new constitutional form.

A threatened estate: the new generation of Governors had to confront problems from other sources too, particularly as a counter-effect of that prized Mill Hill element which will be covered separately – the Foundation's 135 acres themselves. It was not a 'town v. gown' situation; more a mix of endemic vandalism, or accident – as for example the burning down of the ancient Gears Cricket Pavilion in 2002, or a brazen assumption that these green spaces were part of the public weal, and open for dog walkers and ramblers. Such incursions underscored the fact that the School's lack of endowment made its management a task of continuing vigilance for the Director of Administration and Finance. Peculiarly, under Incorporation, he and the 'Company' Chairman were the only two officers legally empowered to deal with these issues; problems ranged from Green Belt/ Barnet Unitary Development Plan concerns, and the local Residents Association's attempts to create a cycle route down Wills Grove, to claims on the School's lands from the unrelated 'Belmont Riding Stables', and the Foundation's attempts to close the Cinder Path as a right-of-way. Following the Dunblane tragedy of 1996, schools were also under renewed pressure from the DfES to safeguard pupils' welfare, with which the so-called 'Right to Roam' was in conflict. Boys could visit the Broadway in twosomes, the girls only in threesomes. The impact of the new offence of 'Corporate manslaughter' was a further burden.

Happenings: sequentially, two early events were the formal inspections in 2001 by both the ISI on its six-year programme, and by the Barnet Local Authority, the good outcomes marking the successful resolution of the surmised 'battle' metaphor of the preceding years. The former highlighted two 'moments of quality': in 30 per cent of the 168 inspected classes progress was *well above expectation*; *the quality of teaching observed... was very good or outstanding in 44% of lessons... and good in another 30%...* The judgement was that *more progress* [is] *made between Year 9 and GCSE than... in the independent schools as a whole. The quality of pupils' learning'... was good or very good... in 76% of observed lessons in the sixth form.*

The most noticeable events were the bold Ten-Year Plan projects to which the Court continued to commit the Foundation during these opening years of the century. An obvious linking element was the new line of railings of 2001 on The Ridgeway frontage, marrying with the entrance gates to an ever-busier car park, and Cedars (1997). Following further enhancements to the Stoa of 2000/1, with a landscaped fountain, the first major build was at Belmont: the Jubilee Dining Hall/ classroom block of September 2002. The 2003/4 project, creating the indoor Angela Rumbold Pool, within the re-landscaped Buckland Memorial complex, including new Fives Courts, epitomised the consultative care

New beginnings: (i) the Master's successor as Head, Lynn Duncan; (ii) John Hawkins, Master of Belmont, talking to parents in Jubilee Building, 2002 (originally to be named after Rooker Roberts); (iii) Sir Robert Balchin, Court Chairman, lays Foundation Stone for new Bicentennial Classroom Building, October 2005. *12.f*

which Mill Hill needed to take with every change to the environment, and the vital importance of demonstrating that facilities were also benefiting the community – a direct consequence of Government policy towards the Independent Schools. Once initial agreement on the design had been obtained through the Local Consultative Advisory Committee, and the Barnet Senior Planning Officer, two meetings were convened, bringing in representatives of the MHPS and local residents. There then ensued several more stages before building could begin: the Pool was opened in 2005.

Other significant events in the years 2000-5 included: the Head's sabbatical in Europe and USA in summer 2003; a prompt reaction to the SARS epidemic of 2003, scoring a clean sheet for Mill Hill; the naming of the former School Housemaster's lounge as the Crick Room; a new public Lecture Series, including parliamentary writer Ben McIntyre and historians Andrew Roberts and David Starkey, and the decision not to attempt to set up a satellite School in the Pacific Rim. Dent was superseded from the year 2003 by MoD facilities in various parts of the UK, on sites friendly to both sexes, the proceeds dedicated to a new Bursary for children of Northern *OM*s. Two VI Form Directors, James Fields and Lesley Sharples, were appointed from September 2004; the new 'Café 6' in the SFC was the first symbol of this new role. The key event, however, was the corporate re-structuring of 2004, whereby the Heads of 'Belmont Mill Hill Preparatory School' and 'Grimsdell Mill Hill Pre-Preparatory School', now reported to the Headmaster of the whole Foundation; this facilitated the Trinity as a 'seamless garment' with common standards and interlocking staffs, enabling the Foundation to offer continuity of education from 3 to 18. The successor in 2004 to the Director of Administration and Finance, Beverley Morgan (a widely respected, long-serving facilitator of the new Foundation), was Bruce Fraser; his title reverted to that of Bursar.

Bicentennial reconfiguration: *Headmasters have powers at their disposal with which Prime Ministers have never been invested.* Winston Churchill's famous aphorism has positive relevance for the culminating building decisions of Mill Hill's 200 years. A £280K IT-heavy total refurbishment of the Marnham Block in 2003 under the

Proposed Bicentennial Favell Building, for 2007: architects' model. *12*.g

Court's Estates Committee, was led successively by *OM* surveyor-Governors Eric Harvey and Graham Chase (both the only serving Governors to have ever played rugby against the School). This then enabled the Head to plan the most ambitious programme ever undertaken, the £10m Bicentennial Building Project, reconfiguring the dreary 19th-century buildings between that Block and the Chapel. After the publication of this History, Mill Hill will be commemorating the events of the Bicentennial Year 2006/7 in a companion brochure, thus only sketches can be included here; by 2007/8 this project will hopefully contain many novel, state-of-the-art classrooms, equal to the high standard now displayed to their senior partner both at Belmont and Grimsdell. It should offer fresh perspectives to the School's functional heart, a revolutionary gateway into a re-landscaped Quad.

s.ii *Plus ça change?*

Yet up to this **Territorial Era 8**, for any Millhillian on a fleeting visit and conditioned by earlier images, Mill Hill might still have given an impression of unchangeability, with many constant rituals, such as summer's white flannels and the thwack of stout willow to leather orb on a peaceful Park. For the Armistice Day ceremony through the Gate of Honour (now held on a day that allows the attendance of the preponderant 'Day' culture, both staff and pupils), a comparable passing Mill Hill Village visitor would still observe much that was familiar, with reassuring human silences, despite a non-stopping traffic flow; on an autumnal Top Field, mêlées of familiar chocolate and white rugby kit in action, across that open vista of the Quad. Surely, '*c'est la même chose*'? Indeed, as if to emphasise that impression, growing signs of a rediscovery of the traditional: scholarships named after *OM*s – Todd (sports) – won in 2002 by a golfer, Helmore (music), and Ward (art); the slow return of the Octagon to its more discreet origins; and more significantly, a doubling of *OM* parentage to 20 in 2003, a renewal of a once-proud generational linkage vitiated by geography, social mobility, and the reputation of some recent troubled decades.

At second glance, however, the differences quickly surface: staff with academic hoods from an array of universities, now, like their pupils – in gender, race and colour – reflecting the "precious humans" of a multi-cultural Britain: no longer the now narrow-seeming male 'WASP'-ish homogeneity of even a quarter-century ago. While all now walked unconcernedly on a once-sacrosanct Top Terrace, there were code-locked gates to the car park, to inhibit both ingress and egress. The once infamous School House corridor was now termed the Priestley Corridor (see **Fig.H**, p.52); The 'Large' Stage ("Marnham Up") now formed Room B1.

That sense of difference was further evidenced on the periodic charity-funding 'Alternative Uniform Days', and more so on Sundays when the 70 or so overseas pupils were organised by a teacher for outings and other activities. Another discontinuity – a blue livery outweighing vestigial signposting in chocolate-and-white, the old livery consigned to the sporting arena; indeed, at least one House tie, Cedars, had forsaken chocolate for blue as the binding colour. A blue-kitted world of mixed 'Pre-Preppers' scampered, where once walked, usually more sedately, groups of brown/grey-branded male Winterstokers, the liberation of a martlet from the school crest on the Pre-Prep letterhead, flying free on its own cloud – a new young Millhillian spirit. Pupils' school numbers were now four-figure, no longer just triple.

The territory: while the old Quad was marked out for netball and basketball, the second 'Quad', the Stoa, had matured to form a new social epicentre,

Style and status at the Pre-Prep: (i) the IAPS certificate, the first ever awarded to a Pre-Prep and new (revolutionary) letter-head. (ii) Pauline Bennett-Mills , and (iii) (below) new classroom; *12.h*

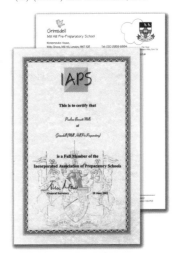

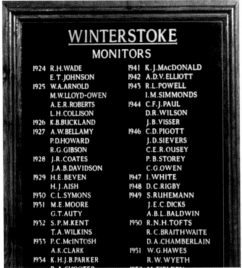

WINTERSTOKE	
MONITORS	
1924 R.H.WADE	1941 K.J.MacDONALD
E.T.JOHNSON	1942 A.D.V.ELLIOTT
1925 W.A.ARNOLD	1943 R.L.POWELL
M.W.LLOYD-OWEN	I.M.SIMMONDS
A.E.R.ROBERTS	1944 C.F.J.PAUL
L.H.COLLISON	D.R.WILSON
1926 K.B.BUCKLAND	J.B.VISSER
1927 A.W.BELLAMY	1946 C.D.PIGOTT
P.D.HOWARD	J.D.SIEVERS
R.G.GIBSON	C.E.R.OUSEY
1928 J.R.COATES	P.B.STOREY
J.A.B.DAVIDSON	C.G.OWEN
1929 H.E.BEVEN	1947 I.WHITE
H.J.AISH	1948 D.C.RIGBY
1930 C.L.SYMONS	1949 S.RUHEMANN
1931 M.E.MOORE	J.E.C.DICKS
G.T.AUTY	A.B.L.BALDWIN
1932 S.P.M.KENT	1950 R.N.H.TOFTS
T.A.WILKINS	R.C.BRAITHWAITE
1933 P.C.McINTOSH	D.A.CHAMBERLAIN
A.K.CLARK	1951 W.G.HAWES
1934 K.H.J.B.PARKER	R.W.WYETH

From sole flag-bearer for 13-18 year old Boarding boys, to the co-ed Trinity with a 15-year span: last vestiges of converted Winterstoke House – (i) Heads of House honours board on School Dining Room wall; (ii) plaque in Wills Grove marked 80th anniversary of founding, opening by Tim Phillips, September 2004. *12.i*

rounded-off to the north-east with the new Piper Library (replacing the Squash Courts – *virtus* again making way for *musas*). The picture was enhanced successively by the 1999 Music Studios, the fountain centrepiece, Duncan Beckman's abstract sculpture in 2004 and, alongside, the redesignated Winterstoke Library/ Learning Resource Centre. The Octagon was transformed in 2001 with its first-ever floor covering. The ancient Tite stonework, internal and external, was specially treated, looking no doubt even better than the original. The All-Weather Pitch (aka "Fishing Net") formed an additional resource. There was much improvement in the Houses, and at Belmont, with its handsome new brick-paved Quad.

Those Armistice Day processions, long since too big to be held within one Chapel, were now also normally diverted to The Large and the Theatre, the Lower School thereby retracing steps historically; (in 2000, for the first time, held in the adjacent St Paul's School due to the Chapel repairs). The Chapel was graced by a millennial enshrinement of 21st-century icons (a mobile phone, photographs of new staff and pupils, coins and papers) in the re-formed interior buttresses. On every building's doors, there was a coded security lock, where once a key, or no lock at all, would have sufficed; closed-circuit cameras watched strategic positions: in tandem, a radio-linked Security Officer patrolled these open grounds, an ever-present alert to their exposure to outsiders. Steel fire escapes added unaesthetic excrescences that would have shocked the classically severe Sir William Tite to the marrow.

On The Ridgeway, where once it was safe to stroll in the road (and dominate as a School preserve with paper-chases and 'Cross-Countrys'), now at end-of-school hours, not just a few Murray boys at the bus stops, but a surge of the majority Day population, most of them in cars. Behind the atmosphere, where pre- and post- the Second World War, planes from Hendon Aerodrome or passing tanks from the Middlesex Regiment Barracks momentarily drowned out all the noises of the School, there now came an insistent hum, overwhelming the sound of the trains: the traffic of the M1 down in the valley, a reminder that in this new century parental accessibility to motorways was a key determinant in the choice of a school within the M25.

Outward signs: even greater signs of difference lay closer to hand, in the detail of the denizens of the present-day School, emulating their teenage peer-groups everywhere. Pupils texted, or 'rapped' – out of lessons – in convergent, Thames Valley estuarine English, on fashion-accessory mobiles; privileged older pupils drove into the Car Park, some with personalised number-plates, many with generously audible in-car stereo, or CD/DVD. Everyone had a 'Colour' to wear, whether School blazer, pullover, skirt, House scarf, umbrella, crested School tie, or an odd, defiantly sported, Old Belmontian or, from 2001, an Entrance Scholars tie; (for even more privileged members, the highly symbolic MHSSSC tie was the first to incorporate OMC colours in its stripes – silver, blue, red and yellow). On occasions when *OMs* came back (a status redefined since co-education as potentially open to former pupils up to 18 of any of the three schools), among the males fewer MHS or *OM* ties were seen than of old, with hair tints, designer-stubble or, surprisingly, suits, the generationally-binding emblems of young male adulthood; among the females, catwalk-fashion freedom and chic.

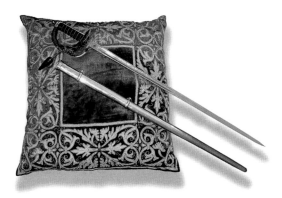

In concerts, where trebles, baritones, and basses once called the tune, and by definition limited the productions in the Chapel – aided by a few sturdy female voices from the ranks of the Matrons and the masters' wives – today the vocal range was extended by young sopranos, altos and contraltos – some in trousers, not skirts – giving access to the full span of the world's music, previously attainable only through the ensembles or the instrumentalists. Whilst never wishing to become a narrowly-channeled 'Musical School', Mill Hill's high standards were symbolised in 2001 in the first-ever Composition Prizes, commemorating *OM* composer Inglis Gundry: adjudicator Tarik O'Regan, Composer in Residence at Cambridge University, described himself as *stunningly impressed* by the entries, demonstrating mastery of a new language – that of music. On the performance of two Chamber Groups at their 2001 Conference in Oxford, the Incorporated Society of Musicians commented on these Millhillians' *commitment and musical awareness*.

Those markers for change were even stronger on what remained a 'MHS' Foundation Day, conducted every October, a fortnight after a repositioned *OMs* Day: a Sports Hall audience no longer containable in The Large, let alone riskable on the Quad, by virtue of the autumnal timing. There was a list of subject-prizes unimaginable to earlier generations – IT, Manufacturing, English as a Second Language, a IV Prize for Design Technology, the Harvey Cup for Charity Fundraising. From 2002, a 'Cowing' Award, embracing in 2003 a new Berwin Sword, was bestowed on the top CCF cadet; from 2004, an OMC Prize, initiated to rebuild the linkage between the Club and all former pupils. There was now more openness between age-groups, with pupils on easy terms with academic staff, who used first names for all boys and girls, a MacAlpine move reinforced by his successor. An Anti-Bullying Audit showed a seismic difference compared with the era described in Chapter IX. In verbal usage, an oddity: the term "boys" now lamely replaced by "the children", not even "the School" – a 19th-century throw-back.

CCF in today's MHS:
(i) first (eponymous) Berwin Sword presentation, Foundation Day 2003.
(ii) Drum Major's sashes, new v. old; *12.j*

s.iii The Millennium Diary

Yet these are all still historically loaded perceptions. To the here-and-now Millhillians, the paradigms have to be quite different, the memories newly furnished. To build such a countervailing picture, an unusual experiment had been conducted at the start of the first term of the new century – the Millennium Diary Project. Samples of every sector of the School's constituency were asked to note their experiences. Those observations yield much food for thought. (House acronyms, and MHS Forms – IV, Remove, V, LVI, UVI – are included). Although the Diary was geared to the Main School, some work overlapped onto Belmont and the Pre-Prep; many comments could equally apply to any of the three schools.

The sensation of January 2000 was quickly assimilated. Matt Halstead [WM/Rem] wrote: *I was saying 'happy millennium' instead of 'happy new year'... seeing all my friends from other houses for the first time this century was weird!* Re-entry itself was more of an event. Carly Warwick [SH/LVI] confessed: *Surprisingly, I'm looking forward to getting back.* Hoda Hosseini [CD/V] reflected: *Compared with the last millennium there have been large changes, but it felt like a normal day.*

Sleepiness was universal, especially for those from overseas, like BB Head of House, Dong Ju Lee [UVI]: *Wake up at 5.00 because of the 'jet let'* [sic]: *came back from Korea yesterday, feel a bit tired... Breakfast – fish fingers, baked beans, bread, cereals. Good to see my girl friend back from holiday.* For parents, a different perception, for example Mrs Carol Minnis, mother of five boys, of whom four were still at the Foundation: *Ready for the start of the new term. Jonathan is a boarder and had returned the previous evening. The three boys left for school, Richard and Christopher to Mill Hill, and Andrew to Belmont. After three weeks of five noisy boys eating me out of house and home, it is peace at last!*

For one member of staff, Matron Pauline Clark, work began at 07.00 with what would have been unheard-of luxury for earlier generations: *Start going round BB, waking up the students.* By 07.15 Dr Roger Axworthy, Foundation Administrator at Walker House, was at his desk, and by 08.00 was meeting the Works Foreman to plan the day's work. At 08.30 he *telephoned the Pre-Prep and spoke to the Head on legal matters.* By that time, a Classroom Assistant there (and Mill Hill parent), Judi Berkovi, had *dropped the boys at School at 08.00.* Day pupils had to get their cars out early, like Nikki Green [WM/LVI]: *07.30 – drive brother and myself to MHS.*

(i) Sartorial distinction now embraced the arts: the three levels of Music Ties; (ii) Music scholar Owen Bubbers at practice. *12.k*

The all-uniting School-day events followed in quick succession, starting with Registration and House Assemblies by 08.20; for Housemaster Andy Luke [then at Priestley] this was held on the balcony of The Large. School Assembly at 08.50 could be auspicious for some. Kabelo Moyo [MH/UVI] was able to say: *For the first time, walked in as Senior Monitor.* An even bigger thrill for Russian, Maria Hvorostovsky [CD/UVI]: *Got a calendar. Happy to see my name under Monitors... nervous when walking in front of everyone clapping. Headmaster awarded my tie.* Likewise Dong Ju Lee: *Feel good that I am still head of BB, but realise again that I have to do so many things for the House (pressure).* For some academic staff, like Rev. James Fields, an opportunity: *Gave notices about Community Service, which is at last shaping up the way I want it.* Yet the highly committed Head of Music, Richard Allain, is more aware of *acres of tedious announcements falling on fairly tired souls.*

The next punctuation comes at 11.00 – Break time. An exhausted Dong Ju Lee goes *back to House, have a rest, then back up to School.* Carly Warwick *stood outside in the Quad, socialising in the cold.* Kabelo Moyo encountered *chaos in the Tuck Shop yet again. No prefect on duty, but it's now my responsibility. Ask G (though nicely) to do it. He did.* Nikki Green goes up to the VI Form Centre *to see everyone and have coffee.*

Lunch in Hall from 12.30 onwards appeared to arrive not a minute too soon. Although for appreciative Head of Girls' Games Kerrie Carroll, *all the food looks nice,* Maria Hvorostovsky chats to the kitchen staff, *complaining about the food as usual.* Dong Ju Lee rejoices that *it always makes me feel good that I do not have to que* [sic] *for the lunch. School staff priority* [monitors and prefects], *I think, is a very good system!* Hoda Hosseini, strictly-fasting for Ramadan, *spent most of lunchtime in Cedars – have to wait until sunset to eat.* Dominic Sebag-Montefiore [P/LVI] takes the chance of further gossip on the Monitors' Block [see Appendix E: "Millhillisms"].

Other occupations resume at once – (the siesta time of the Jacks' era long since gone – see Ch.VI). At 13.15 Matt Halstead joins a meeting about the Mill Hill Millennium Music & Arts Festival, before going back to House *to pack my books for English.* One of the Music Scholars, preferring anonymity, *started the organ at 13.25 and learnt a Prelude and Fugue by Bach. At last something decent.* Sport and other subsidiary activity enter the frame from 15.00 onwards, but not without problems even for Kabelo Moyo: *Rugby Sevens practice, but no one, including myself* (1st XV Captain) *has their kit, and I'm meant to be setting an example!* Hockey went on for an hour for Matt Halstead and his team-mates: *By 16.00 I could have dropped dead.* Also at 16.00, Carly Warwick played *netball for a bit ... with the boarders,* then home by bus.It should not appear from all this that teaching and learning were squeezed in as afterthoughts; on the contrary, academic staff and pupils alike displayed widespread enthusiasms. IT for all is now a keynote throughout the Foundation: at the Pre-Prep at 10.00, Judi Berkovi was *still listening to readers and supervising half the class, while the other half are having a computer lesson.* For Richard Allain the work was particularly interesting, starting with the IV Form at 10.15 – *our first lesson on computers* [in music]; *at 14.00, V Form session with Sibelius software ... they should all get 'A's.* Hoda Hosseini admired the redesigned buildings: *It really does make a difference. The Music School has been brought into the 21st century. I spend the lesson typing up my composition for the saxophone onto the computer.* At noon, Rev. James Fields had *sorted out what materials I wish to use for the Remove classes this week – we will review the terms ethics and morality.*

The experienced Philip Thonemann, Head of Physics, and one of many teachers clearly building up his students towards a university ambience, wrote thoughtfully: *I have Tutees who are Turkish, Russian, Armenian, African, Indian, Korean, Chinese, and British ... excellent! A double lesson with my UVI ... a delightful group to teach; 8 mature, civilised young people. Nan He* [BB/UVI] *tells me she has got into Cambridge to read Maths ... At 11.00, EMCO* [emergency cover] *for Simon Hughes, Head of Science, who is away for this first week at the Association for Science Education Conference. He is mainly there to find out about the changes to VI Form teaching which are about to occur with the shift to 'AS'* (LVI) *and 'A2'* (UVI) *– a broadening of the curriculum ... 15.00 – the Philosophy Group – 5 to 8 pupils from V Form to Upper VI – meets in the newly refurbished Physics Study Room (the old Todd Library) ... Today we continue last term's discussion on political philosophy – can we give rational arguments for preferring some kind of democracy to a kind of oligarchy or dictatorship ... all the pupils are volunteers, the class is in Activity Time ... definitely a highlight of my week.*

The variety of objectives embraced by the Foundation, and the versatility of its staff, are legion. At 13.30 Nikki Green had *a meeting to*

Sporting experience:.
(i) training on Top Field for 2003 rugby tour;.
(ii) all-rounder and Hockey Captain, Pippa, daughter of Geography master and rugby coach, David Woodrow, in action for the 2002 U15 South of England hockey XI. *12.l*

Atkinson: not an exterior
of the Rev. John, MHS'
first Head Master (none
exists) but an exterior of
the new mixed Day House
which commemorates him:
(r.) sculpture by pupil
Duncan Beckman.
Award of first House Tie
(below) September 2004,
to first Head of House
(see Appendix D). *12.m*

discuss the Ethiopia trip I will be taking in Summer 2000. At 14.00 the Chaplain *went into St Paul's School to have coffee with the Head, Sian Thornton. We discuss partnership ideas for St Paul's and Mill Hill.* There are also examples of the way staff get together to solve a 'cross-functional' problem, bringing considerable resources to bear on an individual's needs: at 17.00, four members of staff come to Collinson to discuss one pupil – his father is unhappy. For one of the four *he is just being a lazy boy – one of many others!* Philip Thonemann, proudly sporting – *qua* Tutor – his House Tie, notes that *we decide that he should change his activities so he can do choir, and that he will have a special set of report grades from his teachers after four weeks.* When that meeting was concluded, Philip switched to agreeing with Belgian pupil, Jordi Grognard [CH/VI], to form a Jazz group.

Evening patterns inevitably varied, although pupils continued to communicate across the cultural Day-Boarding divide, with a good deal of overhang from the day's classes. Drama had been a favourite subject for many pupils: from 19.30 to 20.30, Carly Warwick was watching "The Trial" on TV – *part of my Theatre Studies – a very abstract, weird play.* Nikki Green had a Biology revision: *I've got my module next week and I've got to get a 'B' to get into my first choice university – Birmingham.* Matt Halstead was phoned at 20.30 by *my friend, asking about a Big Band rehearsal tomorrow.* At 19.00 Kerrie Carroll's Boarding House duty [RH] included: *check all pupils in rooms – doing prep, organise UVIs to supervise juniors ... 20.30: prep break-time; 21.00 start the junior boys on their House duties; senior boys – prep time; 21.30 Lights Out – IV Form; 22.00 Removes – Lights Out; 22.30 V Form Lights Out ... Spent time chatting to a homesick IV Former ... since I too am away from home, could give some advice; 23.00 – VI Formers to bed; 23.45 – hand back mobile phone to Housemistress; 00.00 bedtime.*

18.30 at the Minnis household was no doubt a replica of many others: *Richard is taking his A-Levels this summer, so he went to his room to study, grumbling that he was starving. Christopher arrived home with a big grin on his face because he, like Andrew, had no homework ... he has been given the opportunity to have fencing lessons ... 'Ask your father when he gets home' ... 21.30: now the boys are back at school, we have to make sure they go to bed at a reasonable time ... Richard is a sensible boy and knows how much sleep he needs, so we let him 'sort himself out'.* Back 'on the Hill', the Chaplain can *drop in on Boarding Houses, meet a couple of new pupils in the LVI and* [amazingly] *a few parents. Day 1 of the new term is over and we're already right back into the swing of things.*

s.iv The culture: 'competition, co-operation, excellence'

Until 1999, when the creative work of the School began to merit a colourful multi-media publication of its own – *First Impressions*, any text which started life as an overview of the 'culture' of Mill Hill might have still concentrated on sport – and would unquestionably have had at least one of the above words in its title. A *MHM* Editorial of 1974 (echoing Descartes) satirised *Rugbo, ergo sum*; that image was still traceable as late as August 2000, in the obituary of the Millhillian surgeon already encountered, Prof Nigel Kinnear, from *a school noted for its emphasis on sporting excellence*. Although numerically there were still as many potential rugger-playing boys in a school of 600 pupils as there were in the all-male populations of earlier years, rugby football was no longer the standard-bearer. Nevertheless, the competitive urge was seen as beneficial in itself – co-operative, but bringing out inherent individual virtues. The amateur principle, venerated by earlier generations, was subsidiary; this was life-training, at its most Darwinian. Survival or success turned on this derivation of the 'protestant ethic'.

Awardees of the Todd Sports Scholarships, 2003, combining old and new traditions. *12.n*

Sport at Mill Hill: for more than a century, the high point of any Mill Hill year was, for many, the Inter-House rugby programme at the end of the Winter Term; cricket buffs might have given pride of place to the House equivalent on the Park in June, and for many predecessors the athletic sports would have vied for this role, notwithstanding that those contests were always clouded by the presence of the annual examinations. Either way, the spirit of competitiveness was unquestionably enshrined in a sporting event; in her autobiography, Lady Thatcher quotes the typically Millhillian view of her husband, Denis: *The desire to win is born in most of us. The will to win is a matter of training. The manner of winning is a matter of honour.* To the objective question, 'Why sport at all?' the history of Mill Hill has established, and contemporary usage confirms, the case for physical training as one of a school's legitimate functions – or rather the holistic concept of physical education, associated with the era of Maurice Jacks.

Retrospect: some account of the School's sport has already been given; its origins, which give it historical meaning, may usefully be rehearsed here. Even if permeating it was the associated idea that, to quote the legendary cricketer, Denis Compton, it was "only a game", the phrase might at least have summed up the first broad phase which ended prior to 1860. That sentiment would not have described the second, century-long phase – the dominating, Empire-building Public School games cult. Although rugby football (initially, as *Nobis* has revealed, with a round ball) and cricket were competed for continuously beyond Mill Hill's Second Foundation, as were athletics (Sports), and Eton fives, the first official signs of the role of sport among the 21st-century games only came through with 12 successive 'firsts'. Several sports rose, later to decline. Among such cycles may be further cited cycling itself, disappearing by the First World War; gymnastics; boxing; and the unique hockey 'IXs' for "Singlehanded" (see Appendix E).

Qualities: manifestly, games inculcated qualities of character that had wider benefits. (Not for nothing did France adopt rugby football from the British wine-importers in the late 19th century, part of that country's longer-term strategy for building 'leaders' that would eventually help to reverse the humiliations of the Franco-Prussian War of 1870.) It is no accident that many of the bravest exploits of Millhillians in the military conflicts of the 20th century can be credited to the School's leading sportsmen. There is anecdotal correlation between success at games and success in civil careers, particularly but not exclusively of that competitive element that *OM* Sir Michael Bishop flagged up in 1999, which infuses many career fields, from the commercial to the professional: the career of *OM* Nigel Wray,

Fives: internationally competitive and most popular minor sport at MHS and Belmont, now one of the eight unifying games open to both sexes; note new 'colours' vest. *12.o*

portrayed in the media as one of the country's "Awesome Foursome" of property tycoons, is a typical example. Today sport not only enters tertiary education, but yields a multitude of careers in its own right – participative, managerial and entrepreneurial, while still demonstrating its overriding power to evoke patriotism. Yet other careers will be cited below where seeming lack of sporting prowess or of membership of Mill Hill's fleeting political *nomenklatura* has proved no bar to excelling later in a chosen field of activity, whether legal, diplomatic, medical, artistic or even in the broader spheres of business.

The wider culture: new emphases were now being asserted. Whilst needing to be placed in a more balanced social context, Sports Awards were available for the 26 games now played, many achieving top place in the Middlesex or Barnet Leagues. As outlined in Ch.XI, alongside the three 'majors', most minor sports had survived, with for example Eton fives, achieving its own pink 'colours vest'. Other sports had been allowed, or rather forced by timetable pressures, to lapse into the status of informal, non-competitive leisure pursuits.

From 2002, Games lessons were introduced into the mainstream academic timetable, ensuring that all from the IV to the VI Form had at least one afternoon of physical education. From major sports (rugby, hockey, cricket, netball, rounders) choices opened up to embrace minor sports such as tennis, basketball, swimming, badminton, shooting, and further widened out in the V Form to include riding, soccer, squash, Tae Kwon Do, and even dance and "Ultimate Frisbee". Non-timetabled were 'Activities': the popular fives, and scuba diving, go-karting and trampolining. *Mens sana in corpore sano* was taking on a different meaning. For the first time ever, from September 2000, the priority status of the one-time seasonal major game had to be balanced with the equal demands of non-sporting activity – the 'expressive arts' of drama and music, and of Community Service: not a mere administrative change, but one of great import.

VI Form Art class in Art School. *12.p*

Indeed, for well into the 21st century, the popular high spot had been the Inter-House Drama Competition, compressed now by exam pressures into the Autumn Term. Since the late 1980s, the successor to the School House 'hokey-pokey' (which evolved in the 1930s into a full-length play, rivalling the School Play in its production values) had been this keenly-fought annual event, with the senior School allowed to wait up until 11.30 p.m. to cheer the final winning House. Previous application of 'inter-house spirit' had been on the field or the court, in the gym or the water, not on the boards. This aspect of 'culture' could satisfy what was still for Mill Hill the educationally crucial quality of 'spirit', both at the House and School level. As has already been noted, a fourth emerging area of the prevailing culture was Community Service, both at home and overseas. 'Competition, co-operation, and excellence' had new, wider applications and outlets. The plastic arts – design and sculpture – although lacking the team values, also thrived, and led on to a growing field of educational and career options.

The Expressive Arts: Drama had never in fact been just a central 'School' domain: the History has related the School House Gilbert & Sullivan tradition, and the end-of-term cabarets of varying quality in the Boarding Houses. The field of the 'Expressive Arts', above all Drama, was now a force uniting all sections of the School, as well as providing a grounding in a multitude of communications-related work-paths. No longer restricted to that huge old converted Chapel, The Large, theatre could now be taught and practised firstly in the VI Form Centre (SFC), re-designed by David Proudlock in 2002, where the initial performances under the new 'OMADS' banner were staged, again linking Millhillians present and past – "Pygmalion" and "Tom Jones". In 1998, launching the second new venue – the Studio Theatre – a Mill Hill School Arts Society audience had witnessed an astounding mime-balletic musical, "Salome", fresh from its critical acclaim at the Edinburgh 'Fringe'.

One production particularly expressed the liberating spirit infusing the new Mill Hill: the 2002 musical "Cabaret", the most stylish and in both senses the sexiest show yet staged, a combination of the Dramatic and Musical Directorates, and which also witnessed the appearance of a member of the MHS academic staff, Uschi Pulham, in a starring role. It was the first School show to exploit the now smaller Large. The formal portraits of former dignitaries Sir Arthur Pickard-Cambridge, Sir Albert Spicer and Dickie Buckland provided an unintended Brechtian *Verfremdungseffekt* from the walls in the background: their ghosts would have needed a little help to understand all that was going on. This success was topped in 2003 with the four-star acclaim given to Mill Hill's *Théatre Vivant* production of Stephen Berkoff's "Kvetch" at the esteemed Pleasance Courtyard at the Edinburgh Fringe; as a nice compliment, Mill Hill was invited to appear at the Fringe again in 2004 but with a P.G. Wodehouse adaptation. Another aspect of Millhillian performance was the selection of Harry Melling for the part of Dudley in the 'Harry Potter' film series.

The Expressive Arts were a strong feature too of the two junior sections of the Mill Hill Trinity, Belmont having been the first school in the UK to link with the National Youth Music Theatre, through its production of "Salomon Pavey" in 1976, rounded in 2001 with a 25-year celebration in the first joint Mill Hill/ Belmont show – the outstanding "Captain Stirrick", which then toured in Sweden. The picture was one of boys and girls taking responsibility at all levels, from lead roles and writing, to direction and stage management, with just the necessary stabilising admixture of academic staff and outside professional talent to help knit the wholes together.

A contrast was apparent in these first productions of the new century. For the new Millhillians, their future sensory memories of the 'Spirit of Place' (see **s.vi** below) will continue to evoke the customary heady smells of Leichner sticks and greasepaint, but their aural recollections of high-volume 'pop' will be vastly

Drama feats: (i) "Kvetch", MHS as '*Théatre Vivant*' at the Edinburgh Fringe 2003, rated **** by British Theatre Guide; (ii) re-use of The Large for major productions: David Proudlock's stylish "Cabaret", 2002. *12.q*

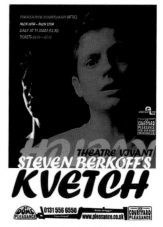

An *OM* in the headlines:
columnist, broadcaster, quiz-
show panellist and author
Sir Simon Jenkins, former
Editor of *The Times*. 12.r

different from earlier generations' experiences of the creaky but
gentle strains of Mendelssohn 78s of "A Midsummer Night's
Dream" on a wind-up gramophone. A pre-war audience would
have equated the smells of theatre with new-mown grass and
flowers, when plays were put on in the garden of "The Grove".
For the miraculous productions conjured out of Shakespearean
'thin air' by Bertie Ricks at St Bees, it was the sea-spray and the
howling of the gales which characterised them.

Yet the fact that all these performances revealed a maturity
that would have been unimaginable for those earlier audiences at
the often-dreaded "School Play" evenings, was not the issue.
Critical in this topical culture, in drama as in music, was that three strands of
Millhillian life welded into one cohesive activity for the first time: age-differences
becoming unimportant compared with talent; the balancing of individual striving and
the desire to excel, with teamwork and commitment to defined goals; and last but in
no way least, both sexes within the School and OMC communities finding an area of
common endeavour across all these one-time boundaries. These are priceless
qualities with which to unite any social group; they provide a binding force in today's
co-educational Mill Hill School, whilst also operating at comparable levels of quality
and dedication both at Belmont and at the Pre-Prep. Sometimes these cultural
activities made their mark in the wider world, for example the performance of the
choral work, '*Salve, Regina*' by Director of Music, Richard Allain, at the 2000 Henry
Wood Proms, with a Mill Hill mention in the programme (emulating the precedent
set by the Gundry 'Heyday, Freedom' suite in 1943): such emergence served to
enhance their importance.

s.v Parental investment in Mill Hill's 'Middle Way'

What of the issue of parental investment in this crucially definitive experience?
A question must now be posed which has been taken as read during this History, and
which can only be partially answered by the endorsing but confidential ISI 2001
Inspection: educationally, what does Mill Hill stand for?

Whilst working within a quite distinct 'philosophy' as to the value which the
Foundation sets out to 'add' for every pupil of any range of ability who passes the
entrance requirements at each stage, Mill Hill has been refreshingly free of the
pedagogic – that is, of philosophising about the science of education itself. That is
not to undervalue the writings of some of the School's Head Masters about particular
aspects of that process: most especially Maurice Jacks in the 1930s, on the value of
physical education; Dr John Whale on the primacy of academic standards, and the
relationship of religion to education; and Michael Hart on the growing European
dimension of British education. Nor is that to ignore the output of members of Mill
Hill's academic staff over the years on their own fields: for example Trevor Chilton
on biology (see 'A Mill Hill Bibliography', p.378).

Theory: guidance abounds. There is the challenging stance of columnist Sir
Simon Jenkins (after *Economist* Deputy Editor Norman Macrae, Sir Michael Bishop
and Mike Corby the fourth *OM* to rate a full-page 'bio' in a national broadsheet: he

was described, in appropriately Millhillian terms, as fostering *a radical, liberating creed of scepticism*): *the test of a school should be its ability to stimulate those who see no point in it, yet who most need the drawing out...* In contrast, and dear to earlier classically trained Millhillians, is Diogenes' politically based dictum: *The foundation of every state is the education of its youth.* In between are views of men from that seed-bed of Mill Hill's intellectual beginnings, Enlightenment figures such as Joseph Priestley, who argued *the concept of human perfectability... all were educable... the teacher's actions must have a necessary effect.* Lord Brougham propounded at the start of the century that saw Mill Hill emerge: *Education makes people easy to lead but difficult to drive, easy to govern but impossible to enslave.*

Vital investment in future learning modes: banks of computers in constant use at all levels. *12.s*

Insofar as definitions occur at all in Mill Hill's context, they tend more towards the jocular and ironic, appearing as populist asides on Foundation Days – *education is what remains when all that you were taught has been forgotten.* There is a long-established custom for such utterances among the world's humorists: from Mark Twain's *I have never let my schooling interfere with my education*, to Emerson's comment about the *hidden curriculum* of the Public Schools in their Victorian heyday: *It is this wise mixture of goodwill in Latin grammar with goodwill in cricket, boating and wrestling that is the boast of English education.*

What this History has identified as Mill Hill's 'Middle Way' has always been pragmatic and implicit, rather than theoretical and explicit – pertaining to the 'sound mind' of the old Latin tag. Over the last 50 years, national debate has swirled frantically around a series of shibboleths – comprehensiveness, streaming, mixed ability classes, and latterly standard curricula, centralisation, privatisation, and assessment, with consumerist concepts entering the fray in the 1990s. The OMC Millennial Celebration booklet of 2 September 2000 surmised that *Mill Hill will remain as a school right through the ebb and flow of society's future political whims.* While not expected to study such classic management text-books as *Organizational Culture and Leadership*, Mill Hill's latter-day Heads have kept their heads, while the political arguments have see-sawed, through no fewer than nine recent Education Acts, asserting what they and their CR believed was right; (see Information Supplement No.3). All three Heads are nevertheless independently career-assessed to ensure that practice reflects policy.

ALIS, YELLIS and League Tables: every autumn from 1993, however, a media event obtruded. All schools' GCSE and A-Level results were ranked in 'Performance Tables' by newspapers, resulting in judgements which owed more to an obsession with statistics than to a genuine scrutiny of the quality of education. Uncomfortably timed, each year these appeared a month before the annual nine-month Admissions process started, and the parent-focused Foundation Day. Historically, these raw League Tables contained surprises, with some erstwhile academically renowned Independents emerging in relatively lowly positions, against the 'beacon' maintained schools; many argued that they merely indicated how selective a school was. If added-value analyses, based on the pioneering Durham University 'ALIS' (A-Level) and 'YELLIS' (Year 11) schemes from the late '90s, had been integrated into the data,

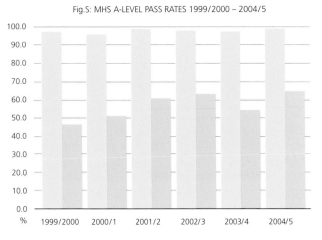

Fig.S: MHS A-LEVEL PASS RATES 1999/2000 – 2004/5

% A-E

% A-B

Oxbridge **A**

International 'Ivy League' **B**

Russell Group
(excl Oxbridge) **C**

All Medicine **D**

Educational Tertiary UK **E**

Unspecified 'GAP' student **F**

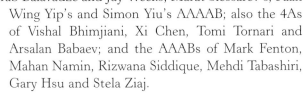

Fig.J(iv) MHS LEAVERS' TERTIARY EDUCATIONAL
DESTINATIONS 2000 – 2005

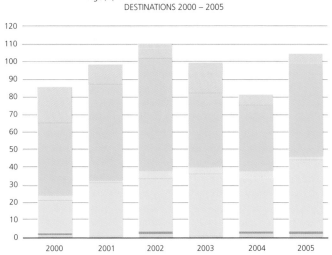

parents would have been better able to make informed choices. The telling factor was that pupils at Mill Hill achieved on average between a half and one whole grade 'higher than expectation'. The Court 'held its nerve', operating, like many others, an explicit policy of setting a hurdle for admission to the Lower VI: 5Bs and 2C scores were asked at GCSE from 2004, this still being deliberately a less stringent entry than that imposed by some competitors, with wider factors taken into account. This presupposed careful discussions with Pre-Prep parents and Belmont parents at Years 6 and 8, so that a move to alternative schools could be effected at those early decision points if advisable. The broad fact remained, however, as the 2004 research by the Assessment and Qualification Alliance showed, that the 240 schools within the HMC were five times more likely to achieve the highest A-L results than state schools.

Although trend-resisting single-sex schools still did better in raw academic terms, these results gave no credit for such aspects of the curriculum as Mill Hill's 'social' training. Despite external pressures for academic gradings, the acid test among Mill Hill parents appeared to be to ignore them, preferring to focus on the breadth of education that Mill Hill offered; nor did they reveal the reason for one parent's warm-blooded comment, *We're hooked on Mill Hill!* (Their musical son had been so bullied at a neighbouring Independent School – higher in the Tables – that he could not wait to get away each day. Mill Hill, in effect, saved him.)

Fig.S shows the A-Level pass rates for the first six academic years of the century, the AB level rising fairly steadily through the period. During this time, Mill Hill maintained a position within the 'top 250' in most of the A-Level League Tables published, with some high individual scores at A and AS levels: Ori Zhiv's AAAAA; the AAAA plus A at AS, of Zurab Balavadze and Jay Weeks; Marat Slessarev's, Faan Wing Yip's and Simon Yiu's AAAAB; also the 4As of Vishal Bhimjiani, Xi Chen, Tomi Tornari and Arsalan Babaev; and the AAABs of Mark Fenton, Mahan Namin, Rizwana Siddique, Mehdi Tabashiri, Gary Hsu and Stela Ziaj.

Destinations: spurred on by UN forecasts of Europe-wide skill shortages, and despite the evidence that the student loan system bore heavily on those less financially supported, tertiary education still remained the norm for some 90 per cent of the VI Form. Millhillians of previous generations might remark on the reduced incidence of 'Oxbridge' in these results. This obscures the fact that the only test had to be 'appropriateness' for the market served. By that standard, self-evidently the Mill Hill of 2006/7 was just as effective as her predecessors. Over 75 trans-national universities of various kinds were chosen by today's pupils, including those rated as a 'top 15' across a range of headings (such as 'Research', and Staff/pupil ratios) by *The Times Good University Guide*: see **Fig.J(iv)**. The 'Russell' Group is worth listing. It embraced not only Oxford, Cambridge, Durham, Edinburgh, Glasgow, LSE, and Imperial, King's and UCL London, but also Birmingham, Bristol, Cardiff, Leeds, Liverpool, Newcastle, Nottingham, Sheffield, Warwick and Southampton. A list of other UK campuses attended by millennial Millhillians was even longer: it included Abertay Dundee, Aston, Brunel, Bradford, Bristol UWE, City, East Anglia, Essex, The European Business School, Exeter, Greenwich, Kent, Leeds Metropolitan, London Guildhall, Loughborough, Middlesex, Nottingham Trent, Portsmouth, QM Westfield, Roehampton, Sheffield Hallam, Surrey, Westminster and St Martin's School of Art. Music institutions included Guildhall, the Royal College and the Royal Academy. Subjects veered from more standard fields such as Japanese and Russian, Medicine, Engineering, Architecture, Law and Accountancy, to courses as newly-compounded as Avionics, Nursing, Operations Management, Hospitality Management, Computer Games Technology, Industrial Design & Technology, Drama Studies, and Investment Banking.

Fig.T: MHS COMMON ROOM: TENURE (YEARS): 20C-21C		
1	L.A.Cane: (1896-1936)..	Music: 40
2 =	A.J.Williams: (1900-1938)..	History: 38
2 =	J.P.Morrison: (1925-1963) ##................................	Classics: 38
2 =	L.R.Bee: (1924-1962)..	Physics: 38
5 =	N.G.Brett James: (1902-1939)............................	History: 37
5 =	W.R.Winfield: (1970-2007)...............................	Languages: 37
5 =	P.S.Bickerdike: (1970-2007?).............................	Maths: 37
5 =	T.W.Corbett: (1971-2008?)...............................	English: 37
9 =	P.J.McAllister: (1926-1962)................................	Maths: 36
9 =	D.M.Hall: (1938-1974) *	Biology/Science: 36
11 =	W.A.Phillips: (1922-1957)...........................	Chemistry: 35
11 =	W.P.Phimester: (1946-1981)........................	History: 35
11 =	A.H.Vine: (1948-1983)..............................	Physics: 35
11 =	G.C.Sutcliffe: (1958-1993).........................	Maths: 35
15 =	V.A.Elliott: (1911-1945) #	English: 34
15 =	H Coates: (1916-1949) #	Maths: 34
17 =	A.R.Clarke: (1906-1938).......................	General: 32
17 =	A.Robertson: (1951-1983)......Physical education: 32	
19 =	J.A.Turnbull: (1947-1978)................	Chemistry: 31
19 =	C.S.Baker: (1947-1978)...........................	Art: 31
19 =	E.Winter: (1952-1983)........................	English: 31

* 31 years teaching, 5 years service, WWII (see Ch.VII)
 # returned, further teaching; ## further teaching; Belmont

Ability and aptitude: the citing of data for the Independent Sector alone should not obscure the fact that Mill Hill has never ignored the significance of the wider national picture. The phrase 'ability and aptitude' was the formula chosen by the Court in 1944 to bring Mill Hill into 'the National System of Education' through the 'Middlesex Scheme'. These would be the selection criteria – not a narrowly intellectual yardstick. Long before the Independents were starting to take note of national standards, and without ever conceding that ultimate independence of judgement which has already been prized as a light-ship amidst a politically fluctuating sea – Mill Hill has always tried to avoid the limitations of a 'closed' Public School system; instead, the School has sought a middle path, bridging the educational duality – in the recruitment of Headmasters, staff or pupils, as well as the curriculum itself. This has been a central feature of 21st-century Mill Hill.

The Common Room: a CR is of course the proving ground for the whole educational process. The teacher's objective – a precious one – is the need to present afresh what are by their nature, tried and tested, established notions, facts, rules. This has been most easily exemplified in the humanities, in the great enduring truths of literature and language, but in its essence it remains true even of the most technical and least historic of taught subjects, such as IT Studies.

One feature has been the CR's composition. With regard to its Old Millhillian element, no fewer than nine such staff returned to teach at MHS: Andrew Welch (1984); Chaplains Rev. Stuart Gibbons (1980-5) and Rev. James Fields from 1998; Richard Veal (1991-4), Austin Vince (1991-8), Lucy Sutton (1991-3), Clive Greenhough (1997-2000), James Orchard (1999-2004), and the first Housemaster to

A 21st-century 'Chief Executive' role was still grounded in the process of teaching: Headmaster William Winfield addresses a new IV Form on 'The History of the School'. *12.t*

be appointed through open advertisement – Andrew Phillips at Collinson, from 2000-04. At the Pre-Prep, Anjali Sicka taught from 1999 to 2003. In past years, however, compared with many schools, very few pupils had 'returned' to this school of strong loyalties – only 0.2 per cent during the first four *RR*s, 1807-2000; (the 1966 Kalton Report showed that nationally 12 per cent returned). As a second factor the longevity of the pre-war CRs will be replicated; several staff will have taught long enough in this one institution not merely to figure in the Mill Hill 'Hall of Fame', with 30 or more years' service, but also to enter 'The 100 Club' (100 terms), see **Fig.T (p.343)**; Col Paul Bickerdike served 34 years in the CCF, 21 years as CO. Most outstanding must surely be the record of the millennial Headmaster, William Winfield, who by April 2005 had served longer as successively Assistant Master and Headmaster (September 1970 to date) than the previous holder of that record, Thomas Priestley (see Ch.III).

A third feature was the increasing spread of the universities represented, despite an ongoing Oxbridge presence. If all staff are included, the 'Oxbridge' (or foreign/ 'Ivy League' equivalent, e.g. Heidelberg, Witswatersrand) total was 60 per cent (90/156) for 1926-83: if the non-degree staff (musicians, arts, war staff at St Bees, and unknowns) are excluded, this figure increased to 87 per cent (75/127), (75/86). Nevertheless in 1957-83 the non-Oxbridge provenances increased from nine (plus 41 non-degree staff) to 45 (plus a mere six non-degree staff); for 1984-2000 the total figures were about 120 non-Oxbridge, 38 Oxbridge, 28 non-degree. The biggest single change was the gender balance, brought into sharp relief in 2003 by the appointment of Mill Hill's first female Acting Head, Judith Herbertson, during William Winfield's sabbatical: by 2005 the male element was only 60 per cent.

Costing the objectives: the down-to-earth Mill Hill approach to education, which these many generations of academic staff have sought to pursue, is one that most pupils, and their parents, can understand and respond to. The stated *Aims of the Foundation* are *to support pupils in the passage from childhood towards adulthood*; the Warwicker survey, quoted in the first Prospectus of the new millennium, included the parental comment, *The School creates adults who feel good about themselves*. Most signally the Head of the first stage, the Pre-Prep, has declared *A love of learning* as her yardstick. John Hawkins, the Master – and the master-mind – of the highly successful Junior School at Belmont up to his retirement in 2004, set out this credo for parents: *our first concern is for the individual. We aim to develop the interests and talents of each child so that he or she feels wanted and valued.*

These objectives have relevance for the independent, Europe-oriented education which parents here and around the world still choose to pay for, out of hard-earned income, despite the existence of a free British 'national' school system. The Mill Hill of the present century endeavours, consciously, continuously, to justify the faith that parents have placed in the three establishments: the aim is to bring out at each unfolding stage the 'ability and aptitude' inherent in each child, with awareness that those attributes could easily remain undeveloped in a narrower, lower quality system, with larger classes of mixed ability, under less dedicated staffs.

Cost-based fee increases for this rounded education kept in line with inflation over the past 10 years; nevertheless, merely to keep a Day pupil at the main School, an annual post-tax income of probably some £20,000 would be required. Owners of businesses, and the self-employed, were now therefore the most typical of parental career-patterns; parental companies ranged from a flourishing newsagency in London, to an international computer firm. A total investment of some £163,000 (Day) or £199,000 (Boarding) would now have to be made for a three-stage 15-year pupil schooltime.

Benefits of the single foundation: the value for parents has been continuity and consistency throughout the primary and secondary educational process. In return the Foundation could now plan its fee income for a decade ahead, assuming that some 60 per cent of entrants to the Pre-Prep went on to become pupils at the senior School, a benefit never possible in any earlier era, and one undreamt-of for most businesses. Under the DAF's regime of tight financial discipline, the Court remit for an average 6 per cent surplus on fee income was achieved. The paramount need was to keep the Foundation's resources competitive; parents could see the results of their financial contribution all around them.

One major corporate difference from all preceding endowment-starved eras lay in the sourcing of capital projects through to 2006: 75 per cent of the new Development Plan was internally-generated from the Foundation's revenue surpluses; see **Fig.U**. In this long period of capital regeneration, the Governors had to consider a range of options for funding new developments; potentially one way was to borrow on the money markets. Another lay in the skilful disposal of assets; this might have included the historic "Grove" in the 1980s, but for the stance of the Life Governors, further proof of the value of that still ongoing and watchful Millhillian stewardship.

A third source has been the letting activities managed via the wholly-owned Mill Hill School Enterprises Ltd, varying from Camp Beaumont holidays, to location facilities for photographic or dramatic work such as the 'Inspector Morse', 'William and Mary' and 'Rosemary and Thyme' TV series; films such as 'Indiana Jones and the Temple of Doom', 'Neverland', featuring J.M.Barrie pre-Peter Pan; or the use of Collinson and St Bees House for the "Powers" TV series.

The fourth source lay in spontaneous benefactions, ranging from the anonymous generosity of a former second-generation hockey-playing *OM* and *OB*, to help pay for the All-Weather Pitch, to *OM* Richard Grimsdell, and to *OM* Arthur Baldwin; on his death in 2001, he bequeathed £400,000 to fund bursaries, and some years earlier his brother Matthew covered, *inter alia*, the cost of restoring the Belmont Chapel Clock. Of comparable importance was the £69,000 contributed by the Rose Foundation for Drama facilities, Collinson, the Café 6 development and the Pre-Prep rear extension; also the bequest by *OM* R.S.Duncan. These gifts were supplemented by individual fund-raisers, for example Peter Woodroffe, who set himself a £1million target. OMC Presidential Appeals formed a sixth area – refurbishing Chapel lighting and the Gate of Honour, and funding new Bursaries.

MILL HILL SCHOOL FOUNDATION
FIVE YEAR AVERAGE % SURPLUS ON GROSS FEE INCOME
PER MANAGEMENT ACCOUNTS 1976 TO 2000

Fig.U GRAPH OF THE FOUNDATION'S AVERAGE ANNUAL SURPLUSES SINCE MID-1980S ILLUSTRATED THE FINANCIAL INTEGRITY WHICH UNDERLIES THE SUCCESS OF THE CURRENT ERA.

Portico provides background for cast of TV series, 'Rosemary & Thyme', 2004. *12.u*

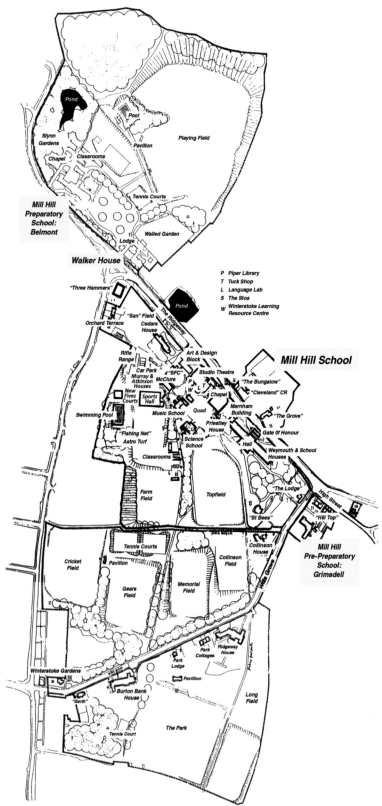

Fig.D(v) MILL HILL TOPOGRAPHY 2006/7

To these could be added special Appeals, such as those for the Partnership projects in Ethiopia, Nicaragua and India, or that organised by Prof Stephen Holt and the author in memory of Dr J.S.Whale. An eighth aspect of this vital task came from various sub-organisations of the Foundation such as the OBA, and the Friends of Belmont. Surprisingly, there has been no general Bicentennial Appeal. Sometimes, sadly, potential offerings were allowed to slip through the hands, or be denied because of 'strings attached', or because a donor's apparent intention had been contested by his heirs. In terms of contributing to the general income of the School, the many historic Trusts and charitable funds should also be mentioned, some formerly run in conjunction with the OMC. Many now agglomerated into a single fund, which usually embraced scholarship purposes, forming an annual £15,000 income.

Each Foundation Day, successive Court Chairmen reminded fellow Governors of their overriding duty to deliver quality, not simply in the opportunities offered by the Foundation's visible features, but more particularly through objectively measurable results, to launch those young Millhillians into the next stage in their careers. That end-purpose will be the cardinal note for this 200-year History. Before that, however, this chapter has to address the one supreme 'intangible' asset that a school life 'on the Hill' has always provided.

s.vi 'The Spirit of Place'

The History's concluding chapter is an appropriate place to pay some homage to what is perhaps the most unifying of all the continuities that have typified Mill Hill – the unique territorial environment. To link to a concept identified in the Introduction, this is the prime example of that *conmoción* that brings together the Foundation's generations and sexes.

The rural nature of Mill Hill's rolling pastures is still embodied in their abundant bird-life – not least the Canada Geese that daily proclaim their right to cross from the Sheepdip to Cedars and back. However, apart from families of House cats and dogs, Mill Hill's ecology has also encompassed other mammals over the 200 years, ranging from the resident wildlife, and the occupants of the School Farm – sheep, cattle, horses, donkeys, pigs and fowl – to occasional deer, and, exotically, an official mongoose and an unofficial marmoset.

Some two years before the Millennial Diary, a comparable project had been conducted with Belmont and the Pre-Prep. The aim: to set down the sensory impact of what Arthur Koestler called the "Eldorado Island", as experienced through those fresh Millhillian minds, and to compare these ideas with the writings of members of earlier generations. It has evolved naturally to become a centrepiece of the chapter.

Whatever the structural and 'cultural' changes that have occurred, the ambience which underlies them has been a constant. Although location is ultimately only one factor in a corporate strategy, and no Governing body can afford to take it for granted, yet the Foundation's territory is special by any measure. Of the three areas of the topographic Mill Hill District, the School's 'Mill Hill' stands out in comparison with the Broadway, and 'Mill Hill East', among all those delights picked out in the *Book of London's Villages: the real Mill Hill... lies around the heights of The Ridgeway; its foliage is of an altogether more luxuriant kind, its spaces more spacious, its vistas longer... Mill Hill has stayed a village girdled by woods and green fields.*

Peter Collinson's "Paradise of Delight": for the former pupils, staff and Head Masters who have spent time on this astonishing rural island, already alluded to as the classicists' *rus in urbe*, it has not been the prosaic facts, or artifacts, of Mill Hill that flashed 'upon the inward eye' when they found themselves far from home, or in time of war: it was the sights, sounds, smells, tastes – the overall 'feel' of these beautiful 135 acres themselves, which dominated. This capacity of Mill Hill to evoke a special nostalgia among her departed occupants was at its most intense at the time of the enforced separation at St Bees, and, as Science master Trevor Chilton emphasised – appropriately — at the Collinson House centenary in 2003, it is a recurrent theme in Mill Hill recollections. The splendours of The Ridgeway date from pre-Mill Hill School days, when the world-famous naturalist, the Quaker merchant Peter Collinson, retreated "from the Hurries of the Town" to "My Garden situate on a Hill north of London," looking from "its High Elevation... 40 or 50 Miles round Mee on the Busie Vain World below"; 18 months before his death in 1768, he could rejoice to a correspondent even closer to him than the American Benjamin Franklin or Thomas Bartram – the celebrated Swedish botanist, Carl Linnaeus: *My Garden is now a Paradise of Delight.*

'*Vieille et toujours renaissante*': the ceaseless international movement of seedlings, plants and letters to and from the 18th-century 'Hill' has been echoed in the flow of ideas and pupils of the three succeeding centuries. Sometimes the outside observer can express deeper meanings. The WWII *Book of Remembrance* reproduced the comment of the Anglophile French writer, André Chévrillon, invited to the Park one typically sunny summer afternoon between the wars, to watch that very English game as perpetually incomprehensible to most of Mill Hill's contemporary friends from France, Germany and elsewhere in Europe, as it was then to him – *le cricket: Je voulais surtout vous dire quel délicieux souvenir je garderai de notre promenade sous vos grands chênes séculaires, aux abords de la pelouse de cricket. On était là au coeur de la vieille et toujours renaissante Angleterre.*

As seen from the Pre-Prep: the History bears witness to just a few aspects of this corner of that *old and ever renascent England* that have caught the senses of "Pre-Preppers", Belmontians, and Millhillians over the years. A simple love of these aspects characterises both ends of the age-scale. It can be seen at its purest through the imaginations of those taking their 'first Step' through the 15-year Mill Hill experience, the six-year-old top year, as expressed through a project which Pauline Bennett-Mills set her future Belmontians. They had to record what they could see from the third-floor windows in Wills Grove, looking out on the grounds and the Totteridge fields. They were also asked to describe their walks through the grounds, hopefully with a touch of Harry Potter magic in their eyes. Six-year-old Robert Murad wrote: *I can see beautiful pink flowers, trees with leaves on top...* The walk offered excitements to these future Mill Hill pupils, making them precociously aware of what went on there. Daniel Douglas wrote: *We see the squirrels. Sometimes we see people playing fives. We saw a tree that queen [sic] Elizabeth had planted...*

"The sense of Belmont is always golden": this phrase of young William Wolfson introduces an echo of this youthful vision at the other end of The Ridgeway, through a project for Form 6H: 'The Sights, Sounds and Smells of Belmont'. The

Continuity amidst continuing change: traditional Park Cricket field and Pavilion facing Burton Bank lawn; (far l. foreground – new oak commemorates 1945-95 OMC Reunion). *12.v*

accompanying pictures show a remarkable corporate feeling for 'the flag', boding well for future holistic 'Millhillianness'; their words also evoke the humour of daily life. Twelve-year-old Tom Walters recalled: *the howls of laughter whistling into my ears, the scratching of pen on paper, the creak of the chair, the tick-tock of the clock, the ring-ring of the bell signalling the end of a period… at the end of the day, your[e] thinking things couldn't get any closer to paradise… It doesn't – Home work!* Katherine Wood vividly conjured up the history room – *I can always smell a wei[r]d smell, like when you walk into a museum… I can hear trees rustling in the breeze.* Alex Bruh had mixed perceptions: *Breakfast takes up the smell in the morning. Even the screaming children make Belmont a nice place…* First days left strong images. Michael James unconsciously echoed Arthur Koestler: *the most enormous trees in my life… the whole of Belmont is like an island of paradise.* All Darshan Allirajah's senses came into play: *A strange vapour browsed into my nostrils. It was a sort of coffee/ bacon smell. A very pleasant odour… I felt a coarse sandy surface that turned out to be a brick wall. I had one final glimpse at the trees, the gravel path, the leaves and the wall, and I knew I would see these things time and time again.* Alexander Barnes summed up the general sentiments, in words that were no doubt manna to the ears of the Master and his team: *The sights, sounds, smells and tastes are so extraordinary… they make you feel so welcome.*

"Mill Hill is a very beautiful place": many Millhillians have tried to set down something of the indefinable 'spirit of place' on paper; yet as the *OM* scientist Bernard Noltingk has observed in his autobiography, people remember differently. For some it will be the sounds, whether man-made or natural, that give rise to the strongest associations. For others, like Noltingk, it was that deep-seated reptilian part of the brain, the sense of smell, that comes readily to mind. Arthur Baldwin remembered *the smell of the distemper that was used on the inside walls of the Marnham Block, most evident after the holidays… the smell of the hot glue pot in the 'Carp'… the taste of the mugs of cocoa and slices of bread handed out in the Tuck Shop* [then on the Quad] *at morning break time.* Another *OM*, "Sam" Micklem, (last generation of the Nonconformist family already referred to earlier) recalled *sitting in the sun by the Buckland Pool sniffing the lavender and reading* Wuthering Heights. *Every scent of lavender I get brings that happy summer back, Heathcliff and Cathy and all.*

Some of these olfactory experiences have been the province of particular groups or eras. To the male Millhillian from 1911 through to the latter part of the century, the evenings before "Corps" had their own inimitable smells, later to be renewed in military service: drying green "Blanco" over radiators; boot polish applied liberally to black boots, with Dubbin on the insteps; the odour of drying soap illegally applied inside khaki trousers to preserve the crease; Brasso on brasswork. The acrid smell of cordite evoked for many the martial rifle ranges that have contrasted with the peaceful Mill Hill scene since the First World War. Whilst "Corps" was the inclusive majority experience, other School smells were exclusive to minorities. For the noses of the now extinct Young Farmers Club, there still

Not a girls cohort in a boys' school, but an integrated community:
(i) bedsits at Cedars House, in its all-girl phase up to 2005; (ii) netball on the Quad; (iii) CCF co-training creates a new fashion.
12.w

Voluntary service, vital element in Mill Hill's wider education. Annual working visits to Ethiopia – staff group at Soddhu village; (below): Group of children welcoming a Millhillian as a teacher. *12.x*

remain the farmyard emanations – especially the piggeries – located out of sight and sense, save only during a very strong wind, on the far side of Farm Road. Other typical smells were those of the glue and balsa wood of the Model Aeroplane Club, the oil and grease of the Model Railway in the roof of Ridgeway, and the dankness of the converted air-raid shelters on Top Field, used for Hobbies Hour on Sundays. For non-scientists, there was simply one all-pervading smell from the Science Block, a mixture of sulphur, gas, and formaldehyde; to the inhabitants of that mysterious world each smell had specific connotations.

'The glorious background of ancient trees': when all allowance is made for sound, smell, taste and touch, the visual qualities of the Mill Hill scene remain the most universally experienced. Familiar chords were struck in Dr Murray's sylvan time. The first *MHM* of June 1873 waxed poetic about one of those typical vistas: *the glorious background of ancient trees ... bounded by the view of Harrow Hill and the bluish outlines of more distant trees beyond.* Memories went back farther still, to a lost world of freedom. In 1875, Lloyd Tayler had compared the then present with the 1840s of Thomas Priestley's time, marvelling that there were *still elms in front of the School, and a fig-tree against the wall near to the Head Master's study ...*

Headmasters, Governors, staff and Millhillians alike have spoken eloquently about the horizon spreading out from the key vantage points – the Portico, Top Terrace, the top floors of Collinson, the Science School, or the Art Block; some vistas have emerged unexpectedly, like the view of "The Fishing Net" from the windows of McClure House, beloved by Housemistress Berinda Banks. Roy Moore wrote of *the memories of the green days in summer.* Lord Justice Cyril Salmon, Guest of Honour on Foundation Day 1971, underlined a quality (also close to the hearts of a body with whom the School has always maintained close links, the MHPS) – the sense of privilege conferred by what he feelingly described as *these lovely surroundings ... the mist rising in the valley in autumn, the cricket field in high summer, the incomparable sunsets bathing the Portico in the rays of the setting sun – these and so many other sights and sounds play a great part in your lives ...*

Some treasures are more intimate, more subtle. For Trevor Chilton, there is one favourite corner. What had hitherto been one of the patches of Mill Hill's ancient wild meadowland and long grass, bounded by Wills Grove and the BB and Collinson paths, where it was possible to lie down of a summer's afternoon and read a book and forget everything, the School needed to create a new playing field. Round the newly formed borders of that transformation – Memorial Field – has evolved a feature that most would not even perceive: *a wonderful example of a characteristic English mixed woodland – oak, lime, and birch.*

Benedictus, benedicat: for a final all-enveloping view –
even a benediction – on Mill Hill's setting, there is no more
fitting source than Dickie Buckland, a true son of Mill Hill,
and one of her greatest conservers. In a letter of 3 September
1922, when staying at "The Grove", Dickie wrote: *I have been
walking along the terraces in the moonlight – Mill Hill is a very
beautiful place. Just a hundred years ago I suppose a few enthusiasts
were walking in the same moon and wondering how they could help
England to pioneer the world to a wider view of things. They built a
Greek Portico and adopted the great trees which Collinson had
planted and thanked God and took courage. Forty years on the whole
place was derelict and the ancestors of the owls that are hooting
tonight were beginning to be wise about new ruins they might haunt.
But there was a spirit about the place that had no taste for becoming
a ghost and somehow... Mill Hill burgeoned into a new spring.*

New Piper Library, with
Thomas Piper portrait, seen
from passage-way to restyled
Winterstoke Learning
Resource Centre. *12.y*

Ten years further on, his Diary quotation for 1932,
recorded in the commemorative booklet produced at his
death in 1947, and inscribed on the plaque in the Memorial
Garden, also takes the trees as its very characteristically
Millhillian metaphor: *I do not know what the result of what I have
tried to do for Mill Hill may be, but somehow I hope I have planted trees in the right places and
that in a hundred years or so a few of them at least will be left to tell God of my good intentions.*
Another decade later, *a propos* the Middlesex Scheme (see Ch.VIII), in a letter of
1943, Dickie Buckland once again took inspiration from the natural setting, in a
message as full of relevance for the 21st century, as it was then, in the midst of war:
*If Mill Hill becomes a centre of living education untramelled by the dead wood of the past, and
filled with that kind of sap which draws its vigour from the soil of Britain as a whole and not
from certain cultivated parts of it, then we shall be serving a great purpose and justifying the
faith of those great founders who, like the Pilgrim Fathers, commenced their set adventure in the
name of freedom in all things of the spirit and cared nothing for class distinctions and party
politics.*

At first sight, to a less attuned 21st-century newcomer, these sentiments might
seem sententious; yet they symbolise the deep convictions of the many cadres of
men and women who over Mill Hill's first two centuries have worked to conserve the
best of the past, in order the better to serve the present and the future. This is the
authentic Mill Hill voice: it links back to the origins, yet the vision is ever ahead,
inspired by 'the spirit of place'. Indeed, this might seem a good note to sound at the
conclusion of this History of the first 200 years. However, it cannot be the last word.
That must lie with the sole end-purpose of this complex system of thought, planning
and investment – the Millhillians themselves. Unless all the privileged tradition and
community effort produce good, fulfilled citizens, and happy, fruitful lives, it would
be thought a glorious failure. *Valete* yet *Salvete!*...

s.vii *Valete, Salvete:* out into the world

'Destinations', **Fig.J(iv)** p.342, marked one aspect of a school's ultimate effectiveness. Yet once the immediate academic achievement has been examined, how to evaluate the 'product'?

Among the many traditional career fields featured throughout the School's story, two examples will serve – the law and medicine. Mill Hill has counted no fewer than three contemporary members of the Supreme Court of Judicature: The Rt Hon Lord Justice Stephen Sedley in the Court of Appeal, and The Hon Mr Justice Roger Toulson and The Hon Mr Justice Roger Buckley in the High Court. In medicine, by 2002, the Medical Register listed a former physician to the Royal Household, Sir John Batten; Dr Colin Barnes, former President of the European League Against Rheumatism; and Prof Robert Kendell CBE, former Chief Medical Officer for Scotland and President of the Royal College of Psychiatrists; the latter's untimely death pointed up a sadly unique example of the sole career where a member of the academic staff – Donald Hall – could in peacetime survive the death of an outstanding former pupil in the same field (both being also, incidentally, Cambridge Double Firsts).

Yet this History would not rest its case on the "dominance" of various walks of life claimed under the title of some other Public School publications. The impact on which Mill Hill has prided herself is of a more pervasive, but in its own way no less self-confident, kind. One measure, if statistics were available, would be to trace through the later careers of pupils from overseas in their countries of origin, to try to assess the benefit of these far-flung Millhillians for Britain's relations with the world.

If success in worldly terms over the past 50 years were the be-all and end-all, attention would turn to such works of record as Debrett's *People of Today*. For example in the author's copy, 75 Millhillians were named in 1992; in the edition of 1997, the list had risen to 82, despite the omission of such eminent names as the opera composer Inglis Gundry; it listed 34 Oxbridge men, no women as yet, and showed a heavy bias not only towards the law and medicine, but also to academe, with a sprinkling of politics and authorship, and above all to the world of business.

If a 'public service' orientation were required – for example Oxford's prestigious Ashmolean Museum – where Prof Nicholas Mayhew is Deputy Director and the late Dr. Roger Moorey was Keeper of Antiquities – the present Headmaster's Millennial copy of *Who's Who* lists some 30 Millhillians. Even more distinguished have been the small group of OMs picked out for membership of the same year's publication of the *International Who's Who*, including some names that have already appeared in these pages: Sir Michael Bishop, Prof Philip King, Sir Simon Jenkins, the theologian, Rev. Prof Charles Cranfield, and again Prof Robert Kendell. If a combination of business and sport were the focus, the country's most capped player in his time, Michael Corby, already met in Ch.IX, would be the 'star'.

Yet however meritorious and headline-worthy, are these the really significant measures? Moreover, as Guest of Honour at the 2004 Foundation Day, Rt Hon Chris Patten, emphasised, is not the concept of 'success' such a relative one, that it would only serve to divide? Recent recorded Millhillian career-paths in fact make up a fascinating A-to-Z. Careers range from **A**gricultural Economist, or Artist/Blacksmith, to **W**oman Police Officer (a "Whoopsie") or Web Designer; from **C**ounter-tenor, or Crime Intelligence Analyst, to **Y**outh Theatre performer; from **E**quine Veterinarian, or Exhibition Designer, to **Z**ookeeper.

This brief overview demonstrates the sheer diversity – an echo of that Gladstonian "aliveness" – that Mill Hill's young men and women now pursue. In some instances an individual will today combine two or more careers, some 'non economic', a model impossible to predict in any of Mill Hill's proactive, yet inevitably limited Career Counselling programmes, geared now more to selecting the correct University course, with a view to options for a subsequent career.

This conditioning for the achievement of happy and satisfying careers and lives in the round has to be Mill Hill's ultimate justification. The question posed at the start of this chapter seems to be in the process of being well answered: at the opening of the 21st century, a financially sound educational enterprise is giving *public benefit* – not to some diffuse 'market', but to the people it serves – parents, pupils and the wider community – in a way that gives reassurance for the future.

Sources for Ch.XII include: s.i; ii: R.Boyd, *Independent Schools – Law, Custom & Practice* (1998); *Guidelines for Governors* (ISC); *News of the World* 12.xi.1995; *Edgware & Mill Hill Times* 13.xii.2001; D.Enright, *The Wicked Wit of Winston Churchill* (2001).

s.iii: thanks to Diary contributors/ Judith Herbertson, Dep HM.

s.iv: obit, *Irish Times*, 5.viii.2000, Prof N.A.Kinnear MB, BCh, BAO, FRCSI, [1919-25]; Margaret Thatcher, *Downing St Years* (Harper Collins, 1993).

s.v: S.D.Jenkins [1956-60], 'Why GCSEs are cheating our children'. *Times*, 28.viii.2000 & *Observer*, 17.xii.2000; *Independent*, 31.xii.1988 ref N.A.D.Macrae [1937-42]; *Sunday Times*, 15.i.1989, ref M.D.Bishop [1955-7]; *D.Telegraph*, 9.ix.2000, ref M.W.Corby [1953-8]. E.H.Schein, *Organizational Culture & Leadership* (San Francisco, 1985) – input, P.B.Armitage [1952-8]. [Calculation of post-tax disposable income for 2004/5 based on Day fee of £12,582, and a tax rate of 30 per cent.]

s.vi: Ltr, Peter Collinson, Linnean Soc Archive, via, 15.iv.1999, Alan Armstrong, Hatfield, MA, USA, author of *Forget not Mee and my Garden...* (2002, Am. Philosophical Soc. 2002, USA); ltr, 25.iv.1766, No 174, to Linnaeus: "I survey my Garden with Raptures, to see the Infinite Variety with which the Great Creator has enriched the Vegetable World... my Garden is now a Paradise of Delight'. N.G.Brett James, *Life of Peter Collinson* (1926) #; Lewis W.Dillwyn ed, *Hortus Collinsonianus, account...*, Plants cultivated by the late Peter Collinson FRS (pte. circ., Swansea, 1843)#; J.Hingston Fox, *Dr John Fothergill & his Friends* (1919) [incl evidence ref final transplantation by Collinson of his famous Peckham garden to

Mill Hill, 8.iv.1749; Jean O'Neill, *Country Life*, 21.v.1981, 1442/4, 'Plants for an Intire Stranger': Peter Collinson's Contribution to 18th Century Botany' #; Hazel le Rougetel, 32-9 'Philip Miller/ John Bartram Botanical Exchange' [source unidentifiable] #; T.Aldous, *Illustrated London News: Book of London's Villages* (Random House Gp, 1980); "Trees", Natural History Society, (Mill Hill, 1957) N.L.Jackson, "Survey of the Woods and Grounds of Belmont.. European Year of the Environment & Belmont's 75th Anniversary" (Belmont, 1987), & M.Newcombe, (Belmont, 1998) #; M.Flanagan, 'The Grounds at Mill Hill School', Royal Botanic Gardens, Kew (1988) #; Tree Surveys, Walker House, MHS #; ltr 16.vii.1990, Dr C.D.Pigott [1941-6], Dir, Cambridge U, Botanic Gdn, #; *MHM* 1971, speech, L.J.Salmon [1917-22]. Thanks to John Hawkins & Pauline Bennett-Mills, projects by BMT & Pre-Prep, Summer 1998; advice from HM Alastair Graham [MHS] & Gordon Smith [BMT] and A/Ms Donald Hall, Edward Stanham, Trevor Chilton, Chris Sutcliffe; corr with N.S.Farrow [1927-30]; A.M.Macfarlane [1944-8]; A.M.Micklem [1946-51]; A.B.L.Baldwin [1945-9]; T.Longville, Maryport; The *MHPS*. Noltingk *op cit*. P.Hobhouse, *Plants in Garden History...* (Pavilion, 1997 edtn).

Envoi: Sir Winston Churchill, *The Unrelenting Struggle* (1942), q. in *Transactions, Ryl Historical Soc, 2001,* v.XI, 6th, 180; Sir Percy Cradock, *In Pursuit of British Interests...* (John Murray, 1997); Gathorne-Hardy, *op cit*; S.Bungay, *op cit*.

Other *OM* references: D.Allirajah [2000-5]; A.Babaev [2001-3]; Z.Balavadze [2000-4]; M.O.T.Baldwin [1947-52]; Maria Baneeva [1997-2000]; A.E.J.Barnes [1961-6]; C.G.Barnes [1949-54]; J.Batten [1938-42]; D.Beckman [1999-2004]; J.Berwin [1999-

2004]; V.Bhimjiani [1995-2000]; M.Bishop [1955-7]; N.G.Brett James [1894-8]; A.Bruh [2000-5]; R.W.B.Buckland [1878-84]; R.Buckley [1952-7]; G.F.Chase [1967-72]; X.Chen [2000-2]; A.B.Cowing [1951-6]; C.E.B.Cranfield [1929-33]; R.S.Duncan [1965-70]; M.Fenton [1995-2000]; J.T.Fields [1973-8]; S.F.Gibbons [1947-52]; G.M.R.Graham [1952-7]; Nikki Green [1998-2000]; C.Greenhough [1969]; J.Grognard [1999-2000]; I.Gundry [1918-22]; Tanika Gupta [1980-2]; M.Halstead [1998-2003]; E.Harvey [1946-51]; Nan He [1999-2000]; F.G.Helmore [1834-6]; S.C.Holt [1948-54]; Hoda Hosseini [1997-2002]; G.Hsu [2000-3]; Maria Hvorostovsky [1998-2000]; M.James [2000-5]; S.D.Jenkins [1956-61]; R.E.Kendell [1948-53]; P.K.King [1947-52]; N.A.Kinnear [1919-25]; Amy Lee [1997-2001]; D.J.Lee [1995-2000]; Sheryl Lee [1995-7]; H.Marnham [1874-80]; N.J.Mayhew [1961-6]; H.Melling [2002-prsnt]; A.M.Micklem [1946-51]; Minnis family – S.E. [1993-8], – J. [1997-2002], – R. [1995-2000], – C. [1998-2003], – A. [2000-3]; P.R.S.Moorey [1951-6]; K.Moyo [1996-2000]; R.Murad [1965-70]; M.Namin [1996-2001]; B.E.Noltingk [1931-5]; J.Orchard [1988-93]; A.R.B.Phillips [1968-73]; O.Sander [1998-2003]; D.Sebag-Montefiore [1996-2001]; S.J.Sedley [1952-7]; Anjali Sicka [1991-3]; R.Siddique [1999-2001]; M.Slessarev [1995-2000]; A.Spicer [1858-63]; Lucy Sutton [1981-3]; M.Tabashiri [2001-3]; L.Tayler [1840-6]; D.Thatcher [1928-32]; A.F.Todd [1885-92]; C.Tornari [1997-2002]; R.G.Toulson [1959-64]; R.J.Veal [1982-7]; A.E.Vince [1978-83]; Kamelija Vrangalova [1998-2002]; T.Walters [2000-5]; H.F.Ward [1877]; Carly Warwick [1999-2001]; J.Weeks [2000-4]; P.M.Woodroffe [1942-5]; W.Wolfson [2000-5]; Katharine Wood [2000-3]; N.W.Wray [1961-6]; F.W.Yip [2001-3]; S.Ziaj [1999-2003]; S.Yiu [2000-4].

The contemporary School prospectus underlines the Mill Hill Chapel's ongoing central,
multi-faith role. Director of Music, Richard Allain, rehearses School Choir,
with the 1986 Mander Organ in the background; it replaced
the original Vowles installation of 1898. *12.z*

Envoi

Political power is now lying in the hands of a vast and mobile electorate, with scanty regard for tradition or history ... Men discover a change of attitude towards the law as law, a decline of reverence for institutions as institutions. The fact that this quotation from a speech by Lord Morley was prefaced with the phrase *The public school is on its trial now*, could be as readily understood in the context of the challenge facing the Independent Schools at the opening of the 21st century, as it was when first expressed to a Millhillian audience: the occasion was the 34th Annual Dinner of the OMC, at the Princes' Restaurant, on 25 October 1912, in celebration of the 21st anniversary of the Headship of that other authentic, enduring voice of Mill Hill, Sir John McClure.

The speaker was the guest of honour, a Wykehamist friend of McClure's, Sir Robert Morant, until recently civil service Head of the Board of Education, who went on to draw from what then seemed an imminent challenge, a moral, and a role, for the future pupils of Mill Hill, just as contemporary HMC meetings are re-asserting the contribution made by the Independent Schools as a whole: the evolving State depended on *men and women with courage, energy and will, with open, supple, teachable intelligence, who must also have developed the power of making these qualities effectively felt ...*

The sense of being on trial, challenged by a fast-changing world, is no new phenomenon: it dominated the thinking of a Mill Hill facing the end of the second millennium, just as it rightly governs the minds of the Foundation which now looks to the third. The Charity Commission's sharper focus on the need for the 'public benefit' and 'wider [financial] access' to flow from charitable status is but one example of that challenge; it was further emphasised in a report by the Joint Committee on the Draft Charities Bill in 2004. Even though the Foundation's representative body, the ISC, may claim that Independent Schools' parents render a £2 billion tax bonus to the Exchequer, these pressures will not go away.

The later Sir John McClure's unwavering response to that 1912 speech also rings out with a message of the same relevance to today's Mill Hill as were so many of his pronouncements recorded by this History: *A school which stands for what Mill Hill School stands for can never die ... the best is yet to be.*

The former Chairman of the Court, Dame Angela Rumbold, recorded a more complex view: *Notwithstanding the demands that the future may bring, the total educational experience that is Mill Hill's 'Middle Way' has demonstrated the resilience and a capacity to develop which are key to any enterprise. I believe the liberal heritage of Mill Hill School, underpinned by the concept of a co-educational Foundation taking pupils from 3-18 will ensure its continued success. At the same time I hope that it will serve the local community, enabling a broad spectrum of the pupil population to achieve their true potential and meet the challenges and expectations of the 21st century.* In his inaugural address to the Old Millhillians Club in 2004 her successor, Sir Robert Balchin, added a further dimension: *Throughout its almost-two hundred years of existence, Mill Hill School has encountered many vicissitudes, has triumphed over those occasional difficulties to which all schools are prone, and has continued to provide an excellent education for the young people entrusted to it by parents, no just from North London, but from all over the world. We would be foolish indeed, however, to think that the present government is not inimical to independent schools: it clearly is. In the coming decade we could face the most testing time yet of the School's history. I hope not, but, as long as I remain Chairman of its Court, I pledge that we shall meet such challenges that come, head-on and well prepared – and that Mill Hill will emerge as strong as it has ever been.*

If at the outset of this long journey the horizons of Mill Hill's founding fathers were happily insular, yet infused by the values of the English Enlightenment, quietly trustful of God's world, that certainly cannot be predicted even for the year of grace 2007. Too much has happened in between for this History to offer the kind of unquestioning, very British perspective on the 'Public School' and its world which that first Brett James story of 1907 seemed to radiate. Even the third revised and popular version of 1938, albeit written both in the consciousness of the War of 1914-18, but also against a sense of the clouds that were gathering once more over Europe – even then the view that emerged was uncomplicated, rooted in the inviolability of Mill Hill's ideals.

The story of the events, people, buildings, setbacks and achievements, which form the first 200 years of Mill Hill's history is now enshrined in print: the ending of each era, in Tanika Gupta's phrase, providing the *new beginning* to the next. It still seems to embody the historic precepts – humanity and tolerance balanced with principle, innovation balanced with a commitment to excellence. These are in fact very 21st-century virtues: the full circle has been turned.

Looking to the future, perhaps two prophecies can be made: the Mill Hill School Foundation has the will to survive, and to do so positively – that at least has been firmly evinced over the centuries. Moreover, when the 250th anniversary of Mill Hill's foundation is celebrated, it may well be told through other media, and to new audiences for whom the millennial generation, male and female, is but a distant, even unfamiliar memory.

History with its flickering lamp stumbles along the trail of the past, trying to reconstruct its scenes, to revive its echoes, and kindle with pale gleams the passions of former days: so does Winston Churchill highlight the limitations of the historian's craft – indeed this was an important theme of one of the new century's Prestige Lectures, by historian Andrew Roberts.

Yet for all those unknowable future members of the wider Mill Hill Community, it must be hoped that this narrative will prove to have been something more than Coleridge's *lantern on the stern, which shines only on the waves behind us.* It is no accident that those lines were deliberately quoted by a different kind of professional from those hundreds of educational practitioners who have sought to teach and guide Millhillians over the centuries: they were in fact used by a representative of a calling that is no stranger to Mill Hill's story, a distinguished diplomat of the late 20th century, Sir Percy Cradock, in a notable memoir about an institution 'of limited resources, a glorious but imprisoning past, an uncertain future'. His subject was Britain and her 'Interests': they might as easily have been applied – if the extremity of that parallel is acceptable – to Mill Hill, or at least to the embattled Mill Hill of the 1970s to 1990s.

The motivation behind that work was to proclaim the real purpose of all good history: *to urge the mind to aftersight and foresight*. In Mill Hill terms: will those with responsibility for the Foundation's future governance be able to carry forward the good things from the past and present, but thereby also avoid some of its mistakes? They will undoubtedly only be able to do so in the context of their time, of their 'market' as it will then present itself, and of the educational parameters that will by then need to prevail.

The *flickering lamp, the lantern on the stern*, have illuminated many good things in Mill Hill's evolution. They have also flashed a passing beam on the problems encountered along the way, when what the School 'stood for' appeared to be in conflict with that ever-renewing principle – adaptation to appropriateness.

Welcoming self-criticism, this History has sought to avoid that self-congratulatory fate rightly castigated elsewhere by Public Schooldom's historian as a *series of paeans*. In the enduring words of the same Head Master whose spirit was first invoked earlier, the History has *thought backwards*, yet now, with confidence, looks – and *lives – forwards* to times that are yet to be.

Those times, their leaders, and their pupils will surely continue to radiate that ongoing vitality which the Gladstonian title to this History describes – *an Institution strikingly alive*.

They will as surely embody the successive subscripts that have accompanied Mill Hill's historic Coats of Arms: not only constantly seeking to improve on what has gone before – *Excelsior* – but also thereby serving and fulfilling the time-honoured, mutually enriching goals, in the deepest sense of both concepts in that ancient Mill Hill device – *et virtutem et musas*.

Appendix A

ABBREVIATIONS

The History uses these abbreviations where appropriate (see also Appendix E & Supplement 1), also abbreviations common in both World Wars. Current MHS usage shown [] where different.

ABC   Anti-Bullying Council
ADC   Aide-de-camp
AGBIS Assctn of Governing Bodies of Independent Schools
AGR   Assctn of Graduate Recruiters
AHM   Assctn of Headmistresses (fmr)
A/HM   Acting Headmaster
AKC   Associate, King's College, LU
A/L   "A" Level exam
ALIS   Advanced Level Information Service
alt   alternative
A/M   Assistant Master/ Mistress (see M)
APS   Assisted Places Scheme
Assctn Association
BB   Burton Bank House
BBP   Borough Boarding Places
BJ/1, 2, 3: Brett James' Histories: 1- 1909; 2- 1923; 3- 1938
BMT   Belmont MH Prep S.
Bps Boarding pupils
Bt.   Baronet
c   circa, approximately
c.   centre
[19]C century
C   College (alt: Coll)
CD   Cedars House
CE   Common Entrance examination
CH   Collinson House [C]
Ch.   Chapter
CoG   Court of Governors
corr   correspondence
CR   Staff Common Room, fmr Masters' Common Room (MCR)
C/T   'Composite Treasurer'
CU   Cambridge University
DAF   Director of Administration & Finance
DBE   Order of the British Empire, Dame Commander; [BEM, Br. Emp. Medal; OBE, Officer, CBE, Commander; KBE, Knight Commander]
DD   Doctor of Divinity
DES   Dept for Education & Skills (fmr Dept for Education & Science)
DfEE   Dept for Education & Employment
DfES   Dept for Education & Skills
DL   Deputy Lieutenant [of a County]
DLitt Doctor of Literature
DNB *Dictionary of National Biography* (New *DNB*: 2002+)
DPhil Doctor of Philosophy, aka DPh
Dps Day pupils
dscn   discussion
FCO   Foreign & Commonwealth Office
F&DC   Finance & Development Cmttee, alt to:
FGPC   Finance & General Purposes Cmttee
FEIS   Fellow of the Educational Institute of Scotland
fmr   formerly
Fps Female pupils
FRAS   Fellow, Ryl Astronomical Soc
FRHS   Fellow, Ryl Horticultural Soc
FRHistS Fellow, Ryl Historical Soc
FRPS   Fellow, Ryl Photographic Soc
FRS   Fellow, Ryl Soc
FSI   Fellow, Chartered Surveyors Institute (now FRICS)
GBA   Governing Bodies Assctn
GBGSA Governing Bodies of Girls' Schools Assctn
GCE   General Certificate of Education
GCSE   Gen. Cert. of Secondary Education
GDST   Girls Day School Trust (fmr GPDST)
gggs   great-great-grandson
GMs   Governors' Minutes
Gov.   Governor
HC   Higher Certificate exam

HoD   Head of a teaching Dept
HM   Head Master: later – Headmaster
HMC   Headmasters' & Headmistresses' Conference
HoH   Head of House (pupil)
HS/M   House-Master, House-Mistress
HT   House Tutor
IAPS   Incorporated Assctn of Preparatory Schools
ISBA   Independent) Bursars Assctn
ISCis Schools   ) Information Service;
ISC   "   ) Council (fmr ISJC)
ISI   "   ) Inspectorate
ISJC   "   ) Joint Council
JP   Justice of the Peace
KC   King's Counsel
l.   left
LEA   Local Education Authority
LLD   Doctor of Laws
LoN   League of Nations
LU   London University
M   Master of BMT
Mc   McClure House
MH/MY Murray House [M]
MHHS   Mill Hill Historical Soc
MHM *"The Mill Hill Magazine"*
MHPS   Mill Hill Preservation Soc
MHS   Mill Hill School
MHSSSC MH Sports & Social Club
MHV   Mill Hill Village
MIDYIS Middle Years Information Service
Min   ordained Minister
MO   Medical Officer
MoEd   Ministry of Education
Mps Male pupils
MusB   Bachelor of Music
MusD   Doctor of Music
MxCC   Middlesex County Council
NLCS   North London Collegiate S
OB   Old Belmontian
OBN   'Old Boy Network'
OC   Officer Commanding
OM   Order of Merit
OM   Old Millhillian (also *)
OMC   Old Millhillians Club
OS   Ordnance Survey
OU   Oxford University
PA   Personal Assistant
PC   Member of the Privy Council (aka Rt Hon.)
'pc'   politically correct
PhD   Doctor of Philosophy
PH   Priestley House [P]
PHSE   Personal, Health & Social Education
PM   Prime Minister
Prof   Professor
pt   part
QC   Queen's Counsel
r.   right
R.A.   Ryl Academician
Rev.   The Reverend
RH   Ridgeway House [R]
RR   School Register(s) [RR1: 1807-1926; RR2: 1926-57; RR3: 1957-83; RR4 : 1983-2000]
Ryl   Royal
SBOMA St Bees Old Millhillians Assctn
SC   School Certificate exam
S/Sch School
SCOEG [later AGR] Standing Conf. of Employers of Graduates
SCR   Scrutton House
SFC   VI Form Centre
SH   School House [S]
mS   Senior monitor
2M   Second Master
SMT   Senior management team
Soc   Society
SRN   State Registered Nurse
TES   Times Educational Supplement
TSR   Hon. School Treasurer

U   University
WM   Weymouth House
WK   Winterstoke House [WH]
YELLIS Year 11 Information Service
YFC   Young Farmers Club

War Terminology/ Decorations/ Medals

AB   Able-bodied Seaman
AC2   Aircraftsman 2nd Class
AEF   American Expeditionary Forces
AFC   Air Force Cross
AFS   Auxiliary Fire Service
ARP   Air Raid Precautions
ATS   Auxiliary Territorial Service (women)
AWOL   Absent without leave [US orig]
Brig   Brigadier
Brig Gen Brigadier Gen
Capt   Captain
CCF   Combined Cadet Force
Col   Colonel
Codr   Commander
CSM   Company Sgt Maj
DFC   Distinguished Flying Cross
DSO   Companion, Distinguished Service Order
Fl Lt Flight Lt
FO   Flying Officer
Gen   General
Gp Capt Group Captain
GSM   General Service Medal
K.i.a. Killed in action
LAC   Leading Aircraftsman
LDV   Local Defence Volunteers (pre HG, Home Guard)
LI   Light Infantry
Lt   Lieutenant
Lt Col Lieutenant-Col
(M)   Military, aka Mil
Maj   Major
MAP   Ministry of Aircraft Production
MC   Military Cross
MiD   Mentioned in Despatches
MM   Military Medal
MSM   Meritorious Service Medal
Nazi   National Socialist (German)
NS   National Service
O/C   Officer Cadet
O/S   Ordinary Seaman
PO   Petty Officer
P/O   Pilot Officer
POW   Prisoner of War
PSI   Permanent Staff Instructor
Pte   Private
RA   Ryl Artillery
RAF   Ryl Air Force
Regt   Regiment
RFA   Ryl Fleet Auxiliary
RFC   Ryl Flying Corps
RM   Ryl Marines
RMA   Ryl Mil Academy, Sandhurst, fmr RMC
RN   Ryl Navy
ROC   Ryl Observer Corps
RQMS   Regmntl Quartermaster Sgt
RSM   Regmntl Sgt Maj
SHAEF Supreme HQ, Allied Expeditionary Forces Europe
SOE   Special Operations Executive
Sqn Ldr Squadron Leader
SSI   Senior Staff Instructor
Stalag POW Camp (German)
TD   Territorial Efficiency Decoration
VD   Volunteer Officers' Decoration
WAAF   Women's Auxiliary Air Force
Wg Cdr Wing-Commander
WO   Warrant Officer
WOSB   War Office Selection Board
WRNS   Women's Royal Naval Service
WWI   First World War 1914-18
WWII   Second World War 1939-45

Sources: *Oxford Companion to Military History* (2002), also *Who's Who.*

Appendix B

THE LEADERS OF THE FOUNDATION 1807-2007

1. MILL HILL SCHOOL

Headmaster/ Principal Tutor ('Principal')

1 1807-10: Rev. John ATKINSON, (b175?, d1821) *from:-* Homerton Coll, (Hackney, now CU).

2 1811-18: Rev. Maurice PHILLIPS, Aet. 44; (b1767, d1822) *from:-* Tutor, Rotherham Coll; *to:-* Cng Min. \#

3 1819-June '25: Rev. Dr John HUMPHRYS LLD, Aet. 61; (b1758, d1837) *from:-* Cng Min, Southwark, and MHS School Secretary.

4 1825-Dec '27: Dr James CORRIE MD, Aet. 33; (b1792, d1855) *to:-* resume career, medicine.

5 1828 Jan-June: George Samuel EVANS MA (later Rev. Dr, & the Hon.), MA Glasgow, LLD, Aet. 26; (b1802, Gloucester d1868, Australia); *from:-* U; *to:-* Prn., North End Acad, Hampstead, thence political career, Australasia: (see Ch.II).

(After six months with no Head Master, July-Dec 1828, for the ensuing 20 years a dual management formula was attempted):-

Chaplain/Domestic Superintendence

1828-31: Rev. Thomas Blundell *from:-* Baptist Min, Prn.

*1831: [A.D.McLAUGHLIN]

1831: Rev. Henry Lea Berry MA, Glasgow U, Prn., Gov., *OM*, Aet. 24; Prn. (b1807, d1884).

1831-38: Rev. Wm. Clayton Aet. 46; 46; Prn. (b1785, d1838) Cng Min, Saffron Walden. \#

1838-46: Rev. Henry John Crump (b1803, d1846); Prn, *from:-* Cng Min, Weymouth *to:-* own S, Lechlade. \#

1846-52: Rev. Samuel England, Aet.35; Prn. (b1811, d1886) *from:-* Cng Min, Royston *to:-* Walthamstow.

Head Master & Classical Master

6 1829-31: Aet. 42 (b1786, d1861) Robert CULLEN *from:-* Eton Coll.

7 1831-Sept '34: Rev. H.L.BERRY.

8 1834 October-September 1852: Thomas PRIESTLEY Aet. 43; (b1792, d1864) *from:-* Rotherham Coll, *to:-* ret. \#

Headmaster/ Principal

9. Dec 1852-'60: Rev. Philip SMITH BA, LU, *OM*, Aet. 41; (b1812, d1884) *from:-* 'Prof', New C, LU, *to:-* writer. \#

10 1860-63: Rev. Dr William Flavel HURNDALL MA, LU, PhD. Heidelberg U, Aet. 30; (b1830, d1888) *from:-* Fellow, University C, LU to foundation of own rival S, The Cedars, Rickmansworth.

11 1863-64: Rev. Philip Chapman BARKER MA, LLB, LU, Aet. 35; (b1828, d1904) *from:-* Cng Min: *to:-* Cng Min, Chester.

12 1864-68: Rev. George Donald BARTLET MA, Aberdeen U, Aet. 41; (b1823, d1906) *from:-* HM, own S, *to:-* HM, Solsgirth Hse, Highgate.

[**13**] 1869: (Prof A.S.WILKINS: 1 day) [Year of New Foundation]

14 1869-86: Dr Richard Francis WEYMOUTH MA, DLitt, LU. (b1822, d1902); Aet. 47; *from:-* HM, Portland Grammar S, *to:-* ret, writer. \#

15 1886-91: Charles Arthur VINCE MA *from:-* Fellow, Christ's C,CU & A/M Repton S, Aet. 31; (b1855, d1929); *to:-* teaching/ writing. \#

16 1891-18 Feb '22: John David McCLURE (later Dr, then Sir) Aet. 32: (b1860, d1922), MA, LLD, MusD, Holly Mount C, Bury, & Trinity C, CU, 1882-85: *from:-* Prof of Astronomy, Queen's C, LU. \#

*1912-13: [Dr Arthur S.WAY MA, DLitt, London] during Dr McClure's 2-term sabbatical: for much of this time N.G.B.James acted as HM, *vice* A.J.Williams, *vice* Dr Way.

*1922: [Albert John Williams MA], 2M: 2 terms

17 Sept 1922-Dec '37: Maurice Leonard JACKS MA, Aet. 28; (b1894, d1964); *from:-* Bradfield C, & Fellow, Tutor & Dean, Wadham C, OU; *to:-* Dir, Dept, Eductn, OU, 1938-43, 44-51. \#

18 Jan 1938-May '40: Dr Thomas Kingston DERRY MA DPhil, Aet. 34; (b1904, d2001), Kingswood S, Queen's C, OU, *from:-* Repton, HD, History, *to:-* BBC European Srvce, teaching, writing. \#

*[March-May] 1940: [Victor Elliott MA], 2M; Carlisle Grammar S, & Jesus C, OU.

19 May 1940-Aug '43: Arthur J.ROOKER ROBERTS MA. *OM*. Aet. 58; (b1882, d1943), Jesus C, CU, *from:-* ret. \#

20 September 1943-April '44: M.L.JACKS seconded *from:-* Oxford for 2 terms: back *to:-* Dept of Education, OU.

21 April 1944-Mar '51: Rev. Dr John Seldon WHALE MA, Aet. 48; Caterham S, St Cath's.Soc, OU, & Magdalene C, CU, DD Glasgow U; (b1896, d1997), *from:-* Pres, Cheshunt C, CU *to:-* resume international academic & writing career. \#

22 April 1951-July '67: Roy MOORE CBE, MA, AKC, Aet. 43; Judd S; Fellow, King's C, LU, (b1908, d1992) *from:-* HM, Lawrence Sheriff S, Rugby: *to:-* U of California. \#

*1961-2: [John Morrison MA, JP], 2M, during Sabbatical of Roy Moore: City of London S, St. Cath's. C, CU.

23 Aug 1967-July '74: Michael HART CBE, MA, (b1928-), Aet. 39; Collège Français, Berlin, & Keble C, OU; *from:*- School HS/M, Shrewsbury; *to:*- Inspectorate of Schools, & HM, the European S, Luxembourg. #

24 Aug 1974-Aug '78: Alan Fraser ELLIOTT MA, OU, (b1929-) Aet. 45; *from:*- HS/M, Marlborough C, *to:*- Classics A/M, Brecon.

*Aug 1978-July '79: [William Allan Phimester TD, MA], Jesus C, OU] (b1921, d2002): *from:*- 2M & HD, History & Politics, *to:*- resume duties. #

25 Aug 1979-Aug '92: Alastair Carew GRAHAM MA. Aet 47; (b1932-); Winchester, & Gonville & Caius C, CU, *from:*- HS/M, HD, Modern Languages, Eton C *to:*- ret. #

26 Aug 1992-July '95: Euan Archibald MacFarlane MacALPINE (b1940-). Aet. 52; Cranleigh S, & Edinburgh U & Liverpool U, *from:*- HM, Bedales S, *to:*- ret & Chairman, Not-For-Profit Landowners Group, Strathspey.

*July 1995-March '96: [William Richard Winfield].

27 1996-2007: William WINFIELD MA, (b1947-). Aet 48; William Ellis S, & Clare C, CU; *from:*- Deputy HM, and Director of Studies, HD Modern Languages.

*2003 May-July: [Judith Herbertson, A/HM, fmr Dep HM, MA], *vice* sabbatical of Wm Winfield: Perse S, Nottingham U.

2. MASTERS/HEADS OF BELMONT, MILL HILL PREPARATORY SCHOOL 1912-2007

1912-1937: Arthur James Rooker Roberts.

1937-1966: Arthur Edward Rooker Roberts MA *OM*, (b1907, d1988), Jesus C, CU, *from:*- Marlborough C, *to:*- ret.

1966-1973: James Burnet MA, JP, (b1930-), Gonville & Caius C, CU, *from:*- Clifton C Prep. S, *to:*- HM, Edinburgh Acad Prep. S.

1973-1980: Peter Foster BA (b1923, d1997) LU, *from:*- HM, King Henry VIII Prep. S, Warwick *to:*- Asst. Archaeologist, Warwicks. Cnty Mus.

1980-1991: Gordon Smith MA, Dip Ed., (b1933-), Trinity C, OU, *from:*- HM, Brighton C Junior S, *to:*- ret, & Archivist, Belmont.

1991-2004: last 'Master': John Hawkins BA, Cert Ed. (b1947-), Westminster C, OU, & Sorbonne, *from:*- HM, Caterham Prep S., *to:*- *locum* Prep Head, then educational consultancy.

2004-prsnt: first 'Head' and internal appointment: Mrs Lynn Duncan BSc (LU), (b.1952-), *from:*- Deputy Head, BMT.

3. GRIMSDELL, MILL HILL PRE-PREPARATORY SCHOOL 1995-2007

1995-prsnt: Mrs Pauline Bennett-Mills, Cert. Ed. [b1949-], Bishop Otter C., (now pt of Sussex U) *from:*- Deputy Head, Jnr Dept, Notting Hill & Ealing High S, GDST.

APPENDIX C:

BUILDING MILL HILL

Although the names occur within the text, listed here are eight main categories of those who, apart from Heads/ Acting Heads (Appendix B), helped to 'build' Mill Hill both strategically & aesthetically; ([*..-.] = yrs at MHS); (u/k)= unknown.

s.1 Presidents of the School

This honorary office, first attempted in time of Thomas Scrutton/ Dr Weymouth, with unsuccessful invitation to Earl Granville (1871), was brought to fruition by Gov Sir Ryland Adkins, MP [1875-80], to connect the School 'on high':-

1914-1927: Viscount Bryce of Melbourne (paved the way for HRH Prince of Wales to officially open new Science Block, 1924).

1927-33: Rt Hon Sir Albert Spicer Bt MP [*1858-63]

1933-57 The first and last Earl of Athlone KG, PC, GCB, GMMG, GCVO, DSO, FRS, personal ADC to the Queen, Chancellor of LU [fmr Pr. Alexander of Teck]: (assisted Sir Frederic Sellers to invite HM Queen Elizabeth II to 1957 Sesquicentennial).

s.2 Vice-Presidents

Again started by new Treasurer, Thomas Scrutton, and through the time of John McClure, a range of V-Ps was introduced, to spread the School's re-burgeoning name; most were distinguished in the public life of the country. From 1869, these included various MPs (eg William Woodall MP). The year 1889 included Sir Edward Baines and Rt Hon. Sir Thomas Chambers QC, MP; 1892 listed Samuel Morley MP, Dr John Storrar and Rev. F.W.Gotch LL.D. 14 were added later- Thomas Barker DL JP [1840-3]; Henry M.Bompas QC MA; Alex Brown FRS, MD, DSc, FRCP [1853-4]; Sir Samuel Davenport KCMG LLD. [1830-1]; Edward Dawson LLB, JP [1842-7]; Jos. Hardcastle MA, JP [1829-30]; Sir Kingsmill Key [1829-32]; Thos. Micklem JP; Sir William Roberts FRS, MD, BA [1845-6]; Henry Spicer BA [1849-54]; Dr R.Thorne-Thorne FRS, MB [1857-9]; Thos. Walker; W.H.Wills DL, JP [1842-7] and Dr James Murray (1903). The practice survived to the 1930s, in the persons of Lord Winterstoke's two nieces (see Ch.VI).

s.3 Chairmen of the Court

Before 1896, the Honorary Treasurer was the central figure in the Committee/ Court's affairs, but only 'taking the Chair' at meetings. Even after this, he acted (pace Nathaniel – "Nath." – Micklem in regard to R.W.B.Buckland) as'Gideon' [= famous Judge of ancient Israel] 'Achates' [= faithful lieutenant of Virgil's Aeneas] to the now Chairman. From 1909 (Sir Albert Spicer) until 1999 there was also an unofficial courtesy role for a Vice-Chairman. The Court's Chairmen are now commemorated on the walls of the former School HS/M House. (Style given as at career peak):-

1896-1911 Lord Winterstoke of Blagdon DL, JP, MP [*1842-7]

1911-1922 Rt Hon Sir Albert Spicer Bt JP, MP [*1858-63]

1922-1944 "Nath." Micklem QC, LLB, BCL, MP [*1866-8, 1870-1]

1944-1951 Prof Sir Arthur Pickard-Cambridge DLitt, LLD, FBA

1951-1968 Rt Hon Lord Justice Sellers MC, LLD

1969-1976 Marshal of the Royal Air Force Sir Dermot Boyle GCB, KCVO, KBE, AFC

1976-1979 Rt Hon Lord Justice Orr OBE

1979-1981 Hon Mr Justice Kempster CBE, QC, BCL [*1936-42]

1982-1989 Prof Sir Cyril Philips PhD, Hon DLitt, Hon LLD

1989-1995 Rt Hon Lord Slynn of Hadley PC, MA, LLM

1995-2004 Rt Hon Dame Angela Rumbold DBE, MP

2004-prsnt Sir Robert Balchin DL

s.4 Governors:

title evolved from 'Members of the Committee'– 1819. First 9 MP Governors were William Tite MP (1864) after 45 years MHS service; W.H.Wills MP (1880+); Albert Spicer; T.A.Herbert [1878-81]; A.E.Hutton [1878-84]; N.Micklem; Sir Ryland Adkins; Sir Alfred Hopkinson KC. After 1945, the MxCC had the power to appoint six 'Governors by invitation': MPs included F.Messer, Dudley Smith. 1948: first of 6 females – Mrs M.R.Forbes JP. Individual Governors identified within chapters.

s.5 Hon. Treasurers, Bursars/ Directors of Finance, Patrons

Hon. Treasurers: # dates as First Register 1926; (>= partially accurate inscriptions as on Treasurers Pew, Chapel). Function became redundant on Incorporation as a Company, 1998.

1807-30# Favell, Samuel (1806-35 >)

1830-54# Piper, Thomas (1835-51 >) [*1811-7]

1854-63 Coombes, Thomas (1851-63 >)

1863-96# Scrutton, Thomas U. (1863-95 >) [*1840-2]

1896-99 Gunn, Ernest (1895-99 >) [*1870]

1899-1945# Buckland, Richard W.B. (1899 >) [*1878-84]

1941-51 ('Composite Treasurer': see Appendix E)

1945-56 Moore, Harold (1945-51 >) [*1889-94]

1956-59 Viney, Oscar (1951-59 >) [*1900-3]

1959-88 Walker, T.Dickson, MBE FCA (1959- >) [*1926-9]

1987-95 Constantine, Hon Roy, FCA [*1950-3]; Jt. 1987-8

Bursars:

1896-1903 Tucker, Henry (combined with role of Librarian)

1903-06 Watson, David

1907 James, Norman G.B. [*1894-8]

1907-09 Tucker, Henry

1909-10 Andrews, William [*1884-7]

1911-16 Gluenicke, Lt Col George

1916-37 Gifford, John

1937-44 Mitchell, Lt Col John D. CMG, DSO [*1895-9] amends RR2)

1944-46 Morrison, John P. JP MA

1946-60 Horne, Capt H.M.

1960-72 Symons, Jack F., OBE

1972-87 Webb, E.H. (Ted)

Dir of Administration & Finance, (& Secretary to Court 1998-2004):

1987-2004: Morgan, Lt Col Beverley MSc BA FCMA FCCA

Bursar: 2004-prsnt. Fraser, Bruce BsBA MBA

s.6 Trustees and Patrons

Similarly many individuals have been elected as Trustees, up to Incorporation in 1998. From 1999-prsnt, the first 'Patron' was elected: Walker, T.Dickson MBE FCA.

s.7 'No.2, No.3, No.4'

The function of the senior team working under the Head Master is underplayed in school histories, yet over the last 100 years, as schools grew more complex, its structure has become an ever more vital element in the whole. At the School, the 'No.2' title has evolved from a 'Vice-Master' through the traditional 'Second Master', seen rather as a custodian of the School's 'ethos' and only as a cover for the Head's absence; then latterly to a more administrative role, through to the current 'Joint Deputy Head'. By the 1990s a 'Third Master' had been introduced, the vital 'Director(s) of Studies' having evolved in the 1980s. From1990s there was also a formal 'Senior House Master' role. If this system works well, it can act as a lubricant, a two-way channel, between the CR (it has its own staff-representative, two-year electable Chairman – a very different role) and the Headmaster. The 'No.2' was traditionally in his 'gift', but from 1996 onwards has been claimed as the Court's prerogative, like that of the Chaplain appointment. Although in earlier times it acted as a predominantly conservative force, on several occasions,

(e.g. during time of E.P.Stanham vis-a-vis Roy Moore, during 1960s), it was the means of advising the HM that certain matters, in the opinion of the CR, needed more – or less – attention (e.g. discipline); nowadays unless the role is proactive, it is not working. Can also act as a stabilising element in HM's favour, (e.g. 1940, when V.A.Elliott stood by the then increasingly beleaguered Head, Dr Derry).

This list complements that given for the HMs, and Acting Heads, in Appendix B. In the 20th century, seven Second Masters or Deputy Heads performed as Acting Head, actually running the School in the absence, for various reasons, of the nominal HM: A.J.Williams, (N.G.Brett James vice A.J.Williams), V.A.Elliott, J.P.Morrison, W.A.Phimester, W.R.Winfield and Judith Herbertson. List also includes one appointment as 'Vice-Master' of the School.

'Vice-Master' 1875-1881 – Rev. R.Harley, MA, FRS; HS/M, BB.

Second Master:

1897-1919 E.W.Hallifax MA

1921-1938 A.J.Williams MA, FRHistS

1938-1943 V.A.Elliott MA (& Deputy HM)

1943-1946 H.Coates MA [amends RR2]

1946-1963 J.P.Morrison MA, JP

1963-1972 E.P.Stanham MA

1972-9, 1980-1 W.A.Phimester MA, TD

1981-1983 A.Robertson DPE

1983-1991 G.C.Sutcliffe MA

Deputy Head Master:

1992-1995 W.R.Winfield MA	
1995-1999 T.T.Dingle BSc	
1996-2003 Judith Herbertson MA	Joint Deputy Heads
1999-2004 J.Johnson-Munday MA	
2003-prsnt Jane Sanchez MA	
2004-prsnt A.C.Gaylor BA	
2001-prsnt P.J.P.McDonough MA	[External]

s.8 The Mill Hill School Foundation's Architects & Designers

'C/P' = reference in Cherry/Pevsner, (see Sources):-

Aikman, (u/k): Buckland memorial window, Chpl (1948).

Barnsley, Hewitt & Mallinson: Bicentennial Building.

Bentham, P.G.: Sculptor, WWII names, Gate of Honour (1949).

Briggs, M.S. [*1896-9]: revised Gears Cricket Pavilion (1911); The Vineries (1911); Winterstoke Gardens houses (1911); McClure Music S (1913); Winterstoke Hse redesign (1924). Advisor: WWII names, Gate of Honour (1947); Chpl extension (1951-5); [Memorial Field sign (1953)]; Buckland Pool tablet, raising. First OM Architect to MHS; (see RIBA Archive: 'BRMS', 81 boxes & Bibliography).

Brown, Vincent & Partners: architects, Faculty Blocks (1987).

Champneys, B.: Chapel. RIBA Gold Medallist (1912) – most nationally distinguished of Architects so far retained by Mill Hill, despite fact of Tite's preceding role as twice PRIBA. Considered as one of the top architects of 19C, one of the most respected members of the secular 'Queen Anne' movement. First work was a church, St Luke's, still extant in Kentish Town; designed Mansfield C, OU, which recommended him to MHS; other work is best seen in a continuous series of buildings, Newnham C, CU. 'Among the private schools, the outstanding buildings of the 1890s onwards are at Mill Hill; a chapel..., a library and other buildings, all in a spirited Free Classical manner': C/P.

Collcutt, T.E.: RIBA Gold Medallist (1902) & PRIBA (1906-8), important in 'Arts & Crafts' movement; Consultant Architect, 1898+; partner, Collcutt & Hamp. Working earlier for Collinson (no known relation to P.Collinson) & Locke, fashionable furniture-makers, developed attention to detail, helped create for MHS 'comfortable and kindly buildings'. Chemical Labs/ (between third Chpl & Swimming Bath) (1898), Collinson Hse (1903), Scriptorium (1902/3), Tuck Shop (1902), fmr Winterstoke Library (1907), Marnham classrooms (1905), Ridgeway Hse (1911). Best remembered for Wigmore (fmr Bechstein) Hall; D'Oyly Carte – Savoy Hotel (first Strand & Thames facades) & Ryl English Opera Hse (now Palace Theatre); Imperial Inst, Kensington (now destr); Houses at Eton C. C/P.

Crompton, W.E.V. [*1882-3]: "Thatched [cricket] Pavilion", old 1st XI field, Gears (1897), (destr by vandalism, 2002).

Dalgleish, K., FRIBA **& Pullen**: rebuilding of The Large (1949); Art & Workshop Block (1960).

FDA: Angela Rumbold Indoor Pool (2005).

Gordon, A. & Prtnrs: "Hill Top" site – conversion to 10 staff houses (1970s); VI Form Building; Murray Hse. C/P.

Gray, A.S. [* 1916-22]: Park Cricket Pavilion (1925).

Greenwood, S., formerly Chief Architect, John Laing & Son: 1971-2: RH dormitory heating (1971).

Hamp, S.H.: Gate of Honour: C/P – 'Mill Hill has a rather good restrained Beaux Arts archway...' (1919-21); Science Block (1924/5); new BB (1935); WWII war damage restorations, Dining Hall, House plans: >1948: partner, Collcutt & Hamp 1906+.

Hayward, C.F.: first Burton Bank (1874).

Howard, H.M.: [*1956-60]: Greek Mural, Classics Room.

Hughgates Ltd: Sports Hall (Design & Build contract, 1983).

Lloyd, M: Belmont Chpl stained glass window (2000).

Murray, G.W.: original painted ceiling, Gate of Honour (1920).

Paine, J. the younger: Belmont Villa, for P.Hammond (1760s).

Powell & Moya: Belmont classroom blocks (1989).

Rawlins, Darcie ARC FPBS: Designer, plaque to Cecil Goyder, Science Block (1988).

Rooke, A Bradley: Natural History & Museum buildings (1898).

Smith, T.R.: Sanatorium (1877); new SH classrooms (1880). C/P.

Soutar, J.C.S.: Belmont, extensions (1923); cloisters and quadrangle (1928-9).

Stock, J. Stock Wolstencroft, (DAF revived practice of retention as Consultant Architects, with Project Management role): Sports Hall (1983); Mill Hill Pre-Prep (conversion from Winterstoke, 1995); Cedars Hse (conversion from Old San, 1997); Studio Theatre (conversion from Old Gym) & extension of Sports Hall & 'Fishing Net' Spectator Stand (1998); Michael Bishop Music Studios, & extension of Art, Design & Technology Building (1999); The Stoa, & new Piper Library – conversion of fmr Squash Courts (2000-2); Belmont Multi-Purpose Hall, Classroom Block & Quad, redesign of Cleveland (CR) & fmr SH HS/M's House forming first Governors' Conference (Crick) Room (2002).

Sutcliffe, Col: renovation, Belmont (1940), "The Grove" (1948).

Taylor Pearce: Gate of Honour updating/ refurbishment (2001):

Letter cutter – Philip Surrey; Conservators (roof/ gold leaf) – Rian Kanduth, Layla Collier, Paul Newall.

Tite, (Sir) W.: School Hse (1825/7), 2nd Chpl (1833).

William Tite's role in obtaining assignment to build the most famous, most frequently depicted building in the MHS complex is set out in Ch.II. Best known – Royal Exchange building (1844), as well as for long line of railway stations. First of two Architects retained by MHS who become PRIBA (1861-3), (1867-70), and first of three RIBA Gold Medallists (1856).

Tubbs, R.S. [*1925-30]: Cleveland MCR – adaptation (1956). Known for 1951 Festival of Britain buildings, Thames Sth Bank).

White, E.H.: 'Garden Architect' for levelling of Park and other playing fields (1923-4).

Wills, F.: Headmaster's (= St Bees) House (1896).

Woods of Taplow Ltd: Buckland Garden (1949).

Sources: corr with T.D.Walker, *MHS Properties* (Mill Hill, pte circ, 1990) #; corr/dscns with Lt Col B.Morgan (DAF), & fmr A/M Fabian Watkinson, member – the Victorian Society; RIBA Library & Entrance Hall Wall of Honour; C/P – Cherry/ Pevsner, *Buildings of England...*, London: North op cit; Gray, *Edwardian Architecture*, op cit;); Stamp & Avery, *Victorian Buildings of London 1837-1887* op cit; valuable inputs on Collcutt from Joe Shaw, husband of RH HM/M, Lindsay Farrant.

APPENDIX D:

Our Mansion has Many Houses

In 2002, the trend for option against the 'boarding experience' appeared to reverse, re-emphasising its continuing appeal. Indeed, for still a majority of the 15,000 boys and girls, who have attended Mill Hill (inevitably less so in the case of Belmont) in common with other schools with a historic Boarding ethos, their sharpest personal memories, and the legends that dominated their schooldays, centred round the parallel life of **'the House'**. That is one of the paradoxes of any Boarding school History. Above all, if Boarders (*Bps*), the allegiance of being an 'Old Burton Banker' or an 'Old Collinsonian' took pride of place as an individual's 'Mill Hill identity'; if a House itself may have ceased to exist, its passing can seem like a bereavement: (for one 1920s Old Winterstoker the change to Grimsdell Pre-Prep was a *disgraceful degradation*).

Each House acquired its own 'character', partly as a function of its current inhabitants, but partly due to its history, and to its geography – both internally, and in relation to the Main School centre. In McClure's time and up to the 1960s, the oldest House, SH, almost felt itself synonymous with Mill Hill School as a whole; the further away from the centre, the stronger the sense of separate identity (eg the first BB, see Ch.IV. Above all, the physical layout affected 'character': Houses like CH, or WK (formed from an original Vicarage), with centrally-located kitchens, seemed more like a domestic home, than Houses with long corridors – School, or even BB. Houses also had strong if biassed perceptions of each other; e.g. the non-hierarchical (still characteristic) regime of pre-1943 CH made **BR** comment (see Appendix E): *under the influence of the present [HS/M], CH has been notorious for its dissociation from the true spirit and tradition of the School... There is no fagging and no distinction of years to speak of...* The nature of a House could turn on pure chance: e.g. originally, in 1944, Dr Whale had designated C.M.Meade-King, not L.R.Bee, for BB.

Here the History records a time-profile of the formal Houses, as well as of each of the dwellings where MHS pupils 'lived-in', 1807-2007, a surprising list – 35 locations (25 at Mill Hill, 10 at St Bees); this is supplemented with a summary of a once-vital inward-looking factor, the House colours: (inter-competing – scarf, tie, square (to 1970s), vest (to 1939); 'prefectorial staff'). At key stages of growth, many properties acted in the role of what would now be thought of as 'Boarding Houses', in addition to those regarded as proper Houses. In 1909/1910 a sharp distinction was drawn between 'Hostels' and Boarding Houses: the former including the new RH (1911), the latter covering the original SH, and the first Out-House, BB.

The 1900-1910 GMs and RR1 also show an initial allocation of boys during the McClure growth period, prior to the building of CH and RH, and pre-WWI, to the 'Waiting-Hostels' of "West Grove" (still at the top of Hammers Lane); "Christowell", "Erlesmere" and "Haslemere" (both these latter houses also still in Hammers Lane, opposite Lower Gears, were rented for £100 p.a. from Mr Pitt); a further adjacent House, "Opawa" (rented for £45 p.a. from Mrs Isaacs, 1907), was connected with "Haslemere" (see below).

Some Boarders also lodged within the private quarters of the SH Master, on occasion 14, if an extra bedroom was used for 5 more boys. For some 207 boys, this was the sum total of their residence throughout their time at 'Mill Hill', (in the same way that 128 boys – and staunch Old Millhillians – only knew the School under a St Bees identity).

Strictly speaking all Houses should be termed Hostels since from 1915 by Resolution of the Court they were run on the 'Hostel' system, fees going into the 'central purse'. However for good semantic reasons, 'Houses' became the phrase: 'Hostel spirit' and 'Head of Hostel' would not have had the same ring.

The three School Houses that were formed and to whom new boys were first allocated in 1907-9 were Scrutton, Weymouth, and Priestley (on the merging of Priestley with Scrutton, on the exile to St Bees, a *MHM* ascribed the birth-year to 1914); however the Register continued to also show 'SH' – School House – as the overall 'House' for some boys at the same period. When House-'Ties' (= matches), rather than 'Dormitory' or 'Form' Ties, became the norm for internal competitions, there was much discussion about how to break down SH – fluctuating between 110 and 122 boys – into competitive, but manageable entities: the first experimental solution had been to describe teams as School House 'NW', 'East', and 'Octagon', although this idea had the disadvantage that boys would move dormitories and locations, and so continuity was destroyed.

The next approach was to follow other Public Schools, despite the lack of precedent in the fact of the first BB in Burtonhole Lane never having been called 'Harley's' when Rev. Harley started to build this first Out-House in 1874: this proposal was to name them after the House Tutors. By now RH had come into existence (1911), and the Minor Houses – 'Hasle', 'Erles.'– would disappear – 1913-15. McClure's own suggestion was to call them simply 'A', 'B', and 'C', but it was quickly realised that it would be confusing for 'B' to have to play 'BB'. The 'authorities', as the *MHM* always humorously but mysteriously described them, decided to retain the three existing MHS figures within the permanent formulae of [SH] 'Scrutton', [SH] 'Priestley' and [SH] 'Weymouth', although there is no reference in the Minutes. The final stage was then to drop the prefix 'School House' altogether, although it was always implied, to facilitate the role of senior 'Vice-Master(s)' for SH, *pro parte* the Headmaster; *vide* the SH House photograph of 1914, with McClure and his three Tutors.

The reincarnations of the Houses evacuated to St Bees (see Ch.VII) are in square brackets ["Tomlin", "Eaglesfield", "Grindal", "Seacote", "Seacroft"], as well as the names of the Out-Houses which supplemented that limited accommodation, eg ["Fern Bank" @]. Because of the would-be ending of *Dps* status upon the departure to Cumberland, apart from two Day Boys at St Bees, and the subsequent merging of Houses due to suddenly reduced numbers, many boys in 1939/40 (as earlier) carried two House names in their Valete slips, eg Murray & Collinson, Priestley & Scrutton, CH/BB, (= a transference from one to the other. Names of Housemasters/ Housemistresses are mostly omitted, the Registers being the proper place for that topic.

Several Houses were planned but never executed: thus in 1908, after "The Grove" was purchased, one idea mooted was to sell BB, and erect a new Boarding House on the "Grove" site. In 1944 there was a Seven-Year Plan to convert the Marnham block into a 'Master's House for 40 Boys', and to create three new Boarding Houses of 50 boys each; R.W.B.Buckland suggested that one House might be a Junior College for 200 16-18-year olds. These ideas were never then realised.

The ladies will, it is to be hoped, forgive this outline of the early Houses for being written from the 'receivers' point-of-view: that is how it was. They will take some wry amusement in the fact that to the experienced retrospective eye of the year 2006/7, 'boys-only' has a distinct ring of 'Boys Own' about it.

[Mrs Abbey's @]: St Bees overflow Out-Hse.

"Arrandene": property of parents of an OB, Mr & Mrs Fordham, Wise Lane, temporary accommodation for BMT and MHS boys, together with the "Sani", and Mrs Elliott's, 1923-4, before WK finally available, after builders' strike.

["Ashley House" @]: St Bees Out-Hse, former YH, Finkle St.

Atkinson (ATK): first 21st-century mixed Day Hse, formed in Sept 2004 from the overgrown McClure, IV, V, VI Forms; occupying top floor of same building: (Colours: thick choc. thick cream, med pale blue.)

Burton Bank (BB): **1.** old, Sept 1875+, 1.25 miles away, at Burtonhole La; **2.** New, planned, 1924, for its ultimate site, before WK was built; 1935+, Wills Grove; **3.** ["Eaglesfield"] but initially partly with CH at ["Grindal"]; **4.** Reunited, Autumn 1941; **5.** Spring 1943, co-located with SH, ["Seacote"]; **6.** Third Hse to go co-educational, in 1980. Initially, girls dormitory was on second floor, separated from boys dormitory by a curtain; then upper floor was luxuriously converted into bed-sits for girls only, followed, 1988, with conversions on 1st floor, bringing girls' total to 13. (Colours: thick maroon, v.thin white ('wht'), thin chocolate ('choc'), v. thin wht).

Cedars (CD): (aka 'IKEA House', by reason of its modern style). **1.** First 13-18 all-girl *Bps* Hse, built and opened, September 1997, within frame of former Sanatorium, named in honour of Peter Collinson's Cedars of Lebanon. **2.** 2000: + *Dps*. **3.** 2005+: mixed Day House. (Colours: (tie): medium navy blue, v.thin wht, thin red, v.thin white; (scarf): thick navy blue, thin wht, thick red, thin grey. Second Hse colours to omit traditional MHS 'choc'. "San" first suggested as a Hse, 1947, by W.C.Ramsay.

"Christowel", in Hammers Lane: served briefly as a Waiting-Hostel 1901-05 before CH was built, 1903. (Colours as SH).

Collinson (CH): **1.** First Out-Hse built within grounds, 1903; **2:** 1939-42 [Grindal], **3.** 1943-5, ["Eaglesfield"]. **4.** At Mill Hill, sole male-only *Bps* Hse up to 21st century. **5.** Sept 2000: first/only group of male IV Form *Dps*. **6.** First 6 V/VI Form girl *Dps* Sept 2001, at "St Bees"; all dorms converted into study bedrooms – Stage 1 refurbishment, (on CD model); old nomenclature – JCR, SCR, Quiet Room – remains. (Colours: Thick choc, thin wht, v.thin choc, thin pink).

["The Crescent, No 3" @]: leased from Sgt Brown, St Bees School PTI, 1944, for 7 boys boarding with Mr & Mrs Taylor, Miss Hess.

('DB': the designation for male *Dps* from at least 1881 – 25 boys in 1900s – until formation of MY, 1933. Sometimes boys went on to become *Bps*, thus they will be shown in the Registers as, e.g., 'DB, CH', 'M, CH', etc.).

(Mrs Elliott's: SH HS/M's Hse again, temporary home for WK boys, Nov 1924). (HS/M's private quarters in SH ended 2002.)

"Erlesmere" (aka **Erlsmere**): Waiting-Hostel for 10-18 *Bps*, in Hammers Lane, run by A/M W.A.Andrews as HS/M, 1901 to 1915, in relation to first CH, then RH. (Colours as SH).

["Fern Bank" @]; St Bees overflow Out-Hse in Finkle Street.

["Grindal" @]: former St Bees School Hse, (see Ch.VII); named after Grindal, Archbishop of Canterbury.

"Haslemere": Waiting-Hostel for 7 *Bps*, Hammers Lane, 1902-13, in relation to RH. (Colours as SH).

McClure (MC): **1.** Formally formed 1971 (alt. names – 'Priestley', 'Buckland', 'Ramsay', 'Jacks'), largest Hse of its time, c.115; **2.** 1976, first *Dps* Hse with *Fps*, VI Fm; **3.** 1998 IV Fm *Fps*. (Colours: thick choc, v.thin black (later dk blue), thin wht, v.thin black; girls tie 1998, thick dk blue, v. thin choc, thin wht, v.thin choc).

Murray (M/ MY/MH): **1.** First Hse for male *Dps*, identified 1933, to provide basis for 'house spirit': at one point, Dec 1936, largest Hse, at 45; (folded on exodus to St Bees, where initially no *Dps*), but later **2.** + *Dps*: (amends RR2); **3.** Re-formed 1945, basement, Marnham Block; **4.** 1955 to 'old Rifle Range', Farm La., idea of W.Skinner, HoH, only Hse move part-funded from own 'Pound' (APP E); **5.** 1971 to new building, new Quad; **6.** 1994 relocated to rooms of fmr History Dept, below SFC; **7.** 1984-6 co-ed LVI/UVI Hse; **8.** *The last bastion of masculinity*; male *Dps* only. (Colours: thick choc, thin wht, thick choc, thin yellow).

"Opawa": semi-detached Hse of A/M D.Watson as HS/M, in Hammers Lane, 'Waiting-Hostel' for 7-9 *Bps*, amalgamated with/ to be known as "Haslemere", growth period 1902-1911.

Priestley (Priestl./PH): **1.** Games-competitive div of SH from 1909 (3T); **2.** After departure to St Bees, 1939, *Bps* to Scr./Wey.; **3.** First new Hse for *Dps*, 1975+, (location as post-war MY); **4.** Girls *Dps* 2003; **5.** Upper floor Cedars. (Colours: Thick choc, thin wht, thick navy blue, thin wht).

["The Retreat" @]: St Bees overflow Hse, Finkle Street.

Ridgeway (RH/ R): named after old 'Ridgeway House' on the Ridgeway, Peter Collinson's home: (see Ch.I). Originally 4 sites considered (at that stage described as a Hostel to indicate the differing form of funding from the first Out-Hse, BB): (a) land opposite old *King's Head* pub, at top of Wills Grove; (b) the eventual site; (c) land beyond San, along the Ridgeway; (d) what the Committee originally thought the 'most satisfactory' site until School Architect proposed otherwise – land at the side of "The Grove", facing the School. Six phases of usage, first three as male-only *Bps* Hse – **1.** 1911-39, MHS; **2.** 1939-45 ["Seacroft"]; **3.** 1945-77, MHS; **4.** From 1977 (3T) first to take VI Form female *Bps*; **5.** Reverted to male *Bps* in 1990s, with strong international flavour; **6.** 2000+: Reintroduced VI Form female *Bps*; largest Hse, 2003+. (Colours: thick choc, v.thin wht, thin purple, v.thin wht).

St Bees: 1. First dedicated girls-only VI Form Boarding Hse, from 1986, initially 7 girls+. (Colours: as former Weymouth, although attached to CH: hence need for new Weymouth colours); **2.** Became 11-13 Boarding Hse for BMT pupils, 1997+; **3.** 1999+ converted to co-ed Boarding, 11-13; **4.** Sept 2000+, reallocated to MHS, attached to CH, with 11 male *Bps*. (Originally the dedicated Head Master's Hse for the then Dr & Mrs McClure; re-named in 1945 as married A/Ms' quarters).

(The Sanatorium: temporary accommodation, WK boys, Nov 1924).

School (SH/ S): **1.** As fledgling School's sole *Bps* Hse 1807-1875, still main Hse 1875-1907, HS/M as 'Vice-Master' *vice* HM; **2.** 1907-9+, divided into component Hses, RRs showing boys in 'SH', + Priestley, Scrutton and Weymouth; **3.** St Bees: 1942 (3T)+ reverts as sole Hse – ["Seacote"]; **4.** 1943 – SH overflow dorms in ["Tomlin"] and ["Seacroft"]; **5.** From 1945+ again divided into SCR/WEY for games purposes. **6.** From 1980, a mixed *Bps* Hse, with Girls' dormitories ranged to the W. end of first floor; **7.** Sept 1989: IV Form male *Dps* entry; **8.** Sept '95: all male *Dps*, plus ex-WK male *Bps* VI Formers. **9.** Sept 1999: girl *Dps* IV Form entry – all mixed *Dps*. **10.** 2001: historic ending of SH as HS/M's, 176 years. (Colours: as fmr SCR).

Scrutton (Scrut./ SCR): **1.** First sub-div SH, founded 1907 (3T); **2.** Sprte at St Bees up to 1942 (3T); **3.** Male *Dps* from 1945 to 1976; **4.** Combined with WEY for sport, 1976+, thereafter defunct, as name thought risible. (Hse Colours: thick blue-green, thin wht, v.thin choc, thin wht).

["Seacote" @]: hotel taken over as SH/ classrooms, St Bees.

["Seacroft" @]: large private house at St Bees, housing RH; also one SH dorm, 1943+.

['SH Hostel': reference to pre-Hostel 1923-4 before building of WK, see "Arrandene"].

"Sunnyside": some boys boarded with Dr Murray, see Ch.IV.

["Tomlin" @]: former St Bees Prep School Boarding Hse, home for WK; also 1943+ one SH dorm.

["Vale View", 1 @]: opposite Seacote, attic for 6-8 boys, 1944.

"The Vineries", Milespit Hill: 5 boys boarded here, 1922+, pre WK, before Lady McClure took up residence, as gift of Court.

"West Grove" 1891: a pre-Hostel, at top of Hammers Lane, fmr property of School Doctor.

Weymouth (Weym./ WM): **1.** Male *Bps* sub-div, SH: 1909 (1T)+. **2.** ["Seacote"] St Bees – still separate part of SH up to 1942 (3T); **3.** 1945+ male *Bps*; **4.** 1977: merged with SCR, forming new SH. **5.** 1993: re-inaugurated under first-ever female HS/M, mixed *Dps*, incl all MHS VI Form girls; junior section all-male. **6.** 1998+: new male HS/M, Anthony Armstrong; arrival of IV Form (13+) girl *Dps*, fully co-ed: (2003 – new 10th birthday). (Colours: traditional: medium pale blue, v.thin choc, thin wht, thick choc, thin wht, v.thin choc; new, 1993+, thick dark blue, thin wht. v.thin choc, thick green, v.thin choc, thin wht).

Mr Williams' House: First use of private House of SH HS/M, Mr Williams, 1907-1911, to accommodate from 7 to 14 boys, pre RH .

Winterstoke (WH/ WK): **1.** 1924-1939 & 1945-95 originally mooted as 'Home Field' after name of grounds in which this fmr Vicarage lay; **2.** 1939-45 St Bees ["Tomlin"]: **3.** Only Hse, male-only *Bps* (of many considered for this fate over the years) to move out of use for MHS, being re-converted to become Foundation's third educational 'arm', associated with *OM* benefactor, "Grimsdell". Mixed Pre-Prep, 1995+. Only Hse to have an eponymous GWR locomotive name-plate, commemorating Lord 'Winterstoke', adorning its walls – 'lost' when converted to Pre-Prep). 80th birthday commemoration plaque in Wills Grove, 2004. (Colours: thick grey, thin wht, thick choc, thin wht).

Winterstoke Gardens, Nos 10/11: c.1911; **No 3:** 1922+, one term by T.F.Jackson, part of post-WWI build-up of *Bps*, pre SH Hostel, pre WK 1924.

BELMONT (see Appendix H): 80 years after Thorowgood Academy at "Hill Top" (see Ch.II), and prompted by *MHM* article of 1905, N.G.Brett James was first to initiate idea for a Junior/ Preparatory School in "Bittacy House", 1907. CoG agreed in principle for an under-14 Dept as 'a desirable departure' for Mill Hill, but bad drains killed project. Hse colours denoted by clothes-'patches' only. Sole extension of Junior School's boarding accommodation was at "Arrandene" (see above), 1923, [at St Bees, all *Bps*, accommodated in St Helen's].

Sources include: *GM*s; RRs 1,2,3,4; *Caught in the Web of Words*; Hse Notes in *MHM*s, 1923+; A.J.Rooker Roberts' Newsletters to Parents, 1940-3; supplemented by recollections of *OM*s, HS/Ms, HS/Ms' wives, HTs (who actually led the three School Hses at various times), and Matrons; also families of HS/Ms, who experienced those houses in an entirely different way, during term time & above all during vacations. Only three Hses have yet produced their own Histories: WK to coincide with ceasing to 'trade' as a Hse of the School, 1995; BB to celebrate its 125th anniversary in 1999/2000; and CH its centenary in 2003. The author is grateful to current and former HS/Ms, G.C.Sutcliffe, R.Axworthy, H.Barnes and A.Phillips for permission to quote from these Histories, and to other HS/Ms and their partners, for memories.

APPENDIX E

Selections from Supplement 1: "The Book of Millhillisms"

As Supplement 1 demonstrates in greater detail, the histories of the Public Schools emphasise how, like army regiments, they develop their own language. Although this may not be the stuff of major historical study for the world at large, it has sociological interest, forming part of the 'socialisation' which the Public Schools were meant to provide. "The Book of Millhillisms" forms a separate companion publication to this History; it is nevertheless of as much fascination to Mill Hill insiders as the 38-page book of Winchester College 'Notions' is to Wykhamists, in that in a certain sense it also embodies the School's History. Such a list is also essential to any reader of the *MHMs*, where contemporary phraseology did not need to be explained to its audience. As society itself evolves, so do such terms and customs. A 1930 *MHM* confidently asserted that "people still use the time-honoured phrases". Yet buildings and grounds have changed their usage over time: people forget, or misremember – an additional value derived from a Glossary. This selection covers most unusual phrases used in the History, as well as some that space precluded from inclusion in the text.

Although Belmont also has its place in this context, the richness of the School's stock is the main focus here. Her great lexicographer, Sir James Murray, and his Head Master, Dr Weymouth, would both have delighted in it as an aspect of their beloved field of 'philology'.

Some phrases were part of the MHS and BMT that went up to St Bees in 1939, but did not return with them in 1945/6. Language, and attitudes, are constantly evolving. As the survey of 800 teenagers by Dillons and Oxford Dictionaries (*Guardian*, 18 July 1997) underlined, 'Teenspeak' was evolving faster than anyone could comprehend in the late 20C, and arguably, the exclusivity of such language in the future will more likely relate horizontally across all groups and classes, the 'barrier' being age-related, rather than specific to a particular institution.

Omitted from "The Book" are: (i) Sports trophies, colours details; (ii) aspects of School Governance, e.g. The Jacks Trust; (iii) most ongoing Foundation land/ buildings; (iv) anachronistic terms of general 19C use; (v) nicknames of individuals (see Supplement 2: "A Gallimaufry of Mill Hill Characters"); (vi) words which if in their original use may have appeared to be 'vernacular', eg 'barging' (1911), are nowadays common usage, and understandable.

KEY (see also 'Abbreviations'):-

>: new expressions requiring indoctrination by later generations of Millhillians/ Millhilliennes/Belmontians (but not yet Grimsdellians). There will inevitably be omissions, as new words will emerge, while many current phrases will become incomprehensible to future members of the Mill Hill 'Trinity'.

Or.: where given, original 'Murray Dict.' version is offered.

(189.) indicates an early *MHM* where expression occurs.

*: language used in first History (1909) as a matter of course, or as a conscious/Indexed '*argot*', but today unknown, or

has changed meaning. That first History saw no need for a Glossary.

'D': a source in the *Dictionary of Oxford and Cambridge*, 1885.

prob: probable meaning, but no firm evidence.

GT: indicates first attempt at a Glossary, identified by George Timpson at the Sesquicentennial, 1957.

AE: occurrence in the Alec Eason Diaries [1901-5].

JB: occurrence in Jere Brierley [1908-13] Diary 1912/13.

BR: occurrence in Record compiled 8 Feb 1943 at St Bees by sM Tony Blair [1938-43], a unique resource for pre-WWII customs. although not infallible (eg wrong origination for "Fishing Net").

Cross-refs are to chapters of MHS History.

"Ads.."/ "Adsum": original expression used at roll-call/line-up, following general Public School practice, through to 1930s: one of many practices disrupted by the St Bees move, although still in use in SH in 1948.

anamorphose: '*to distort into a monstrous projection*': word introduced by Murray in 1876 *MHM* article, subsequently to achieve immortality both for word and medium, in pages of Murray/ *Oxford English Dictionary*: '*Shakspeare (sic) might have seen this very picture, or, if not, some other in which a skull was thus anamorphosed, in which 'looking awry', a 'shape' of grief was found* [Cp. Rich II, 2 ii 22]'. (see Ch.IV).

Badges: 1) Monitor's – evolved from badge invented by Sir J.Clure for identifying boys on his continental trips [Source: D.Ousey – 22.vi.1998]; 2) OMC Franklin's. First title-holder, A/M David Franklin (see also monitors, sM).

Beating the Bounds: secret BMT ceremony at end of last day of Summer term, led by senior boarding HS/M: group of senior Leavers traced course of Bounds, armed with sticks, special dances and song, finally breaking their sticks on BMT Cedar.

'beats'>: late 20C pastime, passing smaller boys being swiped at haphazardly by passing older boys, or on other special occasions eg birthdays: outlawed by HM, 1995.

"Bee": girl in St Bees Hse 1986-96.

Beating-machine: School Hse monitors, c1950, had a machine designed to beat: it was purloined by boys and destroyed. See 'Beating' (Supplement 1). (G.Henderson).

Bell: 1914 School Bell was located on wall by Loggia; was muffled by boys at end of Summer Term 1950, after edict by HM that all boys should obey call of the bell on the final morning: result no one attended line-up. (H.Syers).

Benedictus, Benedicat: traditional pre-meal Grace, in use post-war, see Ch.X, APP F. Once rendered by a facetious jazz-loving Monitor at St Bees as: 'Benny Goodman, Benny Carter'.

blazers: (i) School: navy blue, crest on pocket, or tweed Sports Jacket (SJ), coincided with underlying swings between greater freedom & greater discipline. Blazer introduced by 1901: **AE**; replaced by SJs 1933, re-introduced 1939, again replaced by SJs, St Bees, re-introduced 1945; again replaced by SJs, mid-1960s, again re-introduced 1996; (ii) Colours Blazer-stand: pre-WWII, provided (with 30 pegs) on path onto Topfield, where both competing School Rugby Teams hung their blazers, tassels of caps showing in breast pocket: **BR**.

'bog Jacket'>: see blazer; grey tweed jacket, standard in 1996: nick-named 'bog' because of its lavatorial smell when wet, due to rain. (In Teenspeak – see above – 'bogging', meaning 'horrible', was already passing out of favour by 1997).

bootman */ bootroom/ 'Jock's (Boot) Hole' (1918, 1920): at first, corner of former enclosed play-ground, to west of old SH, ostensibly for Jock Hindes, servant, to do boot-cleaning; used by fags as 'boot-boys' (1917), in fact haunt of 'glutinous gourmandisers' on Sunday afternoons,

(1913), and thus a minor political centre viz. 'Boot-Hole Union Rules' (1909). Later, 1920s, basement of Marnham block, about whose custodian the saying ran: "*You can't have your boots done til Thursday. Cos Why? Cos I aint got no nails*".

bumps >: another late 20C practice, banned in 1995, of throwing a boy up and and down in the air, on occasion eg of birthdays, or to signal some minor deviation from accepted behaviour, bumps or whacks being given as body moved downwards.

Buttonholes: privilege, see monitors: **BR**. Still extant 21C, usually white carnation, also offered to Governors, Visitors.

Cadre, The: Arduous Training Company of CCF: officer training section after 2 compulsory years (see Ch.IX).

call-over *: late 19C/ early 20C term for lining up to call out names at specified times: up to mid 20C, Day Boys also had to attend at 4 pm, to ensure they had not 'sloped off'.

car: rule pre-WWII that no boy allowed in a car, thus boys used to ride round standing on side running-board: **BR**. Late 20C: car use allowed as privilege within legal limits.

'Cardboard Shack': pre-fab House for MRY, pre 1962, Farm Rd.

Carp *: Carpenter's 'Shop', (i) in room, W end of SH corridor; (ii) edge of Quad; (iii) site below Science Block; (iv) shed in Farm Lane; (v) in BMT orchard yard: ash Singlehanded sticks were made/ bought, there. Also available for boys' carpentry: open Sunday afternoons for Hobbies.

'cattlemarket' >: 1980s, Hse dances with girls' schools.

century bats: cricket bat awarded to century-maker (1934); alt £3.3 credit at Blenheim Steps, also to bowler of 7 wickets in a match: **BR**.

chant: extended singing of the words 'Mill Hill', compulsory for boys watching 1st XV match on lower side of Topfield.

'chinky run'>: visit, Chinese take-away, MH Broadway – 1988.

chocolate and white: chosen as colours, New Foundation by A/M H.J.Tucker, with boys G.van Someren & C.Bodley, 1870; attempt to retain as notepaper colour for SH only, 1918. Choc. & white – medieval symbolism, brown = grief, white = holiness, thus *MHM* translates choc. & white = 'pious melancholy'. Being superseded as Foundation colour for blue, 1990s; retained for MHS sport.

Choir Garden(s) *: site of Music School, noted both for flowers, and illicit but major school fights, 1900s, (1920).

Cinder Path: early 20C name for now asphalted right of way extending from Wills Grove (The New Road), past CH back entrance, down to Hammers Lane; by 1970s, 'the snake path'>.

clapping: apparently a MHS 'lust' (1909), displayed on any suitable celebratory occasion; eg at tea, both teams leaving premises, field; 'time-honoured practice' in 1945 +, if major teams won their matches that day. Clapping into tea, from line-up to grace: team members distinguished by not clapping.

Colours: (i) School, sport only – cap, tie, scarf, square, blazer, sports kit, bootlaces: triple colours for all three major sports not uncommon, quadruple colours extended, 1939, when Athletics Team beat all-comers, and status raised as one-off to major sport: **BR**; worn for one year only – if rewarded, could be worn permanently; monitors could wear at any time except Chpl; (ii) Hse – tie, scarf, square, vest **BR**, umbrella: awarded for inter-Hse competitiveness, Hse ties wearable on any half-holiday, but if 1st Match at home, only if won for that sport. Always sporting until 1950, when awarded for Hse Choir by RH; competition extended to Drama, 1990s, and Hymn-singing, work (1997); (iii) Hse: also awarded exceptionally, as Hse Tie, Scarf or 'Square' to HS/Ms, or to a Matron (RH, 1940), even (WK) to one HM, Dr Whale, 1951 (see Ch.VIII). See 'learning the colours'; (iv) failure to afford special Shooting VIII tie, 1980s, but Middlesex Rifle Assctn ties (MHS affiliated) awarded by I.C.Brownlie, in lieu.

Common-Room rugby: eg at BB – 'played in CR in gymshoes or socks, consisting of all-in fights, no tackling, and touch end wall for try': **BR**.

Copy: standard punishment up to mid-20C, copying out a printed copperplate line on a Copy 'Block'; after circumvention at St Bees, line changed regularly from standard line – "What makes life dreary is the want of occupation". 'Criminals' signed their name, collected Copy next morning, ... completed by prep that evening.. if neglected, doubled'. **BR**. Prefect's Copy: one side, 19 lines; Monitor's Copy – double. 10 Copies in a half-term led to an automatic beating (6), and a 'Perm': **BR**.

Coronation Oak: planted after ret by Maurice Jacks, Mar 1938, plus tablet (now lost), for Coronation of K George VI, 1937: 'top of the bank at northern end of the running track, adjacent to SW corner of Music S' (1938).

Crown Cottages: 5 cottages (17 properties by 1944) for staff, early 19C brick, on the Ridgeway, painstakingly acquired by MHS over the years, sold in 1990: No 1, "Fuchsia"; No 2 "Bakers"; No 3 "Inkwell" (after inkwells which formed path, laid by earlier A/M); No 4 "Barn"; No 5 "Millers".

'Crump stuff': derisory name for scripture primer used by chaplain, Rev. Crump, mid 19C, to teach MHS boys.

Crumpites *: girls at a School on the Ridgeway 'opposite the School' (run by Rev. Crump's sister), who used to attend MHS Chpl and lectures, to delight of the boys.

Dame Janet's Gate GT: wrought-iron gate in old brick wall on the Ridgeway, former (dangerous) drive up to HM's Hse, opened by Dame Janet Stancomb-Wills, niece of Ld Winterstoke; led to re-named 'Dame Janet's Garden'; 1928. **GT**.

"Dirge, The">: name for 20C 2-tone rugger chant: "Mill-Hill!".

Doctor's Pond *: 'the Hollow', pond beyond Peter Collinson's old garden, 'just above' site of 'beautiful clump of Scotch firs' near 'far goal-posts' on 'Top Field', and thus 'outside the school property', where boys could take a muddy dip, almost deep enough for an A/M, H.J.Tucker (1869-73, 1893-1907), to dive in, and earlier for Dr Weymouth to learn skating, only to fall and break his leg in the early 1870's, (**prob**. hence name); (1920). Site of a well; filled in during 19C.

Dramatic, The: early 20C name for MHS Dramatic Society, founded 1876 as a *Corps Dramatique*.

'Drive'>: 1950s/1960s term unknown in pre WWII or in immediate post-WWII period; 'out-of-character behaviour'... 'going on a drive'... 'pulling out all the stops by way of good deeds and good behaviour and even good academic work to achieve high office', or first rung on ladder – Hse Pre; (C.Fox, 1998).

"dungeons/ infernal regions/ purgatory/ catacombs" *: space under rotting floorboards, old SH Form V classroom, where boys (i) could hide from A/M during classes, with hilarious results; (ii) be sadistically banished by older bullies; (E.R.Tanner 1875); (iii) still in evidence, 1970s (Paul Bickerdike, 2001).

Exeat: (aka Exeant) permission to go out singly, 1920+; Saturday exeat: out with parents; Sunday exeat: home from after Chapel for lunch, back for School tea. School caps worn out of bounds, pre WWII.

Fagging: eulogised, **BR**, as *the backbone of the Public Schools, and plays the most important part in the social education of boarding schools*: chores performed by new non-Scholars, in return for end-of-term payment (2/6d+) from 'fagmaster', a monitor or prefect in the Hse; also in

some Hses, less common, and less sanctioned, for any boy in an older year. Could include: cleaning shoes/ boots, CCF boots and blancoing (green) CCF belts and gaiters; carrying piles of schoolbooks to, and from, Hse/ S (no mean task in pre-1935 BB); making tea at week-ends, massaging legs of 1st XV team-member, errands to Blenheim Steps, waking fagmaster in morning: **BR**. 'Bell fag': bell-ringing duty, to wake Hse, pre-breakfast: 1950s. Personal fagging ended by Roy Moore (see Ch.IX), replaced by general Hse Duties, later 20C.

'First night singing' (1904): MHS & BMT, practice of making new boys sing a song on their first night, while objects thrown at them, theoretically stopped by 1904, but still in being under Maurice Jacks, 1930s, and possibly also WWII+ in some Hses.

"Fishing Net": former Athletics field, and still main Hockey pitch, so-named not because of its shape, nor because it was situated below the old 'Carp' shop, but because the 1924 cricket captain, famous W.H.Sobey, put up a net *for some sort of cricket practice, The Fishing Net it was dubbed*" (*MHM* article by A/M T.A.Williams, June 1930). > 'Fishnet'/ 'Astro'.

Football, footer (1918) *: terms for 'rugger', up to early 20C; [usage of '-er' at end of an abbreviated first syllable originated at Harrow, 1870s, spread up to Oxford by 1880s, and thence throughout the Public School world; eg 'nailer'= footballer good at tackling (1918)].

Foundation Day, New: annual prize-giving to mark New Foundation of 1869, replaced 'Public Day', 'New' later omitted.

"Full fig": sM's complete morning dress – top hat, tail-coat, wing collar, white gloves: (H.E.Beven: 1920s).

Galleries, Chapel: (i) 'Old Boys': 1898/ (1918) opposite Organ, later, Hse Prefects (1945); (ii) 'Visitors', over entrance = 'New Boys Gallery', for IV Forms & Removes: **BR**.

GC: (i) 'Good Conduct' in first MH Register, where 'Ga.' is the abbreviation for (ii) the Games Committee. First known appearance in the *MHM* of 1880s. when the 'GC' was elected by votes, first from all boys, then from names nominated by three votes. Initially denoted simply a debt of the Committee, later extended to property of the committee, on behalf of the school, in 1880s : 'G.C. horses', 'GC oil' (1904), 'GC board' (1910), and so to embrace any property, actions: G.C.Kippers, Food, Chairs, cap, nag, (1923). Final stage – synonymous with the School itself: "how long it took the G.C. to puzzle the length of the Junior Road Race"; "How typical of the G.C.!", (1923); 'the G.C. did us proud" (1925). In the words of David Tinker (1983), '*the social life of the School*', regardless as to whether the Committee was involved. Still used in the 1970s(+), as in: 'The G.C. life', 'at G.C.'; evolved into single word, pronounced 'Geece', 1980s; by 1990s out of use at the School, but used by OMs, 1998. Suffered temporary schizophrenia during St Bees time, used both for the buildings left back at Mill Hill, and also for the Body of the School in exile.

'Gilly/gillie-Roar' gillyroar' *: one of MHS's 'lost' sounds; hard 'G', [first appears in **JB**, 1912]. See *MHM* 1923/4: *Art Room... where... la belle gillie-roar flourishes.* Imitated by Donald Hall as "Woop woop woop waaaay!", by Donald Batty as a rising bird-like crescendo of "warrk, Warrk, WARRK, WOOOW!', and by Lewis Wild as 'Wuh- Wuh- Wuh- Wuh- WHOOOAAA OOOAOH!': i.e. a loud four/five-part call made by boys: (i) "as a group effort shouted derisively for purpose of intimidation [Lewis Wild], eg to bait 'baitable' Masters when they made a mistake; few of the better disciplinarians (Coates, Elliott) were ever 'baitable'; (ii) in Assembly if unpopular announcements were made; [Will Weir: 1924-'8]; (iii) to celebrate scoring of a try/ goal; or, pre WWII, presence of those who had won colours; or as a

welcome, eg arrival of Mrs Roberts at St Bees station, 30 May 1940; (iv) on the be-suited, be-capped, top-hatted Sunday walks; (v) as a sing-song ending to CU OM Dinner (1933), with Auld Lang Syne and "Three Loud Cheers for Mill Hill" (School Song). Attempt was made to stop custom in Maurice Jacks' time, but it continued beyond the exodus to St Bees; not mentioned in **BR**, 1943; unknown after 1945. Associated with an A/M, **prob**. F.M.Gilbert 1904-10, or poss. C.M.Gilray 1910-2 [R.Stanger 1919-23, *MHM* 1986].

'Great Northern': (i) the now Mill Hill East, erstwhile steam, railway station; (ii) name extended to describe the steepest part of Bittacy Hill from at least 1877, up which boys returning from holiday might have to walk on foot, getting out of the coaches, as horses could not manage incline.

'Grimsdellian' >: term tentatively coined 8.v.1998, for pupils of Mill Hill Pre-Prep at "Grimsdell", now theoretically and potentially all embraced as 'Old Millhillians', late 1990s.

'guff': verbal cheek to any senior, common from at least early 1900s, (1904): (*has ousted cheek of late years*); lasted beyond 1953, unknown in 1996. Became incorporated into some *OM* family sayings: ('guffy little skwits' – a humorous commonplace of the Batty family shorthand for years). [**Or**.: Murray Dict 1889: US slang – 'empty talk, nonsense, blather – guff and nonsense']. (Cp. 'nip' [Marlborough]; 'jank' [Clifton].

'Heads of the School': mid-19C custom briefly revived by Maurice Jacks, to give status, comparable to that of the sports heroes, to the two senior academics on Classical/Modern, and Maths/Science sides.

Headmaster: title arbitrarily introduced in 1990s; replacing 'Head Master' ('Head Master's Court: 20C tennis court, in grounds of 'St B's' Hse). (Also used earlier).

'Head Master's House': **1.** 1807-1825: Ridgeway Hse, The Ridgeway. **2.** 1825-1896: SE end of SH, [SH HS/M's Hse >2001]. **3.** 1896-1939: [now "St Bees House"]. **4.** 1939-1944: *Seacote Htl*, St Bees, Cumbria. **5.** 1944-5: *Abbot's Court Htl*, St Bees. **6.** 1945+: "The Grove", at first suggestion of W.C.Ramsay, whilst Dr Whale favoured returning it to usage as unmarried Masters' flats, soon converted to idea; 1947 – thought should be knocked down – 'dry rot everywhere'. **8.** 1948: Park Lodge, Wills Grove, 5 mo.

"hipe": example of new vocabulary introduced with OTC (1911), familiar to all 20C ex-service personnel: perceived sound from orders as in "Stand at hipe!" (=ease); "Order hipe"! (= arms).

'hitting-off': optional permuting Copies for beatings, 1920s to 1960s, form of punishment preferred by some hardened offenders.

Hockey: originally, mid to late 19C, denoted 'playground (Singlehanded). Real Hockey introduced as major sport 1901, following popularisation by Blackheath and Teddington Clubs etc c.1860+; had to be denoted as 'Double-handed' Hockey; sticks had circular ridges c.2" above ground level, to stop opponent's stick riding up into face (J.Cranwell).

Honours Boards: lists of university scholarship winners, painted white on double row of large green boards, SE wall, The Large, into disuse – WWI, still in situ – WWII, while School at St Bees. Some Hses maintained own Boards, now lost, eg WK; SH boards still in upper corridor, 1990s. Board of former Science award-winners kept in Science Block, 1997+.

'horse boxes': name for Visitors' seats, transversely either side of entrance to Chapel: **BR**.

House Copy: minor punishment within Hse, awardable by 'School staff' down to level of 'Hse Pre.s', for untidiness, ragging, guff, talking in Prep, in fact anything displeasing to 'staff'.

Jubilee Alley: double line of hornbeams planted N edge of new Fishing Net, below Music School, donated by OMs and Teaching Staff, in honour of Silver Jubilee of K George V (see Ch.VI).

King's Head, The: former ancient pub, out of bounds, opposite end of Wills Grove, on the Ridgeway, bought and owned by School, used at one stage in early 19C for meetings of Visiting Committee, once destined as site for a petrol station, worsened during 'Corps' grenade attacks: demolished as unsafe in late 1940s, site of present private house, same name.

Kissing Gate: former entrance to path by Collinson Field from RH, abolished Dec 1961, to minimise delays for RH boys.

learning the colours/ colours tests: new boys had to learn all school colours, names and initials of monitors, first teams, numbers of Portico pillars, etc, and be questioned on them, sometimes standing on tables, practice still entrenched 1950+.

line-up: queue pre-meals/ Chapel/ Assembly, whole School, first A-Z, then Form order, calling "adsum" as passing through 'Barrier'; at BMT, line-up in playground. >'Registration'.

Lyke Wake Walk >: walk of 40 miles from Dent, following old route for disposal of dead; those completing wore special tie.

Make-Ups: lists of teams ranked by deemed merit, for award of different levels of colours, pinned on 'screens' below Loggia. Experiment by John Visser, 1944, to change system to Groups within teams – not proceeded with.

"mare" >: nightmare, N.London teenage expression of 1990s, much used at MH, = awful.

Masters' Lawn: gardens overlooking Top Terrace, originally out of bounds to all except A/Ms, Mtrs.

Meatsafe>: colloquial for Todd Memorial Lectern in Chapel.

Memorial Field: rugby pitch (former meadow below Collinson Field) proposed by N.S.Farrow, and created, 1950, from WWII Restoration & Memorial Fund, originally (1947) envisaged in fields below "Rosebank", to NE of the Ridgeway; Also Memorial Tennis Courts, above Gears.

Middlesex Boys: name for the boys from County Grammar Schools who entered MHS under Bursary Scheme 1945 onwards.

Monitorial: formal beating by each of the monitors.

Monitors' Garden: *the Farm Road ... skirts that desolate No Man's Land...* (1933); stretch of land, once famed for flowers, at foot of steps in the line of former public Footpath across Top Field, weeded over but well-known in 1920s, existing nominally 1945+, but then unknown to many OMs, and wrongly remembered in **BR**: *Monitors always had [Sunday] buttonholes which they picked from "The Monitors' Garden" near the Chapel.*

morning dress: privileged dress for mntrs for Sunday Chapel, or other special occasions (eg visit of HM Queen Elizabeth 1957): black tailcoat, waistcoat, striped trousers, and sedate tie, usually grey; late 1920s/ early 1930s, mntrs also wore white spats over their black shoes, a topical fashion, and carried umbrella or School staff's silver-topped cane (see Ch.VII). Up to 1920s, kit bought and kept for life; in the 1945-50 era, on loan. 'Taking the tails' (1923), accompanied by 'toppers' up to 1930s. Abolished as anachronistic by Michael Hart, late 1960s.

Museum*: Natural History Museum formed under encouragement from Dr Murray in 1880s, and centre for Natural History Soc, in own building next to site of present Marnham Block; re-created when site was so re-designated 1905 in rooms opposite to Chapel, unknown 1945+, due to space pressures; see Ch.VII.

"Name, Boy?": traditional accosting of any new boy by any senior boy, usage through to 1950s.

Octagon(s): (i) SH central concourse: in late 19C, the expression also in the plural, as the design comprises two such shapes; (ii) designation of one of 3 SH teams, (1913), pre break-down into teams from the 3 already-named SH Hses.

'Old Boy': thought by author of *Networks* not to be used until *Haileyburian Magazine* 1868, but in fact used by MHS in 1840s.

OM: (not to be confused with acronym for the Order of Merit; Old Mancunian; the 1920s *Officine Meccanice* car marque); or an eponymous Swedish conglomerate.

Omnichit>: 1996+, form for instant noting by any member of academic Staff of bad, or good, points in a pupil's behaviour.

"out of bounds": variable according to regime, much restricted by Maurice Jacks, after relative freedom under John McClure; 1945+, delineated by Village War Memorial, north path of the Ridgeway, Blenheim Steps, east path of Wills Grove, RH path, boundaries of Park, and new BB, barrier at foot of Wills Grove, hedge on Hammers Lane, Cinder path, lower edge of Farm Field, Fishing Net, edge of Sanatorium Field.

'Perf': standard perforated Notebook used by late 1920s and into post-WW2 era (1934).

'pill, give the, a root': *MHM* 1904: kick a football.

"PJS", The>: the so-called but secret Practical Joke Society, probably founded in 1970s, following remark by new, unpopular HM: *I like a joke*; boys took him at his word, and keys were obtained to all rooms; foreclosed by a HS/M in 1990s, who found the duplicate keys of the PJS, and moved out its ring-leaders.

playground *: original name for Quad, Square; covered-in source beyond west end of original Tite building of 1825+, where former outside lavatories stood, north of Loggia; *They may make as much noise as they like here!*: Weymouth to Tucker, 1869. (1920). Playground cricket *: daringly dangerous cricket played in old playground, 19C, with 'big oak bludgeon', wicket marked 'on the wall between the windows that looked across to 'Mother's'; bowler lobbed 'rubber ball', then tried to hide behind stone pillars of building, score according to number of walls hit, purpose also to hit bowler, (1920). Later as Quad Cricket up to at least 1950s.

Points: post 1945-system for amassing points for Hse, in Hse Points Comp., through athletic activity: if no games prowess, achieved by running round Park, one point per round.

Potato garden: formerly on site of Buckland Pool.

'Pound': (i) impounding of belongings if left lying around, regained by beating; (ii) general Hse Fund from minor charges eg for going to W.C. during prep, but see Appendix D. Head of JCR in CH, 1920s, was beaten for not raking in enough!

privileges: based mainly on year system:- (i) mS could also wear a white pullover: **BR**; (ii) monitors: elect [sic] new monitors/ prefects, coloured shirts/ socks, wear anything in outside breast pocket, monitors' tie/ square, cap (brown velvet, silver braiding, brown tassel, monogram), carry umbrella, have tea in Tuck shop "inside café": **BR**. (iii) school prefects: coloured pullovers, Sunday white tie, Staff stick (black cane, silver knob), late for meals: **BR**. Also (iv) only 1st XV colours could cross Top Field – school prefects allowed, if accompanied by a monitor; (v) only 1st XI players could walk in front of Park Pavilion in summer terms, unless playing in matches; (vi) only Colts upwards could wear 'Wings'; (vii) 2nd Year VI and those taking HC: excused Sunday walk: wear collar/ tie on Sunday p.m.; read at Breakfast/ Tea: **BR**.

PSRE/ PSHE>: Personal, Social and Religious Education, later Personal, Social and Health Education (subject taught).

'Puke, The' >: 1980s, derisory term for the VI Form Centre.

"Quis?": habit of offering objects not wanted by owner, 1945+; reply *Ego* shouted as loudly as possible, often cause of punishments (e.g. to both father (1912) & son Bewsher (1950s).

'R.A.S.B.O.': Royal Society for the Abolition of Burocratic Organisations: mock-anarchic soc., mid 1950s, (see Ch.IX).

Rose Piazza: area round ATD Block >; usage 1980s.

rugger: term coming into use, via Oxford, 1919, standard in AJRR's Belmont Reports 1919+, but MHS still using 'football'/ 'footer', at same time. OMs by then wrote of 'Rugby Football'.

"Sack!" *: whispered call for boys collectively to finish off any stale bread in the bowls, so that fresh bread could then be brought in by the maids, mid-19C.

SATB: abbreviation all-but incomprehensible to any Millhillian pre 1980s – Sopranos, Altos, Trebles, Basses – divisions of choir between girls' and boys' voices, in co-educational era.

School cap: brown velvet, with white band, worn by all Years when outside Bounds, on legitimate business, up to WWII; post WWII, worn by new boys and day boys outside MHS, up to mid 20C.

School songs *: (i) collective singing at end of term up to and through Dr McClure's time: (ii) MHS never formed attachment to her own 'School Song', although several were written in early 1900s, including unpopular "Fill the Cup, Fill" (1902), and L.A.Cane's "Hurrah for the Worth of Mill Hill", (words by Rev. H.C.Carter, OM, father-in-law of Dr J.S.Whale), sung at end of term concerts for short period from 1903.

"Scotts": privately owned provision shop, now "The Grove" before the 'GC' built a Tuck Shop (1890s), where tea would be taken, and food bought: run by Mrs Scott and two daughters.

Scrip/ Script: **GT**: names for corrugated-iron Murray Scriptorium, after transporting it from "Sunnyside", then post 1902 fire, properly built, NW end; used first for daily papers post WWI; converted to computer room, 1980s. Several versions, see Ch.IV.

SDR: Staff Dining Room, SH corridor, SW side, later 20C.

SFC>: Sixth Form Centre.

Shout, The: Monday break-time, weekly CR gathering for notices by HM, 1992+.

Singlehanded: GT, AE: [SHD]: MH's unique game, played as a popular, serious all-year sport, with large solid rubber ball, c. 3", later 2" diameter, officially 9-a-side but unlimited in 'break', by dorms and classes); played as Hse knock-out tournament, and against OMs: 1st, 2nd & 3rd IX colours awarded. Rules: **BR**: (i) "no bullying-off – ball was hit in along centre from touch"; (ii) "if ball went past goal-line, ball thrown up from where it went out, and one member of each side tried to get it as it came down"; (iii) " 'Sticks' was permissible"; (iv) "if caught cleanly, could be thrown at goal"; (v) if goalkeeper held on caught ball too long, could be chargeable by opponents. Created own culture, *vide* 1920s poem: 'The 1st Dragoons at Poona would infinitely sooner, Play single-handed Polo – a sort of solo polo, Than Single-handed chukka with a Team that wasn't pukka': (D.Clifford). At St Bees, SHD played on sands 1939, 1944 (see Ch.VII) (cf. Rossall Hockey, double-handed, also on sands, own rules, wef 1870s). SHD introduced by Maj.A.Addison Smith, Aldershot, WWII; brought back to MHS, 1945, when smaller harder ball used. Thought dangerous, allowed to go out of fashion by P.Hodgson, Hockey Coach, also because Hockey technique, and Rules, were being undermined by SHD; *MHM* ref, SHD House

Match, 1960; by 1962/3 reference to 'Quad Hockey'. Eventual loss of SHD unlamented. See Ch.IX: 'Hockey'.

"Skippers": former Quaker Meeting House> 19C shop owned by Mr Skipper, a carrier> Rosebank Farmhouse and owned by School, hence legal entity – Rosebank Ltd – OMC owned; **AE**.

'snitching': part of 'year system': boy of lower 'year' listening to conversation of boy of higher year, as in: "Snitching, Boy? Snitch off!" [Or: 'snitch = nose, an informer'].

Staff: odd 'GC' term for all levels of boys' authorities (eg School Staff, Hse Staff), confusingly co-existent with (merely!) 'academic' Staff, now needing to be so designated, as 'A/Ms' anachronistic: (1909); still in use 2001+.

straws: straw 'boaters' in use 30 years prior to 1909, hung on hooks on rows of wooden rails in SH corridor, purpose then already forgotten by boys (1920); visible in Hse photos, 1970s; still used by occasional OMs.

swagger/swag: thin army cane, monitorial beatings, WWII+.

'thousand-pounders, The': former SH outside lavatories, by Loggia, converted to create new Bursar's offices, late 20C.

Top Field/ top-field/ topfield: **GT**: (i) former MHS cricket field, now School's main rugby field (once crossed by public footpath – story of a mother pushing her loaded pram across, during a match); (ii) also name of BMT's main rugby field.

Town Club: OMs Club, Whitehall Court, Horse Guards Parade, SW1; founded 1932/3, closed 1969 due to lack of demand, and costs. Site for many valuable events, incl OMs' Literary Society 1950s, Governors' Meetings during WWII, etc. Famed servants: "Young", WW1 under-age volunteer, and "Polish Joe".

Tunnel: underground passage linking BMT building to drive exit.

'vill': abbreviation for Mill Hill Village, early 20C.

'Walker': term used until the early 1990s for local pupils who were attached to a Boarding Hse eg BB, but arrived at breakfast and went home at night, usually after first Prep.

White Tie Club: way of describing membership of school prefects body, from the white tie worn on Sundays only, up to 1970s; thereafter (prob) worn by monitors only until superseded by monitors' maroon/martlets tie, mid-1980s; once worn by whole school, on Sundays, as at Rugby, until abandoned, c. WWI.

'Windsor Castle half': theoretically extant 19C tradition: award of half-holiday if Windsor Castle could be espied from Top Terrace, last I claim Windsor Castle, 3 June 1976 (GF): A/M Tony Vine claimed c1967/8: Michael Hart disallowed as too time-wasting; (C.Fox):- last attempt, James Fox, mS c.1989. (Alastair Graham: 27.x.98:– very early in the day and with haze up by Chapel time quite incapable of corroboration... public exams would have prevented an instant holiday, but... I would only have granted a deferred planned one anyway).

Wings: much envied rugger and hockey shorts with pockets: 20C.

Year system: finely graduated scale of rights and duties, found in all closed societies, from monasteries/ convents to the Services, to put newcomers in their place, and not threaten elders: 1st year – blazer done up by middle button only; 2nd year – hands in pockets, much prized in winter; 3rd year – all blazer buttons undone or all done up; 4th year – could walk round arm-in-arm (**BR**), also collars turned up, see countless Team/ Hse Photos, sign of disdain for all, coincident with entry into Lower VI Forms. At one time rumoured privilege for senior monitors to: (a) marry; (b) keep an elephant. At its height pre/ post St Bees and into 1950s; eventually ended by Michael Hart. See Networks: All [public]

schools... had an unbelievably obscure system regulating... buttoning of jackets... putting of hands in pockets... carrying of umbrellas.

Special thanks to Gowen Bewsher, Donald Hall, Tony Blair, Dick Walker, Stanley Farrow, Paul Hodgson, Alastair Graham, William Winfield, and to T.Heald/ Hodder & Stoughton, for permission to quote from Networks, Who We Know and How to Use Them (1983)].

Full list in Information Supplement 1.

APPENDIX F

Classical Heritage: Mill Hill's Inscriptions & Quotations

This Appendix has a single function, a task unnecessary for earlier classically-grounded generations of Mill Hill – translations for the Latin phrases that are: (i) part of the School's tradition; and (ii) quotations used in the text. Translations based – sometimes loosely – on those provided, courtesy of MHS HD Classics (1987-prsnt), Stephen Plummer BA.

(i) Classical phrases in the MHS tradition

Excelsior. [first School motto]: "Higher" (see Ch.IV).

Et virtutem et musas: (ambiguous) "Both Excellence and Culture"; "Both character and learning"; "character and culture" (MLJ); "Courage and learning" (Lord Wetherill, 1996); humorously – "Manners and music taught here"; adopted 1895 as motto for Rev. Samuel Lavington's Anglo-Chinese College, Tientsin; (see Ch.VI, also G.F.Timpson, op cit).

Benedictus, benedicat; ... Benedicto benedicatur. Grace said by monitors before and after all meals, discontinued by 1970s, when Grace no longer said, due to self-service queuing: "May the Blessed [One] bless", "May the Blessed [One] be blessed".

(ii) Quotations used in text

Ch.IV: *Hoc unum facio*: [Dr Murray's watchword] "I [have to] do this one thing."

Ch.VI: *Grates persevere dignas non opis est nostrae*: dedication by A.J.Williams, 2M, to M.L.Jacks, (MHM 1938): "It is not within our power to repay you worthy thanks." [Virgil, Aeneid 1.600]

Ch.VII: *Semper memores opis datae*: SBOMA's dedication on window of St Bees Chapel, 1997, commemorating hospitality of St Bees Community to Mill Hill during WWII: "Always mindful of the help given".

"Oderint dum metuant": saying of 2M, J.P.Morrison, written over Classics Room door at St Bees: "Let them hate [me] provided they fear [me]."

Ch.XII: *Rus in urbe*: "[Of the] countryside [yet] in the city".

(iii) Buildings/ chapel & furniture:

Chapel – McClure (external plaque):

In piam memoriam/ Joh. David McClure/ M.A. LL.D. D.Mus./ per XXXI Ann. Rectoris/ huius scholae dilectissimi/ cui voluntate/ studio viribus/ impensis inserviit dum cel/ tenui amplissimam redderet/ idem artis musicae peritus/ astronom disertе professus/ necnon leporibus sermonis/ atque orationis insignis/ humanitatis diligentiaeque/ omnibus exemplo factus/ praeterea in educatione/ populari opt. de civ. meritus/ obiit die XVIII Feb. MCMXXIII/ annos LXII natus.

"To the devout memory of John David McClure MA, LLD, MusD, beloved Head Master of this school for 31 years, which he served with willingness, enthusiasm and great energy until he raised the school from a humble status to a very distinguished position. He was also skilled in the art of music, spoke eloquently about astronomy, as well as being distinguished with wit in conversation and speech; he became an example of humanity and industry to everyone and in addition was most deserving of his fellow citizens [with regard to] popular education. He died on 18th February 1922, aged 62."

Chapel – Jefferiss Plate:

In memoriam Johannis Fredrici Jefferiss qui hujus scholae alumnus amans amatus praematura morte abreptus est. Natus III Apr. MCMXXVII obiit V Mart. MCMXLV.

"To the memory of John Frederick Jefferiss, a loving and beloved old boy of this school, who was snatched away by an early death: born 3rd April 1927, died 5th March 1945."

McClure Music School:

In honorem I.[J] D.MacClure [sic] MA Mus Doc LL.D per XXI iam annos summo in schola Millhilliana imperio perfuncti hanc. aedem Musis dedicatam aedificandam curaverunt euisdem scholae alumni A.D. MCXII.

"In honour of J.D.McClure MA, MusD, LLD, who has now held the position of Head Master of Mill Hill School for 21 years, the old boys of the same school saw to the construction of this building dedicated to Music in 1912."

Gate of Honour:

PIIS PATRIAE SERVATORIBUS SERVATI MEMORES D.D.D.

"Those who have been saved remember and give, devote and dedicate [this memorial] to those loyal saviours of their country."

SDR, School House:

Framed Punch cartoon of 1906, prefacing first MHS History:-
At genus immortale manet multosque per annos stat fortuna domus.

"But the immortal race survives and may the good fortune of the [Foundation] be better preserved for many years."

Portico: commemorative message, buried 1825

Aspiante Deo/ Precibusque nomine Divini sospitatoris habitis/ Gymnasii/ in juventutis liberalem institutionem eorum qui/ Ab Ecclesia Anglicana legi coelesti et propria conscientia/ Notu se libere Dissentire adstrictos existimant/ Fundamenta jecit/ SAMUEL FAVELL AERARII CUSTOS Adsistentibus/ ROGERIO DAWSON ADJUTORE FISCALI/ Atque viris rerum Administrationi praepositis/ Pastoribus ecclesiarum Josepho Berry, Georgio Clayton,/ Josepho Hughes Artium Magistro, Johanni Pye Smith Sacrae/ Theologii Doctore et professore, Johanni Townsend,/ Alexandro Waugh,/ Sacrae Theologiae Doctore et Johanni Yockney: Necnon civibus admodum colendis/ Georgio Bacchus, Roberto Bousfield, Josepho Bunnell,/ Thoma Carter, Jacobo collins,/ Olintho Gregory,/ Utriusque juris Doctore,/ Josepho Guteridge, Gulielmo Alers Hankey,/ Samuelo Luck kent, Rogiero Lee, Ebenezere Maitland,/ Abrahamo Mann, Nathianele Roberts, Thoma Piper./ Nathianele Muggeridge, Gulielmo Sabine, Thoma Smith,/ Gulielmo Lepard Smith, Georgio Stevenson, Henrico Waymouth,/ Et architecto Gulielmo Tite;/ Die Ante Kalendas Julii sexto decimo/ Annoque sexto Regni Georgii Quarti/ Ac reparati orbis MDCCCXXV.

"On the 16th June, in the sixth year of the reign of George IV and the restoration of order, 1825, with God's help and with prayers offered in the name of the Divine Redeemer, the foundations of this Grammar School for the liberal education of the sons of those who believe that, by heaven's law and their own conscience to acknowledge, they are bound of their own accord to dissent from the Church of England, were laid by Samuel Favell, Esqre., Treasurer, attended by Roger Dawson, Esqre., Sub-Treasurer, and the Committee and the fathers of the churches – Joseph Berry, George Clayton, Joseph Hughes MA, John Pye Smith, Professor and Doctor of Holy Divinity, John Townsend, Alexander Waugh, Doctor of Divinity, and John Yockney: the following citizens were committed to give great assistance as well: George Bacchus, Robert Bousfield, Joseph Bunnell, Thomas Carter, Jacob Collins, Olinth Gregory, a Doctor of both Laws, Joseph Gutteridge, William Alers Hankey, Samuel Luck Kent, Roger Lee, Ebenezer Maitland, Abraham Mann, Nathaniel Roberts, Thomas Piper, Thomas Muggeridge, William Sabine, Thomas Smith, William Lepard Smith, George Stevenson, Henry Waymouth and the Architect William Tite ..."

Science School, Entrance Hall:

Hoc aedificium naturae rerum investigandae atque explicandae causa exstruendum curaverunt huius scholae alumni comitum et amicorum haud immemores qui pro suis pro patria pro virtute dimicantes mortem obierunt MCMXIV – MCMXIX.

"The old boys of this school saw to the construction of this building for the investigation and explanation of Science, mindful of their contemporaries and friends who died fighting for their own people, for their country and for righteousness, 1914-1919."

OMC Presidential Regalia

Medallion: *Pro summa fide amor.*

"The greatest affection in return for the greatest loyalty".

Gavel: *Hunc si quis audet capere malleum mano sit ventris illi robur aere durius: quid? intus aere durius frustrum latet bis coctum et aevo iam diuturno rigens.*

"If anyone dares to take this gavel in his hand let him have a stomach stronger than cast iron. Why? Inside lies hidden a piece of biscuit [which is itself] harder than iron."

APPENDIX G

Money Values: 1807-2004

This statistical series is only a guide to the changes in the value of money over Mill Hill's three centuries; it gives the amount of money required at March 2004 to purchase goods bought by £1 at the dates shown. Thus £38.51 would have been required in March 2004 to have the same purchasing power as £1 in 1807.

The figures are derived from the Retail Prices Index, based on January 1987 = 100. Data in the period to 1914 has been taken from source 'Phelps Brown, E.H. and Hopkins S.V. (1981), Seven Centuries of the Prices of Consumables, compared with Builders' Wage-rates', Economica'.

A snapshot for 1870, according to Claire Tomalin (*The Invisible Woman*, Viking, Penguin Group, 1990, p.280) to be compared with the items in Dr Weymouth's cash book (see Ch.IV), provides a more vivid insight: average weekly wage less than £1; London cab ride one shilling a mile; a comfortable London house rentable for £50 p.a.; and the fact that a young lawyer, typical of Mill Hill's evolving middle-class constituency, could get married on a £250 income: this, when extrapolated to mid-career, would compare with an MHS *Bps* fee (age 14) of £81.

As at March 2004:-

£1 in 1807 = £ 38.51	£1 in 1917 = £ 29.14
£1 in 1817 = £ 36.01	£1 in 1927 = £ 30.52
£1 in 1827 = £ 44.43	£1 in 1937 = £ 33.14
£1 in 1837 = £ 47.01	£1 in 1947 = £ 24.96
£1 in 1847 = £ 43.72	£1 in 1957 = £ 15.51
£1 in 1857 = £ 42.70	£1 in 1967 = £ 11.70
£1 in 1867 = £ 40.83	£1 in 1977 = £ 4.00
£1 in 1877 = £ 41.32	£1 in 1987 = £ 1.73
£1 in 1887 = £ 57.55	£1 in 1997 = £ 1.17
£1 in 1897 = £ 57.07	£1 in 2003 = £ 1.05
£1 in 1907 = £ 53.31	

APPENDIX H

Belmont's History: an overview

Space precludes a detailed review of Belmont, although in relation to its market, the Preparatory School has over the years played as formative a role as the Main School; it provided from its ranks many future leaders of comparable schools, most recently Belmont itself: from Gordon Smith's time no less than seven staff went on to lead other IAPS establishments. This Appendix summarises the relationship between Belmont and the School. *OM* Brian Boys had first suggested in 1947 that the School should buy Belmont, but "drastic economy" precluded it; one of the elements that started to achieve a true balance during this time was the

well-debated relationship between the two. The story of how Mill Hill has served pupils below the age of 13 is also, for much of the past century, the history of Belmont (or as it might have been, 'Bittacy House', if Brett James' idea of 1905 had been pursued). In retrospect, 12 organisational/management stages can be discerned:

1. 1807-1912 Boys below 13 admitted from the start, e.g: W.Lepard Smith b.1795, [1807+, age 12; Edward Williams, b.1800, [1808+, age 8; W.H.Ibotson b.1805, [1810+, age 5; P.H.Smith (son of Rev. John Pye Smith) b.1804 [1811+], age 7 – Later, Junior Classes (Forms 1, 2 and 3) within MHS. **2.** 1912-1919 Belmont as the separate Junior Hse to MHS. **3.** 1919-1963 Junior S, broadly 'independent' of MHS; this embraced the period 1945-65 when Belmont had to be excluded from the Middlesex Scheme due to its 'ownership for profit' status. **4.** 1963-1966 MHS ownership: Belmont Master now salaried. **5.** 1966-1985 Roberts family dynasty ends, ('old contract'); included participation in the APS. **6.** 1985+ 'New contract' of management, MHS and Belmont. **7.** 1987-1995 Day pupils (boys) only. **8.** 1995+ Co-educational; **9.**1996+, 100% co-educational. **10.** 1.i.1998+ Formal incorporation within the Mill Hill School Foundation. 1997+: temporarily resumed part-Boarding, in St Bees Hse, MHS. **11.** 2002+ All Day pupil population. **12.** Sept 2004+ First 'Head' (succeeding last 'Master') reports to Mill Hill School Foundation Headmaster.

That debate, re-surfacing in the 1980s, had started half-way through 'Stage **3**', with Belmont's return from Cumbria, in 1946. There was much short-sighted discussion then, as later, during 'Stage 5', as to whether Mill Hill 'needed' a Junior S at all, with divergence on rights of either to influence the other: whether from Belmont, to expect follow-on if CE was passed, (if no longer on a preferential basis) or from MHS, to demand right to exclude on the basis of academic standards or general suitability – the Head Master's historic, and HMC-safeguarded right of selection.

Later, in 1996, this sift was embodied in a separate and preceding Mill Hill School Entrance Exam. Only a few perceptive voices were raised during that first review period, and fortunately a majority in the more recent review, to proclaim the future pattern: the inevitable interdependence – even a symbiosis, of the two establishments.

Sequence of Mastership dates sometimes cut across these phases; first signal change had been that of 1966. Until then Roberts family influence was all-pervasive. "AJ" personified the tradition, in Richard Buckland's words, of *the responsible father of a family – the essence of a Boarding school*. Boys identified with the members of that family, young and old, who attended the school as pupils; before term was born, Rona, the youngest, was first 'Belmontienne'.

As the *OM*, and OB, Graham Patterson recalled in his 83rd year, from his days there, the three islands on the little lake were called, at least during the 1920s, Arthur, Rona, and Mary, after AJ's children. At bedtime on Sundays, before the Epilogue, AJ, and following in his footsteps, his son and successor, Arthur – "AE" – (father of third generation *OM*, future golfer Stephen Roberts) would give readings from popular novels.

It was very much a *Just William* kind of life, broken only by exeats to the Village on Wednesdays and Saturdays, parental visits, outings, and occasional unsanctioned break-outs via the broken fence at the end of the wood to the north-west, to buy deliciously contraband sweets at a sweet shop 100 yards below the convent on Holcombe Hill. (See also Chs.V, X).

A culminating signal change was the appointment wef September 2004 of Mrs Lynn Duncan as the first 'Head' of 'Belmont, The Mill Hill School Preparatory School', succeeding the last 'Master', John Hawkins; she was also the first female Head, and first internal appointment.

APPENDIX I

LIST OF FIGURES

The geographical constituency from which MHS has drawn pupils is shown as series of blocks with 5 cols. RRs are patchy ref. parental domicile; best inferences are made; no ethnic distinctions are drawn – father living in India = Col.5; Japanese mother living in Mill Hill = Col.1. Blocks highlight intake patterns; apart from example for 1945, 3T (see Ch.VIII), 6-year 'cohorts' even out yr-to-yr fluctuations.

APPENDIX J

PICTURE CREDITS & DETAILS OF PERSONALIA

KEY: all items in MHS Archive (#), & all photos by MHS
History photographer Peter Lloyd [1936-40], unless
otherwise stated.

* = Courtesy acknowledgement:

@ = author's collection.

<commissioned artist, where known>.

Personalia: all groups l.-to- r., & from back row to front.

[...] = MHS dates, except for large groups;

stndg = standing; std = seated.

Introduction

b   *M.R.W.Berry, [1943-7] from family of *C.D.L.
Smith [1938-43]; 1941 Water colour, <A.J. Rooker
Roberts>, HM MHS 1940-3.

c   <Frank Ogilvie> [1874-6].

d   *Evening Standard*, 27.ii.1953; * R.Gardner; A.Bush
(A/M, later HD English, 1937-9, 1945-58);
RQMS Crouch (1937-1958).

e   One of a series of First Centennial paintings, 1907:
<H.E.Tidmarsh>.

f   Nobel Prize for Medicine & Physiology: *
F.H.C.Crick
[1930-4]: jt award with Profs Watson and Wilkins.

g   <Ken Jackson> 1983: names of subscribers,
back of canvas.

h   Series of 50, 'Famous Public Schools', W.D.&
H.O.Wills. c.1907: Chairman, Lord Winterstoke,
[1842-7]: @.

i   <James Gunn RA>.

j   <G.L.E.Wild> OB & [1927-30]>.

k   Winterstoke Hse 1924-1995, named after Lord
Winterstoke; Pre-Prep School 1995 to date, named
after R.L.Grimsdell [1927-31].

n   H.Ward [1877].

o   *The Joint Grand Gresham Committee: Royal
Exchange Panel Painting No 8: National Peace
Thanksgiving Service on the steps of St Paul's
Cathedral, 6 July 1919 by <FRANK O.SALISBURY>
(Presented by Sir Horace Marshall, Lord Mayor,
1919); AofC Randall Davidson, BofL Arthur
Winnington-Ingram.

Ch.I

1.a   Busts on mantelpiece: S.Favell, Rev. Dr John Pye
Smith; oils on wall: T.Piper, T.Priestley, Sir J.McClure.

1.b   T.D.Walker [1926-9].

1.c   *Sheila Hume, *The Dissenters of Mill Hill*;
Key: 1. Hendon Park; 2. Highwood Hse;
3. Highwood Ash; 4. Holcombe Hse; 5. Belmont;
6. "The Grove"; 7. "Sunnyside", (now "Murray
Hse"); 8. "Rosebank"; 9. Old "Ridgeway Hse"
(site of MHS); 10. "Clock Hse"; 11. "Jeannettes";
12. "Littleberries" (leading to Burtonhole Ln, first
site of BB Hse).

1.d   Samuel Favell, buried Bunn Hill Fields, London.

1.e   <The brothers Ng>; [1975-9, 1981-6]; * late
R.Calder, *1000 Years of Mill Hill*; Hendon
Crprtn Plaques.

1.f   *A.Bryant, *Years of Victory* 1802-12,
(Harper Collins, 1944).

1.g   <J.Miller>, engraving from John Fothergill,
Some Account of the Late Peter Collinson ...
(Linnean Soc, 1770).

1.h   Architect's elevation: * British Library, ADD.
31323 AAA f374v. (See also Source Notes, Ch.II.)

1.i   *A.Armstrong, *Forget Not Mee and My Garden ...*,
American Philosophical Soc, (Philadelphia, 2002): @.

1.k   Oil c1807.

Ch.II

2.a   <MHS Art Master, G.Renton, 1819-60>.

2.b   <J?.Blood>. 1817.

2.d   <F.M.Holborn> [1897-8].

2.e   *RIBA Library Photographs Collection.

2.h   *Rona Bagnall.

2.i   *Melbourne Chronicle* Archive, via Mrs Helen
Riddiford, descendant of family of Harriet Riddiford.

2.j   *Mrs Helen Riddiford, New Zealand.

2.k   <Photographic Partners>; I.F.Luckin [1922-5].
(iii) *M.D.Henderson [1946-50].

Ch.III

3.a   *<Peter van den Berg>.

3.b   <Thomas Phillips RA>: presented by former pupils,
celebrating Priestley's 25 years on MHS staff.

3.c   *Punch*.

3.d   'Son of Econchatti, King of the Red Hills', from
*A Narrative of the Early Days & Reminiscences of
Oceola Nikkanochee* [1843-4], publr Hatchards,
(1844).

3.e   <Frank Ogilvie>; T.U.Scrutton [1840-2];
T.E.Scrutton [1870-3].

3.f   W.H.Wills (Lord Winterstoke) [1842-7].

3.g   <M.S.Briggs> [1896-9].

3.h   *Clive Smith, *Mill Hill As It Was* (MH, c.1973)

3.i/j   H.Shaw [1811-7]; * W.B.Faherty, *Henry Shaw, his
Life and Legacy*, (Columbia, USA, 1987).

3.k   P.Smith [1829-34?].

3.m   Having been stolen earlier, chairs were rediscovered
in Mill Hill auction rooms by Lt Col B.Morgan.

3.n   Early photos, * Ingrid Penny, gd dtr of <A.B.Eason>
[1901-5].

Ch.IV

4.a   A/Ms (possibly from messrs Harley, Charpentier,
Emery, Ferrier, Leslie, Montini, Nettleship, Payne,
Scott-White, Tucker or Wood), with mtrs, now
unidentifiable.

4.b   *Punch*.

4.c   *Punch*: allusion to Wonder of the Ancient
World, 'The Colossus of Rhodes': Gladstonian
policy themes – Sound finance, liberal Foreign
Policy, Electoral Reform, Retrenchment, Peace.

4.d   *<W.Holl>, National Portrait Gallery, London,
Reg No. 39117; W.H.Salt [1847-8]; G.Salt [1847-9],
E.Salt [1847-54], H.Salt [1849-55], T.Salt [1853-5].
C.Aspin, *The Woollen Industry*, Aylesbury; Mayor of
Bradford at opening of Mill 1853: *from his
immense profits ... he built ... [800] houses, a
church ... an institute and a park.*

4.e   Coat of Arms 'No 2' of 1869: MHS initials in middle
of cross: Biblical motto introduced by Dr Weymouth,
Et virtutem et musas replacing Longfellow/
Arthurian *Excelsior*.

4.f   Sir James Murray, A/M, MHS 1870-85; * Maj Colin
Ruthven-Murray [1933-7], family collection.

4.h   (ii) First champion 1885: S.R.Trotman [1883-6].

4.i   @. Designer of new Rumbold Pool Building: <FDA>.

4.j   Series of engravings <E.?Burrows>, late 19C.

4.k   <Sidney Paget>.

4.l   <'English School'>, 19C: *painted at the request of
former pupils*.

Ch.V

5.a   J.D.McClure, Kathleen M.J.McClure (m.J.E.Ousey
[1894-8]), Mrs M.McClure, L.C.J.McClure, Keith
A.J.McClure [1901-5].

5.c   *RIBA Library Photographs Collection, London.

5.d   (l.): Sir Albert Spicer MP PC [1858-63], Governor;
(r.) Dr McClure.

5.e   <H.E.Tidmarsh>: one of five, First Centennial poster.

5.f   1895: SHD Personnel unknown.

5.g   *Barnet Local Archive.

5.h   (ii) <C.Fisicaro>.

5.i   c1900: gymnast (r.): A.J.Rooker Roberts as pupil
[1893-1900]; (c.) stairs down to "Jock's Hole"
(Bootroom): see Appendix E.

5.k   Stndg: A.F.F.Hall [1911-7]; A.C.Pearse, mon, [1910-
5], K.i.a. N.Russia, 1919 (MHS memorial: OTC Staff
Sergeant's Malacca Sticks); K.Gammon [1910-5];
also in picture: R.G.Scarr [1909-15]. Vehicle hire –
C.Evans, MHV butcher.

5.l   1912: <M.S.Briggs> FRIBA, architect.

5.m   1913: Academic staff, std (7th from l.):
F.R.McLellan, ANO, "Buster" Brown, Dr & Mrs Way,
Acting HM; N.G.Brett James [1894-8] SH HS/M;
ANO; V.A.Elliott (HT).

5.n   (i) Research, G.Bewsher, *Nobis*: all 10 boys served,
three were killed [+], plus C.F.Batty [1909-14] (see
Acknowledgements). Stndg: I.M.Campbell +[1909-
14], K.V.Hooper [1909-15], W.M.James +[1909-14].
Std: I.E.Owen +[1909-15], L.Whittome [1909-14]
(see Ch.II), W.M.Williams, Capt +[1909-14],
C.S.Anton, R.Theobald +[1908-15], J.W.H.Trenchard
+[1911-5]. (ii) Stndg: C.P.M.Wright [1912-8], L.W
Butcher [1914-8], J.G.Anton [1910-4], H.S.Sly
[1912-7], J.A.Ewards [1917-9], D.Tennet [1913-7],
I.E.Furlong [1916-8]; std: W.C.Ramsay [1912-8],
E.MacLennan [1911-7], R.H.Dummett [1913-8]
Capt, E.S.Burrow [1912-7], A.S.Buckley [1913-8];
squatting: V.Owen Jones [1913-9], W.D.Gibbs
[1913-8], F.Morris [1913-8].

5.o   *D.Tennet [1913-7]: from (r.) 3rd XV (blue velvet,
white tassel & braiding);through (l.) 2nd XV
(brown tassel, white braiding, tassel &
monogram); to (c.) 1st XV (silver tassel, braiding,
monogram & six 'arcs').

5.p   *Barnet Local Archive, Hendon.

5.q   Biography by Kathleen Ousey (née McClure), (1927),
McClure of Mill Hill.

5.r   GoH – stndg: Minister – Rev. Arnold Thomas
[1861-2]; (l.) R.W.B.Buckland [1878-84]; (c) prob
F.Lapthorn, Pres OMC (elected previous night); Sir
J.McClure, Gen Horne; (group, r.) incls V.A.Elliott.

Ch.VI

6.a   (c.) Portico and School Hse; (r.) fmr St Paul's
Vicarage (future Winterstoke Hse, 1924);
(extr r.) Head Master's Hse (future St Bees Hse,
1945); (c.l.) Marnham Block (showing fmr Chapel,
later The Large, as part of LH NW-facing wing);
Fives Courts; (l.) Gym, Armoury, Tuck Shop,
Winterstoke Library, Script, McClure Music School
(lwr l.) Farm & Farm Road; (lwr c.) Carp Shop &
Aviary (pre-Science School) with future
"Fishing Net".

6.b   Stndg: K.T.Liang [1914-5]; R.E.F.Peill [1900-4];
G.K.Chou [1907-10]; W.N.Douglas [1916-7];
K.C.Cheng [1909-12]; Dr P.T.Liang [1908-13]. Std:
Dr P.K.Liang [1908-11]; Rt Hon Sir Albert Spicer &
Chrmn of Govrnrs, doing world tour [1858-63];
Dr S.Lavington Hart, Principal [1876].

6.c 1939: F.C.A.Cammaerts [1936-40].

6.d Fmr mtrs' tie: thick choc, thin white,thick choc, thick white, thin choc, thick white; CUOMC, *T.J.Wright [1934-9]; OUOMC, *G.Elyot Rowland [1938-41].

6.e Prince of Wales had known Maurice Jacks at OU. OTC boy is prob D.Petts [1921-4].

6.h ©*'The Dean & Chapter of Westminster'. F.R.Dimbleby [1927-31]; (an A/M was said to have predicted that *he would either finish up 'on the wireless', or in prison!*).

6.i W.Murray Wood [1931-5].

6.j Informtn, Museum of Rugby, Twickenham: England beat France 11-5, 22.ii.1930: Back row in photo: A.E.Freehy (Ref), H.P.Jacob (Blackheath: wing), Peter Howard (*OM*s/OU: [1922-8]: lock), J.W.Forrest (U.S., RN: 2nd row fwd), B.H.Black (OU: second row fwd), J.G.Askew (full back), H.Rew (Army/Exeter: prop fwd); Middle row:- J.S.R.Reeve (Quins: wing), A.H.Bateson (Otley: prop. fwd); J.S.Tucker (Capt: Bristol: hooker), H.G.Periton (Waterloo: flanker), H.Wilkinson (Halifax: flanker). Front:- M.Robson (OU: centre three qtr), Roger Spong (*OM*s [1918-24]: fly half), Wilf Sobey (*OM*s [1918-24]: scrum half), A.L.Novis (Blackheath: centre three qtr). Match report incls:- England's fortunes changed for the better, in the 38th minute when Sobey escaped from the base of the scrum, drew the French full-back and passed to Reeve who scored ...
After half-time ... proficient tactical kicking by Sobey countered the advances of the Championship contenders. Later, ten minutes from the end of the match, the indefatigable Sobey dodged away on the blind side of the scrummage backed up by Periton. The Waterloo flanker marked [sic] the final try... [Match Report 169].

6.m *F.H.C.Crick [1930-4]; other wrld-clss scientists wtng prsntn: Max Perutz & Sir John Cowdery Kendrew (Chem.); Maurice Wilkins & James Watson (Crick's co-winners): 1962.

6.n 1923: C.W.Goyder CBE [1920-4]: W.H.Brown (1908-38, 1940).

6.o Roland Hse, Stepney Green, London E; Alford Hse, Lambeth.

6.p *MHM, Daily Express*.

6.r J.H.Todd [1880-4], fmr Gov.

6.s (i) *A.D.V.Elliott [1937-42].

Ch.VII

7.a *H.W.Gauntlett [1939-44].

7.b K.Whitehorn, dtr of CH HS/M, Alan Whitehorn: article 'And So to Bed', * *Observer Review*; (m. the late Gavin Lyle, writer).

7.c (ii) Lino cut <H.D.Krall> [1937-41]; *MHM* March 1941. (iii) * D.J.Turner [1939-43].

7.d M.P.Lloyd [1936-40]; [* Mrs Edna Middleton explains the 'Tuck shop' lineage: Mrs Hale, later 'Mrs Reid', was running the all-comers Village Shop in 1939, next to "Grindal"; her daughter married Mr Middleton,and the wife of their son, James, became the "Mrs Midd" of MHS legend; "Mrs Midd"'s son, Maurice, and his wife, Edna, preserve the famous Mill Hill autograph book, with its many now historic names and illustrations, displayed at the 2003 SBOMA AGM.]

7.e *Rona Bagnall.

7.f *Illustrated Sporting & Dramatic News*, 3pp feature, 'Mill Hill Boys in Cumberland', in series, 'Public Schools in a New Setting', 10.xi.1939.

7.ghi *News Chronicle* feature on MHS, Nov 1940.

7.j <J.Scott Paterson> [1942-6]; poster * Richard Stout, St Bees Garage, custodian of SBOMA Visitors' Book; from M.R.W.Berry, from Maurice Middleton, son of "Mrs Mid".

7.k *SBOMA Chairman, M.R.W.Berry [1943-7]. Stndg: "Tom" Jackson, "Scailes" McAllister, "Bertie" Ricks, "Boz" Bee, "Patsy" Taylor, "Mog" Morrison. Std: "The Baron" Whitehorn, "Slimy" Coates, "Pips" Phillips MC.

7.l @.

7.m J.G.Dean, Mr Huggan, A.N.Schofield, C.Davies, D.W.Dixon, P.J.Schofield, J.A.Smith, J.D.Reid, I.Adams, F.W.H.Auty, J.E.Williams, R.N.Davies, G.T.Auty, B.Farrow, M.W.Avison, J.J.Huggan, D.Leath (fell to death, St Bees Head, first day at MHS), I.Hutchinson, C.Teale, J.L.Dixon, I.White, R.J.Nettleton, M.C.Sweetman, P.O.Walker: *MHM* 520, 1988: Sept 1943.

7.n (i) Stained-glass window, <Christine Boyce, 1997>; (iv) *(Peter van den Berg); Museum of the Royal Air Force: Fl Lt D.O.Street [1935-40], Fl Lt C.D.Swain [1926-9].

7.p *T.J.Wright [1934-39].

7.oqr *Audrey Raymond, nurse at MHEH.

7.t * National Portrait Gallery, London, <Daniel Farson> Reg No. P289; B.K.Martin [1914-6].

Ch VIII

8.b N.Micklem QC [1866-8, 1870-1].

8.d @ Dr Frederick Cronheim, MHS A/M Languages & Librarian 1945-62; Heidelberg U, & art historian, as 'F.M.Godfrey'.

8.e (i) <C.S.Baker>, HD Art, MHS 1947-78. (ii) H.E.Ricks, BMT 1923-39 MHS 1941-61; HS/M MRY 1945-61; (unidentifiable fairies!), A.M.Hutt, A.B.L.Baldwin, M.R.Lackie, R.H.L.Coleman, E.W.Brenchley, (x,x,x); front row: I.F.Fairburn, M.S.Gedye, M.D.Henderson, R.A.Melluish, N.R.White, H.E.R., M.R.Crowder, G.R.Isaac, A.G.Cosgrove, G.Morgan, A.W.Ramsay, S.Ruhemann, author, S.T.Sargrove.

8.f R.W.B.Buckland [1878-84].

8.g Stage cast included: Cecil Trouncer, Robert Flemyng, Denholm Elliott, Joan Hickson. @.

8.h *British Film Institute, London; (Greta Gynt thrilled assembled audience by 'kicking off' at outset).

8.j *J.Roberts [1945-50]; (W.J.G.Roberts [1973-8], Karen Roberts [1979-81], Fiona M.Roberts [1980-2], R.S.W.Roberts [1980-4]). For rugby record, see Information Supplement No.6.

8.k *MHM*, December 1938.

8.l Peter van den Berg.

8.m J.E.Williams [1945-49]; R.M.Aye Maung [1945-50], A.M.Flutter [1946-50], J.A.Coombs [1945-50], A.W.Ramsay [1944-9].

Ch.IX

9.b * Tom Hustler/National Portrait Gallery, London, <Dorothy Wilding> X24407: N.B.Hartnell [1914-9].

9.c C.B.Salmon [1917-22].

9.d *T.M.Rothery [1946-51].

9.e (i) * Sport & General: incls (back rw) P.W.Hemmings [1947-52]; P.S.Semlyan [1951-6], W.Skinner [1949-55]; (middle) B.Higginson [1950-5], A.E.Kirkland [1950-5], J.S.Parrott [1950-5], M.Spettigue [1951-6]; behind Gen Horrocks, CSM D.K.R.Buck [1947-52]; (front) S.Hibberdine [1950-5], R.M.Coates [1948-53]; (ii) *MHM*.

9.f (*Stdg*): A.R.Dyer [1954-9], S.W.Whyte [1955-60], H.M.Saunders [1954-9], P.B.Armitage [1952-8], T.D.Phillips [1954-60], R.H.Goude [1953-8], C.D.Parker [1953-8],; (*Std*): A.J.Ferryman [1954-9], L.P.Scammell [1953-8], M.W.Corby [1953-8], Capt A.D.B.Webster [1953-8], A.M.Garden [1953-8], B.K.Na'isa [1952-8].

9.g *T.D.Phillips [1954-9].

9.h *P.King [1947-52]; photograph <Jorge Lewinski>. In foreground, wood and steel sculpture "Shogun" (1981); background (r) "Barbarian Fruit", steel/aluminium (1964).

9.i R.S.Tubbs [1925-30].

9.j *A.G.Peters [1955-60]; C.M.T.Bowring, ANO, Biology Lab Drawing: <B.Dunglinson> [1953-7]. The six MHS fires were: (i) Script 1900s; (ii) Large (1909); (iii) Science Block (1920s); (iv) WWII incendiary raid; (v) Science Block (1957); (vi) Gears Cricket Pavilion (2002).

9.k *Frankfurter Allgemeine Zeitung*, 3.vii.1957: A.P.B.Figgis [1953-7], HMQ, R.B.Bennett [1952-7], F.D.Higgs [1952-7] sM *, E.C.S.Ivens [1952-7], A.Scobie [1953-7], RM, I.G.H.Halstead [1952-7], G.M.R.Graham [1952-7]; @ — serendipitous consequence of MHS' sending author to post-WWII Germany — cutting spotted by father of host family.

Ch.X

10.a <P.K.C.Jackson> 1989.

10.b <Catharine Brennand>, 1998: gift to *Join-Lambert*, Rouen.

10.c Rev. H.Starkey, 1957-80, Chaplain; A.P.Hodgson 1955-78, HS/M RH 1973-9, Hockey Coach; A.Prosser-Harries HD Geography, HS/M McClure 1974-6: *MHM* 1969 Spr.

10.e *Ingram Cleasby, *Dentdale 2000...* (2000); J.B.Fox [1924-6]; P.O.Walker [1916-20].

10.f Conductor: S.J.Barlow, HD Music 1957-73.

10.g S.J.Slater [1962-7]: *MHM* 1968 Sept.

10.h *MHM* 1968 Mar.

10.i *J.P.Bolton [1936-40], S.Byles ?, P.Wykes ?, P.J.D.Envers [1943-7].

10.k <Photographic Partners>: (i) * *Punch*: SCR Dining Room, MHS (see Appendix F); [Sir] O.Seaman [1874-8]; (iii) Table: @.

10.m SSI CSM P.F.Maloney MSM (1951-71); Marshal of the Royal Air Force Sir Dermot Boyle (see Appendix C); CCF CO Sqn Ldr D.M. ("Masher") Franklin, 1959-90, HS/M Collinson 1974-85.

Ch.XI

11.a *Coach I.C.Brownlie: (stndg) G.W.Jones [1971-6.], C.A.Briggs [1971-5], M.J.Dolamore [1971-6]; (std) L.B.J.Sargrove [1971-4], L.J.Scott [1971-5], T.D.Tinker [1970-5] Capt, J.G.R.Howard [1971-6], A.Weavers [1969-74].

11.b *Stdg*: S.K.Chua [1972-7]; R.Foulger [1972-7]; T.D.Williams [1972-7]; *Std*: R.M.J.Blackburn [1972-7]; M.G.Johnson [1972-7]; S.J.Rosenkranz [1972-7]; D.M.Allen [1972-7].

11.c <Linda Nichol> 1992.

11.d <June Allison> 1994.

11.e   See *MHM* 1999 for story of names.

11.f   Sir Denis Thatcher [1928-32]; Jerome Evans [1983-7]; Sarah Rymer [1986-8], Clare Watkiss [1985-7] (later, 2004, Governor), who said she was going to read French at Durham U – response *Oh my dear, what a luxury*. See *MHM* 1987 Jy.

11.g   Sir Robert Telford.

11.h   J.G.Bewsher [1948-53].

11.i   *Julian Stock.

11.k   (ii) * <Claude Fisicaro>.

11.n   M.D.Bishop [1955-7].

11.o   stdg: E.S.Harvey [1946-51], H.James [1967-72], Mrs Pauline Bennett-Mills (HM, Pre-Prep), John Hawkins (M of BMT), A.L.Poole [1942-6], R.L.Stewart, Sir Sydney Chapman, Lt Col Beverley Morgan (DAF), chief 'architect' of the complex Incorporation process, one of the four Executives of the new company,1983-2004; std: W.Skinner [1949-56], Prof Potts, J.Roberts [1945-50], Rt Hon Dame Angela Rumbold DBE (Chairman, 1995-2004), William Winfield (HM MHSF 1996 to prsnt), J.G.Bewsher [1948-52], G.M.R.Graham [1952-7].

Ch.XII

12.a   <Claude Fisicaro>; <Peter van den Berg>.

12.b   E.Winfield, T.Mackenzie, A.Majrekar, J.Fitzpatrick, Zara Letz, K.Tija, O.Telvi, T.Northover: [2002-prsnt].

12.c   (i) CH: * *Mill Hill & Edgware Times*: Trevor Chilton 1985-2000, Snr HS/M 1996-2000, Andrew Phillips 2000-prsnt, [1968-73], Snr HS/M 2003-prsnt; David Franklin 1974-85; Tony Turnbull 1960-74, Donald Hall 1945-60 (major contributor of reminiscences for this History); Katharine Whitehorn, *vice* Alan Whitehorn HS/M 1929-45. (ii) @ WEY: Dep HoH J.Berwin [1999-2004] (later HoH and recipient of first Berwin Sword, and also the Ramsay Award), sM Angela Lam, HoH N.Ho, Weymouth HS/M Dr Tony Armstrong.

12.d   *Mill Hill & Edgware Times*.

12.f   (i) John Hawkins, M BMT 1991-2004; (iii) Sir Robert Balchin 2004-present, Ch of CoG.

12.h   *Pauline Bennett-Mills, HM MHS Pre-Prep 1995-prst; l. Georgia Barnett; r. Nikul Parekh.

12.i   <Peter van den Berg>: @ T.D.Phillips [1954-60]..

12.j   (ii) *OC i/c CCF, Lt Col H.Barnes: Sword presented in honour of late Lt Col A.B.Cowing [1951-6].

12.k   Music ties 1st, 2nd, 3rd colours; O.Bubbers [1999-2004].

12.l   (i) Oliver Sander [1998-2003] Michael James [2000-5].P.Woodrow [2000-5]; subsequently also S. of Engl. U17, 2003/4.

12.n   Joanna & Tom Audley, Emma Allen [2002?-prsnt].

12.o   *S.Plummer: <Peter van den Berg>. A.Beckman [2002-prsnt], W.Hughes [2002-prsnt], J.Coakley [2002-prsnt], N.Krendel [2000-prsnt] (Capt of Eton Fives).

12.q   * David Proudlock, HD Drama 2000-prsnt. (i) "Kvetch" 2003: D.Sharman; (ii) "Cabaret", 2002: incls R.Greene, [1999-2004].

12.r   S.D.Jenkins [1956-60]; declined to use title, Jan 2004.

12.s   C.Minnis [1998-2003].

12.t   W.R.Winfield HM MHS # 1996-prsnt.

12.u   *Carnival Productions: Felicity Kendal; Anthony Andrews; Pamela Ferris. MHS as 'Stagford Lodge School', Berkshire.

12.v   <Peter van den Berg>.

12.w   (i)Sophie Hamedani; (iii) CCF Cadets: Maria Baneeva, Kamelija Vrangalova, Amy Lee, Sheryl Lee.

12.x   Ethiopia visit leaders: Rev. James Fields [1973-8], MHSF's second Presbyterian Chaplain, 1998-prsnt; Soddho host, Emanuel; Judith Herbertson, Dep HM MHS, 1996-2003; Rev. Paul Hunt, MHS Chaplain 1993-8 & Priest-in-Ordinary to HM the Queen. (Below):

12.z   Richard Allain, HD Music (1994-prsnt). (First organ was in the 1832 Chapel.)

Bibliographical Note

The History of Religious and Political Dissent,
Rational Dissent, the English Enlightenment,
and the Origins of Mill Hill School.

For this school history, the convention of a general bibliography is better observed
through the Mill Hill Bibliography and the end-of-chapter sources, where detailed references are given.
This Bibliographical Note is for those who may wish to explore the main sources for the arguments in Chapter I.

17th-19th century background: J.Israel, *Anglo-Dutch Moment: Essays on the Glorious Revolution and its World Impact* (Camb. 1991); D.Jarratt, *Britain 1688-1815* (1965); J.H.Plumb, England in the 18th Century (1950); R.H.Brissenden ed., *Studies in the 18th Century* (Canberra, 1968); A.S.Briggs, *The Age of Improvement* (1959); R.Porter, *English Society in the 18th Century* (1982); J.B.Owen, *The 18th Century* (1974); M.Dorothy George, *London Life in the 18th Century* (1925); R.E.Schofield, *The Enlightenment of Joseph Priestley...* (Penn., USA, 1997); *Annual Register, 1807*; A.Bryant, *The Years of Endurance 1793-1802, Years of Victory 1802-1812* (1944); E.Halévy, *England in 1815: History of the English People in the Nineteenth Century* (1961); J.Pollock, *Wilberforce* (1977); Linda Colley, *Britons: Forging the Nation 1707-1837* (1994). For evidence of the Calvinist boarding concept of the *Collegium*, eg Sarospatak & Debrecen in E.Hungary, see M.E.Osterhaven, *Story, Sarospatak Academy* (1987).

The English Enlightenment: K.Haakonssen, Prof of Philosophy, Boston U, USA, *Enlightenment and Religion, Rational Dissent in 18th Century Britain* (Cambridge, 1996), particularly the Editor's Introduction, and Ch.2, 'The Emergence of Rational Dissent' (R.K.Webb), Ch.5, 'The Contribution of the Dissenting Academies to the Emergence of Rational Dissent' (D.L.Wykes), Ch.6, 'Rational Dissent and Political Opposition in England, 1770-1790' (J.Seed), and Ch.7, 'Law, Lawyers & Rational Dissent' (W.Prest); R.Porter & M.Teich, *The Enlightenment in National Context*, particularly Ch 1, 'The Enlightenment in England', and 'Afterword' (Cambr. 1981); S.Deane, *French Revolution and Enlightenment in England, 1789-1852*, Ch.8, 'English Dissent and the Philosophes ...' (Cambr. USA, 1989); R.Porter, 'The British Enlightenment: Then and Now', Ryl Hist. Soc. meeting, 8.xi.2000.

France in the Enlightenment, (1998) ('Enlightenment France'). 'Enlightenment & Dissent', passim; J.Aikin, *Address to the Dissenters of England in Their Late Defeat* (1790); J.Priestley, *A View of the Principles & Conduct of the Protestant Dissenters with Respect to the Civil & Ecclesiastical Constitution of England* (1769); A.Bewell, *Wordsworth & the Enlightenment: Nature, Man & Society in the Experimental Poetry* (New Haven, USA, 1989); O.P.Grell & R.Porter, (eds) 'Toleration in Enlightenment Europe' (Cambridge, 2000);

R.N.Stromberg, *Religious Liberalism in 18th Century England* (1954); U.Henriques *Religious Toleration in England 1783-1833* (1961); S.Schaffer, 'Status & Mind: Enlightenment & Natural Philosophy', in G.S.Rousseau (ed.) *The Languages of Psyche: Mind & Body in Enlightenment Thought* (Berkeley, 1990);

The History of Religious Dissent: S.Palmer ed, *The Nonconformist's Memorial, being an Account of the Lives, Sufferings & Printed Works of the Ministers Ejected from the Church of England, chiefly by the Act of Uniformity, Aug. 24 1662* 3 vols, orig by E.Calamy (1802-3); H.Smith, *The Churchman's Answer to the Protestant Dissenter's Catechism...* (1795); D.Bogue & J.Bennett, *History of the Dissenters from the Revolution in 1688 to the year 1808* 4 vols, (1808); B.Brook, *The Lives of the Puritans* (1813); R.W.Dale, *History of English Congregationalism* (1907); B.A.Millard [1876-8], *The Great Ejectment of 1662 & the Rise of the Free Churches* (1912), *Congregationalism* (1912); D.Coomer, *English Dissent under the Hanoverians* (1946); R.N.Stromberg, *Religious Liberalism in 18th Century England* (Oxfd, 1954); W.Stevens, 'Oxford's Attitude to Dissenters 1646-1946', BQ, xiii (1949); D.W.Bebbington, *Evangelicalism in Modern Britain...* (1989); J.Munson, *The Nonconformists: In Search of a Lost Culture* (1991); A.H.Lincoln, *Some Political & Social Ideas of English Dissent 1763-1800* (Camb. 1937); B.L.Manning, *The Protestant Dissenting Deputies* (1952); M.R.Watts, *The Dissenters* (Oxford 1995); C.R.Cole & M.E.Moody, *The Dissenting Tradition* (Athens USA, 1975); D.Davie, *A Gathered Church, the Literature of the English Dissenting Interest 1700-1930* (1978); K.Higham-Smith, *Churches in England from Elizabeth I to Elizabeth II* (1997); C.Binfield, *So Down to Prayers: Studies in English Nonconformity 1780-1920* (1977), *A Congregational Formation...* (1996); E.Routley, *The Story of Congregationalism* (1961); Ursula Henriques, *Religious Toleration in England 1787-1833* (1961); B.G.Worrall, *The Making of the English Church* (1988), Chs.1/8; H. de Selincourt, *The Cricket Match* (1924).

Political dissent: A.J.P.Taylor *The Trouble-Makers: Dissent over Foreign Policy 1792-1939* (1957); Inge Scholl, *Die Weisse Rose* (1955); E.Bethge ed, *Dietrich Bonhoeffer: Letters and Papers from Prison* (1953).

A Mill Hill Bibliography

Mill Hill and Millhillians in Print

A surprisingly high 1% of Millhillians (c.150 out of the c.15,000 over the 200 years) have put pen to paper, or currently mouse to word-processor, ranging from prize-winning novels, music scores and poetry, to politics, history, and often arcane textbooks, see (B) below. Of these usually only one work per writer will be listed in this mini-Bibliography; it illustrates the "aliveness" of the History's title, offering a further aspect of Mill Hill's 'product'. Using 'Millhillians' in its widest sense, Old Belmontians are also included.

At (C) are listed members of all the academic staffs who have also been writers, a further aspect

of the Foundation's intellectual activity. Some authors have also occurred legitimately as Sources at the end of the History's chapters, or in the Bibliographical Note, which must be consulted for wider literary/ historical references.

First,(A) lists general book references, MHS; (publishers are listed in chapter sources).

NB: (i) the Short-title form is used;

(ii) ".." = *nom-de-plume*;

(iii) # = in MHS Archive Collection;

(iv) [1..-..] or * = pupil's years at MHS;

(v) @ = member of MHSF academic staff.

A. Reference in print to Mill Hill or MHS-related figures
*[Includes works by Millhillians * and/or academic staff @].*

Aldous, T.	*ILN... Book of London Villages* (1980)
Alford, B.W.E.	*W.D. & H.O.Wills... Development of... UK Tobacco Ind... 1786-1965* (1973) [G.A.Wills [1870-2]; H.H.Wills [1871-2]; W.H.Wills [1842-7]
Armstrong, A.	*Forget Not Mee and My Garden...* (USA, 2002)
(author unknown)	*Lavington Hart of Tientsin** [1976] (Livingstone Press 1947)
Aveling, T.	*Memorials of the Clayton Family* (1867)
Beaconsfield, Earl (Disraeli)	*Endymion* (1878) [MHS, 70]
Bewsher, J.G.*	*Nobis* (Mill Hill, 1979) #
Binfield, C.	*Et Virtutem et Musas: Mill Hill School and the Great War*, chapt. in Studies in Church History, v.20, Church & War, Ecclesiastical Hist. Soc. #; *So Down to Prayers: Studies in English Nonconformity 1780-1920* (1977)
Binney, T.	*@Education, two Sermons at Mill Hill... 1842, 1847* (1847)
Block, W.	*Mill Hill to Congo* (1909) (S.R.Webb [1882-4])
Blundell, Rev.T.	*@ Narrative of the Appointment of [TB] to the chaplaincy of the [PDGS/MH], and the causes of his removal* (1831)
Bradford, E.E.	*Stories... at our Great Public Schools* (1908)
Bradley, H.	*Sir James Murray...* (1919)
Brickhill, P.	*Great Escape* (1979) [Stalag Luft III]
Burgon, J.W.	*Lives of Twelve Good Men* (1888) (Bishop Wm. Jacobson [1815-19])
Calder, R. Collier, J.W. & Calder, R.	*Mill Hill, A Thousand Years Of History* (Angus Hudson in assoc. with MHHS (1993)# *Story of Mill Hill* (MH,1991)
Cesarani, D.	*Arthur Koestler, The Homeless Mind* (1998)
Clayton, W.	*@ Rural Discourses* (1814)
Clifford, D.*	*St Bees Remembered* (OMC, 1997)
Dale, R.W.	*Mill Hill School Nonconformist Education* (an address... New Foundation Day... (1889)
Dimbleby, J.	*Richard Dimbleby** (1975)
Eysenck, H.J.	*Dimensions of Personality: Record of Research carried out with H.T.Himmelweit* (1947) *Rebel With a Cause...* (1990)
[MHS	as the MHEH]
Faherty, W.B.	*Henry Shaw, His Life and Legacies,* (Columbia, USA, 1987) # (H.Shaw [1811-17])
Flower, B.	*Statement of Facts relative to the conduct of J.Clayton...* (1808)
Foot, M.R.D.	*S.O.E., an Outline History 1940-6* (1990) ([F.C.A.Cammaerts [1933-6])
Gathorne-Hardy, J.	*Public School Phenomenon 597-1977,* (1977) #
Gribbin, J.	*Science, A History...* (2002) (F.H.C.Crick [1930-4]).
Hall, W.A.N.*	*An Autobiography* (1901)
Hampden-Cook, Rev. E.*	*Register of Mill Hill School 1807-1926* (MH, 1926) #
Haworth, P.	*Under Cover* (1950) [F.H.C.Cammaerts]
Helmore, F.	*Memoir of the Rev. Thomas Helmore* (1896) ([T.Helmore [1825-8])
Hume, S.	*Dissenters of Mill Hill* (2000)
Humphrys, Rev. J.	*@ Committee of the [PDGS/MH] brought before the Bar of the Dissenting part of the Religious Public...,* (1825)
Innes, P.R.	*The Bengal Regiment* (1885) # [1840-2]
Jacks, Dr L.P.	*Life & Letters of Stopford Brooke* (1917) # *Confession of an Octogenarian* (1942)
James, N.J.B.*	*@ History of Mill Hill School:- 'BJ1'* (1909); 'BJ2' (1923); 'BJ3'(1938); *Life of Peter Collinson* (1926) #
Johnson, R.A.	*New City, Old Bridge* (1981) (I.F.Luckin [1922-5])

Jones, M. *Social Psychiatry: A Study of Therapeutic Communities* (1952) [MHS as MHEH 1939-45]

Kenworthy, J.D. *Fisherman's Philosophy* (1933) [St Bees: owner of "Seacroft", RH 1939-45]

La Fargue, T.E. *China's First Hundred* (1942) (P.T.Liang [1908-13])

Mantle, J. *Mr Copperad, Life & Work of Basil Tanner* [1920-3], (1998).

Martin, B.Kingsley* *Father Figures: A First Vol. of Autobiography 1897-1931* (1966) [Sir John McClure, HM 1891-1922].

Matthews, A.G. *Diary – Cambridge Minister* (H.C.Carter [1899-94])

Medway, J. *Memoirs... of John Pye Smith* (1853)

Micklem, N.* *The Box and the Puppets* (1957)

Morgan, E.S. *Benjamin Franklin* (Yale, 2003)

Murray, K.M.E. *Caught in the Web of Words* (Yale, 1978)

Murray, W.G.R.* *Murray the Dictionary Maker* (Wynberg, 1943) New Grove Dictionaries: ... Music (1980); ... Opera (1997)

Oak, B.H. *Mill Hill, A History...* (Edinburgh, 1994)

Oceola Nikkanochee* *written by his Guardian* (1841)#

Ogilvie, V. *The English Public School* (1957)

Orme, W. *Address... to the Young Gentlemen of [PDGS/MH] on appointment of Rev. H.March to religious charge of that establishment* (1826)

Ousey, K.M.J. *McClure of Mill Hill* (1927)#

Owen, B. *(With Popski's Private Army)* (1993) [see Shaw below]

Peniakoff, V. *Popski's Private Army* (1950)

Pevsner, N. & Cherry B. *Buildings of England: London 4 North* (1998)

Pugh, R.B. *Victoria History... Counties...: v.1* (1976)

Raven, J.C. *Mill Hill Vocabulary Test* (1944) [MHS as EMH]

Roberts, A. *Eminent Churchillians* (1994) (J.R.Tanner [1874-8]); (F.R.Dimbleby [1927-31]).

Shaw, W.B. Kennedy *Long Range Desert Group. The Story of its Work in Libya 1940-3* (1945) # (Lt. Col. J.R.Easonsmith, DSO, MC: [1923-26])

Shorter, E. *A History of Psychiatry...* (1997) [MHS as MHEH]

Smith, C.R. *Mill Hill As It Was* (1960?)

Smith, G. *@Belmont, MHS Junior S, 1912-1994* (MH 1994) #

Spicer Family *Albert Spicer, 1874-1934, A Man of His Time* (1938) # (Sir A.Spicer [1858-63])

Spooner, P. *Night Fighter Ace* (1997) (Braham, OB)

Stowell, W.H. *Memoir of... R.W.Hamilton* (1850) [1807-10]

Sutcliffe, G.C. *@Winterstoke House 1924-1995...* (1995)#; *A History of Burton Bank 1875-2000* (1999)#; *A History of Collinson House 1903-2003* (2003)#

Thatcher, C. *Below the Parapet...* (1996) and.

Thatcher, M. *Downing St. Years* (1993) (D.Thatcher [1928-32])

Timpson, G.F.* *Et Virtutem, Essays on Mill Hill* (MH, 1957) # *Kings & Commoners, Studies in British Idealism* [Signor Vesti, Q-M Fleming] (1936) *Sir James A.H.Murray, A Self-Portrait* (Gloucester, 1957) #

Tinker, H. *A Message from The Falklands; The Life and Gallant Death of David Tinker, Lieut RN, From His Letters and Poems compiled by Hugh Tinker* (1983) (D.Tinker [1970-5]).

Wakeford, J. *The Cloistered Elite* (1969)

Walker, T.D.* *Mill Hill School Properties* (1990)# [pte circ].

Watson, J.D. *The Double Helix: A Personal Account of the Discovery of the Structure of DNA* (1968, rev edtn 1996) (F.H.C.Crick [1930-4])

Webster, F.A.M. *Our Great Public Schools* (1937) #

Wells, Rev A.* *An Address Delivered in the Chapel of the Protestant Dissenters Grammar School, Mill Hill, on Occasion of Public Day, June 18th 1845*

Williamson, D. *Gladstone the Man* (1898) [MHS] (ed) *William Ewart Gladstone, Statesman and Scholar* (1898)

Winchester, S. *Surgeon of Crowthorne* (1998) [OED/ Murray] *Meaning of Everything...* (2003)

Wolrige Gordon, Anne *Peter Howard, Life and Letters* (1969) (P.D.Howard [1922-8]).

B. Other books by Millhillians

Adeney, Dr W.F. *Constantine to Charles the Great* (1887)

Armitage, P.B. *Political Relationship & Narrative Knowledge* (2000)

Ashton, R.S. *Austrian Ideas of Religious Liberty* (1881)

Autant-Lara, C. *La Rage dans le Coeur* (1984)

Bains, Prof W. *Genetic Engineering... Almost Everybody* (1993)

Bardsley, J. *Hospital Facts & Observations* (1830)

Barker, E.A. *Nquonquolha* (18..)

Beatson, B.W. *Ancient History* (1864)

de Beer, E.S. *Diary of John Evelyn* (1955)

Bendall, G. *King Charles* (1909)

Berry, M.R.W. *A Sunlit, Intimate Gift* (2002) #

Birks, Prof T. *Modern Rationalism* (1854)

Blumenthal, H. *Studies in Plotinus...* (1993)

Bodley, J.E.C. *Cardinal Manning* (1912)

Boyd, Dr J.P. *Nitrous Oxide & Oxygen* (1900)

Brain, W.R. *Tea with Walter de la Mare* (1957) #

Braithwaite, R. *Palmerston & Africa...* (1996) #

Bramham, W/Cdr *Scramble* (1961) [J.R.D.Bramham: OB]

Bridgett, T.E. *Life of Blessed John Fisher* (1888)

Briggs, M.S. *Puritan Architecture and its Future* (1946)

Bruce, J.C. *Bayeux Tapestry* (1856)

Buckingham, L. *Mary, Queen of Scots* (1844)

Bull, Dr T. *Maternal Management of Children* (1848)

Butler, F.H. *Through Lapland with Skis & Reindeer* (1917)

Carter, H.C. *Hurrah for the Worth of Mill Hill!* (1902?)

Challis, J. *Practical Astronomy* (1879)

Chase, J.C. *Mission & Destiny of France* (1854)

Clifford, Rev. P. *Ecumenical Pilgrimage* (1998) #

Colebrook, F. *William Morris, Master Printer* (1897)

Conder, F.R. *Recollections of English Engineers* (1868)

Cook, J.T. *How to Work Insurance Agencies* (1909) #

Craig, R.D. *Trees & Woods* (1866)

Crick, Prof F.	*What Mad Pursuit...* (1989)
Crowder, Prof M.	*Cambridge History of Africa ed.,* (1978)
Curwen, J.F.	*Castles... Cumberland & Westmorland* (1932)
Davenport, J.M.	*Lords Lieutenants & High Sherrifs* (1871)
Davidson, J.	*Axminster during the Civil War* (1851)
Dawson, C.W.	*Khaki Courage* (1917)
Dimbleby, F.R.	*The Frontiers are Green* (1943) #
Dodds, G.E.	*Is Liberalism Dead?* (1920)
Downing, C.	*Life & Personality of Shakespeare* (1911)
Dunlop, Brig J.	*A Short History of Germany* (1957)
Eason, A.B.	*Prevention of Vibration & Noise...* (1923)
Epps, Dr J.	*Life of Dr John Walker* (1830)
Eve, H.W.	*Notes to Scott's Waverley* (1876)
Ferguson, D.W.	*Life of Capt Robert Knox* (1880s)
Foster, A.	*Elementary Lessons in Chinese* (1887)
Gervis, H.	*Arms & The Doctor* (1920)
Gibbon, R.P.	*African Items* (1904)
Goldman, P.	*Victorian Illustration...* (1996)
Goyder, G.A.	*The Responsible Worker* (1975)
Gray, C.	*Diary of a Barrister* (1850)
Gray, A.S.	*Edwardian Architecture* (1985)
Griffiths, Dr F.	*Dermatology* (1866)
Gundry, I.	*Gallileo* (1996) [last of 15 operas]
Gunn, H.M.	*Nonconformity in Warminster* (1853)
Gupta, Tanika	*The Waiting Room* (play: 2000)
Gurney, T.A.	*Church... First Three Centuries* (1911)
Haddon, Prof A.	*History of Anthropology* (1910)
Hamilton, Prof I.	[Nine operas]; *Commedia* etc (1980s)
Hamilton, R.W.	*John Ely's Memoir* (1848)
Hankinson, C.J.	*Belgians at Home* (1901) ["Clive Holland"]
Harley, H.	*"Oh Susannah!"* (1897) ["Mark Ambient"]
Hartnell, N.	*Silver and Gold* (1955)
Helmore, Prof H.	*Lightfoot's Horae Hebraidicae...* (1889)
Helmore, T.	*Cathechism of Music* (1878)
Henderson, M.D.	*The Forgiveness Factor* (1999)
Herbert, Rev. T.	*Realistic Assumptions... Modern Science* (1879)
Hill, P.G.	*Napoleon III* (1869)
Holborn, J.G.	*Architecture of European Religions* (1909)
Holt, Prof S.C.	*Common Market... Theory & Practice* (1967)
Hood, W.C.	*Criminal Lunatics* (1854)
Hourani, A.H.	*Arabic Thought in the Liberal Age* (1962)
Hourani, C.A.	*Unfinished Odyssey, Lebanon & Beyond* (1984)
Howard, P.D.	*Guilty Men* (1939) [with M.Foot, P.Cudlipp] *That Man Buchman* (1946)
Hutton, H.	*English Liturgy* (1848)
Jacobsen, Bish.W.	*Bishop Sanderson's Works* (1854)
James, T.S.	*History... Presbyterian Chapels* (1854)
James, E.A.B.	*Repeat My Signals* (1943)
James, N.G.B.	*Growth of Stuart London* (1935)
Jenkins, Sir S.	*England's Thousand Best Churches* (1999)
Jones, N.A.	*World Tanks & Reconnaisance...* (1984)
Kendell, Prof R.	*Role of Diagnosis in Psychiatry* (1975)
Kitts, E.J.	*In the Days of the Councils* (1912)
Lay, H.N.	*The Opium Question* (1893)
Lefever, R.M.H.	*Kick The Habit...* (2000)
Lethem, G.J.	*Colloquial Arabic* (1914)
Link, fam	*A Memoir* (1920)

Leonard, Prof G.	*Nobler Cares* (1909)
Lincoln, A.H.	**Some Political & Social Ideas of English Dissent 1763-1800* (1938)
Maddox, Dr E.H.	*Clinical Uses of Prisms* (1889)
Mallett, R.	*Poems from Beyond* (1920)
Marshall-Andrews. R.	*The Palace of Wisdom* (1989)
Martin, B.K.	*Triumph of Lord Palmerston...* (1925)
Mather, J.	*Socialism Exposed* (1839)
Mather, R.C.	*Christian Missions in India* (1856)
Mather, C.	*Selections in Hindustani* (1858)
Medhurst, Sir W.	*Foreigner in Far Cathay* (1872)
Melville-Ross, A.	*Shadow* (1984)
Micklem, N.	*Ultimate Questions* (1955)
Millard, E.C.	*South America... Neglected Continent* (1894)
Millard, B.A.	*The Great Ejectment of 1662 & the Rise of the Free Churches* (1912)
Mo, T.	*Brownout on Breadfruit Boulevard* (1995)
Montgomery, R.J.	*Examinations... Evolution...* (1966)
Morgan, G.E.	*Dreams & Realities* (1902)
Morris, D.E.	*Pilgrim Through This Barren Land* (1972)
Morrison, Hon J.	*Chinese Commercial Guide* (1834)
Moore, G.	*Body & Mind* (1847)
Nash, W.	*A Lawyer's Life on Two Continents* (1920)
Newth, G.S.	*Chemical Analysis* (1898)
Nicholson, I.	*Wales: Its Part in the War* (1920)
Noble, J.	*Facts for Liberal Politicians* (1880)
Noltingk, B.E.	*Dissenting Conformist* (1998)
Nutter, S.B.	*History of the Cambridge Baptists* (1912)
Partridge, J.A.	*Making of the American Nation* (1866)
Piper, T. (Jnr)	*Digest of the Building Acts* (1856)
Pye-Smith, Dr P.	*Diseases of the Skin* (1893)
Renshaw, C.B.	*The Humour Club* (1924)
Ridley, W.	*Kamilaroi...Australian Native Dialects* (1877)
Roberts, Sir W.	*Digestion & Diet* (1891) [wrote 99 books]
Roberts, A.J.R.	*The Bird Book* (1903)
Robinson, Prof T.	*Bible for African/Asian Christians* (1939)
Rogers, P.H.	*Superhuman Origin of the Bible* (1874)
Ropes, A.R.	*"Lilac Time"* (1922) ["Adrian Ross"]
Satow, Sir E.	*English-Japanese Dictionary...* (1919)
Scott, B.	*Morality of London* (1884)
Scott James, R.	*Modernism & Romance* (1908)
Scrutton, Hon T.	*Laws of Copyright* (1882)
Seaman, Sir O.	*Interludes of an Editor* (1929) [Punch]
Seaton, J.	*Great Circle Sailing Made Easy* (1850
Shaw, H.	*Vine & Civilisation* (St Louis, 1884)
Sherring, C.A.	*Western Tibet...* (1906)
Sibree, J.	*Hegel's Philosophy of History* (trans 1857)
Spalding, H.	*Suvoroff* (1890)
Spicer, Sir A.	*Australia* (1911)
Stark, Dr B.P.	*Determination of Epoxide Groups* (1969)
Stephenson, H.	*Ceramic Pottery* (1912)
Stewart, A.W.	*Manual... Practical Chemistry* (1924)
Stibbe, P.G.	*Return Via Rangoon* (1947)
Stirling, W.F.	*Orange Groves* (1935)
Stock, E.E.	*Land of the Lords Marchers* (1912)
Sykes, G.F.H.	*Pupils' Geography* (1882)
Talfourd, Sir T.N.	*Vacation Thoughts & Rambles* (1845) #
Tanner, Prof J.	*Mr Pepys* (1926)
Thorne, R.	*Practical Guide...Rd Tfc Claims* (1988)
Thorpe, Dr W.H.	*Learning & Instinct in Animals* (1956)
Trotman, S.R.	*Inorganic Chemistry* (1900)

Tubbs, R.S. *Living in Cities* (1942)
Tucker, H. *Songs of Love & Nature* (Sth Africa, 1910) #
Walker, Prof E. *History of Southern Africa* (1959)
Ward, H.F.E. *Five Years with the Congo Cannibals* (1890)
Wardill, Dr W.E. *Pseudoconalgia* (1921)
Waylen, J. *History of the House of Cromwell* (1880)
Waylen, H. *Mountain Pathways* (1909)

Webb, S.R. *A Young Congo Missionary* (1897) #
Webb, B. *Taxation of Profit & Gains* (1965)
Weightman, H. *To...Gladstone, Clerical Disabilities* (1870)
White, E. *Number in Nature* (1885)
Wood, E.G. *Defenders of Our Empire* (1919)
Wyld, J. *A Time of War* (1854)

C. Works by MHSF Heads & Members of Academic Staff

Allain, R.P. *Salve Regina* choral work, (2002)
Armstrong, Dr A. *Balzac, Early Works...*(Thesis, 1992)
Axworthy, Dr R. *London Merchant Community...* (Thesis, 2000)
Brown, W.H. *On the Nature of Things* (NY 1950) #
Chilton, T.W. *Applied Plant Science* (2002)
Cronheim, Dr F. *Student's Guide to Early Italian Painting 1250-1500* (1956) ["F.M.Godfrey"]
Derry, Dr T.K. *The European World* (1950); *A History of Scandinavia* (1979)
Flecker, J.E. *Hassan* (1922)
Hart, M. *E.E.C. & Secondary Edctn... U.K.* (1975)
Hurndall, Rev. W. *Pulpit Memorials...* (1878)
Jacks, M.L. *Physical Education* (1938); *The Education of Good Men* (1955)
McClure Sir J. *Devotional Services... for use in Mill Hill School Chapel* (1895) #
Murray, J.A.H. *A New English Dictionary on Historical Principles... with the assistance of many scholars and Men of Science* (1888+) [Refs to: Rev. R.Harley @, T.E.Scrutton*, P.H.Pye-Smith*, Dr R.F.Weymouth @, etc.]
Murray, W.G.R.* 3 MHS school songs, Osborn, + G.F.A.@
Pye Smith, Rev. J. (sel. from over 20 works): *On Sacrifice of Christ...* (to patrons ... of Protestant Dissenters Acadmy, Homerton (1813); *Protestant Dissenters Catechism...*

1814); *Reasons of Protestant Religion* (1815); *On relationship between holy scriptures and some points of geological science* (1839)
Quadling, D.A. *Mathematical Analysis* (1955); *Introduction to Advanced Mechanics* (1962)
Ryland, J.E. (@1825-31: biographer)
Smith, Rev P.* *History of the World* (1863)
Vince, Rev C.A. *Christian Conduct, Sermons...* [MHS] (1890); *John Bright* (1898)
Way, Dr A.S. *The Fall of Troy* (1913)
Weymouth, Dr R. *Early English Pronunciation* (1874); *Resultant Greek Testament* (1886); *New Testament in Modern Speech* (1st ed 1902)#
Whale, Rev. Dr J.S. (sel. from over 30 published works): *The Crown Rights of the Redeemer* (1934); *Christian Doctrine: Eight Lectures delivered in U of Cambridge to undergraduates of all Faculties* (Cambridge, 1941); *Protestant Tradition... Interpretation* (1955); *Christian Reunion: historic divisions reconsidered* (1971)
Winfield, W.R. *Vocational French* (1984)
Winter, E. The Allerdale Years ... (2003)
Wormell, C.P. & Budden, F.J. *Mathematics through Geometry* (1964)

General Index

PEOPLE INDEX

KEY: This Index includes individuals referred to in the text, mainly under group headings: MHSF Presidents; Court Chairmen; Hon Treasurers & Secretaries; MHS Head Masters & Wives; Chaplains; Director of Admin & Finance/ Bursars; Housekeepers/ Lady Residents/ Matrons; Admin staff/ fmr servants; Heads of State; distinguished visitors/ Guests of Honour; architects retained; Heads of other schools; writers/ authors quoted; individuals in the field of the Arts; *MILLHILLIANS* (OMs) (*) of all three schools; Governors and other individuals if significantly associated with MHSF history and/or referred to in the text. Otherwise, *see* End-of-Chapter Notes, and/or Bibliography; for other themes/ points *see GENERAL INDEX.*